A COMPLETE WHO'S WHO OF NEWCASTLE UNITED F.C.

By PAUL JOANNOU

Published by
POLAR PRINT GROUP LTD

DEDICATION
To those players who have worn the famous black'n'white shirt.
They have stirred the Geordie crowd for over a century.

First published in Great Britain by
Polar Print Group Ltd
2, Uxbridge Road, Leicester LE4 7ST
England

Text © Copyright 1996 Paul Joannou
Design © Copyright 1996 Polar Print Group Ltd

ISBN 1 899538 03 8

Edited by
Julian Baskcomb

Assistant Editor
Julia Byrne

Design & Layout
Neill Staniforth

Printed and Produced by
Polar Print Group Ltd
2, Uxbridge Road, Leicester LE4 7ST
Telephone: (0116) 2610800

Photographs and illustrations are courtesy of:
Newcastle United FC, Associated Sports Photography, Empics Ltd., Colorsport, Sporting
Pictures, David Munden Photography, Newcastle Chronicle & Journal, Garth Dykes and Ian
Horrocks.
Many of the photographs reproduced are from original material in the archives at Newcastle
United FC who also retain the rights to official photocall pictures from the modern era taken by
the appointed Club Photographer. Most remaining photographs are from the private collection
of the author or from albums owned by various Newcastle supporters or former players. We
have been unable to trace the sources of all these pictures, but any photographer involved is
cordially invited to contact the publishers in writing providing proof of copyright.

Dust Jacket Photographs:
Front Cover (L to R): Alan Shearer, Jack Thomas, Kevin Keegan, Les Ferdinand.
Back Cover (L to R Top): Bill McCracken, Peter Beardsley, Willie McFaul.
Middle: Jackie Milburn, Bob McKay, Alf McMichael.
Bottom: Hughie Gallacher, Malcolm Macdonald.

FOREWORD

by Robson Green

I love going to the match, watching and supporting Newcastle United. Along with my dad, we both enjoy the spectacle at St James Park immensely, just like everyone else at Gallowgate. We all obtain tremendous pleasure seeing United perform and watching all those personalities to have worn the famous black'n'white stripes. Some of them great, some of them good and those who ..... well, let's say need a bit of coaching!

My dad had a tough life as a miner, working six days a week most of the time. And his father did the same too. There were thousands of others like them on Tyneside. The Geordie working man demanded, as Pele once said: "Beautiful Football" from Newcastle United; football to give an afternoon of pleasure, shouting themselves hoarse supporting The Toon, an outlet from the grind down the pit or in the shipyard. Industries may have changed now, but we still demand the same.

I first saw United in season 1973-74. Dad used to take me and he always said to watch out for Newcastle's centre-forward Malcolm Macdonald. And I quickly found out why. Supermac was something special. I have never seen anyone like him. He was my first hero, a striker who made the fans go wild when in full flow heading for goal.

But every Newcastle United team needs other players besides the superstars. I also loved to watch Paddy Howard at the back. And I quickly likened to Alan Kennedy too. Soon Paul Gascoigne and Peter Beardsley started to display their talents, and football will probably not see their like again when they call it a day.

Newcastle supporters always like hero figures to look up to. I am no different. And there is nothing wrong with that. We are proud of our Geordie heritage and feel good when United have the very best in a black'n'white shirt. None more so than in recent years as Kevin Keegan has formed a stunning line-up of quality, playing entertaining football. Indeed, "Beautiful Football".

This book covers all our heroes as well as the not so well-known names, players just as important in the development of Newcastle United over the years. It is a fascinating study of the men who have played for the Magpies.

Robson Green

ACKNOWLEDGMENTS

In a work of this magnitude I am most indebted to many, many people. Football enthusiasts from all corners of the country have provided vital clues on career details. Individuals from South Africa, North America and Australia, as well as throughout Europe have assisted in the accumulation of information.

Firstly my thanks to Sir John Hall, his directors and to Freddie Fletcher at St James Park for their agreement to publish this book on the club's behalf. To the staff of Newcastle United who I have turned to for assistance over the years; Ken Slater, Tony Toward and secretary Russell Cushing who has allowed access to official documents from 1892, an invaluable source of accurate knowledge.

The excellent facilities of the City Library's local history department in Newcastle have been a central point of reference, while the columns of the north east's media have been a cornerstone to research. Many members of the Association of Football Statisticians have kindly helped, as well as fellow club historians around the country. I am grateful for their individual response and for their books on their respective clubs.

Kind replies from the stars themselves are appreciated. Most have been very enthusiastic. Players like Frank Brennan, Charlie Crowe, Alan Kennedy and Jim Pearson, as well as many less well known characters like Carl Wilson, John Shiel, Kevin Todd and Reg Evans. And sadly some who have since passed away; famous names like Jackie Milburn, Joe Harvey, Duggie Wright and Len White to name a few of many. Contact has also been made with former managers, coaches and Chairmen; Gordon Lee and Gordon McKeag are two of several to have given run downs on their career.

The players' families have been also most helpful. From well known names like Lawrie McMenemy who confirmed blood relations with United's schemer Harry, and music star Jimmy Nail who did likewise with 'Peter' Mooney, to relatives of Billy Aitken, Tom Niblo, Andy Aitken, Stan Seymour and Colin Veitch, again just a handful of many spoken to.

The following people have assisted in various ways, several, authors of books researched. My thanks to all. A special thank you to Newcastle supporters Steve Corke and Alan Candlish. And to journalist and long-standing friend, Paul Tully.

A Armstrong, A Appleton, A Ambrosen, P Attaway, S Adamson, F Arrighi, R Borthwick, R Barton, S Basson, T Brown, D Brassington, A Bluff, M Brodie, J Byrne, G Binns, D Batters, G Blackwood, M Braham, G Chalk, C Calder, P Coyde, S Cheshire, T Carder, T Conway, J Crooks, C Cameron, D Clarebrough, M Cooper, T Clapham, T Collings, T Campbell, A Crabtree, R Calley, J Cross, J Cavanagh, P Crate, M Davage, G Dykes, M Dix, D Downs, W Donna, B Dalby, G Davies, P Daw, R Dean, J Diamond, J De Graaf, J Duffy, J Edminson, J Eastwood, J Esther, D Easterby, C Elton, A Fiddes, P Freeman, M Featherstone, C Freddi, D Farmer, G Firth, K Farnsworth, T Frost, G Frome, J Farrier, G Frame, J Ford, F Furness, R Goodwin, A Groom, I Garland, M Golesworthy, J Gibson, R Graham, H Glasper, R Goble, D Goodyear, R Gilbert, J Hunter, D Holley, B Hugman, A Hardisty, B Hunt, J Harding, R Harnwell, R Hockings, R Harris, P Harrison, J Helliar, A Hogg, J Harris, M Hartley, R Howland, A Howland, D Hepton, L Hughes, B Hobbs, L Hewitt, W Hume, S Inglis, M Jones, A Jones, M Jackman, P Jones, M Jarred, M Jay, T Jones, D Johnson, A Jobson, P Jeffs, J Jeffery, M Kirkup, H Keevans, J Kent, B Knight, N Kaufman, D Lamming, E Law, J Litster, R Lindsay, E Lee, J Lawson, S Marshall, T Matthews, G Macey, P Mason, C Martin-Jenkins, E MacBride, A McDonald, I Morrison, H Mason, J Murray, K McCarra, W Marwick, L McMenemy, J McAllister, D McGlone, W McLure, J McKay, M MacDonald, G Mortimer, S Marland, K Mouldon, A Mitchell, W Moorman, C Matheson-Dear, J Maddocks, Millwall FC Museum, D Nannestad, I Nannestad, G Noble, M Neasom, J Northcutt, J Nail, J Norman, A Oliver, M O'Connor, P O'Connor, F Ollier, O Hall Oldsen, O Phillips, N Price, B Pead, M Purkiss, M Roberts, P Rundo, J Rollin, M Robinson, R Redden, J Retter, D Robinson, A Ravenhill, I Ross, J Rickaby, S Renauld, D Smith, G Smailes, W Swann, P Soar, G Sheridan, J Slater, M Stein, J Staff, R Shoesmith, S Searl, N Sands, R Simpson, D Steele, S Smith, M Simons, G Stephanides, P Taylor, R Triggs, T Thwaites, D Turner, F Tweddle, D Ticehurst, G Upton, A White, J Waugh, K Warsop, S Woodhead, D Watson, A Ward, B Watson, J Wilkie, P Woods, M Watson, D Woods, C Wilson, N Wratten, R Wells, J Ward, J Waters, A Wilkie.

Finally a thank you to actor and United supporter Robson Green for his Foreword and to Julian Baskcomb at Polar Publishing for his commitment to this extensive work of almost 1000 biographies as a companion text to 'United: The First 100 Years & More'. His willingness to issue another top quality volume in terms of design and production is appreciated.

Paul Joannou, Club Historian
Edinburgh, October 1996

CONTENTS

Bill McCracken (Ireland), Colin Veitch (England) and Jimmy Howie (Scotland), three international players who lined up for United during the early part of this century.

INTRODUCTION

THE MEN WHO MADE UNITED

The Black'n'White Alphabet is a comprehensive who's who of Newcastle United Football Club and covers a biographical history of every player to wear a black'n'white shirt. All players who have appeared in senior competitive football since United's pioneers Newcastle East End entered action in the Northern League for season 1892-93 are included, a total of over 930 individuals.

When the much smaller first edition of this text was published by Newcastle United Supporters Club in 1983, books covering histories of football clubs and their players were very much a rarity. Over a decade later and soccer literature at long last has boomed, with books published on almost every club. Detailed who's who volumes have become a popular way of recording those players who have thrilled, and at times infuriated, the millions of spectators who watch the sport.

This book features not only all the well known names in United's past, but also all those less famous players to appear for the club, researched down to every last man, whether they played four or 400 matches.

In the period of research, on and off over the last 15 years, piecing together information from numerous sources and slowly identifying a career from birth to death (where applicable) is in many ways like a huge jig-saw. It has occasionally been very time consuming and is not yet complete. More work is needed. There are still a handful of the club's early personalities who are frustratingly difficult to trace information on; contemporary newspapers before the turn of the century being at times scant of hard information, and notoriously contradictory.

Gathering information on United's stars past and present is a lifetime's work; players will come and go, facts will continue to be unearthed in an attempt to obtain a comprehensive biography. And over the coming years I will continue to record information and try to contact former players themselves, or their families. If readers have any further details or photographic material, this will be gratefully received at St James Park or through the publisher. This will be utilised in the club archive and in any follow up editions of this book.

In a text with such a huge amount of data, I have tried hard to eradicate mistakes. Football writing in the past has been prone to error, many carried through the years from volume to volume. United's inter-war full-back Billy Hampson has been noted for decades as the oldest man to appear in an FA Cup final, for United in 1924. Indeed he is so described in the current Rothman's Yearbook, even though mistakenly noted as Walter (his brother Walker - another error). This however, is wrong, as when Norwich City historian Mike Davage checked his birth certificate Hampson ended up being two years younger! In summary a great deal of effort has gone into checking and re-checking facts and figures, and also to confirm the many queries which have arisen. However, while every care has been taken it is maybe inevitable in a work containing so much material that errors have slipped the net. Corrections will be welcome on any entry.

This book is a text that will give nostalgic pleasure, reviving memories. It is also though a historical research document for present and future generations - a history of the 'Men Who Made United'.

... and the dog! Rex, the club's Great Dane mascot early this century.

NOTES ON THE TEXT

Every effort has been made to produce a comprehensive biography, including not only information during the player's period at Gallowgate, but also details of his overall career, and wider life, away from Tyneside.

Appearances and goals for each player are the total for all first-class competitive games, ie Football League (including Play Offs and Test Matches), Northern League, FA Cup (including qualifying games and annulled fixtures), FL Cup and European tournaments. Wartime league and cup matches are included, as are appearances in sundry competitions such as the Texaco Cup, Anglo-Scottish & Italian Cups, as well as Mercantile, Simod, Full Members Cup, Zenith competition and Charity Shield games. These are classed as 'Other' appearances. Friendlies, minor and local matches such as hospital cup fixtures and the like are not included, neither are abandoned and postponed fixtures. However the Football League season prior to World War Two in 1939-40 is. Substitute appearances are given, noted in parenthesis. They are correct up to the end of the 1995-96 season. Where appearances and goals are quoted in the text, they are generally league and cup totals unless stated. Many hours have been spent checking anomalies in these statistics. The vast majority have now been resolved.

Debuts for Newcastle United are indicated. All fixtures are the player's first senior appearance for the club in league or cup football inclusive of substitute entries. The career section of each biography tracks the players' movements in consecutive order on leaving school. Schools football has been omitted except for international honours, while loan deals are noted as the season in which the transaction took place. For easy reference, the dates at the beginning of each biography, eg 1946-1948, refer to the years the player joined and left United.

Club titles are those at the point in time, eg Birmingham City will be noted as that title from 1945 to date, and as Small Heath from 1888 and Birmingham from 1905 to 1945. For clarity the change from Newcastle East End to Newcastle United has been shown as May 1892, even though the Newcastle United title did not come into being until some time later. Transfer fees quoted are generally those as recorded in the club's official Player Ledgers or Minutes of Board Meetings. Otherwise fees are those appearing in the press or other publications.

Honours achieved have been correlated up to the close season of 1996. This section gives each player's major achievements during his career and the year for each honour always represents the second-half of the season in which the honour was obtained, eg 1925 represents the 1924-25 season. For those players who have taken part in championship or promotion sides, a minimum of ten games (including substitute appearances) has been used for qualification, however in some cases the player may not have received a medal for any title success.

International appearances are covered in detail, although honours do not include sundry representative fixtures such as Navy or RAF selections. International trial games are included with the span of appearances noted, eg 1923-29. Also included is success achieved on the continent where traced. Secondary competitions such as the Texaco Cup or Anglo-Italian Cup are not included in this section.

Additional sections at the rear of the book cover those players who did not graduate to league or senior cup action. These include war-guest players and those personalities who played in competitions like the Anglo-Scottish or Simod Cup without appearing in league or cup football for United. Also included are many of the players to have taken to the field for United's pioneers Newcastle East End and West End from 1882 to 1892. The club's managers and first-team coaches are covered also, as are Newcastle United's Chairmen.

Inevitably readers will, especially from younger generations, compare players from the Twenties decade with those say of the Seventies, or names from the Thirties to those from the turn of the century. Bobby Cowell will be compared with Frank Clark or Bill McCracken. Andy Aitken may be grouped with Frank Brennan and Philippe Albert as to who was the best centre-half. It has to be remembered that during the development of the game, several changes have occurred to alter the style of play and tactics of football, while additionally in several cases although the positional label remains the same, ie full-back or centre-half, the actual function of that position has altered considerably.

Andy Aitken was a centre-half of repute in United's golden Edwardian era; to compare him with Frank Brennan is impossible. Centre-half play in Aitken's day was far from the tough, physical defenders' role in Brennan's. In Aitken's case they were skilful half-backs who were more like a midfield creator of today.

The soccer spectrum can be divided into largely three eras. Prior to 1925 the field of play was split into a 2-3-5 formation; two full-backs acting solely as defenders and rarely crossing the half-way line; three half-backs working both as creators and defenders; and five forwards consisting of two wingers who usually stuck hard to their touchline, one centre-forward with two inside men alongside.

During this period the offside law was such that pairs of full-backs, notably led by United's Bill McCracken, were able to almost catch forwards offside at will. Football was becoming quite unbearable to watch in many cases, and in 1925 an expected change in the offside law occurred and with it an important change in the role of the centre-half and to a lesser extent, of inside-forwards.

Now that the two full-backs could not cope with defending duties alone, the centre-half was turned into a defensive player, a stopper in the middle of the rearguard. The line-up became 3-2-5. The remainder of the formation was mainly as before, but with the two inside-forwards dropping back to give the now under-strength wing-half-backs a helping hand in midfield.

This system lasted for over 40 years, until Sir Alf Ramsey's wingless system dramatically changed the face of English soccer in 1966. The advent of the double centre-half system, the near eradication of wingers and total change in labelling of players evolved. Gone were inside-forwards and wing-halves, now midfield men and strikers reigned supreme. Three systems became popular; 4-4-2, 4-3-3 and lesser used 4-2-4. With no out and out wingers the two full-backs became attack minded and the overlapping back became nationally known. Currently football is played in much this format, although we have seen the re-introduction of wide players and a three centre-half game which has evolved a wing-back role. And we now see formations packing midfield in a 4-5-1 or 3-5-2 layout.

So when reading through this Alphabet of United's players remember how soccer has changed over the years and what role players had in their own era. Remember too the other factors which have altered; the initiation of the modern ball, new remedies for injuries, streamlining of kit and not least the huge influx of money into the game. An important factor to also note is the decline of reserve football. In years gone by United's second eleven were of a standard equivalent to the present day Second or Third Divisions and attracted gates of up to 20,000. The individuals who perhaps only played a handful of senior games on the record sheet were still, by modern standards, fine players.

Abbreviations used:

(a) = away fixture

am, or, amat = amateur

app = apprentice, or youth training scheme or equivalent

app.(s). = appearance(s)

asst = assistant

b. = born

Brit = Great Britain

c = circa

CBE = Commander of the British Empire

champs = champions

Chair = Chairman

Co = County

cs = close season

CW = Colliery Welfare FC

d. = died

Dir = Director

div = division

EC = European Champions Cup

ECWC = European Cup Winners Cup

EL = Eire League

Eng = England

Eur = European

FA = Football Association

FAAC = FA Amateur Cup

FAC = FA Cup

FAT = FA Trophy

FAV = FA Vase

FAVC = FA Victory Cup

FAYC = FA Youth Cup

FC = French Cup, or, Football Club

FL = Football League

FLa = FL abandoned fixture

FLC = Football League Cup

free = free transfer

FrL = French League

FrLC = French League Cup

FWA = Football Writers Association

gl.(s). = goal/goals

(h) = home fixture

ICFC = Inter Cities Fairs Cup

IC = Irish Cup (before nation split)

IL = Irish League(before nation split)

Irel = Ireland(before nation split, or, combined side)

Jnrs = junior appearances, or, junior club

LMA = League Managers Association

(m) = honours when a manager

MBE = Member of the Order of the British Empire

(N) = North; indicating FL division or war league

NIC = Northern Ireland Cup

NIL = Northern Ireland League

N.Irel = Northern Ireland

NL = Northern League

NPL = Northern Premier League

nr = near

OBE = Officer of the Order of the British Empire

PFA = Professional Footballers Association

PL = Premier League

pmt = permanent transfer

pro = professional

prom = promotion

qv = cross reference

(S) = South; indicating FL division or war league

SC = Scottish Cup, or, social club when affixed to club

sch = schoolboy

Scot = Scotland

SL = Scottish League

SLC = Scottish League Cup

SJC = Scottish Junior Cup

SnL = Southern League

SQC = Scottish Qualifying Cup

sub = substitute

SVC = Scottish Victory Cup

Switz = Switzerland

UEFAC = UEFA Cup

unoff = unofficial

u21 = under 21

u23 = under 23

VC = Vauxhall Conference

WC = World Cup

wg = war guest

WL = Welsh League

WrC = War Cup

WsC/WshC = Welsh Cup

ADAMS, George

Role: Left-half 1896-1897
5' 10"
b. Ayrshire

CAREER: Kilmarnock Mar 1889/Cowlairs cs 1892/Kilmarnock Oct 1894/UNITED Feb 1896/Hebburn Argyle cs 1897/ Southern League football 1899/ Darlington St Augustine 1903.

Debut v Loughborough Town (a) 7/3/1896

Although a good young prospect at St James Park after impressing United's officials with some splendid displays north of the border, George Adams was deputy to the powerful Jimmy Stott for most of his stay on Tyneside and had little opportunity to claim a regular first team place.

Appearances:
FL: 13 apps. 1 gl.
Total: *13 apps. 1 gl.*

AGNEW, William Barbour

Role: Left-back 1902-1904
5' 8"
b. New Cumnock, near Kilmarnock,
16th December 1880
d. 20th August 1936

CAREER: Afton Lads(New Cumnock)/Kilmarnock Nov 1900/UNITED May 1902 £200/ Middlesbrough June 1904/ Kilmarnock Sept 1906/ Sunderland May 1908/ Falkirk Sept 1910 to 1912/ Third Lanark trainer Aug 1913/East Stirlingshire Sept 1913.

Bill Agnew

Debut v Stoke (h) 6/9/02

But for the eminent names of Carr, McCombie and McCracken, William Agnew would have had a far more fruitful stay at St James Park. A defender of the finest pedigree, he was well built and brave in combating attacks. Bill operated in both full-back roles during his career and was the first of only a handful of men to appear for all three of the north east's major clubs. The blond-haired Agnew made a big name for himself during his second spell at Kilmarnock when he was capped for his country.

Appearances:
FL: 43 apps. 0 gls.
FAC: 1 app. 0 gls.
Total:
44 apps. 0 gls.
Honours:
3 Scot caps 1907-08/2 SL caps 1907-08/ Scot trial app. 1908

AITKEN, Andrew

Role: Half-back 1895-1906
5' 8"
b. Ayr, 27th April 1877
d. Ponteland, nr Newcastle upon Tyne, 15th February 1955

CAREER: Elmbank/Ayr Thistle/Ayr Parkhouse 1894/UNITED July 1895 (Kilmarnock loan 1898-99)/Middlesbrough player-manager Oct 1906 £500/Leicester Fosse Feb 1909, becoming player-manager Apr 1909/Dundee player May 1911/ Kilmarnock June 1912/retired due to a groin injury Jan 1913/Gateshead Town manager June 1913/Arsenal scout.

Debut v Loughborough Town (h) 7/9/1895 (scored once)

Andy Aitken

One of the early game's most prominent players, Andy Aitken was known as 'Daddler'. He was well respected for his drive, stamina, attacking ability and head play - a central midfielder who always supported his forwards. Aitken took part in United's inaugural First Division game during 1898 and skippered the side on many occasions. He was only a teenager when he first appeared for the Magpies, but quickly made an impression and was a tremendous asset to the club during their rise to become Football League champions.

One biography of the day noted Aitken as being, "of the bustling type", while another recorded him as, "lean, lissom, artistic in method and touch". Colleague Alex Gardner once said, "He may lack physique, but for clever headwork and terrier-like persistency he would be hard to beat". Aitken was extremely adaptable and arguably the club's most versatile player, operating in every position except goalkeeper for Newcastle. He was also often capped by Scotland, and led out his country too. A former grocer's boy, Aitken was a player above the ordinary, one of the elite in football before World War One. He later became a publican for a time, residing on Tyneside to his death. Andy was related to Alex Gardner through marriage; the two United stars wed sisters who were 'Tiller Girls' of the time.

Appearances:
FL: 316 apps. 33 gls.
FAC: 33 apps. 8 gls.
Total: *349 apps. 41 gls.*
Honours:
14 Scot caps 1901-11/Scot trial app. 1901-10/ FL champs 1905/FAC finalist 1905, 1906/ FL div 2 prom 1898.

AITKEN, Robert Sime

Role: Midfield 1990-1991
6' 0"
b. Irvine, 24th November 1958

CAREER: Ayr United Boys' Club/Glasgow Celtic Boys' Club/Glasgow Celtic June 1975/ UNITED Jan 1990 £500,000/St Mirren player-coach Aug 1991 £150,000/Aberdeen asst player-manager June 1992 £100,000, becoming manager in Feb 1995.

Debut v Leicester City (h) 13/1/90

After 667 senior games for Celtic, Scotland's captain Robert Aitken arrived on Tyneside as something of a veteran, but with the inspirational qualities United's side needed at the time. Nicknamed 'Roy', the 31 year-old commanded respect and had a remarkable debut for the Magpies, leading the side to a terrific 5-4 victory over Leicester after being 4-2 behind. Big and tough, Roy never shirked from a challenge and was far more skilled on the ball than many critics gave him credit for. Aitken mainly operated in midfield for United, but also appeared in central defence, and his whole-hearted displays almost took

the black'n'whites to promotion in 1989-90, United failing in the play-offs. A regular for Scotland, he led his country in the 1986 World Cup finals and was indispensable to Celtic, lifting trophy after trophy at Parkhead including a Scottish double in 1988, Celtic's centenary year. He was though, a fiery player at times, once sent-off in a Scottish Cup final, and by the time he joined the Magpies had become something of a victimised player in his native country. With a change in manager Aitken was discarded by United's new boss, Ossie Ardiles, when perhaps his vast experience was exactly what Newcastle's young side needed. Also known as 'The Bear', Roy represented Great Britain schools at basketball before concentrating on a career in football.

Appearances:
FL: 56 apps. 1 gl.
FAC: 6 apps. 0 gls.
FLC: 2 apps. 0 gls
Other: 1 app. 0 gls.
Total: *65 apps. 1 gl.*
Honours:
57 Scot caps 1980-92/16 Scot u21 caps 1977-85/Scot youth app./Scot schools app./ SL champs 1977, 1979, 1981, 1982, 1986, 1988/SC winner 1977, 1980, 1985, 1988, 1989/SC finalist 1984/SLC winner 1983, 1996(m)/SLC finalist 1977, 1978, 1984, 1987, 1993.

Roy Aitken

AITKEN, William John

Role: Outside-right 1920-1924
5' 9"
b. Peterhead, 2nd February 1894
d. Dunston, Gateshead, 9th August 1973

CAREER: Kirkintilloch Harp 1914/ Kirkintilloch Rob Roy 1915/Queen's Park Sept 1917/Glasgow Rangers Aug 1918 (Port Vale loan 1919-20)/UNITED May 1920 £2,500/Preston North End June 1924 £1,000/ Chorley Sept 1926/Norwich City Dec 1926 £175/Bideford Town player-trainer Sept 1927/ Juventus (Italy) c1929/AS Cannes (France) Oct 1930/Stade de Reims (France) 1933/ Retired and returned to Tyneside 1936/ Brussels (Belgium) player-trainer c1946/ Brann Bergen (Norway) player-trainer 1948/ Retired c1950.

Debut v West Bromwich Albion (h) 28/8/20

A typical winger of his day, clever, fast, and good enough to appear in the Anglo-Scots versus Home Scots fixtures, Aitken scored plenty of goals over the border, but struggled to find the net in England where he concentrated on being a provider. With the Magpies, he had his best season during 1920-21 when Newcastle ended in fifth position in the First Division table. The Scot lost his place in United's side during the first half of the 1924 FA Cup winning season when he found both Jimmy Low and Willie Cowan ahead of him in team selection. Aitken left St James Park for Deepdale soon after the trophy arrived on Tyneside. In 1929 he won the Morpeth sprint and also took part in the prestigious Powderhall Run, while during World War Two he was employed at the giant Vickers Armstrong factory alongside the Tyne. His many years on the continent, where he won honours with Cannes, had made Billy fluent in French and Italian and, when he finally called a halt to his long playing career, he took up the role of representative at a north-east wine and spirit merchant. He resided on Tyneside until his death. It is recorded that the Scot possessed a fiery temperament; once, when starved of the ball during a game, he kicked it out of the Gallowgate stadium in disgust when it finally came his way!

Appearances:
FL: 104 apps. 10 gls.
FAC: 6 apps. 0 gls.
Total: *110 apps. 10 gls.*
Honours:
Scot trial app. 1920-21/French champs 1932/ French Cup winner 1932.

ALBERT, Philippe

Role: Centre-half 1994-date
6' 3"
b. Bouillon, Belgium, 10th August 1967

CAREER: Dematter (Belgium)/Standard Bouillon(Belgium)/RSC Charleroi (Belgium) 1986 £12,000/KV Mechelen(Belgium) cs 1989/ RSC Anderlecht(Belgium) cs 1992/ UNITED Aug 1994 £2.65m.

Debut v Leicester City (a) 21/8/94

Philippe Albert

Established Belgian international Philippe Albert had been a long term target of Newcastle United and during the 1994 World Cup finals in the USA, Kevin Keegan saw Albert stand out as a special talent. Within weeks of the Magpies' boss returning from the States, Albert became a United player. Cool and confident on the ball, he was a defender who could attack with menace in the continental fashion, striding forward from the middle of defence with style. A tough and no-nonsense stopper too, Albert possesses an exquisite left-foot and much of Newcastle's passing game starts from his control and distributive vision at the back. A European thoroughbred, he appeared for his country in both the 1990 and 1994 World Cups. Albert immediately became a crowd favourite at St James Park with his classy style and was just starting to take the Premiership by storm when an unfortunate training mishap forced him onto the sidelines for over six months with a cruciate ligament injury. Dangerous at free-kicks and corners, Albert can hit a venomous shot and returned to help Newcastle's assault on the Premier League crown in 1996. Brought up in the Ardennes, Albert is Flemish speaking with a first class command of English.

Appearances:
PL: 36(4) apps. 6 gls.
FAC: 2 apps. 1 gl.
FLC: 6(1) apps. 2 gls.
Eur: 4 apps. 0 gls.
Total: 48(5) apps. 9 gls.
Honours:
37 Belg caps 1987-date/Belg Lg champs 1993, 1994/Belg cup winner 1994/Belg cup finalist 1991, 1992/Belg Player-of-the-Year 1992.

ALDERSON, John Thomas

Role: Goalkeeper 1913-1919
6' 0"
b. Crook, Co. Durham, 28th November 1891
d. Sunderland, 17th February 1972

CAREER: Crook Jnrs/Shildon Athletic/ Middlesbrough amat July 1912/Shildon Athletic/UNITED Feb 1913 £30/Crystal Palace May 1919 £50/Pontypridd July 1924/Sheffield United May 1925/Exeter City May 1929/ Torquay United trainer Nov 1930/ Worcester City Sept 1931-Apr 1932/ Crook Town.

Debut v Woolwich Arsenal (h) 25/1/13

Known as Jack to football fans of his era, John Alderson became a noted, consistent goalkeeper who made his name away from Gallowgate. A reserve to Jimmy Lawrence at St James Park, he also had tough competition from two other professional 'keepers at Gallowgate in Sid Blake and William Mellor. As a consequence he moved on following World War One and, being posted to London when in the services, signed for Crystal Palace where he quickly became something of a legend appearing over 200 times for the Eagles. Alderson was noted for his ability to stop penalties - he once saved two spot-kicks in the same match - and was good enough to play for England, even though he was out of the top division. Once retired from the game, Jack became a farmer residing in the north east.

John Alderson

Appearances:
FL: 1 app. 0 gls.
Total: *1 app. 0 gls.*
Honours:
1 Eng cap 1923/FL div 3 champs 1921/ 1 SnL app. 1920/1 WL app. 1925.

ALDERSON, Stuart

Role: Outside-right 1965-1967
5' 9"
b. Bishop Auckland, 15th August 1948

CAREER: Evenwood Town/UNITED Aug 1965 £50/York City June 1967 free to cs 1968/ Ashington/West Auckland asst-manager 1980 becoming treasurer and general manager to date.

Debut v Burnley (h) 10/9/66

Stuart Alderson was a teenage debutant for United, unexpectedly thrown into league action at a time of poor results when the Magpies were struggling to steer clear of relegation from the First Division. A rival of Bryan Robson at St James Park, Alderson found it difficult to cope with the rigours of a

relegation dog-fight and quickly returned to Central League soccer. It was 'Pop' Robson who soon flourished in the Magpie line-up, and Alderson drifted onto the non-league scene. Stuart lives in County Durham and is employed by Hydro Polmor Plastics in Newton Aycliffe.

Appearances:
FL: 3 apps. 0 gls.
FLC: 1 app. 0 gls.
Total: *4 apps. 0 gls.*

ALLAN, Richard

Richard Allan

Role: Outside-right 1897-1898
5' 8"

CAREER: Preston North End/Chorley/Dundee 1896/ UNITED May 1897/Bristol St George cs 1898.
Debut v Walsall (a) 11/9/1897

Richard Allan, a very business-like forward, rarely wasted the ball and was a regular in United's successful promotion side in 1898. Along with Willie Wardrope, he was one of the chief providers for centre-forward Jock Peddie that season, but was discarded for the Magpies' debut in the First Division.

Appearances:
FL: 24 apps. 4 gls.
FAC: 5 apps. 0 gls.
Total: *29 apps. 4 gls.*
Honours: *FL div 2 prom 1898*

ALLAN, Stanley James E.

Role: Inside-forward 1908-1911
5' 10"
b. Wallsend, 28th December 1886
d. Wallsend, 4th May 1919

CAREER: Wallsend/Sunderland/UNITED June 1908/West Bromwich Albion May 1911 £150/Nottingham Forest June 1912/ Retired 1913.
Debut v Leicester Fosse (h) 5/9/08

A fringe player at St James Park, Stanley Allan began his career as a half-back, but ended playing at either inside or centre-forward. Commonly known as Jack, he was fast, strong and of the old-fashioned bustling breed. Allan had a good scoring run in season 1908-09 as a stand-in for Albert Shepherd, when he grabbed five goals in eight games following his debut. Moving to West Brom, Allan was still unable to command a regular place although he helped Albion to the 1912 FA Cup Final, appearing in the semi-final replay. He joined the RAMC on the outbreak of war in 1914 and served throughout the hostilities, only to die aged just 31 of pneumonia within two weeks of his safe return to Tyneside.

Appearances:
FL: 15 apps. 5 gls.
Others: 1 app. 1 gl.
Total: *16 apps. 6 gls.*

ALLCHURCH, Ivor John M.B.E.

Role: Inside-forward 1958-1962
5' 10"
b. Swansea, 16th December 1929

CAREER: Plesmarl Jnrs/ Swansea Town May 1947/ Shrewsbury Town guest during army service/ UNITED Oct 1958 £28,000/ Cardiff City Aug 1962 £15,000/ Swansea Town July 1965 £6,500/ Worcester City cs 1968/ Bishoptown/ Haverford West/ Pontardawe Athletic.

Debut v Leicester City (h) 11/10/58 (scored twice)

One of the finest inside-forwards to appear in post-war football, Ivor was a distinguished schemer who played on either the right or left, and who turned out in over 700 first-class games. A goalscorer too, Allchurch was deadly within shooting range and scored over 250 goals. Establishing himself as a player of special ability with Swansea and Wales, Ivor moved into the big-time, and the First Division when he transferred to Newcastle for a new club record fee. A gentleman on the field with a complete repertoire of skills, he played with bundles of panache and possessed a hypnotic body swerve as well as a deceptive turn of speed. Ivor stroked the ball around with precision and grace, and was a master of the long pass as he linked alongside Len White with menace for United. Immediately he became a crowd favourite on Tyneside, yet his time at Gallowgate was destined to coincide with a period of decline for United, and Allchurch couldn't stop the club slipping into the Second Division in 1961. Ivor held the record for international appearances for his country for many years - including the 1958 World Cup - his younger brother Len was also a Welsh international, while another brother, Sid, appeared for the Welsh at amateur level. Allchurch was awarded the MBE for his services to the game in 1966; he was United's top paid star at £60 per week after the abolition of the maximum wage. He later resided in Bishopton, near Swansea and played local football into his 50th year when employed as a storeman.

Appearances:
FL: 143 apps. 46 gls.
FAC: 8 apps. 4 gls.
FLC: 3 apps. 1 gls.
Total: *154 apps. 51 gls.*
Honours:
68 Wales caps 1951-66/4 WL apps.
1951-54/WsC winner 1950, 1964, 1965,
1966/WsC finalist 1956, 1957.

ALLEN, Edward

Role: Left-back 1900-1901
b. Montrose, c. 1875

CAREER: Dundee Wanderers Sept 1896/ Millwall Athletic Oct 1899/UNITED Aug 1900/Dundee May 1901/Watford July 1902/ Dundee 1903 to c.1905.

Debut v Stoke (h) 15/9/1900

Purchased from London club Millwall at the start of the 1900-01 season, Edward Allen was deputy to Dave Gardner and Charles Burgess and found it difficult to make a first team place his own. He did turn out in four games for the club, as well as in several friendlies, but was released during the summer of 1901. When in the capital, Allen took part in Southern League Millwall's giant-killing run to the FA Cup semi-final of 1900. Newcastle were suitably impressed with the Scot's form in this headlining cup run and quickly brought him north.

Appearances:
FL: 4 apps. 0 gls.
Total: *4 apps. 0 gls.*

ALLEN, Geoffrey Barry

Role: Outside-left & Coach 1964-1974,
1979-1981
5' 7"
b. Walker, Newcastle upon Tyne,
10th November 1946

CAREER: UNITED Apr 1964/Retired Mar 1970 due to injury/UNITED asst-coach Mar 1970 to June 1974/Gateshead coach 1974/ North Shields manager 1977/UNITED asst-coach July 1979/Mansfield Town coach July 1981 to Jan 1983.

Debut v Norwich City (h) 25/4/64

A down to earth Geordie from the Scrogg Road area of Walker, Geoff Allen was a most unlucky player with injuries. But for a persistent cruciate ligament

Geoff Allen

problem he would have no doubt made a big name for himself in United's First Division - and Inter Cities Fairs Cup side. It was in the club's very first European fixture against Feyenoord in 1968 that Allen made the headlines. He destroyed the Dutch giants with a brilliant display of wing play, but a few weeks later was on the treatment table with a bad leg injury which wrecked his career when only 24 years old. At one time one of the youngest ever players to appear for the club, rosy-cheeked Allen later returned to Gallowgate as coach.

Appearances:
FL: 22 apps. 1 gl.
FAC: 1 app. 0 gls.
FLC: 1 app. 0 gls.
Eur: 2 apps. 0 gls.
Total: *26 apps. 1 gl.*
Honours:
Eng youth app. 1965.

ALLEN, John

Role: Centre-forward 1898-1901
5' 10"
b. Bishop Auckland

CAREER: Bishop Auckland/ UNITED amat Jan 1898 to 1901 when he returned to local football.

Debut v Darwen (h) 15/1/1898

A well-built youngster, Allen deputised at centre-forward for the established Jock Peddie during the club's first promotion campaign in 1897-98. Apart from his single appearance for the Magpies, he was always considered a reserve and played out his career in United's Northern Alliance side. He was signed from Bishop Auckland illegally, without their permission, and United were censored and fined £10 while secretary Frank Watt was suspended for a period. Allen, meanwhile, had his league registration with the black and whites revoked.

Appearances:
FL: 1 app. 0 gls.
Total: *1 app. 0 gls.*

ALLEN, John William Alcroft

Role: Centre-forward
1931-1934
5' 10"
*b. Newburn,
Newcastle upon Tyne,
31st January 1903
d. Burnopfield, Co Durham,
19th November 1957*

CAREER: Prudhoe Castle/Leeds United Feb 1922/Brentford Aug 1924/Sheffield Wednesday Mar 1927/UNITED June 1931 £3,500/Bristol Rovers Nov 1934 £200/ Gateshead Aug 1935 £100/Ashington 1936/ Retired Feb 1936.

Debut v Liverpool (h) 29/8/31

An aggressive, bustling leader with a deadly left foot shot, Jack Allen arrived back on his native Tyneside after plundering 85 senior goals in only 114 league and cup games for Sheffield Wednesday. He was the Owls' leading goalscorer for two years in succession as the Tykes twice lifted the championship trophy. During his early months at St James Park though, Jack struggled and failed to live up to his big billing, but slowly found his form

Jack Allen

and by the time United set off on a Wembley FA Cup run in 1932, Allen was the Magpies' danger man. He netted seven crucial goals, including two in the famous 'Over the Line' final with Arsenal which earned him immortality in football history. Jack had also been involved in another highly controversial cup goal in the 1931 semi-final for Sheffield Wednesday against Huddersfield. His brother Ralph, turned out for Brentford and Charlton Athletic, and Jack remained in the north east after retirement becoming a noted publican at The Travellers Rest in Burnopfield to his death.

Appearances:
FL: 81 apps. 34 gls.
FAC: 9 apps. 7 gls.
Others: 1 app. 0 gls.
Total: *91 apps. 41 gls.*
Honours:
FL champs 1929, 1930/FAC winner 1932.

ALLEN, Malcolm

Role: Striker or Midfield 1993-1995
5' 8"
b. Deiniolen, Caernarfonshire, 21st March 1967

CAREER: Watford app July 1983, pro Mar 1985(Aston Villa loan 1987-88)/Norwich City Aug 1988 £175,000/Millwall Mar 1990 £400,000/UNITED Aug 1993 £300,000/Retired due to injury Dec 1995/Gwynedd Council coach and development officer July 1996.

Debut v Tottenham Hotspur (h) 14/8/93

Malcolm Allen

Rejected by Watford and then Manchester United as a trialist, Malcolm Allen received another chance at Vicarage Road and carved out a decent career in the game. Making his Football League debut in November 1985, he made only four senior appearances under Graham Taylor's guidance before being called up by Wales for his international debut. Skilful on the ball with a sure pass and shot, Allen arrived at Gallowgate as cover for the injured Peter Beardsley as United embarked on their inaugural season in the Premier League. He made a good start in a black'n'white shirt and found the net with confidence, but Malcolm was then badly injured and found himself on the sidelines for almost a year with a knee ligament problem, this after a lengthy spell out of action when at Carrow Road. By the time he returned to fitness, Allen not only found several multi-million pound stars at St James Park ahead of him for a first-team place but soon suffered an injury relapse which forced him to leave the game aged 28 after seven operations on his knee. He took up a post in north Wales as a Welsh FA Schools Coach in the summer of 1996. Malcolm's younger brother Gavin appeared for the Welsh Under-21 side and for Tranmere Rovers.

Appearances:
PL: 9(1) apps. 5 gls.
FLC: 3 apps. 2 gls.
Total: *12(1) apps. 7 gls.*
Honours:
14 Wales caps 1986-94/1 Wales B app. 1991/6 Wales youth apps./1 FL app. 1993.

ALLON, Joseph Ball

Role: Centre-forward 1984-1987
5' 11"
b. Washington, 12th November 1966

CAREER: UNITED app, pro Nov 1984/ Swansea City cs 1987 free/Hartlepool United loan Oct 1988, pmt Nov 1988 £12,500/ Chelsea Aug 1991 £200,000(Port Vale loan 1991-92)Brentford Nov 1992 £275,000/ Southend United Sept 1993 exch/Port Vale Mar 1994/Lincoln City July 1995 £42,500/ Hartlepool United Oct 1995 £50,000.

Debut v Stoke City (h) 1/12/84

As a youngster, blond-haired Joe Allon scored almost 120 goals for United's reserve and junior sides in less than 150 games, and

Joe Allon

overshadowed Paul Gascoigne in the same Magpie line-up as Newcastle's kids won the FA Youth Cup. An 18-year-old debutant who should really have been given a better chance in the club's senior line-up, he rivalled two other centre-forwards, Cunningham and Whitehurst, both of whom registered mediocre records in a Magpie shirt. Allon was released by manager Willie McFaul, even though he had been the club's overall leading scorer in each of the previous three seasons. Joe earned a second opportunity in the top flight, this time with Chelsea after becoming the top striker in the Fourth Division in 1990/91, but again his chances were limited and he drifted around the lower divisions for the remainder of his career - but always grabbing goals. Despite his travels, Joe was a United man through and through and once remarked, "When I bleed, I bleed black and white". His brother Paul appeared for non-league Whickham in the 1981 FA Vase final.

Appearances:
FL: 9 apps. 2 gls.
FLC: 1 app. 0 gls.
Total: *10 apps. 2 gls.*
Honours:
Eng youth app. 1985/
FAYC winner 1985/
FL div 4 prom 1988, 1991.

ANCELL, *Robert Francis Dudgeon*

Role: Left-back 1936-1944
5' 10"
b. Dumfries, 16th June 1911
d. Monifieth, nr Dundee, 5th July 1987

CAREER: Mid-Annandale jnrs/St Mirren Feb 1930/UNITED Aug 1936 £2,750/ Carlisle United war-guest 1939-40/ Blackpool war-guest 1941-42/ Rochdale war-guest 1941-42/ Blackburn Rovers war-guest 1941-43/ Derby County war-guest 1943-44/ Burnley war-guest 1945-46/Aberdeen war-guest/Dundee player-trainer July 1944 £150/ Aberdeen player-trainer 1948/Berwick Rangers player-manager 1950/Dunfermline Athletic manager 1952/Motherwell manager cs 1955/Dundee manager Mar 1965/Dundee asst-coach Sept 1968/Nottingham Forest scout Oct 1969.

Debut v Barnsley (h) 29/8/36

Bobby Ancell was a great favourite with the St James Park crowd in the years leading up to World War Two. Slightly built, he was a sound and capable defender who contested with footballing skills and anticipation rather than brawn. Cool headed, he was likened to the famous inter-war full-back, Warney Cresswell in style, one of the elite of his day. Ancell was persuaded to join the Magpies by manager Tom Mather at Dumfries railway station where the pair underwent negotiations as the trains went by. Bobby later became a noted manager north of the border, especially when in charge of Motherwell

Bobby Ancell

for a decade, where he created the 'Ancell Babes', a side which included Ian St John. During the war he served in the RAF as a training instructor and guested for a number of clubs as he travelled around the country. Ancell resided alongside the Tay following retirement.

Appearances:
FL: 97 apps. 1 gl.
FAC: 5 apps. 0 gls.
War: 53 apps. 0 gls.
Total: *155 apps. 1 gl.*
Honours:
2 Scot caps 1937/1 Scot war cap 1940/SC finalist 1934/SL Div 2 prom 1936, 1955 (m).

ANDERSON, Andrew L.

Role: Outside-left 1908-1912
5' 8"
b. Glasgow

CAREER: Ashfield jnrs/St
Mirren/UNITED May 1908
£350/Third Lanark May 1912
£100/Leicester Fosse July
1914/Abercorn 1919.

Debut v Woolwich Arsenal (a) 12/9/08

Andrew Anderson came to Tyneside
with good reviews from his days in
Paisley with St Mirren. An unselfish
winger who always played for the
team, he performed well for United.
Anderson shared the flanker's berth
with another noted Scot of the time,
George Wilson, the pair often playing
together at inside and outside-left as
Newcastle lifted the title in season
1908-09. On the fringe of a Scotland
cap, Andrew was fast and direct rather
than tricky.

Appearances:
FL: 61 apps. 5 gls.
FAC: 6 apps. 2 gls
Others: 1 app. 0 gls.
Total: 68 apps. 7 gls.
Honours:
FL champs 1909/SC finalist 1908.

ANDERSON, John Christopher Patrick

Role: Right-back or Centre-half & Coach
1982-1992
5' 11"
b. Dublin, 7th November 1959

CAREER: Stella Maris(Dublin)/West
Bromwich Albion Nov 1977/Preston North
End Aug 1979/UNITED Aug 1982 free/
Retired due to injury Jan 1992/Berwick
Rangers manager June 1992/UNITED asst-
coach Sept 1992/Dunston Federation
Mar 1993/Whitley Bay Dec 1993/Dunston
Federation 1994 - cs 1994/Later appearing in
local Sunday football notably for Blakelaw SC
and Walbottle Masons.

Debut v Blackburn Rovers (a) 1/9/82 (sub)

John Anderson

United received grand service from John Anderson following his arrival on a free transfer during the summer of 1982. Released by Gordon Lee at Preston, the Dubliner proved United's ex boss wrong as he became a huge terrace favourite with his gutsy, never-say-die attitude on the field. Versatile at full-back, central defence or in the midfield anchor role, John had few of the finer skills on the ball, but was a workmanlike and honest professional respected by his team-mates. Consistent and reliable, he missed only one game during the Magpies' promotion campaign of 1983-84. An ankle injury picked up in a friendly match troubled him for almost four years and eventually forced him to quit after a decade at St James Park. John had a well supported testimonial fixture in April 1992 (13,780) and later remained in the north east working for local radio and assisting Newcastle Kestrels women's football club. Anderson played Gaelic football as a teenager and was also at Manchester United for trials.

Appearances:
FL: 285(16) apps. 14 gls.
FAC: 14 apps. 0 gls.
FLC: 17 apps. 1 gl.
Others: 6(1) apps. 0 gls.
Total: *322(17) apps. 15 gls.*
Honours:
16 Eire caps 1980-89/1 Eire u21 cap/
Eire youth app./FL div 2 prom 1984.

ANDERSON, Stanley

Role: Right-half 1963-1965
6' 0"
b. Horden, Co Durham, 27th February 1934

CAREER: Horden CW/Springwell United/ Sunderland am. June 1949, pro Feb 1951/ UNITED Nov 1963 £19,000/Middlesbrough player-coach Nov 1965 £11,500/ Middlesbrough manager Apr 1966/ AEK Athens (Greece) coach Jan 1973/ Panathinaikos (Greece) coach May 1974/ Queens Park Rangers asst-coach, then asst-manager June 1974 to Nov 1974/ Manchester City scout Dec 1974/ Doncaster Rovers manager Feb 1975/ Bolton Wanderers coach Nov 1978, becoming manager Feb 1980 to May 1981/ Occasional scout, including for Newcastle United.

Debut v Cardiff City (h) 9/11/63

Stan Anderson

A cultured, whole-hearted half-back, Stan Anderson was something of a legend at Roker Park for over a decade, holding the Reds' match record for several years. Sunderland, Newcastle and Middlesbrough skipper, he made a total of over 600 appearances for the north-east's three senior clubs. When 29 years old, Stan joined the Magpies in a shock move which stunned Wearside, the beginning of Joe Harvey's push to rejoin the First Division elite. Anderson was a key purchase, and during the 1964-65 Second Division championship programme the former England international was a driving force. A brilliant short-term buy, Anderson led the side by example and oozed class on the ball. He was a past captain of the England Under-23 line-up and travelled with the country's party to the 1962 World Cup finals in Chile, although always as second choice to the likes of Moore, Robson, Clayton and Flowers. A former apprentice plasterer and plumber, Anderson was rejected by Middlesbrough as a youth, only to return as a veteran, while he was once sent off when wearing the white shirt of England, in 1957. He later resided in the Doncaster area.

Appearances:
FL: 81 apps. 13 gls.
FAC: 2 apps. 1 gl.
FLC: 1 app. 0 gls.
Total: *84 apps. 14 gls.*
Honours:
2 Eng caps 1962/1 Eng B cap 1957/
6 Eng u23 caps 1954-57/
3 Eng schools app. 1949/
2 FA apps. 1962/
FL div 2 champs 1965/
FL div 2 prom 1964/
FL div 3 prom 1967 (m).

ANDERSON, William Ronald

Role: Goalkeeper 1946-1948
6' 0"
b. Ponteland, nr Newcastle upon Tyne, 20th September 1927
d. Co. Durham 1995

CAREER: Dinnington 1943/ Throckley CW 1946/UNITED Oct 1946 £25/Annfield Plain cs 1948/ Local soccer until retirement through injury 1953.

Debut v Leicester City (h) 19/4/47

Ron Anderson, a miner in the local pits, impressed United's officials whilst appearing in the strong North Eastern League just after World War Two. He joined St James Park's staff as a part-time professional and had to compete with several other goalkeepers on United's books, notably Garbutt, Swinburne, Theaker and later Jack Fairbrother. Brother of Bob Anderson, 'keeper for Crystal Palace and both Bristol clubs during the Fifties, Ron was just 18 years old when he made his only appearance for the Magpies. For many years Anderson lived in Peterlee.

Appearances:
FL: 1 app. 0 gls.
Total: *1 app. 0 gls.*

APPLEYARD, William

Role: Centre-forward 1903-1908
5' 10"
b. Caistor, nr Cleethorpes, 1878
d. Newcastle upon Tyne, 14th January 1958

CAREER: Cleethorpes Town/Grimsby Tradesmen/Grimsby Town July 1901/ UNITED Apr 1903 £700/Oldham Athletic June 1908 £350, joint deal with F.Speedie/ Grimsby Town Nov 1908/Mansfield Mechanics 1909, retiring shortly afterwards.

Debut v Blackburn Rovers (a) 18/4/03

A terror to goalkeepers, Bill Appleyard was a well-built striker weighing over 14 stone who led United's forwards with much gusto during the early part of the Magpies' Edwardian dominance. In complete contrast to Newcastle's other more cultured players, Bill couldn't be classed as a brilliant stylist, but battled away up front and was a clinical finisher in front of goal, especially on the

APPLEBY, Matthew Wilfred

Role: Centre-half 1990-1994
5' 10"
b. Middlesbrough, 16th April 1972

CAREER: Nunthorpe/UNITED app cs 1989, pro Apr 1990(Darlington loan 1993-94)/ Darlington June 1994 free/Barnsley July 1996 £250,000.

Debut v West Bromwich Albion (h) 27/10/90

Matty Appleby was tracked as a teenager by both Middlesbrough and Hartlepool and, although he had trials at both clubs, chose to join United's junior staff. The Teesside youngster impressed manager Ossie Ardiles at a time of a youthful imprint on United's side, and Appleby was given an extended run in the club's Second Division line-up. Assured on the ball, to an extent that he

Matty Appleby

right. He also aimed to put the then unprotected opposing 'keeper in the net as well as the ball, and was involved on several occasions in fierce goalmouth skirmishes. A former North Sea fisherman, Appleyard was given the nickname of 'Cockles' and just missed an England cap, chosen as reserve for the international with Scotland in 1908. Bill was also a fine billiards player, being the footballers' champion, and often gave exhibition displays around the north east. Appleyard registered Newcastle's first FA Cup hat-trick, against his old club Grimsby in 1908. After retiring from the game, he returned to Tyneside and worked at the Vickers factory, living in the city's west-end.

Appearances:
FL: 128 apps. 71 gls.
FAC: 17 apps. 16 gls.
Others: 1 app. 1 gl.
Total: *146 apps. 88 gls.*
Honours: *FL champs 1905, 1907/ FAC finalist 1905, 1908.*

appeared at times too casual, Matty looked to be a good prospect until the intense pressure of a relegation fight affected him. When Kevin Keegan took control of affairs he was soon back in the reserves and, following a bad ankle injury, moved to Feethams. With Darlington Matty appeared at Wembley in 1996 in an unsuccessful bid to gain promotion to Division Two. His younger brother, Richie, was also given a contract by the Magpies and the pair appeared together in the Anglo-Italian Cup campaign of 1992-93.

Appearances:
FL: 18(2) apps. 0 gls.
FAC: 2 apps. 0 gls.
FLC: 2(1) apps. 0 gls.
Others: 2(2) apps. 0 gls.
Total: *24(5) apps. 0 gls.*

ARCHIBALD, John

John Archibald

Role: Goalkeeper
1922-1923
5' 11"
b. Strathaven, Lanarkshire, 27th August 1895

CAREER: Albion Rovers/Reading Aug 1919/Chelsea Jan 1920/Edinburgh St Bernards cs 1921/UNITED Apr 1922 £200/Grimsby Town May 1923 free/ Darlington Mar 1927/Albion Rovers Aug 1928/East Stirlingshire Nov 1928.

Debut v Manchester City (h) 29/4/22

One journalist of the day described John as, "a goalkeeper of consummate coolness and marked ability". He was purchased by United as a successor to the veteran Jimmy Lawrence, but, after only a single appearance in the black'n'whites senior eleven, lost out to rivals Bill Bradley and Sandy Mutch. The Scot did well though at Blundell Park, being a regular for Grimsby over four seasons and clocking up 111 matches as the Mariners won promotion.

Appearances:
FL: 1 app. 0 gls.
Total: *1 app. 0 gls.*
Honours:
FL div 3(N) champs 1926.

ARENTOFT, Preben

Role: Midfield 1969-1971
5' 7"
b. Copenhagen, Denmark, 1st November 1942

CAREER: Bronshoj Boldklub (Denmark)/Greenock Morton Sept 1965/UNITED Feb 1969 £18,000/Blackburn Rovers Sept 1971 £25,000/Returned to Denmark cs 1974/Helsingor IF (Denmark) manager 1977 to 1980, as well as occasional player.

Debut v Tottenham Hotspur (a) 2/4/69

ASKEW, William

Role: Midfield 1990-1992
5′ 6″
b. Great Lumley, Co Durham, 2nd October 1959

CAREER: Lumley jnrs/Middlesbrough Oct 1977/Hull City Aug 1982(Blackburn Rovers loan 1981-82)/UNITED Mar 1990 £150,000 (Gateshead loan 1991-92)(Shrewsbury Town loan 1991-92)/Gateshead cs 1992 free/ Whitley Bay Oct 1994/Spennymoor United/ Workington/Darlington asst-coach 1996.

Debut v Blackburn Rovers (a) 24/3/90

Billy Askew was signed by Newcastle as a 30 year-old to add guile and experience to the Magpies' midfield. A United supporter as a teenager, visiting Wembley as a fan in 1974, it took him almost 13 years to fulfil his ambition of playing for the club. In that time he had been reserve for several years to David Armstrong at Ayresome Park, before making his name in the lower divisions with Hull City. Blessed with bags of energy, he was the proverbial midfield dynamo; small, neat on the ball with lots of stamina. Billy was past his best when he arrived at Gallowgate but was also unlucky with niggling injuries which kept him out of the selection picture.

Appearances:
FL: 7(1) apps. 0 gls.
Total: *7(1) apps. 0 gls.*
Honours:
FL div 4 prom 1983/FL div 3 prom 1985.

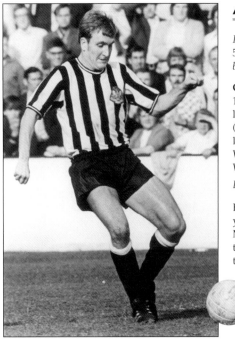

'Benny' Arentoft

A diminutive, but stocky midfield worker, Arentoft excelled in a close marking role during United's first assault on European soccer. Known as 'Benny', he was one of the earliest of Newcastle's foreign imports and proved an astute footballer, able to read the game well and perform to the team's benefit, rather than his own. Capped by his country, Arentoft left his largely amateur domestic football scene with a host of fellow countrymen in an attempt to carve out a future in Scotland but was the only one to succeed south of the border. Arentoft netted in the 1969 Fairs Cup final for United, and later operated at full-back at Ewood Park. An educated man of many talents, Benny later was employed as a senior manager by Copenhagen City Council, while he was also something of an art dealer and part-time journalist, as well as an accountant. He resides in Stenlose near Denmark's capital.

Appearances:
FL: 46(4) apps. 2 gls.
FAC: 3 apps. 0 gls.
Eur: 10(1) apps. 1 gl.
Total: *59(5) apps. 3 gls.*
Honours:
9 Denmark caps 1965-71/Denmark B app./ ICFC winner 1969/ SL Div 2 champs 1967.

Billy Askew

ASPRILLA, Faustino
Hernan Hinestroza

Role: Striker 1996-date
5' 7"
b. Tulua Valle, Colombia, 10th November 1969

CAREER: Estudiantes de Tulua
(Colombia)/Deportivo Cali(Colombia)
1989/Atletico Nacional de Medellin
(Colombia) July 1990/Parma(Italy) cs
1992 £3m/UNITED Feb 1996 £7.5m.

Debut v Middlesbrough (a) 10/2/96 (sub)

The record £7.5 million purchase of Colombian
international Faustino Asprilla was
surrounded in controversy, and at times,
media hysteria. The on-off transfer from
Italian club Parma was a drawn out affair and
had more twists than a
television soap opera, but
in the end the flamboyant
and highly talented
South American arrived
on Tyneside
to link
up with Ferdinand, and later Shearer, to form
United's strike-force. Manager Kevin Keegan
was first attracted to his style and special
ability a year earlier when he stood out for
both Colombia and Parma, United's boss
making the comment: "he is a one-off, a
special player, a big-stage performer".
Nicknamed 'The Black Arrow' in Italy, Asprilla
could be explosive on the field, but with a
sometimes volatile temperament, he
immediately became the focus of tabloid
headlines, for both his brilliance on the ball
creating and scoring goals, and his sometimes
rash retaliation towards defenders who gave
him a rough time. A unique entertainer, he
specialises in an acrobatic somersault
celebration on scoring which delights
supporters. Known as 'Tino', he looks far from
a thoroughbred footballer, being leggy and
loping in appearance, but Asprilla possesses
frightening ability and balance, able to turn
defenders in tight situations. Unorthodox in
style, Tino has deceptive pace over a few yards
and can call on an array of extravagant ball
skills. Able to speak only a few words of
English on his arrival, it took Tino several
months to settle in the north east and adapt
to Premier League soccer. A touch
erratic, he could however turn a
match with a flash of brilliance.
The Colombian appeared in the
1990 and 1994 World Cups, as
well as the 1992 Olympic
Games and was a fans' hero
with Parma as the Italian club
challenged AC Milan at the
top of Serie A. In the news
throughout his career, for
actions both on and off the
field, although much of the
adverse publicity was
exaggerated, he has become
another of Kevin Keegan's
personality signings which has made
Newcastle one of the most talked about clubs
in the country.

Appearances:
PL: 11(3) apps. 3 gls.
Total: *11(3) apps. 3 gls.*
Honours:
*37 (plus) Colombia caps/Colombia Lg champs
1991/Italian Cup winner 1992/Italian Cup
finalist 1995/ECWC winner 1993(as sub)/
ECWC finalist 1994/UEFAC winner 1995/
Colombian Footballer of the Year 1991.*

Faustino Asprilla

AULD, John Robertson

Role: Centre-half & Director 1896-1906
5' 9"
b. Lugar, nr Cumnock, 7th January 1862
d. Sunderland, 29th April 1932

CAREER: Kilmarnock/Lugar Boswell/Third Lanark 1883/Queens Park Nov 1884/ Third Lanark 1886/Sunderland May 1889/ UNITED Oct 1896 to June 1897 when he retired, becoming a United director to 1906.

Debut v Manchester City (a) 17/10/1896 (scored once)

John Auld

A member of the famous Sunderland 'Team of all the Talent', John arrived at St James Park nearing the end of his career, into his thirties and as the first player to be transferred from Wear to Tyne. It was a controversial transaction, as Auld moved to United as a reinstated amateur which meant no fee was due to the Reds, the press noting that the move went ahead "after the childish hubbub of the Wearsiders". Auld played in the centre of midfield and for a season linked well, helping the black'n'whites fashion an eleven to push for promotion. He was in fact the first of three noted Sunderland players from their all-conquering side to assist United in reaching the First Division, the others being Harvey and Campbell. The younger legs of Ghee or Ostler took his place as Auld moved into United's boardroom, the first, and one of only a handful of ex players to do so at St James Park. The Ayrshire product made over 100 appearances for Sunderland including being captain for their first Football League game. A shoe-maker by trade, his early transfer to Wearside is one of the best recorded. Auld received a £150 signing-on fee, £20 for turning professional, £300 in wages for two years - and financial assistance in establishing a boot and shoe shop. He resided in the Roker area to his demise.

Appearances:
FL: 14 apps. 3 gls.
FAC: 1 app. 0 gls.
Total: *15 apps. 3 gls.*
Honours:
3 Scot caps 1887-89/1 unoff Scot app. 1889/ FL champs 1892, 1893/SC winner 1889.

BAILEY, John Anthony

Role: Left-back 1985-1988
5' 8"
b. Liverpool, 1st April 1957

CAREER: Blackburn Rovers app, pro Apr 1975/Everton July 1979 £300,000/UNITED Oct 1985 £80,000/Bristol City Sept 1988 free/ Retired Jan 1992/Everton asst-coach/ Sheffield United asst-coach.

Debut v Aston Villa (a) 26/10/85

John Bailey turned out in over 200 games for Everton before heading for Tyneside. A clever defender who liked to attack down the flank, being a former forward as a teenager, he was the joker of the dressing-room, possessing a typical Scouse sense of humour. John had one good season in United's ranks in 1985-86, before losing his place to local lad Kenny Wharton. Lively and something of an extrovert, Bailey was a useful boxer too, competing in the ABA championships. Before joining the Goodison set-up, John had been rejected by Everton as a kid, but on his return shared in an era of much glory for the Blues.

Appearances:
FL: 39(1) apps. 0 gls.
FAC: 1 app. 0 gls.
FLC: 1 app. 0 gls.
Total:
41(1) apps. 0 gls.
Honours:
1 Eng B cap 1980/
1 FL app. 1980/
FL champs 1985/
FAC winner 1984/
FLC finalist 1984.

John Bailey

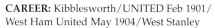

BAIRD, Ian James

Role: Centre-forward 1984-1985
6' 0"
b. Southampton, 1st April 1964

CAREER: Bitterne Saints/St Marys/
Southampton app July 1980, pro Apr 1982
(Cardiff City loan 1983-84)(UNITED loan
Dec 1984 - Jan 1985)/Leeds United Mar 1985
£100,000/Portsmouth Aug 1987 £285,000/
Leeds United Mar 1988 £185,000/
Middlesbrough Jan 1990 £500,000/
Heart of Midlothian July 1991 £350,000/
Bristol City July 1993 £295,000/
Plymouth Argyle Oct 1995 £75,000/
Brighton Aug 1996 £35,000.

Debut v Aston Villa (a) 22/12/84

Ian Baird

Ian Baird was acquired on trial by Jack
Charlton when United were searching for a
target man to play up front alongside
playmakers Waddle and Beardsley. A centre-
forward with a big heart and battling instincts,
he didn't perform too well during his limited
stay at St James Park. Baird did though, take
part in a terrific New Year's Day 'derby' clash
with Sunderland, won 3-1 by the Magpies. A
touch fiery, Ian was booked by referees on
each of his five appearances for Newcastle but,
after returning to the Saints, he served all his
clubs in a professional manner, especially at
Leeds where he helped the Tykes to promotion
and was recognised as Player of the Year in
1988-89.

Appearances:
FL: 4(1) apps. 1 gl.
Total: *4(1) apps. 1 gl.*
Honours:
Eng schools app. 1979/
FL div 2 champs 1990/FL div 3 prom 1996.

BAMLETT, Thomas

Role: Right-back
1901-1904
5' 10"
b. Tyneside

CAREER: Kibblesworth/UNITED Feb 1901/
West Ham United May 1904/West Stanley
1908/Later playing in
local soccer for a number
of years.

Debut v Notts County (a)
3/10/01

Tom Bamlett

A local product, Tom
Bamlett was a noted
Tyneside footballer, but
one who found it hard to
break into United's
developing side during
the opening years of this
century. Competition was fierce at the time
with six or seven players challenging for the
two full-back positions. Able to play on either
flank, Bamlett moved south to Southern
League West Ham in search of regular first-
team football and appeared in the Hammers'
inaugural match at Upton Park in September
1904.

Appearances:
FL: 2 apps. 0 gls.
Total: *2 apps. 0 gls.*

BARBER, Stanley

Role: Left-half 1925-1928
5' 10"
b. Wallsend, 28th May 1908
d. Newcastle upon Tyne, 18th April 1984

CAREER: Wallsend/UNITED Sept 1925 £100/
Bristol City June 1928 £500/Exeter City June
1930/Brighton May 1934 free/retired 1935.

Debut v Burnley (a) 31/3/28

Constantly overshadowed at Gallowgate by
Willie Gibson and Joe Harris, Stan Barber was
a good player nevertheless and turned in
many a decent game for the club's strong
reserve side during the inter-war years,
matches supported with a regular 10,000
attendance. He was a key figure in the
Magpies' North Eastern League title victory in

Stan Barber

1926 and when he received a call up to the senior line-up, never let the side down. Big, strong and rosy-cheeked, he was enthusiastic, a terrific worker in midfield and always a gentleman. He established himself at the other St James Park in Exeter, taking part in a famous giant-killing FA Cup run in 1930-31 and clocking up 127 league and cup fixtures for the Grecians. However, after being noted as one of the best players in the lower divisions, Stan was dogged by illness and never recaptured his eyecatching form. He later returned to Tyneside.

Appearances:
FL: 1 app. 0 gls.
Total: *1 app. 0 gls.*

BARKER, John

Role: Inside-left 1891-1893
5' 9"
b. South of England
d. Newcastle upon Tyne, 1925

CAREER: Newcastle West End c1885/ Newcastle East End Dec 1891/UNITED May 1892/Trafalgar (Newcastle) cs 1893/ Shankhouse Black Watch 1893.

Debut v Middlesbrough (h)
1/10/1892 (NL)

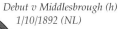

One of the most prominent of Tyneside's pioneer footballers, John Barker served both West End and East End during their formative years on Victorian Tyneside. He was on the field for West End's very first FA Cup fixture in 1886 and took part in their first FA Cup proper tie against Grimsby Town in season 1889-90. Barker also reached three Northumberland Senior Cup finals (1886, 1887 and 1888) and, when he changed allegiance to United's embryo club, took part in Newcastle's first season at St

John Barker

James Park in 1892-93, appearing once, in a Northern League fixture with Middlesbrough. Barker was also a noted cyclist - a popular sport in his day - appearing for the Clarence Bicycle Club. After retiring he managed several pubs; The Turks Head and Albion Hotel included. Barker, who resided in the west-end of the city to his death, was also employed in a local factory and lost an eye in a work accident. John has the distinction of being the first player to be awarded a benefit match staged at St James Park, in April 1891 against Sunderland. He is also recorded as the first man to be sent-off for West End, in a local derby with East End during 1889.

Appearances:
NL: 1 app. 0 gls.
Total: *1 app. 0 gls.*

BARKER, Michael Allan

Role: Left-back 1972-1979
5' 10"
b. Bishop Auckland, 18th December 1955

CAREER: UNITED app 1972, pro Jan 1974/ Gillingham Jan 1979 £65,000/Ferryhill Athletic Apr 1980/Bishop Auckland/USA football/ Hartlepool United Sept 1982.

Debut v West Ham United
(a) 28/2/75

Micky Barker

A forceful, fierce-tackling full-back, Barker was a reserve to Alan Kennedy during most of his time at St James Park. His best season was during the club's relegation from Division One in 1977-78, but he was eventually replaced by first, Kenny Mitchell, then new signing Ian Davies. He moved to the Priestfield Stadium in Kent where he had a solid if not spectacular career with Gillingham and, on his return to the north east, also did well with Hartlepool. Micky once walked out on United after a dispute over wages and worked in a garage for almost a year before returning to Gallowgate. Latterly Barker has been running a public house in Bishop Auckland.

Appearances:
FL: 21(2) apps. 0 gls.
FAC: 4 apps. 0 gls.
FLC: 1 app. 0 gls.
Others: 1 app. 0 gls.
Total: *27(2) apps. 0 gls.*

BARR, J. W.

Role: Right-half 1893-1894

CAREER: Grantham Rovers/UNITED Aug 1893 to cs 1894/Ashington.

Debut v Burton Swifts (a) 23/9/1893

Barr joined United during the summer months of 1893, just after East End had taken over the lease of St James Park from the defunct Newcastle West End. Captain of the Grantham side, he was described in the *Newcastle Daily Chronicle* as being "a well-built youth", noted to have plenty of weight and speed, although "he appears to be rather weak in kicking"! He appeared only once for United, during the club's first Football League season in 1893-94. A reserve to Bob Creilly, he had departed by the close season of 1894. Barr was travelling reserve when United made their Football League debut at Arsenal.

Appearances:
FL: 1 app. 0 gls.
Total: *1 app. 0 gls.*

BARROWCLOUGH, Stewart James

Role: Outside-right 1970-1978
5' 7"
b. Barnsley, 29th October 1951

CAREER: Barnsley app Apr 1967, pro Nov 1969/UNITED July 1970 £33,000/Birmingham City Apr 1978 exch deal with T. Hibbitt & J. Connolly/Bristol Rovers July 1979 £90,000, becoming player-coach cs 1980/Barnsley Feb 1981 £50,000/Mansfield Town Aug 1983 free/Local Yorkshire football cs 1985, becoming Grimethorpe manager c1995.

Debut v Blackpool (h) 29/8/70 (sub)

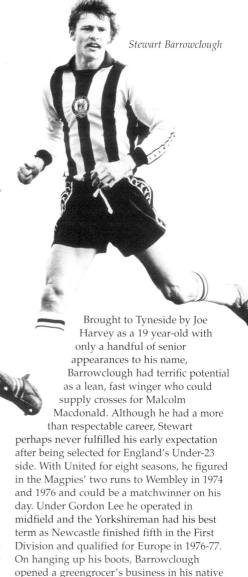

Stewart Barrowclough

Brought to Tyneside by Joe Harvey as a 19 year-old with only a handful of senior appearances to his name, Barrowclough had terrific potential as a lean, fast winger who could supply crosses for Malcolm Macdonald. Although he had a more than respectable career, Stewart perhaps never fulfilled his early expectation after being selected for England's Under-23 side. With United for eight seasons, he figured in the Magpies' two runs to Wembley in 1974 and 1976 and could be a matchwinner on his day. Under Gordon Lee he operated in midfield and the Yorkshireman had his best term as Newcastle finished fifth in the First Division and qualified for Europe in 1976-77. On hanging up his boots, Barrowclough opened a greengrocer's business in his native town. In 1996 he guided Grimethorpe Miners Welfare to Wembley in the Carlsberg Pub Cup.

Appearances:
FL: 201(18) apps. 21 gls.
FAC: 15(7) apps. 2 gls.
FLC: 14(3) apps. 1 gl.
Eur: 4 apps. 0 gls.
Others: 27 apps. 4 gls.
Total: *261(28) apps. 28 gls.*
Honours:
5 Eng u23 caps 1973/FLC finalist 1976/ FL div 3 prom 1981.

BARTLETT, Thomas

Role: Inside-left 1893-1894, 1896-1897
5' 10"
b. Tyneside

CAREER: St Thomas'(Newcastle)/Science & Art (Newcastle)/Arthur's Hill(Newcastle)/ UNITED 1893/Willington Athletic 1894/ Walsall c1895/Willington Athletic/UNITED May 1896 to 1897/Hebburn Argyle.

Debut v Notts County (h) 9/12/1893

Given the nickname of 'Knocker' after his renowned foraging and bustling play, Tom Bartlett was a most popular reserve in United's ranks before the turn of the last century. He was a well-known personality in local Tyneside soccer and in his limited

Tom Bartlett

appearances for United during the club's first league season did very well; the side winning all three games and Bartlett striking a marvellous hat-trick in a 5-1 victory over Lincoln City. Despite this success, he was always second choice to Joe Wallace and soon moved back into local competition. In 1893 Bartlett was selected for the Northumberland County side.

> **Appearances:**
> *FL: 3 apps. 3 gls.*
> **Total:** *3 apps. 3 gls.*

BARTON, David

Role: Centre-half 1975-1983
6' 0"
b. Bishop Auckland, 9th May 1959

CAREER: UNITED July 1975 (Blackburn Rovers loan 1982-83)(Darlington loan 1982-83)/Darlington July 1983 free/ Retired due to injury Mar 1984/Blyth Spartans 1984-85/Coundon 1985-86/Newton Aycliffe manager July 1990/Spennymoor United asst-manager 1993.

Debut v Leeds United (a) 2/1/78

A tall, gangling central defender, ideally built for the stopper's position, David Barton showed lots of promise during his early years with United and looked like developing into a fine centre-half. However, his progress was halted, not only by a succession of injuries but also by being part of a United line-up struggling to come to terms with Second Division football during the early eighties. Predictably nicknamed 'Dick', he was positive at the back and tough-tackling in his prime, but was replaced by Jeff Clarke and missed out on the Keegan-led resurgence at Gallowgate.

David Barton

> **Appearances:**
> *FL: 101(1) apps. 5 gls.*
> *FAC: 2(1) apps. 0 gls.*
> *FLC: 5 apps. 1 gl.*
> **Total:** *108(2) apps. 6 gls.*

BARTON, Warren Dean

Role: Right-back 1995-date
5' 11"
b. Islington, London, 19th March 1969

CAREER: Leyton Orient app 1985/ Leytonstone & Ilford(Dagenham & Redbridge) cs 1987/Maidstone United July 1989 £10,000/ Wimbledon June 1990 £300,000/ UNITED June 1995 £4m.

Debut v Coventry City (h) 19/8/95

Warren Barton became Newcastle United's most expensive purchase and Britain's costliest defender when he moved to Tyneside, although the club smashed the record only two days later during a week of spectacular purchases. Barton was rejected by former Magpie favourite, Frank Clark, when the manager was at Orient, but then attracted attention whilst turning out for Football League newcomers Maidstone United.

The Magpies had tried to sign him in 1990, but wouldn't pay the fee of £300,000 and Barton joined the Dons at Wimbledon instead. Confident on the ball, the rangey blond-haired all-rounder attacks in the Newcastle manner, can defend with resolve, and is also able to perform in midfield. During his time in South London he was picked by England at both 'B' and full level although Warren's full debut for his country lasted barely half an hour - the international fixture in Dublin during 1995 was abandoned due to a riot. Having impressed United's boss Kevin Keegan he completed a move to Tyneside after a persistent chase by the black'n'whites. Warren trained with both Arsenal and Watford as a kid and worked for an accountants' office in the City's Embankment before turning professional.

Appearances:
PL: 30(1) apps. 0 gls.
FAC: 2 apps. 0 gls.
FLC: 5 apps. 1 gl.
Total: *37(1) apps. 1 gl.*
Honours:
3 Eng caps 1995-96/ 3 Eng B caps 1991-95.

Warren Barton

BATTY, David

Role: Midfield
1996-date
5' 7"
b. Leeds,
2nd December 1968

CAREER: Leeds United sch 1983, app 1985, pro Aug 1987/Blackburn Rovers Oct 1993 £2.75m/UNITED Feb 1996 £3.5m.

Debut v Manchester United (h) 4/3/96

When David Batty's career became entangled in argument at Ewood Park following a long injury lay-off, Newcastle were alerted to the possibility of acquiring another international player to give the Magpies' flamboyant side added bite in midfield. The £3.5 million deal was quickly concluded and Batty immediately slipped into the central anchor role, operating just in front of Newcastle's defence. David was an instant hit, both with his manager and the fans who warmed to his battling instincts and immaculate distribution of the ball. Although known for his robust tackling, ball-winning ability and the competitive edge to his game, Batty is a much better player than many judges have given him credit for. Composed on the ball, David rarely wastes possession and can be an intelligent player too, linking and prompting his side forward. A former skipper of the Leeds youth side, David was in the first team at Elland Road by the time he was 18 years old and went on to appear over 250 times for Leeds. Very quickly a big personality with the Yorkshire giants, he helped the Tykes to promotion and then to the Football League title in 1991-92. A regular with England by then, he was controversially sold to Blackburn in a deal that angered Leeds' supporters. An ankle injury robbed Batty of a second championship medal in 1994-95 (5 apps.) with Blackburn, before he settled on Tyneside to be involved in yet another title race with the black'n'whites.

Appearances:
PL: 11 apps. 1 gl.
Total: *11 apps. 1 gl.*
Honours:
17 Eng caps 1991-date/5 Eng B caps 1990-92/7 Eng u21 caps 1988-90/ FL champs 1992/FL div 2 champs 1990.

BATTY, Ronald Robson

Role: Left-back 1945-1958
5' 8"
b. West Stanley, Co. Durham, 5th October 1925
d. West Stanley, Co. Durham, July 1971

CAREER: East Tanfield CW/Quaking Houses jnrs/UNITED Oct 1945 £10/Gateshead Mar 1958 £510, becoming player-manager Oct 1958/He retired in Mar 1960 and occasionally scouted for Bury.

Debut v Portsmouth (a) 2/10/48

Ron Batty

A sound and able defender, especially impressive when under pressure, Ron Batty spent over a decade at St James Park and was held in high esteem by his fellow professionals. Many colleagues considered Ron to be the best left-back at the club during the immediate post-war years. Fierce and hard as they come, Batty was recalled by Jackie Milburn as a player, "who could cut wingers in two with his tackling". He was most unlucky with injuries, and missed out on both the 1951 and 1952 FA Cup finals, while he almost lost out again in 1955. Second choice to Alf McMichael that season, he received a call-up on the Irishman dropping out, only for Batty to break his wrist in the run up to Wembley; fortunately he still played at the twin towers although his arm was heavily strapped. For much of his time at Gallowgate Ron had to battle for the Number Three shirt with McMichael but, when Bobby Cowell was forced to call it a day, switched flanks and found a place at right-back. When in charge at Gateshead, he was manager for much of the season in which the Tyneside club were controversially voted out of the Football League in 1960. Batty later resided in Stanley until his death and was employed as an electrician at the Marley Hill Colliery.

Appearances:
FL: 161 apps. 1 gl.
FAC: 20 apps. 0 gls.
War: 1 app. 0 gls.
Others: 1 app. 0 gls.
Total: *183 apps. 1 gl.*
Honours:
FAC winner 1955.

BEARDSLEY, Peter Andrew M.B.E.

Role: Striker or Midfield 1983-1987, 1993-date
5 '8"
b. Longbenton, Newcastle upon Tyne, 18th January 1961

CAREER: R.Holmes Youth Club/Wallsend Boys' Club 1972/The Fusilier 1977/ Ashington/Carlisle United Aug 1979/ Vancouver Whitecaps(Canada) Apr 1981 £220,000(Manchester United loan 1982-83)/ UNITED Sept 1983 £120,000/Liverpool July 1987 £1.9m/Everton Aug 1991 £1m/ UNITED July 1993 £1.5m.

Debut v Barnsley (a) 24/9/83 (sub)

To many United supporters of the modern generation, Peter Beardsley is recognised as the best player to have pulled on the black and white shirt. And without doubt the locally born striker ranks with the most eminent of men to have played for the club in its long history. Although Peter spent several of his most productive years away from St James Park, on Merseyside with Liverpool and Everton, he never lost his passion for his native Tyneside and boyhood idols, Newcastle United. A brilliant little player, slight of build, who in his role operating just behind the front strikers has proved devastating at both creating and scoring goals, netting over 230 up to the summer of 1996. Possessing lovely ball skills and marvellous vision, as well as tremendous stamina, enthusiasm and work-rate, above all Beardsley has the special quality of finding the net with truly spectacular goals - over and over again. Rarely does he convert a chance by ordinary means. Many come from stunning long range shooting, splendid placement, precision timing or delightful dribbles. With over 100 goals registered for the Magpies the majority are worthy of monthly or even seasonal awards, such are their quality. Beardsley has in fact appeared on United's books in three spells, being released by Bill McGarry as a teenager when at Gallowgate on trial. He also had spells with Gillingham, Cambridge United, Burnley and Oxford before he was picked up by former Newcastle skipper Bob Moncur, manager at Carlisle, and Peter proceeded to make a

Peter Beardsley

name for himself at Brunton Park, a gem among the rough and tumble of Third Division football. He developed further in the United States calypso and had all of 78 minutes of senior football in a five month trial at Old Trafford before being released. Arthur Cox brought him back to the north east to partner Kevin Keegan as Newcastle made sure they returned to Division One in spectacular fashion in 1983. Beardsley's captivating brand of football matured and he became an England regular, an effective partner to Gary Lineker. Peter once netted four goals for his country in an unofficial match against Aylesbury, and he captained England as well as appearing in the final stages of two World Cups, in 1986 and 1990. But Peter clashed with United boss Jack Charlton and the club's stagnation meant he was off to Anfield in search of trophies for a new British record deal. Honours duly came and Beardsley was noted as one of the country's top entertainers, yet following the arrival of new boss, Graeme Souness at Liverpool, he moved across Stanley Park to Everton where he again became a crowd favourite. When Beardsley was 32 years old, he made a dramatic return to St James Park for £1.5m, a fee which proved to be the bargain of the decade. Back alongside Kevin Keegan and later Arthur Cox too, Peter led United's charge on the Premiership as he enjoyed a new lease of life. Now an experienced head went with his all round ability and he skippered the Magpies as they became a new force in the game. United's most capped player for England with 25 appearances, Peter was awarded the MBE for his services to football in 1995 and just missed out on the Footballer of the Year award the previous year. Nicknamed 'Pedro' by his colleagues, Peter Beardsley is a matchwinner supreme, a genius in football boots who always has time for the fans.

Appearances:
FL/PL: 250(1) apps. 103 gls.
FAC: 14 apps. 3 gls.
FLC: 19 apps. 3 gls.
Eur: 4 apps. 2 gls.
Others: 1 app. 0 gls.
Total: *288(1) apps. 111 gls*
Honours:
59 Eng caps 1986-96/1 unoff Eng app. 1988/ 2 Eng B caps 1991-92/1 FL app. 1988/ FL champs 1988, 1990/FL div 2 prom 1984/ FAC winner 1989/FAC finalist 1988.

Peter Beardsley

BEASANT, David John

Role: Goalkeeper 1988-1989
6' 4"
b. Willesden, London, 20th March 1959

CAREER: Old Uffintonians/Legionnaires/
Edgware Town/Wimbledon Aug 1979
£1,000/UNITED June 1988 £850,000/
Chelsea Jan 1989 £725,000(Grimsby Town
loan 1992-93) (Wolverhampton Wanderers
loan 1992-93)/Southampton Nov 1993
£300,000.

Debut v Everton (a) 27/8/88

Dave Beasant became United's costliest
player, along with fellow Wimbledon
defender Andy Thorn, when he moved
north in the summer of 1988. Also
Britain's most expensive 'keeper at the
time, Beasant had made headlines just
prior to signing for the Magpies by
becoming the first man to save a penalty
kick during a Wembley FA Cup final,
against Liverpool in a famous Wimbledon
victory. As skipper of the Dons, he lifted
the trophy and was a central figure in that
club's rise from non-league football to an
established Premiership club. Known as
'Lurch' by his team-mates, he is the tallest
player to turn out for the Magpies, along
with Hislop and Reilly. Dave reached the
England squad with United, but had left
by the time he was called up to play for
his country. Noted for sprinting yards out
of his goal, Beasant could be quite brilliant
at times, yet was always prone to a costly
and embarrassing lapse. Beasant began his
career as a prolific scoring centre-forward
before switching to between the posts. Dave
created a tremendous run of consecutive
appearances, a record bettered by only one
man in the whole of the British game (H. Bell)
when he totalled 394 matches without a gap
from August 1981 to October 1990.

Appearances:
FL: 20 apps. 0 gls.
FAC: 2 apps. 0 gls.
FLC: 2 apps. 0 gls.
Others: 3 apps. 0 gls.
Total: *27 apps. 0 gls.*
Honours:
2 Eng caps 1990/7 Eng B caps 1989-91/
FL div 2 champs 1989/FL div 4 champs 1983/
FL div 3 prom 1984/FL div 2 prom 1986/
FAC winner 1988.

Dave Beasant

BEDFORD, Harry

Role: Inside-forward & Trainer 1930-1932,
1937-1938
5' 8"
b. Calow, near Chesterfield, 15th October 1899
d. Derby, 24th June 1976

CAREER: Grassmoor Ivanhoe(Chesterfield)/
Nottingham Forest Aug 1919/Blackpool Mar
1921 £1,500/Derby County Sept 1925 £3,000/
UNITED Dec 1930 £4,000/Sunderland Jan
1932 £3,000/Bradford Park Avenue May 1932/
Chesterfield June 1933/Heanor Town player-
trainer Aug 1934/UNITED trainer Oct 1937/
Derby County masseur May 1938/Belper
Town manager Jan 1954/Heanor Town
manager Mar 1955 to Mar 1956.

Debut v Leicester City (h) 13/12/30 (scored once)

Harry Bedford was a dashing and fearless centre-forward who scored over 300 goals during his outstanding career between the two world wars. He arrived at St James Park nearing the veteran stage of his footballing days and was played largely out of position at inside-forward. However, Bedford still gave good short term service to the Magpies at a difficult time in the club's history in the aftermath of the controversial sale of Hughie Gallacher. An ex miner, always immaculately turned out both on and off the field, Harry never settled too well in the north east, at either Newcastle or Sunderland, but he came to the

Harry Bedford

region with a formidable record from Blackpool and Derby. He had attracted national attention netting 118 goals in 180 League and cup matches for the Seasiders, being the league's leading scorer in both 1922-23 and 1923-24. There was more a strategic approach to his play up front than force, his neatly placed shots often finding the net, while he once scored four goals for the Football League against the Irish in 1924. Harry was under-rated in an era when there was a galaxy of noted strikers, but he was especially favoured at the Baseball Ground where he became the Rams' leading goalgetter for five years in succession, grabbing almost 30 a season. Before retiring to his home county he was a licensee for a while in Derby, and worked for 23 years in the Rolls-Royce fire service.

Appearances:
FL: 30 apps. 17 gls.
FAC: 2 apps. 1 gl.
Total: *32 apps. 18 gls.*
Honours:
2 Eng caps 1923-25/2 FL apps. 1925-26/
Eng trial app. 1925/FL div 2 prom 1926.

BELL, Anthony W.

Role: Goalkeeper 1973-1975
6 '0"
b. North Shields, 27th February 1955

CAREER: UNITED Mar 1973/North Shields May 1975 free.
Debut v Tottenham Hotspur (a) 7/12/74

Tony Bell was one of first choice goalkeeper Willie McFaul's deputies during the Irishman's extensive dominance of the Number One jersey. The young Tyneside product was called up only once, against Spurs, when his other rival for the 'keeper's position at Gallowgate, Martin Burleigh, was concluding a transfer to Darlington. Bell found the Tottenham forwards on top form at White Hart

Tony Bell

Lane as Newcastle fell 0-3 and didn't get another chance in the Magpie senior line-up, Mick Mahoney being purchased before the season was out. Nevertheless, he proved to be a fine 'keeper in the local Northern League.

Appearances:
FL: 1 app. 0 gls.
Others: 1 app. 0 gls.
Total: *2 apps. 0 gls.*

BELL, David

Role: Right-half 1930-1934
5' 11"
b. Gorebridge, Midlothian, 24th December 1909
d. Monkseaton, Whitley Bay, April 1986

CAREER: Arniston Rangers/Musselburgh Bruntonians/Wallyford Bluebell (Musselburgh) 1929/UNITED May 1930 £150/Derby County June 1934 £700/Ipswich Town Oct 1938/Retired in May 1950.
Debut v Grimsby Town (a) 5/9/31

Daniel Bell

Known as 'Daniel' and a deputy to the tenacious Roddie MacKenzie in United's squad, Scotsman Bell proved to have lots of promise in midfield when called upon. He was, though, a victim of fate. When performing well and impressing United's team selection committee and manager Andy Cunningham, he seriously injured an ankle, then a cartilage, which left him sidelined for a long period. Untiring and always in the thick of the action in the MacKenzie mould, Bell departed following United's relegation from Division One and went on to have a good career at Portman Road, appearing in Ipswich Town's first ever league game in 1938. He totalled 198 games for the Suffolk club and played on until more than 40 years old. After retiring from the game David worked for a period at crane manufacturers Ransome & Rapier in Ipswich, where his immense strength was renowned. He later lived in Monkseaton to his death.

Appearances:
FL: 21 apps. 1 gl.
FAC: 2 apps. 0 gls.
Others: 1 app. 0 gls.
Total: *24 apps. 1 gl.*

BELL, Derek Stewart

Role: Midfield 1981-1983
5' 9"
b. Fenham, Newcastle upon Tyne, 19th December 1963

CAREER: UNITED app, pro Dec 1981/ Retired due to injury Nov 1983/Eppleton CW/Newcastle Blue Star/Gateshead Feb 1985/North Shields Feb 1988/ Gateshead 1988/Bridlington Town June 1993/ Bishop Auckland 1993-94/ Blyth Spartans/Whitley Bay/Berwick Rangers player-coach June 1994/Whitley Bay manager Feb 1995/Blyth Spartans player-asst-manager Nov 1995/Durham City July 1996.

Debut v Blackburn Rovers (a) 1/5/82

Derek Bell had an unfortunate time at St James Park with injuries. Firstly, soon after turning professional, he was in the treatment room for many weeks with a bad ankle knock and then, after showing what he could do in senior action, picked up knee trouble which eventually forced him to quit the Football League. Bell was only 19 years of age and had showed he was a bright prospect, full of running in the middle of the field with plenty of stamina. After leaving the full-time football scene, he was employed in a snooker and golf business then worked with the City of Newcastle's Housing Department. At the same time he continued a career in north east non-league soccer where he won two Northern Premier League titles with Gateshead. Derek was also selected for the FA's England non-league squad in 1989. His father played for Partick Thistle in the Scottish League.

Derek Bell

Appearances:
FL: 3(1) apps. 0 gls.
Total: *3(1) apps. 0 gls.*

BELL, John Russell

Role: Left-half 1956-1962
5' 8"
b. Evenwood, Co. Durham, 17th October 1939
d. Gainford, Co. Durham, 22nd April 1991

CAREER: Evenwood Town/UNITED Oct 1956 £10/Norwich City July 1962 £8,725/Colchester United May 1965/Gainford Town June 1966.

Debut v Luton Town (a) 16/11/57 (scored once)

A former England Boys' reserve who quickly developed through United's junior ranks, Jackie Bell was a fine attacking wing-half with a deadly shot. He was a 17 year-old debutant for the Magpies - netting with virtually his first shot against Luton Town - and showed that he could become a big star with some excellent performances in United's side during the late fifties. His displays were such that he was a reserve to both the England Under-23 and Football League elevens, but never quite broke into the international side. Newcastle's relegation in 1961 saw a new manager appointed at St James Park and, even though Bell had been a regular for three seasons, Joe Harvey didn't include him as part of his plans. Jackie's transfer to Carrow Road was tinged with controversy after Norwich City complained bitterly to the Football Association that United had sold him under false pretences; they hadn't advised City that Bell was a diabetic and consequently the FA cut the £10,000 fee by £1,375. Bell was a former captain of Northumberland Boys and was rejected by Burnley after trials. When he concluded his career, he resided in Gainford, near Darlington. Following an accident whilst working in the building trade, John endured a partial amputation of one of his legs.

Appearances:
FL: 111 apps. 8 gls.
FAC: 6 apps. 0 gls.
Total: *117 apps. 8 gls.*

Jackie Bell challenges Johnny Haynes during United v Fulham in 1960.

BENNETT, Albert

Role: Striker 1965-1969
6' 0"
b. Chester Moor, near Chester-le-Street,
16th July 1944

CAREER: Chester Moor jnrs/Rotherham United app May 1960, pro Feb 1962/UNITED July 1965 £27,500/Norwich City Feb 1969 £25,000/Retired Jan 1971 due to injury/Bury St Edmunds player-manager July 1972/Sprowston Athletic/Thurlton/Yarmouth Town Oct 1979 to May 1981/Sprowston Athletic/Carrow/Quebec Rovers/Sprowston Thursday/Taveners(All East Anglian sides).
Debut v Sheffield Wednesday (a) 28/8/65

Albert Bennett had caught the attention of several big clubs as a noted goalpoacher in three seasons of consistent scoring for Rotherham United; he had netted 70 goals and reached the England Under 23 line-up. Newcastle and Aston Villa led the chase to take the leggy striker into the First Division and Joe Harvey was the manager who succeeded, landing the player who was once on the Magpies' books as a teenage trialist. A colourful and jovial character, curly-haired Albert became a popular player at Gallowgate forming a good understanding with Wyn Davies in season 1967-68 that led to the black'n'whites qualifying for Europe for the first time. Unfortunately by the time that had occurred, Bennett had undergone knee surgery which saw him miss United's debut in the Inter Cities Fairs Cup, and worse, lose his place as partner to Davies, to Bryan Robson. United's first named substitute, Albert is also noted as being responsible for nicknaming Emlyn Hughes, 'Crazy Horse', during a 1967 United-Liverpool confrontation. Known as 'Ankles' himself, due to another injury problem, Bennett was mentioned in dialogue in the famous television programme,

Albert Bennett

'Auf Wiedersen Pet', Oz making reference to Albert as a "great centre-forward"! A former apprentice bricklayer, after quitting the professional scene due to more knee handicaps, Albert had a succession of jobs including working for the prison service and running a catering business as well as even a joke shop on Lowestoft pier. Residing in the Norwich area, he has been a publican for several years.

Appearances:
FL: 85 apps. 22 gls.
FAC: 1 app. 0 gls.
FLC: 3 apps. 1 gl.
Eur: 0(1) app. 0 gls.
Total: *89(1) apps. 23 gls.*
Honours:
1 Eng u23 cap 1965/Eng youth app. 1962

BENNIE, Robert Brown

Role: Right-back & Director
1901-1904, 1930-1945
5' 8"
b. Lanarkshire, 1873
d. Newcastle upon Tyne, 1st October 1945

CAREER: Airdrieonians/Heart of Midlothian/St Mirren 1896/ UNITED May 1901 in a joint deal with R.Orr/Retired due to injury cs 1904/Morpeth Harriers/ UNITED director July 1930 to 1945.

Bob Bennie

Debut v Blackburn Rovers (a) 7/9/01

An honest player and a thoroughly professional individual. Although dogged with a persistent knee complaint which eventually forced his retirement, Bob Bennie was a good all round sportsman too. He was local golf and bowls champion and later became a successful Tyneside entrepreneur. Uncle of the famous Airdrie and Scotland player of the same name during the twenties, Bob also had four brothers who played the game north of the border. He tackled strongly and was a regular choice for the Magpies in season 1901-02. Due to those knee problems he lost his place to firstly, local lad, James Tildesley, then to Scottish international Andy McCombie. Bennie, himself, just missed out on a cap for his country appearing in a trial game in 1901-02. Over 25 years after leaving United as a player he returned to the fold as a director. Bennie lived in the Jesmond area of the city to his death.

Appearances:
FL: 33 apps. 0 gls.
FAC: 4 apps. 0 gls.
Total: *37 apps. 0 gls.*
Honours:
Scot trial app. 1902

BENSON, Robert William

Role: Right-back 1902-1904
5' 9"
b. Whitehaven, 9th February 1883
d. Islington, London, 19th February 1916

CAREER: Dunston Villa/Shankhouse/ Swalwell/UNITED Dec 1902 £150/ Southampton Sept 1904 £150/Sheffield United May 1905 £150/Woolwich Arsenal Nov 1913/ Retired 1914.

Debut v Liverpool (a) 7/3/03

A young miner when he was at St James Park, Bob Benson developed his talent away from Tyneside and was especially noted for his displays at Bramall Lane for Sheffield United where he made over 300 appearances. With competition for United's full-back positions extremely fierce during the early years of the new century, he had a difficult task breaking into the Newcastle side. After famous international Andy McCombie had been purchased from Sunderland, Benson's opportunities were limited to a single game and it was no surprise that he was transferred south. Yet, he proved a point to Newcastle's directors, when he developed into a big, bold defender who represented his country. At over 14 stone, he was a

PROMINENT FOOTBALLERS.

R. BENSON.

WOOLWICH ARSENAL.

Bob Benson

heavyweight full-back, described by one biography of the day as, "a terror to opposing forwards". Bob adopted a curious strategy with penalty kicks in which it is recorded he ran almost the full length of the pitch before walloping the ball as hard as he could! At the age of only 33, Benson met a tragic end. Working in a munitions factory in Woolwich, he had given up football during the First World War, but in February 1916 had gone to watch the Arsenal v Reading fixture. With the Gunners a man short, Benson volunteered to fill in. Hardly fit for such a challenge, he became dizzy on the field and had to depart for the dressing-room where, within a matter of minutes, he died of a burst blood vessel in trainer George Hardy's arms. Benson was buried in an Arsenal shirt.

Appearances:
FL: 1 app. 0 gls.
Total: *1 app. 0 gls.*
Honours:
1 Eng cap 1913/Eng trial app. 1913/1 FL app. 1910/3 unoff Eng app. 1910

BENTLEY, Roy Thomas Frank

Role: Inside-right 1946-1948
5' 11"
b. Shirehampton, Bristol, 17th May 1924

CAREER: Portway/Bristol Rovers am. 1937/Bristol City am. 1938, pro Aug 1941/ Gateshead war-guest 1945-46/UNITED June 1946 £8,500/Chelsea Jan 1948 £12,500/ Fulham Sept 1956 £8,600/Queens Park Rangers June 1961/Reading manager Jan 1963 to Feb 1969/Bradford City scout Mar 1969/ Swansea Town manager Aug 1969 to Oct 1972/Thatcham Town manager/ Reading secretary 1977 to Feb 1984/ Aldershot secretary Jan 1985 to 1986.

Debut v Millwall (a) 31/8/46 (scored twice)

When Roy Bentley joined United immediately after the Second World War, he became the most expensive player signed from the lower divisions. Serving in the navy, he was almost an unknown, Stan Seymour, however, saw a rich talent in the slightly built youngster. Starting off at Bristol Rovers as an office-boy, Roy possessed vision and thought on the ball as well as the natural ability to find the net. He erupted with a bang in a Magpie shirt, netting twice on his debut and scoring 19 goals in his first season. However, he was frequently laid low through ill health whilst in the north east and it was said he never could adapt to the harsher climate. Leaving for Chelsea during United's promotion season and once back in the south, Bentley became a huge personality in the game. He was unorthodox in his method, and when operating at centre-forward became one of the first roving leaders, popping up all over the park to confound defenders. Often raiding from the flanks, Roy packed a tremendous shot in his right-foot and was supreme in the air. He scored goals on a regular basis at Stamford Bridge and

Roy Bentley

skippered the Blues to their only championship victory in 1954-55. He was their leading scorer for eight consecutive seasons and, all told, scored 149 goals in 366 games for the Londoners - one of Chelsea's all time greats. Bentley also recorded an impressive record for England too, scoring nine times in only 12 internationals, including a hat-trick for his country in season 1954-55, while he also represented Great Britain. He appeared, too, in the England side that lost so infamously to the USA in the 1950 World Cup. Bentley was a player who attracted the crowds, one of the elite of the glorious fifties. On retirement Roy settled in Reading. His father was a noted rugby player.

Appearances:
FL: 48 apps. 22 gls.
FAC: 6 apps. 3 gls.
Total: *54 apps. 25 gls.*
Honours:
12 Eng caps 1949-55/2 Eng B caps 1949-50/
3 FL apps. 1949-55/1 FA app. 1953/Great
Britain app. 1956/FL champs 1955/FL div 2
prom 1948, 1959/FL div 4 prom 1970(m).

BERESFORD, John

Role: Left-back 1992-date
5' 6"
b. Sheffield, 4th September 1966

CAREER: Manchester City app
Apr 1983, pro Sept 1983/
Barnsley cs 1986 free/
Portsmouth Mar 1989 £300,000/
UNITED June 1992 £650,000.

Debut v Southend United (h) 15/8/92

Since John Beresford made the long trip from Portsmouth to Tyneside, he has become one of the Magpies' most consistent players. With an attacking flair from his left-back position, he immediately became a hit with the Gallowgate crowd as the Magpies lifted the Division One crown. The Yorkshireman had almost signed for Liverpool before heading for the north east to team up with Kevin Keegan, but once the Anfield deal fell through due to a medical, the Magpies stepped in and neither club nor player has regretted the move. It was with Barnsley that Beresford became a first-team regular after being shown the door at Maine Road by Billy McNeill, and following almost 100 games for Pompey,

including their run to the FA Cup semi-final (he missed a spot-kick in a penalty shoot-out), had become hot property. A former England youth skipper, John was included in both Graham Taylor's and Terry Venables' England squads and has been on the fringe of a full cap, on the bench as a substitute in 1995. A gutsy defender with a cultured left-foot, who is always comfortable on the ball and committed to United's cause. With Southampton as a schoolboy, John's father appeared for Notts County and Chesterfield.

Appearances:
FL/PL: 141(1) apps. 1 gl.
FAC: 12 apps. 1 gl.
FLC: 14 apps. 0 gls.
Eur: 4 apps. 0 gls.
Others: 2 apps. 0 gls.
Total: *173(1) apps. 2 gls.*
Honours:
2 Eng B caps 1994-95/Eng schools app./
Eng youth app. 1984-86/
FL div 1 champs 1993.

John Beresford

BERTRAM, William

Role: Inside-left 1920-1921
5' 7"
b. Brandon, County Durham,
31st December 1897
d. Crossgate, County Durham,
27th October 1962

CAREER: Browney Colliery/Durham City amat 1923/UNITED Apr 1920 £150/Norwich City May 1921 £150/Leadgate Park Aug 1922/Durham City June 1923/Rochdale May 1925 to 1931/Accrington Stanley Oct 1931.

Debut v Manchester City (h) 17/4/20

Never able to break fully into United's senior line-up during the immediate years following World War One, Willie Bertram appeared in the last three games of the 1919-20 season. An accomplished player nevertheless, he was a schemer with a good touch on the ball, in the same mould as future star, Terry Hibbitt. His career began at Durham City's Football League outfit, but it was with Rochdale that Bertram became a noted star. He appeared over 200 times for the Lancashire club, netting frequently in their colours, over 80 senior goals. A pocket dynamo in midfield, Bertram served in the Durham Light Infantry during the war, and on retiring from the game returned to County Durham where he became a publican and later was employed in the Durham coalfield.

Appearances:
FL: 3 apps. 0 gls.
Total: 3 apps. 0 gls.

BEST, Jeremiah

Role: Outside-left 1919-1920
5' 9"
b. Mickley, Northumberland, 23rd January 1901
d. Darlington, 1975

CAREER: Mickley CW/UNITED Dec 1919 £100/Leeds United July 1920 £100/Northern League football 1921/Providence Clamdiggers (USA) Sept 1924/New Bedford Whalers (USA) Sept 1926/Fall River Marksmen (USA) Nov 1929/Pawtucket Rangers (USA) Dec 1929/New Bedford Whalers (USA) Sept 1930/Clapton Orient Aug 1931/Darlington Oct 1933/Hull City Oct 1936/Hexham cs 1937.

Debut v Blackburn Rovers (h) 6/3/20

Jerry Best hailed from a local footballing family of which several relations graced the Football League circuit during the inter-war years. A fast winger with good control, Best rivalled Alex Ramsay for a season as a youngster with lots of promise, but United's management only gave him two opportunities to impress during the first season after the First World War. A versatile player, operating at centre-forward and inside-left too, Jerry moved on soon after and was very popular at Feethams scoring 68 goals in 109 games for Darlington. He later resided in that area, and was one of several inter-war players to sample the American's early experiments with association football. Best appeared in Leeds United's first ever Football League fixture in 1920.

Appearances:
FL: 2 apps. 0 gls.
War: 1 app. 0 gls.
Total: 3 apps. 0 gls.

BETTON, Alec

Role: Centre-half 1931-1934
6' 0"
b. New Tupton, Derbyshire, 28th November 1903

CAREER: New Tupton Ivanhoe/Chesterfield May 1926/Scarborough Town June 1929/UNITED Jan 1931 £500/Stockport County June 1934 to c1935 £600/Scarborough Town trainer cs 1936, asst-trainer 1937 to c1960.

Debut v West Ham United (a) 26/1/31

Alec Betton

Within a few short weeks of showing up well in Scarborough's FA Cup success during 1928-29 and 1930-31, Alec Betton made the leap from Midland League football obscurity to the big-time. Betton was a highly effective stopper who possessed long legs and a powerful frame. Replacing Dave Davidson after the Magpies' Wembley success in 1932, he was commanding in the air and for a season with United, during 1932-33, few centre-forwards got the better of him. Yet the following campaign saw United fail to survive a relegation fight and Betton lost his place. Biographies of the era note Alec as an honourable and sporting defender who, on Tyneside, never received credit from his critics. Prior to entering football, Alec had been a former pit-boy in Derbyshire. Betton was later associated with Scarborough for many years.

Appearances:
FL: 61 apps. 1 gl.
FAC: 2 apps. 0 gls.
Total: *63 apps. 1 gl.*

BIRD, John Charles

Role: Centre-half 1975-1980
6' 0"
b. Rossington, nr Doncaster, 9th June 1948

CAREER: Doncaster United/Doncaster Rovers Mar 1967/Preston North End Mar 1971 £6,000/UNITED Sept 1975 cash-exch for A.Bruce/Hartlepool United May 1980 free, becoming player-coach cs 1983 and manager Oct 1986/York City manager Oct 1988 to Oct 1991/Doncaster Rovers coach 1992/Halifax Town manager Apr 1994.

Debut v Manchester City (a) 30/8/75

The purchase of John Bird was clouded in controversy when Preston officials sold their star player and captain against the wishes of manager, Bobby Charlton. The famous ex England player resigned in protest, yet Bird arrived at St James Park nevertheless and took time to settle in the First Division, finding the transition from the lower divisions a handful at first. He had a torrid debut at Maine Road, United losing 4-0, but the Yorkshireman quickly came to grips with Newcastle's defence. Bird eventually replaced Glenn Keeley at centre-half and on occasion looked a solid defender, especially during season 1978-79 following United's relegation from Division One. Often sidelined through injury, he was replaced by the arrival of Stuart Boam and the development of local youngster David Barton. John took part in two championship sides without qualifying for a medal, with Doncaster in 1969 (Div. 4) and Preston in 1971 (Div. 3).

Appearances:
FL: 84(3) apps. 5 gls.
FAC: 4 apps. 1 gl.
FLC: 4 apps. 0 gls.
Eur: 1(1) apps. 0 gls.
Others: 2 apps. 0 gls.
Total: *95(4) apps. 6 gls.*

John Bird

41

Ralph Birkett

was capped when at Ayresome Park and was extremely popular making 101 appearances and scoring 36 goals; when he joined United, 'Boro supporters were dismayed. In the Second World War he served as an Army PT instructor, and while he was in India for a time also guested for several clubs in England. For many years Birkett has resided in Brixham, Devon.

Appearances:
FL: 23 apps. 3 gls.
FAC: 3 apps. 0 gls.
War: 40 apps. 12 gls.
Total: *66 apps. 15 gls.*
Honours:
1 Eng cap 1936/1 Eng war cap 1941/
2 FL apps. 1936-37/Eng trial app. 1936/
FL champs 1934.

BIRNIE, Edward Lawson

Role: Half-back 1898-1905
5' 10"
b. Sunderland, 25th August 1878
d. Southend, 21st December 1935

CAREER: Sunderland Seaburn/ UNITED June 1898/Crystal Palace May 1905/Chelsea Aug 1906 £100/Tottenham Hotspur July 1910/Mulheim(Germany) player-trainer Aug 1911/Rochdale cs 1912/ Leyton player-manager July 1914/Sunderland asst-trainer & chief scout Aug 1919/Rochdale trainer cs 1921/Southend United manager Jan 1922 to May 1934/Germany coaching/ Newcastle City player-manager.

Debut v Notts County (h) 17/9/1898

BIRKETT, Ralph James Evans

Role: Outside-right 1938-1941
5' 9"
b. Newton Abbot, Devon, 9th January 1913

CAREER: Dartmouth United/Torquay United am. Aug 1929, pro Mar 1930/Arsenal Apr 1933 £2,000/Middlesbrough Mar 1935 £5,900/ UNITED July 1938 £5,900/Darlington war-guest 1939-40, 1945-46/Fulham war-guest 1940-41/Chester war-guest 1941-42/ Middlesbrough war-guest 1941-42/ Chelsea war-guest 1942-43/Reading war-guest 1942-43/Torquay United war-guest 1945-46.

Debut v Plymouth Argyle (h) 27/8/38
(scored once)

A regular scorer from the wing during his entire career, by the time Ralph Birkett appeared for the Magpies he had built a reputation as a quality First Division player. Signing for United when they were rebuilding to make a push to return to Division One, Birkett rejoined his former Arsenal international colleague and close friend, Ray Bowden at St James Park. Stan Seymour had envisaged the pairing would be United's cutting edge, but the Second World War put a swift end to such plans. Possessing a powerful shot, fast and direct, the ever-cheerful Ralph

Newcastle United's utility reserve during the early years of the century, Ted Birnie played in six different positions for the Magpies in his 20 games. His opportunities in the First Division were spread over six seasons; included were full-back, outside-left, centre-forward

Ted Birnie

and his more customary midfield role. He was a key figure in United's Northern League title winning sides of 1903, 1904 and 1905, never letting Newcastle's first-team down when called upon. Birnie looked leisurely on the ball at times but had good command of it and was an intelligent player who rarely wasted possession. After leaving St James Park he had a good spell at Stamford Bridge where he became a tremendous asset to Chelsea's promotion side, clocking up 108 games for the Pensioners, before his playing career was disrupted by a broken leg. Birnie was also noted as one of Southend's most successful managers, being in charge in Essex for over a decade. During his early career, he represented Northumberland County on more than one occasion when training as an engineer in the north east.

Appearances:
FL: 19 apps. 0 gls.
FAC: 1 app. 0 gls.
Total: *20 apps. 0 gls.*
Honours:
FL div 2 prom 1907.

BLACKBURN, Robert

Role: Outside-right 1906-1908
5' 8"
b. Edinburgh, 1885

CAREER: Leith Athletic/UNITED May 1906 free/Aberdeen July 1908/ Grimsby Town May 1909 to 1910.

Debut v Sheffield Wednesday (a) 3/9/06

As one contemporary report noted, Robert Blackburn possessed, "speed, dash and cleverness". He was a deputy to the great Jackie Rutherford at Gallowgate, gaining a call-up to senior action on three occasions in 1906-07 and twice in 1907-08. Blackburn performed well in the club's reserve side that picked up the North Eastern League championship in both of those seasons, but the stocky Caledonian who packed a stinging shot had little hope of displacing United's immense wall of international talent at St James Park and he departed for Aberdeen.

Appearances:
FL: 5 apps. 0 gls.
Total: *5 apps. 0 gls.*

BLACKHALL, Raymond

Role: Right-back 1973-1978
5' 9"
b. Ashington, 19th February 1957

CAREER: UNITED app 1973, pro Aug 1974/ Sheffield Wednesday Aug 1978 £20,000/ IK Tord(Sweden) free cs 1982/ Mansfield Town Oct 1982 to cs 1983/ Carlisle United trial cs 1984/ Blyth Spartans Sept 1984.

Debut v Arsenal (a) 18/3/75

Ray Blackhall

Nicknamed 'Bomber', Ray Blackhall was developed by Newcastle United through the junior sides and broke initially into the first eleven during season 1974-75 and more permanently in 1976-77. He was a tough-tackling defender who liked to go forward and who improved rapidly the more he played in United's First Division side. Was also given a midfield role for the black'n'whites and was often substitute. Released after relegation to the Second Division in 1978, Blackhall flourished under the guidance of Jack Charlton at Hillsborough where he made 140 outings for Sheffield Wednesday, being a regular when The Owls regained their Second Division status in season 1979-80.

Appearances:
FL: 26(11) apps. 0 gls.
FAC: 5(1) apps. 2 gls.
FLC: 0(1) app. 0 gls.
Eur: 1 app. 0 gls.
Others: 1(1) apps. 0 gls.
Total: *33(14) apps. 2 gls.*
Honours:
FL div 3 prom 1980.

BLACKLEY, John Henderson

Role: Centre-half 1977-1979
5' 10"
b. Westquarter, nr Falkirk, 12th May 1948

CAREER: Gairdoch United/Hibernian 1966/UNITED Oct 1977 £100,000/Preston North End July 1979 free/Hamilton Academical Oct 1981, becoming player-manager Oct 1982/Hibernian asst-manager cs 1983, becoming manager Sept 1984 to Nov 1986/Cowdenbeath manager Oct 1987/ Dundee asst-manager Sept 1988, becoming manager to Feb 1992/St Johnstone coach Nov 1993.

Debut v Derby County (h) 8/10/77

John Blackley

In over a decade operating in the Scottish scene, John Blackley was recognised as one of Scotland's most accomplished players. Cool and assured, he was a skilful centre-half who liked to play alongside a big partner in the middle of the back four. Blackley had the ability to set attacks moving with accurate distribution and the vision of a midfield player. On several occasions during the seventies the Scot had been linked with big moves south of the border, including one with United's boss Joe Harvey, before he eventually moved to England being purchased by one of Harvey's successors, Richard Dinnis, at a time of crisis at St James Park. By then John was 29 years old and reaching the end of his career, but he still displayed his almost casual and arrogant approach to the game. At St James Park, United fans were attracted to his play almost immediately, voting him Player of the Year, but his undoubted talent was unable to halt a United slide which saw the club drop into the Second Division and thereafter Blackley was more often than not found in the treatment room. Nicknamed 'Scoop' north of the border, he took part in Scotland's World Cup quest in 1974.

Appearances:
FL: 46 apps. 0 gls.
FAC: 5 apps. 0 gls.
FLC: 1 app. 0 gls.
Total: *52 apps. 0 gls.*
Honours:
7 Scot caps 1974-77/4 Scot u23 caps 1970-71/ 1 SL app. 1972/SLC winner 1973/ SLC finalist 1969, 1975/SC finalist 1972.

BLAKE, Sidney

Role: Goalkeeper 1905-1906, 1909-1914
5' 10"
b. Whitley Bay

CAREER: Willington Athletic/Whitley Athletic Oct 1904/UNITED Jan 1905/ Queens Park Rangers cs 1906/Whitley Athletic 1907/North Shields Athletic 1908/ UNITED May 1909 £30/ Coventry City May 1914 free/ Retired 1918/Coventry City trainer cs 1920.

Debut v Notts County (a) 14/4/06

Although Sid Blake made his United debut at outside-left, he later changed his role into that of a goalkeeper and became a secure and trustworthy custodian. Unfortunately, during his stay with Newcastle, the Magpies had internationals in Albert Gosnell and Jimmy Lawrence as rivals in both positions and Sid found chances in the senior team limited. Blake's best season with United was during 1911-12 when Lawrence was injured for nine games. He tried his luck in the Southern League with both QPR and Coventry City, during both clubs' pre Football League days, but Blake ended back in his native north east where he was a well known local player.

Sid Blake

Appearances:
FL: 14 apps. 0 gls.
FAC: 1 app. 0 gls.
Total: *15 apps. 0 gls.*

BLANTHORNE, Robert

Role: Centre-forward 1908-1910
6' 1"
b. Rock Ferry, Birkenhead, 8th January 1884
d. 1965

CAREER: Rock Ferry/Birkenhead/Liverpool 1906/Grimsby Town cs 1907/UNITED May 1908 £350/Hartlepools United Dec 1910.

Debut v Bradford City (h) 2/9/08

Signed as a replacement for the popular Bill Appleyard during the summer of 1908, Bob Blanthorpe had cruel luck in his Tyneside career. On his very first appearance, and as it turned out his only outing, he broke his leg and was out of action for almost a year. He had impressed United's directors after grabbing 14 goals in 28 league matches for the Mariners - and five in one FA Cup match against Carlisle. Well-built in the Appleyard mould, he stood over six feet tall and was a most assertive leader who could have become quite a star in a black'n'white shirt. After his injury Blanthorne was never the same marksman again, and by the time he was nearing fitness, United had completed the signing of England leader Albert Shepherd.

Appearances:
FL: 1 app. 0 gls.
Total: *1 app. 0 gls.*

BLYTH, Thomas Hope

Role: Centre-forward 1896-1898
6' 0"
b. Seaham Harbour, nr Sunderland,
16th October 1876
d. Ryhope, nr Sunderland, 16th December 1949

CAREER: Durham University/UNITED 1896 to 1898/Later becoming a Durham FA & FL referee/coached Old Bedens (Sunderland).

Debut v Burton Swifts (h) 27/3/1897 (scored once)

Thomas Blyth had only a brief stay with Newcastle United during the years leading up to the turn of the century. As understudy to top scorer Richard Smellie in United's Second Division team for season 1896-97, he was once called upon to lead the Magpies' attack. He did well, netting a goal in Newcastle's 2-1 victory over the now defunct club, Burton Swifts in front of 4,000 at St James Park. While he was on United's books, Blyth was training to become a teacher and later attended both the Universities of London and Durham. For many years he was a schoolmaster in Sunderland at The Bede School. Apart from his teaching profession, Thomas was also a Sunderland councillor, Freemason and keen sports enthusiast, as well as a life governor of Sunderland Orphanage. During World War One he fought at Arras and Ypres as a signaller in a siege battery. Nicknamed 'Tosh', he lived on Wearside to his death.

Appearances:
FL: 1 app. 1 gl.
Total: *1 app. 1 gl.*

Thomas Blyth

BOAM, Stuart William

Role: Centre-half 1979-1981
6' 1"
b. Kirkby in Ashfield, nr Mansfield,
28th January 1948

CAREER: Kirkby Boys' Club/Mansfield Town
July 1966/Middlesbrough June 1971 £50,000/
UNITED Aug 1979 £140,000/ Mansfield Town
player-manager July 1981 to Jan 1983/
Hartlepool United Mar 1983/Guisborough
Town player-manager Aug 1983/Occasional
scout, including for Newcastle United 1989-90.

Debut v Chelsea (h) 1/9/79

For over five years Stuart Boam had been the
linchpin of Middlesbrough's defence at a time
when the Teesside club possessed a fine side.
Tall and commanding at centre-half, Boam
was a formidable defender who, alongside
Willie Maddren, was respected in the First
Division. He appeared 378 times for the Reds
and was once tipped for an England cap.
When he opted for the short journey to join
United, he was over 30 years old, but still
helped give a shaky Magpie back-four
experience and stability for two seasons in
their bid to climb out of Division Two. Able to

dominate a centre-forward and rugged with it,
he was a born leader, captaining all his clubs.
He possessed neat skills on the ball too.
Turned down by Nottingham Forest as a
teenager, Stuart was recommended to his
home town club, Mansfield by former United
pre-war star Sammy Weaver. A former
toolmaker, Boam proceeded to make a big
name for himself with the Stags (213 games),
and later managed the club too. Stuart
afterwards resided in Kirkby and was
employed as a manager for Kodak.

> **Appearances:**
> *FL: 69 apps. 1 gl.*
> *FAC: 5 apps. 0 gls.*
> *FLC: 3 apps. 1 gl.*
> **Total:** *77 apps. 2 gls.*
> **Honours:**
> *FL div 2 champs 1974*

BODIN, Paul John

Role: Left-back 1991-1992
6' 0"
b. Cardiff, 13th September 1964

CAREER: Chelsea am. 1981/Newport County
app 1981, pro Jan 1982/Cardiff City Aug 1982/
Merthyr Tydfil Aug 1985/Bath City Aug 1985/
Newport County Jan 1988 £15,000/Swindon
Town Mar 1988 £30,000/Crystal Palace Mar
1991 £550,000(UNITED loan Dec 1991-Jan
1992)/Swindon Town Jan 1992 £225,000 to
cs 1996/Reading cs 1996 free.

Debut v Port Vale (h) 7/12/91

Newcastle's supporters only saw a fleeting
glimpse of Welsh international Paul Bodin
during a month's
loan deal in season
1991-92. He was
tried by manager
Ossie Ardiles for six
games but, despite
showing some
exciting attacking
ideas down the left
touchline, wasn't
offered a permanent
transfer. Returning
to Crystal Palace, he
quickly rejoined
Swindon Town
where he displayed
all his best football,   *Paul Bodin*

as a regular for the Robins in over 250 games. Bodin also netted many goals in his career, several from the penalty spot, including the last-minute winner to gain Swindon promotion to the top flight in a thrilling 4-3 Wembley play-off victory over Leicester City in May 1993. He did, however, miss one crucial spot-kick for Wales in a World Cup qualifying tie.

Appearances:
FL: 6 apps. 0 gls.
Total: *6 apps. 0 gls.*
Honours:
23 Wales caps 1990-95/1 Wales u21 cap 1983/7 Wales youth apps./FL div 1 prom 1993/FL div 3 prom 1983/ FL div 2 prom 1996.

BOGIE, Ian

Role: Midfield 1985-1989
5' 7"
b. Walker, Newcastle upon Tyne, 6th December 1967

CAREER: Wallsend Boy's Club/UNITED app 1985, pro cs 1986/Preston North End Feb 1989 cash-exch for G.Brazil/Millwall Aug 1991 £145,000/Leyton Orient loan Oct 1993, pmt Dec 1993/Port Vale Mar 1995 £50,000.

Debut v Luton Town (a) 30/8/86

One of several bright young hopefuls developed through the club's youth policy during the eighties, Ian Bogie was a midfield find with a sure touch on the ball and an eye for the opening in the mould of Paul Gascoigne, whom he had followed through the ranks. The media in fact dubbed the local lad, the new Gazza, but Bogie never lived up to that unfair billing. Small and stocky, he showed United's fans nice skills on his limited outings, but was unable to stamp his authority on the

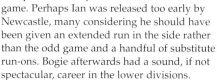
Ian Bogie

game. Perhaps Ian was released too early by Newcastle, many considering he should have been given an extended run in the side rather than the odd game and a handful of substitute run-ons. Bogie afterwards had a sound, if not spectacular, career in the lower divisions.

Appearances:
FL: 7(7) apps. 0 gls.
FAC: 1(2) apps. 0 gls.
FLC: 0(1) app. 0 gls.
Others: 3(1) apps. 1 gl.
Totals: *11(11) apps. 1 gl.*
Honours:
Eng schools app.

BOLTON, Hugh

Role: Inside-right 1905-1906
5' 8"
b. Port Glasgow

CAREER:
Clydeville/Port Glasgow Athletic 1902/UNITED May 1905/Everton Jan 1906/Bradford Park Avenue Dec 1908/ Greenock Morton cs 1910.

Debut v Sheffield United (a) 2/12/05

Hugh Bolton

Hugh Bolton appeared only once for United during the 1905-06 season, as stand-in for established schemer Jimmy Howie. Yet the young Scot was to be quickly picked up by Everton, United's main rivals during the Edwardian era, and amazingly faced the Magpies in the same season's FA Cup final. He went on to become a favourite at Goodison Park turning out on 87 occasions for the Blues and always had a keen eye for the goal. Bolton could strike the ball hard or place it accurately and netted 34 goals for Everton. He started his career in the Scottish League with the old Port Glasgow club.

Appearances:
FL: 1 app. 0 gls.
Total: *1 app. 0 gls.*
Honours:
FAC winner 1906/FAC finalist 1907.

BOOTH, Curtis

Role: Inside-left 1913-1920
5' 11"
b. Gateshead, 12th October 1891
d. Amsterdam, Netherlands, 29th October 1949

CAREER: Wallsend Elm Villa/UNITED Nov 1913 £15/Leeds City war-guest 1915-16/ Norwich City Sept 1920 £800/Accrington Stanley player-manager June 1923 to May 1924/Erfurt(Germany) June 1925/Racing Club de Paris(France) 1933/Turkish FA head-coach Sept 1936/Later coaching on the continent in Holland and Egypt.

Debut v Sheffield Wednesday (h) 9/9/14

Curtis Booth was a popular local forward in North Eastern League soccer who earned a contract at St James Park before the outbreak of the First World War. He was unfortunate to have just made the breakthrough at Gallowgate in season 1914-15 when the hostilities halted his eye-catching progress. Booth served with the Durham Light Infantry and was injured fighting at Villers Bretouneux but, once recovered, he started brightly in the Magpies' side in the first season after peace was restored. Vying for the inside-forward position with another local product, Andy Smailes, he lost out and moved south to conclude his playing days with Norwich City and Accrington, where he was Stanley's first manager in the Football League. On his debut for the Lancashire club he had to retire after only 20 minutes due to a knee ligament problem, and didn't play again. Booth later became a respected coach overseas, residing in the Netherlands to his death.

Curtis Booth

Appearances:
FL: 34 apps. 6 gls.
War: 8 apps. 5 gls.
Total: 42 apps. 11 gls.

BOTT, Wilfred

Role: Outside-right
1934-1936
5' 7"
b. Featherstone, nr Pontefract, 25th April 1907

CAREER: Edlington CW/Doncaster Rovers Mar 1927/ Huddersfield Town Mar 1931 £1,000/ UNITED Dec 1934 £1,000 plus T.Lang/ Queens Park Rangers May 1936 £750 to 1940/ Lancaster Town/Aldershot war-guest 1939-40/Brighton war-guest 1939-40/ Chelsea war-guest 1939-40/ Queens Park Rangers war-guest 1940-41/Colchester United c1945.

Debut v Bury (h) 1/1/35 (scored three)

On joining Newcastle United Wilfred Bott made immediate headlines by striking a marvellous hat-trick on his first outing in a black'n'white shirt. A flier, he was very fast and always willing to cut in from his wing berth and fire a shot at goal. With outstanding displays for Huddersfield totalling 26 goals in 115 games and including an important role in the Terriers' championship runners-up spot in season 1933-34, Bott had caught the attention of several clubs. He replaced the ageing Jimmy Boyd in United's side, but after only two seasons moved on to join QPR where he became a terrace favourite, again grabbing goals from the wing, this time 42 in 102 appearances.

Appearances:
FL: 37 apps. 11 gls.
FAC: 7 apps. 4 gls.
Total: 44 apps. 15 gls.

BOTTOM, Arthur Edwin

Role: Inside-right 1958
5' 10"
b. Sheffield, 28th February 1930

CAREER: Sheffield YMCA/Sheffield United
Apr 1947/York City June 1954/UNITED
Feb 1958 £4,500/Chesterfield Nov 1958
£5,000/Boston United cs 1960/
Alfreton Town.

Debut v Everton (a) 22/2/58 (scored twice)

Purchased at a time of crisis at St James
Park, Arthur Bottom gave good short
term service to United when they were
fighting to remain in the First Division
during season 1957-58. He came into the
Magpies' side when they were 19th in the
table and immediately made an impact
netting a brace of goals on his debut and
seven more for the rest of the season in
only eight games. Bottom linked with Len
White up front and saved United from
the drop. A battling, aggressive striker, he
was strong and forceful in attack and a
legendary figure at Bootham Crescent,
being York's goalgetter during their FA
Cup exploits in the mid-fifties. Arthur led
the line when the Tykes reached the FA
Cup semi-final in 1955 and faced the
black'n'whites. They very nearly caused a

huge upset by reaching Wembley and
Bottom's display against United greatly
impressed the club's directors. He had an
explosive record, scoring 105 goals in 158
senior outings for York and was the Third
Division North's leading marksman in 1954-55
with 31 goals - still a club record for York, and
netted another eight goals in the FA Cup.
When United signed Welsh maestro Ivor
Allchurch, Bottom found himself frozen out as
the White-Eastham-Allchurch trio came
together. He was unfortunate and moved on,
although his goals tally perhaps proved he
deserved better. Arthur was once a ball-boy at
Bramall Lane; he appeared on six occasions as
Sheffield United won the Second Division title
in 1952-53.

> **Appearances:**
> *FL: 11 apps. 10 gls.*
> **Total:** *11 apps. 10 gls.*

BOWDEN, Edwin Raymond

Role: Inside-forward 1937-1939
5' 10"
b. Looe, Cornwall, 13th September 1909

CAREER: Looe/Plymouth Argyle am. cs 1926,
pro June 1927/Arsenal Mar 1933 £7,000/
UNITED Nov 1937 £5,000/Retired 1939.

Debut v Southampton (h) 6/11/37

A forward full of
grace and style,
Charlie Buchan noted
Bowden as being "a
great player with the
ball". Making his
name in the fabulous
Arsenal side of the
thirties, Ray Bowden
dovetailed so well
with Joe Hume in the
Gunners' line-up that
they formed
England's right flank
too. He arrived at St
James Park late into
his career, in a bid to
revitalise a Magpie
eleven who, up to his
arrival, had made
hard work of getting

Ray Bowden

49

out of the Second Division. Appearing at both inside-left or right and despite being sidelined with injury and illness, Bowden certainly inspired United when he was in the mood but, like many of the stylish greats, lacked consistency. Of a rather frail physique, mild-tempered and a gentleman on the field, Ray oozed class and could turn a game with a single pass. Once a clerk in Plymouth, as a junior he scored 10 goals in one game and 100 in a season for Looe and was immediately snapped up by Argyle. With the Pilgrims he bagged 87 goals in 153 games and at Arsenal 47 in 136 matches. Bowden also scored a hat-trick on the very last day of his senior career,

netting three for United against Swansea Town just prior to war being declared. He later ran a sports outfitters business in Plymouth.

Appearances:
FL: 48 apps. 6 gls.
FAC: 4 apps. 0 gls.
War: 3 apps. 3 gls.
Total: *55 apps. 9 gls.*
Honours:
6 Eng caps 1935-37/2 FL apps. 1935-36/
1 unoff Eng app. 1935/FA app. 1931/
Eng trial app. 1938/FL champs 1934, 1935/
FL div 3(S) champs 1930/FAC winner 1936.

BOWMAN, J.

Role: Outside-right 1893-1894
b. Scotland
Debut v Woolwich Arsenal (a) 2/9/1893

Signed in August 1893 from Dundee East End, Bowman was described in the local press as being one of the best forwards on Tayside. He appeared only once for the Magpies, in the historic inaugural Football League meeting with Arsenal that took place in the capital and ended in a 2-2 draw. Bowman did not stay on Tyneside long, leaving before United's first league season, 1893-94, was completed. He was a reserve for established forwards Crate and Quinn.

Appearances:
FL: 1 app. 0 gls.
Total: *1 app. 0 gls.*

*Jimmy Boyd left
& illustrated right*

BRACEWELL, Paul William

Role: Midfield 1992-1995
5' 8"
b. Heswall, Cheshire, 19th July 1962

CAREER: Stoke City app 1978, pro 1980/ Sunderland June 1983 £225,000/ Everton May 1984 £250,000/Sunderland Aug 1989 loan, pmt Sept 1989 £250,000/ UNITED June 1992 £250,000/ Sunderland player-coach May 1995 £50,000.

Debut v Southend United (h) 15/8/92 (scored once)

When Kevin Keegan made a transfer swoop for 30 year-old Sunderland captain, Paul Bracewell during the summer of 1992, both Tyne and Wear were stunned. Bracewell had just led the Roker side out at Wembley in the FA Cup final and was the cornerstone of the Reds' line-up. But United's boss pulled off a marvellous deal, bringing the highly experienced England midfielder to Gallowgate to provide the Magpies' new side with a bargain-priced anchor man. Having a steadying influence, Paul's gritty determination knitted perfectly with his

BOYD, James Murray

Role: Outside-right 1925-1935
5' 10"
b. Glasgow, 29th April 1907
d. Bournemouth, 22nd March 1991

CAREER: Petershill jnrs/Edinburgh St Bernards Oct 1924/UNITED May 1925 £600/Derby County May 1935 £1,000/Bury Jan 1937/Dundee Oct 1937/Grimsby Town June 1938/Leyton Orient war-guest 1943-44/Brighton war-guest 1943-44/Retired Mar 1947 and coached in Sweden/Newcastle United scout Aug 1949/Middlesbrough scout.

Debut v Cardiff City (a) 20/9/26

Jimmy Boyd had a consistent if not headlining career at St James Park. Never the flamboyant type, but a thoroughly professional team-man who ran up and down the right wing supplying accurate crosses, he was noted for his penetrating far post ball and ability to snatch a goal himself.

During season 1931-32, Boyd grabbed 23 goals from the wide position and was a key player in the Magpies' run to FA Cup glory. A regular for United in six seasons after taking over from Tommy Urwin, he spent a decade on Tyneside. Always immaculately turned out, on and off the pitch, during his early career he was the subject of a legal test case over the signing of amateur players by senior clubs in Scotland. A dressing-room joker, Boyd kept United's thirties stars smiling with a stream of humorous pranks. Afterwards a Physical Education instructor, in later life Jimmy became an expert indoor bowls player and represented England. He lived into his eighties, residing in Westbourne.

Appearances:
FL: 198 apps. 58 gls.
FAC: 16 apps. 5 gls.
Others: 1 app. 1 gl.
Total: *215 apps. 64 gls.*
Honours:
1 Scot cap 1934/FAC winner 1932.

simple yet efficient distribution of the ball. It was, however, at Goodison Park that Bracewell had found most success, in an enterprising midfield alongside Reid, Steven and fellow United colleague Kevin Sheedy, the foursome became the engine room behind Everton's success. Unlucky to appear in four FA Cup finals and lose them all, he was also unfortunate to undergo over a dozen

Paul Bracewell

operations during his career, including a cancer scare at St James Park but Bracewell always bounced back to prove a welcome asset. Cool and composed, he was a vital cog in the resurgence of Newcastle United.

Appearances:
FL/PL: 64(9) apps. 3 gls.
FAC: 6(2) apps. 0 gls.
FLC: 3(1) apps. 1 gl.
Others: 2 apps. 0 gls.
Total: *75(12) apps. 4 gls.*
Honours:
3 Eng caps 1985-86/13 Eng u21 caps 1983-85/FL champs 1985/FL div 1 champs 1993, 1996/FL div 2 prom 1990/FAC finalist 1985, 1986, 1989, 1992/ECWC winner 1985.

BRADLEY, George Joseph

Role: Right-half 1938-1946
6' 0"
b. Maltby, South Yorkshire, 7th January 1917

CAREER: Maltby Hall Old Boys/ Rotherham United Mar 1937/UNITED Nov 1938 £820/Hull City war-guest 1940-41/Bradford City war guest 1941-42/ Rotherham United war-guest 1943-45/ Arsenal war-guest 1944-45/Millwall Sept 1946 £1,000/Guildford City Aug 1950.

Debut v Blackburn Rovers (a) 19/11/38

George Bradley had the makings of a decent player when he stood in for the established Jimmy Gordon, but was one of a group of youngsters to have their careers in the game ruined by the outbreak of the Second World War. He lost his best footballing years to the hostilities and, by the time the Yorkshireman had returned to St James Park as peace was restored, found a new batch of youngsters ahead of him. Moving to Millwall, he did well at The Den appearing on nearly 100 occasions for the Lions. Bradley afterwards resided in Guildford.

Appearances:
FL: 1 app. 0 gls.
War: 20 apps. 1 gl.
Total: *21 apps. 1 gl.*

BRADLEY, Robert

Role: Right-back 1927-1929
5′ 10″
b. Washington, 16th September 1906
d. Carlisle, 18th February 1934

CAREER: Bishop Auckland/UNITED Mar 1927 £100/Fulham May 1929 £125/Tunbridge Wells Rangers June 1930/Carlisle United Aug 1932 to his death.

Debut v Leicester City (h) 7/4/28

An amateur player at Gallowgate for a time, Robert Bradley arrived on the staff with a big reputation having played for famous non-leaguers Bishop Auckland. Understudy to Alf Maitland during his stay on Tyneside, Bob was chosen for a single Football League appearance before

Robert Bradley

moving to Craven Cottage. He later became a noted servant to Carlisle United and was skipper of the side when he died suddenly aged only 27. Bradley made 70 appearances prior to his untimely death which occurred shortly after playing for the Cumbrians at Chester. Complaining of stomach pains he travelled back to his lodgings and the following morning was found dead in his bed. A post-mortem determined death was from natural causes.

> **Appearances:**
> *FL: 1 app. 0 gls.*
> **Total:** *1 app. 0 gls.*

BRADLEY, William

Role: Goalkeeper 1914-1927
6′ 0″
b. Wardley, Gateshead, 1st March 1893
d. North Shields

CAREER: Dunston Wednesday/Fatfield Albion/Jarrow Caledonians Oct 1911/Portsmouth Mar 1912/UNITED Apr 1914 £300/Ashington May 1927 to Feb 1929/North Shields Feb 1930, becoming a director in Mar 1933.

Debut v Preston North End (h) 1/11/19

A goalkeeper who gave United fine service before and after the First World War, Bill Bradley was reserve to Jimmy Lawrence as a youngster but claimed the 'keeper's jersey for himself during the early years of the twenties. As United embarked on a Wembley FA Cup run in 1924, Bill found himself second choice again, this time to the veteran Sandy Mutch who had been signed from Huddersfield. Bradley looked like losing out on a medal until Mutch was injured in the last league fixture before the Wembley appointment and missed the final. In stepped Bill Bradley to play the game of his life against Aston Villa as United lifted the trophy. Tall and thin, Bradley could be a commanding goalkeeper on his day. He served in the Tank Corps during the Great War and later ran a profitable hen ranch on Tyneside. For many years he resided in North Shields and ran a newsagents business.

> **Appearances:**
> *FL: 133 apps. 0 gls.*
> *FAC: 10 apps. 0 gls.*
> *War: 4 apps. 0 gls.*
> **Total:** *147 apps. 0 gls.*
> **Honours:**
> *FAC winner 1924.*

BRADSHAW, Darren Shaun

Role: Centre-half 1989-1992
5′ 11′
b. Sheffield, 19th March 1967

CAREER: Sheffield Wednesday app/Matlock Town/Chesterfield trial Aug 1987/Matlock Town/York City Nov 1987 £2,000/UNITED loan Aug 1989, pmt Sept 1989 £10,000/Peterborough United May 1992 free(Plymouth Argyle loan 1994-95)/Blackpool Oct 1994 £65,000.

Debut v Swindon Town (a) 30/12/89

Tall and pacy, Darren Bradshaw possessed ideal qualities for the central defender's position. Although a bright prospect as a

Darren Bradshaw

teenager, a broken leg at Hillsborough ruined his early career, but he received a chance of top football again when he was recommended to United by his former boss at York, Bobby Saxton who was assistant manager at St James Park. Darren was initially on loan at Gallowgate as a 22 year-old and impressed manager Jim Smith during a month's trial earning a full time contract. The blond-haired Bradshaw was never a regular in United's line-up, competing with Scott and Appleby at centre-half and Stimson and Neilson at full-back but he was versatile, appearing on the right or left of defence and was used as cover across the back line. He was appointed captain whilst playing at Peterborough. His younger brother, Carl appeared with both Sheffield clubs, Manchester City and Norwich. Prior to entering football Bradshaw had been a power station boiler engineer.

Appearances:
FL: 33(6) apps. 0 gls.
FAC: 2(1) apps. 0 gls.
FLC: 3 apps. 0 gls.
Others: 2 apps. 0 gls.
Total: *40(7) apps. 0 gls.*
Honours:
Eng schools app./Eng youth app. 1984.

BRANDER, George Milne

Role: Outside-left 1952-1954
5' 9"
b. Aberdeen, 1st November 1929

CAREER: Aberdeen East End/Raith Rovers/ UNITED Mar 1952 £1,850/Stirling Albion Jan 1954 £750/Arbroath/Fraserburgh/ Huntly/Elgin City 1959.
Debut v Derby County (h) 1/11/52

George Brander stepped into the role of the great Bobby Mitchell on the few occasions his fellow countryman was sidelined through injury. Brander was fast and skilful, but had to be content to watch his contemporary dominate the left wing position for his entire stay on Tyneside. All his appearances for the Magpies were in season 1952-53, and George afterwards continued his career back in Scottish football residing in the north east of the country.

George Brander

Appearances:
FL: 5 apps. 2 gls.
Total: *5 apps. 2 gls.*

BRAYSON, Paul

Role: Striker 1994-date
5' 6"
b. Newcastle upon Tyne, 16th September 1977

CAREER: Walker Central/UNITED app July 1994, pro Aug 1995.
Debut v Bristol City (h) 4/10/95 (FLC)

Paul Brayson has scored almost 100 goals in reserve and junior football during his two seasons on Newcastle United's staff. Nicknamed 'Brassy', the Tyneside youngster is

Paul Brayson

highly thought of within the corridors of St James' Park and has a natural touch in front of goal. Small, slightly-built and boyish-looking, Brayson earned a call-up as an 18 year old for his senior baptism in a League Cup tie during 1995-96. Quiet, direct and thoughtful in attack, Paul has been a regular at the Football Association's training complex at Lilleshall and has also reached his country's youth side, and is possibly destined to become the latest in a long line of home-grown stars. Brayson was brought up in the shadows of the old Gallowgate pylons and attended Rutherford School in the city's west end. He once netted eight goals in a match against Hartlepool juniors.

Appearances:
FLC: 1 app. 0 gls.
Total: *1 app. 0 gls.*
Honours:
Eng youth app. 1996.

BRAZIL, Gary Nicholas

Role: Striker 1989-1990
5' 11"
b. Tunbridge Wells, 19th September 1962

CAREER: Crystal Palace app 1978/Sheffield United Aug 1980 free(Port Vale loan 1984-85)/ Preston North End Feb 1985 £20,000 (Mansfield Town loan 1984-85)/UNITED Feb 1989 £250,000/Fulham loan Sept 1990, pmt Nov 1990-cs 1996 £110,000/Cambridge United trial Aug 1996/Barnet Sept 1996 free.

Debut v Coventry City (a) 11/2/89

At Newcastle as the black'n'whites struggled, initially to stay in Division One, then to get out of the Second Division, Gary Brazil was often named as substitute but never given an extended opportunity in either attack or midfield. In his 27 games for the Magpies,

Brazil started only eight fixtures, and perhaps should have been given more of a chance by managers Willie McFaul and Jim Smith. Captain of Preston when he joined United, he had netted over 50 goals for the Deepdale club and was recognised as one of the top players in the lower divisions. Becoming frustrated at the lack of first-team action on Tyneside, Gary moved south and was an instant hit at Craven Cottage. He quickly became a favourite and totalled over 250 outings for the Thames outfit. During the early part of his career, Gary took part in Sheffield United's promotion from Division Three in 1983-84 making eight appearances.

Appearances:
FL: 7(16) apps. 2 gls.
FAC: 0(1) app. 0 gls.
FLC: 1(1) apps. 1 gl.
Others: 0(1) app. 0 gls.
Total: *8(19) apps. 3 gls.*
Honours:
FL div 4 prom 1987.

Gary Brazil

Frank Brennan puts a stop to a Blackpool attack during the 1951 FA Cup final.

BRENNAN, Frank

Role: Centre-half 1946-1956
6' 3"
b. Annathill, nr Coatbridge, 23rd April 1924

CAREER: Coatbridge St Patricks 1940/
Airdrieonians am. Feb 1941/UNITED
May 1946 £7,500/North Shields Mar 1956,
becoming coach/British Council coach,
including in Singapore and Trinidad/

North Shields manager Apr 1967/
Darlington coach 1970, becoming manager
Aug 1971 to Nov 1971/South Shields coach
Feb to Oct 1972.

Debut v Millwall (a) 31/8/46

A tremendous centre-half for Newcastle
United, Frank Brennan is rated the best
to have played for the Magpies in over
a century of football. Known as the
'Rock of Tyneside', he was cool-headed,

steady and tough - a no nonsense defender who formed a terrific bond with the Geordie supporters for a decade. A towering 6'3", weighing over thirteen and a half stone and wearing size 12 boots, he was fast for such a big man and possessed all the necessary attributes for combat with the opposition. Frank relished a duel with the big-name centre-forwards of his era and often came out on top, being the king-pin to United's defence as they first won promotion then lifted the FA Cup two years in succession. By the time the black'n'whites reached Wembley again in

1955, Brennan had become entangled in a dispute with the club's hierarchy, an unsavoury affair which led to protest meetings, speeches at the Union Congress and the Scot's eventual departure from the first-class game. Brennan later travelled the world as a coach for the British Council and then successfully led North Shields to Wembley. For many years he ran a sports outfitters business close to St James Park and later retired to live in Whitley Bay. During his early days at Gallowgate he was employed as an electrical engineer at Hartley Main Colliery.

Appearances:
FL: 318 apps. 3 gls.
FAC: 29 apps. 0 gls.
Others: 2 apps. 0 gls.
Total: *349 apps. 3 gls.*
Honours:
7 Scot caps 1947-54/3 unoff Scot caps 1946-47/FAC winner 1951, 1952/FL div 2 prom 1948/FAAC winner 1969(m).

BROADIS, Ivan Arthur

Role: Inside-right 1953-1955
5' 9"
b. Isle of Dogs, London, 18th December 1922

CAREER: Finchley/Northfleet/Millwall war-guest 1940-41/Manchester United war-guest 1942-44/Tottenham Hotspur war-guest 1944-46/Blackpool war-guest 1944-45/Carlisle United war-guest 1944-45/Bradford Park Avenue war-guest 1944-45/Carlisle United player-manager Aug 1946/Sunderland Jan 1949 £18,000/Manchester City Oct 1951 £25,000/UNITED Oct 1953 £17,500/Carlisle United player-coach July 1955 £3,500/Queen of the South June 1959/Retired playing 1960, coached to 1962.

Debut v Sheffield United (a) 31/10/53

Ivan Broadis was a creative, fast thinking inside-forward who possessed a lethal shot yet, although a well-respected player during the fifties, he never fitted in too well at Gallowgate. That was due perhaps to a poor relationship with the club's board and trainer Norman Smith. Outspoken, Broadis was once quoted as saying, "I know what people say about me. That I'm hard to please. That I'm a rebel. Better to speak your mind than be a slave". Known commonly as 'Ivor', he arrived at St James Park to boost United's creative ability on the field and rivalled fellow international Reg Davies for the Number 8 shirt. Broadis scored twice on his home debut and at times showed a mastery in everything he did. Appearing in the 1954 World Cup finals, he had a fine record in an England shirt grabbing eight goals in 14 appearances, but after displaying some good form in United's FA Cup run in 1955,

Ivor Broadis

was left out of the Wembley line-up and moved on within weeks of the Magpies' victory. During the Second World War Ivor was a commissioned officer, a navigator with a Dakota squadron, and also played for a number of sides on service, doing especially well with Spurs, netting 38 goals in 83 games. On the restoration of peace, Broadis became, at 23 years of age, the youngest player-boss at Brunton Park and later sold himself to Sunderland. He always had a close tie with Carlisle though, and by the time he retired and had completed a second spell with the Cumbrians he had clocked up over 250 games for the club. Afterwards Ivor became a sports journalist, initially on Tyneside with *The Journal*, then back in Cumbria with the *Cumberland News* and *Evening News & Star*, residing in the Carlisle area.

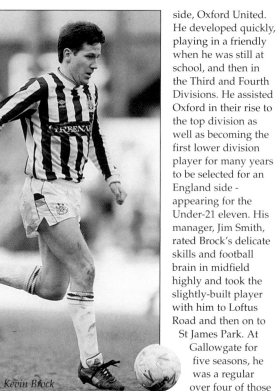

Kevin Brock

Appearances:
FL: 42 apps. 15 gls.
FAC: 9 apps. 3 gls.
Total: *51 apps. 18 gls.*
Honours:
14 Eng caps 1952-54/3 FL apps. 1952-53/ 4 FL(N) apps. 1956-58.

BROCK, Kevin Stanley

Role: Midfield 1988-1994
5' 9"
b. Middleton Stoney, nr Bicester, 9th September 1962

CAREER: Oxford United May 1979/Queens Park Rangers Aug 1987 £260,000/UNITED Dec 1988 £300,000 to June 1994 free(Cardiff City loan 1993-94)/Cambridge United trial July 1994/Stockport County trial Sept 1994/Stevenage Borough Nov 1994/Yeovil Town Feb 1995/Rushden & Diamonds cs 1995.

Debut v Wimbledon (h) 10/12/88

Although a much sought after schoolboy star, courted by a string of big clubs including Manchester United, Everton and Spurs, Kevin Brock preferred to sign for his home town

side, Oxford United. He developed quickly, playing in a friendly when he was still at school, and then in the Third and Fourth Divisions. He assisted Oxford in their rise to the top division as well as becoming the first lower division player for many years to be selected for an England side - appearing for the Under-21 eleven. His manager, Jim Smith, rated Brock's delicate skills and football brain in midfield highly and took the slightly-built player with him to Loftus Road and then on to St James Park. At Gallowgate for five seasons, he was a regular over four of those years and at times looked a very good player always liable to find the net. He just missed out on promotion in the play-offs of 1990 when he had his best season for United. But Brock was also often on the sidelines through injury or illness during the latter period of his career with the Magpies and maybe lacked the determination to reach the very top. He wasn't part of either Ossie Ardiles' or Kevin Keegan's plans and was handed a free transfer. Brock once appeared in goal during an emergency for United, against Birmingham City during the club's championship season in 1993. Whilst with Oxford he totalled 305 senior games and was also a noted local cricketer.

Appearances:
FL: 137(10) apps. 14 gls.
FAC: 11 apps. 1 gl.
FLC: 7 apps. 1 gl.
Others: 7(1) apps. 1 gl.
Total: *162(11) apps. 17 gls.*
Honours:
4 Eng u21 caps 1984-86/1 Eng B cap 1988/ Eng schools app. 1978/FLC winner 1986/ FL div 2 champs 1985/FL div 3 champs 1984.

BROWN, Alan

Role: Striker 1981-1982
5' 11"
b. Easington, County Durham, 22nd May 1959

CAREER: Easington/Sunderland Sept 1976(UNITED loan Nov 1981-Jan 1982)/ Shrewsbury Town July 1982/Doncaster Rovers Mar 1984 £35,000 to 1986.

Debut v Chelsea (a) 7/11/81

Arriving at St James Park from Wearside on an eight week trial deal, Alan Brown quickly made an impression on United's supporters forming a fruitful partnership with Imre Varadi. He was a bustling front man who put himself about and with his devastating pace was a considerable handful for defenders. However, to the surprise of many, the blond-haired striker was not retained by Newcastle and returned to Roker Park amidst controversy, some claiming he was injured with hamstring and back problems, whilst others noted that United had no cash to purchase him. Later in the season United brought David Mills to Tyneside as his replacement. Brown had been a 17 year-old debutant for Sunderland, while the Reds had also just pipped United for his signature from

Alan Brown

school. At the end of his career Alan achieved promotion to Division Three with Doncaster in 1983-84 (9 apps.).

Appearances:
FL: 5 apps. 3 gls.
Total: *5 apps. 3 gls.*
Honours:
FL div 2 prom 1980.

BROWN, Harry

Role: Inside-left 1906-1907
5' 8"
b. Northampton, November 1883
d. Basingstoke, 9th February 1934

CAREER: St Sepulchres(Northampton)/ Northampton Town 1902/West Bromwich Albion Nov 1903 £200/Southampton Apr 1905/UNITED July 1906 £380/Bradford Park Avenue Oct 1907 £250/Fulham Mar 1908/ Southampton Sept 1910/Woolston Nov 1913.

Harry Brown

Debut v Birmingham (a) 8/9/06 (scored three)

Although purchased as a stand-in for Scottish international Ronald Orr, from the start Harry Brown shone in a black'n'white shirt. He netted a marvellous hat-trick on his debut and finished the 1906-07 season a league championship medal holder with 22 games to his name. Slightly-framed and small, but deceptively quick off the mark, he could unleash a fierce shot. Harry though only remained on Tyneside for a little over a year, before heading for Yorkshire after being displaced by United's international stars of the time. Brown earlier had performed well with the Saints, scoring 31 goals in 81 senior fixtures for Southampton. After retiring he became a publican as well as a greengrocer, both in the Southampton area. Sadly later in life, in 1933, he contracted a virus which attacked the optic nerve causing the loss of his sight. The illness quickly spread and he died within a few months aged 50.

Appearances:
FL: 24 apps. 8 gls.
Others: 1 app. 2 gls.
Total: *25 apps. 10 gls.*
Honours:
FL champs 1907.

BROWN, Malcolm

Role: Right-back 1983-1985
6' 2"
b. Salford, 13th December 1956

CAREER: Bury app 1973, pro Oct 1975/Huddersfield Town May 1977 free/UNITED July 1983 £100,000/ Huddersfield Town June 1985 £45,000/ Rochdale Feb 1989/Stockport County July 1989/Rochdale Aug 1991 free to cs 1992.

Debut v Leicester City (a) 25/8/84

Malcolm Brown was rated as the best defender in the lower divisions when he was purchased by Arthur Cox for a big fee. He was part of a double full-back signing along with John Ryan, both players arriving in a bid to boost Newcastle's promotion campaign for 1983-84. As it turned out, Brown missed the whole of

Malcolm Brown

that wonderful Keegan-inspired season and didn't make his debut for fully twelve months due to a snapped Achilles tendon injury sustained in training, and this after not missing a fixture for the Terriers in 259 games - a five year record! A cheerful and resilient personality, Brown bounced back to become a regular in United's return to Division One, but surprisingly was allowed to move back to Leeds Road in the summer of 1985 for a knock-down price. He proceeded to appear on over 400 occasions for the Yorkshire club. At 6'2" and over 13 stone he was a powerful defender and the tallest full-back to appear for the Magpies.

Appearances:
FL: 39 apps. 0 gls.
FAC: 2 apps. 0 gls.
FLC: 4 apps. 0 gls.
Total: *45 apps. 0 gls.*
Honours:
FL div 4 champs 1980/FL div 3 prom 1983/ FL div 4 prom 1991.

BROWN, Noel

Role: Outside-right 1907-1908
Debut v Aston Villa (h) 8/4/08

Joining Newcastle United from local football in 1907, Brown deputised for England international Jackie Rutherford in the Magpies' senior line-up only once, during season 1907-08. That wasn't a happy afternoon for United as Villa won 5-2 on Tyneside during the black'n'whites' preparations for the FA Cup final.

Appearances:
FL: 1 app. 0 gls.
Total: *1 app. 0 gls.*

BROWNLIE, John

Role: Right-back 1978-1982
5' 10"
b. Caldercruix, Lanarkshire, 11th March 1952

CAREER: Pumpherston jnrs/Hibernian Apr 1969/UNITED Aug 1978 cash-exch deal for R.Callachan/Middlesbrough July 1982 £30,000 (Valaudus (Finland) loan 1983-84)/ Hartlepool United Aug 1984 free/Berwick Rangers Aug 1985/Blyth Spartans Jan 1986/Ashington player-coach/Cowdenbeath asst-manager Nov 1987, becoming manager to May 1992/Clyde asst-manager cs 1992/ Meadowbank Thistle manager Dec 1993 to Feb 1994/ Clyde asst-manager 1994 to Sept 1996.

Debut v Cambridge United (a) 2/9/78

Right-back John Brownlie was a highly respected player on the Scottish beat, like his international colleague at Easter Road, John Blackley, who also made the journey over the border to sign for the Magpies. At his peak in the early seventies, Brownlie was out of action for over a season with a badly broken leg and never quite regained the impressive form that had made him the target of nearly every top English club. By the time John had signed for the Magpies, he was attempting to resurrect a career that had stagnated. Brownlie became a favourite of United's fans very quickly, showing glimpses of a quality player in an ordinary Magpie eleven. He was always willing to surge forward in the modern style and could pack a cracking shot. With his permed hair style, fashionable in the early eighties, he was Newcastle's most exciting

BRUCE, Alexander Robert

Role: Striker 1974-1975
5' 8"
b. Dundee, 23rd December 1952

CAREER: Dundee jnrs/Preston
North End May 1970/UNITED Jan
1974 £150,000/Preston North End
Sept 1975 cash-exch for J.Bird/Wigan
Athletic asst-player-manager cs 1983
free/Retired as player Apr 1985.

Debut v Southampton (a) 5/2/74

After striking plenty goals for
Preston, Alex Bruce was purchased
for one of Newcastle's biggest fees
and in the middle of United's 1974
FA Cup run to Wembley. Being cup-
tied with the Deepdale club, he rarely
received an opportunity in Joe
Harvey's first team that season, and
afterwards found it almost
impossible to break the Macdonald-
Tudor front combination. Neither tall
nor powerful, the ginger-haired Bruce
relied on positional play and quick
thinking to convert a goal chance. He
returned to Preston without
reaching double figures in
any of his three seasons at
St James Park, and although
he won an Under-23 cap for
his country when on
United's books, has
ultimately to be regarded
as an expensive flop. Bruce
though, found his touch
again with the Lilywhites
as the Third Division's
leading scorer in 1977-78,
hitting 157 goals in 363
league matches, not far off
Tom Finney's club record.
Alex afterwards resided in
that town where he was
employed as a leisure centre manager. Bruce
scored in Newcastle's Texaco Cup final success
over Southampton in 1975.

Alex Bruce

John Brownlie

player in season 1979-80. An injury
saw him out of the reckoning for a
long period, then a dispute with the
club over terms saw the Scot depart
just as the Magpies were ready to
take off; Brownlie headed for
Middlesbrough just as Kevin Keegan
was set to sign for Newcastle. John
was capped by Scotland before his
20th birthday, whilst his elder
brother appeared for Partick Thistle.

Appearances:
FL: 124 apps. 2 gls.
FAC: 7(1) apps. 1 gl.
FLC: 4 apps. 0 gls.
Total: *135(1) apps. 3 gls.*
Honours:
7 Scot caps 1971-76/5 Scot u23 caps 1972-76/
1 SL app. 1972/SLC winner 1973/
SLC finalist 1975/SC finalist 1972.

Appearances:
FL: 16(4) apps. 3 gls.
Others: 4 apps. 1 gl.
Total: *20(4) apps. 4 gls.*
Honours:
1 Scot u23 cap 1974/FL div 3 prom 1978.

BULLOCH, Hugh Cairns

Role: Centre-half 1935-1936
5' 10"
b. Larkhall, Lanarkshire, 2nd June 1908

Hugh Bullock

CAREER: Royal Albert/Greenock Morton Jan 1931/Portadown 1932/UNITED Nov 1935 £1,325/New Brighton Sept 1936 free/ Portadown player-manager Dec 1937/ New Brighton May 1938 to Sept 1939.

Debut v Nottingham Forest (h) 30/11/35

A report of the day noted Hugh Bulloch as, "one of the outstanding players in Irish league football". A defender who could turn defence into attack, Bulloch impressed United manager Tom Mather and directors Oliver and Rutherford in the Irish Gold Cup semi-final. He captained Portadown to success in the tournament and Newcastle quickly brought him to Tyneside to compete for the centre-half position alongside Dave Davidson and former England captain, Tony Leach. The balding Bulloch was unfortunate to pick up an injury soon after making his debut for the Magpies and, once recovered, never regained his place. He later did well on Merseyside with New Brighton, an inspiration to their defence during the club's Football League days.

Appearances:
FL: 5 apps. 0 gls.
Total: *5 apps. 0 gls.*

BURGESS, Charles

Role: Right-back
1900-1901
5' 10"
b. Montrose, 1874

CAREER: Montrose 1894/Dundee 1895/ Millwall Athletic May 1898/UNITED May 1900/Portsmouth May 1901/Montrose cs 1903.

Debut v Nottingham Forest (h) 1/9/1900

Charles Burgess was a tall, powerful and robust defender who appeared as a regular during the 1900-01 season. Although performing consistently that year, Burgess was never a favourite of the Tyneside fans and it is recorded he received some typical terrace abuse during his short stay at St James Park. As a consequence he moved during the

Charles Burgess

summer to appear successfully in the Southern League, then in the days before the formation of the Third and Fourth Divisions. One pen picture in 1903 noted he, "tackles with extreme resolution, and will take the risk of rushing among a crowd of players to get the ball".

Appearances:
FL: 30 apps. 0 gls.
FAC: 1 app. 0 gls.
Total: *31 apps. 0 gls.*
Honours:
SnL champs 1902.

BURKE, Richard

Role: Right-back 1946-1947
5' 10"
*b. Ashton, nr Manchester,
28th October 1920*

CAREER: Droylsden/Blackpool Feb 1939/UNITED Dec 1946 £3,250/Carlisle United Aug 1947 £1,350 to May 1949/ Ashton United 1953.

Debut v Plymouth Argyle (h) 7/12/46

Starting his career with Blackpool prior to the outbreak of the Second World War, Dick Burke had made his debut in the Football League a matter of months before his contract was cancelled due to Hitler's advances in Europe. Consequently his promising career was ruined and he didn't return to Bloomfield Road action for over five years. In the transitional 1945-46 programme, Burke's displays caught the eye of Stan Seymour's scouting network and he signed for the Magpies to add a bit of experience to rub off onto the club's youngsters. He rivalled one of those kids, Bobby Cowell, for a season before Cowell showed he was to become a star of the future. A competent rather than brilliant defender, Burke travelled across the Pennines and continued to appear for Carlisle for two seasons (78 apps.) before moving into non-league football.

Appearances:
FL: 15 apps. 0 gls.
FAC: 2 apps. 0 gls.
Total: *17 apps. 0 gls.*

BURLEIGH, Martin S.

Role: Goalkeeper 1968-1974
5' 11"
b. Durham, 2nd February 1951

CAREER: Willington/UNITED Oct 1968/Darlington Dec 1974 £8,000/ Carlisle United June 1975/ Darlington Aug 1977/ Hartlepool United Oct 1979 £8,000 to cs 1982/ Bishop Auckland Nov 1982/ Spennymoor United July 1983 to Dec 1983/Langley Park 1984.

Debut v Leeds United (a) 26/12/70

Martin Burleigh

Deputy to Irish international Willie McFaul, Martin Burleigh began his career at St James Park following good displays in the Northern League. After waiting four years to gain possession of United's green 'keeper's jersey, the unlucky Martin fractured a finger in a clash with Mick Channon but in his few appearances for the club the well-built Burleigh showed he was a good player to call upon and a goalkeeper who could command his area. Trouble in keeping his weight to an acceptable level, coupled with McFaul being at his peak during the early seventies, meant Burleigh's future was likely to be elsewhere and he was replaced by Mick Mahoney as understudy as Martin moved to Feethams. He was on the substitutes' bench for United's 1970-71 European campaign. Burleigh later resided in Ferryhill and is employed in the decorating trade.

Appearances:
FL: 11 apps. 0 gls.
Others: 4 apps. 0 gls.
Total: *15 apps. 0 gls.*

BURNS, Michael Edward

Role: Striker or Midfield 1974-1978
5' 7"
b. Preston, 21st December 1946

CAREER: Preston North End/Chorley/
Skelmersdale United am. 1965/Blackpool
May 1969/UNITED June 1974 £170,000/
Cardiff City player-coach Aug 1978 £72,000/
Middlesbrough Sept 1978 £72,000, becoming
asst-coach July 1981 to Nov 1982/
PFA Education Officer Feb 1984, later
becoming Chief Executive of the FL & PFA's
Further Educational Vocational Training
Society, based in Manchester (now the
registered charity, Education in Football).

Debut v Coventry City (h) 17/8/74

When Micky Burns joined the staff in the close
season of 1974 following impressive figures at
Blackpool of 62 goals in 203 matches, he
became United's most expensive signing next
to Malcolm Macdonald. Only 5'7" tall, but full
of trickery and the natural touch of a goalscorer
in front of goal, Burns scored a stunning effort
on his first appearance at St James Park in a
Texaco Cup match against Middlesbrough. In a
marvellous solo run from the half-way line he
went past several defenders before slipping the
ball into the net. A versatile forward, he
initially operated on the wing, but Burns'
relationship with Joe Harvey had started poorly
and it wasn't until Gordon Lee took over that
the player flourished. Intelligent and thoughtful
with the ball, he then became more of an out
and out striker, just behind the front runners,
and often found the net as United reached
Wembley in 1976 and qualified for Europe the
following season. He was a central figure in the
so-called players' revolt that ended with
Richard Dinnis being given the manager's job,
and on Dinnis' departure, Burns left quickly
along with many of the side. An educated
individual, holding a degree in economics,
Micky exchanged a teaching career to sign for
Blackpool after being recognised as one of the
top amateur players in the country. On retiring
from the game, Burns was a key promoter of
the Youth Training Scheme (YTS) and football's
links with the community. He became an
important member of the PFA's staff in
Manchester, residing in Wrightington.

Appearances:
FL: 143(2) apps. 39 gls.
FAC: 17 apps. 5 gls.
FLC: 14 apps. 4 gls.
Eur: 4 apps. 0 gls.
Others: 11 apps. 3 gls.
Total: *189(2) apps. 51 gls.*
Honours:
*1 Eng am. cap 1969/FAAC
finalist 1967/FLC finalist
1976/FL div 2 prom 1970.*

*Micky Burns attacks Derby defenders Todd
and McFarland in a 1977 league meeting.*

BURNS, Michael Thomas

Role: Goalkeeper 1927-1936
5' 10"
b. Leeholme, County Durham, 7th June 1908
d. Newcastle upon Tyne, September 1982

CAREER: Chilton CW/UNITED Sept 1927
£100/Preston North End July 1936 £400/
Ipswich Town May 1938/Norwich City
war-guest 1939-40/Retired playing
May 1952.

Debut v Blackburn Rovers (h) 1/10/27

After once being converted to a forward
for conceding too many goals, Mick
Burns developed into a steady
goalkeeper and served Newcastle for
nine seasons. At a time when the
Magpies had three or even four senior
'keepers on the books, Burns was never
recognised as a first choice, although he
turned out on 30 occasions in season
1928-29, his best term. He initially battled
with Willie Wilson for the position, then
international 'keeper Albert McInroy as
well as Norman Tapken. When Burns
joined Preston he quickly found himself
thrust into the biggest game of his life, as
stand-in for Harry Holdcroft in the 1937
FA Cup final against Sunderland. He
later played for many years with Ipswich
Town, being on the field for the East
Anglians' inaugural match in the
Football League. A dependable 'keeper
and thoroughly professional, curly-
haired Micky's last game was in October
1951 when he was almost 44 years old;
only a handful of players have been
older when appearing in post-war
football. After retiring from the game,
Mick lived on Tyneside where he was
caretaker at a Roman Catholic school in
Newcastle.

Appearances:
FL: 104 apps. 0 gls.
FAC: 3 apps. 0 gls.
Others: 1 app. 0 gls.
Total: *108 apps. 0 gls.*
Honours:
FAC finalist 1937.

BURRIDGE, John

Role: Goalkeeper & Coach 1989-1991, 1993-date
5' 11"
b. Workington, 3rd December 1951

CAREER: Workington Town app Apr 1967, pro Jan 1970/Blackpool Apr 1971 £10,000/ Aston Villa Sept 1975 £100,000(Southend United loan 1977-78)/Crystal Palace Mar 1978 £65,000/Queens Park Rangers Dec 1980 £200,000/Wolverhampton Wanderers Sept 1982 £75,000(Derby County loan 1984-85)/ Sheffield United Oct 1984 £10,000/ Southampton Aug 1987 £30,000/UNITED Sept 1989 £25,000/Hartlepool United trial July 1991(Falkirk loan 1991-92)/Hibernian Aug 1991 free/Barrow 1993/UNITED Aug 1993 part-time player & goalkeeping coach to date/Scarborough Oct 1993/ Lincoln City Dec 1993/Enfield Feb 1994/Aberdeen Mar 1994/ Dunfermline Athletic Oct 1994/Falkirk Dec 1994/ Dumbarton 1994-95/ Manchester City Nov 1994/Notts County Sept 1995/Witton Albion Oct 1995/Darlington Nov 1995/Gateshead Jan 1996/Grimsby Town Jan 1996/Durham City Mar 1996/Gateshead Mar 1996/Queen of the South Mar 1996/Purfleet Mar 1996/Blyth Spartans Aug 1996.

Debut v Ipswich Town (a) 7/10/89

John Burridge has undergone a remarkable career in the game, appearing for more than 30 different clubs in a long playing span of almost 30 years. He started as a teenager with then Football League side Workington in 1967(FL debut in 1968-69) and since has appeared throughout England and Scotland in over 800 senior matches, later in his career becoming something of an emergency call-out 'keeper, filling in for clubs with a goalkeeping problem. Always super-fit, Burridge lived for playing football. He was agile and brave, and ever an extrovert, entertaining supporters with brash warm-up routines. At Newcastle when 37 years old, the club's oldest post-war player, John always regarded United as one of his favourite clubs since supporting them as a boy - he later became Kevin Keegan's goalkeeping coach. This after being handed a free transfer by Ossie Ardiles, although winning the club's Player of the Season award for the previous 1990-91 campaign.

Confident and dedicated as they come, John has an infectious personality and has been a popular player at all his venues. Known the nation over as 'Budgie', he unusually appeared for Manchester City against United in season 1994-95 when on the Magpies' staff; he was also sub for the black'n'whites when aged over 40. Burridge resides in Durham city, and his son has played for The Wasps and Great Britain at ice-hockey.

Appearances:
FL: 69 apps. 0 gls.
FAC: 7 apps. 0 gls.
FLC: 4 apps. 0 gls.
Others: 4 apps. 0 gls.
Total: *84 apps. 0 gls.*
Honours:
FLC winner 1977/FL div 2 champs 1979/ FL div 2 prom 1983/SLC winner 1992.

John Burridge

BURTON, Alwyn Derek

Role: Centre-half 1963-1973
5' 11"
b. Chepstow, Monmouthshire, 11th November 1941

CAREER: Bulwark Youth Club Sept 1957/
Newport County Dec 1958/Norwich City
Mar 1961 £11,000/UNITED June 1963
£37,500/Retired due to injury 1973.

Debut v Derby County (h) 24/8/63

Impressing manager Joe Harvey in several
displays for Norwich against the
black'n'whites, including a 5-0 FA Cup
hammering by the Canaries in 1963, Ollie
Burton became one of United's costliest
purchases at the time. Signed as a wing-
half, the Welshman eventually operated as
a defensive stopper when the style of
football changed after the 1966 World Cup.
A versatile player for the Magpies, Burton
also played at right-back, in midfield and even
at centre-forward. He took time to settle in the
north east and didn't gain a permanent position
in United's side until Newcastle had returned
to the First Division in 1965. With rivals like
Anderson, Iley, Thompson and later, Moncur
and McNamee, Ollie always had stiff
competition at Gallowgate but he did hold the
Number 5 shirt during the club's Inter Cities
Fairs Cup success. Characterised by ginger hair
and a high pitched yell on the field, Burton was
a tough footballer, but one who could play a bit
too. He also possessed a tremendous drive
which unfortunately was never used to its full
potential at Gallowgate. On United's books for
ten years, he was unlucky with injuries, a knee
problem in January 1972 later forcing his early
retirement. A well supported testimonial took
place in November 1973 (35,873) and
afterwards Burton returned to Norfolk where
he resided in Diss. He was employed in public
relations for firstly Rothmans, then brewers
Hurlinam before concentrating on a catering
business in Diss. Burton became the first
Newcastle substitute to enter the field in
September 1965, while he also was the first sub
to score for the club two years later.

Appearances:
FL: 181(7) apps. 6 gls.
FAC: 9 apps. 0 gls.
FLC: 7(1) apps. 2 gls.
Eur: 18(1) apps. 0 gls.
Others: 5 apps. 0 gls.
Total: *220(9) apps. 8 gls.*

Ollie Burton

Honours:
9 Wales caps 1963-72/
5 Wales u23 caps 1961-65/Wales schools app./
FLC winner 1962/ICFC winner 1969.

BUSBY, Vivian Dennis

Role: Striker 1971-1972
6' 0"
b. Slough, Bucks, 19th June 1949

CAREER: Terries (High Wycombe)/Wycombe
Wanderers 1966/Luton Town Jan 1970
(UNITED loan Dec 1971-Feb 1972)/Fulham
Aug 1973 £25,000/Norwich City Sept 1976
£50,000/Stoke City Nov 1977 £50,000(Sheffield
United loan 1979-80)/Tulsa Roughnecks (USA)
Mar-Nov 1980/Blackburn Rovers Feb 1981
£40,000/York City player-coach Aug 1982,
becoming asst-manager 1984/Sunderland
asst-manager May 1987/Manchester City
scout Dec 1991/Hartlepool United manager
Feb 1993 to Nov 1993/Afterwards a scout for
several clubs including Southampton and
West Bromwich Albion/Sheffield United
asst-coach Dec 1995.

Debut v West Bromwich Albion (a) 11/12/71
(scored once)

A former goalscoring partner to Malcolm
Macdonald at Luton, Viv Busby was
unfortunate to have his short loan period at St
James Park coincide firstly with a lay off due
to influenza, then with the club's biggest

humiliation in their modern history, a defeat at Hereford United in the FA Cup. The tall and silky striker had scored for United in his first two outings and consequently found himself in the line-up that took to Edgar Street on that fateful February afternoon in 1972. That historic defeat was never going to help Viv's chances of a contract at Gallowgate and although Busby didn't play badly during his sojourn north, he was sent back to Kenilworth Road. He proceeded to prove that he was a useful, if not brilliant, striker elsewhere, notably at Fulham where he had trials earlier as a teenager. Busby was part of the Londoners' FA Cup giant-killing side and scored some crucial goals on their run to Wembley. Following his spell as boss of Hartlepool, Viv resided in the north east for a period becoming a football analyst for local radio. His younger brother, Martin, appeared for Queens Park Rangers.

Appearances:
FL: 4 apps. 2 gls.
FAC: 1 app. 0 gls.
Total: *5 apps. 2 gls.*
Honours:
FAC finalist 1975.

BUTLER, Joseph William

Role: Left-back 1960-1965
5' 7"
b. Newcastle upon Tyne, 7th February 1943

CAREER: UNITED Sept 1960/Swindon Town Aug 1965 £5,500/Aldershot Mar 1976/ Whitney Town.

Debut v Manchester City (a) 4/4/64

Joe Butler

Small in stature, Joe Butler was one of the club's early youth products developing alongside the likes of Bob Moncur, Frank Clark and David Craig. A ninety minute worker, he appeared for United's reserve and junior sides at both full-back and wing-half, but it was at left-back that he was selected for all his appearances in season 1963-64. Butler stood in for George Dalton, but saw Frank Clark leap ahead of him to take over Dalton's role in time for the Magpies' promotion to Division One. Joe was transferred to Swindon where he became a noted servant to the Robins, totalling over 350 games in a versatile fashion; in midfield, attack or in defence. He showed much courage and determination and was part of the famous Swindon side that reached Wembley as a Third Division club in 1969 and defeated the mighty Arsenal. Joe later settled in Wiltshire and runs a taxi firm in Swindon.

Appearances:
FL: 3 apps. 0 gls.
FLC: 1 app. 0 gls.
Total: *4 apps. 0 gls.*
Honours:
FLC winner 1969/
FL div 3 prom 1969.

Viv Busby

CAHILL, Thomas

Role: Left-back 1951-1955
5' 9"
b. Glasgow, 14th June 1931

CAREER: Vale of Leven/UNITED Dec 1951
£750/Barrow Aug 1955 to c1964.

Debut v Cardiff City (h) 25/12/52

Having played well in front of
watching United scouts in the Scottish
junior leagues, Tommy Cahill was
given an opportunity to join the
Magpies, but very much as a reserve.
He was third choice at left-back behind
Ron Batty and Alf McMichael, two
tremendous servants to the club, and
therefore given very limited
opportunity in Newcastle's first team.
A dogged fighter in defence, Cahill did
very well at Holker Street, in Barrow's
Football League side, making over 300
outings for the west coast outfit, good
enough to appear for the divisional
select eleven. His son Tommy appeared for
United's juniors in the early seventies without
making the grade.

Appearances:
FL: 4 apps. 0 gls.
Total: *4 apps. 0 gls.*
Honours:
FL div 3(N) app. 1957.

CAIE, Alexander S.

Role: Right-half 1901-1903
5' 10"
b. Aberdeen, 1878
d. Lowell, Massachusetts, USA, November 1914

CAREER: Victoria United(Aberdeen)/
Woolwich Arsenal Feb 1897/Bristol South End
May 1897/Millwall Athletic Mar 1900/
UNITED May 1901/Brentford cs 1903/
Motherwell July 1904 £30/Westmount
(Canada)/Sons of Scotland(Canada)/
Rosedale (Canada) to death.

Debut v Notts County (a) 3/10/01

A well built, powerful half-back at over 13
stones, Alex Caie was versatile enough to play
in most outfield positions during his career
and in four different roles for Newcastle.
Apart from right-half, Caie also operated at
left-half, centre-
forward and inside-
left. He arrived
from London after a
fine spell with
Bristol City's pioneer club (114 apps. 64 goals)
to take over the role of Tommy Ghee following
consolidation in the First Division at the turn
of the century. He was
effective for a season, in
1901-02, but when Alex
Gardner landed on
Tyneside, Caie moved
on and eventually
emigrated to North
America, where he was
later killed in a railway
accident. Colin Veitch
once noted Caie, who
was known as 'Big
Sandy', as being, "hard
as nails" and "stout of
heart".

Sandy Caie

Appearances:
FL: 31 apps. 1 gl.
FAC: 4 apps. 0 gls.
Total: *35 apps. 1 gl.*

CAIRNS, Thomas

Role: Inside-left 1914-1916
5' 10"
b. Chopwell, nr Gateshead
d. France, 1916

CAREER: Newcastle City/
UNITED Sept 1914 £20 to death.

Debut v Aston Villa (h) 28/4/15

Tom Cairns was one of the many who sadly
sacrificed their lives during the First World
War. He was one of the first of United's
players to respond to Lord Kitchener's call for
men at arms, joining the RFA and reaching the
rank of corporal. He fell fighting in the
trenches in France. Cairns had deputised for
Curtis Booth in the final fixture of the 1914-15
season - the last before war enforced a close-
down on football - and played his part in a
fine 3-0 victory. Tom was one of six United
players in the club's 1915 squad who died in
the hostilities.

Appearances:
FL: 1 app. 0 gls.
Total: *1 app. 0 gls.*

CAIRNS, William Hart

Role: Centre-forward 1933-1944
5' 9"
b. Newcastle upon Tyne, 7th October 1912
d. Grimsby, 9th January 1988

CAREER: Holborn Rangers/Stargate Rovers/
UNITED May 1933 £25/Chester war-guest
1940-41/Liverpool war-guest 1940-41/
Mansfield Town war-guest 1941-42/
Nottingham Forest war-guest 1941-42/
Chesterfield war-guest 1942-43/Notts County
war-guest 1942-43/Sunderland war-guest
1944-45/Gateshead Nov 1944 free/Grimsby
Town May 1946/Retired cs 1954, becoming
Grimsby Town asst-trainer for a period.

Debut v Bury (h) 1/1/35

Thrustful and bustling, Billy Cairns did well for
Newcastle in the years leading up to the Second
World War. Getting a chance in the senior line-
up after relegation in 1933, he firstly partnered
Jack Smith, then took over in the leader's shirt to
good effect. In season 1936-37 he grabbed 16
goals, while in the campaign before the war,
Billy hit the net on 20 occasions. Big hearted, one
thirties scribe noted him as, "a high spirited, hell
for leather, shoot on sight centre-forward,
determined to score no matter the risk". He was
strong, hard to push off the ball and was always
a danger in the air. He twice scored four goals in
a single game for the Magpies, and once netted
five against Halifax Town during the wartime
programme of 1939-40. After a record season at
Redheugh Park with Gateshead when he scored
42 goals, Billy started the post-war part of his
career with Grimsby. Cairns didn't retire from
the game until he was over 40, appearing for the
other black and whites at Blundell Park with
distinction. He found the net 129 times in 231
senior games for Grimsby and was skipper of
the Mariners for a period. His father and
grandfather were noted runners on Tyneside,
while Billy can claim to be the first Magpie
centre-forward to actually wear the now famous
Number 9 shirt, this when numbers were
introduced in 1939. For a while he returned to
Tyneside, then spent the rest of his life in
Cleethorpes, a noted publican for 30 years.

Appearances:
FL: 87 apps. 51 gls.
FAC: 3 apps. 2 gls.
War: 23 apps. 14 gls.
Total: *113 apps. 67 gls.*

Billy Cairns

CALLACHAN, Ralph

Role: Midfield 1977-1978
5' 10"
b. Edinburgh, 29th April 1955

CAREER: Heart of Midlothian 1971/UNITED Feb 1977 £100,000/Hibernian Aug 1978 cash-exch for J.Brownlie/Greenock Morton Sept 1986/Meadowbank Thistle Nov 1986/Berwick Rangers 1988, becoming manager 1990 to 1992.

Debut v Bohemians (a) 14/9/77 (UEFAC)

Scot Ralph Callachan can count himself unlucky to have landed at St James Park at the wrong time. The transfer from Tynecastle was completed between the departure of Gordon Lee and the appointment of Richard Dinnis, and amidst rumours that he was actually signed by the directors. A midfield player with the typical vein of Scottish ball skills to the fore,

Ralph Callachan

Callachan had a stylish look but never fitted into a relegation fight during season 1977-78. He was given few opportunities by Dinnis and by the time Bill McGarry had taken over the hot-seat, Callachan had resigned himself for a return to Scotland. With Hibs, Ralph did well as he had done on the other side of Edinburgh at Tynecastle. He was highly rated north of the border and served the capital's senior clubs for almost 15 seasons. Callachan later went into business in Edinburgh running several pubs.

Appearances:
FL: 9 apps. 0 gls.
Eur: 2 apps. 0 gls.
Total: *11 apps. 0 gls.*
Honours:
Scot youth app/Scot amat cap 1973/
SL div 1 champs 1981/SC finalist 1976, 1979.

CAMBELL, T.

Role: Outside-right 1894-1895
Debut v Darwen (a) 1/9/1894

A former Northumberland County player, Cambell appeared in the first two games of the 1894-95 campaign for United, but then was replaced and did not regain a first-team place. Some sources have his surname spelt as 'Campbell', but official club record books note it as above.

Appearances:
FL: 2 apps. 0 gls.
Total: *2 apps. 0 gls.*

CAMERON, Hugh Gibson

Role: Outside-left 1951-1952
5' 8"
b. Burnbank, Lanarkshire, 1st February 1927

CAREER: Burnbank Athletic/Clyde 1946/Torquay United May 1948 free/UNITED Apr 1951 £4,500/Bury Mar 1952 £500/Workington Oct 1953/St Mirren Aug 1956 free to c1958.

Debut v Liverpool (h) 3/11/51

A stand-in for Bobby Mitchell on two occasions during the 1951-52 FA Cup winning season, Hugh Cameron was quick and tricky, but never could threaten the stranglehold his fellow Scot held on the number 11 shirt at Gallowgate. He later proceeded to perform well with Bury and Workington before returning to the Scottish League.

Hugh Cameron

Appearances:
FL: 2 apps. 0 gls.
Total: *2 apps. 0 gls.*

CAMPBELL, John Middleton

Role: Centre-forward 1897-1898
5' 9"
b. Renton, Dunbarton, 19th February 1870
d. Sunderland, 8th June 1906

CAREER: Renton Union/Renton/Sunderland
cs 1889/UNITED May 1897, joint deal with
J.Harvey £40/Retired after dismissal Oct 1898.

Debut v Woolwich Arsenal (h) 4/9/1897
(scored once)

An important member of Sunderland's famous
'Team of all the Talent' during the years before
the turn of the last century, Johnny Campbell
was a magnificent forward in his day and at
his peak was the Football League's leading
goalgetter on three occasions in four seasons
between 1892 and 1895. Stocky and bustling,
all told the Scot netted 150 times in 215 league
and cup games for the Wearside club and
played a key role in the Reds lifting three
championship trophies. Campbell arrived at
Gallowgate very much as a player of
experience nearing the end of his career, but
still with much to offer to a Magpie side
aiming to join Sunderland in the First
Division. And Johnny did his job, in a first-
class way with his 'do or die' attitude during
United's promotion year in 1898. As
Newcastle's first year in Division One opened,
Campbell fell out of favour with United's
directors after he decided to take over The
Darnell public-house with the aim of a career
once he had retired. This was strictly against
the board's rules at the time and, after a long-
running, controversial saga, the club
dismissed the player. Campbell's impressive
career was ended and he concentrated on a
business in the licensing trade in the north-
east. To many judges of his Victorian era it
was a mystery why this potent centre-forward
never played for his country. He was on the
fringe of international selection several times
but never got to pull on the blue shirt of
Scotland. Campbell has the distinction of
being on the field for both Newcastle's and
Sunderland's inaugural First Division fixtures.
His brother, R. Campbell, was appointed
secretary at Roker in 1896.

Appearances:
FL: 26 apps. 10 gls.
FAC: 3 apps. 2 gls.
Total: *29 apps. 12 gls.*

Johnny
Campbell

Honours:
FL champs 1892, 1893, 1895/FL div 2 prom
1898/FL(N) app. 1893/SC winner 1888.

CANNELL, Paul A.

Role: Striker 1972-1978
5' 11"
b. Newcastle upon Tyne, 2nd September 1953

CAREER: UNITED June 1972/Washington
Diplomats(USA) Feb 1978 £40,000/
Memphis Rogues(USA) Nov 1979/Calgary
Boomers (Canada) 1980/Detroit Express(USA)
Jan 1981/Washington Diplomats(USA) Apr
1981/North Shields 1981/Mansfield Town Jan
1982/Berwick Rangers May 1983/Blyth
Spartans Jan 1984 to Apr 1984/
SC Vaux Jan 1986.

Debut v Manchester City (a) 27/3/74

As a teenager Paul Cannell was a much
coveted prospect at Gallowgate. A schoolboy
star, he rose quickly through United's junior
ranks and, on the departure of Malcolm
Macdonald to Arsenal in 1976, was given a
regular striker's role by manager Gordon Lee.
The dark and moustached Cannell was quick
off the mark and performed well, striking 12
goals alongside Alan Gowling and Micky
Burns as Newcastle qualified for Europe in

season 1976-77. But the internal strife which followed affected the young Tynesider and, on the appointment of Bill McGarry, Cannell was part of a mass clear-out. He continued his career in North American football where he was a big hit, appearing alongside such world megastars as Pele and Cruyff. Cannell gave up a place at Durham University to sign professional for Joe Harvey but later returned to settle on Tyneside. He was employed by Vaux Brewery for a while before running Zoots nightclub and afterwards a publishing company. Latterly he has become a publican on Tyneside as well as a coach to local youngsters.

Appearances:
FL: 47(1) apps. 13 gls.
FAC: 5 apps. 0 gls.
FLC: 7(1) apps. 4 gls.
Eur: 3 apps. 1 gl.
Others: 5(1) apps. 2 gls.
Total: *67(3) apps. 20 gls.*
Honours:
Eng schools app./FLC finalist (sub, no app.) 1976.

Paul Cannell

CAPE, John Phillips

Role: Outside-right 1930-1934
5' 8"
b. Carlisle,
16th November 1911
d. Carlisle, 6th June 1994

CAREER: Penrith/Carlisle United May 1929/UNITED Jan 1930 £1,750/Manchester United Jan 1934 £2,000/Queens Park Rangers June 1937/Carlisle United 1939/Scarborough Town cs 1946/Carlisle United Oct 1946 to Feb 1947, becoming asst-trainer for a period.

Debut v Leicester City (a) 18/1/30

Jackie Cape, a strong and rugged player, was in and out of the Magpies' line-up during his five season stay on Tyneside. Joining United as a teenage part-timer for a hefty fee from Carlisle - money which was used to construct a roof on the Brunton Park Scratching Pen - Cape had only appeared on a handful of occasions in senior action, but was seen as a bright prospect for future years. It was described at the time that, "he would run like a deer" for the ball if it was pushed in front of him and Cape did at times realise his potential, but never consistently enough to become the big star many had hoped. A sturdy winger at nearly 13 stone, Cape was overshadowed by Jimmy Boyd at St James Park, yet had one or two memorable moments in a black'n'white shirt including scoring the single goal that defeated Chelsea when St James Park's record attendance was set in 1930, and also a stunning hat-trick in a 7-4 victory over Manchester United. It was the Old Trafford side Cape joined after his stint with Newcastle was over and with the Reds, as well as with QPR, he performed with note assisting Manchester United to promotion in 1936. Jackie was an apprentice electrician before he signed for the Magpies, a job he reverted to during the Second World War. After retiring from the game he resided in his home town for the rest of his life. Jackie's uncle, Jack Nixon, was a director of Carlisle United.

Appearances:
FL: 51 apps. 18 gls.
FAC: 2 apps. 2 gls.
Total: *53 apps. 20 gls.*
Honours:
FL div 2 champs 1936.

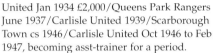

CARLTON, William

Role: Right-half 1926-1929
5' 8"
b. Washington, 15th July 1908
d. Co. Durham, 1973

CAREER: Washington CW/UNITED Sept 1926 £20/Merthyr Tydfil May 1929/West Stanley Sept 1930/Ashington Nov 1931/ Annfield Plain Aug 1933.

Debut v Liverpool (h) 3/12/27

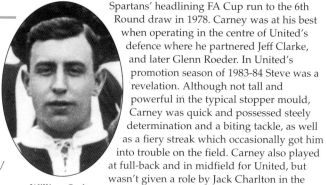

William Carlton

With Newcastle United at the time of a League Championship victory in 1927, dark-haired local youngster William Carlton was given few chances to impress due to the Magpies' established stars. He was third choice for the right-half midfield position behind Joe Harris and Roddie MacKenzie.

Appearances:
FL: 5 apps. 1 gl.
FAC: 1 app. 0 gls.
Total: *6 apps. 1 gl.*

CARNEY, Stephen

Role: Centre-half 1979-1985
5' 10"
b. Wallsend, 22nd September 1957

CAREER: Dudley jnrs/North Shields/ Blyth Spartans 1977/UNITED Oct 1979 £1,000 (Carlisle United loan 1984-85)/Darlington July 1985 free/(Rochdale loan 1985-86)/ Hartlepool United Mar 1986 to May 1986/ Tow Law Town Sept 1986/Blyth Spartans Mar 1987 to c1990/Newcastle Blue Star(Newcastle RTM)manager 1992 to Apr 1996.

Debut v Fulham (h) 1/12/79

Plucked from the rough and tumble of non-league football with Blyth Spartans, Steve Carney arrived late onto the Football League circuit as a 22 year-old along with Alan Shoulder, after the pair had been instrumental in the

Steve Carney

Spartans' headlining FA Cup run to the 6th Round draw in 1978. Carney was at his best when operating in the centre of United's defence where he partnered Jeff Clarke, and later Glenn Roeder. In United's promotion season of 1983-84 Steve was a revelation. Although not tall and powerful in the typical stopper mould, Carney was quick and possessed steely determination and a biting tackle, as well as a fiery streak which occasionally got him into trouble on the field. Carney also played at full-back and in midfield for United, but wasn't given a role by Jack Charlton in the Magpies' First Division line-up. As a youngster Steve was with West Bromwich Albion for a short spell, and he exchanged an electrician's job for that of a professional footballer when he signed for the black'n'whites.

Appearances:
FL: 125(9) apps. 1 gl.
FAC: 9 apps. 0 gls.
FLC: 6 apps. 0 gls.
Total: *140(9) apps. 1 gl.*
Honours:
FL div 2 prom 1984.

CARR, Franz Alexander

Role: Outside-right 1991-1993
5' 7"
b. Preston, 24th September 1966

CAREER: Blackburn Rovers app 1982/ Nottingham Forest Aug 1984 £100,000 (Sheffield Wednesday loan 1989-90)(West Ham United loan 1990-91)/UNITED May 1991 £250,000/Sheffield United loan Jan 1993, pmt Jan 1993 £180,000/Leicester City loan Sept 1994, pmt Oct 1994 £100,000/Aston Villa Feb 1995 cash-exch deal £250,000/Reggiana (Italy) trial Sept 1996, pmt Oct 1996 free.

Debut v Charlton Athletic (a) 18/8/91(scored once)

Small, direct and a potential matchwinner on the right-wing, Franz Carr had been a teenage star under Brian Clough at Nottingham Forest and had played for England at school, youth and Under-21 level. He took part in two League Cup runs to Wembley, but perhaps lacked the necessary genuine craft to complement his exceptional pace to become a top quality forward. In and out of Forest's

Franz Carr

CARR, John

Role: Left-back 1897-1922
5' 10"
b. Seaton Burn, Northumberland, 1876
d. Newcastle upon Tyne, 17th March 1948

CAREER: Seaton Burn/UNITED Nov 1897, becoming asst-trainer 1912/Blackburn Rovers manager Feb 1922 to Dec 1926.

Debut v Nottingham Forest (a) 2/12/1899

Jack Carr was one of the most celebrated locals to perform for Newcastle United. He started as a left-half with United then, on the arrival of Peter McWilliam in the senior side, moved to left-back where he displayed a physical and rugged style, typical of the day. Carr was a noted player, picked for England, who took part in a treble of league title wins with the Magpies as well as reaching three FA Cup finals. Sound and judicious in his football, Jack was also a fine cricketer appearing for the Northumberland County side. Carr spent the whole of his playing career with Newcastle and appeared for the club over 13 seasons. However, he didn't take too well to management, suffering embarrassing FA Cup defeats at Ewood Park before returning to Tyneside and becoming a licensee. For many years he was a publican near the Greenmarket in Newcastle.

Appearances:
FL: 252 apps. 5 gls.
FAC: 25 apps. 0 gls.
Others: 1 app. 0 gls.
Total: *278 apps. 5 gls.*
Honours:
2 Eng caps 1905-07/Eng trial app. 1907/
1 FL app. 1907/FL champs 1905, 1907, 1909/
FAC winner 1910/FAC finalist 1905, 1906.

eleven, he was picked up by Ossie Ardiles as a 24 year-old and for a time looked to be finding a level of consistency until a bad knee injury put him out of action for many months. Kevin Keegan was in charge by the time Carr was available for selection, but within a few weeks Robert Lee was purchased as his replacement and the winger was off to Bramall Lane. From then on it was a struggle to claim a regular place at any of his clubs. Nicknamed 'Roadrunner' on Tyneside, he was a flier and, as a teenager, was good enough to be offered an athletics scholarship in the USA.

Appearances:
FL: 20(5) apps. 3 gls.
FLC: 2(2) apps. 0 gls.
Others: 3(1) apps. 0 gls.
Total: *25(8) apps. 3 gls.*
Honours:
9 Eng u21 caps 1987-88/Eng schools app./
Eng youth app. 1984-86/FLC winner 1990.

CARR, John Robert

Role: Left-half 1894-1898
5' 10"
b. Newcastle upon Tyne

CAREER: Science & Art(Newcastle)/UNITED Nov 1894/Kilmarnock May 1898/Tyneside minor soccer 1900.

Debut v Crewe Alexandra (h) 25/12/1895

A commendable Tynesider, the son of a local councillor, Jack Carr made his first appearance for the Magpies in a 6-0 St James Park victory over Crewe on Christmas Day 1895. A vigorous, efficient amateur Jack was a stand-in for the powerhouse of Jimmy Stott at half-back and his handful of matches in the United first-team were spread over three seasons. Carr departed the scene to enter University in Glasgow when he also turned out for Kilmarnock, assisting in their Second Division title success in 1899 (6 apps.). He later returned to his native north east, and became a well known player in local circles for many years.

> **Appearances:**
> *FL:* 4 apps. 0 gls.
> **Total:** 4 apps. 0 gls.

CARR, Kevin

Role: Goalkeeper 1976-1985
6' 2"
b. Morpeth, 6th November 1958

CAREER: Burnley trial/UNITED July 1976/Carlisle United July 1985 after loan period(Darlington loan 1986-87)/ Hartlepool United Oct 1987/ Middlesbrough briefly cs 1988/Blyth Spartans Aug 1988/ Bedlington Terriers July 1989.

Debut v Queens Park Rangers (a) 10/12/77

Local product Kevin Carr, a one club man with Newcastle United for almost 10 years after signing for the black'n'whites following a trial at Burnley, was given a contract by Gordon Lee. For a long time Carr was reserve to Mick Mahoney, then Steve Hardwick, but eventually earned the Number One jersey for himself in season 1980-81 when he was voted

Player of the Year. Tall and agile, Kevin produced a level of sound goalkeeping for a period before a new rival appeared on the scene in the shape of Martin Thomas. Of a similar standard, Carr shared the custodian's role during Newcastle's promotion campaign in 1983-84, but eventually lost his place to the Welsh international. When Kevin retired from the game he opened a trophy business before joining the Northumbria Police. He played football for the England Police XI in 1991 and presently resides in Northumberland.

> **Appearances:**
> *FL:* 173 apps. 0 gls.
> *FAC:* 13 apps. 0 gls.
> *FLC:* 9 apps. 0 gls.
> **Total:** 195 apps. 0 gls.
> **Honours:**
> *FL div 2 prom 1984.*

Kevin Carr

CARTWRIGHT, Peter

Role: Midfield 1979-1983
5' 7"
b. Newcastle upon Tyne,
23rd August 1957

CAREER: Dudley Welfare jnrs/
North Shields 1978/UNITED June
1979 £2,000(Scunthorpe United loan
1982-83)/Darlington Mar 1983 to cs
1984/Blyth Spartans Sept 1984 to cs
1987/Middlesex Wanderers tour
combination in 1985 and 1986.

Debut v Charlton Athletic (a) 25/8/79
(sub)

One of three bargain captures from
the local non-league circuit around
the same period, dark-haired Peter
Cartwright, like Shoulder and
Carney, gave Newcastle good short
term service. A former trainee civil
engineer, Peter turned his mind to
professional football as a 21 year-old
after an outstanding performance in
the Northumberland Senior Cup
final at St James Park during 1979.
He quickly burst onto the scene,
netting on his second outing in a
derby with Sunderland at Roker
Park. Short but with plenty of
running and stamina, Cartwright
was a midfield worker and became a
regular for season 1979-80. His
ability on the ball was always
limited, but in the dog-fight to
escape the Second Division, he
performed with credit. Peter also had trials
with Middlesbrough and Nottingham Forest
before he ended up at Gallowgate. Back in local
football after he left the Magpies, Cartwright
was selected for the England non-league squad
in 1985. He later became a mathematics teacher
in Blyth. During his spell at Feethams,
Cartwright became one of the quickest-ever
substitutes to take the field, coming on after
only five seconds of play against Chester in
1983.

Appearances:
FL: 57(8) apps. 3 gls.
FAC: 1 app. 0 gls.
FLC: 0(3) apps. 1 gl.
Total: *58(11) apps. 4 gls.*

Peter Cartwright

CARVER, Jesse

Role: Centre-half 1936-1939
5' 10"
b. Aigburth, Liverpool, 7th July 1911

CAREER: Blackburn Rovers amat Dec 1927,
pro June 1928/UNITED June 1936 £2,000/
Bury Apr 1939 £850/Huddersfield Town asst-
trainer 1945/Xerves (Holland) coach 1946/
Netherlands FA coach 1947/Millwall coach
Sept 1948/Juventus(Italy) coach 1949/
Marzotto (Italy) 1949/Genoa (Italy) coach
1951/Valdagno (Italy) coach 1952/West
Bromwich Albion manager Apr 1952 to Dec
1952/AC Roma(Italy) coach 1953/Coventry
City manager June to Dec 1955/Lazio (Italy)
coach Jan 1956 to 1957/Internazionale (Italy)

coach 1957-58/Sweden national coach cs
1958/Tottenham Hotspur coach Oct 1958 to
Mar 1959/Later in Portugal (1959-61) and USA
(1962-3)coaching.

Debut v Barnsley (h) 29/8/36

Jesse Carver made his Football League debut
in 1930 and was developed as a youngster of
note at Ewood Park having captained his
country as a schoolboy in 1913. A sturdy and
effective pivot in defence, he made 146 first
class appearances for Blackburn and was a
keen student of the tactical game which later
served him well during a long career as a
distinguished coach. Joining Newcastle as part
of a rebuilding process, Carver was a regular
for two seasons in the black'n'whites side,
before a near disastrous fall into Division
Three saw his place taken by the up and
coming Jimmy Denmark. War ended his
playing career but the Merseysider then
started on a quite remarkable career on the
Continent, especially in Italy where he became
something of a legend. Taking Juventus to the
Italian title during his first season made him a
much-coveted coach and he hopped from club
to club, including brief stays back in England.
At one time when he joined Coventry he was
recognised as, "the highest paid manager in
the Football League". But his footballing brain
and methods were too far ahead of their time
on home soil, and it was throughout Europe
that Carver was revered the most. A cheerful
but strict character, he was dubbed the "Iron
Sergeant" in Italy for his qualities of discipline
and motivation. As a teenager, Jesse started
out as a butcher's assistant and was also a
champion weight lifter. He returned to
England in the sixties to retire.

Appearances:
FL: 70 apps. 0 gls.
FAC: 6 apps. 0 gls.
Total: *76 apps. 0 gls.*
Honours:
Eng schools app./Italian champs 1950(m).

Jesse Carver

CASEY, Thomas

Role: Left-half 1952-1958
5' 8"
b. Comber, Northern Ireland, 11th March 1930

CAREER: Comber/Clara Park(Belfast)/Belfast
YMCA/Bangor/Leeds United May 1949/
Bournemouth Aug 1950/UNITED Aug 1952
£7,000/Portsmouth June 1958 £8,500/Bristol
City Mar 1959 £6,000/Gloucester City player-
manager cs 1963/Inter Roma(Canada)/
Swansea Town coach c1965 to Oct 1966/
Distillery manager cs 1967/Everton asst-coach
July 1972/Coventry City coach 1974/Grimsby
Town manager Feb 1975 to Nov 1976/Later
coaching in Iceland and Norway, also
managing the Northern Ireland youth side.

Debut v Burnley (a) 6/9/52

A human dynamo
on the field, Tommy
Casey was a 90-
minute man with
lots of stamina and
endeavour. He
wasn't stylish or
fancy on the ball,
but effective in his
midfield destroyer's
role. Tenacious and
full of vigour, Casey
was the iron-man of
Northern Ireland's

Tommy Casey

noted 1958 World Cup line-up that reached the
quarter-finals. Recommended to the Magpies
by former stalwart, Bill McCracken, Casey
spent six seasons in United's squad, his best
campaigns being 1952-53, 1955-56 and 1956-57.
A rival to Charlie Crowe, he stepped into his
contemporary's place for the 1955 Wembley
showpiece following Crowe's unfortunate
injury. Tommy was quite a traveller during his
career and when he quit football was later self-
employed as a fishmonger in Portbury near
Bristol. In total, Casey appeared over 400
times in league and cup football.

Appearances:
FL: 116 apps. 8 gls.
FAC: 16 apps. 2 gls.
Others: 2 apps. 0 gls.
Total: *134 apps. 10 gls.*
Honours:
*12 N.Irel caps 1955-59/NI youth app./
FA Cup winner 1955.*

CASSIDY, Thomas

Role: Midfield 1970-1980
5' 11"
b. Belfast, 18th November 1950

CAREER: Glentoran/UNITED Oct 1970
£25,000/Burnley July 1980 £30,000 to cs 1983/
Apoel Nicosia(Cyprus) Nov 1983, becoming
manager June 1985 to Nov 1988/Gateshead
commercial manager Oct 1990 to May 1991/
Gateshead manager Nov 1991 to Nov 1993/
Glentoran manager June 1994.

Debut v Southampton (a) 7/11/70

After being signed by Joe Harvey as a player
of promise, Irish international Tommy Cassidy
took some time to find a regular place in
Newcastle's side. But when he did earn a
position, Cassidy showed he had subtle skills
on the ball for a well built man, and the ability
to thread passes through the opposition's
defence to create a goalscoring opportunity. At
the peak of his form as United headed for
Wembley in 1974 and 1976, and as the
Magpies qualified for Europe, Tommy linked
well in midfield alongside the likes of Terry
Hibbitt and Tommy Craig. Appearing for the

Tommy Cassidy

Irish in the 1982 World Cup in Spain, Cassidy spent a decade at St James Park and was always liable to find the net from the edge of the box. During his period on Tyneside he also had a spell in South Africa appearing for the Lusitano club, while in between football appointments he ran a newsagency in the Newcastle suburbs of Benwell and Gosforth and worked for local radio. At one stage during Cassidy's period in Cyprus, he was banned from the game by UEFA after unfounded allegations of corruption against his Apoel club. Before joining United, Tommy had trials with Manchester United and had played in European competition with Glentoran.

Appearances:
FL: 170(10) apps. 22 gls.
FAC: 22(1) apps. 1 gl.
FLC: 17(2) apps. 3 gls.
Eur: 3 apps. 0 gls.
Others: 13(1) apps. 2 gls.
Total: *225(14) apps. 28 gls.*
Honours:
24 N.Irel caps 1971-82/FAC finalist 1974/FLC finalist 1976/FL div 3 champs 1982/NI Lg champs 1970/ NIC winner 1996(m)/Cyprus Lg champs 1986(m)/Cyprus cup winner 1984/Cyprus cup finalist 1986(m).

CHALMERS, William

Role: Inside-right 1928-1931
5' 9"
b. Bellshill, Lanarkshire

CAREER: Queens Park 1922/Glasgow Rangers May 1924/UNITED Mar 1928 £2,500/Grimsby Town May 1931 £1,000/Bury June 1932/Notts County May 1936/Aldershot June 1938, becoming trainer during World War Two and acting manager/Ebbw Vale manager June 1943/Juventus(Italy) coach 1948/Bury asst-trainer Sept 1949.

Debut v Leicester City (h) 7/4/28 (scored once)

William Chalmers was an elegant player who always looked to have the ability to reach the very top of the game. United's Andy Cunningham claimed he was "among the best inside-forwards who have been prevailed upon to leave Scotland". Hailing from the same Scottish town as Hughie Gallacher, he followed the famous centre-forward to St James Park and played alongside his more celebrated contemporary in United's eleven. Scoring on his debut, in a 5-1 defeat, Willie performed well in season 1928-29 netting eight goals in 19 appearances when he delighted the Newcastle crowd with flashes of brilliance. Possessing a light physique, Chalmers was a crafty schemer, who perhaps lacked the bite and determination to succeed. After moving into the lower divisions, he became a big favourite with fans at Gigg Lane. When coaching in Italy, he was succeeded at Juventus by another United player, Jesse Carver.

Appearances:
FL: 41 apps. 13 gls.
FAC: 1 app. 0 gls.
Total: *42 apps. 13 gls.*
Honours:
SL div 2 champs 1923.

William Chalmers

CHANDLER, Albert

Role: Right-back 1925-1926
5' 10"
b. Carlisle, 15th January 1897
d. Carlisle, 28th January 1963

CAREER: Dalston Beach Reds/Carlisle
jnrs/Derby County Aug 1919/UNITED
June 1925 £3,250/Sheffield United
Oct 1926 £2,625/Northfleet Nov 1929/
Manchester Central Feb 1930/Holmstead
(Carlisle) cs 1930/Queen of the South
cs 1931.

Debut v Bolton Wanderers (a) 29/8/25

Bert Chandler

At times, Bert Chandler could be a steady defender who displayed moments of brilliance not usually associated with full-backs during the inter-war years. Appearing on 183 occasions for Derby, he was especially noted for a sliding tackle but, after taking over from Billy Hampson for the 1925-26 season, lost his place to Alf Maitland as the Magpies went on to lift the title the following term. He faithfully served in both world wars, commissioned in the Machine Gun Corps, and later resided in Carlisle. During his stay at Bramall Lane, Chandler was censored for financial irregularities over Players' Union subs and ultimately blacklisted by the Football League as a player whose "registration is to be refused". As a result he was unable to continue a career in league soccer.

Appearances:
FL: 33 apps. 0 gls.
FAC: 3 apps. 0 gls.
Total: *36 apps. 0 gls.*

CHANNON, Michael Roger

Role: Striker 1982
6' 0"
b. Orcheston, nr Salisbury, 28th November 1948

CAREER: Shrewton/Southampton app Mar
1964, pro Dec 1965/Manchester City July 1977
£300,000/Southampton Sept 1979 £200,000/
Caroline Hills(Hong Kong) cs 1982/UNITED
Sept 1982 free/Bristol Rovers Oct 1982/
Norwich City Dec 1982/Portsmouth Aug
1985/Finn Harps Oct 1986/Retired 1987.

Debut v Middlesbrough (h) 8/9/82 (scored once)

Mick Channon was recognised as one of the top strikers in Division One during the seventies and early eighties, finding the net over 300 times, including 21 for England when he played on many occasions alongside Kevin Keegan. It was the Keegan link that brought him to Tyneside during the first month of the 1982-83 season. With his career drawing to a close, 33 year-old Channon teamed up with his former Saints colleague in a trial deal but, although Mick scored on his debut in a local derby with Middlesbrough, he wasn't retained by manager Arthur Cox. As it turned out, Channon gave good service to Norwich City afterwards. Developing alongside Ron Davies at The Dell, Channon was a potent attacker, able to hold the ball up and possessed vision and a natural awareness to find the net. Tall and well-balanced, with pace and control to run at defenders, he holds the Saints'

goalscoring record of 223 league and cup strikes in 596 games. He twice captained his country, and after leaving the game became a celebrated racehorse trainer at Lambourn, residing in Hampshire.

Appearances:
FL: 4 apps. 1 gl.
Total: *4 apps. 1 gl.*
Honours:
46 Eng caps 1973-78/
1 unoff Eng app. 1976/
9 Eng u23 caps 1971-72/
3 FL apps. 1973-77/
FAC winner 1976/
FLC winner 1985.

Mick Channon

CLARK, Albert Henry

Role: Right-half 1948-1949
5' 10"
b. Ashington, 24th July 1921

CAREER: North Shields/UNITED Jan 1948
£850/North Shields Mar 1949 free.
Debut v Sheffield United (h) 11/12/48

Impressing United's manager George Martin
following a series of good displays for North
Eastern League club, North Shields, Albert
Clark was given an opportunity to join the
Magpies, albeit very much as a reserve to
skipper Joe Harvey. He assisted Newcastle's
second string to the Central League
championship, but only managed a single
appearance in the senior team before moving
back to Appleby Park.

> **Appearances:**
> *FL: 1 app. 0 gls.*
> **Total:** *1 app. 0 gls.*

CLARK, Frank Albert

Role: Left-back 1962-1975
6' 0"
b. Highfield, nr Gateshead, 9th September 1943

CAREER: Sunderland sch/Preston North End
sch/Highfield/Crook Town 1960/UNITED
Oct 1962 £200/Nottingham Forest May 1975
free/ Sunderland asst-manager July 1979/
Nottingham Forest asst-coach Aug 1981/
Orient asst-manager Oct 1981, becoming
manager May 1983 and managing director Nov
1986/Nottingham Forest manager May 1993.
Debut v Scunthorpe United (a) 18/4/64

Frank Clark served his apprenticeship as a
laboratory technician before signing
professional terms for Newcastle United, this
after declining a full-time career with
Sunderland and Preston. He appeared as an
amateur for Crook, where he reached
Wembley in the Amateur Cup final, but Clark
had a bad start at St James Park, breaking his
leg. However, Frank battled his way back and
was handed the left-back shirt when George
Dalton faded from the scene. In his first full
season, when Clark was an ever-present, the
Magpies lifted the Second Division trophy and
for the next ten years the solid and
dependable defender was an automatic choice

for manager Joe Harvey, totalling 457 league
and cup games - the most by any United
player in post-war football. Neither
flamboyant nor volatile, Clark had the perfect
professional temperament and simply
shrugged off criticism from some sections of
United's crowd. He was totally dedicated to
United's cause appearing also at centre-half
during his last three seasons. At the end of the
1974-75 campaign, when Harvey resigned the
manager's post, club skipper Clark was
handed a controversial free transfer, although
many considered he still had much to offer the
club. Clark moved to join Brian Clough at the
City Ground and proceeded to win a
championship and European Cup medal. He
then started a learning period in management
eventually ending up back alongside the Trent
in charge of Forest. A fine cricketer too, Frank
Clark has never lost his affection for the
Magpies and is deservedly recognised as one
of the club's best servants. He was given a
well supported testimonial fixture in 1976
(19,974). Frank was appointed Chief Executive
of the Managers' Association in 1992.

> **Appearances:**
> *FL: 388(1) apps. 0 gls.*
> *FAC: 26 apps. 0 gls.*
> *FLC: 19 apps. 1 gl.*
> *Eur: 23 apps. 0 gls.*
> *Others: 29(1) apps. 1 gl.*
> **Total:** *485(2) apps. 2 gls.*
> **Honours:**
> *1 FL app. 1970/3 Eng youth app. 1962/1 Eng
> amat cap 1962/FL champs 1978/FL div 2
> champs 1965/FL div 2 prom 1977/FAC finalist
> 1974/FLC winner 1978, 1979/EC winner
> 1979/ICFC winner 1969/ FAAC winner 1961/
> FL div 4 prom 1989(m)/FL div 2 prom
> 1994(m)/LMA Manager of the Year 1995.*

Frank Clark

JAMES R. CLARK

CLARK, James Robinson

Role: Inside-left 1921-1924
5' 8"
b. Bensham, Gateshead, 20th October 1895
d. Gateshead, September 1947

CAREER: Annfield Plain/Jarrow/
UNITED Dec 1921 £350/Leeds United
May 1924 £300/ Swindon Town June
1925/Greenock Morton Dec 1926/
Ashington Mar 1927 to c1928/Dublin
to retirement.
Debut v Chelsea (h) 27/1/23

The lesser known of the two JR Clarks on
Newcastle's books at the same time,
James was very much on the fringe of
United's side and deputy to Tom
McDonald as the club lifted the FA Cup
in 1924. He was part of the Magpies'
reserve side that won the North Eastern
League title in 1923, and later appeared
in Scotland and Ireland before returning
to Tyneside. Clark lived in the area to his
death, for many years working at the
Wright-Anderson steelworks.

> **Appearances:**
> *FL: 11 apps. 2 gls.*
> **Total:** *11 apps. 2 gls.*

CLARK, John Robert

Role: Inside-right 1923-1928
6' 0"
b. Newburn, Newcastle upon Tyne,
6th February 1903
d. Newcastle upon Tyne, 1977

CAREER: Spencers Welfare/Hawthorn
Leslie/Newburn Grange/Newburn/Prudhoe
Castle/UNITED Feb 1923 £130/Liverpool Jan
1928 £3,000/Nottingham Forest July 1931 to
May 1932/North Shields Aug 1932, becoming
player-coach Sept 1937.

Debut v Huddersfield Town (h) 7/4/23
(scored once)

Known as Bob and a very popular
Novocastrian figure between the two wars
famed for his entertainment quality, Robert
Clark was a hefty forward, over 14 stone, and
once described as, "skilful but slow". He
possessed a ferocious shot and formed a 'Little
and Large' partnership alongside Hughie
Gallacher for several seasons, including part of
the championship campaign of 1927. The
Tynesider used his big frame well and
defenders never relished a meeting with this
6' 0" giant of a man. Newcastle United were

Bob Clark fires in a shot against Arsenal
at Highbuy watched by Hughie Gallacher.

reprimanded by the Football Association for playing Clark in a friendly match before the club had actually signed him. When he retired from the game, Bob resided on Tyneside, in Newburn, to his death.

Appearances:
FL: 77 apps. 16 gls.
Total: *77 apps. 16 gls.*
Honours:
FL champs 1927.

CLARK, Lee Robert

Role: Midfield 1988-date
5' 7"
b. Wallsend, 27th October 1972

CAREER: UNITED app cs 1988, pro Nov 1989.
Debut v Bristol City (a) 29/9/90 (sub)

An England player at schools, youth and Under-21 level, Lee Clark has been associated with Newcastle United since captaining the national side on a regular basis as a teenager. Given his chance in the Magpies' senior side initially under Ossie Ardiles in season 1990-91, Lee soon was recognised as a star of the future. With short cropped hair, at times even shaven, Clark has astute vision and combines long passes with short accurate interplay. Following United's promotion to the Premiership, in which Lee was an ever-present and played a leading role as an attack minded schemer, Clark found himself frustrated at not getting a regular place in Kevin Keegan's line-up. Injured with a broken foot for many weeks, he was on the transfer list for a period, yet the Tynesider never wanted to leave the club he has always supported. Clark eventually gained an anchor role in midfield until the arrival of David Batty again put him on the sidelines. Very much the fan's favourite, a local lad from Walker who has made good in the footsteps of Waddle, Beardsley and Gascoigne. Clark once netted a hat-trick in 1987 for England Boys against Italy at Wembley, while he picked up the nickname of 'Gnasher' in the St James Park dressing-room.

Appearances:
FL/PL: 144(26) apps. 21 gls.
FAC: 12(1) apps. 2 gls.
FLC: 16 apps. 0 gls.
Eur: 1(2) apps. 0 gls.
Others: 4 apps. 1 gl.
Total: *177(29) apps. 24 gls.*
Honours:
11 Eng u21 caps 1992-94/
Eng youth app./Eng schools app./
FL div 1 champs 1993.

Lee Clark

CLARKE, Jeffrey Derrick

Role: Centre-half & Coach 1982-1987, 1988-date
6' 1"
b. Hemsworth, nr Pontefract, 18th January 1954

CAREER: Manchester City app Aug 1971, pro Jan 1972/Sunderland June 1975 cash-exch deal/UNITED July 1982 free(Brighton loan 1984-85)/MKE Ankaragucu (Turkey) cs 1987/ Whitley Bay Feb 1988/UNITED Community Officer Nov 1988, becoming asst-coach cs 1993.

Debut v Queens Park Rangers (h) 28/8/82

Jeff Clarke

Watson to Manchester City from Roker Park. Jeff had several good seasons with the Reds, but missed out on their promotion celebrations due to injury. Unluckily the same happened to the Yorkshireman at Gallowgate, when he was sidelined for the finale as Keegan, Beardsley, Waddle and Co reclaimed the club's Division One status in 1984. Regaining fitness, Clarke played an important role in Newcastle's consolidation in the First Division during 1984-85 and 1985-86 before injury again saw him out of action. Jeff headed for a brief stay in Turkey, and on his return to St James Park worked his way up the coaching ladder to take charge of the Magpies' reserve eleven. Clarke qualified as a physiotherapist under a PFA scheme in 1995.

Appearances:
FL: 124 apps. 4 gls.
FAC: 5 apps. 0 gls.
FLC: 5 apps. 1 gl.
Total: *134 apps. 5 gls.*
Honours:
Eng schools app./Eng youth app./FL div 2 champs 1976/FL div 2 prom 1984.

CLARKE, Raymond Charles

Role: Centre-forward 1980-1981
5' 11"
b. Hackney, London,
25th September 1952

CAREER: Tottenham Hotspur app May 1968, pro Oct 1969/Swindon Town June 1973 £8,000/Mansfield Town Aug 1974 £5,000/Sparta Rotterdam(Netherlands) July 1976 £80,000/Ajax (Netherlands) cs1978/ Club Brugge (Belgium) July 1979/ Brighton Oct 1979 £175,000/ UNITED July 1980 £180,000/ Retired due to injury Aug 1981.

Debut v Sheffield Wednesday (a) 16/8/80

A free transfer signing from Sunderland, blond-haired Jeff Clarke arrived on Tyneside at the same time as the first Kevin Keegan bandwagon began. He proved a marvellous capture and an effective stopper at the heart of United's defence claiming the majority of high balls. Ideally built, with composure and good distribution from the back line, he was part of the deal that took England centre-half Dave

Ray Clarke only took part in six months' action for Newcastle United following a transfer from the Goldstone Ground after a successful period in Dutch and Belgian football. Clarke had made a reputation for himself as a dangerous leader with Mansfield netting 57 goals in a little over 100 matches, and was the Fourth Division's top goalpoacher in 1975. That earned him a move to the

Ray Clarke

Continent and by the time he joined mighty Ajax, was at the peak of his form, winning the double in the Netherlands. He netted 26 league goals for the Dutch giants in 1978-79 before moving across the border to Belgium where he also helped his side to the league title before returning to England. Ray moved to Tyneside as a replacement for Peter Withe, but never lived up to his billing. Not a power packed centre-forward in the Newcastle United tradition, but quick and positive, Clarke relied on neat touches, lay-offs and positional play in the box. He was a former England schools trialist, but never made the grade at White Hart Lane. Injured after only seven months with the black'n'whites, a knee problem forced his retirement from the game in 1981 and he later resided for a period in East Anglia, before becoming an hotelier on the Isle of Man.

Appearances:
FL: 14 apps. 2 gls.
FAC: 4 apps. 1 gl.
Total: *18 apps. 3 gls.*
Honours:
Eng youth app. 1971/FL div 4 champs 1975/
FAYC winner 1970/Dutch Lg champs 1979/
Dutch cup winner 1979/
Belgium Lg champs 1980.

CLIFTON, Henry

Role: Inside-forward 1938-1946
5' 8"
b. Newburn, Newcastle upon Tyne,
28th May 1914

CAREER: Lintz Colliery/Annfield Plain July 1932/West Bromwich Albion amat Sept 1932/Scotswood Dec 1932/ Chesterfield Aug 1933/UNITED June 1938 £8,500/Chelsea war-guest 1940-41/ Grimsby Town Jan 1946 £2,500/Goole Town cs 1949/Sutton Town Oct 1951.

Debut v Plymouth Argyle (h) 27/8/38
(scored once)

For a season Harry Clifton looked to be a buy of distinction in black'n'white colours. In the campaign of 1938-39 he bagged 17 goals from either the inside-right or left positions and was set to be a focal point in the Mather-Seymour regeneration of Newcastle United. War put an end to that plan and all but ruined Clifton's football career. Harry's best years were lost to the conflict, but he did manage to appear for his country in a wartime international. Clifton had become hot property at Chesterfield with bustling and tenacious

displays as the Spireites won honours in 1935-36. He had a lively sense of anticipation in the box and was an eyecatching player, special enough to be one of the great Jackie Milburn's favourites as a lad. On peace being restored in 1945, Clifton was United's club skipper but was eased out of the St James Park scene by the many developing youngsters, including Milburn. Harry returned to Tyneside after his career was over and resided in Throckley, a regular at the Bank Top Club for many years.

Appearances:
FL: 29 apps. 15 gls.
FAC: 6 apps. 2 gls.
War: 42 apps. 27 gls.
Total: *77 apps. 44 gls.*
Honours:
1 Eng war cap 1940/
FL div 3(N) champs 1936.

CLISH, Colin

Role: Left-back 1961-1963
5' 11"
b. Hetton-le-Hole, County Durham, 14th July 1944

CAREER: UNITED Jan 1961/Rotherham
United Dec 1963 £5,000/Doncaster Rovers
Mar 1968 exch deal/Retired due to injury
1972/Gainsborough Trinity.

Debut v Sheffield United (a) 2/10/61 (FLC)

Colin Clish

Stocky blond-haired defender Colin Clish, who developed alongside Bob Moncur and David Craig in United's talented Youth Cup-winning side of 1962, was neat and tidy at his game and always tried to play football. He skippered the successful junior line-up but was later unfortunate to have Frank Clark as a rival for the left-back spot. Manager Joe Harvey chose to nurture Clark as a First Division defender rather than Clish, and a transfer to Millmoor quickly followed. A twice broken leg eventually forced him to leave the Football League and he afterwards joined the British Transport Police becoming a railways detective in the Doncaster and Grantham area. Colin made his Magpie debut as a 17 year-old and appeared over 150 times for Rotherham, and more than 100 for Doncaster.

Appearances:
FL: 20 apps. 0 gls.
FAC: 2 apps. 0 gls.
FLC: 1 app. 0 gls.
Total: *23 apps. 0 gls.*
Honours:
FL div 4 champs 1969/
FAYC winner 1962.

COLE, Andrew Alexander

Role: Centre-forward 1993-1995
5' 11"
b. Nottingham, 15th October 1971

CAREER: Parkhead Academicals
(Nottingham)/Emkals (Nottingham)/Arsenal
sch Oct 1985, app July 1988, pro Oct 1989
(Fulham loan 1991-92)/Bristol City loan Mar
1992, pmt July 1992 £500,000/UNITED Mar
1993 £1.75m/Manchester United Jan 1995
cash-exch deal with K.Gillespie £7m.

Debut v Swindon Town (a) 13/3/93 (sub)

Andy Cole was purchased by Kevin Keegan as a virtual unknown centre-forward who had lots of potential, being an FA graduate from the Lilleshall Academy and a player who had appeared for the England Under-21 side. Yet the 21 year-old Cole had not then completed a full season in regular first-team action and many in the game gasped at the club record fee Newcastle paid for the player. Keegan though had made a master stroke signing. Immediately the lithe and agile leader started to dominate the headlines throughout a short but quite amazing spell at St James Park. From his first showing at Gallowgate the goals started to flow in abundance and Cole became dubbed the most lethal hot-shot in the country as Newcastle regained their top-flight status. With devastating pace, positional sense and expert placement of his shot, Andy was simply lethal in the box and United's scintillating approach play, especially when paired with Peter Beardsley, made sure Cole had plenty of chances to find the net. In season 1993-94 his goals ratio for much of the campaign reached a tremendous 100% - a goal a game - and he finished the year by clocking up 41 goals in only 45 outings, thereby smashing the long-standing club record held by Gallacher and Robledo. Not particularly well built for the centre-forward's role, the whippet-like Cole became a cult figure in the tradition of the club's famous Number 9 heroes, yet the Nottingham-born star shunned publicity and didn't take to the limelight. Just as Cole was further developing his raw talent into a certainty for an international cap, earning a place on the England substitutes' bench, his manager decided to sell to rivals Manchester United in a national record transfer valued at £7 million, although the fee was later noted as £6.25m. It was a transaction

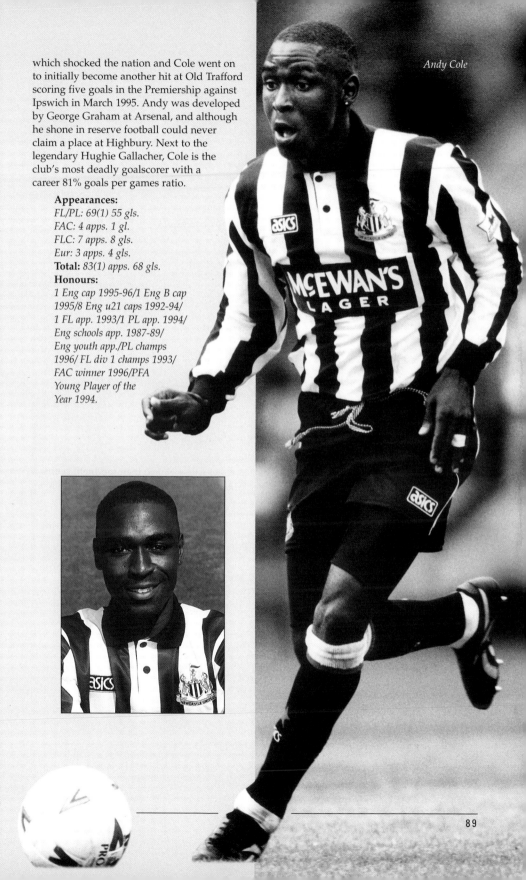

Andy Cole

which shocked the nation and Cole went on to initially become another hit at Old Trafford scoring five goals in the Premiership against Ipswich in March 1995. Andy was developed by George Graham at Arsenal, and although he shone in reserve football could never claim a place at Highbury. Next to the legendary Hughie Gallacher, Cole is the club's most deadly goalscorer with a career 81% goals per games ratio.

Appearances:
FL/PL: 69(1) 55 gls.
FAC: 4 apps. 1 gl.
FLC: 7 apps. 8 gls.
Eur: 3 apps. 4 gls.
Total: *83(1) apps. 68 gls.*
Honours:
1 Eng cap 1995-96/1 Eng B cap 1995/8 Eng u21 caps 1992-94/ 1 FL app. 1993/1 PL app. 1994/ Eng schools app. 1987-89/ Eng youth app./PL champs 1996/ FL div 1 champs 1993/ FAC winner 1996/PFA Young Player of the Year 1994.

COLLINS, James

Role: Inside-right 1892-1893, 1895-1897
5' 9"
b. Scotland, 1872
d. Rochester, Kent, 2nd January 1900

CAREER: Newcastle East End c1888/
Newcastle West End Jan 1891/
UNITED May 1892/Nottingham Forest cs
1893/ UNITED cs 1895 £20/Sheppey
United cs 1897/Chatham c1899 to death.

Debut v Sheffield United (a) 24/9/1892 (NL)

James Collins

A mobile and
dangerous forward
on the football field,
James Collins
assisted United and
their pioneers during
the very early years
of the club's
development,
including the
Tynesiders' days in
the Northern League.
Coming to the region
from north of the
border to earn his
living in the game, he
was a versatile player
appearing in both
inside positions and
on the wing for
Newcastle. Well
known and admired in the region, Collins
was quiet and inoffensive off the park, yet
could be an aggressive individual on it.
Sadly, he died of tetanus after being
injured when turning out for southern
club Chatham. He was in East End's line-
up for their very first fixture at St James
Park against Celtic in September 1892.
Collins also represented Northumberland
during his stay on Tyneside, while he
skippered the East Enders during his first
period based at the Chillingham Road
ground.

> **Appearances:**
> *NL: 10 apps. 1 gl.*
> *FL: 34 apps. 9 gls.*
> *FAC: 8 apps. 2 gls.*
> **Total:** *52 apps. 12 gls.*

CONNELL, John

Role: Inside-right 1896-1897
5' 10"
b. Scotland

CAREER: St Mirren 1894/Galston/
UNITED Oct 1896 to cs 1897.

Debut v Manchester City (a) 17/10/1896

Connell was a noted Scottish League player,
fancied by Newcastle United's directors after
several good displays in front of their
watching scouts. He had appeared on 33
occasions for Paisley's St Mirren before
heading south and was described in the
Scottish Referee magazine as being "a young
player, smart and tricky". Taking the place of
the veteran Collins in season 1896-97 as the
Magpies attempted to gain promotion,
Connell was a regular choice, but wasn't
retained for the following year. He was good
enough to represent the Scots in inter-league
action in 1894-95 against the Irish.

> **Appearances:**
> *FL: 24 apps. 3 gls.*
> *FAC: 1 app. 0 gls.*
> **Total:** *25 apps. 3 gls.*
> **Honours:**
> *1 SL app. 1895.*

CONNELLY, Edward John

Role: Inside-left 1935-1938
5' 8"
b. Dumbarton,
9th December 1916
d. Luton, 16th February 1990

Eddie Connelly

CAREER: Rosslyn jnrs June 1934/UNITED
Mar 1935 £90/Luton Town Mar 1938 £2,100/
West Bromwich Albion Aug 1939/
Dunfermline Athletic war-guest/Luton Town
war-guest 1945-46/Luton Town Apr 1946/
Leyton Orient June 1948/Brighton Oct 1949/
Retired May 1950.

Debut v Walsall (a) 11/1/36 (FAC) scored once

Eddie Connelly made his Football League
debut with United as a teenager and was
destined for a great career. Possessing heaps of
talent, he was a marvellous ball-player, typical
of many celebrated Scots of the day. Bursting
onto the scene in the Magpies' Second

Division campaign of 1935-36, he stepped in for the injured Harry McMenemy and on his day could be a matchwinner. However, before he had left Tyneside he was often criticised for overdoing the clever tricks, and for also occasionally losing his cool on the field. At Kenilworth Road Eddie became a firm favourite of supporters for a brief period, while later in his career, when with West Bromwich Albion, he again was a popular star, but was once banned for life by the FA after being sent off twice for wartime misdemeanors, which were then punished heavily. Later he was reinstated but retired from soccer due to injury. Afterwards Connelly resided in Luton.

Appearances:
FL: 25 apps. 8 gls.
FAC: 5 apps. 1 gl.
Total: *30 apps. 9 gls.*

CONNOLLY, John

Role: Outside-left 1978-1980
5' 9"
b. Barrhead, nr Glasgow, 13th June 1950

CAREER: Glasgow United 1966/St Johnstone Jan 1968/Everton Mar 1972 £75,000/ Birmingham City Sept 1976 £70,000/UNITED Apr 1978 exch deal/Hibernian Sept 1980 free/Gateshead Jan 1982/Blyth Spartans player-manager Nov 1982/Gateshead Nov 1983/Whitley Bay manager Feb 1984 to Sept 1984/Later, Ayr United part-time coach 1995.

Debut v Millwall (a) 19/8/78

Signed as part of Bill McGarry's rebuilding plans after Newcastle's relegation from Division One, John Connolly looked for a season to be an effective player in a black'n'white shirt. Linking well on the left wing and in midfield with United's strikeforce of Peter Withe and Alan Shoulder, Connolly was prominent as the Magpies reached the top of the Second Division and looked as though they would regain their First Division place. But the team's good form vanished in the promotion run-in and with it went John's hopes of a sustained period at Gallowgate. Tricky and always liable to cut inside and have a go at goal, Connolly had recovered from a twice broken leg at Goodison Park after making his name as a forward who had grabbed 55 goals at Muirton with St

Johnstone. Very talented, but inconsistent and often injured, Connolly possessed a neat body swerve and jink to beat his man. After a spell on the north east non-league circuit, John worked for Vaux Breweries then returned to his native Scotland and was

John Connolly

employed as advertising manager for *Golf Monthly* magazine. His sons Stuart and Graeme both joined Ayr United.

Appearances:
FL: 42(7) apps. 10 gls.
FAC: 0(1) app. 0 gls.
FLC: 1 app. 0 gls.
Total: *43(8) apps. 10 gls.*
Honours:
1 Scot cap 1973/2 Scot u23 caps 1971-73/ SL div 1 champs 1981/SLC finalist 1970.

COOPER, Edward

Role: Outside-right 1913-1919
5' 8"
b. Walsall, 1891

CAREER: Stafford Rangers/Glossop May 1912/UNITED Mar 1913 £1,300/Rochdale cs 1919/Notts County July 1920 £500 to cs 1921 free.

Debut v Blackburn Rovers (h) 15/3/13

Edward Cooper

The First World War divided Edward Cooper's career in two, like many unlucky footballers of his era. He was a patient and talented deputy to Jackie Rutherford at Gallowgate, filling in for the famous England international in the years up to the outbreak of the Great War. His best turn-out was 1913-14 when he totalled 14 games, while in the first season after peace was restored he made 11 appearances. By then Rutherford had departed, but Cooper was frustrated to find new signing Willie Aitken ahead of him for the first-team wing position. Despite this, Ed was a crowd pleaser with plucky displays down the touchline. During World War One, Cooper was with the West Yorkshire regiment in France.

Appearances:
FL: 45 apps. 2 gls.
FAC: 1 app. 0 gls.
War: 10 apps. 2 gls.
Total: *56 apps. 4 gls.*

COOPER, Joseph

Role: Half-back 1952-1959
5' 7"
b. Gateshead, 15th October 1934

CAREER: Winlaton Mill/
UNITED Sept 1952 to 1959 free.

Debut v Preston North End (a) 12/9/53

A part-time professional at St James Park, Joseph Cooper worked as a factory machinist, and found it extremely difficult to find a first-team place although he could play at both right or left-half-back and deputised for two noted United skippers in Bob Stokoe and Jimmy Scoular during his lengthy period in reserve. Joe was 18 years of age when he made his debut, but never managed more than two outings in any one season for the club.

Appearances:
FL: 6 apps. 0 gls.
Total: *6 apps. 0 gls.*

CORBETT, Robert

Role: Left-back 1943-1951
5' 8"
b. Throckley, Newcastle upon Tyne, 16th March 1922
d. Newcastle upon Tyne, October 1988

CAREER: Throckley Welfare/UNITED Aug 1943 £25/Middlesbrough Dec 1951 £9,000/Northampton Town Aug 1957 to 1958.

Debut v Barnsley (h) 5/1/46 (FAC)

Bobby Corbett

Not always first choice at left-back for Newcastle United, Bobby Corbett had stiff competition for the first team shirt in Doug Graham, Benny Craig, Ron Batty and Alf McMichael, but the Tynesider was an honest player who earned selection as the Magpies reached Wembley in 1951. A former winger, Bobby switched to operate as a full-back with pace who loved to attack and could cross an accurate ball from the flanks. He was one of Stan Seymour's youthful wartime products along with Jackie Milburn, Ernie Taylor and Bobby Cowell. Corbett, who hailed from a local sporting family and, like many of his generation, from the coal pits of the region, was a cheerful, happy character who always played his football with a smile. On his retirement, he lived in North Walbottle on Tyneside.

Appearances:
FL: 46 apps. 1 gl.
FAC: 14 apps. 0 gls.
War: 61 apps. 0 gls.
Total: *121 apps. 1 gl.*
Honours:
FAC winner 1951.

CORNWELL, John Anthony

Role: Midfield or Full-back 1987-1988
6' 0"
b. Bethnal Green, London, 13th October 1964

CAREER: West Ham United sch/Leyton Orient app July 1981, pro Oct 1982/UNITED Dec 1987 £50,000/Swindon Town Dec 1988 £50,000/Southend United Aug 1990 £45,000 (Cardiff City loan 1993-94)(Brentford loan 1993-94)(Northampton Town loan 1993-94).

Debut v Southampton (h) 26/9/87

A blond-haired utility player who operated largely in midfield for United, but also at full-back and in the centre of defence too. Londoner John Cornwell joined the Magpies after 227 league and cup outings for Orient where he was a product of Frank Clark's local junior network. At 23 years of age, he had the opportunity to develop at a top club, but found it difficult in a side that initially couldn't maintain a promotion challenge. His best season was in 1987-88 before moving to Swindon a year later. Always giving 100% effort, he continued to be a valued player in lower circles.

Appearances:
FL: 28(5) apps. 1 gl.
FAC: 1 app. 0 gls.
FLC: 3 apps. 0 gls.
Others: 4(2) apps. 0 gls.
Total: *36(7) apps. 1 gl.*
Honours:
FL div 3 prom 1991.

John Cornwell

COWAN, John

Role: Midfield 1967-1973
5' 10"
b. Belfast, 8th January 1949

CAREER: Crusaders (Belfast)/UNITED Jan 1967 £300/Drogheda United (Eire) player-manager Aug 1973/Darlington Aug 1975 to 1976/Lusitano (South Africa) manager July to Sept 1976/Queen of the South July-Sept 1976.

Debut v Burnley (a) 1/11/69

The dark-haired, slimly-built John Cowan was rarely given an opportunity to show his stylish ability in United's first eleven. Although capped by Northern Ireland against England at Wembley when in United's Central League side, John appeared in the Magpies' midfield during only two seasons

John Cowan

out of the seven he was on the St James Park staff. Nicknamed 'Seamus' by his colleagues, he was out of action with a bad knee injury for a long period. After retiring from the game he resided on Tyneside, opening a trophy business for a spell with former team-mate Jimmy Smith. Latterly John has run Trend Trophies in Burradon.

Appearances:
FL: 6(3) apps. 0 gls.
FLC: 0(1) app. 0 gls.
Total: *6(4) apps. 0 gls.*
Honours:
1 N.Irel cap 1970/N. Irel youth app.

COWAN, William Duncan

Role: Inside-right 1923-1926
5' 10"
b. Edinburgh, 9th August 1896

CAREER: Tranent jnrs/Dundee Jan 1920/UNITED July 1923 £2,250/Manchester City May 1926 £3,000/St Mirren May 1927/Peebles Rovers Mar 1929/Northfleet Nov 1929/North Shields Feb 1930/Hartlepools United Sept 1930/Darlington Oct 1930/Bath City July 1931.

Debut v Sheffield United (h) 8/9/23

A midfield creator who was an important cog in United's FA Cup victory in 1924, the tall, slim William Cowan was elegant and effective, the type of player who could make time and space for himself. With ability in both feet, Cowan consequently filled in on the left side of the pitch too and, possessing a potent shot which frequently tested the opposition's goalkeeper, was always able to score goals. Although at the height of his form as United embarked on their Cup run during the 1923-24 season, his career peaked when he starred at Wembley for United and then, a fortnight later, for his country against England. His performances during the following campaign however dipped alarmingly and, after being barracked by the Gallowgate crowd, Cowan was quoted as saying, "I would rather drop into minor football than remain here". The Scot soon departed, to Maine Road, to be replaced by fellow countryman Bob McKay as Newcastle began a championship winning campaign. One pen picture of the day noted Willie as being, "a mazy dribbler with the leather".

Appearances:
FL: 87 apps. 23 gls.
FAC: 14 apps. 5 gls.
Total: *101 apps. 28 gls.*
Honours:
1 Scot cap 1924/Scot trial app. 1924/FAC winner 1924.

1437 W. COWAN

COWELL, Robert George

Role: Right-back 1943-1956
5' 9"
b. Trimdon Grange, County Durham, 5th December 1922
d. Newcastle upon Tyne, 11th January 1996

CAREER: Trimdon/Blackhall Colliery/UNITED Oct 1943 £10/ Gateshead war-guest 1945-46/ Retired due to injury 1956.
Debut v Barnsley (h) 5/1/46 (FAC)

A solid defender, brave and tremendously quick to make up lost ground, ex-miner Bobby Cowell dominated the Number Two shirt at St James Park for nearly a decade after being signed as a youngster during World War Two. Appearing in three seasons of wartime soccer, Cowell made his first league appearance for the Magpies in the home Second Division fixture with Newport County during 1946, a game that produced the record Football League scoreline of 13-0. He saw off challenges from Craig, Burke and Fraser and made the right-back spot his own, playing in every one of the club's 25 FA Cup-ties that saw the trophy brought back to Tyneside on three occasions. Celebrated for off-the-line clearances, including a famous moment in an FA Cup final, Bobby was on the fringe of an England cap and one of the few attacking full-backs of the era. Jackie Milburn once remarked that he, "was the best uncapped full-back I've known". The quietly-spoken Cowell was injured during a friendly in Germany during the summer tour of 1955 and was forced to quit the game prematurely. A very popular player with the grass-roots fans, in 1956 he was given a testimonial fixture which saw 36,240 turn up to give him a send-off. Afterwards he resided in Ponteland on Tyneside, frequently watching United's fortunes for the next 40 years. Although Bobby appeared over 400 times for the black'n'whites, he never found the net.

Appearances:
FL: 289 apps. 0 gls.
FAC: 38 apps. 0 gls.
War: 81 apps. 0 gls
Others: 1 app. 0 gls.
Total: *409 apps. 0 gls.*
Honours:
FL div 2 prom 1948/ FAC winner 1951, 1952, 1955.

Bobby Cowell

John Craggs

CRAGGS, John Edward

Role: Right-back 1964-1971, 1982-1983
5' 8"
b. Flinthill, County Durham,
31st October 1948

CAREER: UNITED Apr 1964/
Middlesbrough Aug 1971 £60,000/
UNITED July 1982 free/Darlington cs
1983 free to cs 1985/Crook Town 1987/
Hartlepool United asst-coach Dec 1988,
caretaker-manager Nov 1989.

Debut v Everton (a) 1/10/66

With United in two spells, John Craggs had
an association with the Magpies which
spanned eight seasons. Joining the club as a
teenager in 1964, he was unfortunate to
develop in the shadows of David Craig
and, despite his long period at Gallowgate,
infrequently received an opportunity.
Overlapping with style and vision, his best
returns were in 1968-69 and 1969-70, when
Craggs was also involved in the club's
European success, playing in the semi-final
against Rangers and on the bench in the
final. But for Craig's tremendous
consistency, John would have earned the
right-back spot, yet had to depart the scene
to make sure of regular Football League
action. However, at Ayresome Park, Craggs
enjoyed a consistent period himself,
appearing on 473 occasions, many as
captain, during a decade with
Middlesbrough. With a solid frame, calm
assurance and a polished style on the ball,
he rejoined United for a short period at the
end of his career and appeared alongside
Kevin Keegan in a black'n'white shirt. John
was only 17 when he first played for
United, and 33 when he started
his second spell. He later
resided in Yarm, running a
sports shop on Teesside.

Appearances:
FL: 60(4) apps. 1 gl.
FAC: 2 apps. 0 gls.
FLC: 1(1) apps. 0 gls.
Eur: 5 apps. 0 gls.
Total: *68(5) apps. 1 gl.*
Honours:
Eng youth app. 1966-67/FL div 2
champs 1974/ICFC winner
1969(sub, no apps.).

CRAIG, Albert Hughes

Role: Midfield 1987-1989
5' 8"
b. Glasgow,
3rd January 1962

CAREER: Yoker Athletic/Dumbarton 1981/Hamilton Academical Aug 1986 £10,000/UNITED Feb 1987 £100,000(Hamilton Academical loan 1987-88) (Northampton Town loan 1988-89)/Dundee loan Dec 1988, pmt Jan 1989/Partick Thistle 1992/Falkirk Jan 1996.

Debut v Luton Town (h) 7/2/87

Albert Craig joined United as a 25 year-old midfielder who had risen to become headline news in Scotland with a series of dramatic displays for Hamilton. In the space of a few short weeks, he netted four goals in a derby against Motherwell, scored again opposing Celtic, then turned in a superb performance in a shock cup defeat of Rangers at the end of January 1987. Newcastle scouts were suitably impressed and paid a six-figure fee to bring the part-timer to Tyneside. Craig gave up his job in a friend's television shop and turned his attention to the big time in England.

Benny Craig

However, manager Willie McFaul's vision of Craig's ability to become a top class link man never materialised. Unable to come to terms with the pace of English First Division soccer, Craig struggled and totalled just a handful of games for the Magpies. At a big financial loss to United, he eventually returned north of the border where he became a key player for Partick Thistle. At the start of his career Albert turned out on more than 150 occasions for Dumbarton.

Appearances:
FL: 6(4) apps. 0 gls.
FAC: 1(1) apps. 0 gls.
Others: 2 apps. 0 gls.
Total: *9(5) apps. 0 gls.*
Honours:
SL div 1 prom 1992

CRAIG, Benjamin

Role: Right or Left-back & Coach 1938-1982
5' 7"
b. Leadgate, Co. Durham, 6th December 1915
d. Newcastle upon Tyne, 18th January 1982

CAREER: Medomsley jnrs/Leadgate/Ouston jnrs/Eden Colliery/Huddersfield Town Jan 1934/UNITED Nov 1938 £4,000/Chelsea war-guest 1941-42/Retired July 1950, becoming asst-coach and later asst-physio to his death.

Debut v Blackburn Rovers (a) 19/11/38

Benny Craig was a loyal servant to Newcastle United for over 40 years; a shrewd, sound-kicking full-back and a respected and likeable character behind the scenes. Able to play on both flanks, Craig rivalled Joe Richardson for a defender's role before the war and, after losing some of his best years to the fighting, returned to lend an experienced head in the Magpies' promotion line-up of 1948. On retirement Craig worked alongside his former rival, Richardson, for all of three decades in the inner corridors of St James Park, a pairing which was at the very heart of the club. Benny coached Newcastle's FA Youth Cup success in 1962 and helped enormously in the development of future stars Craig, Moncur and Alan Suddick along with a host of other youngsters in the Magpies' emerging junior set-up at the time. During the war he served with the Royal Artillery and spent most of his active service in the Mediterranean including the landings at Anzio when he won the Military Medal. As a teenager Benny had trials with Sunderland and Arsenal before entering senior football at Leeds Road where he earned a Wembley place in 1938 appearing in Huddersfield's FA Cup defeat by Preston. Craig was originally a brick moulder in Consett.

Appearances:
FL: 66 apps. 0 gls.
FAC: 1 app. 0 gls.
War: 55 apps. 0 gls.
Total: *122 apps. 0 gls.*
Honours:
FL div 2 prom 1948/FAC finalist 1938.

CRAIG, David James

Role: Right-back 1960-1978
5' 10"
b. Comber, Northern Ireland, 8th June 1944

CAREER: Boys Brigade/UNITED app Aug 1960, pro Apr 1962/Blyth Spartans cs 1978 free/Retired Nov 1978, occasionally appearing in local football, including Dunston Mechanics 1983-84.

Debut v Bournemouth (a) 6/11/63 (FLC)

Recognised by many judges to be one of the best defenders in the game during the sixties and seventies, David Craig stands alongside the likes of McCracken, Hudspeth and Cowell as the club's most consistent full-back. Joining United's apprentice scheme after a trial at Scunthorpe, and as a raw teenager from Ulster, he rapidly caught the eye of Joe Harvey after starring in the club's Youth Cup success of 1962. Craig was in many ways a complete footballer, dependable and able to recover quickly when in defence, intelligent and positive going forward. He also had a steady character that never gave his manager a problem. David was a thorough professional and is one of only seven individuals to total over 400 league and cup games for the Magpies. One of those players was Craig's partner for many a season, Frank Clark, a duo that served United well for 13

campaigns, the majority in the top flight. Had it not been for several injuries that kept Craig out of action - including both 1974 and 1976 Wembley appearances - the Irishman would have come close to Jimmy Lawrence's long-standing appearance record. Although sidelined for the 1974 FA Cup final, he received a runners-up medal for appearing in eight of the previous fixtures en route to the final. A regular member for the Northern Ireland international squad, he was a one-club man with the black'n'whites. A crowd of 21,280 attended his testimonial match in 1975. David is the only United player to appear in both of the Magpies' European campaigns of 1968-71 and 1977-78. Craig later resided on Tyneside and ran a newsagency chain as well as a heating company and, for a while, a milk business.

Appearances:
FL: 346(5) apps. 8 gls.
FAC: 22 apps. 3 gls.
FLC: 17(1) apps. 1 gl.
Eur: 21 apps. 0 gls.
Others: 23 apps. 1 gl.
Total: *429(6) apps. 13 gls.*
Honours:
25 N.Irel caps 1967-75/2 N.Irel u23 caps 1965-67/1 All-Irel app. 1973/FL div 2 champs 1965/FAYC winner 1962/ ICFC winner 1969.

David Craig

CRAIG, Derek M.

Role: Centre-half 1969-1975
6' 0"
*b. Ryton, nr Gateshead,
28th July 1952*

CAREER: UNITED app May 1969, pro Aug 1969(San Jose Earthquakes(USA) loan cs 1975)Darlington Sept 1975/ York City May 1980 to cs 1982/ Brandon United Nov 1982.

Debut v Arsenal (a) 6/10/71 (FLC)

Derek Craig

Tall, slender centre-half Derek Craig was plunged into the senior line-up at a time of injury crisis at Gallowgate. Regular centre-backs Ollie Burton, Bob Moncur and John McNamee were sidelined, and new signing Pat Howard was cup-tied, so in stepped the untried Craig for a difficult League Cup tie at Highbury, home of the reigning champions. The evening went badly for the youngster, the Gunners netting four times and Craig didn't get another opportunity in Joe Harvey's line-up apart from a Texaco Cup outing. However, he became one of the most respected defenders in the Fourth Division appearing almost 200 times for the Feethams club.

Appearances:
FLC: 1 app. 0 gls.
Others: 1 app. 0 gls.
Total: *2 apps. 0 gls.*

CRAIG, Thomas Brooks

Role: Midfield 1974-1978
5' 7"
*b. Penilee, Glasgow,
21st November 1950*

CAREER: Avon Villa/Drumchapel Amateurs 1965/Aberdeen 1966/Sheffield Wednesday May 1969 £100,000/UNITED Dec 1974 £110,000/Aston Villa Jan 1978 £270,000/ Swansea City July 1979 £150,000/Carlisle United Mar 1982, becoming asst-manager July 1982/Hibernian player-coach Oct 1984 £6,000 to Dec 1986/Glasgow Celtic coach 1987, becoming asst-manager and afterwards on the Parkhead staff as chief-scout and later, head-of-youth to Oct 1994/Aberdeen asst-manager May 1995/Also Scotland FA u21 coach.

Debut v Carlisle United (a) 26/12/74

During the early part of his career, ginger-haired Tommy Craig was wanted by Celtic, Liverpool and West Ham United as a schoolkid and later became the most expensive teenager on record when he moved from Pittodrie to Hillsborough for a six figure sum. The short but stocky Craig's undoubted potential somewhat stagnated with Sheffield Wednesday in 233 games, a quality player in a team which slipped to the Third Division. It wasn't until he moved back to the top in black'n'white colours that the talent of Tommy Craig was fully realised. Tommy was capped by Scotland when at St James Park as he became an influential United player. Replacing the popular, but injured Terry Hibbitt in Newcastle's midfield, Craig had an educated

Tommy Craig

left foot, always prompting and probing, while he could hit a short pass accurately and place a telling long ball which could win a match. He possessed a stinging drive too which brought several picture goals and was also a penalty-kick expert. Replacing the sidelined Geoff Nulty as skipper of the Magpies' Wembley eleven in 1976, Craig also captained his national side at Under-21, Under-23 and youth level, and is one of only a handful of Scots to have appeared at every level of international football for his country. The internal strife which resulted in Richard Dinnis' managerial reign at Gallowgate, eventually led to Craig's departure for a record club fee to Villa Park. His brother, John, also appeared for Aberdeen. Tommy later became a respected coach in Scotland.

Appearances:
FL: 122(2) apps. 22 gls.
FAC: 13 apps. 3 gls.
FLC: 11 apps. 2 gls.
Eur: 4 apps. 2 gls.
Others: 5 apps. 0 gls.
Total: *155(2) apps. 29 gls.*
Honours:
1 Scot cap 1976/9 Scot u23 caps 1974-76/
1 Scot u21 cap 1977/Scot youth app./
Scot schools app./FLC finalist 1976/
WsC winner 1981.

CRATE, Thomas

Role: Forward 1892-1895
5' 9"
b. Ayrshire

CAREER: Newcastle East End cs 1891/ UNITED May 1892/Hebburn Argyle Feb 1895/Blyth Town Mar 1895/Seaton Burn 1896/Morpeth early 1897/Ashington Apr 1897.

Debut v Sheffield United (a) 24/9/1892 (NL)

Tom Crate

One of the club's foremost pioneers, Tom Crate appeared in Newcastle's first game at St James Park against Celtic, and United's Football League baptism with Arsenal. Additionally Tom took part in East End's initial FA Cup proper fixture with Nottingham Forest in 1892. Crate also has the distinction of netting the Tynesiders' first goal in league action against the Gunners, although some sources credit the historic strike to Willie Graham after "a scrimmage" in the Londoners' box. Crate appeared in all five forward positions for United during Newcastle's first three years of existence following East End's move from Heaton to St James Park. He was always able to find the net, scoring 12 goals in the inaugural 1893-94 league programme. But the Scot left the club under a cloud, released after a dispute over wages. He continued his career in local football helping Ashington to the East Northumberland title in 1898.

Appearances:
FL: 39 apps. 14 gls.
NL: 10 apps. 2 gls.
FAC: 2 apps. 1 gl.
Total: *51 apps. 17 gls.*

CRAWFORD, James

Role: Midfield
1995-date
6' 0"
b. Chicago, USA,
1st May 1973

CAREER:
Bohemians(Dublin) 1991/UNITED Mar 1995 £75,000 (Rotherham United loan 1996-97).

Debut v Bristol City (h) 4/10/95 (sub)(FLC)

Jimmy Crawford

Jimmy Crawford earned himself a full-time contract with Premiership Newcastle United after impressing manager Kevin Keegan in a trial period on Tyneside towards the end of the 1994-95 season. The 21 year-old could play wide or in a more conventional midfield role and was quickly handed a senior debut in the Coca-Cola Cup meeting with Bristol City. Before joining the Magpies, Crawford had a trial period at Villa Park in Birmingham. Settling and developing well on Tyneside, Jimmy has skippered United's reserve line-up and was included in the Republic of Ireland's squad during season 1995-96.

Appearances:
FLC: 0(1) app. 0 gls.
Total: *0(1) app. 0 gls.*

CREILLY, Robert

Role: Right-half 1889-1895
5' 10"
b. Scotland

CAREER: Dunmore/Newcastle East End 1889/UNITED May 1892/ Hebburn Argyle cs 1895 to 1897, later with other local sides.

Debut v Sheffield United (a) 24/9/1892 (NL)

Like his team-mate Tom Crate, Scot Bobby Creilly was a stalwart of the East End side that dominated the local scene and eventually saw off the challenge of West End to become Tyneside's premier club. He also appeared in Newcastle United's first fixture at St James Park and saw action in their first Football League tussle as well as East End's inaugural gallant run to the early rounds of the FA Cup proper. Tough and uncompromising at half-back, Creilly was also a touch fiery and temperamental, once suspended in 1894 for two weeks for using bad language on the field at officials, while in 1891 he stormed off the park due to his colleagues' lack of effort! A versatile individual he generally operated in midfield, but also turned out in other roles, including goalkeeper for East End. He was selected for the Northumberland County side during those early Victorian years and was a well known figure on Tyneside. Later in life during the Edwardian era Creilly fell upon hard times and was noted as being in, "destitute circumstances". Records show that Newcastle United forwarded a gift of five guineas to help him out but in March 1905 he was, "removed to Coxlodge Hospital", then a well-known sanatorium in Newcastle. Some sources have his surname spelt, Crielly.

Appearances:
FL: 54 apps. 1 gl.
NL: 9 apps. 1 gl.
FAC: 5 apps. 0 gls.
Total: *68 apps. 2 gls.*

CROPLEY, Alexander James

Role: Midfield 1980
5' 8"
b. Aldershot, 16th January 1951

CAREER: Edina Hearts(Edinburgh)/ Hibernian July 1968/ Arsenal Dec 1974 £150,000/Aston Villa Sept 1976 £125,000 (UNITED loan Feb to Mar 1980)/Toronto Blizzard(Canada) July 1981/ Portsmouth Sept 1981/Hibernian Sept 1982/ Retired 1984.

Debut v Wrexham (a) 9/2/80

One of Scotland's big money exports south of the border, Alex Cropley had proved with Hibs that he was an exciting talent and a tenacious midfielder who possessed vision and loved to have a go at goal. Cropley though had an unfortunate start to his career in England, breaking a leg after only nine games for the Gunners. It took many months before he returned to fitness and by then any chance of making an impression at Highbury was lost. More injuries followed and he arrived at St James Park on loan, desperate for another opportunity to resurrect his career and rediscover his sparkle. The lightweight Cropley was only on Tyneside a matter of weeks yet never revealed his gifted

Alex Cropley

talent in the club's Second Division line-up. Yet another serious injury, this time when at Fratton Park, virtually ended his first-class career. Raised in Edinburgh, although born in deepest England, Alex is one of only a few Englishmen to have played for the Scottish full international side. He had trials with Chelsea before joining the Easter Road set-up as a teenager. His playing career over, Cropley later opened a public-house near to Hibernians' ground. Alex's father John appeared for Aldershot between 1947-54.

Appearances:
FL: 3 apps. 0 gls.
Total: *3 apps. 0 gls.*
Honours:
2 Scot caps 1972/
3 Scot u23 caps 1972-74/
FLC winner 1977/SLC winner 1973/
SLC finalist 1975.

CROSSON, David

Role: Right-back
1972-1975
5' 9"
*b. Bishop Auckland,
24th November 1952*

CAREER: UNITED
app cs 1972, pro Nov
1972/Darlington Aug
1975 free/Crook Town
cs 1980.

Debut v Manchester United (a) 13/4/74

A junior development, blond-haired David
Crosson was stand-by for David Craig over
two seasons, in 1973-74 and 1974-75. Well-built
and strong-tackling, he deputised ably when
asked, but was never going to become
anything but a reserve in United's Division
One line-up. He also often appeared in
midfield in the Magpies' Central League side
and with Darlington totalled over 120
matches.

Appearances:
FL: 6 apps. 0 gls.
FLC: 0(1) app. 0 gls.
Others: 3 apps. 0 gls.
Total: *9(1) apps. 0 gls.*

CROWE, Charles Alfred

Role: Left-half 1944-1957
5' 8"
*b. Walker, Newcastle upon Tyne,
30th October 1924*

CAREER: Wallsend St Lukes/
Heaton & Byker Youth Club/
UNITED Oct 1944 £10/Mansfield
Town Feb 1957/Retired cs 1958/
Whitley Bay manager 1958 to
1960/FA staff coach to 1967.

Debut v Barnsley (h) 5/1/46 (FAC)

A tenacious, hard-working wing-
half who never gave up the
challenge for United's cause in
all of 13 seasons, Charlie Crowe
arrived at St James Park as a
youngster during the Second
World War and was developed
alongside Jackie Milburn and
Bobby Cowell. Although he

appeared as a regular in 1945-46, he didn't
find a position in Newcastle's first-class line-
up until season 1949-50, being a mainstay of
the Magpies' Central League title victory in
1948. Crowe had tough competition for senior
action, with firstly Norman Dodgin, then Ted
Robledo and Tommy Casey as rivals. A player
who rarely took the headlines, Crowe got on
with the rough and tumble in the middle of
the field as a spoiler of the opposition's tactics
and winner of the ball, while he was also used
to good effect as a marker. He unluckily
missed out on the 1955 FA Cup victory at
Wembley due to an ankle injury. United
captain for a spell in 1954-55, he qualified as
an FA Coach under Walter Winterbottom
when on the club's books, teaching the game
extensively in the north east. Charlie later
resided in Longbenton and became a licensee
for a spell, also working at the giant Civil
Service complex in the city to his retirement.
At one point in his career he was appointed
manager of Cairo side Zamelek, only for the
Arab-Israeli war to erupt and prevent him
taking up the position.

Appearances:
FL: 178 apps. 5 gls.
FAC: 14 apps. 1 gl.
War: 24 apps. 1 gl.
Total: *216 apps. 7 gls.*
Honours:
1 FL(N) app. 1958/
1 FA app. 1955/FAC winner 1951.

CROWN, Lawrence

Role: Left-back 1926-1927
6' 0"
*b. Fulwell, Sunderland,
25th February 1898
d. Newcastle upon Tyne,
6th July 1984*

CAREER: Furness
Athletic/Sunderland All
Saints/Redcar/South Shields
Apr 1922/UNITED Mar 1926
£2,750/Bury May 1927 £750/
Coventry City July 1928/
Retired cs 1931.

*Debut v Huddersfield Town (h)
6/3/26*

Charlie Crowe

Known as Lawrie to his colleagues, Crown was a steadfast and gentlemanly character who had built up a fine reputation at Horsley Hill, during the days of Football League soccer at South Shields. Tall and powerful, he always played the game fairly and was deputy to Frank Hudspeth for a year before moving to Gigg Lane. At Coventry, Lawrie was appointed captain and was a regular for three seasons totalling 117 appearances. After retiring from the game he returned to his earlier occupation, as a draughtsman in the Wear shipyards, and later resided in Wideopen.

Appearances:
FL: 2 apps. 0 gls.
Total: *2 apps. 0 gls.*

CRUMLEY, Robert J.

Role: Goalkeeper 1903-1907
5' 11"
b. Lochee, Dundee, 1878

CAREER: Lochee United/UNITED May 1903/Dundee cs 1907 £50.

Debut v Sheffield Wednesday (a) 26/4/05

Bob Crumley gained recognition when in the army with the Gordon Highlanders, winning the Army Cup, but due to the dominance of fellow Scot Jimmy Lawrence in United's goal, he had few opportunities in Newcastle's senior eleven. He did though take part in the Magpies' title season in 1904-05 (1 app.) and the club's reserve success in the Northern League and North Eastern League, as well as the local Northumberland Senior Cup. Crumley liked to fist the ball away in the style of the day, and later became a respected goalkeeper back in Scotland with Dundee, playing alongside two other ex United players - MacFarlane and Fraser - as the Tay club lifted the Scottish Cup after defeating Clyde in a three game final. His brother James was also a custodian, for Dundee Hibs, the forerunner of Dundee United, while his son pulled on a Darlington shirt during the twenties.

Appearances:
FL: 4 apps. 0 gls.
Total: *4 apps. 0 gls.*
Honours:
SC winner 1910.

CUMMINGS, Robert Douglas

Role: Centre-forward 1954-1956, 1963-1965
5' 10"
b. Ashington, 17th November 1935

CAREER: New Hartley/UNITED May 1954/ Ashington Nov 1956/Aberdeen 1960 £2,000/ UNITED Oct 1963 £5,000/Darlington Oct 1965 £3,500/Hartlepools United Mar 1968 £2,500/ Port Elizabeth(S.Africa) June 1969.

Debut v Northampton Town (h) 26/10/63

Robert Cummings was on the St James Park books on two occasions, firstly as a junior who didn't make the grade, then as a decent centre-forward who played his part in the club's Second Division title victory in 1965. Not big, nor powerfully built, nevertheless Bobby possessed fine positional sense, was good in the air and found the net with important goals. He later had an invaluable spell at Feethams, leading the Quakers to promotion

Bobby Cummings

for the first time ever and then did the same with Hartlepool, making a hat-trick of north-east promotion successes. After leaving Gallowgate as a youngster, he impressed everyone by becoming Ashington's record goalscorer with 60 goals in 1958-59. Cummings had the odd experience of leading United's attack five days before his transfer to the Magpies - as a guest in Alf McMichael's testimonial fixture. He clinched the move after scoring a terrific goal. Bobby twice broke a leg during his career but was the epitome of a hard working professional who rarely took the headlines.

Appearances:
FL: 43(1) apps. 14 gls.
FLC: 1 app. 0 gls.
Total: *44(1) apps. 14 gls.*
Honours:
FL div 2 champs 1965/
FL div 4 prom 1966, 1968.

CUNNINGHAM, Anthony Eugene

Role: Centre-forward 1985-1987
6' 2"
b. Kingston, Jamaica, 12th November 1957

CAREER: Kidderminster Harriers/ Stourbridge cs 1977/Lincoln City May 1979 £20,000/Barnsley Sept 1982 £85,000/Sheffield Wednesday Nov 1983 £100,000/ Manchester City July 1984 £90,000/ UNITED Feb 1985 £75,000/ Blackpool Aug 1987 £25,000/Bury Aug 1989 £40,000/Bolton Wanderers Mar 1991 £70,000/Rotherham United Aug 1991 £50,000/ Doncaster Rovers July 1993 free, becoming player-coach Nov 1993 and caretaker-manager Dec 1993/Wycombe Wanderers Mar 1994 free/Gainsborough Trinity cs 1994/ Retired 1995.

Debut v Manchester United (h) 9/2/85

Big Tony Cunningham very quickly became a crowd favourite at Gallowgate due to his splendid work-rate and attitude to the game, never shirking a challenge and never hiding from the action. Cheerful, tall and leggy, his skills on the ball were limited, yet Cunningham was still a handful in the lead role. He was never going to become one of Newcastle's great centre-forwards, but will be remembered as an honest striker at a time when manager Jack Charlton preferred to

utilise a long ball game. Leaving the West Indies as a seven year-old, Tony became an errant traveller; his career peaked with Lincoln City where he made his name scoring 32 goals in 123 appearances, and at Hillsborough where he also did well. His short stays with giants Manchester City, Sheffield Wednesday and the Magpies gave him a taste of top level football, and by the time he was ready to hang up his boots, Cunningham had made over 500 senior outings. He then concentrated on a career in law, becoming employed as a legal executive in Lincoln.

Appearances:
FL: 37(10) 4 gls.
FAC: 1(1) apps. 0 gls.
FLC: 2 apps. 2 gls.
Total: *40(11) apps. 6 gls.*
Honours:
FL div 2 prom 1984/
FL div 4 prom 1981, 1992.

Tony Cunningham

CUNNINGHAM, Andrew Nisbet

Role: Inside-right & Manager 1929-1935
6' 0"
b. Galston, Ayrshire, 31st January 1890
d. Scotland, 8th May 1973

CAREER: Galston Riverside Rangers
1906/Newmilns 1907/Kilmarnock June
1909/Glasgow Rangers Apr 1915 £800/
West Ham United war-guest 1915-19/
UNITED Feb 1929 £2,300, becoming player-
manager Jan 1930, manager May 1930/
Resigned May 1935/Dundee manager
June 1937 to May 1940.

Debut v Leicester City (a) 2/2/29

One of the 'All Time Greats' of Scottish
football, Andy Cunningham appeared
almost 450 times, scoring nearly 200 goals,
for Rangers during the Ibrox club's twenties
heyday. Tall and golden-haired, he was an
elegant inside-forward able to operate right
or left with superb ball control, positional
sense and passing ability, as well as a
vicious shot that all goalkeepers feared.
When Cunningham headed over the border
for Tyneside he was over 38 years of age,
and thought to be the oldest player to make
his debut in the English league. He arrived
very much as United's first manager
designate, quickly graduating to player-
boss and outright manager, although the
club's directors still had a big say in team
matters throughout his reign. Scoring on his
international debut and captain of Scotland,
he was a fine tactician and great thinker on
the game. Andy led the Magpies to
Wembley victory, but alas also to relegation
and obscurity in the Second Division. After
leaving football he spent many years as a
sports journalist with the *Scottish Daily
Express* and was once noted during the
inter-war years as, "brainy, breezy and
bowler-hatted".

Appearances:
FL: 12 apps. 2 gls.
FAC: 3 apps. 0 gls.
Total: *15 apps. 2 gls.*
Honours:
*12 Scot caps 1920-27/Scot trial app. 1911-
24/10 SL apps. 1912-28/SL champs 1920,
1921, 1923, 1924, 1925, 1927, 1928/
SC winner 1928/SC finalist 1921, 1922/
FAC winner 1932(m).*

CURRY, Thomas

Role: Wing-half 1912-1929
5' 8"
b. South Shields, 1st September 1894
d. Munich, Germany, 6th February 1958

CAREER: South Shields St Michaels/South
Shields Parkside/UNITED Apr 1912 £20/
Stockport County Jan 1929 free/Carlisle
United trainer July 1930/Manchester United
trainer June 1934 to his death.

Debut v Arsenal (a) 30/8/19

A sergeant with the Royal Engineers in the
Great War, Tom Curry was a good all-round
player who served United well for 12 seasons
after being spotted as a teenager in the
Northern Alliance. At home in either right or
left-half roles, Curry was a regular in United's
side during the years immediately after World
War One as the black'n'whites challenged for
honours. Tom was good enough to be selected
for the Football League eleven, showing much
ability in both link play and foraging in
midfield. He unluckily missed out though on
the 1924 success at Wembley after playing in
five of the games during the Magpies' FA Cup

run. He then also couldn't find a place for much of the 1927 championship campaign and had to be content to wait on the sidelines as a reserve. Curry retired and entered the sphere of coaching, eventually becoming an important backstage aid to Matt Busby at Old Trafford during the 1940s and 1950s, but tragically was a victim of the Munich Air Disaster which claimed the lives of so many noted footballers in 1958.

Tom Curry

Appearances:
FL: 221 apps. 5 gls.
FAC: 14 apps. 0 gls.
War: 13 apps. 0 gls.
Total: *248 apps. 5 gls.*
Honours:
1 FL app. 1920/Brit Olympic
XI trainer 1948.

CURRY, William Morton

Role: Centre-forward 1953-1959
5' 8"
b. Walker, Newcastle upon Tyne,
12th October 1935
d. Mansfield, 20th August 1990

CAREER: UNITED Oct 1953/Brighton July 1959 £13,000/Derby County Sept 1960 £12,000/Mansfield Town Feb 1965 £10,000/ Chesterfield Jan 1968 £2,000(Boston United loan 1968-69)/Worksop Town coach June 1969/Boston United manager Feb 1971 to May 1976/Sutton Town manager May 1977 to May 1980.

Debut v Manchester United (a) 23/10/54

Bill Curry

Very often Bill Curry looked the part in United's forward line, either at centre-forward or inside-left. Although not a big man, he was a danger in the air and quick on the floor with punch in the kill. A dour fighter, Bill would also battle hard for the ball and opposing defenders always knew they

had been in a contest. He was an outstanding product of Newcastle schools football and became the first United player to graduate from the club's new junior set-up, the N's. As a teenager Bill once netted eight goals for the kids' side in a FA Youth Cup victory. Like many players of his era, National Service affected his progress at Gallowgate, being away from the scene for a long period, but he did appear for the Army Select eleven and scored five goals against the Navy in 1958. Despite being the first Newcastle player to be chosen for the England Under-23 side, Bill was destined to be second choice to Len White at St James Park at an age when he needed first-team action. Moving on, he scored goals at all his clubs; 76 with Derby, 29 for Brighton and 57 at Mansfield. Cousin to George Luke who also appeared for the Magpies, the pair attended the same school in Walkergate. After leaving the game, Bill set up a window cleaning business in Mansfield.

Appearances:
FL: 80 apps. 36 gls.
FAC: 8 apps. 4 gls.
Total: *88 apps. 40 gls.*
Honours:
1 Eng u23 cap 1958.

DALTON, George

Role: Left-half or Left-back 1958-1967
5' 8"
b. West Moor, nr Newcastle upon Tyne,
4th September 1941

CAREER: UNITED Nov 1958/Brighton June 1967 free/Birmingham City coach May 1970/ Coventry City physiotherapist Jan 1976 to date.

Debut v Leicester City (a) 11/2/61.

George Dalton

Highly thought of at St James Park, at one stage of his United career George Dalton was tipped as an England player after a series of eye-catching displays in a black'n'white shirt during seasons 1962-63 and 1963-64. Cool-headed and with a constructive football brain for both defending and setting attacks going, Dalton was a popular character, but a clash with Leeds United's Johnny Giles in a match at Elland Road during Easter 1964 ruined his career. A badly fractured leg from that tackle put Dalton out of action for over a year and as a consequence his place went to the young Frank Clark. Dalton only appeared once more for the Magpies after that unfortunate injury and never displayed the same promise again. As a teenager he made his senior baptism as a half-back, a position he favoured during his early years in Joe Harvey's first eleven. Dalton actually netted an own-goal on his debut after only six minutes of play. After retiring he resided in the Midlands giving long service behind the scenes to Coventry City.

Appearances:
FL: 85 apps. 2 gls.
FAC: 2 apps. 0 gls.
FLC: 7 apps. 0 gls.
Total: *94 apps. 2 gls.*

DAVID DAVIDSON

DAVIDSON, David Leighton

Role: Centre-half 1930-1937
5' 10"
b. Aberdeen, 4th June 1905
d. Tynemouth, May 1969

CAREER: Garthdee(Aberdeen)/Aberdeen Argyle/Forfar Athletic/Liverpool July 1928/ UNITED Jan 1930 £4,000/Hartlepools United June 1937 £50/Gateshead Oct 1937/Retired cs 1938/Whitley Bay manager 1945/Ashington manager 1955 to cs 1963.

Debut v Huddersfield Town (a) 1/2/30

After a slow start in United's ranks, Dave Davidson claimed the centre-half shirt from former England captain Jack Hill and developed into a strong and dependable stopper during an exciting FA Cup run to Wembley in 1932. Rugged rather than brilliant on the ball, Davidson had been watched by United as a youngster yet was passed over only for Liverpool to sign him. After appearing in every game but one of the successful league and cup 1931-32 programme, Davidson picked up an injury and wasn't an automatic choice again, having a succession of new centre-halves as rivals. Although not tall for the central defender's role, Dave possessed a terrier-like attitude and indomitable spirit, as well as a biting tackle. Before turning to football, the Scot had worked as an attendant in a mental institution. Dave resided in Monkseaton on Tyneside, becoming a respected local football personality and at one time ran a masseur's business in Whitley Bay.

Appearances:
FL: 128 apps. 0 gls.
FAC: 16 apps. 0 gls.
Others: 1 app. 0 gls.
Total: *145 apps. 0 gls.*
Honours:
FAC winner 1932.

Dave Davidson

DAVIDSON, Thomas

Role: Left-back 1901-1903
6' 0"
b. *West Calder, Midlothian, 1875*

CAREER: Dykehead/Bury
1894/Millwall Athletic June
1900/UNITED May 1901/
Brentford cs 1903 to 1905.

Debut v Sunderland (h) 28/9/01

A tall, powerful defender, gritty
and determined, Tom Davidson
was a regular at left-back during
the 1901-02 season. One description noted him
as, "strong as a lion, cool and reliable". He
was a celebrated player in Bury's ranks, at a
time when the Lancashire club were a force in
the First Division and FA Cup. Eventually
though, Davidson lost his place at Gallowgate
to new signing William Agnew. His brother
Bob appeared for both Glasgow
Celtic and Manchester City, also
starting his career at Scottish
club, Dykehead.

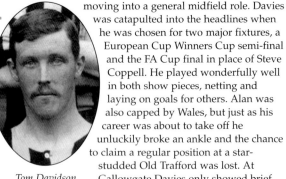

Tom Davidson

Appearances:
FL: 38 apps. 0 gls.
FAC: 5 apps. 0 gls.
Total: *43 apps. 0 gls.*
Honours:
FAC winner 1900.

DAVIES, Alan

Role: Midfield 1985-1987
5' 8"
b. *Manchester, 5th December 1961*
d. *Horton, nr Swansea,*
4th February 1992

Alan Davies

CAREER: Mancunian jnrs/Manchester United
sch Sept 1977, app July 1978, pro Dec 1978/
UNITED July 1985 £50,000(Charlton Athletic
loan 1985-86)(Carlisle United loan 1986-87)/
Swansea City Aug 1987 free/Bradford City
June 1989 £135,000/Swansea City Aug 1990
exch deal, to death.

Debut v Southampton (a) 17/8/85

Born in England of Welsh parents, Alan
Davies had a meteoric rise to fame as one of
Manchester United's modern 'babes'.
Developed at Old Trafford from a schoolboy,
he started as a skilful outside-right later

moving into a general midfield role. Davies
was catapulted into the headlines when
he was chosen for two major fixtures, a
European Cup Winners Cup semi-final
and the FA Cup final in place of Steve
Coppell. He played wonderfully well
in both show pieces, netting and
laying on goals for others. Alan was
also capped by Wales, but just as his
career was about to take off he
unluckily broke an ankle and the chance
to claim a regular position at a star-
studded Old Trafford was lost. At
Gallowgate Davies only showed brief
glimpses of his true capabilities and
after further injury problems, soon moved into
a lower grade of football, serving Swansea
with note. Tragically, Alan Davies became
overwhelmed by personal problems and
committed suicide, being discovered dead in
his car on the same day as he was due to play
for the Swans against Cardiff.

Appearances:
FL: 20(1) apps. 1 gl.
FLC: 2(1) apps. 0 gls.
Total: *22(2) 1 gl.*
Honours:
11 Wales caps 1983-90/
6 Wales u21 caps 1982-83/
Wales youth app/FAC winner
1983/FL div 4 prom 1988.

DAVIES, Ellis Reginald

Role: Inside-right or left
1951-1958
5' 8"
b. *Cymmer, Glamorgan,*
27th May 1929

CAREER: Cwm Athletic/Southampton
amat/Southend United July 1949/UNITED
Apr 1951 £9,000/Swansea Town Oct 1958
cash-exch deal for I.Allchurch/Carlisle United
June 1962 £4,000/Merthyr Tydfil July 1964/
Kings Lynn player-manager 1965/Bayswater
United(Australia) player-coach/
Ascot(Australia) player-coach.

Debut v Wolverhampton Wanderers (h) 6/10/51
(scored once)

A slightly built inside-forward who played on
both flanks to equal effect. Reg Davies had a
sudden burst of speed over ten yards that
could prove penetrating around the

Reg Davies

DAVIES, Ian Claude

Role: Left-back 1979-1982
5' 8"
b. Bristol, 29th March 1957

CAREER: Cleveland jnrs(Bristol)/Norwich City app July 1973, pro Apr 1975(Detroit Express(USA) loan cs 1978)/UNITED June 1979 £175,000/Manchester City Aug 1982 free(Bury loan 1982-83)(Brentford loan 1983-84)(Cambridge United loan 1983-84)/ Carlisle United May 1984/Exeter City Dec 1984/Bath City cs 1985/Yeovil Town/Bury Town/Diss Town/Bristol Rovers Aug 1985/ Swansea City Nov 1985 to Feb 1986/ Gloucester City Nov 1987.

Debut v Oldham Athletic (h) 18/8/79

Ian Davies had been Norwich City's youngest ever debutant at Carrow Road - 17 years and 29 days old - but at the time of joining United had accumulated only 34 appearances for the Canaries. A defender full of potential though, and with a cultured left-foot, he was level-headed with an inclination to join the attack. Ian was a regular for two seasons before being discarded by Arthur Cox in favour of local talent Kenny Wharton. Perhaps lacking the pace and defensive bite to develop into a top class player, Davies afterwards drifted around the Football League and non-league circuit returning to his native south-west England. A fine cricketer too, he was on Somerset's books before making a career in professional soccer.

Appearances:
FL: 74(1) apps. 3 gls.
FAC: 1 app. 0 gls.
FLC: 6 apps. 1 gl.
Total: *81(1) apps. 4 gls.*
Honours:
1 Wales u21 cap 1978.

opposition's box, and an inventive telling pass. A team-man first and foremost, Reg had fellow international Ivor Broadis as his main rival at St James Park and then saw two more noted players take over his role, George Eastham and Ivor Allchurch, as he moved to Wales. Part of Newcastle's side for eight seasons without ever being an automatic choice, Reg was Newcastle's 12th man for the 1952 FA Cup final but unluckily missed out in 1955; although picked to play he developed tonsillitis and had to step down. Davies emigrated to Perth, Australia in 1971, appearing for Western Australia against New Zealand at the age of 47, and playing on until his 50th year. As a former soprano choir boy with the Steffans Silver Singsters, he had toured with the Great Britain choir.

Appearances:
FL: 157 apps. 49 gls.
FAC: 13 apps. 1 gl.
Others: 1 app. 0 gls.
Total: *171 apps. 50 gls.*
Honours:
6 Wales caps 1953-58/
FL div 4 prom 1964.

Ian Davies

DAVIES, Ronald Wyn

Role: Centre-forward 1966-1971
6' 1"
b. Caernarfon, 20th March 1942

CAREER: Caernarfon Boys' Club/Llanberis/Caernarfon Town 1958/Wrexham Apr 1960 £500/Bolton Wanderers Mar 1962 £20,000 plus player/UNITED Oct 1966 £80,000/Manchester City Aug 1971 £52,500/Manchester United Sept 1972 £25,000/Blackpool June 1973 £25,000 (Crystal Palace loan 1974-75)/Stockport County Aug 1975/Arcadia Shepherds (S.Africa) 1975-76/Crewe Alexandra Aug 1976/Bangor City Aug 1978.

Debut v Sunderland (h) 29/10/66

Although the formidable figure of Wyn Davies never became one of the Magpies' goalscoring machines, his contribution to United's cause for five years as the club stormed Europe was immense, and it made him a cult hero on Tyneside. After a long chase and contest with Manchester City for his transfer from Second Division Bolton, where he had netted 74 goals in 170 games, Davies immediately became a crowd favourite at centre-forward. He cost the black'n'whites a record fee but the big Welshman repaid the amount several times over. An ideal target man in the Number 9 shirt, Davies was noted for his considerable aerial menace and nicknamed 'Wyn the Leap' for his stunning jumping ability. He led United's line like few before or since, with ability to hold up the ball and bring his partners, notably Albert Bennett and Bryan Robson, into play. Davies created space for others and Robson, in particular, flourished as a top goalgetter. Wyn was able to soak up a physical battering by

defenders, especially from continentals who couldn't handle him at all. Davies was a brave player and on many occasions soldiered on even though injured and in pain. Not the best individual with the ball at his feet, and his goal tally can only be regarded as modest, yet Wyn Davies will be recalled with esteem by every United supporter who witnessed his whole-hearted displays. He was the key factor in United's Inter Cities Fairs Cup victory in 1969, and remains the club's top goalscorer in European football with ten goals. Also given the tag of 'The Mighty Wyn' or 'Welsh Flier', before setting out on a football career he had worked in a Welsh slate quarry. After retiring, Wyn settled in Bolton working for a local bakery.

Appearances:
FL: 181 apps. 40 gls.
FAC: 8 apps. 3 gls.
FLC: 3 apps. 0 gls.
Eur: 24 apps. 10 gls.
Total: *216 apps. 53 gls.*

Honours:
34 Wales caps 1964-74/4 Wales u23 caps 1963-65/2 Wales youth app 1960/ICFC winner 1969/FL div 4 prom 1962.

Wyn Davies

DAY, William

Role: Outside-right 1962-1963
5' 9"
b. Middlesbrough, 27th December 1936

CAREER: Sheffield Wednesday amat/South Bank/Middlesbrough May 1955/UNITED Mar 1962 £12,000/Peterborough United Apr 1963 £6,000/Cambridge United 1964/ Retired 1965.

Debut v Scunthorpe United (h) 17/3/62 (scored once)

Billy Day was a popular winger at Ayresome Park scoring 21 goals in 131 league and cup matches for Middlesbrough. However, a broken leg meant he lost his place in the Reds' line-up and Billy moved up the north east coast to try his luck with the Magpies. Day's short period at St James Park was not a productive one; he was overshadowed by the emerging teenage talent of Alan Suddick as manager Joe Harvey attempted to fashion a side to challenge for promotion. Billy later became a bookmaker at Cleveland Park.

Billy Day

Appearances:
FL: 13 apps. 1 gl.
FAC: 1 app. 0 gls.
Total: *14 apps. 1 gl.*
Honours:
1 FA app. 1959.

DENMARK, James

Role: Centre-half 1937-1946
6' 1"
b. Glasgow, 13th May 1913

CAREER: Tollcross Clydesdale/Parkhead jnrs/Third Lanark 1931/UNITED May 1937 £2,550/Middlesbrough war-guest 1941-42/ Queen of the South Mar 1946 £707/Ashington player-manager Nov 1948.

Debut v Barnsley (h) 1/9/37

A big kicking stopper, very powerful in the air and in the tackle, Jimmy Denmark made a deep impression on United's directors following commanding displays in the Scottish League with Third Lanark. He was skipper of the Glasgow side and led them to the Scottish Cup final against Rangers in 1936. An inspiration on the field, he arrived at Gallowgate to rival Jesse Carver just prior to the Second World War so didn't have a sustained period to develop his career further. He was though, an important factor in Newcastle's dramatic escape from relegation to the Third Division for the first time in 1938.

Jimmy Denmark

Appearances:
FL: 51 apps. 0 gls.
War: 54 apps. 0 gls.
Total: *105 apps. 0 gls.*
Honours:
SC finalist 1936/
SL div 2 champs 1935.

DENNISON, Robert Smith

Role; Inside-left 1929-1934
6' 0"
b. Amble, Northumberland, 6th March 1912

CAREER: Radcliffe Welfare United/UNITED May 1929 £10/Nottingham Forest May 1934 £1,400/Fulham June 1935/Northampton Town war-guest 1939-45, pmt 1945 £450/ Northampton Town asst-coach, then manager Mar 1949/Middlesbrough manager July 1954 to Jan 1963/Hereford United manager Dec 1963/Coventry City scout Dec 1967, becoming asst-manager Dec 1968, and various other roles including caretaker-manager Mar 1972 to retirement in 1978.

Debut v Sheffield United (h) 18/2/33

From a large Scots family that settled in Northumberland, Bob Dennison joined United as a promising youngster and admitted later in life that he was "just an ordinary player". Dennison had fierce competition for a first-team place at St James Park and by the time

Bob Dennison

he was ready for senior action had the immense talent of Harry McMenemy as a contemporary playmaker. Later, moving to half-back, Bob turned out in seasons 1932-33 and 1933-34 before travelling south in search of regular football. He afterwards served Northampton well as both player (246 apps.) and manager, while Dennison was also in charge at Ayresome Park for eight and a half seasons - the longest serving Middlesbrough boss - introducing the likes of Brian Clough and Alan Peacock to 'Boro colours. His son, Richard, was secretary at Coventry City, Port Vale and Gillingham, while his elder brother Jack, turned out for Coventry just after World War One. Following a long period with the Highfield Road club himself, Dennison settled in Kent, residing in Westgate near Thanet.

Appearances:
FL: 11 apps. 2 gls.
Total: *11 apps. 2 gls.*
Honours:
SnL div 1 champs 1965(m).

DEVINE, Joseph Cassidy

Role: Inside-right or left 1930-1931
5' 7"
b. Motherwell, 8th September 1905
d. Chesterfield, 9th May 1980

CAREER: Motherwell Watsonians/Cleland jnrs/Bathgate/Burnley May 1925 £250/ UNITED Jan 1930 £5,575/Sunderland Jan 1931 £2,597/Queens Park Rangers May 1933/ Birmingham City Jan 1935/Chesterfield May 1937 to 1938, becoming coach to cs 1950.

Debut v Huddersfield Town (a) 1/2/30

Joe Devine was a terrace favourite at Turf Moor before the deal that brought him to Tyneside. Having scored 29 goals in 121 matches for Burnley he was a useful inside man, at home either right or left of the centre-forward. Fair-haired, Devine boasted superb ball control and an eye for goal. He joined United at a time of crisis when the club were rock bottom of the First Division with relegation staring them in the face. But Devine went to work partnering Hughie Gallacher, netted eight goals in 16 fixtures and greatly assisted the club's climb to safety; included was a crucial goal which earned victory in the last fixture of the season against West Ham United. Surprisingly though, after impressing many, Joe couldn't claim a place the following term and moved to Roker Park and on to Loftus Road where he was appointed captain. On leaving the game, Devine

Joe Devine

settled in the Chesterfield area running The Peacock public house in Cutthorpe. He was related to Joe Cassidy who appeared with Glasgow Celtic.

Appearances:
FL: 22 apps. 11 gls.
Total: *22 apps. 11 gls.*
Honours:
1 FL app. 1927.

DICKSON, Charles

Role: Outside-left 1894-1895
5' 7"
b. Dundee

CAREER: Dundee/Preston North End c1892/UNITED Sept 1894 £5/Loughborough Town cs 1895 to c1896.

Debut v Burslem Port Vale (a) 6/10/1894 (scored once)

Although fleet of foot, Charles Dickson was unable to gain a place in the fine Preston side that made a big imprint on the early days of Football League action, but when he joined United the Scot displayed much vigour and zest up front. Noted as a "crack forward", he was adaptable in a wide or inside role. Dickson made a headlining start in a black'n'white shirt, netting on his debut then powering goals in each of his next three outings too. When United failed to gain promotion at the end of the 1894-95 season, he joined league newcomers Loughborough and Willie Wardrope became his effective replacement at Newcastle. His transfer to United is recorded in great detail in the club's Minutes; £5 went to agent Peter Allan and £5 to Dundee, the club who held his registration, while his wages were £2 per week with a £5 bonus.

Appearances:
FL: 21 apps. 12 gls.
FAC: 2 apps. 0 gls.
Total: 23 apps.
12 gls.

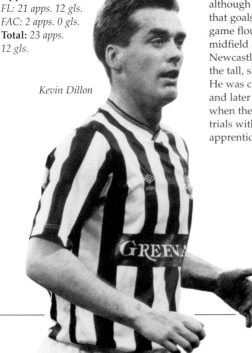

Kevin Dillon

DILLON, Kevin Paul

Role: Midfield 1989-1994
6' 0"
b. Sunderland, 18th December 1959

CAREER: Birmingham City app June 1976/Portsmouth Mar 1983 £200,000/UNITED June 1989 free/Reading cs 1994 free/Wycombe Wanderers on trial Aug 1994/Brentford on trial Sept 1994/Stevenage Borough Oct 1994/Yeovil Town Feb 1995.

Debut v Leeds United (h) 19/8/89

With plenty of experience at gaining promotion into the First Division, Kevin Dillon joined United's staff approaching the end of a career that had seen him noted as one of Birmingham City's biggest prospects during an era of better fortunes for the St Andrews club. The Wearsider developed through the Blues' ranks and was a 17 year-old debutant in 1977 alongside the likes of Trevor Francis and former United players; Hibbitt, Connolly and Howard. However, Dillon's early years were clouded by a fiery streak, often landing him in trouble on and off the field. Totalling 212 matches for Brum over six seasons, he holds the unmerited distinction of being sent-off at St James Park, Ayresome Park and Roker Park! At his best, Kevin was a mobile and direct midfield player, always liable to find the net clocking up over 60 goals in his career - although during his spell with the Magpies that goalscoring touch deserted him. Dillon's game flourished once Roy Aitken arrived in midfield and during season 1989-90, when Newcastle missed promotion in the play-offs, the tall, slim Kevin had an effective campaign. He was captain of Jim Smith's side for a while, and later gave Reading a steadying influence when they reached Division One. Kevin had trials with Tottenham Hotspur before signing apprentice forms for Birmingham.

Appearances:
FL: 62(1) apps. 0 gls.
FAC: 6(1) apps. 0 gls.
FLC: 3 apps. 0 gls.
Others: 3 apps. 0 gls.
Total: 74(2) apps. 0 gls.
Honours:
1 Eng u21 cap 1981/1 Eng youth app 1978/FL div 2 champs 1994/FL div 3 champs 1983/FL div 2 prom 1980, 1987.

DIXON, Edward Stanley

Role: Inside-right 1914-1923
5' 9"
b. Choppington, Northumberland,
26th May 1894
d. Bedlington, Northumberland,
13th August 1979

CAREER: Barrington Albion/UNITED Feb
1914 £5/Blackburn Rovers Mar 1923 £1,100/
Hull City May 1926 to cs 1930/East Riding
Amateurs.

Debut v Liverpool (h) 1/4/14

A sturdy, talented inside-forward, extremely
versatile across the forward line, Ed Dixon
had his career at St James Park divided by
the First World War, playing for the club
before and after the hostilities. After serving
in the Engineers' Corps, in season 1919-20
he commanded the inside-right position for
the Magpies and was good enough to be
reserve for both England and the Football
League sides. Apart from that productive
season, he struggled to claim a permanent
place, although Ed always fitted smoothly
into the team when called upon over the
next three seasons. The highlight of his
career with Newcastle was a stunning hat-
trick against Chelsea in 1919. At Anlaby
Road in Hull, Dixon made 107 appearances
for the Tigers. When he retired Ed became a
cinema manager in Hull, later returning to
his native Bedlington.

Appearances:
FL: 49 apps. 7 gls.
FAC: 4 apps. 3 gls.
War: 8 apps. 0 gls.
Total: 61 apps. 10 gls.

DOCKING, Stanley Holbrook

Role: Inside-left 1934-1938
5' 10"
b. Chopwell, nr Gateshead, 13th December 1914
d. Newcastle upon Tyne, 27th May 1940

CAREER: Birtley/UNITED Aug 1934
£5/Tranmere Rovers May 1938 £1,100/
Hartlepools United war-guest 1939-40.

Debut v Fulham (h) 19/1/35

A powerful, bustling forward and well built,
at one stage weighing in at 14 stone, Stan
Docking would invariably take the direct
route for goal despite the numbers of
defenders in his path. Stan packed a hot shot
and was a big goalgetter in the Magpies'
recently installed Central League side during
the thirties. In seasons 1936-37 and 1937-38 he
was called-up for several first-team outings,
but was never going to displace the
established stars. When Stan moved to
Merseyside, Newcastle inserted a clause in the
transfer deal that if he helped Tranmere,
"retain their place in Division Two", the
Magpies would receive an extra £100. Rovers
finished bottom in 1938-39 and United didn't
get another penny. Docking died during the
Second World War. Serving as an aircraftsman
in the RAF, he was on leave at
his home in Whitley Bay
when he contracted
septicaemia and
died suddenly of
heart failure.

Appearances:
FL: 21 apps.
3 gls.
Total: *21 apps.*
3 gls.
Honours:
Eng schools app.

Stan Docking

DODDS, John T.

Role: Outside-right or left 1906-1908
5' 9"
b. Hexham, October 1885

CAREER: Northern Star(Hexham)/UNITED Mar 1906/ Oldham Athletic Aug 1908 £100/ Heart of Midlothian June 1909 £50/ Merthyr Tydfil cs 1910 to 1913.

Debut v Woolwich Arsenal (h) 16/4/06

Local product John Dodds deputised for international wingers Gosnell and Rutherford at St James Park, making four of his five outings during the Tynesiders' league title victory in 1906-07. He also took part in the club's reserve championship success in the North Eastern League during that same season, and again twelve months later. He was one of three Magpie players - Appleyard and Speedie being the others - who moved to Oldham in the summer of 1908. Dodds was unfortunate to pick up an injury in only his second game for the Latics, and, when fit, sustained another knock. He only made eight appearances before trying his luck in Scotland.

Appearances:
FL: 5 apps. 0 gls.
Total: *5 apps. 0 gls.*

DODGIN, Norman

Role: Left-half 1940-1950
5' 11"
b. Sheriff Hill, Gateshead, 1st November 1921

CAREER: Ouston jnrs/Whitehall jnrs/ UNITED Aug 1940/Reading June 1950 £5,000/ Northampton Town Sept 1951/Exeter City Apr 1953, becoming player-manager to Apr 1957/Yeovil Town manager June 1957/Barrow manager Sept 1957/Oldham Athletic manager July 1958 to May 1960.

Debut v Chesterfield (h) 3/9/47

Norman Dodgin was a sound half-back and a player's player, always aiming to perform for the team. Tall and composed on the ball, he lost the best years of his career to the Second World War, although he gained a lot of experience appearing in wartime services football both at

Norman Dodgin

home and abroad, including in Italy where he caught the eye of AC Milan. A former bricklayer, Norman took part in United's promotion success in 1948 and was a regular in the club's initial season back in the First Division. He gave way to the younger Charlie Crowe in 1950 after a dispute with trainer Norman Smith. Dodgin hailed from a footballing pedigree; his brother, Bill, played for and managed a string of clubs, while he is uncle to Bill junior, who also appeared for and managed Football League sides. After quitting the game, Norman ran a newsagency in Dawlish, near Exeter.

Appearances:
FL: 84 apps. 1 gl.
FAC: 2 apps. 0 gls.
War: 46 apps. 1 gl.
Total: *132 apps. 2 gls.*
Honours:
FL div 2 prom 1948.

DONALDSON, Andrew

Role: Centre-forward 1943-1949
6' 0"
b. Newcastle upon Tyne, 22nd March 1925
d. Peterborough, 20th June 1987

CAREER: South Benwell(Newcastle)/Vickers Armstrong(Newcastle)/UNITED Sept 1943/ Middlesbrough Jan 1949 £17,500/ Peterborough United cs 1951/Exeter City Sept 1953/Peterborough United 1955 to 1958.

Debut v Leicester City (h) 19/4/47

Tall, leggy, and once described as being, "built like a greyhound", Andy Donaldson was the scoring force behind United's Central League championship victory in 1948 when he netted

33 goals. A danger in the air, the former Newcastle schools' forward was a direct rival to Jackie Milburn as the pair started to make an impression at St James Park in season 1948-49. And for a while it was Donaldson

Andy Donaldson

who looked the more likely to remain at St James Park, but Milburn just edged the vote and Andy moved to Teesside for what was then a big fee. After struggling to impress with Middlesbrough, it was with non-league Peterborough that Donaldson made his mark. In the Posh annals it is recorded he "established himself as one of the all time great players and crowd favourites at London Road". As Peterborough developed as a top non-league side, eventually reaching Football League status, and becoming FA Cup giant-killers of renown, Donaldson was an effective leader of the attack. After retiring, he lived in Peterborough to his death.

Appearances:
FL: 19 apps. 6 gls.
War: 12 apps. 3 gls.
Total: *31 apps. 9 gls.*

DONALDSON

Role: Inside-right 1894-1895
Debut v Newton Heath (h) 13/4/1895

A local player who was on United's staff for the 1894-95 season, Donaldson gained an opportunity for the last two games of the Second Division campaign, including the club's record defeat, a 0-9 reverse at Burton Wanderers. He left Newcastle during the summer of 1895.

Appearances:
FL: 2 apps. 0 gls.
Total: *2 apps. 0 gls.*

DONNACHIE, Joseph

Role: Outside-left 1905-1906
5' 9"
b. Kilwinning, Ayrshire, 1885

CAREER: Rutherglen Glencairn/Albion Rovers/Greenock Morton Mar 1905/ UNITED June 1905/Everton Feb 1906/ Oldham Athletic Oct 1908 £250/ Glasgow Rangers Mar 1919 £800/ Everton Aug 1919/Blackpool June 1920/Chester player-manager 1921.

Debut v Birmingham (h) 9/9/05

Smart and fast, as well as being bow-legged, Joe Donnachie was a Scot with potential when he signed for the Magpies, but found it almost impossible to break into the club's near all international side. He did win reserve honours with the black'n'whites, yet Joe was forced to continue his career elsewhere and became an international player himself after some sterling displays for Oldham as they finished runners-up in the First Division. Totalling almost 250 senior games for the Latics, he played on both flanks, was direct and always liable to create an opening. Donnachie also has the distinction of being one of only a handful of Roman Catholics to appear for Rangers. He later was publican at the Mariners Arms Inn near Chester's Sealand Road stadium. His son, also Joe, was on Liverpool's books, but was killed in a wartime flying accident.

Appearances:
FL: 2 apps. 0 gls.
Total: *2 apps. 0 gls.*
Honours:
3 Scot caps 1913-14/Scot trial app 1913-14/ FL div 2 prom 1910.

DOUGLAS, Angus

Role: Outside-right 1913-1918
5' 9"
b. Lochmaben, Dumfries, 1st January 1889
d. South Gosforth, Newcastle upon Tyne,
14th December 1918

CAREER: Castlemilk/Lochmaben Rangers/
Chelsea May 1908/UNITED Oct 1913 £1,100
to demise.

Debut v Burnley (a) 1/11/13

A great favourite at Stamford Bridge for five
seasons (103 apps. 12 goals), Angus Douglas
was an entertainer on the field, fast and clever
on the ball, and by all accounts especially
liked by the Londoners' female contingent of
fans. With Jackie Rutherford's departure,
Douglas was purchased to replace one of
Tyneside's best loved players of the era, and to
the Scot's credit he fitted into the right-wing
position well. The First World War, however,
ended his footballing career and after
surviving the fighting on the continent Angus
returned to Tyneside, only to fall victim to the
national influenza epidemic. Douglas died
after contracting pneumonia.

> **Appearances:**
> *FL: 49 apps. 2 gls.*
> *FAC: 7 apps. 0 gls.*
> **Total:** *56 apps. 2 gls.*
> **Honours:**
> *1 Scot cap 1911/FL div 2 prom 1912.*

DOWSEY, John

Role: Inside-right 1924-1926
5' 11"
b. Gateshead, May 1905
d. Costock, Nottinghamshire, 27th October 1942

CAREER: Hunswick Villa/UNITED June 1924
£10/West Ham United May 1926 £250/Carlisle
United Aug 1927/Sunderland Nov 1927/Notts
County Feb 1929/Northampton Town Nov
1931 to 1934.

Debut v Tottenham Hotspur (h) 14/11/25

A noted forward in Tyneside's non-leagues,
John Dowsey was given a chance by
Newcastle's directors just after the club had
lifted the FA Cup in 1924. Known as 'Jack', he
never threatened his senior professionals in
United's colours and only made a handful of

Angus Douglas

appearances in season 1925-26, standing in for
Willie Cowan while he was tried at centre-
forward. Dowsey however, was still a threat in
reserve soccer as United's second string lifted
the North Eastern League title. He netted 54
goals in two seasons for the club before the
Hammers took him to east London, but again
the Geordie found it difficult to claim first
team football, making just a single appearance
for the Upton Park outfit before moving on
again. Jack found a permanent place with
Notts County (103 games) and at the County
Ground, Northampton where he dropped
back to play a wing-half role.

> **Appearances:**
> *FL: 3 apps. 0 gls.*
> **Total:** *3 apps. 0 gls.*

DRYDEN, John

Role: Outside-left 1932-1934
5' 9"
b. Broomhill, Northumberland, 21st August 1908
d. Northumberland, 16th September 1975

CAREER: Ashington/UNITED Sept 1932
£175/Exeter City May 1934 free/Sheffield
United May 1935/Bristol City cs 1936/Burnley
May 1938/Peterborough United cs 1939.

Debut v Leeds United (h) 14/1/33 (FAC)

Johnny Dryden was only allowed to leave St James Park because of the special talent of Tommy Pearson. Dainty on his feet, Johnny possessed skill and pace, being a deputy to Tommy Lang before Pearson emerged. From a footballing family, his brother (J.G. Dryden) was on Manchester City's staff during the mid thirties, while Johnny is also related to the famous Milburn clan.

Appearances:
FL: 5 apps. 1 gl.
FAC: 1 app. 0 gls.
Total: *6 apps. 1 gl.*

DUFFY, Alan

Role: Striker 1966-1970
5' 6"
b. Stanley, County Durham, 20th December 1949

CAREER: UNITED Aug 1966, pro Mar 1967/Brighton Jan 1970 £8,000/Tranmere Rovers Mar 1972/Darlington Aug 1973 to cs 1974/Evenwood Town/Consett/Later minor County Durham football.

Debut v Manchester United (a) 21/9/68

A product of Newcastle's excellent sixties junior set-up, Alan Duffy climbed through the ranks to reach senior status alongside Alan Foggon and Keith Dyson. Although not tall or

powerful, Duffy was a quick and nimble striker, who was a reserve to Bryan Robson. As a teenager he was noted as a future star but, unlike his two more famous contemporaries in the junior ranks, Duffy didn't claim many appearances and was transferred south. His grandfather, Albert Bell, appeared for Leeds United and Accrington Stanley.

Appearances:
FL: 2(2) apps. 0 gls.
Total: *2(2) apps. 0 gls.*
Honours:
Eng youth app 1968.

Alan Duffy

DUFFY, Christopher Francis

Role: Outside-left 1906-1908
5' 7"
b. Jarrow, 1885

CAREER: Jarrow/St Marys College (Hammersmith)/Brentford Jan 1905/ Middlesbrough Oct 1905/UNITED Aug 1906/ Bury May 1908 £100/North Shields Athletic July 1914/Leicester City Dec 1919 to Aug 1920/Chester-le-Street.

Debut v Sheffield United (a) 8/12/06

Although born on Tyneside, Chris Duffy attended school in Hammersmith, gaining a first-class education. He was a noted sportsman and turned to soccer after winning several prizes as a sprinter. Returning to his native north east, Duffy was purchased to give the Magpies cover on the wing and did a sound job, although he was rarely given much scope in the senior eleven. However, he appeared on seven occasions in the club's league championship win in season 1906-07, and when at Gigg Lane held an automatic place totalling over 100 games for the Shakers. On retiring from the game, Chris became a schoolteacher on Tyneside, holding the position of headmaster at St Alyoysis and St Dominics Schools in the city's west-end.

Appearances:
FL: 16 apps. 1 gl.
Total: *16 apps. 1 gl.*

DUNCAN, Adam Scott Mathieson

Role: Outside-right 1908-1913
5' 9"
b. Dumbarton, 2nd November 1888
d. Helensburgh, 3rd October 1976

CAREER: Dumbarton Oakvale/Dumbarton Corinthians/Clydebank jnrs/Shettleston jnrs/Dumbarton Nov 1905/UNITED Mar 1908 £150/Glasgow Rangers May 1913 £600/ Manchester United war-guest 1918-19/ Glasgow Celtic war-guest 1918-19/Partick Thistle war-guest 1918-19/

Dumbarton July 1919/Cowdenbeath cs 1920/ Retired 1922/ Hamilton Academical manager July 1923/Cowdenbeath manager July 1925/ Manchester United manager June 1932/ Ipswich Town manager Sept 1937, becoming secretary Aug 1955 to May 1958.

Debut v Everton (a) 4/4/08

A distinguished personality of pre-war football, both as a player and manager, Scott Duncan was a swift, ball-playing winger, typical of his native breed. He could be intricate at dribbling and one biography described him as "one of the most stylish wingers in Britain". Although at St James Park for six seasons, he took time to settle on Tyneside and spent the first few campaigns chiefly as a reserve, but he appeared in the club's championship success in 1909 and really came into his own in season 1910-11 when his sparkling form saw him just miss a Scotland cap. The son of a Dumbarton butcher, 'Archie', as he was known, worked in a solicitor's office before heading to Tyneside and during World War One served as a signalling instructor in the Royal Field Artillery. He later became an outstanding manager on both sides of the border, taking Manchester United to promotion and developing into something of a legend at Portman Road, steering the then little known non-league side, Ipswich Town, into the Football League. Duncan had a long career in the game and lived into his nineties, residing in the Scottish resort of Helensburgh.

Scott Duncan

Appearances:
FL: 73 apps. 10 gls.
FAC: 8 apps. 1 gl.
Total: *81 apps. 11 gls.*
Honours:
Scot trial app 1910-11/FL champs 1909/FL div 2 champs 1936(m)/FL div 3 champs 1954(m)/FL Long Service Award 1957.

DUNCAN, John Gilhespie

Role: Centre-forward
1950-1953
5' 11"
b. Glasgow, 10th December 1926

CAREER: Partick Avondale 1948/Ayr United 1948/ UNITED Nov 1950 £8,250/Retired due to injury June 1953.

Debut v Preston North End (a) 8/9/51

John Duncan

John Duncan was a versatile player who possessed an exciting talent. Purchased by United as a defender to be groomed for the future, Duncan made his early outings in Newcastle's colours at right-back, but when he was converted into the centre-forward's role, he created headlines by netting twice against Aston Villa. Big-hearted and full of gusto, John was, however, soon afterwards sidelined with a bad knee injury and it took months of recuperation before he attempted a comeback. He did that as a goalkeeper, but the injury forced him to call a halt to his career. Duncan then moved back to Ayr where he ran a haulage business.

Appearances:
FL: 5 apps. 3 gls.
Others: 1 app. 0 gls.
Total: *6 apps. 3 gls.*

DYSON, Keith

Role: Striker 1967-1971
5' 10"
b. Blackhill, County Durham, 10th February 1950

CAREER: UNITED app 1967, pro Aug 1968/ Blackpool Nov 1971 cash-exch for A.Green/ Retired due to injury Mar 1976/Lancaster City 1979, becoming player-manager cs 1980.

Debut v Tottenham Hotspur (h) 28/9/68

Appearing for United's senior line-up as an 18 year-old, Keith Dyson was a highly thought of prospect, good enough for international recognition during season 1969-70 when he netted 12 goals for the Magpies. With ability to shield the ball and turn in confined spaces, Dyson created chances for himself in the box and could finish with accuracy. For a while he looked likely to develop into a top First Division striker appearing in several of the Magpies' European fixtures. But, like his teenage partner Alan Foggon, the player never lived up to his early star billing and moved to Bloomfield Road as part of the deal that brought Tony Green to Gallowgate. In five seasons with Blackpool, Keith grabbed 32 goals in 104 outings before a knee injury halted his career. Well qualified academically, Keith later began a career in insurance, eventually returning to the north east and settling near Hexham.

Appearances:
FL: 74(2) apps. 22 gls.
FAC: 4 apps. 1 gl.
FLC: 1(1) apps. 1 gl.
Eur: 13(1) 2 gls.
Others: 0(2) apps. 0 gls.
Total: *92(6) apps. 26 gls.*
Honours:
1 Eng u23 cap 1970/Eng schools app.

Keith Dyson

EASTHAM, George Edward O.B.E.

Role: Inside-right or left 1956-1960
5' 8"
b. Blackpool, 23rd September 1936

CAREER: Bispham Church/Highfield Youth Club/Ards amat, pro 1956/UNITED May 1956 £9,000/Arsenal Nov 1960 £47,500/Stoke City Aug 1966 £30,000/Hellenic (S.Africa) player-manager Feb 1971/Stoke City Oct 1971, becoming asst-player-manager Dec 1972/ Retired Feb 1975/Stoke City manager Mar 1977 to Jan 1978.

Debut v Luton Town (h) 6/10/56

A midfield master who linked with his colleagues through precision passing, George Eastham came from footballing stock; his father George, appeared for Bolton and England and elder brother, Harry, for Liverpool and Newcastle during wartime football. Blond-haired and slightly built

George Eastham

almost to the point of looking frail, Eastham played alongside his father in Ireland before being spotted as a player with huge talent by United scout Bill McCracken. Stan Seymour quickly brought the 19 year-old to Tyneside, developing the youngster rapidly and he flourished alongside the Welsh maestro Ivor Allchurch in midfield. Playing equally well on the left or right, George was a new star, but after becoming a regular for the young England side and almost a certainty for an full cap, Eastham became embroiled in a major dispute with the Magpies; an unsavoury affair over, firstly money and a club-house, then eventually the basic right of a footballer to ply his trade wheresoever he chose. George stood up for his principles and, backed by the Players' Union, took football's antiquated authorities and rule-book - as well as Newcastle United - to the High Court and won an historic litigation battle to free, as the media then called footballers, the 'soccer slaves'. By the time the long legal process was resolved (in 1963), Eastham had been granted his wish to leave Newcastle, joining the Gunners for a club record fee and the second most expensive man in British football. At Highbury he was another success totalling 223 appearances for the Londoners. United lost a special player, one who earned England recognition like his father, making the Eastham duo the only father and son pair to appear for their country. George was included in both the 1962 and 1966 World Cup squads, but was more often than not a deputy for England. Eastham played on until he was over 35 years old, inspiring Stoke to Wembley success and their first major trophy victory in which he scored the winner. Before moving to Ireland as a teenager, George was an apprentice joiner and he had trials with Blackpool and Bolton. He later emigrated to South Africa and settled in Johannesburg operating a sportswear company. For his services to the game he was awarded the OBE in 1975.

Eddie Edgar

Appearances:
FL: 124 apps. 29 gls.
FAC: 5 apps. 5 gls.
Total: *129 apps. 34 gls.*
Honours:
19 Eng caps 1963-66/5 unoff Eng app 1961-66/7 Eng u23 caps 1960/3 FL app 1960-67/3 NIL app 1955-56/FLC winner 1972.

EDGAR, Edward

Role: Goalkeeper 1973-1976
5' 11"
b. Jarrow, 31st October 1956

CAREER: UNITED Oct 1973/Hartlepool United July 1976 to Mar 1979/N.American football/Gateshead Jan 1980/London City(Canada) cs 1980.

Debut v Derby County (a) 6/3/76 (FAC)

Ideally built for the goalkeeper's position, Eddie Edgar was reserve to Mick Mahoney in Gordon Lee's squad but only once was called upon to deputise for United's first choice, and that in an important FA Cup tie. Immediately following the club's League Cup final defeat at Wembley in 1976, the Magpies travelled to the Baseball Ground to face Derby County with a

long absentee list. Edgar came into a patched up side that lost 4-2 in the sixth round stage of the competition. After quitting the English circuit he appeared in Canada as an outfield player. Eddie totalled 75 league outings for Hartlepool.

Appearances:
FAC: 1 app. 0 gls.
Total: *1 app. 0 gls.*

ELLIOTT, David

Role: Midfield 1966-1971
5' 8"
b. Tantobie, County Durham, 10th February 1945

CAREER: Gateshead 1960/Sunderland app 1961, pro Feb 1962/UNITED Dec 1966 £10,000/Southend United Jan 1971/Newport County player-manager July 1975 to Feb 1976/ Bangor City player-manager 1977/Newport County Nov 1978/Bangor City player-manager 1978 to 1984/Cardiff City asst-coach/ Caernarfon Town.

Debut v Tottenham Hotspur (a) 31/12/66

During the festive period of the 1966-67 season with United struggling to climb away from the First Division relegation zone, manager Joe

Dave Elliott

Harvey made a critical decision to sell Alan Suddick in order to raise cash to purchase three players who effectively saved the black'n'whites' hide. One of those men was Dave Elliott, a compact, chunky midfielder who had been on the fringe of the Sunderland side for several seasons. With stamina and tackling ability, he boosted the Magpies'

lightweight midfield. Elliott gave United excellent service for a short period, helping the club go on to qualify for a European place for the first time. Replaced by Benny Arentoft in the midfield worker's role as Newcastle appeared in the Inter Cities Fairs Cup, Elliott moved to serve Southend well, clocking up 194 games for the Roots Hall club. Also a fine local cricketer, Elliott later resided in Anglesey, running a sports shop in Bangor. He took that non-league club to the Northern Premier League title in 1982.

Appearances:
FL: 78(2) apps. 4 gls.
FAC: 2(1) apps. 0 gls.
FLC: 3 apps. 0 gls.
Eur: 3(1) apps. 0 gls.
Total: *86(4) apps. 4 gls.*
Honours:
WsC finalist 1978/NPL champs 1982(m).

ELLIOTT, Robert James

Role: Left-back or Midfield 1989-date
5' 10"
b. Gosforth, Newcastle upon Tyne, 25th December 1973

CAREER: Wallsend Boy's Club/ UNITED sch cs 1989, pro Apr 1991.

Debut v Middlesbrough (a) 12/3/91 (sub)

Robbie Elliott had trials with Manchester United before the Magpies snapped him up from the renowned Wallsend Boys' Club. A 17 year-old debutant, Robbie is a versatile player with excellent distribution who has appeared at full-back, central defence and midfield for United, always showing a cool and mature

assurance on the ball. Despite being dogged by serious injury in which he suffered from cruciate ligament, shin splints and medial ligament problems, the richly-talented Elliott bounced back to become an England Under-21 player, one to compete with Kevin Keegan's team of internationals. And after sitting on the bench for much of the 1994-95 and 1995-96 seasons, Elliott forced his way into first-team action. In a match against West Ham United, along with Steve Watson, Robbie holds the distinction of being the youngest full-back pairing selected by the Magpies. In summer 1996 he was the subject of a six-figure transfer bid by Blackburn but the move fell through when Elliott failed the club medical. His elder brother, John, was also on United's books but was released without breaking through.

Robbie Elliott

Appearances:
FL/PL:
42(8) apps. 2 gls.
FAC: 6(2) apps. 0 gls.
FLC: 3 apps. 0 gls.
Others: 1 app. 0 gls.
Total: *52(10) apps. 2 gls.*
Honours:
2 Eng u21 caps 1996-date/Eng youth app.

ELLISON, Raymond

Role: Right or Left-back 1968-1973
5' 7"
b. Newcastle upon Tyne, 31st December 1950

CAREER: UNITED May 1968/Sunderland Feb 1973 £10,000/Torquay United May 1974 free/ Workington Town July 1975/Gateshead Feb 1977/Tow Law Town/Whitley Bay player-coach June 1980/Alnwick Town manager Nov 1983 to 1984.

Debut v Derby County (h) 2/10/71

One of United's many home grown full-back discoveries during the sixties and seventies, Ray Ellison stood in for both David Craig and

Ray Ellison

Frank Clark during the 1971-72 season and always gave a sound if not spectacular display. However, the emerging talent of Alan Kennedy and Irving Nattrass from the junior ranks saw Ellison surplus to manager Joe Harvey's requirements and the Tynesider headed for Roker Park and on to the south-west with Torquay. He later returned to the north-east and became a taxi driver.

Appearances:
FL: 5 apps. 0 gls.
FLC: 1 app. 0 gls.
Others: 1 app. 0 gls.
Total: *7 apps. 0 gls.*

EVANS, Reginald

Role: Outside-left 1956-1959
5' 9"
b. Consett, County Durham, 18th March 1939

CAREER: UNITED Mar 1956 £25/Charlton Athletic Mar 1959 exch for J.Ryan/Ashington July 1960 to 1962.

Debut v Wolverhampton Wanderers (a) 20/9/58

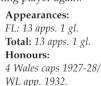

Reg Evans

A hard-hitting forward who liked to raid from the wing, Reginald Evans had tough competition for the Number 11 shirt at Gallowgate at the time, with no fewer than four rivals in McGuigan, Luke, Punton and Bobby Mitchell. Likened to the great Jimmy Mullen of Wolves, he was unfortunate to be injured on a tour of Ireland after just breaking into the United line-up. A damaged ankle hindered the rest of his St James Park career and Reg tried his luck at The Valley after a swop deal with 'Buck' Ryan, but again couldn't break into the first eleven on a regular basis. He returned to the north east, living in his native Consett, and for over 30

years was employed by Newcastle Breweries at their complex, a mere goal-kick away from St James Park.

Appearances:
FL: 4 apps. 0 gls.
Total: *4 apps. 0 gls.*

EVANS, Thomas John

Role: Left-back 1927-1929
6' 0"
b. Maerdy, Glamorgan, 7th April 1903

CAREER: Maerdy/Aberdare Athletic Sept 1924/Clapton Orient May 1924/UNITED Dec 1927 £3,650/Retired due to injury May 1929/Clapton Orient June 1930 free/Merthyr Town 1932.

Debut v Arsenal (a) 10/12/27

The first Welsh international to appear for Newcastle United and only the second Welshman ever, Tom Evans was purchased as a replacement for the ageing Hudspeth shortly after the championship trophy was lifted in 1927. A tall and athletic full-back, Tom was an exceptionally skilled defender who could fight for the ball and had caught the eye in FA Cup ties for Orient against the Magpies. Evans though, didn't have the best of times at St James Park being the target of sections of the crowd, while he had atrocious luck with knee injuries. He was on the sidelines during most of his stay on Tyneside, eventually calling it a day in the close season of 1929. However, he did make a comeback but Tom, nicknamed 'Con' by his team-mates, was never the same battling player again.

Appearances:
FL: 13 apps. 1 gl.
Total: *13 apps. 1 gl.*
Honours:
4 Wales caps 1927-28/
WL app. 1932.

Tom Evans

FAIRBROTHER, John

Role: Goalkeeper 1947-1952
6' 0"
b. Burton upon Trent, 16th August 1917

CAREER: Burton Town/Preston North End
Mar 1937/Blackburn Rovers war-guest
1939-43/Burnley war-guest 1940-41/Chester
war-guest 1942-43/UNITED July 1947 £6,500/
Peterborough United player-manager June
1952/Coventry City manager Dec 1953 to
Oct 1954/Israel FA coach/Consett manager
c1961/Gateshead manager June 1962/
Peterborough United manager Dec 1962
to Feb 1964.

Debut v Plymouth Argyle (h) 23/8/47

John Fairbrother was a well-built,
confident and stylish goalkeeper
who made great studies of
positioning and the shooting styles
of attackers during his career.
Known as 'Jack', he was a
renowned humourist in
United's dressing room
always ready with a grin or a
practical joke. Due to the Second
World War, Fairbrother did not make
his Football League debut until he
was approaching 30 years of age,
having to be content with wartime soccer
in which he was good enough to appear for
the Football League select team. Taking over
from Garbutt and Swinburne, Jack was
United's regular 'keeper over four
seasons until a broken collar
bone forced him out of the
Magpie eleven allowing
the younger Ronnie
Simpson to take his
place. He was a safe
custodian for
Newcastle, some
judges
considering he
was good enough
for an England
cap during his
heyday at the end
of the forties. A
former policeman
during the war - for
a time he wore white

Jack Fairbrother

police gloves on the
field as a gimmick -
Fairbrother later
entered
management and
became a bright young manager until tragedy
struck when he was in charge at Highfield
Road. Jack's wife was killed after a domestic
accident and he was left a widower with two
young children. A nephew of England and
Everton player, George Harrison, Fairbrother
later resided in Titchmarsh near Kettering,
Northamptonshire.

Appearances:
FL: 132 apps. 0 gls.
FAC: 12 apps. 0 gls.
Total: *144 apps. 0 gls.*
Honours:
*1 FL app. 1942/FL div 2 prom 1948/
FAC winner 1951/WrC winner 1941.*

FAIRHURST, David Liddle

Role: Left-back 1929-1946
5' 8"
b. Blyth, 20th July 1906
d. 26th October 1972

CAREER: New Delaval Villa/Blyth
Spartans/Walsall June 1927/UNITED Mar
1929 £1,750/Hartlepools United war-guest
1939-40/Wrexham war-guest 1943-44/Retired
May 1946/Birmingham City trainer and
physio July 1946.

Debut v Derby County (a) 27/4/29

Curly-haired Dave Fairhurst was a
stout-hearted, reliable defender
rather than a flamboyant footballer.
He was at his best under pressure
in the thick of the action and for
a decade served the
black'n'whites with credit. A
former Tyneside pit lad, Dave
had trials at St James Park
before moving to sign for
Walsall, but United brought
him back to his native north
east after a spell in the
Midlands. Dave replaced Bob
Thomson at left-back and
became an automatic choice as
the 1930s began. During the
Magpies' FA Cup run to
Wembley in 1932 he was an ever-

present and it wasn't until the Second World War approached, and Fairhurst was well into his thirties, that the club found a replacement. The sturdy Dave reached the England side, while he occasionally appeared at right-back as well as once taking to the wing when he was injured yet still managed to net two goals against Nottingham Forest. From a family of footballers, his father, William turned out for non-league Spartans also, while brother, Bill appeared for Southport, Nelson and Northampton.

Appearances:
FL: 266 apps. 2 gls.
FAC: 18 apps. 0 gls.
Others: 1 app. 0 gls.
Total: 285 apps. 2 gls.
Honours:
1 Eng cap 1934/
FAC winner 1932.   *Dave Fairhurst*

FASHANU, Justinus Soni

Role: Centre-forward 1991
6' 1"
b. Hackney, London, 19th February 1961

CAREER:
Shropham/Attleborough/Peterborough United/Norwich City app Sept 1977, pro Dec 1978(Adelaide City(Australia) loan cs 1980)/ Nottingham Forest Aug 1981 £1m/ (Southampton loan 1982-83)/Notts County Dec 1982 £150,000/Brighton June 1985 £115,000/Retired due to injury 1986/ Los Angeles Heat(USA) player-manager/ Edmonton Brickmen(Canada) July 1988/ Manchester City trial 1988-89, pmt Oct 1989/ West Ham United Nov 1989/Ipswich Town trial Feb 1990/Leyton Orient Mar 1990/ Southall player-coach Mar 1991/UNITED trial Oct 1991/Leatherhead Nov 1991/Toronto Blizzard(Canada)/Torquay United Dec 1991, becoming asst-manager June 1992 to Jan 1993/Airdrieonians Feb 1993/Trelleborg (Norway) cs 1993/Heart of Midlothian July 1993 to Feb 1994/ Toronto(Canada) and USA coaching 1994.

Debut v Peterborough United (a) 29/10/91 (FLC)(sub)

At one stage in his career, Justin Fashanu was one of the country's biggest names when he moved from Carrow Road to Brian Clough's Nottingham Forest for £1 million, at a time when a seven figure transfer sum was rare. Hitting the headlines as Norwich City's leading marksman - winning BBC Match of the Day's Goal of the Season award in 1980 - his move to the big-time with the Reds was unproductive, Fashanu not seeing eye to eye with Forest's controversial boss. The tall, muscular striker never fulfilled the promising·talent that earned him England Under-21 and B honours, partly due to troublesome knee injuries. He moved around from club to club, eventually landing at St James Park as a 31 year-old in a bid to resurrect a floundering career. Given a chance by Ossie Ardiles, his stay with United was short - only 11 days - and his deceptive skill and explosive shooting of ten years before had all but vanished. A former Barnado's Boy of African parents, Fashanu is a past ABA heavyweight finalist and before concentrating on a footballing career was a steel erector. His brother John also starred with Norwich City and later Wimbledon and England.

Appearances:
FLC: 0(1) app. 0 gls.
Total: 0(1) app. 0 gls.
Honours:
1 Eng B cap 1980/
11 Eng u21 caps 1980-83/
Eng youth app. 1979.

Justin Fashanu

FEENEY, Wilfred Thomas

Role: Inside-left 1930-1932
5' 8"
b. Grangetown, near Middlesbrough,
26th August 1910
d. Teesside, 5th March 1973

CAREER: Whitby United/UNITED Dec 1930
£25/Notts County June 1932 £500/Lincoln
City June 1933 exch/Stockport County Feb
1934/Halifax Town Aug 1934/Chester May
1937/Darlington Feb 1938 to cs 1939.

Debut v West Ham United (h) 30/1/32

A deputy to United schemer Harry
McMenemy, Wilfred Feeney made all his
appearances for the Magpies during the club's
FA Cup winning season of 1931-32. A popular
reserve, he possessed neat skills, but also a
temperament that at times could explode on
the field. After leaving Gallowgate Wilf
proceeded to have a useful career in the Third
Division.

Appearances:
FL: 4 apps. 1 gl.
Total: *4 apps. 1 gl.*

FELL, James Irving

Role: Outside-left 1962-1963
5' 10"
b. Cleethorpes, 4th January 1936

CAREER:
Waltham(Grimsby)/Grimsby Town
amat, pro Apr 1954/Everton Mar
1961 £18,500/UNITED Mar 1962
£3,000 plus G.Heslop/Walsall July
1963 £5,000/Lincoln City Dec 1963/
Boston United Jan 1966 to cs 1969/
Skegness Town 1969/Ross Group FC
1970.

Debut v Middlesbrough (a) 7/3/62

Tall and direct, Jimmy Fell had a turn
of speed that frightened full-backs.
One of the Mariners' finds during the
late fifties, he played on 174 occasions
for Grimsby netting 35 goals before
catching the attention of Everton. But
it was at Blundell Park that Fell
played his best football, although for
a season with the black'n'whites -
1962-63 - he did look to be an
effective winger, scoring 16 goals and
becoming the Magpies' top scorer.
But after that fine showing, Jimmy
dropped out of favour with manager
Joe Harvey and was replaced by
Colin Taylor. When he retired, Fell
returned to the Grimsby area and was
employed in a local sports centre. His
son, James junior, began a Football
League career with Grimsby too.

Appearances:
FL: 49 apps. 16 gls.
FAC: 2 apps. 0 gls.
FLC: 2 apps. 1 gl.
Total: *53 apps. 17 gls.*

FERDINAND, Leslie

Role: Centre-forward 1995-date
5' 11"
b. Notting Hill, London, 8th December 1966

CAREER: Viking Sports/Southall/Hayes/
Queens Park Rangers June 1986 £15,000(plus
£590,000 when he joined Newcastle)(Brentford
loan 1987-88)(Besiktas(Turkey) loan 1988-89)/
UNITED June 1995 £6m.

Debut v Coventry City (h) 19/8/95 (scored once)

Prior to becoming United's record purchase at
the time for a fee of £6 million, Les Ferdinand
had been one of the outstanding strikers in the
country. Tall, strong, powerful and composed
on the ball, he leads the attack with genuine
menace. With an excellent all round game,
judges consider him one of the most complete
English strikers of his generation; Ferdinand's
pace, aerial ability and stinging shots are all
features of his play. Les was
something of a late developer
in the game, appearing on the
London non-league scene
before being picked up by
QPR. However, it was not
until he had been on loan to
Brentford and to Turkish
outfit, Besiktas, that
Ferdinand was introduced on
a regular basis at Loftus
Road. He made a huge
impact in Istanbul netting 21
goals in 33 games, including
the winning strike in the
Turkish cup final against
Fenerbahce. Then once back
in London Les began to
impress in domestic football
too. Scoring 90 goals for
Rangers and reaching the
England side, striking on his
debut against San Marino,
Kevin Keegan tracked his
power-play for 15 months
before securing his signature,
in the end as a replacement
for Andy Cole. At once the 28
year-old Londoner took to the
mantle of becoming the
Magpies' new 'Number 9
Hero'. The spearhead to
Newcastle's title challenge in

1995-96, he netted 29 goals and landed the
Player of the Year award, becoming the first
United player to do so. Before turning
professional, Ferdinand had a number of jobs
including those of decorator, van driver and
car cleaner. Brought up streetwise in Notting
Hill of West Indian parents, his cousin Rio
signed for West Ham United in 1995, while
Les has developed into a first class
ambassador for the club; always immaculately
turned out and able to communicate with the
media, all very much a part of being a modern
superstar.

Appearances:
PL: 37 apps. 25 gls.
FAC: 2 apps. 1 gl.
FLC: 5 apps. 3 gls.
Total: *44 apps. 29 gls.*
Honours:
*10 Eng caps 1993-date/1 unoff Eng cap 1996/
FA Vase finalist 1986/Turkish Cup winner
1988/PFA Player of the Year 1996.*

Les Ferdinand half of a £21m strike force with Alan Shearer.

FEREDAY, Wayne

Role: Outside-left 1989-1990
5' 9"
b. Warley, nr Birmingham, 16th June 1963

CAREER: Queens Park Rangers app Sept 1980/UNITED May 1989 £400,000/ Bournemouth Nov 1990 £150,000/West Bromwich Albion loan Dec 1991, pmt Feb 1992 £60,000/Cardiff City Mar 1994 free/Telford Oct 1995 to Dec 1995.

Debut v Leeds United (h) 19/8/89

It was during season 1980-81 that Wayne Fereday made a name for himself as a new teenage star at Loftus Road. He enjoyed an impressive first outing, netting twice on his Football League debut and developed well with QPR, pulling on his country's shirt at Under-21 level. Lithe and extremely quick, one of the fastest players on the circuit, he appeared on 242 occasions for the Londoners before heading

Wayne Fereday

north to team up with his previous manager Jim Smith at St James Park. Able to take on defenders and get in a dangerous cross, Wayne however, did not do his reputation justice, rarely showing his previous form on Tyneside, often being on the sidelines through injury. Fereday also operated at full-back and moved south as part of the deal that brought Gavin Peacock to Gallowgate. After leaving the game in 1995, he resided in Poole.

Appearances:
FL: 27(6) apps. 0 gls.
FAC: 1 app. 0 gls.
FLC: 3(1) apps. 0 gls.
Others: 1(2) apps. 0 gls.
Total: *32(9) apps. 0 gls.*
Honours:
5 Eng u21 caps 1985-86/
1 FL app. 1988/FL div 2 prom 1993.

FERGUSON, Brian James

Role: Midfield 1979-1980
5' 11"
b. Irvine, Ayrshire, 14th December 1960

CAREER: Mansfield Town app 1977/UNITED Jan 1979/Hull City Dec 1980 free/Goole Town Aug 1982/Southend United Aug 1983/ Chesterfield loan Oct 1984, pmt Dec 1984/ Skegness Town cs 1986.

Debut v Burnley (h) 7/4/80 (sub)

Youngster Brian Ferguson was handed an opportunity in United's midfield during the closing weeks of the 1979-80 season. Brought to Tyneside by assistant manager Peter Morris, who worked with the Scot at the Field Mill Ground in Mansfield,

Brian Ferguson

Ferguson stepped in for Nigel Walker and Peter Cartwright, showing promise with plenty of enthusiasm and stamina. However, manager Bill McGarry, along with his successor Arthur Cox, didn't give Brian another run in the senior eleven. At Boothferry Park he appeared 37 times for Hull City and afterwards was a regular when Chesterfield lifted the Fourth Division title in 1984-85.

Appearances:
FL: 4(1) apps. 1 gl.
Total: *4(1) apps. 1 gl.*
Honours:
FL div 4 champs 1985.

FERGUSON, Robert Burnitt

Role: Left-back 1955-1962
5' 10"
b. Dudley, nr Newcastle upon Tyne, 8th January 1938

CAREER: Dudley/UNITED May 1955/Derby County Oct 1962 £4,000/Cardiff City Dec 1965 £5,000/Barry Town player-manager Dec 1968/ Newport County player-manager July 1969

£250, dismissed as manager Nov 1970, but remained as player until cs 1971/Ipswich Town asst-coach July 1971, becoming coach and manager Aug 1982 to May 1987/Al Arabi(Kuwait) manager June 1987/ Birmingham City asst-manager June 1989 to Jan 1991/Colchester United coach Apr 1991/ Coventry City scout 1991/Sunderland coach June 1992 to May 1993.

Debut v Manchester City (h) 7/4/56

Bobby Ferguson's 12 appearances for the Magpies were spread over nine seasons, being an able stand-in for Irishman Alf McMichael when the noted international was at his peak. From a footballing background, both his father, Bobby, and uncle, Eddie, turned

Bobby Ferguson

out in senior football, for West Bromwich Albion and Chelsea respectively while another uncle, Luke Curry, played for Bury. Although Ferguson made his debut as a 17 year-old, he was given little opportunity at St James Park, but grasped his chance at both Derby and Cardiff, and later became a respected coach, notably at Portman Road as assistant to Bobby Robson. A former England Boys' trialist and apprentice electrician at Seaton Burn pit, when on National Service with the Commandos, Ferguson represented the Army select eleven.

Appearances:
FL: 11 apps. 0 gls.
FAC: 1 app. 0 gls.
Total: *12 apps. 0 gls.*

FERRIS, Paul James

Role: Outside-left
& Physiotherapist 1981-1986, 1993-date
5' 8"
b. Belfast, 10th July 1965

CAREER: Lisburn jnrs/UNITED Nov 1981/ Gateshead Sept 1986 free/Port Vale on trial Oct 1986/North Shields Feb 1988/Barrow Aug 1989/Whitley Bay Aug 1990/Retired Nov 1991/UNITED asst-physio Oct 1993.

Debut v Blackburn Rovers (a) 1/5/82 (sub)

Many United supporters who watched him play thought Paul Ferris should have been given an extended opportunity in the Magpies' first eleven instead of sitting on the substitutes' bench for long periods. Signing for Newcastle as a youth fresh from Northern Ireland,

Paul Ferris

Ferris was highly rated as a teenager and quickly reached the fringe of firstly, Arthur Cox's side, then Jack Charlton and Willie McFaul's team. He became the club's youngest ever debutant at the time, aged 16 years 294 days old, but the management resisted selecting him for more than one full match, although he came on as a replacement in 12 outings, and was named on many occasions without getting into the action. Fast and marauding on the flank, Paul had good control, but was unluckily one of those players who didn't get the break at the right time while he also received a bad medial ligament injury which kept him on the treatment list for nine months. He subsequently moved to a lower grade of football reaching Wembley with non-league Barrow in 1990. Ferris later returned to St James Park and was appointed assistant physiotherapist by his former skipper Kevin Keegan after a spell at the Freeman Hospital in a similar role.

Appearances:
FL: 1(10) apps. 0 gls.
FLC: 0(2) apps. 1 gl.
Total: *1(12) apps. 1 gl.*
Honours:
N.Irel youth app./FAT winner 1990.

FIDLER, Albert

Role: Goalkeeper 1929-1930
5' 11"
b. Newcastle upon Tyne, 1906

CAREER: Spen Black'n'White/Gosforth British Legion/UNITED Aug 1929 £25 to May 1930/Newburn.

Debut v West Ham United (a) 9/9/29

A reserve guardian with Newcastle who had showed up well in local Tyneside football, Albert Fidler was the third choice 'keeper for a season at Gallowgate, behind Albert McInroy and Micky Burns. Called upon on five occasions during the 1929-30 season at a time of injury crisis, he

Albert Fidler

had the harrowing experience of conceding five goals on his debut at Upton Park against West Ham United. Fidler later returned to the north east semi-professional scene.

Appearances:
FL: 5 apps. 0 gls.
Total: *5 apps. 0 gls.*

FINDLAY, John

Role: Right-half 1905-1906
5' 9"
b. Scotland

CAREER: Knibshill United/UNITED cs 1905/Vale of Leven 1906.

Debut v Bolton Wanderers (h) 23/12/05

Brought down from Scottish junior football on recommendation of the club's large scouting network north of the border, John Findlay deputised for Alex Gardner in United's formidable Edwardian line-up during season 1905-06. A midfielder with plenty stamina, the local press noted he was "a capable understudy" who was "cool and steady". A Scottish junior cap, he returned north within a year and continued his career in his native country.

Appearances:
FL: 2 apps. 0 gls.
Total: *2 apps. 0 gls.*
Honours:
Scot junior app.

FINLAY, John

Role: Left-half & Trainer 1909-1930
5' 10"
b. Riccarton, Kilmarnock, 19th October 1892
d. Newcastle upon Tyne, 31st March 1933

CAREER: Airdrieonians/UNITED May 1909 £775, retiring May 1927 and becoming asst-trainer to 1930.

Debut v Blackburn Rovers (a) 4/9/09

Known more commonly as 'Jock' on Tyneside, John Finlay was a grand servant to United for 14 seasons as a player. Arriving at St James Park as a talented teenager who had appeared for the Scottish League side, Finlay made his debut as a 16 year-old, one of the club's youngest ever players. During the years up to World War One, he was reserve to two great Scots, Peter McWilliam and Jimmy Hay but then, after peace was restored, found a place himself in United's attractive side of the early 1920's. A team-man, he worked hard and rarely placed a pass astray. Jock was on the fringe of a full Scotland cap, while he later gave the Magpies valuable service coaching youngsters in the club's North Eastern League side. On leaving the game,

Jock Finlay

Finlay went into business in Newcastle and on his death in 1933 his ashes were scattered from the top of Scafell in the Lake District.

Appearances:
FL: 153 apps. 8 gls.
FAC: 8 apps. 0 gls.
War: 12 apps. 1 gl.
Total: *173 apps. 9 gls.*
Honours:
1 SL app. 1909/
Scot trial app. 1920.

FLANNIGAN, David

Role: Left-half 1928-1929
5′ 10″
b. Glasgow, 1906

CAREER: Third
Lanark/UNITED June 1928
£2,500/East Stirlingshire
May 1929 free.

Debut v Aston Villa (a) 15/9/28

David Flannigan was a much sought after
youngster when United secured his signature
from now defunct Glasgow club Third Lanark.
Although possessing plenty of skill on the ball
Flannigan lacked the stamina and pace to
succeed in the English league. He appeared on
a handful of occasions in season 1928-29 as a
stand-in for Joe Harris, but received few
opportunities thereafter.

> **Appearances:**
> *FL: 3 apps. 0 gls.*
> **Total:** *3 apps. 0 gls.*

FLEMING, James Brown Montgomerie

Role: Centre-forward 1911-1913
5′ 8″
b. Musselburgh, 8th March 1884
d. Belgium, 18th August 1917

CAREER: Edinburgh St
Bernards/UNITED Apr 1911 £250/
Tottenham Hotspur May 1913
£300/Armadale Thistle cs 1915
to demise.

Debut v Tottenham Hotspur (a)
23/11/12

A bright and breezy Scot, who
crossed the border as a reserve to
United's talented Edwardian side,
James Fleming made a great start in
a black'n'white jersey, netting four
times on his debut during a tour
match against Koln. He was given
an opportunity in season 1912-13,
being tried along with several
others when Albert Shepherd was
badly injured. Like many of his
fellow countrymen, Fleming had

James Fleming

good skills but lacked the pace and aggression
to fill the leader's role on a regular basis. He
was a deputy at White Hart Lane too, while
his brother, Bill, was also on Tottenham's
books just prior to World War One. Sadly,
Fleming was killed in action while serving as a
major in the East Yorkshire regiment during
trench warfare on the Continent.

> **Appearances:**
> *FL: 4 apps. 0 gls.*
> **Total:** *4 apps. 0 gls.*

FOGGON, Alan

Role: Striker 1965-1971
5′ 9″
b. West Pelton, County Durham,
23rd February 1950

CAREER: UNITED app Aug 1965, pro Nov
1967/Cardiff City Aug 1971 £25,000/
Middlesbrough Oct 1972 £10,000/Rochester
Lancers(USA) Apr 1976/Hartford
Bi-Centennials(USA) June 1976/Manchester
United July 1976 £40,000/
Sunderland Sept 1976 £25,000/
Southend United July 1977
£15,000(Hartlepool United loan
1977-78)/Consett Aug 1978/
Whitley Bay.

Debut v Arsenal (a) 10/2/68

Alan Foggon was potentially a
star find who had developed
through United's junior set-up
during the late sixties. For a
while the youngster looked like
solving Newcastle's problem
wing position when he hit the
First Division scene during
season 1968-69. The teenager
perhaps characterised the era;
he was trendy with long
flowing hair and had a
somewhat untidy appearance
on the field - socks down and
shirt outside his shorts. But
Foggon also showed he had the
ability to destroy defences with
direct running at pace and he
linked well with Wyn Davies
and Bryan Robson in United's
attack. Alan could play wide or
inside, and was on the fringe of
a regular place as the Magpies

lifted the Inter Cities Fairs Cup, scoring a wonderful goal during the final in Budapest. He reached the young England set-up and saw off more experienced rivals Jim Scott and Jackie Sinclair before losing his way at Gallowgate through erratic form. He appeared for several clubs afterwards and was a big hit under Jack Charlton at Ayresome Park becoming Middlesbrough's top scorer, recording 49 goals in 136 matches, as the Teessiders were promoted to Division One. A former England schools sprint champion, Foggon became a publican in Spennymoor for a period before entering a career with a security company on Tyneside. Alan is one of only a handful of players who have turned out for the north east's three major clubs.

Appearances:
FL: 54(7) apps. 14 gls.
FAC: 4 apps. 0 gls.
FLC: 1(1) apps. 0 gls.
Eur: 10(3) apps. 2 gls.
Total: *69(11) apps. 16 gls.*
Honours:
Eng youth app. 1968/FL div 2 champs 1974/ FL div 4 prom 1978/ICFC winner 1969.

Alan Foggon

FORD, David

Role: Outside-left 1969-1971
5' 7"
b. Sheffield, 2nd March 1945

CAREER: Sheffield Wednesday Jan 1963/UNITED Dec 1969 cash-exch deal for J.Sinclair/ Sheffield United Jan 1971 exch deal for J.Tudor/Halifax Town Aug 1973 to cs 1976.

Debut v Ipswich Town (h) 20/12/69 (scored once)

At the time of joining Newcastle United, David Ford was the latest acquisition in attempts to find a consistent wide player to give service to big Wyn Davies at centre-forward. Having made a name for himself at Hillsborough, a key figure in Wednesday's run to Wembley in 1966, Ford had become one of football's most promising players until a fatal car accident intervened. His fiancee was killed and David was badly hurt with knee and scalp injuries and it took the England Under-23 player some time to recover. Stockily built with powerful legs, Ford was quick and always able to find the net with potent shooting, but at Gallowgate he only gave Tyneside glimpses of his form with the Owls. It wasn't long before he returned to Sheffield in a deal that saw 'keeper John Hope also head for Bramall Lane and John Tudor arrive in the north east. On retiring from soccer Ford ran a heating business in his native city.

Appearances:
FL: 24(2) apps. 3 gls.
FAC: 1(1) apps. 0 gls.
Eur: 3 apps. 0 gls.
Total: *28(3) apps. 3 gls.*
Honours:
2 Eng u23 caps 1967/ FL div 2 prom 1971/FAC finalist 1966.

David Ford

FORD, Joseph Charles

Role: Centre-forward 1931-1934
5' 5"
b. Canongate, Edinburgh, 20th September 1910
d. Leith, April 1951

CAREER: Rosewell Rosedale/UNITED May 1931 £40/Partick Thistle Jan 1934/ Leith Athletic Feb 1934/ Gala/ Benford(Edinburgh) player & secretary.

Debut v Grimsby Town (h) 16/1/32

Joe Ford

Joe Ford captivated United's reserve crowds with his twinkling feet and audacious play in front of goal. Much likened to Hughie Gallacher in style as well as build, he was extremely popular on Tyneside and nicknamed 'Hughie' after Newcastle's recently departed centre-forward hero. One of the smallest players ever to turn out for the club, Joe was described as having "the heart of a lion", and had the ability to take on a whole defence. With everything going well for the little Scot, Joe came in on his debut for Jack Allen but tragically was carried from the field, albeit to a rousing and sympathetic reception, after sustaining a double fracture of his leg. And this after his landlady gave Joe a 'lucky foot' to put in the stocking of his United strip for good luck! Ford took a long time to regain fitness and never recaptured his previous eyecatching form, nor a place in the Magpies' first eleven. In the Merchant Navy during the war, on hanging up his boots Joe spent a lengthy period in local football in Midlothian, and was employed at the Holyrood Brewery of William Younger. Ford resided near to Easter Road and died of tuberculosis.

Appearances:
FL: 1 app. 0 gls.
Total: *1 app. 0 gls.*

FORSTER, William Birkett

Role: Right-back 1932-1938
5' 7"
b. Walker, Newcastle upon Tyne, 28th May 1909

CAREER: Howdon British Legion/UNITED May 1932 £25/Southend United Aug 1938 £150/Bristol Rovers July 1939.

Debut v Burnley (h) 8/2/36

A strong and thoughtful defender who had good positional sense, William Forster was reserve to Joe Richardson at St James Park and never let the side down although deputising only occasionally. However, he became an important figure in the club's second eleven as they moved from local football into the national Central League.

Appearances:
FL: 3 apps. 0 gls.
Total: *3 apps. 0 gls.*

FOULKES, William Isaiah

Role: Inside or Outside-right 1951-1954
5' 7"
b. Merthyr Tydfil, 29th May 1926
d. Hoole, Chester, 7th February 1979

CAREER: Cardiff City amat Feb 1945, pro June 1945/Winsford United/Chester May 1948/UNITED Oct 1951 £11,500/Southampton Aug 1954 £12,500(Winsford United loan 1955-56)/Chester July 1956 £1,000/ Hyde United cs 1961.

Debut v Huddersfield Town (a) 13/10/51

Billy Foulkes was a compact, strong and stocky forward who had a dramatic rise to fame after joining United. He moved from the lower leagues to St James Park for a large fee, and made his debut in the First Division within three days of his arrival. A week later came his first international outing against England, Billy scoring after four minutes with his first kick of the ball! Big in character, Foulkes continued making headlines for that 1951-52 season, ending a quite amazing six months by helping the Magpies lift the FA Cup at Wembley - an ever-present in United's cup run. He possessed a stinging shot and was versatile, operating on the wing or at inside-forward, but after that bright opening Billy's face never quite fitted at Gallowgate.

He moved to The Dell but suffered a back injury soon after and the Saints complained to the Football League requesting the transfer be reversed; the dispute was ruled in Newcastle's favour. Foulkes soon moved back to Wales, serving Chester well in over 170 games, and then resided in that city running a milk-bar in the tourist centre.

Appearances:
FL: 58 apps. 8 gls.
FAC: 10 apps. 1 gls.
Total: *68 apps. 9 gls.*
Honours:
11 Welsh caps 1952-54/FAC winner 1952/ WsC finalist 1958.

Billy Foulkes

FOX, Ruel Adrian

Role: Outside-right 1994-1995
5' 6"
b. Ipswich, 14th January 1968

CAREER: Witton United 1980/Ipswich Town sch/Norwich City sch Oct 1983, app Aug 1984, pro Jan 1986/UNITED Feb 1994 £2.25m/ Tottenham Hotspur Oct 1995 £4m.

Debut v Wimbledon (a) 12/2/94

Ruel Fox became the first of Newcastle United's multi-million pound men as they reinforced their position as one of the game's superclubs during 1994. Small and tricky, Fox could be a handful for any defence and operates in the modern style, on either the right or left-wing or in midfield. Rising to prominence with over 200 games in Norwich City's entertaining line-up that did so well in the UEFA Cup, Ruel was an immediate hit with United's crowd, showing delightful ball skills as he gave service to Andy Cole in the box. Elevated to the edge of the full England set-up, winning B honours, Fox also could be relied upon to grab goals, especially when cutting in from the touchline to hit a drive. However, the addition of David Ginola to Kevin Keegan's international squad, meant Fox could only claim a substitute's place as the 1995-96 season began. Fox wanted first-team action and soon moved on to White Hart Lane for nearly double the fee Newcastle had paid the Canaries.

Appearances:
FL/PL: 56(2) apps. 12 gls.
FAC: 5 apps. 0 gls.
FLC: 3 apps. 1 gl.
Eur: 4 apps. 1 gl.
Total: *68(2) apps. 14 gls.*
Honours:
2 Eng B caps 1994-95.

Bob Foyers

Ruel Fox

attitude towards his game during season 1895-96. Short and well-built, Bob was a touch temperamental and was often in trouble with Newcastle's hierarchy. He was stripped of the captaincy after "misconduct" in December 1895 and later censored for being "worse for liquor"! Not surprisingly perhaps, he left the club soon after, replaced by White and Jackson. By profession, Foyers was a mechanical engineer.

Appearances:
FL: 34 apps. 0 gls.
FAC: 5 apps. 0 gls.
Total: *39 apps. 0 gls.*
Honours:
2 Scot caps 1893-94/Scot jnr app./
SC winner 1895/SJC winner 1889, 1890.

FRANKS, Albert John

Role: Wing-half 1953-1960
5' 10"
b. Boldon, County Durham, 13th April 1936

CAREER: Jarrow Police/South Tyne jnrs/ Boldon CW/Sunderland/UNITED Dec 1953 £50/Glasgow Rangers Mar 1960 £6,500 (Greenock Morton loan 1961-62)/ Lincoln City Nov 1961/Queen of the South Jan 1964/ Scarborough player-manager June 1964 to Dec 1965.

Debut v Luton Town (a) 16/2/57

A tall, powerful, barrel-chested half-back who operated equally well on the right or left side of the field, Albert Franks also possessed the stamina to last the hard slog of 90 minutes in the midfield battleground. An ex police cadet and captain of the Durham youth side, Albert began his career at St James Park as a stand-in for either Jimmy Scoular or Tommy Casey, but by season 1957-58 had earned a place for himself. With a mighty long throw too, Franks proved

Albert Franks

FOYERS, Robert

Role: Left-back 1895-1897
5' 9"
b. Hamilton, Lanark, 22nd June 1868
d. Glasgow, 16th August 1942

CAREER: Burnbank Swifts c1888/Edinburgh St Bernards 1889/Heart of Midlothian Aug 1890/Edinburgh St Bernards 1890/UNITED Aug 1895 £100/Edinburgh St Bernards Apr 1897/Clyde cs 1897 to Oct 1897.

Debut v Loughborough Town (h) 7/9/1895

Bob Foyers settled at Gallowgate from Scotland with a reputation for defensive expertise. An experienced international north of the border, he was appointed captain of United and showed a relentless and shrewd an effective player for two seasons displaying progressive use of the ball, before moving to Scotland to join Rangers - one of only a few Englishmen to have signed for the Ibrox club up to that time. Also a fine cricketer, Franks was unfortunate to be forced to spend 18 months of his time at St James Park on National Service, a period of this in Germany where he represented the RAF. He later resided in Chester-le-Street, where he was employed as a security manager.

Appearances:
FL: 72 apps. 4 gls.
FAC: 3 apps. 0 gls.
Total: *75 apps. 4 gls.*

FRASER, John

Role: Outside-left 1899-1901
5' 11"
b. Dumbarton, 10th November 1876
d. 1st October 1952

CAREER: Dumbarton 1896/Motherwell 1897/Notts County Jan 1898 £70/UNITED June 1899/St Mirren cs 1901/Southampton May 1902/Dundee cs 1905, becoming player-manager/Chelsea scout 1919, becoming asst-manager to 1925.

Debut v Everton (h) 9/9/1899

A workmanlike, courageous and lively winger who packed a thundering shot at goal, John Fraser was a hefty forward, tall and weighty, but possessed splendid command of the ball. Known as 'Jack', he took over from the popular figure of Willie Wardrope at St James Park and had two good campaigns in a black'n'white shirt as the last century closed.

John Fraser

He was good enough to be on the fringe of an international call-up, reaching Scottish trial games. Fraser later became a firm favourite at The Dell, scoring a hat-trick on his debut for the Saints, while at the end of his playing career back in Scotland, he turned in brilliant performances for Dundee which earned him a Cup medal and eventually that Scottish cap.

Appearances:
FL: 49 apps. 9 gls.
FAC: 3 apps. 0 gls.
Total: *52 apps. 9 gls.*
Honours:
1 Scot cap 1907/1 SL app. 1902/
Scot trial app. 1901-07/SC winner 1910/
SC finalist 1897/SnL champs 1903, 1904.

FRASER, Robert

Role: Right-back 1946-1950
6' 0"
b. Glasgow, 23rd January 1917

CAREER: Dunoon Athletic/Ashfield (Glasgow)/Hibernian Aug 1937/UNITED Dec 1946 £3,750/Retired July 1950, becoming a United scout to 1958.

Debut v Nottingham Forest (h) 1/1/47

Cool and versatile in defence, Bob Fraser appeared for United mainly at full-back, but also filled in at centre-half. After serving in the Glasgow Highlanders in Germany during the war, Bob was purchased at a time of an injury pile-up and the experience Fraser had gained in pre-war football served United well, especially during the club's promotion success in 1947-48 when he totalled 20 games. A broken foot put Bob out of action and eventually the younger Bobby Cowell replaced Fraser in United's side. After scouting for a while, he concentrated on a stockbroking business as well as running a sports wholesale company on Tyneside, residing in Ponteland. Robert's brother, William, appeared for Partick Thistle.

Bob Fraser

Appearances:
FL: 26 apps. 0 gls.
FAC: 1 app. 0 gls.
Total: *27 apps. 0 gls.*
Honours:
FL div 2 prom 1948

FROST, Arthur Douglas

Role: Centre-forward 1939
5' 10"
b. Walton, Liverpool, 1st December 1915

CAREER: New Brighton amat July 1938,
pro Aug 1938/UNITED Mar 1939 £2,515/
New Brighton Oct 1939/Wrexham war-guest
1941-43/Southport war-guest 1942-44/
Tranmere Rovers war-guest 1942-46/
New Brighton war-guest 1944-45/
South Liverpool player-manager 1946.

*Debut v Sheffield Wednesday (h) 11/3/39
(scored once)*

Arthur Frost showed Newcastle United's
scouts that he was a player with plenty of
potential when appearing for New Brighton's
Football League outfit in season 1938-39. Frost
was a much-wanted youngster - 18 goals in 23
games - but by the time he had moved to
Tyneside and quickly gained a chance in the
Magpies' first-team, the Second World War
had all but started and his footballing career
was effectively ruined. Cool and intelligent in
the leader's role, Frost always played for the
team in an unselfish fashion.

Appearances:
FL: 5 apps. 1 gl.
Total: 5 apps. 1 gl.

GALLACHER, Hugh Kilpatrick

Role: Centre-forward 1925-1930
5' 5"
*b. Bellshill, Lanarkshire, 2nd February 1903
d. Gateshead, 11th June 1957*

CAREER: Tannockside Athletic 1919/
Hattonrigg Thistle 1919/Bellshill Athletic
Mar 1920/Queen of the South Dec 1920/
Airdrieonians May 1921/UNITED Dec
1925 £6,500/Chelsea May 1930 £10,000/
Derby County Nov 1934 £2,750/Notts
County Sept 1936 £2,000/Grimsby Town
Jan 1938 £1,000/ Gateshead June 1938
£500/Retired Sept 1939.

Debut v Everton (h) 12/12/25 (scored twice)

Hughie Gallacher is considered by many to
be the greatest centre-forward of all time.
Although a mere 5' 5", he was a handful
for any defence possessing awesome strike
power. Hughie could shoot with either
foot, dribble with the ball, head, tackle,
forage and also frequently lose his cool on
the field. A record of netting a formidable
total of 463 goals in 624 senior matches
speaks for itself, while Gallacher is
United's most potent attacker of all
time with a strike-rate of over 82% in
his 174 outings. Newcastle tracked
the Scottish leader for many months
before landing his signature for a
new club record fee, and very nearly
the biggest in the country at the time.
Immediately Hughie took Tyneside
by storm, hitting goals by the dozen
and at the same time developing into
one of the biggest cult figures
Tyneside has witnessed. On, and off
the field - where he became
something of a playboy - Gallacher
was worshipped by Magpie
supporters, and when he skippered
the club to the league title in 1927,
bagging a season's record 39 goals
in only 41 games, the Scot could do
no wrong. Yet Hughie was a
temperamental character, often in
trouble with referees, directors and,

Hughie Gallacher

at times, the police, which just added to the amazing life story of this wizard of the leather. Although the Scot was the Magpies' top goalgetter in each of his five seasons with the club, his relationship with United's directors was never too healthy, and in the summer of 1930 Hughie was sold to Chelsea for a vast fee to the outcry of Tyneside. Protests were many, and on his return to St James Park with the Londoners for the first home fixture of the new season, Newcastle fans packed into Gallowgate to see their past idol. A record crowd of 68,386 was recorded with another 10,000 locked out and for the next decade, and more, Gallacher continued to be held in esteem. He made an impression on all his other clubs too, notably Airdrie - when the Diamonds were next best to Rangers in Scotland - Chelsea and Derby County. A regular for Scotland for over ten years, he netted 23 goals for his country in only 20 games, while he was a star in the famous Wembley Wizards match in 1928. He also scored five goals for the Scottish League in one contest, one of four occasions when he bagged five in a game. Brother-in-law to United's George Mathison, after a long playing career Gallacher settled in Gateshead employed in a number of roles from sports journalist - once being banned from St James Park for his outspoken remarks - to factory worker. Following a series of personal problems, Gallacher committed suicide by throwing himself in front of the York to Edinburgh express train. The *Newcastle Journal's* headline noted, "Hughie of the Magic Feet is Dead". Football will never see another quite like 'Wee Hughie'. His sons, Hughie junior and Matty, both had spells with the black'n'whites without making the grade.

Appearances:
FL: 160 apps. 133 gls.
FAC: 14 apps. 10 gls.
Total: *174 apps. 143 gls.*
Honours:
20 Scot caps 1924-35/
6 Scot unoff app 1935/
1 Scot jnr app. 1921/
2 SL app. 1925-26/
1 Scot trial app. 1925/
FL champs 1927/SC winner 1924.

Hughie Gallacher

GALLACHER, John Anthony

Role: Outside-right 1989-1992
5' 10"
b. Glasgow, 26th January 1969

CAREER: East Kilbride YC/Derby County
app 1985/East Kilbride YC/Falkirk cs 1987/
UNITED May 1989 £100,000/Hartlepool
United July 1992 free/Kettering Town 1993-94/
Gateshead 1994/Berwick Rangers 1994-95.

Debut v Leeds United (h) 19/8/89 (scored once)

A nephew of Alex Ferguson and former
schoolboy trialist at Manchester United, slimly
built John Gallacher signed for the Magpies
after only 16 outings in senior football for
Falkirk. Homesick, and rejected at the Baseball
Ground under Arthur Cox, Gallacher moved
out of the full-time game to take on a career in
insurance until he received another chance at
Brockville Park. His rise to the top was then
meteoric as he played out of his skin in front
of watching Newcastle officials - netting five
goals in six games. Fast and direct and always
able to find the net, Gallacher had a stunning
start with United in season 1989-90, showing
matchwinning potential down the flank.
However, a stress fracture to his shin halted a
blossoming career. The injury took many
months to clear up and John was never quite
the same exciting prospect again, and drifted
quickly out of the picture.

Appearances:
FL: 22(7) apps. 6 gls.
FAC: 2 apps. 0 gls.
FLC: 3 apps. 1 gl.
Others: 3 apps. 1 gl.
Total: *30(7) apps. 8 gls.*

John Gallacher

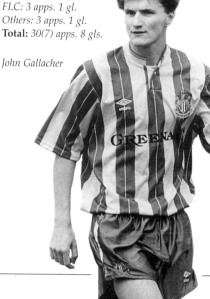

William Gallantree

GALLANTREE, William Leslie

Role: Outside-right 1931-1936
5' 5"
*b. East Boldon, County Durham,
25th December 1913*

CAREER: Harton Colliery/UNITED amat
June 1931, pro Sept 1931 £20/Aldershot Town
May 1936 free/Gateshead July 1937 to 1939.

Debut v Liverpool (a) 7/1/33

William Gallantree was a small but
particularly strong winger who spent his
time at St James Park as deputy to first,
Jimmy Boyd, then Wilf Bott and Tim
Rogers. Direct and plucky, he was
unlucky to break his leg in 1935 during
a Central League fixture which
hampered his chances of a regular
place in United's Second Division
line-up. After the Second World
War Gallantree resided near
Durham City.

Appearances:
FL: 9 apps. 2 gls.
Total: *9 apps. 2 gls.*

141

GARBUTT, Eric John Edward

Role: Goalkeeper 1939-1951
5' 11"
b. Scarborough, 27th March 1920

CAREER: Hartlepools United/
Billingham/UNITED Jan 1939
£100/Retired cs 1951 due to
injury.
Debut v Millwall (a) 31/8/46

Two serious injuries suppressed
what would have been a fine career
for Eric Garbutt. With plenty of stiff
competition for places in United's
ranks from Fairbrother and Swinburne,
Garbutt firstly broke a hand, then a leg which
saw him out of action for many weeks and
ultimately brought a premature conclusion to
his career. At his best, Eric was always alert
with fine anticipation and he commanded
respect from his colleagues, many noting him
as the pick of Newcastle's immediate post-war
custodians. Garbutt served in the RAF during
World War Two and later appeared on 17
occasions during United's promotion
campaign in 1947-48.

Eric Garbutt

Appearances:
FL: 52 apps. 0 gls.
FAC: 1 app. 0 gls.
War: 1 app. 0 gls.
Total: *54 apps. 0 gls.*
Honours:
FL div 2 prom 1948.

GARDNER, Alexander

Role: Right-half 1899-1910
5' 8"
b. Leith, 1877
d. South Shields, 1952

CAREER: Leith Ivanhoe/Leith Athletic
1897/UNITED Nov 1899/ Retired 1910/
Blyth Spartans 1911.
Debut v Preston North End (h) 25/11/1899

Although there were few better midfielders
than Alex Gardner at the time, he remains the
only one of United's Edwardian greats not to
be capped. A regular for the black'n'whites for
almost a decade, his colleague Colin Veitch
noted him as "the best half-back who never
got an international cap". Gardner reached

Scottish trial fixtures but, to Tyneside's
dismay, was always overlooked. Consistent
throughout his long stay at St James Park,
the Scot was a versatile player, starting off
at inside-forward or outside-right, before
switching to the heart of midfield just
before United began to dominate the
game in the mid 1900's. He specialised
in the low, direct pass, forming a near
telepathic understanding with Jackie
Rutherford on the right flank, a feature
of United's play in that era. Captain of
United on many occasions, Gardner broke
his leg in 1909, an injury which curtailed
his career. In his early days with the
Magpies - during November 1901 - he was
out of action for some time whilst recovering
from scarlet fever, a killer virus during the
early part of the century. Nicknamed 'Punky',
he signed his name as, 'Alick' and later ran the
North Terrace and Dun Cow public-houses
close to St James Park up to his death.

Appearances:
FL: 279 apps. 22 gls.
FAC: 34 apps. 4 gls.
Others: 1 app. 0 gls.
Total: *314 apps. 26 gls.*
Honours:
Scot trial app. 1900-06/FL champs 1905,
1907, 1909/FAC finalist 1905, 1906, 1908.

Alex Gardner

GARDNER, Andrew

Role: Outside-left 1902-1903
5' 8"
b. Oban, Argyllshire, 26th September 1877

CAREER: Kilbarchan Victoria/Kilbarchan/ Clyde c1895/Grimsby Town May 1901/ UNITED Sept 1902/Bolton Wanderers May 1903/Brighton cs 1904/ Queens Park Rangers cs 1905/Carlisle United cs 1907/Johnstone Apr 1908/Carlisle United Jan 1909.

Debut v Liverpool (h) 8/11/02

One of a trio of unrelated players with a similar surname at Gallowgate during the same era. The lesser known of the three, Andrew Gardner was still a respected player around the turn of the century. He replaced the popular Richard Roberts in United's side, but only appeared for two months in their first eleven during season 1902-03 before another hugely favoured player, Bobby Templeton, arrived to take his place. Some sources have Gardner born in Glasgow (17/4/1877).

Appearances:
FL: 9 apps. 3 gls.
FAC: 1 app. 0 gls.
Total: *10 apps. 3 gls.*

GARDNER, David Richmond

Role: Left-back 1899-1902
5' 8"
*b. Glasgow,
31st March 1873
d. Longcliffe, nr Matlock,
5th November 1931*

CAREER: Third Lanark 1896/UNITED May 1899/Grimsby Town May 1902 £250/West Ham United cs 1904/Croydon Common Sept 1907, becoming manager Feb 1910, then trainer and occasional player to cs 1916/Leicester City trainer Aug 1919 to his demise.

Debut v West Bromwich Albion (a) 2/9/1899

A great favourite with the spectators, Dave Gardner was an intelligent and elegant defender. He was something of a gentleman on the field too - a rarity for a full-back in those years - and he always played to the crowd, possessing a trick that he used over

and over again of back-heeling the ball to fool his opponent. Winning one cap for his country, he was on the fringe of more honours while Dave also captained United, and all his other clubs too. He also took part in West Ham's first game at Upton Park in September 1904. Gardner died whilst playing golf alongside his Leicester City colleagues.

Appearances:
FL: 76 apps. 2 gls.
FAC: 2 apps. 0 gls.
Total: *78 apps. 2 gls.*
Honours:
1 Scot cap 1897/1 Scot unoff app. 1898/ Scot trial app. 1900.

GARLAND, Peter James

Role: Midfield 1992
5' 9"
*b. Croydon, Surrey,
20th January 1971*

CAREER: Tottenham Hotspur app July 1987, pro cs 1989/UNITED Mar 1992 £35,000/ Charlton Athletic Dec 1992 £35,000(Wycombe Wanderers loan 1994-95)/Leyton Orient July 1996 free.

Debut v Millwall (h) 18/4/92 (sub)

One of Kevin Keegan's earliest signings as manager of United, Peter Garland had never started a first-team fixture for Spurs, but had been on the bench on several occasions. When the former teenage international was given the opportunity to move to Gallowgate, the Londoner had the chance to impress and claim a regular position in United's developing side. Able to turn out at full-back or in midfield, Garland though, found he was again in the shadows never quite showing the form that warranted an extended run. Tenacious and mobile, he moved back to the capital and proceeded to have a decent career at The Valley with Charlton where he claimed over 50 outings.

Appearances:
FL: 0(2) apps. 0 gls.
Others: 0(1)app. 0 gls.
Total: *0(3) apps. 0 gls.*
Honours:
Eng youth app. 1988.

GARNHAM, Alfred

Role: Left-half 1934-1939, 1942-1943
5' 9"
b. Birtley, nr Gateshead, 22nd June 1914

CAREER: Fatfield Albion/Herrington CW/
Birtley/UNITED Apr 1934/Queen of the
South Aug 1939/UNITED war-guest 1942-43/
West Stanley player-manager c1946/
Retired 1950 due to injury.

Debut v Norwich City (a) 7/12/35

A hearty local player who attempted to claim
a first-team place in three different roles with
United, at left-back, left-half and right-half, Alf
Garnham had two good seasons in 1935-36
and 1936-37, but was always recognised as a
reserve afterwards. He was a dour performer,
but one who never let the Magpies down.
After retiring from the game he worked on
Tyneside, later residing in Perkinsville near
Chester-le-Street. Garnham served as a fire
officer in Dumfries during the war.

Appearances:
FL: 45 apps. 1 gl.
FAC: 5 apps. 0 gls.
War: 1 app. 0 gls.
Total: *51 apps. 1 gl.*

Alf Garnham

GARROW, Herbert Alexander

Role: Goalkeeper 1960-1963
6' 3"
b. Elgin, 24th January 1942

CAREER:
Fochabars/UNITED Feb
1960 £1,150/Horden CW
June 1963 free/South
Shields 1965/Scarborough
cs 1972/Retired cs 1974/
Bishop Auckland Sept
1978/Newcastle Blue Star
cs 1980 to 1982/Blyth
Spartans briefly/Whitley
Bay briefly.

Herbert Garrow

Debut v Blackburn Rovers (h) 26/11/60

The tall, vastly built Herbert Garrow was, at
over 14 stone, one of the most powerfully
framed players to have served the Magpies.
With Bryan Harvey, then Dave Hollins, ahead
of him in selection at St James Park, as well as
having Stuart Mitchell as a rival for the
Number One position, Garrow's opportunities
in the senior eleven were limited. He did,
though, have a noted career in local football,
being a well-known and popular character in
Northumberland and Durham for over two
decades. He also reached Wembley with
Scarborough in 1973 and was dubbed Man of
the Match in the FA Trophy final. Residing on
Tyneside, Garrow was employed as a housing
inspector for the City of Newcastle local
authority.

Appearances:
FL: 4 apps. 0 gls.
Total: *4 apps. 0 gls.*
Honours:
FAT winner 1973.

GASCOIGNE, Paul John

Role: Midfield 1980-1988
5' 10"
b. Dunston, Gateshead, 27th May 1967

CAREER: Redheugh Boys' Club 1979/
Dunston jnrs/UNITED sch 1980, app June
1983, pro May 1985/Tottenham Hotspur July
1988 £2.3m(plus £350,000 later)/ Lazio(Italy)
May 1992 £5.5m/Glasgow Rangers July 1995
£4.3m.

Debut v Queens Park Rangers (h) 13/4/85 (sub)

A phenomenon of the nineties, Paul Gascoigne became the British game's biggest personality with a brand of entertainment on and off the field reserved only for a few gifted individuals. Paul began his headlining career as the precocious young star of the black'n'whites FA Youth Cup victory in 1985. He quickly earned a place in Newcastle's senior eleven as a teenager who possessed an array of skills and flair that rapidly had the whole country taking notice. Gascoigne always wanted to be involved in the action and added to his superb vision, passing, shooting and dribbling skills, was his strength and workrate as well as the ability to tackle - rare for his type of ball player - all of which turned him into almost a complete footballer. The only negative aspect of his game was the tendency to sometimes be rash, temperamental and even self-destructive. Known universally as 'Gazza', he developed into perhaps the second 'Clown Prince of Soccer', after Len Shackleton a generation before. With colourful displays on the park and plenty of antics off it, Gascoigne became Tyneside's most famous modern son and it was a huge disappointment when he left for London and White Hart Lane in a new British record deal. He flourished into a megastar under Terry Venables at Spurs and became an England regular. Then, after a protracted transfer and fitness saga following a crippling self-inflicted cruciate knee ligament injury collected in the 1991 FA Cup final, he eventually headed for Rome and Serie A giants, Lazio. Dogged by various injury problems throughout his career, Paul recovered from these long term setbacks and has latterly become a favourite at Ibrox with Rangers. Always the showman keen to put a smile on the faces of supporters, Gascoigne won the prestigious BBC Television Sports Personality of the Year award in 1990. He also hit the record charts with a remake of the Geordie classic, *Fog on the Tyne*, is preserved in wax at Madame Tussaud's, and even now is rarely out of the news for long. Once turned down by Ipswich Town and Middlesbrough after a trial, Gazza began at St James Park on a youth training scheme.

Appearances:
FL: 83(9) apps. 21 gls.
FAC: 4 apps. 3 gls.
FLC: 8 apps. 1 gl.
Others: 4(1) apps. 0 gls.
Total: 99(10) apps. 25 gls.
Honours:
*43 Eng caps 1989-96/4 Eng B caps 1988-90/
13 Eng u21 caps 1987-88/FAC winner 1991/
FAYC winner 1985/SL champs 1996/
SC winner 1996/PFA Young Player of the Year
1988/SPFA & SFWA Player of the Year 1996.*

Paul 'Gazza' Gascoigne

GASKELL, Alexander

Role: Centre-forward 1953-54
5' 10"
b. Leigh, nr Manchester, 30th July 1932

CAREER: Manchester Amateurs/Southport
Nov 1952/UNITED Oct 1953 £5,000/
Mansfield Town June 1954 £3,500/Grantham
May 1956/Tranmere Rovers June 1957 to cs
1958/Rhyl/Wigan Rovers/Winsford United
Dec 1961.

Debut v Middlesbrough (h) 26/12/53

One of the best strikers in the lower divisions,
Alex Gaskell was purchased as a forward to
groom into a star of the future at St James
Park, but in the end it was a deal that never
bore fruit. Gaskell was given only one
opportunity in United's first-team, a Boxing
Day derby against Middlesbrough in season
1953-54 when he stood in for Jackie Milburn.
Without making an impact in senior football,
Gaskell later resided in Cheshire.

Appearances:
FL: 1 app. 0 gls.
Total: *1 app. 0 gls.*

GAYLE, Howard A.

Role: Striker 1982-1983
5' 11"
b. Liverpool, 18th May 1958

CAREER: Liverpool app June 1974, pro Nov
1977(Fulham loan 1979-80)(UNITED loan Nov
1982 to Jan 1983)/Birmingham City loan 1982-
83, pmt June 1983 £50,000/Sunderland July
1984 £70,000/Dallas Sidekicks(USA) cs 1986/
Stoke City Apr 1987 free/Blackburn Rovers
Aug 1987 £5,000/Halifax Town Aug 1992/
Carlisle United on trial Oct 1992/Accrington
Stanley Sept 1993.

Debut v Cambridge United (h) 27/11/82

An injury to Kevin Keegan led to the arrival of
Howard Gayle on a loan deal during the
winter of 1982. One of Liverpool's shadow
eleven, Gayle had only appeared on a handful
of senior occasions for the Reds, but was still
recognised as potentially a quality player,
much like Kevin Sheedy who left Anfield and
developed into one of the best. Gayle could
operate in a wide role, or up front, as well as
in midfield, and he caught the eye of many

United supporters. However, while the
Merseysider didn't do badly at St James Park,
he drifted in and out of games and manager
Arthur Cox failed to be impressed. Howard
possessed pace and explosive shooting - only
rarely used - and also a hot temper. He later
served Sunderland and Blackburn with credit.
Gayle played in one of Liverpool's European
Cup semi-final ties, against Bayern Munich in
1981 and was a substitute in the final against
Real Madrid but was not called to action.

Appearances:
FL: 8 apps. 2 gls.
Total: *8 apps. 2 gls.*
Honours:
*3 Eng u21 caps 1984/FLC finalist 1985/
EC winner 1981(sub, no app).*

Howard Gayle

GAYNOR, Thomas

Role: Centre-forward 1990
6' 1"
b. Limerick, 29th January 1963

CAREER: Limerick City/Doncaster Rovers
Dec 1986/Nottingham Forest Oct 1987
£25,000 (UNITED loan Nov to Dec 1990)/
Millwall Mar 1993 to cs 1993.

Debut v Watford (h) 24/11/90

Tommy Gaynor

Tommy Gaynor arrived on Tyneside as an emergency replacement for striker Mark McGhee who was sidelined through injury. The tall Irishman had a good first touch and combined well up front but, like many of United's on-loan players, never persuaded the club's management to immediately rush for the cheque-book. Tommy had made a name for himself at the Belle Vue Ground before being fancied by Brian Clough. Although never a regular with Forest, he appeared in over 50 matches for the Trent club before heading for London and The Den.

Appearances:
FL: 4 apps. 1 gl.
Total: *4 apps. 1 gl.*
Honours:
FLC winner 1989.

GHEE, Thomas

Role: Right-half & Trainer 1897-1920
5' 11"
b. Kilmarnock, 1873

CAREER: Kilmarnock cs 1893/Darwen Jan
1894/St Mirren Dec 1894/Kilmarnock Apr
1895/UNITED May 1897/Retired 1902,
becoming asst-trainer and backstage aid
to 1920.

Debut v Woolwich Arsenal (h) 4/9/1897

Close to international recognition, Tommy Ghee was said to have signed for United at a Paisley bar. The Scot helped United to promotion and took part in Newcastle's initial First Division match, becoming one of the club's mainstays as they developed in the big-time. Skipper of the Magpies, Tommy was a whole-hearted character, a big personality and a driving force on the field who possessed courage and tenacity; it was recorded he would, "stop the opposition at all costs". Ghee was tough and uncompromising and his rugged style linked perfectly with Jack Ostler and Jimmy Stott in midfield, a combination which served the black'n'whites with distinction. A great all-round sportsman, Ghee was proficient at both swimming and water-polo, then a popular pastime. Tommy later suffered from a leg injury which permanently affected his walk. Helping behind the scenes, he resided on Tyneside and also looked after the players' billiard room at St James Park.

Appearances:
FL: 134 apps. 3 gls.
FAC: 10 apps. 1 gl.
Total: *144 apps. 4 gls.*
Honours:
Scot trial app. 1899/FL div 2 prom 1898.

Tommy Ghee

GIBB, Thomas

Role: Midfield 1968-1975
5' 10"
b. Bathgate, 13th December 1944

CAREER: Wallhouse Rose/Armadale Thistle
1963/Partick Thistle 1963/UNITED Aug 1968
£45,000/Sunderland June 1975 free/
Hartlepool United May 1977 free to July 1979.

Debut v Sheffield Wednesday (a) 14/8/68

Tommy Gibb was purchased by boss Joe Harvey as a reserve midfield player, one to be groomed for the future. Yet the Scot grasped an early chance in a black'n'white shirt due to injuries and proceeded to secure his midfield role for the next four seasons. In doing so Tommy created a club record, appearing in 171 successive games. Slim with plenty of running power, Gibb was a terrific worker in the Magpies' blossoming European line-up. He did the simple things well on the ball, while he also had the ability to make late, telling runs into the box. Tommy never really received all the credit he deserved from fans on the terraces, yet was widely respected in the dressing-room by his colleagues. After leaving the game he returned to his native West Lothian where he managed a public house in Armadale for a while, then entered the haulage business. Gibb netted a well-remembered 25-yard screamer on his home debut against Chelsea, while he appeared on eight occasions when Sunderland lifted the Second Division crown in 1976.

Tommy Gibb

Appearances:
FL: 190(9) apps. 12 gls.
FAC: 8(3) apps. 0 gls.
FLC: 12 apps. 1 gl.
Eur: 24 apps. 3 gls.
Others: 17(5) apps. 3 gls.
Total: *251(17) apps. 19 gls.*
Honours:
1 Scot u23 cap 1968/FAC finalist 1974/ ICFC winner 1969.

GIBSON, Colin Hayward

Role: Outside-right 1948-1949
5' 11"
b. Normandy on Tees, 16th September 1923
d. 27th March 1992

CAREER: Penarth Pontoons/Cardiff City Aug 1942/UNITED July 1948 £15,000/Aston Villa Feb 1949 £17,500/Lincoln City Jan 1956 £6,000/ Stourbridge July 1957 to 1958.

Debut v Everton (a) 21/8/48

A dashing, blond, slimly-built forward, Colin Gibson played on the wing or inside with pace, style and panache throughout the immediate post-war years. Newcastle were impressed with his sparkling

Colin Gibson

performances for Cardiff City (over 150 games) and brought him to Tyneside for what was then a near record fee. The former dockyard marine engineer had one season in United's colours, 1948-49, before losing his place. But his was a talent that many clubs admired and, after turning in two brilliant performances against Aston Villa, he moved to Birmingham within 24 hours. Becoming a crowd-pleaser with Villa, he scored 26 goals in 167 games for the Claret and Blues and graduated into the England set-up. Gibson eventually retired to the Stourbridge area where he moved into the licensing trade, managing a succession of pubs in the Midlands.

Appearances:
FL: 23 apps. 5 gls.
FAC: 1 app. 0 gls.
Total: *24 apps. 5 gls.*
Honours:
1 Eng B cap 1949/
1 FL app. 1949/
FA app. 1949/
FL div 3(S)
champs 1947.

GIBSON, James

Role: Centre-forward 1959-1961
6' 0"
b. Belfast, 4th September 1940

CAREER: Linfield/UNITED Jan 1959
£6,000/Cambridge United July 1961
free/Luton Town Feb 1965 to 1966.

Debut v West Ham United (h) 30/3/59

Jimmy Gibson was recommended to
Newcastle as a buy for the future by former
hero, Jackie Milburn, who rated the raw Irish
youngster highly. A teenager when he moved
to Tyneside, Gibson was something of a full
blooded, tearaway type of leader. Jimmy
though, only received a chance in United's
first-team on two occasions, deputising for
Len White and Bill Curry. He perhaps lacked

guile, but did well
when he moved
into the Southern
League with
Cambridge United,
hitting 35 goals in
his first season and
later earning
another chance in
the Football League
at Kenilworth
Road.

Appearances:
FL: 2 apps. 1 gl.
Total: *2 apps. 1 gl.*

Jimmy Gibson

GIBSON, Robert James

Role: Outside-right 1911-1912, 1919-1920
5' 7"
*b. Scotswood, Newcastle upon Tyne,
1887*

CAREER: Middlesbrough Sept
1910/UNITED Aug 1911 £50/
Lincoln City May 1912 £35/ Third
Lanark May 1914/UNITED 1919
to 1920.

Debut v West Bromwich Albion (h) 7/10/11

After appearing in most of
Middlesbrough's First Division fixtures
during season 1910-11, young Geordie
Robert Gibson was brought back to his native
Tyneside by United to act as cover to Jackie

Robert Gibson

Rutherford. He made only two outings in his
single season with the Magpies before being
transferred to Lincoln City where he failed to
make the grade. Gibson returned briefly to St
James Park after World War One, appearing in
the Northern Victory League.

Appearances:
FL: 2 apps. 0 gls.
War: 1 app. 0 gls.
Total: *3 apps. 0 gls.*

GIBSON, William M.

Role: Left-half
1923-1929
5' 8"
*b. Larkhall, Lanarkshire,
21st July 1898*

CAREER: Cadzow
St Annes/ St Anthonys
(Glasgow)/ Larkhall/Ayr United Oct 1919/
UNITED Nov 1923 £2,500/ Birmingham City
trainer May 1929.

Debut v Preston North End (a) 17/11/23

W. GIBSON

A talented Scottish ball player who possessed
near perfect distribution in midfield, Willie
Gibson hailed from a famous footballing
pedigree. Son of the illustrious Neil Gibson of
Rangers and Scotland, he had two other
brothers of note in the game as well. Gibson
became a regular in the Magpies' line-up in
season 1923-24 and was prominent in both
United's FA Cup and championship victories
in that era. Although appearing to be
duck-footed, he proved an important
link-man able to forage for the ball
in defence, while he was also
quick to set up Newcastle's
attack. After he retired from the
game, Gibson returned to
Tyneside and was employed as
a baker in Newcastle.

Appearances:
FL: 124 apps. 2 gls.
FAC: 18 apps. 2 gls.
Total: *142 apps. 4 gls.*
Honours:
*FL champs 1927/
FAC winner 1924.*

GILFILLAN, Robert I.

Role: Centre-forward 1959-1961
5' 9"
b. Cowdenbeath, 29th June 1938

CAREER: Dundonald/Cowdenbeath
1956/UNITED Oct 1959 £4,000/St Johnstone
Jan 1961 £4,000/Raith Rovers Dec 1961/
Southend United July 1963/Doncaster Rovers
Nov 1965 £40,000/Northwich Victoria player-
coach cs 1971.

Debut v Bolton Wanderers (h) 24/10/59

Bobby Gilfillan

Bobby Gilfillan had
an eye-catching
record in the Scottish
League at
Cowdenbeath and
United's scouts noted
his name to United
boss Charlie Mitten.
Small and thin,
Bobby arrived at
Gallowgate as cover
for Len White and
only rarely was
handed the Number
9 shirt in senior
action. And when
White was badly
injured Gilfillan was overlooked and didn't
get the call-up, moving shortly afterwards
back to Scotland. He later had a good spell at
the Belle Vue Ground, where he was a regular
for six seasons, topping 200 games for
Doncaster.

Appearances:
FL: 7 apps. 2 gls.
Total: *7 apps. 2 gls.*
Honours:
FL div 4 champs 1966, 1969.

GILLESPIE, Keith Robert

Role: Outside-right 1995-date
5' 10"
b. Larne, Northern Ireland, 18th February 1975

CAREER: West Bangor/St Andrews Boys'
Club (Belfast)/Manchester United sch 1989,
app July 1991, pro Jan 1993(Wigan Athletic
loan 1993-94)/UNITED Jan 1995 £1m.

Debut v Sheffield Wednesday (a) 21/1/95 (sub)

Arriving in the north east as part of the
dramatic multi-million pound deal that sent
Andy Cole to Old Trafford, Keith Gillespie
quickly showed the football world he was no
make-weight in that transaction. The young
Northern Ireland international proved he had
the ability to become a huge name in his own
right. Fast and direct, with a cutting edge to
become a matchwinner on the right touchline,
Keith had greatly impressed manager Kevin
Keegan before the Cole deal in a series of
matches against the Magpies. Starring in
United's successful side of 1995-96, Gillespie
possessed balance and control on the ball and
searing pace running at defenders, qualities
that could destroy the opposition. Rapidly
endorsed as a terrace favourite, Gillespie gave
United a contrasting option on the flank to
their other wide player, David Ginola when
the Magpies challenged for the championship
trophy in 1995-96. A former Youth Cup winner
who was connected with Alex Ferguson's Old
Trafford side when he was 14, Keith has
played for his country at every level, gaining
his full cap when he was only 19 years old.

Appearances:
PL: 41(4) apps. 6 gls.
FAC: 3 apps. 2 gls.
FLC: 4 apps. 1 gl.
Total: *48(4) apps. 9 gls.*
Honours:
*12 N.Ireland caps
1995-date/1 N.Irel
u21 app./N.Irel youth
app./N.Irel schools
app./FAYC winner
1992, 1993.*

Keith Gillespie

GILLESPY, Toby

Role: Inside-right or left 1893-1894
5' 8"
b. Tyneside

CAREER: Arthur's Hill (Newcastle) 1888/UNITED cs 1893 to cs 1894/Hebburn Argyle 1894 to 1895.

Debut v Lincoln City (a) 7/10/1893

Local product Toby Gillespy was signed as a professional following the disbandment of city club, Arthur's Hill, and just as United entered Football League soccer in 1893. A versatile forward who stepped into action on four occasions in United's inaugural league season, Gillespy afterwards returned to local football turning out for Hebburn Argyle, a home for several of United's pioneers.

Appearances:
FL: 4 apps. 0 gls.
Total: *4 apps. 0 gls..*

GILLESPIE, William F.

Role: Left-back 1927-1929
5' 8"
b. Fife, 29th October 1903

CAREER: East Fife/UNITED May 1927 £1,500 /Bristol Rovers May 1929 free/ St Mirren 1930/ East Fife Oct 1930.

Debut v Manchester United (h) 21/1/28

Scot William Gillespie crossed the border as a replacement for United's veteran defender Frank Hudspeth. He had just appeared in East Fife's 3-1 defeat at the hands of Celtic in the 1927 Scottish Cup final, but had been impressive throughout their run to Hampden Park. However, the Scot never quite shone in English football and was replaced by another of his countrymen in Bob Thomson.

Appearances:
FL: 9 apps. 0 gls.
Total: *9 apps. 0 gls.*
Honours:
SC finalist 1927.

GINOLA, David

Role: Midfield 1995-date
5' 11"
b. Gassin, Cote d'Azur, France, 25th January 1967

CAREER: St Maxime Boy's Club (France)/ OGC Nice (France) 1982 to 1983/ SC Toulon (France) 1985/Matra Racing Paris (France) 1988/Brest Armorique (France) 1990/Paris St-Germain (France) 1991/UNITED July 1995 £2.5m.

Debut v Coventry City (h) 19/8/95

The £2.5 million signing of David Ginola set United's fanatical 'Toon Army' alight with expectation during the close season of 1995. Born on the Mediterranean coast, near St Tropez, Ginola came to Tyneside as a player of experience with Paris St-Germain, having reached three European semi-finals, including the Champions' Cup in 1994-95. Appearing in almost 400 senior games before crossing the Channel for England, Ginola was clearly a virtuoso of the very highest quality possessing both balance and poise. Tall, with a near-perfect physique, the Frenchman arrived with a reputation for being something of a pin-up star who could entertain but also deliver the goods and, it was hoped, would turn the Magpies into a trophy-winning outfit. That did not quite materialise but Ginola made a huge impact on English football and was in contention for the Player of the Year award at the end of the 1995-96 season. Known as 'Il Magnifique' in France, David was the mainstay of the Parisiens' midfield as they won domestic honours. Possessing tremendous technique and style on the ball, he operates wide on the left and can use both feet to deliver telling crosses and passes. English defences learned they had only one way to stop Ginola - by hunting in packs of two or even three men to swamp his trickery. Largely overlooked by his own national side since coming to England, Ginola is at times erratic and perhaps does not work back as much as some might wish, yet he can set the crowd roaring in delight with his special brand of skills on the flank and an uncanny ability to

GODDARD, Paul

Role: Centre-forward 1986-1988
5' 9"
b. Harlington, Middlesex, 12th October 1959

CAREER: Queens Park Rangers app 1976, pro July 1977/West Ham United Aug 1980 £800,000/UNITED Nov 1986 £415,000/Derby County July 1988 £425,000/Millwall Dec 1989 £800,000/Ipswich Town Feb 1991 free, becoming coach May 1994, caretaker-manager Dec 1994, asst-coach 1995.

Debut v Leicester City (a) 8/11/86

Paul Goddard commanded record club fees when he joined West Ham United, Newcastle and Millwall. Not a tall and powerful centre-forward in the traditional mould, Goddard was small, but knew how to control and shield the ball, and had the poacher's instinct in front of goal. Developing through the ranks at Loftus Road, it was at Upton Park on the other side of London where Goddard really flourished. He appeared on 213 occasions for the Hammers, netted 71

goals and was a key man in West Ham's promotion and League Cup run in season 1980-81. However, a dislocated shoulder forced him to the sidelines and by the time Paul was fit again his place had been taken by Frank McAvennie. Newcastle jumped at the chance to bring the quality striker north and immediately Goddard repaid the Magpies' hefty fee by netting 11 precious goals, including seven in seven consecutive games, which saved the Geordies from the First Division trapdoor in 1987. Nicknamed 'Sarge' after his Boys' Brigade days, Goddard had a

David Ginola

race away with the ball under complete control. During the early part of his career, David quit the game to concentrate on studying law in Nice, only to be given a second chance in football with Toulon. Charming and articulate with the looks of a film star, he also acted as a model for Italian fashion-house Nino Cerutti, while Ginola won the National Hairdressers Federation 'Male Head of the Year' award in 1996! His father was also a professional footballer in France.

Appearances:
PL: 34 apps. 5 gls.
FAC: 2 apps. 0 gls.
FLC: 4 apps. 0 gls.
Total: 40 apps. 5 gls.
Honours:
20 France caps 1990-date/France B app./5 France u21 app. 1988-89/FrL champ 1994/FC winner 1993, 1995/FC finalist 1990/FrLC winner/French Footballer of the Year 1994.

Paul Goddard

GOODWILL, Thomas

Role: Outside-left 1913-1916
5' 7"
b. Bates Cottages, Northumberland, 1894
d. Thiepval, France, 1st July 1916

CAREER: Seaton Delaval / UNITED May 1913 £100 / Killed in action during the First World War.

Debut v Everton (h) 13/9/13

A former miner, Tommy Goodwill was the archetypal working-class hero. Graduating from local football, he gained a chance with the black'n'whites and made such an impression in the club's reserve eleven that he quickly succeeded Scottish international George Wilson on the left wing. He was a quick 'mover and could accurately cross the ball as well as delight the crowd. Goodwill was hailed as a new star as he became a regular for United in the two seasons before the Great War halted football in 1915. Like so many of the game's players he volunteered for action on the continent, signing up for the somewhat elite 'Newcastle Commercials', the 16th Northumberland Fusiliers Battalion, along with United colleagues Dan Dunglinson and Stan Hardy. Sadly Goodwill and Dunglinson were both killed in the terrible opening battle of the Somme. Their battalion was ordered to attack the fortress village of Thiepval and as the Commercials left the trenches at walking pace, Germans opened fire with machine-guns and shells; Goodwill was fatally hit by shrapnel. He fell a few yards from his team-mate who was shot to pieces. It is thought that one of the figures on the Barras Bridge War Memorial in Newcastle features Tommy Goodwill, while his name is engraved on the memorial at Thiepval, one of 73,412 men who have no known grave at that hamlet in France.

Appearances:
FL: 52 apps. 4 gls.
FAC: 8 apps. 3 gls.
Total: *60 apps. 7 gls.*

willingness to play for the team and was admired by United's supporters. But his family never settled on Tyneside and he soon returned south. Goddard has one of the shortest careers in an England shirt on record - 50 minutes - scoring on his only appearance as substitute against Iceland.

Appearances:
FL: 61 apps. 19 gls.
FAC: 6 apps. 3 gls.
FLC: 3 apps. 1 gl.
Others: 2 apps. 0 gls.
Total: *72 apps. 23 gls.*
Honours:
1 Eng cap 1982/1 Eng B cap/8 Eng u21 caps 1981-83/FL div 2 champs 1981/ FL div 1 champs 1992/FLC finalist 1981.

GORDON, James

Role: Right-half 1935-1945
5' 7"
*b. Fauldhouse, West Lothian,
23rd October 1915
d. Derby, 29th August 1996*

CAREER: Wishaw
jnrs/UNITED Apr 1935
£140/Middlesbrough Nov
1945 £3,500, becoming asst-
coach cs 1955/Blackburn
Rovers coach 1961/Derby
County coach cs 1969/
Leeds United coach July
1974 to Sept 1974/
Nottingham Forest coach
Jan 1975/Retired May
1981.

*Debut v Oldham Athletic (a)
27/4/35*

Jimmy Gordon was one of
the best players around
during the immediate
years before the Second
World War broke out in
1939. Joining United after
being the star of the 1935
Scottish Junior Cup semi-
final in front of manager
Andy Cunningham, Jimmy
was a polished wing-half.
He was frequently tipped for Scottish caps in
1937 and 1938, but was unlucky to break his
fibula when almost a certainty for his first call-
up. Sure, effective and rarely flustered,
Gordon was tenacious to the point that one
colleague noted him as "the terror of
forwards", while he also
specialised in a long throw. Jimmy
turned out for the Magpies often
during the war, but was unable to
command a first-team place at St
James Park after the hostilities due
to the many rising youngsters. He
headed for Ayresome Park where
he continued to perform with
distinction in 253 games for 'Boro.
It was on Teesside that the Scot first
made contact with Brian Clough,
Gordon becoming the third
member of the celebrated Clough
and Peter Taylor management team
that lifted several trophies during

Jimmy Gordon

the seventies. He once led
Nottingham Forest out at Wembley
in a League Cup Final, a generous
gesture and acknowledgment of
Gordon's influence behind the
scenes by Clough. Jimmy afterwards
resided in Derby; latterly suffering
with Alzheimer's Disease he died in
August 1996.

Appearances:
*FL: 132 apps. 2 gls.
FAC: 11 apps. 1 gl.
War: 111 apps. 18 gls.*
Total: *254 apps. 21 gls.*

GORRY, Martin C.

Role: Left-back 1976-1978
5' 10"
b. Derby, 29th December 1954

CAREER: Barnsley app 1972, pro
Nov 1973/UNITED Oct 1976
£50,000(Stockport County loan
1977-78)/Hartlepool United
July 1978 free to cs 1980/Shildon
Oct 1980.

*Debut v Manchester City (a) 26/12/77
(sub)*

With less than a year of senior
experience to his name, Martin
Gorry was purchased by United
manager Gordon Lee as a prospect to be
developed into a First Division defender. But
the £50,000 fee, a hefty sum for an unknown in
1976, was not in the end justified as Gorry
managed only a single appearance, as a
substitute for John Blackley at Maine Road.

Martin struggled to push
regular full-backs
Kennedy and Nattrass,
and their successors
Brownlie and Mitchell.
With Hartlepool he was
voted Player of the Year
in his first season with the
club totalling over 50
appearances at the
Victoria Ground.

Appearances:
FL: 0(1) app. 0 gls.
Total: *0(1) app. 0 gls.*

Martin Gorry

GOSNELL, Albert Arthur

Role: Outside-left & Trainer
1904-1910, 1919-1921
5' 10"
b. Colchester, 10th February 1880
d. Norwich, 6th January 1972

CAREER: The Albion(Colchester) cs 1898/
Colchester Town/New Brompton cs 1901/
Chatham cs 1902/UNITED May 1904 £10/
Tottenham Hotspur July 1910 £100/
Darlington cs 1911/Port Vale cs 1912 to 1915/
UNITED asst-trainer 1919/Norwich City
manager Jan 1921 to Mar 1926/Colchester
Town trainer cs 1926.

Debut v Middlesbrough (h) 5/11/04

A lively winger for a big
man who weighed in at
over 12 stone, Albert
Gosnell boasted a
consistent cross and
good shot but never got
on too well with
United's spectators,
probably as a result of
him replacing their
favourite, the
flamboyant Bobby
Templeton. Gosnell was
exactly the opposite in
character to Templeton;
steady, reliable and
thoroughly a team man. And
he was, despite the problems
encountered with the boo-boys, a
very effective player for United as they won
the championship in 1904-05 and 1906-07 and
justified his England selection. By the time the
Magpies had lifted their next title two years
later, Gosnell was only given a sparse run in
the side and was replaced, to the fans' delight,
by another Scottish maestro, George Wilson.
Gosnell had the best years of his career on
Tyneside and after leaving the game scouted a
little and then became a licensee in Norwich.

Albert
Gosnell

Appearances:
FL: 106 apps. 15 gls.
FAC: 18 apps. 3 gls.
Others: 1 app. 0 gls.
Total: *125 apps. 18 gls.*
Honours:
1 Eng cap 1906/Eng trial app. 1906/
FL champs 1905, 1907/FAC finalist 1905, 1906.

GOURLAY, Archibald Murdoch

Role: Midfield 1988-1992
5' 8"
b. Greenock, 29th June 1969

CAREER: Greenock Morton
1987/UNITED Mar 1988
£50,000(Greenock Morton
loan 1989-90)(Gateshead
loan 1991-92)/Motherwell
Apr 1992 free/Gateshead/
Linfield/ Hartlepool United 1993/Whitley Bay
cs 1994/Morpeth Town player-coach Mar 1995.

Debut v Luton Town (a) 3/12/88 (sub)

Archie Gourlay was only 19 years-old
when he joined Newcastle as a
skilful forward from Scottish
football. With only two games
to his name for Morton,
Gourlay was clearly the
unfinished article when he
arrived on Tyneside, but
possessed the look and style
that prompted Ossie Ardiles
to note him as "one of the
most talented players on our
books". Archie never
fulfilled his potential and
was almost totally restricted
to Central League football and
at one stage couldn't even get to
train with the senior pool. Slightly
built, he operated up front as well
as in midfield.

Appearances:
FL: 2(1) apps. 0 gls.
FLC: 0(2) apps. 0 gls.
Total: *2(3) apps. 0 gls.*

GOWLING, Alan Edwin

Role: Striker 1975-1978
6' 0"
b. Stockport, 16th March 1949

CAREER: Manchester University/Manchester
United amat Aug 1965, pro Aug 1967/
Huddersfield Town June 1972 £65,000/
UNITED Aug 1975 £70,000/Bolton Wanderers
Mar 1978 £120,000/Preston North End Sept
1982 free/Retired Aug 1983.

Debut v Ipswich Town (a) 16/8/75

Alan Gowling

Gangling, awkward-looking front-runner Alan Gowling never appeared overly skilful or even epitomised most fans idea of a footballer, but was nevertheless an extremely effective striker for the Magpies. A university graduate in economics, Gowling was a star youngster at Old Trafford, playing alongside established names like Charlton and Best, either in midfield or up front. Skipper of the England Under-23 side, Alan moved to Leeds Road for a record fee, but suffered two successive relegation seasons with Huddersfield as they plunged into the Division Four graveyard. His goalscoring record was still a good one - 61 for the Terriers - and it prompted Gordon Lee to rescue Gowling and place him alongside Malcolm Macdonald as Newcastle began the 1975-76 season. The partnership worked and the tall, lean Gowling ended up top scorer with 30 goals. His deceptive skill on the ground and power in the air proved a menace as United reached Wembley and afterwards qualified for the UEFA Cup. A bust-up with the Magpies over the sacking of Richard Dinnis led to Gowling moving on, to Bolton for another record fee. He later became Chairman of the PFA (1980-82) and was on the Management Committee from 1975 to 1984. He once scored four goals in a single match for both the Magpies and

Manchester United, while he turned down a place at Cambridge University to turn professional at Old Trafford. On retiring from the game, Gowling entered business in Lancashire and is General Manager of Seldon Research, a chemical manufacturing company.

Appearances:
FL: 91(1) apps. 30 gls.
FAC: 15 apps. 8 gls.
FLC: 9 apps. 7 gls.
Eur: 3 apps. 3 gls.
Others: 4 apps. 4 gls.
Total: *122(1) apps. 52 gls.*
Honours:
1 Eng u23 cap 1972/Eng sch app/Eng youth app/Eng amat app/British Olympic app. 1968/FA app. 1985/FL div 2 champs 1978/FLC finalist 1976.

GRAHAM, Douglas

Role: Left-back 1940-1950
5' 10"
b. Ashington, 15th July 1921
d. Newcastle upon Tyne, 10th November 1993

CAREER: Barrington United/UNITED war-guest 1939-40, pro Aug 1940 £20/ Middlesbrough war-guest 1941-42/Preston North End Nov 1950 £8,000/Lincoln City Dec 1951/St Gallen (Switzerland) player-coach July 1957/ Gateshead coach c1965.

Debut v Millwall (a) 31/8/46

Douglas Graham

A bricklayer-cum-joiner at Barrington Colliery, Douglas Graham was converted from a centre-forward to a stylish defender and was able to operate on the right or left flank. Graham was unfortunate to lose the best years of his career to World War Two. Nicknamed 'The Duke' on account of his immaculate attire, Graham also played with class on the field. On the resumption of peacetime football, he was part of United's promotion team in 1948 until a bad injury put him out of the side. He also helped Lincoln City to promotion, being skipper of the Imps. At Sincil Bank, he gave City over five years' splendid service totalling more than 200 outings. Graham married United coach, Norman Smith's daughter, and was an accomplished sprinter. Residing in Newcastle, he later worked for a Tyneside car dealer .

Appearances:
FL: 71 apps. 0 gls.
FAC: 3 apps. 0 gls.
War: 90 apps. 1 gl.
Total: *164 apps. 1 gl.*
Honours:
FL div 2 prom 1948/
FL div 3(N) champs 1952.

GRAHAM, John R.

Role: Outside-left 1901-1903
5' 7"
b. Newcastle upon Tyne

CAREER: Workington Diamonds/UNITED
Nov 1901/Bradford City Aug 1903 to cs 1905.

Debut v Bury (h) 28/12/01

A stand-in for regular winger Richard Roberts
during the 1901-02 season, John Graham was
"quick witted and dexterous on the green"
according to one Edwardian critic. But in
Newcastle's ranks he was always recognised
as a reserve, although Graham had a good
spell with Bradford City as they entered the
Football League scene in 1903.

Appearances:
FL: 6 apps. 0 gls.
Total: *6 apps. 0 gls.*

GRAHAM, Samuel

Role: Outside or Inside-right 1902-1905
5' 6"
b. Galston, Ayrshire,
7th April 1878

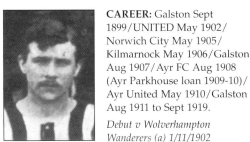

CAREER: Galston Sept
1899/UNITED May 1902/
Norwich City May 1905/
Kilmarnock May 1906/Galston
Aug 1907/Ayr FC Aug 1908
(Ayr Parkhouse loan 1909-10)/
Ayr United May 1910/Galston
Aug 1911 to Sept 1919.

Debut v Wolverhampton
Wanderers (a) 1/11/1902

Sam Graham

Sam Graham had a long career of over 20
years in the game, never reaching great
heights, but the Scot was a most dependable
player especially in Ayrshire football where he

was a well-known figure. At St James Park,
Sam deputised for internationals Jackie
Rutherford, Ronald Orr and Jimmy Howie
across the Magpies' forward line, and always
fitted in adequately, although unjustly
compared to his great contemporaries.
Graham won Northern League Championship
medals with the Novocastrians and was a
member of the Galston side that lifted the
Scottish Qualifying Cup in 1900.

Appearances:
FL: 5 apps. 0 gls.
FAC: 1 app. 0 gls.
Total: *6 apps. 0 gls.*

GRAHAM, William

Role: Centre-half 1892-1899
5' 10"
b. Ayr

CAREER: New
Cumnock/Preston North End
c1888/New Cumnock/ UNITED
July 1892 to Jan 1899 when he
returned to Scotland.

Debut v Sheffield United (a) 24/9/1892 (NL)

One of the Magpies' earliest stalwarts, Willie
Graham arrived from Scotland as Newcastle
East End had just completed their move from
Heaton to St James Park and in essence
became Newcastle United. He appeared in the
club's first fixture at St James Park and then in
the Northern League campaign for the 1892-93
season. And the following programme he was
on the field for the Tynesiders' debut in
Football League soccer, becoming a regular
during those formative years in Division Two.
Graham was a tireless worker in the middle of
the park and an inspiration on the field.
Captain of the club, he organised United's
team plan. When he left Gallowgate in 1899 it
was without the club's permission following a
dispute. His more famous brother, John
Graham, also appeared for Preston. Both men
took part in the Lilywhites' historic first
capture of the Football League title during the
inaugural season of competitive soccer in
1888-89.

Appearances:
NL: 10 apps. 2 gls.
FL: 88 apps. 10 gls.
FAC: 11 apps. 1 gl.
Total: *109 apps. 13 gls.*

GRAVER, Andrew Martin

Role: Centre-forward 1947-1950
5' 9"
b. Craghead, County Durham,
12th September 1927

CAREER: Quaking House jnrs/Willington Athletic/Annfield Plain cs 1947/UNITED Aug 1947 £25/Lincoln City Sept 1950 £5,000/Leicester City Dec 1954 £27,600/Lincoln City July 1955 £26,000/Stoke City Nov 1955 £12,000/Boston United Sept 1957 £1,000/Lincoln City Oct 1958 £2,500/Skegness Town July 1961/Ilkeston Town July 1962/Retired due to injury Nov 1963/Lincoln City asst-coach cs 1964 to Oct 1965, becoming a Lincoln scout.

Debut v Manchester City (a) 21/1/50

A centre-forward with youthful enthusiasm and no little talent, Andrew Graver found it difficult to break out of Newcastle's Central League side during the immediate post-war

Andrew Graver

years. He was given only a single chance in the senior eleven, as a stand-in to Jackie Milburn, but when he moved south in search of a regular first team place, Andy quickly developed into the most potent striker in the lower divisions. A household name in post-war football with Lincoln City, Graver holds the record aggregate scoring total for the Imps; 143 goals in 274 outings during three spells at Sincil Bank. In season 1951-52 when City won promotion, he was the Third Division (North) leading scorer with 36 goals which included netting six in one fixture against Crewe. Fast as well as direct, Andy was a leader who would chase anything that moved up front and commanded club record fees when he moved to Filbert Street and then back to Lincolnshire. His father, Fred, turned out for Grimsby and Leeds during the inter-war years while his brother, Alf was also on Lincoln's books for a time. Later Graver resided in the cathedral city, employed as a financial consultant.

Appearances:
FL: 1 app. 0 gls.
Total: *1 app. 0 gls.*
Honours:
FL div 3(N) champs 1952.

GRAY, Andrew D.

Role: Outside-right 1920-1921
5' 9"
b. Newcastle upon Tyne

CAREER: Jesmond Villa/UNITED Oct 1920 £10/Leadgate Park June 1921 free/South Shields 1921 to 1923.

Debut v Aston Villa (h) 4/12/20

Local product Andrew Gray appeared mainly as a half-back in United's reserve side, but was called up to deputise on the wing for William Aitken during the 1920-21 season. Without pushing the senior players for their place at St James Park, Gray later returned to local football before making a comeback in the Football League with South Shields.

Appearances:
FL: 2 apps. 0 gls.
Total: *2 apps. 0 gls.*

GREEN, Anthony

Tony Green

Role: Midfield 1971-1973
5' 7"
*b. Kinning Park, Glasgow,
30th October 1946*

CAREER: Drumchapel
Amateurs/Kirkintilloch Rob
Roy/Albion Rovers/Blackpool
May 1967 £15,000/UNITED Oct
1971 £150,000 cash-exch for
K.Dyson/Retired due to injury
Dec 1973.

Debut v Everton (a) 30/10/71

The all too brief career of Tony
Green is fondly cherished by
every Newcastle supporter who
saw him play. With United in
the relegation mire, Green landed on Tyneside
from Blackpool as the most expensive Scot on
record after becoming one of the hottest
properties in the country. He made 137
appearances for Blackpool - many in a fruitful
partnership with ex Newcastle star Alan
Suddick. With abilities on the ball that thrilled
the crowd and confounded opponents, the
boyish-looking Scot transformed the
black'n'whites as he combined with Hibbitt in
midfield and Macdonald in attack. Tony
buzzed with enthusiasm, darted into the action
and jinked past players in midfield. He
possessed splendid ball
control, a thundering shot and
a stunning change of pace that
often took him into the danger
zone. Tragically, though, Green
was hampered by injury,
firstly at Bloomfield Road,
then with United after a heavy
challenge against Crystal
Palace saw him stretchered off
with a knee ligament
complaint. Months of surgery
and recuperation followed, but
Tony was forced to quit the
game at an age when he
should have been at his peak.
His manager Joe Harvey was
to say: "It was the saddest day
of my life. He was my very
best buy". Simply to become
the idol Tony Green did in such a short stay on
Tyneside was a remarkable achievement in
itself. After leaving Tyneside, he returned to
the west coast, residing near Poulton-le-Fylde
where he became a schoolteacher. Green also
sits on the Pools Panel.

Appearances:
FL: 33 apps. 3 gls.
FAC: 2 apps. 0 gls.
Others: 3(1) apps. 0 gls.
Total: *38(1) apps. 3 gls.*
Honours:
6 Scot caps 1971-72.

GREENER, Ronald

Role: Centre-half 1951-1955
5' 11"
*b. Easington, County Durham,
31st January 1934*

CAREER: Easington Colliery/UNITED May
1951/Darlington June 1955 free to cs 1967.

Debut v Charlton Athletic (h) 3/10/53

Ron Greener made his inaugural appearance
in United's line-up as a 19 year-old deputy
for Frank Brennan and impressed everyone
with a composed display. In fact Ron hardly
put a foot wrong in his limited first-team
outings, but had to be content to watch
Brennan, then Stokoe and Paterson,
dominate the Number Five shirt. He made
up for the lack of opportunity with the
Magpies by moving to Feethams where he
proceeded to clock up a record total of
games for Darlington; 442
league fixtures and over 500
senior games all told - and
this despite overcoming the
handicap of a broken leg.
Ron performed with
wholehearted endeavour for
the Quakers for more than a
decade and was recognised
as an outstanding pivot in
the lower divisions.

Appearances:
FL: 3 apps. 0 gls.
Total: *3 apps. 0 gls.*
Honours:
FL div 3(N) app. 1957.

GREY, Thomas J.

Role: Centre-half 1908-1910, 1911-1915
5' 11"
b. Whitley Bay

CAREER: Bedlington United/UNITED Jan 1908 £70/Blyth Spartans Apr 1910/UNITED amat cs 1911 to 1915/Newcastle Bohemians 1919.

Debut v Aston Villa (a) 4/4/14

Respected local player Thomas Grey had two spells with United, his latter stay just prior to World War One being the more productive. Grey was then an amateur on Newcastle's books, one of the best in the country, being capped for his country and taking part in the English Wanderers tour to Scandinavia, although he missed out on England's Olympic gold victory in Stockholm in 1912. A stout player who operated when the centre-half role was mainly that of a midfielder, Tom claimed only a single first-team appearance for the Magpies, replacing the injured Wilf Low during season 1913-14.

Appearances:
FL: 1 app. 0 gls.
Total: *1 app. 0 gls.*
Honours:
3 Eng amat caps 1912-14.

GRUNDY, Arnold John

Role: Left-half 1936-1944
5' 8"
b. Whickham, nr Gateshead, 19th September 1919

CAREER: Dunston CWS/UNITED May 1936 £5 to May 1944 free/Liverpool war-guest 1940-41/Southport war-guest 1942-43.

Debut v Bradford City (h) 24/4/37

Arnold Grundy was only 17 years-old when he turned out for the Magpies, one of the youngest debutants on record. He was elevated to United's Second Division side in place of the injured Bill Imrie, but was never going to challenge the former Scottish

Arnold Grundy

international, or his successor Doug Wright, for the senior's jersey. Fast and, like Imrie, tenacious, he started his career at St James Park as an assistant in the club's offices. Inevitably, the outbreak of the Second World War virtually ended his professional career.

Appearances:
FL: 2 apps. 0 gls.
Total: *2 apps. 0 gls.*

GUPPY, Stephen Andrew

Role: Outside-left 1994
5' 11"
b. Winchester, 29th March 1969

CAREER: Southampton 1988/Colden Common(Hampshire)/Wycombe Wanderers 1989/UNITED Aug 1994 £150,000/Port Vale Nov 1994 £225,000.

Debut v Manchester United (h) 26/10/94 (sub)(FLC)

As a 25 year-old who had developed late onto the scene, Steve Guppy joined United after only one full season as a full-time professional. After a ten week trial period at The Dell he hadn't make the grade, but graduated through the non-league ranks with Wycombe, a star of Wanderers' rise under Martin O'Neill from the Vauxhall Conference to Second Division football. Tall and slimly built, Steve proved positive and penetrating and was purchased by Kevin Keegan purely as cover, although he was steadily developing his talents further. When Port Vale made an approach United accepted a profit on the deal - making his stay at Gallowgate one of the shortest on record, a mere four months. An ex bricklayer, Guppy's father was on West Bromwich Albion's books during the fifties.

Steve Guppy

Appearances:
FLC: 0(1) app. 0 gls.
Total: *0(1) app. 0 gls.*
Honours:
FAT winner 1993/VC champs 1993.

Chris Guthrie

GUTHRIE, Christopher William

Role: Centre-forward 1970-1972
6' 1"
b. Dilston, nr Hexham, 7th September 1953

CAREER: UNITED Dec 1970/Southend United Nov 1972 £10,000/ Sheffield United May 1975 £100,000/Swindon Town Aug 1977 £25,000/Fulham Sept 1978 £65,000/ Millwall Feb 1980 £100,000 to cs 1980/Retired due to injury Mar 1982/Witney player-manager July 1982/Roda JC(Holland) 1982/Willem II(Holland) 1982/Helmond Sport (Holland)/Seiko(Hong Kong) Feb 1984/Blyth Spartans Apr 1985/Racing White(Holland) Sept 1985/Ashington commercial manager/ UNITED kit-manager 1989 to Oct 1993.

Debut v Manchester United (h) 23/10/71

A schoolboy star, Chris Guthrie appeared for his country as a teenager, netting seven goals in six matches, and was a prominent goalscorer in United's junior and reserve elevens. Big and powerful, Guthrie had little opportunity though to break the first choice strike force of Macdonald and Tudor at St James Park and it was no surprise when he moved south to further his career. Chris returned to the big-time, commanding substantial fees, doing especially well with Southend (40 goals in 118 games) as well as at Bramall Lane and Craven Cottage. Younger brother of Ron Guthrie, who was with the Magpies during the same era although the pair never appeared in United's first-team together, Chris later rejoined United looking after the kit at St James Park. He became also an international fly fisherman in 1988 and later coached youngsters on Tyneside residing in the region. His son, Chris junior, appeared for Sunderland and Gateshead.

Appearances:
FL: 3 apps. 0 gls.
Others: 1 app. 0 gls.
Total: *4 apps. 0 gls.*
Honours:
Eng schools app/Eng youth app.

GUTHRIE, Ronald George

Role: Left-back 1963-1973
5' 10"
b. Burradon, Newcastle upon Tyne, 19th April 1944

CAREER: UNITED July 1963/Sunderland Jan 1973 £15,000/Ashington June 1975/Gateshead United 1975 free/Lusitano(South Africa) 1976/Blyth Spartans cs 1977/North Shields Sept 1981.

Debut v Aston Villa (a) 20/8/66

Ron Guthrie

A full-back with a biting tackle who had good distribution and was quick to recover, Ron Guthrie was unlucky to be second choice to Frank Clark during his near ten year spell with the black'n'whites. Occasionally used as a midfield power source too, Guthrie enjoyed a lot of crowd support and many would have liked to see the chunky defender find a place in United's side. However, injury didn't help his cause at Gallowgate and Ron was sidelined through two cartilage operations. But after his move to Sunderland he found better fortune, being part of Bob Stokoe's team that lifted the FA Cup. Guthrie is one of only a few modern cup winners to play in every round of the competition, including preliminary stages - a feat recorded when he was with Blyth. After quitting the game, Ron settled on Tyneside and for a time was employed by a local department store.

Appearances:
FL: 52(3) apps. 2 gls.
FAC: 0(1) app. 0 gls.
FLC: 2 apps. 0 gls.
Eur: 3(2) apps. 0 gls.
Others: 3 apps. 0 gls.
Total: *60(6) apps. 2 gls.*
Honours:
FAC winner 1973.

GUY, Alan

Role: Striker 1975-1979
5' 10"
b. Jarrow, 8th September 1957

CAREER: UNITED Sept 1975 (Shrewsbury Town loan 1977-78)/Peterborough United Mar 1979 £10,000, joint deal with A.Smith, to cs 1981.

Debut v Gillingham (a) 1/9/76 (FLC)

A regular junior and Central League scorer for United, Alan Guy lacked the craft and pace to perform at the highest level. Following a handful of opportunities, and once Peter Withe was installed in the striker's role on Tyneside, Alan was transferred to attempt a career in the Third and Fourth Division with Peterborough. Under the guidance of ex Magpie coach Peter Morris at London Road, Guy was converted to a midfield player.

Alan Guy

Appearances:
FL: 3(1) apps. 0 gls.
FAC: 2 apps. 0 gls.
FLC: 1 app. 0 gls.
Others: 1 app. 0 gls.
Total: *7(1) apps. 0 gls.*

HADDOCK, Peter Murray

Role: Central defender 1976-1986
5' 11"
b. Newcastle upon Tyne, 9th December 1961

CAREER: Cramlington Jnrs/UNITED 1976, pro June 1978/ (Dunedin City(New Zealand) loan cs 1985) (Burnley loan 1985-86)/Leeds United July 1986 £45,000/Retired due to injury July 1992.

Debut v Queens Park Rangers (a) 5/9/81

Peter Haddock was an outstanding schoolboy prospect, playing alongside Peter Beardsley for South Northumberland Boys, and he earned an early opportunity in United's first eleven during season 1981-82. Composed on the ball with accurate distribution, he was a regular in defence but the arrival of Glenn Roeder and the emergence of Steve Carney saw Haddock relegated to the fringes of, firstly, Arthur Cox's side and then Jack Charlton's. Peter moved on to join up with Leeds United and at

Peter Haddock

Elland Road found a regular place as the Tykes won promotion back into Division One. Injury, though, hampered his progress thereafter and he was out of action with a knee problem for 18 months. The injury eventually forced his early retirement from the game and Haddock returned to the north east, residing in Seghill. Suffering from a crippling arthritic complaint, a legacy of his football career, Peter opened a sports memorabilia shop and bakery outlet on Tyneside in 1996 and is related by marriage to United's assistant coach and former reserve player John Carver.

Appearances:
FL: 53(4) apps. 0 gls.
FAC: 3 apps. 0 gls.
FLC: 5 apps. 0 gls.
Total: *61(4) apps. 0 gls.*
Honours:
FL div 2 champs 1990.

HAGAN, Alfred

Role: Inside-right
1919-1923
5' 6"
*b. Usworth, Co. Durham,
10th November 1895
d. Sunderland, 1980*

CAREER: Washington Colliery/UNITED May 1919 £10/Cardiff City May 1923 £250/Tranmere Rovers July 1926 to cs 1927/Tyneside local football.

*Debut v Manchester United (a) 20/12/19
(scored once)*

Without having a great deal of height or build, Alf Hagan relied on his considerable ball skills which at times delighted the Tyneside crowd. A good reserve to have on the sidelines, Hagan appeared for United in both inside-forward roles, filling in for injured seniors during the immediate seasons after World War One. A pen picture of the day noted Alf as being "dainty and zealous", while he was always capable of grabbing an opportunist goal. He was the father of Jimmy Hagan, a noted player for Sheffield United and England during the mid 1950s. Alf served with the Northumberland Fusiliers during the hostilities.

Appearances:
*FL: 21 apps. 5 gls.
War: 4 apps. 1 gl.*
Total: *25 apps. 6 gls.*

HAIR, George

Role: Outside-left 1943-1949
5' 4"
*b. Ryton, nr Gateshead, 28th April 1925
d. Peterborough, 24th October 1994*

CAREER: Spen jnrs/UNITED May 1943 £10/Grimsby Town Feb 1949 £6,000/ Peterborough United Aug 1951/Boston United/Spalding United cs 1957.

*Debut v Barnsley (h) 5/1/46 (FAC)
(scored once)*

Claiming much local success before joining the Magpies, George Hair was a winger who could use both flanks, but who generally operated on the left for United. Appearing often during the war leagues for the club, Hair became a Gallowgate favourite with his perky displays, but as peacetime football resumed he was crowded out by the stylish Tom Pearson. Hair, a member of a then rare breed of footballers who wore contact lenses, was one of the club's key figures as the black'n'whites' reserve side won the Central League trophy in 1948. After retiring from the game, George was heavily involved with the Northamptonshire FA, living in the Peterborough area to his death. His son, Michael, became a Football League linesman for a period.

Appearances:
*FL: 23 apps. 7 gls.
FAC: 3 apps. 1 gls.
War: 51 apps. 14 gls.*
Total: *77 apps. 22 gls.*

George Hair

HALE, Kenneth Oliver

Role: Inside-right 1956-1962
5' 7"
b. Blyth, 18th September 1939

CAREER: Newsham Boys' Club/Everton 1955/UNITED Oct 1956/Coventry City Dec 1962 £10,000/Oxford United Feb 1966 £5,000/Darlington May 1968 £5,000, becoming caretaker-manager Jan to Apr 1972/Halifax Town player-coach Jan 1973 £500/Hartlepool United June 1974 to Sept 1976.

Debut v Tottenham Hotspur (a) 28/12/57

Blond-haired, stockily-built Ken Hale possessed good control and vision in midfield and initially was recognised as a reserve to either George Eastham or Ivor Allchurch at St James Park. After a brief spell at Goodison Park, Hale, with only two hours notice, made his teenage debut in front of over 51,000 at White Hart Lane. Once United's two star playmakers had departed Ken, who was versatile on either side of the park, was given an extended opportunity in seasons 1961-62 and 1962-63. In 26 outings, Hale had a good return, claiming fourteen goals, but new manager Joe Harvey decided he could leave as part of rebuilding plans. Ken joined Jimmy Hill's bright and breezy Coventry City set-up and helped them to promotion, a feat he achieved with Oxford too. He became an excellent forager and feeder at this level for over a decade, totalling over 400 senior

games. Ken resided in Seaburn, running a newsagency for a period and later working for Sunderland Health Service.

Appearances:
FL: 30 apps. 15 gls.
FAC: 1 app. 0 gls.
FLC: 4 apps. 1 gl.
Total: *35 apps. 16 gls.*
Honours:
FL div 3 champs 1964, 1968.

HALL, Alexander N.

Role: Centre-forward 1907-1908
5' 10"
b. Peterhead, 26th April 1906

CAREER: Edinburgh St Bernards/UNITED Apr 1907 £200/Dundee Mar 1908 £200/Portsmouth May 1910 to 1911.

Debut v Sheffield Wednesday (a) 7/9/07

Young Scot Alex Hall impressed United's selection committee on a tour of Germany during the summer of 1907 when he netted no fewer than ten goals in only three games, including a five goal strike against Freiburg. But Hall found gaining a place in Newcastle's star-studded side difficult, only standing in occasionally for Bill Appleyard. Alex had a similar physique to Appleyard - he was powerfully built and could hit a rasping shot - and played all his games for United in season 1907-08.

Appearances:
FL: 6 apps. 2 gls.
Total: *6 apps. 2 gls.*
Honours:
SL div 2 champs 1907.

HALL, Ernest

Role: Centre-half 1933-1937
5' 10"
b. Crawcrook, nr Gateshead, 6th August 1916

CAREER: West Wylam/UNITED Sept 1933 £10/Brighton May 1937 £100/Stoke City cs 1939.

Debut v Blackpool (h) 25/4/36

Ernest Hall was United's second-string centre-half, rivalling Dave Davidson and Tony Leach for the stopper's position in Newcastle's side. Ernie was given scant openings to show his true worth, only turning out on two occasions during the 1935-36 Second Division programme, although he was a regular in the Magpies' Central League side at a time when games attracted crowds approaching 20,000 to St James Park.

Appearances:
FL: 2 apps. 0 gls.
Total: *2 apps. 0 gls.*

·HALL, Thomas

Role: Centre-forward
1913-1920
5' 9"
b. Newburn, Newcastle upon Tyne

Tom Hall

CAREER: Newburn/Sunderland Jan 1909/ UNITED May 1913 £425/Leeds City war-guest 1918-19/Gillingham cs 1920, becoming trainer Aug 1926.

Debut v Sunderland (a) 6/9/13 (scored once)

Tom Hall had a headlining first outing for the Magpies, netting against his former club Sunderland in a Tyne-Wear derby at Roker Park. Part of the Reds' championship side, Hall was a play-anywhere forward; on the wing, at inside-forward or in the centre-forward's role, the position he favoured. An industrious leader possessing plenty of dash, Tom became a prolific scorer for the club's reserve side but, although an effective Number 9, didn't quite grab enough goals in senior company when he deputised for Albert Shepherd just before, and just after World War One. Tom did appear over 200 times for Gillingham. His brother, Bertie, joined the club in the inter-war years, but didn't get a first-team outing before appearing for Norwich City.

Appearances:
FL: 54 apps. 15 gls.
FAC: 4 apps. 1 gl.
Total: *58 apps. 16 gls.*
Honours:
FL champs 1913.

HALLIDAY, Bruce

Role: Centre-half 1977-1983
6' 0"
b. Sunderland, 3rd January 1961

CAREER: UNITED app July 1977, pro Jan 1979(Darlington loan 1982-83)/Bury loan Dec 1982, pmt cs 1983/Bristol City cs 1983/ Hereford United June 1985/Bath City cs 1987/ Apia Leichhardt (Australia) 1989/Gateshead Aug 1990/Dunston Federation 1993/Blyth Spartans asst-manager July 1996.

Debut v Chelsea (a) 25/10/80

After a harrowing first outing for United when Newcastle fell 6-0 at Stamford Bridge, Bruce Halliday, who was tough and brisk at the heart of the defence, showed for a period that he was capable of developing into a top centre-half. Maturing quickly, the Wearsider impressed many

Bruce Halliday

for half a season in 1980-81, but loss of form as the following campaign began saw a fellow home-grown product, Peter Haddock takeover in defence and Halliday drifted into the shadows. He later returned to the area to settle, playing non-league football extensively on Tyneside.

Appearances:
FL: 32 apps. 1 gl.
FAC: 4 apps. 0 gls.
FLC: 2 apps. 0 gls.
Total: *38 apps. 1 gl.*

HALLIDAY, William

Role: Inside-left 1927-1928
6' 1"
b. Dumfries, 14th November 1906
d. Dumfries

CAREER: Queen of the South 1922/UNITED Nov 1927 £1,000/Third Lanark June 1928 free/Connahs Quay/Exeter City cs 1930/St Cuthbert Wanderers (Dumfries) 1933.

Debut v Leicester City (a) 26/11/27

Brother of Sunderland idol Dave Halliday, Billy was a tall and powerful forward who came south with an excellent reputation. However, the Scot couldn't adapt to the English game and made only a solitary appearance for the Magpies when he stood in for Tom McDonald. Halliday, though, was a noted player for Queen of the South, claiming 64 games for the Dumfries club, netting 22 goals. On leaving the game, Billy resumed his trade as an electrician residing in southern Scotland until his death.

Appearances:
FL: 1 app. 0 gls.
Total: *1 app. 0 gls.*

HAMILTON, David Stewart

Role: Outside-right 1939-1946
5' 7"
b. Carlisle, 8th February 1919

CAREER: Shawfield jnrs/UNITED May 1939 £200/Southampton war-guest 1943-44/Fulham war-guest 1944-45/Queens Park Rangers war-guest 1945-46/Southend United May 1946 £100 to 1947.

Debut v Nottingham Forest (a) 30/8/39 (FLa)

Blond-haired winger Dave Hamilton had a most unfortunate career. Joining the United staff as a youngster full of promise, he had burst into the black'n'whites' senior team for the start of the 1939-40 season, quickly making an impact and forming a bond with the fans. But, with only three games of the new campaign completed, Germany's invasion of Poland put a stop to the first-class game and Hamilton's senior matches for Newcastle were expunged from the record book. More bad luck followed when he soon afterwards broke his leg in war football and, by the time peace

was restored five years later, Hamilton's career was in tatters. Yet, as a teenager, United saw him as a big star. He shone in the Scottish Junior Cup final and Stan Seymour immediately made a move to bring him to Tyneside and set him on the threshold of what could have been a brilliant career. Serving with the Black Watch, Tyneside Scottish regiment, during the war, Hamilton was one of the thousands evacuated from Dunkirk.

Appearances:
FLa: 2 apps. 1 gl.
War: 8 apps. 1 gl.
Total: *10 apps. 2 gls.*

HAMPSON, William

Role: Right-back 1914-1927
5' 9"
b. Radcliffe, nr Manchester, 26th August 1884
d. Congleton, 23rd February 1966

CAREER: Woolford Wesleyans/Ramsbottom/Rochdale cs 1905/Bury May 1906/Norwich City July 1909/UNITED Jan 1914 £1,250/Leeds City war-guest 1916-19/South Shields Sept 1927/Carlisle United manager Mar 1930 to May 1932/Ashington manager July 1934 to May 1935/Leeds United manager July 1935 to May 1947, becoming chief scout/Norwich City scout Oct 1947/Northumberland FA schools coach.

Debut v Sheffield Wednesday (a) 24/1/14

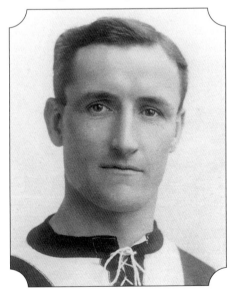

Billy Hampson

Billy Hampson was initially signed by United as cover to the club's noted full backs McCracken and Hudspeth, and consequently took some time to find a regular place. Able to play on either side of defence, he showed fine consistency and eventually took over the right-back role for season 1922-23. Hampson was a stylish and steady defender who, for many years, was thought to be - at 41 years and eight months - the oldest player to have taken part in an FA Cup Final, until his birth certificate was checked, revealing him to be two years younger! Billy played on for another two seasons

George Hannah

in Newcastle's first-team after that 1924 victory at Wembley, but by the time the Magpies embarked on their title campaign in 1927 the veteran Hampson was to play only twice more for the club before moving on, firstly to South Shields, and then to Carlisle where, as boss at Brunton Park, he discovered Bill Shankly. He later had a long spell in charge at Leeds United. During his early football career Hampson once appeared at centre-forward for non-league Norwich and scored twice in an FA Cup giant-killing feat over Sunderland. Billy, whose two brothers, Tom and Walker also played the game during the inter-war years, was an effective cricketer during the summer months.

Appearances:
FL: 163 apps. 1 gl.
FAC: 11 apps. 0 gls.
Total: *174 apps. 1 gl.*
Honours:
FAC winner 1924/War Lg champs 1918.

HANNAH, George L.

Role: Inside-left 1949-1957
5' 8"
b. Liverpool,
11th December 1928
d. Sale, 5th May 1990

CAREER: Everton amat/ Linfield/UNITED Sept 1949 £23,000 in a joint deal with A.McMichael/Lincoln City Sept 1957 £5,000/Manchester City Sept 1958 £10,000 plus player/ Notts County July 1964 £3,000/ Bradford City Oct 1965 £1,000/ Retired May 1966.

Debut v Manchester City (h)
17/9/49 (scored once)

Possessing delightful ball skills, the nine and a half stone and rather frail-looking George Hannah was a joy to watch when on form. He was a one-touch type of schemer, slick on the ball with a quicksilver movement but, like many of his breed, was never an automatic choice at St James Park, although he came into his own between 1952 and 1955; George played a star role in the FA Cup final victory over Manchester City, scoring at Wembley. Having an accurate and sure drive, he was always liable to find the net and at one stage was tipped in some quarters as sneaking an England cap. Hannah resurrected his career when he joined the Maine Road set-up in 1958, playing on until he was nearing 40 years old. As a teenager, he had moved to Ireland when serving with the Royal Ulster Rifles and was spotted, along with Alf McMichael, in the Linfield eleven. On leaving the game he ran a newsagency business in Fallowfield, Manchester for a while, as well as working for British Telecom.

Appearances:
FL: 167 apps. 41 gls.
FAC: 8 apps. 2 gls.
Others: 2 apps. 0 gls.
Total: *177 apps. 43 gls.*
Honours:
FA app 1957-64/1 NIL app. 1950/
FAC winner 1955.

HARDINGE, Harold Thomas William

Role: Centre-forward 1905-1907
5' 7"
b. Greenwich, London, 25th February 1886
d. Cambridge, 8th May 1965

CAREER: Eltham/Tonbridge/Maidstone
United/UNITED May 1905/Sheffield United
Dec 1907 £350/Woolwich Arsenal June 1913
£500/Retired cs 1921/Tottenham Hotspur
asst-coach 1935.

Debut v Sunderland (a) 2/9/05

Harry Hardinge

Harry Hardinge
was a member of
Newcastle's
reserve side for
most of his stay on
Tyneside, but later
developed into a
superb forward,
full of tricks and
good enough to
win an England
cap when at
Bramall Lane.
Nicknamed
'Wally', he stood in
for big Bill
Appleyard in a
black'n'white shirt
during the 1905-06
season and when Sheffield United took a
gamble on his transfer, quickly flourished as a
free-scoring inside-forward and occasional
leader of the attack. An intelligent and strong-
willed character, Hardinge also performed to
the top level at cricket, being a right-hand
batsman of distinction as well as a slow left
arm bowler. He appeared for Kent as a 16
year-old and continued as a noted player from
1902 to 1933, appearing in 607 first class
matches and totalling 33,519 runs including 75
centuries. Harry recorded 1,000 runs in a
season no fewer than 18 times, and in 1921
became a double England international when
he appeared against Australia at Headingley.
After leaving football he joined the well
known sports outfitters and publishers, John
Wisden and Company, becoming a senior
manager. Hardinge served as a Chief Petty
Officer in the Royal Navy air force during
World War One.

Appearances:
FL: 9 apps. 1 gl.
Total: 9 apps. 1 gl.
Honours:
1 Eng cap 1910/1 Eng Test(cricket) app.
1921/County champs(cricket) 1909, 1910,
1913/Wisden Cricketer of the Year 1915.

HARDWICK, Stephen

Role: Goalkeeper 1976-1983
5' 11"
b. Mansfield, 6th September 1956

CAREER: Chesterfield July 1974/UNITED
Dec 1976 £80,000(Detroit Express (USA)
loan cs 1978)/Oxford United Feb 1983
£15,000(Crystal Palace loan 1985-86)
(Sunderland loan 1987-88)/Huddersfield
Town July 1988 free/Boston United 1993.

Debut v Liverpool (a) 23/8/77

Steve Hardwick

A former England youth and amateur
international, Steve Hardwick followed the
line of fine Chesterfield goalkeepers that
produced the likes of Gordon Banks.
Newcastle's record goalkeeper purchase at the
time, Hardwick graduated into his country's
Under-21 squad when at St James Park and
then, following a brief spell in the States, took
over the Number One jersey from Mick
Mahoney. He quickly matured and showed
agility and confidence until a series of lapses

made him, to certain sections of the crowd, something of a villain. But Hardwick also put on the occasional wonderful display, although a lack of consistency eventually cost him his first team position to Kevin Carr. He assisted Oxford in their dramatic rise from the Third Division to Division One totalling 196 appearances, 158 games consecutive, for the Headington club. By the time Steve departed the senior circuit he had made almost 600 outings in league and cup football.

Appearances:
FL: 92 apps. 0 gls.
FAC: 4 apps. 0 gls.
FLC: 3 apps. 0 gls.
Eur: 2 apps. 0 gls.
Total: *101 apps. 0 gls.*
Honours:
Eng youth app. 1974/Eng amat app./FL div 3 champs 1984/FL div 2 champs 1985.

HARDY, Stanley

Role: Inside-left 1911-1918
5' 7"
b. Newcastle upon Tyne, 1890

CAREER: Rutherford College (Newcastle)/UNITED Nov 1911 £20 to 1918/Nottingham Forest secretary May 1929 to Jan 1932.

Debut v Sheffield United (h) 13/12/13

Stan Hardy had no easy task to break into United's exceptional line-up in the years up to the First World War and was unfortunate to be coming to his prime just when his contract was cancelled due to fighting on the continent. A clever midfield player who broke into attack, he joined Lord Kitchener's army - one of the club's first volunteers - signing for the Newcastle Quayside battalion of the Northumberland Fusiliers in September 1914. Rising to the rank of lieutenant in the machine-gun corps, Stan was severely gassed in the trenches and had to retire from soccer as peacetime resumed. Related to the celebrated goalkeeper, Sam Hardy of Nottingham Forest, he later became involved in the administrative side of the game at the City Ground.

Appearances:
FL: 3 apps. 1 gl.
Total: *3 apps. 1 gl.*

HARFORD, Michael Gordon

Role: Centre-forward 1980-1981, 1982
6' 2"
b. Sunderland, 12th February 1959

CAREER: Lambton Star Boy's Club (Sunderland)/Lincoln City July 1977/UNITED Dec 1980 £216,000/Bristol City Aug 1981 £160,000/UNITED Mar 1982 free/ Birmingham City Mar 1982 £100,000/Luton Town Dec 1984 £250,000/Derby County Jan 1990 £480,000/Luton Town Sept 1991 £325,000/Chelsea Aug 1992 £300,000/ Sunderland Mar 1993 £250,000/Coventry City July 1993 £200,000/Wimbledon Aug 1994 £75,000.

Debut v Grimsby Town (a) 26/12/80

A prolific scoring leader in the lower divisions with 40 goals in 115 league games for the Imps, 22-year-old Mick Harford cost United a Fourth Division record fee when he moved back to his native north east. Tall and slim, Mick was a target centre-forward, exceptional in the air and also possessing nice footwork for a big man. Yet, during his brief days on Tyneside under the management of Arthur Cox, Harford wasn't considered the man to replace the powerful play of Peter Withe and Cox quickly discarded his hidden potential. Mick moved to debt-stricken Bristol City for £160,000 but the Robins encountered difficulties with repayment of the transfer-fee instalments. Consequently, en route to St Andrews, the Wearsider made an unusual return to Gallowgate enabling the black'n'whites to recoup monies owed. From then on Mick's career took off. Joining Luton Town, he developed into the very centre-forward Newcastle had been searching for, showing subtle flicks and lay-offs, well-timed and often

Mick Harford

brave runs into the danger zone and ever-threatening going for a cross. Although hindered by knee operations, Harford gained England recognition before becoming an errant traveller during the latter days of his career, always proving something of a thorn to the Magpies whenever he faced United. As a kid Mick had trials at both St James Park and Roker Park.

Appearances:
FL: 18(1) apps. 4 gls.
Total: *18(1) apps. 4 gls.*
Honours:
2 Eng caps 1988-89/1 Eng B cap 1988/FLC winner 1988/FLC finalist 1989/FL div 2 prom 1985/FL div 4 prom 1981.

HARKER, Christopher Joseph

Role: Goalkeeper 1955-1961
5' 10"
b. Shiremoor, Newcastle upon Tyne, 29th June 1937

CAREER: Backworth Welfare 1952/West Allotment/UNITED Mar 1955(Consett loan 1958-59)(Aberdeen loan 1960-61)/Bury Dec 1961 £1,000/Grimsby Town June 1967/Rochdale July 1968 free/Darlington coach July 1970.

Debut v Burnley (h) 28/4/58

After making his debut in United's first eleven Chris Harker was unlucky to be called up for National Service during which time he was involved in a serious road accident that kept him out of football action. Harker really missed the chance of claiming Ronnie Simpson's goalkeeper's jersey and at one stage was third choice behind Bryan Harvey and Stewart Mitchell. Purchased however by former colleague Bob Stokoe, Chris, a former shipyard fitter, became a regular custodian at Gigg Lane, and later with Rochdale where he appeared almost 200 times. Whilst appearing for Bury,

Chris Harker

Chris was involved in the incident which led to the premature end of Brian Clough's playing career with a serious knee injury. Harker later resided in the Darlington area.

Appearances:
FL: 1 app. 0 gls.
Total: *1 app. 0 gls.*
Honours:
FL div 4 prom 1969.

HARRIS, Albert

Role: Outside-right 1935-1936
5' 4"
b. Horden, County Durham, 16th September 1912

CAREER: Herrington Swifts/Hull City May 1930/Blackhall CW cs 1931/UNITED Mar 1935 £100/Barnsley May 1936 £200/Darlington Jan 1937 to cs 1939.

Debut v Fulham (h) 28/9/35 (scored once)

Albert Harris was given a second chance at the Football League scene after completing an unsuccessful spell with Hull City. 'Diddler', as he was known to both colleagues and spectators, had reverted to local north east soccer with the Blackhall Colliery side but caught the eye with penetrating displays on the wing. The Magpies added the short but stockily built outside-right to their squad for the 1935-36 season when he rivalled Wilf Bott.

Albert Harris

With infinite courage and enthusiasm Harris, who could play on both wings and was as fast as they come, did well despite his limited opportunities and later impressed at Feethams with Darlington claiming over 70 games.

Appearances:
FL: 12 apps. 4 gls.
Total: *12 apps. 4 gls.*

HARRIS, Joseph

Joe Harris

Role: Wing-half 1925-1931
5' 8"
b. Glasgow, 19th March 1896
d. Glasgow, 29th October 1933

CAREER: Strathclyde jnrs/Partick Thistle 1913/Middlesbrough Mar 1923 £4,200/ UNITED Sept 1925 £750/York City June 1931 to his demise.

Debut v Liverpool (a) 25/12/25

When he arrived at St James Park nearing the end of his career, Scottish international Joe Harris rivalled both Willie Gibson and Roddie MacKenzie for the half-back role, being equally effective on the right or left side of midfield. Although no stylist, the tenacious Joe was dainty-footed and recorded nine outings during the Magpies' championship success in 1927. He always contributed on the field and was a consistent and commanding player at his peak. He became a regular immediately after United's title success and was a popular individual with the Geordie crowd. Whilst still on York's books, Harris died when only 37 years old in Glasgow Infirmary after a short illness.

Appearances:
FL: 149 apps. 2 gls.
FAC: 8 apps. 0 gls.
Total: *157 apps. 2 gls.*
Honours:
2 Scot caps 1921/Scot trial app. 1921-22/ SC winner 1921.

HARRIS, Neil L.

Role: Centre-forward 1920-1925
5' 7"
b. Tollcross, Glasgow, 30th October 1894
d. Swindon, 3rd December 1941

CAREER: Vale of Clyde/Partick Thistle June 1913/ Distillery war-guest/Kilmarnock war-guest 1916-17/Fulham war-guest 1918-19/ UNITED May 1920 £3,300/Notts County Nov 1925 £3,000/Oldham Athletic July 1927 £400/ Third Lanark Mar 1929 £400/Burton Town player-manager July 1931/Distillery manager May 1932/Swansea Town manager July 1934/Swindon Town manager May 1939 and occasional wartime player 1939-40 to his death.

Debut v West Bromwich Albion (h) 28/8/20

A daring centre-forward, Neil Harris possessed a born eye for an opening and packed a fearsome drive. At just over 5' 7", he was not a big leader, but proved a prolific goalscorer throughout his career and became one of only a handful of players to score over 100 goals for the Magpies. Yet Neil wasn't an instant hit at Gallowgate, having a difficult early period on Tyneside despite striking the net. At one stage he was transfer-listed before finding a rich seam of form which catapulted him to prominence as he led United to Wembley with his goals in 1924 -

N. HARRIS

including scoring in the cup final victory over Aston Villa. His aggressive style was awkward to play against, and he linked well with United's other cup heroes, Seymour and McDonald. Father of John Harris, later Chelsea player and Sheffield United manager, Neil's brother Joshua also appeared for Chelsea as well as Leeds, Fulham and Wolves. Another son, Neil jnr, also appeared for Swindon at the time of his father's management.

Appearances:
FL: 174 apps. 87 gls.
FAC: 20 apps. 14 gls.
Total: *194 apps. 101 gls.*
Honours:
1 Scot cap 1924/Scot trial app. 1924/
3 Scot jnr caps/FAC winner 1924/
FAVC finalist 1919.

HARROWER, James

Role: Inside-right 1961-1962
5' 9"
b. Alva, nr Stirling, 18th August 1935

CAREER: Sauchie Juveniles/Kilsyth Rangers/ Sauchie Juveniles/Bo'ness United/ Hibernian cs 1954/Liverpool Jan 1958 £11,500/ UNITED Mar 1961 £15,000/Falkirk Jan 1962 £3,115/ St Johnstone cs 1963/Albion Rovers 1965.

Debut v Tottenham Hotspur (a) 22/3/61

Jimmy Harrower enjoyed a good rapport with the Anfield crowd before heading for Tyneside after 105 games and 22 goals for the Reds. A player who excited the supporters with his typical Scottish talent, Jimmy was able to split a defence with a single pass, but could be temperamental, often entering into conflict with

Jimmy Harrower

officials. He arrived in a season of relegation troubles and suffered somewhat at Gallowgate; additionally he was alleged to have been purchased by director Stan

Seymour rather than manager Charlie Mitten who did not want the player. As a consequence the small, but heavily-built inside-forward pulled on a black'n'white shirt only six times and quickly drifted back to Scotland where his talents were always appreciated. Jimmy's grandfather and father both took the field for St Mirren.

Appearances:
FL: 5 apps. 0 gls.
FAC: 1 app. 0 gls.
Total: *6 apps. 0 gls.*
Honours:
1 Scot u23 cap 1958/Scot youth app.

HARVEY, Bryan Robert

Role: Goalkeeper 1958-1961
6' 0"
b. Stepney, London, 26th August 1938

CAREER: March Town/Wisbech Town 1956/ UNITED August 1958 £3,000/New York(USA) guest cs 1960/Cambridge City June 1961/Blackpool Mar 1962 £3,000/ Northampton Town Oct 1963 £1,000/ Kettering Town cs 1968 free.

Debut v Wolverhampton Wanderers (a) 20/9/58.

Agile and with a commanding frame, Bryan Harvey was plucked out of non-league football and given the United First Division goalkeeper's shirt after impressing many in Wisbech Town's FA Cup runs from 1957 and 1958. Bryan took over from the injured Simpson and displaced second choice Stewart Mitchell. Sound if not brilliant, Harvey's form suffered, like many of his colleagues, when the Magpies were stuck in a relegation battle during season 1960-61. Newcastle purchased Dave Hollins and Harvey moved on, eventually resurfacing as a key figure in the Cobblers' swift and dramatic rise from Division Four to Division One. He later resided in Northampton.

Appearances:
FL: 86 apps. 0 gls.
FAC: 4 apps. 0 gls.
FLC: 1 app. 0 gls.
Total: *91 apps. 0 gls.*
Honours:
FL div 2 prom 1965.

HARVEY, John

Role: Inside-right & Trainer
1897-1900
5' 4"
b. Scotland

CAREER: Renton/Sunderland 1889/
Clyde Jan 1891/Sunderland 1892/UNITED
May 1897 £40 in a joint deal with J.Campbell/
Retired cs 1899, becoming asst-trainer to c1900.

Debut v Woolwich Arsenal (h)
4/9/1897

A member of the celebrated
Sunderland 'Team of all the
Talent', Johnny Harvey took part
in the Wearsiders' first Football
League campaign as well as United's
inaugural Division One fixture. Arriving at St
James Park, very much as a personality with
experience and guile, he was noted as one of
the best players around who had not won an
international cap.
Nicknamed the 'Little Un',
he was only 5' 4", the
diminutive Harvey
became an influential
figure as Newcastle
gained promotion to the
First Division. He
played across the right
flank of the forward
line, occasionally taking
the leader's role too.
Some sources record his
surname as 'Harvie',
although United's
official archives note it
as 'Harvey'.

Appearances:
FL: 30 apps. 8 gls.
FAC: 5 apps. 2 gls.
Total: *35 apps. 10 gls.*
Honours:
FL champs 1893/FL div 2
prom 1898.

Bryan Harvey

Joe Harvey, a most popular servant to United as both a player and manager

HARVEY, Joseph

Role: Right-half, Coach & Manager
1945-1955, 1962-1989
6' 0"

b. Edlington, near Doncaster, 11th June 1918
d. Newcastle upon Tyne, 24th February 1989

CAREER: Edlington Rangers/Bradford Park Avenue May 1936/Wolverhampton Wanderers Nov 1936/Bournemouth May 1937/Bradford City cs 1938/Bradford Park Avenue war-guest 1941-2/Watford war-guest 1942-43/Aldershot war-guest 1943-45/York City war-guest 1943-45/Hartlepools United war-guest 1944-45/Aberdeen war-guest/Dundee United war-guest/UNITED Oct 1945 £4,250, becoming player-trainer June 1953, trainer Jan 1954/Crook Town trainer 1955/Barrow manager July 1955/Workington manager June 1957/UNITED manager June 1962 to Apr 1975, becoming chief scout and caretaker-manager Aug 1980, remaining associated with the club to his demise.

Debut v Barnsley (h) 5/1/46 (FAC)

A devoted servant to the Magpies for most of his adult life, Joe Harvey was an inspiring captain during the club's post-war glory years, then a popular manager as Newcastle won promotion, lifted a European trophy and reached Wembley. As a player he was lean and strong, a tough, uncompromising wing-half who performed best when the contest was at its most fierce. Harvey was developed in the war leagues, totalling 126 games for Bradford City before Stan Seymour brought the Yorkshireman north to Tyneside as a vital cog in the new Magpie machine. Having been a sergeant-major in the Royal Artillery, Joe then became a driving force on the field for United bellowing instructions all over the pitch as only he could. Skippering the Football League line-up, he lifted the FA Cup twice for United and was a coach at Wembley in 1955, before concentrating on learning the managerial skills in the backwaters of Cumberland. An unsuccessful applicant for the Newcastle manager's position when Charlie Mitten was appointed, he returned to Gallowgate

as boss following relegation in 1961. Harvey rebuilt the club and brought the Magpies out of obscurity and into an entertaining period, his teams always bristling with star names like Wyn Davies, Malcolm Macdonald and Jimmy Smith. While Joe won the Inter Cities Fairs Cup, Harvey always regretted not winning a major domestic trophy for United, and never wavered at the criticism hurled his way during his later days in charge of Gallowgate. In 1977 he was given a well deserved, though belated, testimonial (14,000) and, with nearly 40 years service to his name, remained an active personality at St James Park right up to his death.

Appearances:
FL: 224 apps. 12 gls.
FAC: 23 apps. 0 gls.
War: 33 apps. 1 gl.
Others: 1 app. 0 gls.
Total: *281 apps. 13 gls.*
Honours:
3 FL app. 1948-52/FL div 2 champs 1965(m)/FL div 2 prom 1948/FAC winner 1951, 1952/FAC finalist 1974(m)/ICFC winner 1969(m).

Joe Harvey

Jimmy Hay

HAY, James

Role: Left-half 1911-1919
5' 8"
b. Beith, Ayrshire, 12th December 1880
d. Ayrshire, 4th April 1940

CAREER: Woodside Annbank/Annbank jnrs/Glasgow Celtic trial May 1900/Ayr FC Jan 1902/Glasgow Celtic Mar 1903 £50/UNITED July 1911 £1,250/Ayr United war-guest 1915-18/Heart of Midlothian war-guest 1917-18/Clydebank war-guest 1918-19/Ayr United cs 1919, becoming player-trainer cs 1920/Clydebank manager 1921/Ayr United manager June 1924 to Jan 1926/UNITED scout 1928.

Debut v Bolton Wanderers (a) 2/9/11

The successor to the injured Peter McWilliam had to be an exceptional player and Jimmy Hay was just that. Captain of Celtic and Scotland, he was a naturally gifted midfielder, quick to support his attack and ever effective in spoiling the opposition's play. Jimmy had been one of the mainstays of Celtic's all conquering side north of the

border which lifted six championships in succession, recording 255 senior outings. Nicknamed 'The General' and 'The Man with the Iron Chest', the broad shouldered Hay signed for the Magpies after a dispute over terms at Parkhead. A powerful character on the park, mixing neat skills with anticipation and vigour, Hay was a regular in the black'n'white shirt during four seasons up to World War One, and while he never lifted a trophy with the Magpies, still displayed his obvious qualities. Hay was conscripted into the Royal Field Artillery and after the war became a controversial Scottish manager, often cynical of the game's administrators in his native country. Indeed he was suspended sine-die for a period following a bribery scandal in which he accused directors, officials and referees of illegal dealings. As a teenager Hay had signed for Glossop, but his father refused to let the youngster travel so far south.

Appearances:
FL: 132 apps. 8 gls.
FAC: 17 apps. 0 gls.
Total: *149 apps. 8 gls.*
Honours:
11 Scot caps 1905-14/6 SL app. 1909-11/ Scot trial apps. 1905-12/SL champs 1905, 1906, 1907, 1908, 1909, 1910/SC winner 1904, 1907, 1908, 1911/SC finalist 1909.

HAYNES

Role: Left-back 1894-1895
Debut v Crewe Alexandra (a) 9/3/1895

Seemingly a local player, Haynes stepped into the full-back's role for one appearance during United's second season in the Football League. He remained for the programme with the club, but did not get another opportunity in the senior eleven. However, it is suspected that this player could well be United's goalkeeper J. Hynd. Research indicates that the club's reserve custodian may have taken the position in an emergency. The name 'Haynes' appears in brief local reports of the match, but is not mentioned in the club records. The *Newcastle Evening News* of the day notes that Hynd actually "performed several times at full-back in his younger days".

Appearances:
FL: 1 app. 0 gls.
Total: *1 app. 0 gls.*

HEARD, Timothy Patrick

Role: Midfield 1984-1985
5' 10"
b. Hull, 17th March 1960

CAREER: Everton app, pro Mar 1978/Aston Villa Oct 1979 £100,000/Sheffield Wednesday Jan 1983 £60,000/UNITED Sept 1984 cash-exch for J.Ryan/Middlesbrough Sept 1985 £10,000/ Hull City May 1986/Rotherham United July 1988/Cardiff City Aug 1990 free to cs 1992.

Debut v West Ham United (h) 29/9/84

Brought to Tyneside by Jack Charlton to reinforce United's midfield after the departure of Terry McDermott, Pat Heard was a competent player who fitted into the United manager's plans during his one season in charge during 1984-85. Operating on the left of midfield, Heard had a bright teenage career and was capped by his country but was unable to claim a regular slot at any of his high profile clubs. Pat had, however, been on the bench for Aston Villa when they lifted the European Cup against Bayern Munich.

Appearances:
FL: 34 apps. 2 gls.
FAC: 2 apps. 0 gls.
Total: *36 apps. 2 gls.*
Honours:
1 Eng youth app. 1979/EC winner 1982(sub, no apps.)/FL div 4 champs 1989.

Pat Heard

HEDLEY, George

Role: Outside-left 1907-1908, 1910-1911
5' 11"
b. Newcastle upon Tyne

CAREER: UNITED amat cs 1907/Knaresborough cs 1908/UNITED cs 1910 to 1911.

Debut v Manchester United (h) 12/10/07

George Hedley was a well-known Tyneside amateur and handicap sprinter who was called up once into United's side as an eleventh hour replacement for Bert Gosnell. The arrival of international winger George Wilson saw Hedley frozen out at St James Park, although he returned for a second spell at Gallowgate as a centre-half, but failed to gain first team recognition. George's debut, and only outing, for Newcastle ended in a sensational 6-1 defeat at St James Park by Manchester United. His brother W.Hedley was also on the club's books in the Edwardian period but didn't reach the senior team.

Appearances:
FL: 1 app. 0 gls.
Total: *1 app. 0 gls.*

HEDLEY, Richard

Role: Outside-right 1894-1895
b. Newcastle upon Tyne, 1873
d. Newcastle upon Tyne, 1908

Dick Hedley

CAREER: Marlborough(Newcastle)/Arthurs Hill(Newcastle)/Newcastle Albion/UNITED amat cs 1894 to Oct 1894/Jarrow 1895/ UNITED 1895/Hebburn Argyle 1896.

Debut v Notts County (h) 22/9/1894

Another local league favourite, once described as "spry and fearless" and "the pick of United's reserve forwards", Dick Hedley was one of the ball dribblers of the day who loved to speed down the wing and take on defenders. However, before the Tynesider was able to make a big impression on the Football League scene, an unfortunate clash with Newcastle's hierarchy led to his departure. Hedley was one of several amateur reserves who demanded payment and went on strike. Due to this industrial action the club disbanded the 'A' team and he was dismissed along with several of his colleagues, although Dick made a brief appearance a few months later. He afterwards became seriously ill for a lengthy period and died at the youthful age of 35 years. His widow was given a benefit game at St James Park.

Appearances:
FL: 3 apps. 1 gl.
Total: *3 apps. 1 gl.*

HEDWORTH, Christopher

Role: Centre-half 1982-1986
6' 1"
b. Wallsend, 5th January 1964

CAREER: UNITED app, pro Jan 1982/ Barnsley July 1986 free/Halifax Town July 1988 free/Blackpool Sept 1990 to cs 1992.

Debut v Leeds United (a) 30/10/82 (sub)

Chris Hedworth was a reserve defender who graduated through United's youth set-up under Arthur Cox to make the fringe of the club's senior team. Tall and slim, Hedworth was given a debut in season 1982-83 as the Magpies won promotion, and then further outings in the First Division. However, Chris never looked likely to develop enough to become a top class defender and moved to the lower divisions where he concluded his career. He once found himself between the posts for United in a dramatic 8-1 defeat at Upton Park in season 1985-86; having taken over from the injured Martin Thomas, Chris also had to leave the field with a knock, leaving Peter Beardsley to end up as United's 'keeper.

Chris Hedworth

Appearances:
FL: 8(1) apps. 0 gls.
FLC: 1 app. 0 gls.
Total: *9(1) apps. 0 gls.*

HENDERSON, James

Role: Inside-right 1919-1920
5' 10"
b. Newcastle upon Tyne

CAREER: Scotswood/Cardiff City cs 1913/ UNITED May 1919 £50/Scotswood 1920/ Ashington July 1920/Spennymoor United Jan 1923.

Debut v Arsenal (a) 30/8/19 (scored once)

As a young Geordie, James Henderson was robbed of a career at Ninian Park due to the outbreak of the First World War, but after serving with the Lancashire Fusiliers and on the armistice he started again as a Magpie player. He showed enough talent in pre-season fixtures to be given the inside-right position for the opening game of the 1919-20 campaign at Highbury, and proceeded to net Newcastle's first goal after the Great War had ended. Although smart and fast, he was replaced later in the season by Ed Dixon and afterwards appeared for Ashington in their inaugural Football League season.

Appearances:
FL: 6 apps. 1 gl.
Total: *6 apps. 1 gl.*

HENDERSON, John

Role: Goalkeeper 1895-1897
6' 0"
b. Scotland

CAREER: Clyde/UNITED cs 1895 to 1897

Debut v Loughborough Town (h) 7/9/1895

John Henderson

Burly goalkeeper John Henderson was purchased to take over the custodian's position for the beginning of the 1895-96 Second Division season. Henderson came south from Scotland with a first-class record and gave some sterling displays in his period with the club. However, some reports noted that he had "given alarm to the dodgy hearted" on occasion and John was replaced by Charlie Watts within a year.

Appearances:
FL: 30 apps. 0 gls.
FAC: 5 apps. 0 gls.
Total: *35 apps. 0 gls.*

HENDRIE, John Grattan

Role: Outside-right 1988-1989
5' 7"
b. Lennoxtown, 24th October 1963

CAREER: Coventry City app June 1980, pro May 1981(Hereford United loan 1983-84)/ Bradford City June 1984 free/UNITED June 1988 £500,000/Leeds United June 1989 £600,000/Middlesbrough June 1990 £550,000/ Barnsley Oct 1996 £300,000.

Debut v Everton (a) 27/8/88

United's most expensive winger at the time, John Hendrie settled in the north-east as one of Willie McFaul's several purchases in an attempt to quieten the uproar over Paul Gascoigne's sale. A consistent forward with Bradford City, John had missed only a single game for the Bantams in four seasons and totalled 212 league and cup matches scoring an impressive 59 goals. Recognised as one of the best players outside the First Division, Hendrie was part of McFaul's new side that never blended together, although John himself was an individual success. By the end of the 1988-89 season, relegation and a managerial change was the outcome and, to finance Jim Smith's rebuilding, Hendrie moved on - to Leeds United where he tasted success, as he did at Ayresome Park. John was four times part of a promoted side, although twice relegated too. He was in Bradford City's team when the tragic Valley Parade fire disaster occurred in May 1985.

John Hendrie

Appearances:
FL: 34 apps. 4 gls.
FAC: 4 apps. 0 gls.
FLC: 2 apps. 1 gl.
Others: 3 apps. 0 gls.
Total: *43 apps. 5 gls.*
Honours:
6 Scot youth app./FL div 1 champs 1995/FL div 2 champs 1990/FL div 3 champs 1985/FL div 2 prom 1992.

HESLOP, George Wilson

Role: Centre-half 1959-1962
5' 11"
b. Wallsend, 1st July 1940

CAREER: Dudley jnrs/UNITED Feb 1959/ Everton Mar 1962 part-exch for J.Fell/ Manchester City Sept 1965 £25,000(Cape Town City(S.Africa) loan 1971-72)/Bury Aug 1972 £3,000/Northwich Victoria manager Dec 1977/Bury coach cs 1978 to June 1980.

Debut v Everton (h) 7/11/59

Tall, well-built and blond-haired, George Heslop made his debut for United in an 8-2 victory over one of his future clubs, Everton. George rivalled Bill Thompson as Bob Stokoe's replacement in United's side, but had little joy in a Magpie shirt moving to Goodison Park where he struggled to displace Brian Labone. It was, though, when he joined Manchester City that Heslop enjoyed considerable success, being a rock in their

George Heslop

defence as Joe Mercer and Malcolm Allison fashioned a marvellous line-up at Maine Road. Turning out on 198 occasions, he won championship, cup and European honours and later was a publican in Manchester, at The Hyde Road Hotel, the original home of the Light Blues.

Appearances:
FL: 27 apps. 0 gls.
FAC: 1 app. 0 gls.
FLC: 4 apps. 0 gls.
Total: *32 apps. 0 gls.*
Honours:
FL champs 1968/FL div 2 champs 1966/ FLC winner 1970/ECWC winner 1970.

HEWARD, Harold Aubrey

Role: Left-half 1932-1934
5' 8"
b. Hetton-le-Hole, County Durham,
31st August 1910

CAREER: Herrington Swifts/UNITED Mar
1932 £20/Bradford Park Avenue Aug
1934/Hartlepools United July 1935 to cs 1936.

Debut v Huddersfield Town (a) 11/2/33

Harry Heward was a whole-hearted player,
splendid in the tackle and not prone to
making rash clearances. A ninety minute man,
he never let the Magpies down when called
upon to deputise for John Murray at half-back.
Harry made all his black'n'white outings
during the 1932-33 season before moving to
Second Division rivals Bradford Park Avenue.

Appearances:
FL: 5 apps. 0 gls.
Total: *5 apps. 0 gls.*

HEWISON, Robert

Role: Right-half 1908-1920
5' 8"
b. Backworth, Newcastle upon Tyne,
25th March 1890
d. Bristol, 1964

CAREER: East Holywell Villa/Whitley
Athletic/UNITED July 1908 £10/Leeds City
loan 1914, becoming player-manager to Dec
1919 when he returned to Newcastle/
Northampton Town player-manager May 1920
£250/Queens Park Rangers player-manager cs
1925 to May 1931/Bristol City manager Mar
1932 to Mar 1949/Guildford City manager/
Bristol Rovers scout/Bath City manager
May 1957/ Retired 1961.

Debut v Notts County (h) 8/10/10

Steady midfield exponent Bob Hewison,
despite several injuries, was developed into a
solid but unspectacular professional and a
loyal player, giving United grand service for
three seasons before the outbreak of the Great
War. Bob began at St James Park as a youthful
rival to the renowned Colin Veitch, eventually
replacing the Magpie stalwart. When
Newcastle all but closed down during the First

Bob Hewison

World War,
Hewison teamed
up with the Leeds
City outfit and
spent the four
years appearing for
the Tykes. He won
wartime honours
before becoming
embroiled in the
Leeds City scandal
that rocked the
game in 1919 and
led to his club
being expelled from the Football League.
Returning to Gallowgate, Bob was unable to
find a first-team place and continued his career
in management, later again becoming involved
in controversy at Ashton Gate when he was
suspended during season 1938-39 after an
illegal payment inquiry. Hewison,
characterised by suit and glasses, was
nevertheless a respected manager by that time
and in 1943 was awarded the Football League's
Long Service medal. Hewison also took charge
of the League's representative side.

Appearances:
FL: 67 apps. 0 gls.
FAC: 3 apps. 0 gls.
Total: *70 apps. 0 gls.*
Honours:
War Lg champs 1918/SnL champs
1960(m)/FL Long Service medal 1943.

Fred Heywood

HEYWOOD, Frederick

Role: Inside-left 1900-1902
5' 5"
b. Turton, Lancashire, 1881

CAREER: Turton/UNITED cs 1900/Blackpool cs 1902/Reading cs 1903/Blackpool cs 1904/Turton/Chorley.
Debut v Derby County (a) 16/2/01

A pygmy figure at inside or centre-forward, the slightly-built Lancashire-born Heywood was full of cunning and showed plenty of grit and determination. One account of his style of play noted he had only one objective every time he received the ball; to make a bee-line for goal. His snaky runs were a feature of his play and although he only gained opportunities in one season for the black'n'whites - 1900-01 - Heywood later became a noted figure in Lancashire football.

Appearances:
FL: 13 apps. 3 gls.
Total: *13 apps. 3 gls.*

HIBBERT, William

Role: Inside-forward 1911-1920
5' 8"
b. Golborne, nr Wigan, 21st September 1884
d. Blackpool, 16th March 1949

CAREER: Golborne/Newton-le-Willows/Bryn Central 1904/Bury May 1906/UNITED Oct 1911 £1,950/Sheffield Wednesday war-guest 1917-18/Leeds City war-guest 1917-19/Bradford City May 1920 £700/Oldham Athletic May 1922 £500/Fall River(USA) trainer cs 1923/J & P Coats (Rhode Island, USA) 1925/Valencia (Spain) trainer June 1927/

Wigan Borough trainer May 1928/Burscough Rangers Feb 1930/Budapest FC(Hungary) trainer Aug 1930/Retired 1938.
Debut v Blackburn Rovers (h) 21/10/11

Billy Hibbert cost United a new British record transfer fee when he moved from Lancashire to St James Park. A nimble, enthusiastic and most skilful forward who played in the inside positions as well as leading the attack, the five foot eight inch Hibbert possessed the goal-poacher's instinct and became one of the country's top strikers after topping Bury's scoring list for four years in a row during their First Division years. Signed by United to replace the goalscoring talent of Albert Shepherd, Billy never quite lived up to his billing in terms of goals, yet was a popular player in a black'n'white shirt before and after the war. Capped by England and the Football League, he also took part in the FA's first tour of South Africa in 1910 when he scored an amazing 34 goals during the programme. Hibbert bagged over 200 goals in his career and later travelled the continent teaching the game. After retiring Billy settled in Blackpool.

Appearances:
FL: 139 apps. 46 gls.
FAC: 16 apps. 3 gls.
War: 4 apps. 1 gl.
Total: *159 apps. 50 gls.*
Honours:
1 Eng cap 1910/Eng trial app. 1912-13/1 unoff Eng app. 1910/3 FL app. 1908-11.

HIBBITT, Terence Arthur

Role: Midfield 1971-1975, 1978-1981
5' 7"
b. Bradford, 1st February 1947
d. Ponteland, nr Newcastle upon Tyne,
5th August 1994

CAREER: Leeds United app Apr 1963, pro
Dec 1964/UNITED Aug 1971 £30,000/
Birmingham City Sept 1975 £100,000/UNITED
Apr 1978 exch deal for S.Barrowclough/
Retired due to injury June 1981/Gateshead
July 1981, becoming player-coach Jan 1983,
manager Apr 1986/Durham City asst-manager
Oct 1986.

Debut v Crystal Palace (a) 14/8/71

One of United's best-ever bargain buys, Joe
Harvey picked up Terry Hibbitt for a paltry
fee from Don Revie's Leeds squad during a
period of rebuilding by Newcastle's boss. At
the same time, Malcolm Macdonald arrived on
Tyneside and the Hibbitt-Supermac
combination was to give the Magpies a new
dimension. Although small and frail-
looking, Terry possessed a sweet left foot
and forged a great understanding from
his midfield role with his centre-forward
team-mate, providing accurate long-ball
service to capitalise on Macdonald's pace. A
bubbly and, at times, fiery character, Hibbitt
was quickly adopted by United's supporters,
every bit the hero Macdonald was. On the
fringe of an England call-up as Newcastle
reached Wembley in 1974, Terry was a great
competitor with a lion's heart and always
urged his colleagues on. Injury and the arrival
of new boss Gordon Lee saw him move on,
but Hibbitt returned as captain for a second
spell on Tyneside as Newcastle tried to reclaim
their former status. Another injury forced his
departure from the senior game, but Terry
went on to lift the Northern Premier title with
Gateshead and reach the FA's non-league
England side. After quitting the game, he
became a newsagent and milkman for a while
before settling as manager of a pub in
Ponteland on the outskirts of the city. An
adopted Geordie, Terry Hibbitt cruelly died
of cancer when only 46 years old. His
brother Kenny appeared over
500 times for Wolves during
the same era.

Appearances:
FL: 227(1) apps. 12 gls.
FAC: 15 apps. 1 gl.
FLC: 16 apps. 0 gls.
Others: 33 apps. 5 gls.
Total: *291(1) apps. 18 gls.*
Honours:
*FA app. 1982/FL champs 1969/FAC finalist
1974/ICFC winner 1968/NPL champs 1983.*

HIGGINS, Alexander

Role: Inside-forward 1905-1919
5' 9"
b. *Kilmarnock, 4th November 1885*
d. *Newcastle upon Tyne, 15th March 1939*

CAREER: Belle Vue jnrs/Kilmarnock 1904/
UNITED June 1905 £250/Hull City war-guest
1916-17/Kilmarnock Aug 1919/Nottingham
Forest June 1920/Jarrow player-manager Sept
1921/Norwich City Nov 1921/Wallsend Dec
1922/Berne(Switzerland) trainer 1925/Preston
Colliery Nov 1926.

Debut v Aston Villa (h) 24/3/06

Sandy Higgins

Sandy Higgins came to prominence during United's league title campaign of 1908-09 after being signed from Scotland as a teenager three seasons before. He was one of several versatile players to be groomed as stars of the future on United's books during their Edwardian heyday, and operated at either inside-forward position or at centre-forward. Possessing a marvellous left-foot, he could ghost past defenders with ease and proved himself as a big match player with an abundance of craft. A superb purveyor of passes, Sandy sometimes tended to be rather selfish when in possession, and never quite developed into the household name he perhaps should have become, although he was capped by Scotland and recognised as one of the best forwards around. Son of the famous Kilmarnock and Forest international of the same name, his younger brother joined United in 1910 without breaking through. Sandy missed the 1920 Scottish Cup final due to the death of his father a few hours before the match, however he was still given a medal. Serving in World War One with the Durham Light Infantry, the Scot was awarded the Military Medal and a citation. After retiring from the game Higgins settled on Tyneside running a grocer's business in Byker as well as being employed as a publican in the city.

Appearances:
FL: 126 apps. 36 gls.
FAC: 24 apps. 5 gls.
Total: *150 apps. 41 gls.*
Honours:
4 Scot caps 1910-11/Scot trial app. 1910/FL champs 1909/FAC winner 1910/FAC finalist 1911/SC winner 1920(no app.)

HIGGINS, William

Role: Centre-half 1898-1900
5' 11"
b. *Smethwick, nr Birmingham, 1870*

CAREER: Woodfield/Albion Swifts/
Birmingham St George/Grimsby Town 1892/
Bristol City May 1897/UNITED May 1898/
Middlesbrough May 1900/Newton Heath
Sept 1901 to 1902.

Debut v Wolverhampton Wanderers (h) 3/9/1898

Purchased by United's officials in readiness for the Magpies' debut in the First Division, William Higgins appeared in the club's first ever Division One fixture against Wolves and was an experienced and steady head as Newcastle consolidated their newly found status. With a role in the

William Higgins

centre of midfield, although he also played at full-back and centre-forward for United too, one contemporary report noted he was a "fearless player" and was especially regarded for sweeping passes to the wings as well as his stinging shots at goal. Nicknamed 'Sandy', he had made his name at Grimsby Town where he clocked up 126 games (27 goals). Not only the first captain of Bristol City, he also skippered the black'n'whites and was in contention for international honours.

Appearances:
FL: 35 apps. 3 gls.
FAC: 4 apps. 0 gls.
Total: *39 apps. 3 gls.*
Honours:
1 FL app. 1897.

HILL, John Henry

Role: Centre-half 1928-1931
6' 3"
b. Hetton-le-Hole, County Durham,
2nd March 1897
d. Scotland, April 1972

CAREER: Durham City 1919/Plymouth Argyle Sept 1920/Burnley May 1923 £5,450/UNITED Oct 1928 £8,100/Bradford City June 1931 £600/Hull City Nov 1931, becoming manager Apr 1934 to Jan 1936, and scout 1948-1955.

Debut v Sunderland (a) 27/10/28

Red-haired, tall and lanky, Jack Hill was one of the elite of the twenties decade. Captain of England, as well as United and Burnley, he was a constructive centre-half remembered for his stunning duels with Magpie legend, Hughie Gallacher. It was in fact Gallacher who recommended Hill to United's directors when they were

Jack Hill

searching for a powerful defensive pivot to replace Charlie Spencer. Making 198 outings for Burnley, he was considered by many - including Gallacher - to be the best in the country and Newcastle paid a club record fee when Jack moved back to his native north-east, the Magpies just beating off the challenge of Sunderland for his signature. Always willing to move forward from the back line with a constructive urge, Hill possessed quality distribution and was a towering figure on the field, in both personality and build. After a couple of seasons of grand service, Hill though fell into dispute with United's directors which led to his premature departure. A former miner in the Durham coalfield, Hill began in Durham City's Football League eleven and after a

spell with Scarborough running their pools department moved to Helensburgh on the west coast of Scotland to retire.

Appearances:
FL: 74 apps. 2 gls.
FAC: 4 apps. 0 gls.
Total: *78 apps. 2 gls.*
Honours:
11 Eng caps 1925-29/3 FL apps. 1924-26/1 SnL app. 1923/Eng trial app. 1923-26/FL div 3(N) champs 1933.

HILL, James Matthew

Role: Inside-right 1957-1958
5' 8"
b. Carrickfergus, Northern Ireland,
31st October 1935

CAREER: Carrickfergus YMCA/Carrick Rangers/Linfield 1953/UNITED June 1957 in an exch deal for J.Milburn/Norwich City July 1958 £3,000/Everton Aug 1963 £25,000/Port Vale Oct 1965/Derry City player-manager Mar 1968/Linfield manager Aug 1971 to 1972/Carrick Rangers manager Nov 1988 to May 1991.

Debut v Tottenham Hotspur (h) 31/8/57

Jimmy Hill never blossomed into the player that had been promised at St James Park following his arrival from Windsor Park as part of the transfer which saw Jackie Milburn leave Tyneside. A rival to Gordon Hughes in season 1957-58, Hill was given a run during the first half of the programme, but

Jimmy Hill

then was replaced by Hughes and remained in the Central League side during his short stay at Gallowgate. Jimmy moved to Carrow Road and claimed conspicuous success with Norwich, a key member of the Canaries noted FA Cup giant-killing runs and a goalscorer when City lifted the Football League Cup in 1961-62. Although some considered Hill a luxury, others reckoned he was a match-winner, scoring 66 senior goals in 195 games when at his peak with Norwich. Although Jim played mainly on the right of midfield, or on the wing, for United, he spent most of his career on the left. Capped at every level for Northern Ireland, he was nicknamed 'Tiger'. Hill settled in Carrickfergus and runs a sports shop.

Appearances:
FL: 11 apps. 2 gls.
Total: *11 apps. 2 gls.*
Honours:
7 N.Irel caps 1959-64/2 N.Irel B caps 1958-60/6 NIL apps. 1956-69/N.Irel youth app./ N.Irel schools app./N.Irel amat app./FLC winner 1962/FL div 3 prom 1960/NIC finalist 1971.

HILLEY, David

Role: Inside-forward 1962-1967
5' 9"
b. Glasgow, 20th December 1938

CAREER: Muirend Amateurs/ Jordanhill 1958/Pollock Jnrs 1958/Third Lanark June 1958/UNITED Aug 1962 £40,000 incl S.Mitchell/Nottingham Forest Dec 1967 £25,000/Highlands Park(S.Africa) 1970/ Hellenic (S.Africa) 1973/Scarborough Oct 1975/South Shields cs 1976 to cs 1977/ Bedlington Terriers 1977/Retired 1978.

*Debut v Cardiff City (a) 18/8/62
(scored once)*

As Joe Harvey's replacement playmaker for the departed Ivor Allchurch, Dave Hilley cost United a big fee at the time as a player recognised as one of the best north of the border, unlucky not win a full Scottish cap. Chased by the Magpies for almost two years, the slightly-built Scot took time to bed in United's camp, but by the time Newcastle were to make a push to regain their First Division place in 1964, Hilley had settled into a schemer's role that was to be central to United's championship success. With Scottish skills to the fore, Dave was capable of creating openings and hitting the net on a regular basis, scoring 12 important goals during that trophy-winning season in 1964-65. An automatic choice by Harvey for five years, Hilley later resided on Tyneside in High West Jesmond, becoming a schoolteacher at Oakfield College in Newcastle's west end until his retirement in 1996. He also reported on north east soccer for the *Sunday Post*.

Appearances:
FL: 194 apps. 31 gls.
FAC: 8 apps. 1 gls.
FLC: 7 apps. 1 gl.
Total: *209 apps. 33 gls.*
Honours:
2 Scot unoff apps. 1961-62/2 Scot u23 caps 1961/1 SL app. 1960/Scot schools app./FL div 2 champs 1965/SLC finalist 1960/FAT winner 1976/S. African cup winner 1973.

Dave Hilley

HINDSON, Gordon

Role: Midfield 1968-1971
5' 9"
*b. Quaking Houses, County Durham,
8th January 1950*

CAREER: UNITED Aug 1968/Luton Town
Oct 1971 £27,500(Carlisle United loan 1975-
76)(Blackburn Rovers loan 1975-76)/Hartford
Connecticut(USA) 1976/Evenwood Town cs
1976/Consett, becoming coach Aug 1979/
Spennymoor United Jan 1981/Gateshead Nov
1981/Consett player-coach Jan 1984, becoming
manager June 1984.

Debut v Southampton (a) 15/2/69

Gordon Hindson was a fast and determined
midfield player who began at outside-left in
United's junior and reserve set-up. He was on
the fringes of United's side during the club's
European campaigns but found it difficult to
claim a place, his seven games for the Magpies
being spread over four seasons. Gordon did
well at Kenilworth Road, however, making
almost 100 appearances, including an FA Cup
victory at St James Park
in 1973. Following a
broken ankle, he
departed the Football
League scene,
afterwards serving
local non-league sides
with distinction.
Hindson resided in the
north east and was
employed in
management at
Stanley and, later,
Newburn leisure
centres.

Appearances:
FL: 7 apps. 1 gl.
Eur: 0(1) app. 0 gls.
Total: *7(1) apps. 1 gl.*
Honours:
NPL champs 1983.

Gordon Hindson

HISLOP, Neil Shaka

Role: Goalkeeper 1995-date
6' 4"
b. Hackney, London, 22nd February 1969

CAREER: Baltimore Blast(USA) May 1992/
Reading July 1992 trial, pmt Sept 1992/
UNITED Aug 1995 £1.575m.

Debut v Coventry City (h) 19/8/95

Like most of Kevin Keegan's big money deals,
Shaka Hislop had been a target for several
months before the 6'4" goalkeeper arrived in
Newcastle. Considered the best guardian
outside the Premiership, Hislop is agile and
safe in the air, and in many ways is very
similar in style to his rival Pavel Srnicek.
Although born in London of Caribbean
parents Shaka, whose name originates from a
Zulu king, lived most of his youth in Trinidad.

The son of a lawyer and magistrate, Hislop played teenage football and cricket, alongside Brian Lara, before moving to the USA were he studied mechanical engineering at a Washington university. Awarded a four-year football scholarship, he was spotted by Reading's ex Magpie boss, Mark McGhee while playing in a friendly contest for Baltimore Blast against Aston Villa at the NEC; Shaka turned on a stunning display and was given a chance in the Football League. Hislop rapidly became the Elm Park club's Number One choice, appearing on 126 occasions and helping the Royals to promotion, and then very nearly to the Premier League before Reading lost a Wembley play-off in 1995. Hislop is United's tallest player, along with Reilly and Beasant, and wears size 11 boots and size 11 gloves! His brother Kona appeared for the Magpies' reserve eleven before trying to begin a career elsewhere.

Appearances:
PL: 24 apps. 0 gls.
FLC: 4 apps. 0 gls.
Total: *28 apps. 0 gls.*
Honours:
Trinidad schools app./Trinidad youth app./ FL div 2 champs 1994.

Trevor Hockey

HOCKEY, Trevor

Role: Outside-right 1963-1965
5' 6"
b. Keighley, 1st May 1943
d. Keighley, 1st April 1987

CAREER: Keighley Central 1957/Bradford City app May 1958, pro May 1960/ Nottingham Forest Nov 1961 £15,000/ UNITED Nov 1963 £25,000/ Birmingham City Nov 1965 £22,500/Sheffield United Jan 1971 £50,000/Norwich City Feb 1973 cash-exch deal/Aston Villa June 1973 £38,000/Bradford City June 1974 £12,500/Athlone Town player-manager Mar 1976/San Diego Jaws(USA) Apr 1976/Las Vegas Quicksilvers(USA) Apr 1977/ San Jose Earthquakes(USA) June 1977/ Stalybridge Celtic manager Aug 1977/ Keighley Town manager Oct 1980.

Debut v Cardiff City (h) 9/11/63

During his early days as a footballer, the diminutive Trevor Hockey was a fast-raiding winger and a match-winner on his day but, like many talented forwards, suffered inconsistency. He occasionally appeared as a midfielder for the Magpies as the club won promotion, just when football was changing into the modern style. During the seventies Hockey modelled himself into a midfield general, tenacious and hardworking, and characterised by his long hair and bushy beard. Becoming one of the personalities of that era, Trevor eventually totalled over 600 senior games in a chequered and nomadic career. Relishing a battle on the field, he was charismatic and fiery and, qualifying due to his father's nationality, good enough to win international honours for Wales. The extrovert Trevor once owned a velvet-covered car and played a pink piano in a rock group. Hockey for a time coached in Germany and at Pontin's holiday centres, later running a hotel in his home town. He sadly collapsed and died when only 43 years old after playing five-a-side football. Both his grandfather and father were noted rugby league players.

Appearances:
FL: 52 apps. 3 gls.
FAC: 2 apps. 0 gls.
FLC: 2 apps. 0 gls.
Total: *56 apps. 3 gls.*
Honours:
9 Wales caps 1972-74/FL div 2 champs 1965/FL div 2 prom 1971.

Glyn Hodges

HODGES, Glyn Peter

Role: Midfield 1987
6' 0"
b. Streatham, London, 30th April 1963

CAREER: Wimbledon app Feb 1981, pro Apr 1981/UNITED July 1987 £300,000/Watford Sept 1987 £300,000/Crystal Palace June 1990 £410,000/Sheffield United loan Jan 1991, pmt Apr 1991 £410,000/Derby County Feb 1996 free/Goldon Club (Hong Kong) July 1996.

Debut v Tottenham Hotspur (a) 19/8/87

Completing almost 300 games for the Dons, Glyn Hodges, Wimbledon's first ever full international, was a regular in the line-up that leapt from Division Four to Division One. He was a left sided midfield player with good touch and a stinging shot that frequently tested goalkeepers. However, despite his talents, Hodges only had a brief stay on Tyneside operating wide on the left, a position in which he was never comfortable. After only 86 days as a United player, manager Willie McFaul told the Welshman to train with the juniors and he was allowed to move back to London. Glyn later rejoined his Wimbledon manager Dave Bassett

at Bramall Lane where he displayed his best football. His transfer to Sheffield United was in fact only sanctioned after fund-raising by supporters' clubs.

Appearances:
FL: 7 apps. 0 gls.
Total: *7 apps. 0 gls.*
Honours:
18 Wales caps 1984-96/1 Wales B cap 1991/5 Wales u21 caps 1983-84/3 Wales youth apps./FL div 4 champs 1983/FL div 2 prom 1986/FL div 3 prom 1984.

HODGSON, Gordon H.

Role: Midfield 1971-1974
5' 11"
b. Newcastle upon Tyne, 13th October 1952

CAREER: UNITED June 1971/Mansfield Town May 1974 £8,000/Oxford United Sept 1978 £30,000/Peterborough United Aug 1980 £10,000/Kings Lynn cs 1982.

Debut v Nottingham Forest (a) 8/4/72

A schoolboy find by Newcastle United, Gordon Hodgson had the potential to become a big name in top football. Exceptionally skilful, he developed quickly through the Magpies' junior ranks to push hard for a first-team place, but the wall of quality players in front of him - men like Hibbitt, Smith, Cassidy and McDermott - proved an unmovable obstacle. After a handful of games, plus many outings on the bench, Gordon moved down a couple of leagues where he became one of the best players in the lower divisions, twice skippering Mansfield to promotion and appearing on 213 occasions for the Stags. He was also captain at Oxford and after leaving the game joined the police force in Peterborough.

Appearances:
FL: 8(1) apps. 0 gls.
FAC: 1 app. 0 gls.
Others: 1(2) apps. 0 gls.
Total: *10(3) apps. 0 gls.*
Honours:
Eng youth app./Eng schools app./FL div 3 champs 1977/FL div 4 champs 1975.

Gordon Hodgson

HODGSON, Kenneth

Role: Outside-right 1959-1961
5' 10"
b. Newcastle upon Tyne, 19th January 1942

CAREER: Montague & N.Fenham YC/
UNITED May 1959/Scunthorpe United Dec
1961 £3,000/Bournemouth June 1964/
Colchester United July 1966 £4,000/
Poole 1968.

Debut v Nottingham Forest (h) 14/1/61

As a teenager Ken Hodgson was a bright prospect, versatile across the forward-line, although preferring the outside-right channel. After impressing Charlie Mitten when he netted 54 goals in youth leagues, Hodgson was given a contract at Gallowgate. His chance for first team

Ken Hodgson

action came in the 1960-61 season, a year of relegation strife for Newcastle, when he deputised for Gordon Hughes. With the club's demotion at the end of the programme, Hodgson was not included in their plans and he moved to the Old Show Ground as part of the deal that brought Barrie Thomas north. He began a decent career with Third and Fourth Division clubs, especially with Scunthorpe where he scored 30 goals in 88 league matches. Ken afterwards returned to Tyneside setting up a business in Newcastle distributing hearing-aid equipment.

Appearances:
FL: 6 apps. 0 gls.
FAC: 1 app. 0 gls.
Total: *7 apps. 0 gls.*

HOLLAND, Christopher James

Role: Midfield 1994-1996
5' 9"
b. Whalley, nr Blackburn, 11th September 1975

CAREER: Preston North End 1992/UNITED
Jan 1994 £100,000/Birmingham City loan Sept
1996, pmt Oct 1996 £600,000.

Debut v Ipswich Town (h) 23/3/94

Signed by Newcastle as a youngster to be groomed for the future, Chris Holland hardly appeared in Preston North End's senior side, but had given United's management glimpses of a talented repertoire which prompted the club to pay £100,000 for his services. And such was his progress at St James Park that Chris was appearing for England's Under-21 side within 18 months, a further progression through his country's ranks as Holland had already played for both the schools and youth sides. Furthermore, Chris was called up to train with the full England squad in December 1995. Labelled by some as the second 'Gazza', Holland possesses a striking resemblance and similar style on the field to the England star. He has a good touch on the ball and feeds both short and long passes accurately. In 1995 his blossoming career was threatened following an incident in a Newcastle nightclub; he was sprayed in the face with ammonia, and hospitalised in a fight to save the sight of his right eye. Chris recovered swiftly but couldn't break into United's side and departed to St. Andrews. As a teenager,

he was chased by Everton, Blackburn, Liverpool and Leeds as well as United. On his debut for the black and whites Chris created two goals against Ipswich Town.

Appearances:
PL: 2(1) apps. 0 gls.
FLC: 0(1) app. 0 gls.
Total: *2(2) apps. 0 gls.*
Honours:
7 Eng u21 caps 1995-96/Eng youth app./Eng schools app.

Chris Holland

HOLLINS, David Michael

Role: Goalkeeper 1961-1967
6' 0"
b. Bangor, Wales, 4th February 1938

CAREER: Merrow(Guildford)/Brighton
app Nov 1955, pro Mar 1956/UNITED Mar
1961 £11,000/Mansfield Town Feb 1967
£2,500(Nottingham Forest loan 1969-
70)/Aldershot July 1970 (Portsmouth loan
1970-71)/Romford Sept 1971.

Debut v Tottenham Hotspur (a) 22/3/61

After signing from Brighton as a
replacement for Bryan Harvey, Dave
Hollins had a remarkable opening few
weeks as a Newcastle player. He saved a
penalty on his debut against the eventual
'Double' winners, Spurs, then saw Chelsea
plant six goals past him on his first
appearance at St James Park and finally
witnessed United's relegation from
Division One four weeks later. Agile and
acrobatic, Hollins at times looked a
wonderful 'keeper making a string of
breathtaking stops which earned him
recognition on the international stage for
Wales. But he failed to maintain such a
high standard week in and week out and,
following a dispute with new manager Joe
Harvey over wages, the Magpies brought in
Gordon Marshall as first choice. Hollins was
transferred and served Mansfield with
distinction in 126 games, being part of their FA
Cup giant-killing line-up that reached the
sixth round in 1968-69. Dave came from a well
known footballing family; his father Bill was a
'keeper for Wolves, his brother John was a
household name at Chelsea and another
brother, Roy, turned out for Brighton.
Strangely, Dave and John played international
football for different countries with John
appearing for England. After quitting the
game, Hollins settled in Guildford running a
decorating business, while he also played
bowls for the London Welsh club.

Appearances:
FL: 112 apps. 0 gls.
FAC: 3 apps. 0 gls.
FLC: 6 apps. 0 gls.
Total: *121 apps. 0 gls.*
Honours:
11 Wales caps 1962-66/
2 Wales u23 caps 1960-61.

Dave Hollins

HOOPER, Michael Dudley

Role: Goalkeeper 1993-1996
6' 3"
b. Bristol, 10th February 1964

CAREER: Mangotsfield United/Swansea
City/Bristol City 1983/Wrexham loan Feb
1985, pmt July 1985/Liverpool Oct 1985
(Leicester City loan 1990-91)/UNITED Sept
1993 £550,000(Sunderland loan 1995-96)/free
transfer July 1996.

Debut v West Ham United (h) 25/9/93

Although purchased for £550,000 from
Liverpool to become United's Number One
goalkeeper, Mike Hooper was destined to be
third choice behind Srnicek and Hislop.
Following an initial run in United's
Premiership line-up during 1993-94, the well-
built 6'3" red-haired 'keeper lost form,
confidence and his place to his Czech rival,
Srnicek, Hooper rarely receiving a look-in
afterwards. Prior to heading for Tyneside,
Mike spent most of his career as reserve to

Mike Hooper

Bruce Grobbelaar at Anfield. Hooper had a good season with Liverpool in 1988-89 (17 apps.) and totalled over 50 games for the Reds before joining the Magpies' staff. He had a major disappointment on Merseyside when he was left out of the Liverpool 1992 FA Cup final side in favour of Grobbelaar after appearing in several of the games between the semi-final and final. A keen bird watcher and fell walker, Hooper holds a degree in English taken at Swansea University. Mike had a short loan spell with United's arch rivals Sunderland in season 1995-96.

Appearances:
PL: 23(2) apps. 0 gls.
FAC: 3 apps. 0 gls.
FLC: 2 apps. 0 gls.
Total: *28(2) apps. 0 gls.*

HOPE, George

Role: Centre-forward 1971-1975
5' 10"
b. Haltwhistle, Northumberland, 4th April 1954

CAREER: UNITED app 1971, pro Apr 1972/Charlton Athletic May 1975 free/York City loan Nov 1976, pmt Dec 1976 £1,000/ Wezel Sport(Belgium) May 1978 free.

Debut v Leicester City (a) 10/11/73

On his home debut for Newcastle United, youngster George Hope made all the headlines, scoring the winner in a 3-2 victory. He stood in for the injured Malcolm Macdonald and did reasonably well, considering he was thrown into combat with experienced First Division defenders. George, though, had little chance to find a regular position when Supermac was fit, or to displace John Tudor, so the inevitable transfer soon followed. He didn't make an impression at The Valley, but did a little better with York City claiming 48 games. George had trials with Workington's Football League side before joining United's apprentice scheme. He is presently employed as a car salesman in York.

Appearances:
FL: 6 apps. 1 gl.
Total: *6 apps. 1 gl.*

HOPE, John Williams March

Role: Goalkeeper 1969-1971
6' 0"
b. Shildon, County Durham, 30th March 1949

CAREER: Darlington May 1967/UNITED Mar 1969 £8,000/Sheffield United Jan 1971 exch deal for J.Tudor(Preston North End loan 1973-74)/Hartlepool United July 1975/Stockton coach Oct 1980/Wingate manager cs 1986/ Whitby Oct 1988/Willington manager c1989 to Jan 1991/Hartlepool United asst coach/Darlington coach.

Debut v Manchester City (a) 5/5/69

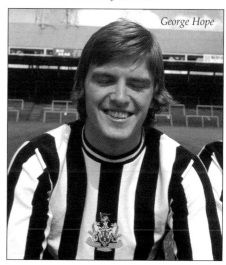

George Hope

John Hope

Arthur Horsfield

John Hope was reserve to international goalkeeper Willie McFaul at St James Park over a period which included United's early years in European football. Hope was on the bench for many of the club's Inter Cities Fairs Cup ties, including the final against Ujpesti Dozsa in 1969. Tall, strong and ideally built for the Number One shirt, he found a regular slot with the Blades at Bramall Lane despite a number of knee operations. John's son, Chris, played with Darlington, Nottingham Forest and Scunthorpe.

Appearances:
FL: 1 app. 0 gls.
Total: *1 app. 0 gls.*
Honours:
ICFC winner 1969(sub, no app.)/
FL div 2 prom 1971.

HORSFIELD, Arthur

Role: Striker 1969
5' 11"
b. Newcastle upon Tyne, 5th July 1946

CAREER: Montague & N.Fenham YC/ Middlesbrough app cs 1962, pro July 1963/ UNITED Jan 1969 £17,500/Swindon Town May 1969 £17,000/Charlton Athletic June 1972 £15,000/Watford Sept 1975 £20,000/Dartford Aug 1977, later becoming coach.

Debut v Southampton (a) 15/2/69

A former Newcastle city schools star at both soccer and athletics, Arthur Horsfield grew up a goal-kick away from St James Park, but began his footballing career further down the east coast at Ayresome Park. He was 22 years old when he returned to Tyneside as a stop-gap purchase and had an unlucky opening for his home town club when he netted on his first outing at Manchester City after just two and a half minutes, only for the game to be abandoned due to heavy rain. Never too fast or flamboyant, Horsfield was nevertheless a good team player always able to strike the ball cleanly. With Charlton he appeared on 156 occasions, all of which were consecutive - a record for the Londoners. He was Division Three's leading marksman in 1972-73 and, when with Swindon Town, netted a hat-trick in the 1969 Anglo-Italian Cup final, twice helping to win the trophy for the Robins. Arthur concluded his career as a centre-half. He later resided in Gravesend, for a period working as a postman and managing a social club.

Appearances:
FL: 7(2) apps. 3 gls.
Eur: 1 app. 0 gls.
Total: *8(2) apps. 3 gls.*
Honours:
Eng youth app. 1964/FL div 3 prom 1975.

HOTTIGER, Marc

Role: Right-back 1994-1996
5' 10"
b. Lausanne, Switzerland, 7th November 1967

CAREER: Renens (Switzerland)/Lausanne-Sports (Switzerland) 1988/FC Sion (Switzerland) 1992/UNITED July 1994 £520,000/Everton Mar 1996 £700,000.

Debut v Leicester City (a) 21/8/94

The first of Kevin Keegan's two signings from the 1994 USA World Cup stage, Marc Hottiger had stood out for Switzerland in that tournament and cost United a bargain fee for an established international full-back. A regular in Newcastle's Premier League side for season 1995-96, Marc could look back on his first season in England with much satisfaction. He showed a cool attitude and ability to link with the attack in the modern wing back style, causing opponents problems down the right flank. Yet, despite a good start on Tyneside, he was squeezed out of contention for a first team

Marc Hottiger

HOUGHTON, Frank Calvert

Role: Wing-half 1948-1953
5' 9"
b. Preston, 15th February 1926
d. Exeter, 19th August 1994

CAREER: Preston North End amat 1942/Derry City 1944/Ballymena United/UNITED Jan 1948 £6,000/ Exeter City June 1953 free, becoming trainer in 1957.

Debut v Leicester City (h) 31/1/48

Frank Houghton will always be remembered on Tyneside for his two goals against Sheffield Wednesday that virtually clinched United's promotion to the First Division in 1948. An honest, slightly-built, play anywhere individual, he tragically lost the best years of his career due to injury and illness. Whilst serving in Ireland with the RAF, Frank was spotted by the Magpies and joined the club just as the black'n'whites were developing a fine set-up. His best season was in 1949-50 when he appeared on 32 occasions in a number of roles, right-half, inside-left and centre-forward. A year later though, Houghton contracted tuberculosis, his weight at one stage dropping to just eight stones. As a result he missed almost three seasons, being sent to Switzerland to recuperate for a time. Unfortunately he then broke his leg, later moving to the other St James Park at Exeter and unluckily fractured his leg once again. Frank once remarked, "my career reads more like a medical chart". Houghton made a home for himself in the south-west country, becoming a well known bookmaker to his demise. He was related to the famous trumpeter of the 1950's, Eddie Calvert, hence his middle name.

Appearances:
FL: 55 apps. 10 gls.
FAC: 2 apps. 0 gls.
Total: *57 apps. 10 gls.*
Honours:
FL div 2 prom 1948.

place by the £4 million signing of Warren Barton, as well as the versatility of local lad Steve Watson. Hottiger was left on the sidelines and, with his international place in danger due to lack of regular action, made a move to Everton, although that transfer was almost jettisoned by problems over work permits. The French-speaking Hottiger can also play in midfield, on the wing, or in the centre of the defence, and captained Switzerland during September 1994.

Appearances:
PL: 38(1) apps. 1 gl.
FAC: 4 apps. 1 gl.
FLC: 6(1) apps. 0 gls.
Eur: 4 apps. 0 gls.
Total: *52(2) apps. 2 gls.*
Honours:
62 Switz caps 1989-96.

Frank Houghton

HOWARD, Patrick

Role: Centre-half 1971-1976
5' 11"
b. Dodworth, Yorkshire, 7th October 1947

CAREER: Barnsley app Apr 1963, pro Oct 1965/UNITED Sept 1971 £23,000/Arsenal Sept 1976 £50,000/Birmingham City Aug 1977 £40,000(Portland Timbers(USA) loan 1978)/ Bury July 1979 free to cs 1982.

Debut v Wolverhampton Wanderers (h) 18/9/71

A blond-haired, forceful stopper centre-half, Pat Howard quickly became a popular character at St James Park following a bargain transfer from Barnsley. Purchased initially as a stand-in for the injured Bob Moncur, Pat's form in the heart of United's defence was so good that he eventually formed a commanding partnership with Moncur. Brian Clough once noted that Howard - at his peak in 1975 - was one of the top five central defenders in the country. Appearing twice at Wembley for the Magpies, Pat was rugged and uncompromising, and made up for a lack of the finer skills by reading the game well and possessing an indomitable will to win. More than a few doubted the wisdom of allowing his departure when he quickly followed Malcolm Macdonald to Highbury. Howard later worked as a Football in the Community officer in Manchester and also for the PFA's

education organisation. In 1988 he was Football Administrator for Salford Council as well as conducting an FA School of Excellence in Manchester. For a period he also opened a snooker centre and sports shop in Bury.

Appearances:
FL: 182(2) apps. 7 gls.
FAC: 23 apps. 1 gl.
FLC: 19 apps. 0 gls.
Others: 37 apps. 1 gl.
Total: *261(2) apps. 9 gls.*
Honours:
FAC finalist 1974/
FLC finalist 1976/
FL div 4 prom 1968.

HOWEY, Stephen Norman

Role: Centre-half 1986-date
6' 2"
b. Sunderland, 26th October 1971

CAREER: UNITED app 1986, pro Dec 1989.

Debut v Manchester United (a) 13/5/89 (sub)

Beginning his career as an out and out striker in over 30 games for the Magpies, Steve Howey's progress in that role had been destined to end up in the lower divisions like many of United's junior developments. But a crucial switch into the heart of United's defence was made in 1991, initially by Ossie Ardiles, but more positively by Kevin Keegan thereafter, and Howey's career took off. Installed in the pivot's role for the 1992-93 championship campaign, he showed that his height and build, as well as his pace, aggression and ball skills, were perfect qualities for the position. His ability to move forward, and distribute accurate passes fitted smoothly into Keegan's tactical plan. And, as a bonus, Howey is always dangerous in attack where his original striker's instincts give United's attack a boost at set pieces. Overcoming a troublesome groin injury which saw the Wearsider out of action after several operations, on and off, for over 12 months, Steve became a regular in Terry Venables' England squad. This after being

Pat Howard

Steve Howey

selected on several occasions for the Under-21 side, but unluckily having to withdraw because of injury. His brother, Lee, appears for Sunderland.

Appearances:
FL/PL: 127(19) apps. 5 gls.
FAC: 11(2) apps. 0 gls.
FLC: 13(2) apps. 1 gl.
Eur: 3 apps. 0 gls.
Others: 5 apps. 0 gls.
Total: *159(23) apps. 6 gls.*
Honours:
4 Eng caps 1995-96/1 unoff Eng app. 1996/ FL div 1 champs 1993.

Jimmy Howie

HOWIE, James

Role: Inside-right 1903-1910
5' 10"
b. Galston, Ayrshire, 19th March 1878
d. London, January 1963

CAREER: Galston Athletic/Kilmarnock May 1898(Galston Athletic loan 1900-01)/ Kettering Town 1901/Bristol Rovers May 1902/UNITED May 1903 £300/ Huddersfield Town Dec 1910 £675/ Queens Park Rangers manager Nov 1913 to Mar 1920/Middlesbrough manager Apr 1920 to July 1923.

Debut v Aston Villa (h) 2/9/03

Recognised as one of the very best inside-forwards in the game during his era prior to World War One, Jimmy Howie was known as 'Gentleman Jim' and possessed a style that oozed finesse. He was a genius at creating opportunities and also at taking chances himself from his midfield role - netting 82 goals for the Magpies during his seven full seasons at Gallowgate. With a peculiar hopping-running action, Howie linked to perfection with Jackie Rutherford on United's right wing, an international pairing that had much to do with the club's three championship winning feats and their first FA Cup victory. Jimmy boasted a remarkable dribble on the ball and, although he wasn't fast, delighted the crowd with flair and entertainment. His younger brother David, was on Newcastle's books just prior to the war, but moved on to have a decent career with Bradford Park Avenue. Following a spell in management, Jimmy resided in London running a tobacconist shop.

Appearances:
FL: 198 apps. 68 gls.
FAC: 37 apps. 14 gls.
Others: 2 apps. 0 gls.
Total: *237 apps. 82 gls.*
Honours:
3 Scot caps 1905-08/1 SL app. 1901/ Scot trial apps. 1903-05/FL champs 1905, 1907, 1909/FAC winner 1910/ FAC finalist 1905, 1906, 1908/ SL div 2 champs 1899.

HUCKERBY, Darren Carl

Role: Striker 1995-date
5' 10"
b. Nottingham, 23rd April 1976

CAREER: Lincoln City app cs 1992, pro 1994/UNITED Nov 1995 £450,000 (Millwall loan 1996-97).

Debut v Chelsea (h) 17/1/96 (FAC)(sub)

Darren Huckerby

On his limited opportunities in United's first eleven, Darren Huckerby has greatly impressed both the Magpies' fans and the club's management. Within a few short weeks the 19 year-old youngster exchanged football in front of a handful of spectators with bottom division club Lincoln City, to that of a packed audience at St James Park, appearing alongside world stars like Ginola and Gullit. Huckerby has pace and the willingness to attack defenders and, although slightly built, possesses a body swerve and control of the ball at speed that tests defenders. He was purchased as cover for Les Ferdinand, and as a player to develop for the future, but Newcastle had to act quickly to secure Darren's signature on the transfer form as Manchester United were also bidding for his raw talents. Whilst at Lincoln he netted eight goals in 28 outings with a direct style and had scored within five minutes of his Football League baptism against Shrewsbury in 1994. As a kid, Darren was rejected by Notts County as being too small.

Appearances:
PL: 0(1) app. 0 gls.
FAC: 0(1) app. 0 gls.
Total: *0(2) apps. 0 gls.*

HUDSON, Raymond W.

Role: Midfield 1973-1978
5' 11"
b. Dunston, Gateshead, 24th March 1955

CAREER: UNITED Mar 1973(Greenock Morton loan 1974-75)/Fort Lauderdale(USA) Mar 1978 £40,000/Brighton Oct 1983 to Nov 1983/Soligen(W.Germany) Jan 1984/ Minnesota(USA) 1986/Edmonton(Canada) c1987, becoming coach in 1989.

Debut v Stoke City (h) 3/11/73 (sub)

Tall, lean and with abundant skill, blond-haired Ray Hudson developed through United's reserve structure to push for a place in the club's first-team just after the Magpies reached Wembley in 1974. With midfield places dominated by experienced seniors, Hudson didn't find it easy to get a regular opportunity but, according to many spectators, showed enough talent on his few outings to warrant an extended run. That never came and 'Rocky', as he was known, moved to the States where he became a big star and displayed a brand of flamboyant football that would have graced the St James Park field. He remained in North America, becoming a sports journalist as well entering business and coaching soccer in Fort Lauderdale, Florida.

Appearances:
FL: 16(4) apps. 1 gl.
FAC: 3 apps. 1 gl.
FLC: 1 app. 0 gls.
Eur: 0(1) app. 0 gls.
Others: 4 apps. 0 gls.
Total: *24(5) apps. 2 gls.*

Ray Hudson

HUDSPETH, Francis Carr

Role: Left-back 1910-1929
5' 9"
*b. Percy Main, nr Newcastle upon Tyne,
20th April 1890
d. Burnley, 8th February 1963*

CAREER: Scotswood/Newburn/Clara Vale
jnrs/North Shields Athletic/UNITED
Mar 1910 £100/Leeds City war-guest
1916-17/Stockport County Jan 1929/
Crook Town Dec 1930 to Jan 1931/Retired
cs 1931/Rochdale trainer July 1933/
Burnley asst-trainer cs 1934/Retired 1945.

Debut v Bradford City (h) 3/12/10

With 472 games to his name, no player has
appeared more for United in an outfield
position in league or cup football than left-
back, Frank Hudspeth. Only goalkeeper
Jimmy Lawrence can claim more matches for
the black'n'whites. Frank was a dependable
defender, good in all departments and a model
of consistency over a 19 year career at St James
Park - record service along with Bill
McCracken, his full-back partner on many
occasions. With his Irish international
colleague, Hudspeth forged the infamous
offside trap which led to a change in the rules;
Frank had a tactical mind like McCracken's
and their joint defensive game at a time of
two-man back lines was a feature of United's
play. The older and more experienced
Hudspeth became, the better a player he
developed into. He was 34 when the Magpies
won the FA Cup in 1924, almost 36 when he
won his first England cap (the oldest debutant
at the time, although he was third choice to
play), and 37 when he was an ever-present in
the club's title victory. United's captain in

many of his games for Newcastle, he was also
something of a penalty-kick expert, striking
home eight in season 1925-26. During the First
World War, Frank served in the Royal Navy as
an able seaman. On hanging up his boots in
1931, he managed a billiards hall in Newcastle
before moving to Lancashire. Hudspeth lived
in Burnley to his death.

Appearances:
FL: 430 apps. 34 gls.
FAC: 42 apps. 3 gls.
War: 10 apps. 1 gl.
Total: *482 apps. 38 gls.*
Honours:
*1 Eng cap 1926/1 unoff app. 1920/
Eng trial app. 1914/FL champs 1927/
FAC winner 1924.*

Frank Hudspeth

Frank Hudspeth shakes hands with Manchester City's skipper Mick Hamill before the 1924 FA Cup semi-final clash.

HUGHES, Gordon

Role: Outside-right 1956-1963
5' 6"
b. Washington, 19th June 1936

CAREER: Fatfield jnrs/Easington Lane/
Tow Law Town/UNITED Aug 1956 £30/
Derby County Aug 1963 £12,000/Lincoln City
Apr 1968 £6,000/Boston United Mar 1971/
Retired Mar 1972.

Debut v Manchester United (h) 8/9/56

Gordon Hughes

Gordon Hughes was a part-timer, still working
as a Fatfield pit-lad, when he was introduced
for his Football League debut by United. He
had been turned down by Middlesbrough,
Sunderland and Workington before Newcastle
took a chance with him, but the Magpies soon
realised they had made a good move and
Gordon was quickly elevated to the First
Division stage. He was extremely fast on the
wing and could clock 100 yards in ten
seconds, but after impressing so well Hughes
unfortunately broke his leg and this injury
kept him out of the action for a long period.
But Gordon bounced back and was a regular
choice for four seasons up to 1961. Stocky with
an effervescent character, he always possessed

an eye for goal and had a direct attitude
towards playing the game. He later did well
for Derby (201 games) and Lincoln (117
games) and in all totalled almost 600 senior
matches in his career. On leaving the game,
Gordon returned to the north east and resided
in Chester Moor.

Appearances:
FL: 133 apps. 18 gls.
FAC: 9 apps. 2 gls.
FLC: 1 app. 0 gls.
Total: *143 apps. 20 gls.*

HUGHES, John

Role: Left-half 1932-1935
5' 8"
b. Tanfield, County Durham

CAREER: Tanfield Lea Institute/UNITED
May 1932 £20/Aldershot May 1935 free/
Hartlepools United cs 1937 to 1938.

Debut v West Bromwich Albion (h) 27/1/34

John Hughes came into Newcastle's first
eleven during the 1933-34 season after an
injury to John Murray, however, with United
struggling to survive a relegation battle, the ex
West Stanley miner could make little headway.
Hughes spent another season with the
Magpies, but travelled south the following
summer where he completed his career in the
lower divisions before the Second World War
erupted. A tireless and unselfish half-back,
John had had trials with Nottingham Forest
before joining the Magpies.

Appearances:
FL: 5 apps. 0 gls.
Total: *5 apps. 0 gls.*

HUGHES

HUGHES, Thomas

Role: Inside-left 1912-1915
5' 7"
b. South Hetton, County Durham
d. France, c.1915

CAREER: Wallsend Park Villa/
UNITED Apr 1912 £80 to his demise.

Debut v Bradford City (a) 8/2/13

Local youngster Tom Hughes was given a
brief taste of Division One football during the
1912-13 season in place of internationals
Stewart and Wilson. Hughes was a small and
compact schemer who, until the outbreak of
World War One, was making good progress
within United's ranks. In the summer of 1914
Tom joined the services and headed to the
continent where, sadly, he was killed in action.

> **Appearances:**
> *FL: 2 apps. 0 gls.*
> **Total:** *2 apps. 0 gls.*

Andy Hunt

HUGHES, William John

Role: Right-half 1908-1910
5' 8"
b. Rhyl, Wales, 1889
d. Rhyl, Wales, 1955

CAREER: Rhyl Athletic/UNITED Mar 1908/
Huddersfield Town Mar 1910 £37/Oswestry
United July 1911/Norwich City June 1912/
Halifax Town/Bradford City Jan 1914 to May
1914.

Debut v Everton (a) 4/4/08

Newcastle United's first Welshman, William
Hughes, was spotted when the Magpies were
on FA Cup training in his native North Wales
resort of Rhyl. More at home in attack, he
appeared for the first-team only once, as a last
minute replacement at right-half. By all
accounts Hughes was a stalwart all-round
athlete, reports noting he "showed really
promising form alike in attack and defence".
During World War One he served in the army
and was awarded the Military Medal, although
the Welshman suffered the consequences of
exposure to mustard gas for the rest of his life.
He later returned to Rhyl, assisting the Welsh
club in various capacities, including
groundsman. As the coxswain of the local
lifeboat, he was a well-known personality in
that town, also operating a fishing boat.

> **Appearances:**
> *FL: 1 app. 0 gls.*
> **Total:** *1 app. 0 gls.*

HUNT, Andrew

Role: Centre-forward 1991-1993
6' 0"
b. Thurrock, Essex, 9th June 1970

CAREER: Ashill/Kings Lynn 1989/Kettering
Town Aug 1990/UNITED Jan 1991 £210,000/
West Bromwich Albion Mar 1993 £100,000.

Debut v Watford (a) 9/3/91 (sub)

In a surprise transfer, Andy Hunt exchanged
the non-league scene of the Vauxhall
Conference with Kettering Town for the big-
time set-up of St James Park. Tall and awkward
to play against and good in possession, Hunt
proved to be a consistent goalscorer in both
reserve and first-team football for the
Tynesiders. Andy had started to develop a

partnership with Mick Quinn before a broken ankle halted his progress, and by the time he was fit again Gallowgate was a very different place with Sir John Hall and Kevin Keegan in charge. Hunt couldn't break into the side and was picked up by West Bromwich Albion. He proceeded to be a regular striker at the Hawthorns, starting with a remarkable hat-trick on his home debut. Andy began as a centre-half and gave up his job in computer systems to turn professional as a 20 year-old.

Appearances:
FL: 34(9) apps. 11 gls.
FAC: 2 apps. 1 gl.
FLC: 3 apps. 1 gl.
Others: 3 apps. 0 gls.
Total: *42(9) apps. 13 gls.*
Honours:
FL div 2 prom 1993.

HUNTER, James Alton

Role: Left-back 1919, 1924-1925
5' 8"
b. Balfron, Stirlingshire, 5th July 1898

CAREER: UNITED 1919/Motherwell Aug 1919/Falkirk/UNITED Jan 1924 £3,500/USA football May 1925.

Debut v Tottenham Hotspur (h) 26/1/24

United purchased James Hunter, who claimed Scottish League honours, as cover to the ageing Frank Hudspeth whose career in 1924 was thought to be coming to an end. But United's veteran continued for several seasons and James had to be content to perform in the club's reserve side for the most part. He was also at St James Park briefly immediately after World War One and was a tactful defender. He had, however, a controversial career; firstly signing for Motherwell without permission from the Magpies who held his registration, then entering into a disagreement with Newcastle's directors. Consequently he was transfer-listed at such a high fee that no one would sign him and, as a result, Hunter emigrated to North America, continuing his footballing career in the States.

Appearances:
FL: 10 apps. 0 gls.
FAC: 2 apps. 0 gls.
Total: *12 apps. 0 gls.*
Honours:
2 SL apps. 1923-24.

Duncan Hutchison

HUTCHISON, Duncan

Role: Centre-forward 1929-1932
5' 7"
b. Kelty, Fife, 3rd March 1903
d. Dundee, January 1973

CAREER: Rosewell/Dunfermline Athletic/ Dundee United cs 1927 free/UNITED Aug 1929 £4,050/Derby County Mar 1932 £3,100 in a joint deal with R.Hann/Hull City July 1934/ Dundee United June 1935 exch deal/Retired 1939/Dundee United director Mar 1953 to 1972.

Debut v Manchester United (h) 31/8/29

Duncan Hutchison, nicknamed 'Hurricane Hutch' after a dare-devil film star, was a household name with the Tannadice club. He had a rip-roaring style at centre-forward, and netted 119 league goals in 196 matches - 27 in 1927-28 and 34 in 1928-29 - the kind of form that ensured a transfer to Tyneside. Rivalling Hughie Gallacher to start with, and replacing him on the United legend's departure to Chelsea, Hutchison was never going to replace the diminutive figure of Hughie, and United struggled to find an adequate substitute. Duncan did well at times, playing in several roles across the forward line, his best effort being an FA Cup hat-trick against Nottingham Forest in 1931. Hutchison later returned to live alongside the Tay, becoming a legendary figure himself - Chairman of Dundee United as well as a popular publican. His younger brother Daniel also turned out for Dundee United during the thirties and played alongside his more famous relation in Dundee's side before the war. It is recorded in the Tannadice annals that Hutchison, like no other, "captured the imagination" of the Tayside public.

Appearances:
FL: 40 apps. 16 gls.
FAC: 6 apps. 5 gls.
Total: *46 apps. 21 gls.*
Honours;
SL div 2 champs 1929.

HYND, John

Role: Goalkeeper 1894-1895
b. Scotland

CAREER: Cowdenbeath/
UNITED Nov 1894 to Apr 1895.

Debut v Grimsby Town (a) 1/12/1894

Goalkeeper John Hynd replaced regular custodian Ward for two months over the winter of 1894-95, during Newcastle's second Football League season. Following a run of nine successive games, Ward regained his place after a 5-3 defeat at the hands of Burton Swifts. The Scot joined United after good reports landed at St James Park following his excellent displays in the East of Scotland v West contest. Hynd stayed with the club for only one season, while he started his career as a full-back and it is suspected he appeared in this role for the club under the name of 'Haynes' (qv).

Appearances:
FL: 9 apps. 0 gls.
Total: *9 apps. 0 gls.*

ILEY, James

Role: Left-half 1962-1969
5' 11"
b. South Kirkby, Yorkshire, 15th December 1935

CAREER: Moorthorpe St Josephs Boys Club/
Pontefract/Sheffield United amat, pro Dec 1952/Tottenham Hotspur Aug 1957 £16,000/
Nottingham Forest Aug 1959 £16,000/
UNITED Sept 1962 £17,000/Peterborough United player-manager Jan 1969 to Sept 1972/
Cambridge United scout 1972/Barnsley manager Apr 1973/Blackburn Rovers manager Apr 1978/Luton Town scout Oct 1978/Bury manager July 1980 to Feb 1984/Exeter City manager June 1984 to Apr 1985/
Charlton Athletic scout/Luton Town scout.

Debut v Plymouth Argyle (h) 8/9/62

Jim Iley

A former colliery lad at Frickley pit before turning professional, Jim Iley made his Football League debut as a 17 year-old part-timer with Sheffield United. He quickly began to be noticed and earned a move to White Hart Lane where he won England honours before moving north again after having difficulty settling in the capital. By the time he arrived at St James Park, Iley was an experienced wing-half who was destined to become the cornerstone, alongside Stan Anderson, of the Magpies' promotion line-up in 1965. The balding Jim was, in many respects, a complete player, possessing good control, versatility, tremendous shooting ability, consistency and a team-man's attitude. Skipper of United before and after Anderson's leadership, Iley was a driving force in midfield and always a danger around the box; he netted a screamer from 20 yards against Bolton Wanderers that sent United back into the First Division. A regular for six seasons, Iley later proved he could manage clubs on a limited budget, although he had a turbulent period of only 172 days at Ewood Park. On leaving the game he resided in the Bolton area, for a while running an Italian restaurant in Chorley. His brother-in-law is the ex England and Rotherham winger, Colin Grainger.

Appearances:
FL: 227(5) apps. 15 gls.
FAC: 9 apps. 0 gls.
FLC: 7 apps. 1 gl.
Eur: 0(1) app. 0 gls.
Total: *243(6) apps. 16 gls.*
Honours:
1 Eng u23 cap 1958/2 FL app 1956-59/
1 FA app 1962/FL div 2 champs 1965.

IMRIE, William Noble

Role: Right-half 1934-1938
5' 11"
b. Methil, Fife, 4th March 1908
d. c.1945

CAREER: East Fife jnrs/Dunnikier jnrs/
St Johnstone 1927/Blackburn Rovers Sept 1929
£4,775/UNITED Mar 1934 £6,500/
Swansea Town July 1938 £1,500/
Swindon Town July 1939 to 1940.

Debut v Sheffield United (a) 17/3/34

The red-haired Bill Imrie was a burly, powerful figure who, apart from being a robust character on the field, was an exceptional talent on the ball too. His wholehearted spirit and gritty determination was blended with a fierce drive as well as the will to get forward to support his strikers. Purchased by United in an attempt to save the club from relegation in season 1933-34, his arrival made an impact but was too late to halt the slide and for the rest of his St James Park career he attempted, as skipper, to lead United out of the mire of Second Division football. A spot-kick expert, versatile at left-half too and possessing a mighty throw, Imrie was a popular personality with Tyneside's faithful during a low point in the club's history. Later he ran a butcher's business in Gateshead. Imrie was a victim of the Second World War whilst serving in the RAF.

Appearances:
FL: 125 apps. 24 gls.
FAC: 3 apps. 0 gls.
Total: *128 apps. 24 gls.*
Honours:
2 Scot caps 1929.

Bill Imrie

INGLIS, John

Role: Outside-left 1893-1894
b. Scotland
Debut v Notts County (a) 14/10/1893

John Inglis arrived on Tyneside in October
1893 from Dalmuir Thistle on trial as United
entered the Football League for the first time
during season 1893-94. He didn't remain in
Newcastle long, appearing on three occasions
as a stand-in for Quinn. The *Newcastle Daily
Chronicle* recorded "he has a splendid
reputation" and "he showed us some smart
doings".

Appearances:
FL: 3 apps. 0 gls.
Total: *3 apps. 0 gls.*

INNERD, Wilfred

Role: Centre-half
1900-1905
5' 9"
b. Tyneside

Wilf Innerd

CAREER: Wallsend Park Villa/
UNITED May 1900/
Crystal Palace 1905/
Shildon Athletic 1909.

Debut v Liverpool (a) 30/3/01

Chiefly a reserve to Andy Aitken at St James
Park, Wilf Innerd responded to a call-up for
First Division action in season 1900-01 and
once during the black'n'whites championship
campaign of 1904-05. He aided the club's
second string win of the Northern League title
on three occasions before he moved south. Wilf
found a place in the Crystal Palace side which
did well in both the Southern League and FA
Cup as giant-killers - including leading the
Eagles in the Londoners' famous success on
Tyneside against the Magpies in January 1907.
He totalled 133 senior games for Palace, a key
figure in midfield, and as captain, during their
formative years. Innerd settled in the north
east following his retirement and lived well
into his eightieth year.

Appearances:
FL: 3 apps. 0 gls.
Total: *3 apps. 0 gls.*
Honours:
SnL div 2 champs 1906.

JACKSON, Darren

Role: Striker 1986-1988
5' 7"
b. Edinburgh, 25th July 1966

CAREER: Melbourne Thistle/Meadowbank
Thistle Aug 1985/UNITED Oct 1986 £240,000/
Dundee United Dec 1988 £200,000/
Hibernian July 1992 £400,000.

Debut v Arsenal (h) 18/10/86 (sub)

Darren Jackson

Darren Jackson was given a chance by
Newcastle after scoring 19 goals as a part-time
professional in his first season with
Meadowbank. Slight of build, but fast and
eager for the ball, Jackson was moved around
from position to position at St James Park,
operating as a striker, in midfield or even at
full-back. Although having the potential to
succeed, reaching the Under-21 squad when
with the Magpies, Darren perhaps wasn't
developed in a manner designed to get the
best out of the player during his stay on

Tyneside. After being transferred back north to Scotland, a move he reluctantly agreed to, Jackson indeed realised his potential by becoming a full international player. He was recognised as one of Scotland's top strikers being a success at both Tannadice and Easter Road.

Appearances:
FL: 53(16) apps. 7 gls.
FAC: 5 apps. 1 gl.
FLC: 5 apps. 1 gl.
Others: 4 apps. 0 gls.
Total: *67(16) apps. 9 gls.*
Honours:
12 Scot caps 1995-date/1 Scot B cap 1995/ SLC finalist 1994.

James Jackson

JACKSON, James

Role: Left-back
1897-1899
5' 9"
b. Cambuslang, Glasgow, 15th September 1875

CAREER: Hamilton Academical/Elmstown Rosebuds(Australia)/Newton Thistle/ Cambuslang 1896/Glasgow Rangers 1896/ UNITED Aug 1897/Woolwich Arsenal May 1899/Leyton player-manager cs 1905/ West Ham United cs 1905/Glasgow Rangers cs 1906/Greenock Morton 1911.

Debut v Woolwich Arsenal (h) 4/9/1897

A steadfast and clever defender, perhaps a decade ahead of his time as a tactician, fair-haired James Jackson was an eye catching player. And he was a rock in United's defence as the Magpies reached promotion to Division One via the Test Matches in 1898. When he was only two years old, Jackson's parents emigrated to Australia and the youngster learnt the Aussie rules version of the game before returning to Scotland in his teens and taking up the association code back in Glasgow. After assisting greatly in Newcastle's consolidation as a force in the game, James moved to Arsenal where he became a noted captain of the Gunners, appearing on 204 occasions, also leading the Londoners into the First Division. A strict teetotaller, Jackson also ran a sports outfitters business outside Highbury and after leaving the game became a blacksmith in Greenock. His two sons played football as well; one was a past skipper of Liverpool, the distinguished Rev. James Jackson, while Archie appeared for Tranmere. James' nephew was Australian Test cricketer, Archibald Jackson.

Appearances:
FL: 62 apps. 1 gl.
FAC: 6 apps. 2 gls.
Total: *68 apps. 3 gls.*
Honours:
Scot trial app. 1905/
FA trial app. 1902/
FL div 2 prom 1898, 1904.

JACKSON, Peter Allan

Role: Centre-half 1986-1988
6' 1"
b. Shelf, Bradford, 6th April 1961

CAREER: Burnley sch 1975/Bradford City
app July 1977, pro 1979/UNITED Oct 1986
£250,000/Bradford City Sept 1988 £290,000/
Huddersfield Town Aug 1990 free/
Chester loan Sept 1994, pmt Nov 1994.

Debut v Aston Villa (a) 25/10/86

Peter Jackson

As captain of Bradford City, Peter Jackson was
a great favourite at Valley Parade totalling
almost 400 senior games for the Bantams. He
was an inspiration on the field; positive,
commanding in the air and able to battle for
the ball. Jackson continued his bond with the
fans when he landed at Gallowgate, being a
popular character with United's black'n white
army right up to the day he left the region in a
return transfer to his home town club. Peter
was Player of the Year in his first season with
Newcastle and his move surprised many on
Tyneside. At the time he was both Bradford's
record sale, and purchase. Jackson was skipper
of City when the Valley Parade fire disaster
occurred in 1985, while he once scored two
own-goals in a Newcastle versus Manchester
United clash in 1987.

Appearances:
FL: 60 apps. 3 gls.
FAC: 6 apps. 0 gls.
FLC: 3 apps. 0 gls.
Others: 3 apps. 0 gls.
Total: *72 apps. 3 gls.*
Honours:
*FL div 3 champs 1985/FL div 4
prom 1982.*

JEFFREY, Harry

Role: Right-back 1892-1895
5' 9"
b. Newcastle upon Tyne, March 1867
d. 1930

CAREER: Newcastle West End Jan 1888/
Drysdale(Newcastle) 1890/Sunderland amat
1890/Third Lanark amat 1890/Newcastle West
End 1890/Newcastle East End Apr 1892/
UNITED May 1892/Retired due to injury
1895/South Shields cs 1897.

Debut v Sheffield United (a) 24/9/1892 (NL)

One of the club's earliest personalities, Harry
Jeffrey was a regular for West End and took
part in United's debut at St James Park against
Celtic and the Tynesiders' first ever league
affair at Arsenal. Strong-tackling, he was
something of a controversial character
within the ranks, once suspended for
two weeks for being, as the club's
Minutes of Meetings note, "a non
trier" while he also received a month's
ban for playing in the close season
without permission. It was reported in
September 1894 that, due to a fracas,
he "will not be seen upon the team
again". Jeffrey sustained a bad leg
injury when at Gallowgate which was serious
enough to force him to quit the top-class
scene. Noted by one biography of his day as a
"stylish and scientific exponent of the game",
Harry is thought to have scored Newcastle's
first penalty kick, against Walsall Town Swifts
in March 1894. Jeffrey also captained
Northumberland as well as West End.

Harry Jeffrey

Appearances:
NL: 7 apps. 0 gls.
FL: 45 apps. 3 gls.
FAC: 3 apps. 0 gls.
Total: *55 apps. 3 gls.*

JEFFREY, Michael Richard

Role: Midfield 1993-1995
5' 11"
b. Liverpool, 11th August 1971

CAREER: Bolton Wanderers 1988/Doncaster Rovers 1991/UNITED Oct 1993 £85,000/ Rotherham United June 1995 £100,000/ Fortuna Sittard (Holland) Dec 1995 £205,000.

Debut v Tottenham Hotspur (a) 4/12/93

Mike Jeffrey

Mike Jeffrey had trials with Sheffield Wednesday and Liverpool before an extended opportunity came his way at Burnden Park, Bolton. Although he netted 19 goals as a striker in 49 games he was released and it was with Doncaster that Jeffrey caught the eye of Kevin Keegan. Totalling over 50 matches for Rovers, he was signed in a deal that saw David Roche move to Belle Vue. Mike became a fringe player in Keegan's squad that established the club as one of the powers of the Premier League. Only rarely given a first eleven outing, the Merseysider always performed with credit in a role either in midfield, or just behind the Magpies' main striker.

Appearances:
PL: 2 apps. 0 gls.
FLC: 1 app. 1 gl.
Eur: 0(2) apps. 0 gls.
Total: *3(2) apps. 1 gl.*

JOBEY, George

Role: Wing-half 1906-1913
5' 10"
b. Heddon-on-the-Wall, nr Newcastle upon Tyne, July 1885
d. Chaddesden, Derby, 9th March 1962

CAREER: Morpeth Harriers/UNITED May 1906 £10/Woolwich Arsenal May 1913 £500/ Bradford Park Avenue June 1914/Arsenal war-guest 1918-19/Hamilton Academical war-guest/Hartlepools United Aug 1919/Leicester City Sept 1919/Northampton Town player-manager May 1920/Wolverhampton Wanderers manager June 1922 to May 1924/ Derby County manager Aug 1925 to May 1941/Mansfield Town manager Jan 1952 to May 1953.

Debut v Bolton Wanderers (a) 20/4/07

One of the prominent names of pre-war soccer, perhaps not as a player, but as a manager, George Jobey was a well known and respected figure for over 30 years. The Tynesider made his first appearance for United in the Magpies' championship celebration game at the close of the 1906-07 season and was for the next six campaigns a squad player, operating in any half-back role as well as at centre-forward. George won a title medal in 1909 and was selected for the 1911 FA Cup final as a replacement for the injured Albert Shepherd. Zealous and dependable, with a tactical mind, it was little surprise that he entered management after World War One, becoming especially noted for his work at the Baseball Ground. He took Derby to promotion, then to within a whisker of the title, The Rams twice becoming runners-up in 1930 and 1936. Jobey loved the transfer market and attracted big names to his club, including Hughie Gallacher, but in 1941

George Jobey

was suspended for life (later lifted) after an FA inquiry into the financial dealings of the Rams; it was found that illegal bonus payments and signing-on fees had been paid to many of the stars Jobey purchased. George holds the distinction of scoring the very first goal at Highbury in 1913 - and afterwards being carried off injured on a milk cart! He later resided in Derby for the rest of his life.

Appearances:
FL: 47 apps. 2 gls.
FAC: 6 apps. 0 gls.
Total: *53 apps. 2 gls.*
Honours:
FL champs 1909/FL div 2 prom 1926(m)/FL div 3(N) champs 1924(m)/FAC finalist 1911.

JOHNSON, Henry

Role: Left-back 1933-1937
5' 10"
b. Walker, Newcastle upon Tyne, 8th August 1913

CAREER: Walker Park/UNITED Aug 1933/
Port Vale June 1937/Hartlepools United cs
1938 to 1939.

Debut v Hull City (a) 13/4/36

Hard and fierce, typical of many full-backs of
the inter-war era, Henry Johnson - more often
referred to as Harry - was a stand-in for David
Fairhurst and collected all his senior outings
during the 1935-36 season. His brother once
had a spell on Chelsea's books.

Appearances:
FL: 5 apps. 0 gls.
Total: *5 apps. 0 gls.*

JOHNSON, Peter Edward

Role: Left-back 1980-1983
5' 10"
b. Harrogate, 5th October 1958

CAREER: Middlesbrough Oct 1976/UNITED
Oct 1980 £60,000/(Bristol City loan 1982-83)
(Doncaster Rovers loan 1982-83)/Darlington
June 1983/Whitby Town Sept 1985/Exeter
City Mar 1985/Crewe Alexandra Oct 1985/
Southend United Sept 1986/Gillingham
cs 1989/Southend United Aug 1990/
Peterborough United cs 1991 to 1992.

Debut v Watford (h) 1/11/80

Peter Johnson arrived on Tyneside as a
replacement for Ian Davies and as Arthur
Cox's first purchase for the Magpies. He
impressed everyone in his opening games for
the club, looking assured and always wanting
to get forward from his left-back position, but
after three months he eventually lost his place
to a revitalised Davies and never saw first-
team action again. Moving into the lower
divisions, however, Peter tasted success at
Exeter and Southend.

Appearances:
FL: 16 apps. 0 gls.
FAC: 4 apps. 0 gls.
Total: *20 apps. 0 gls.*
Honours:
FL div 4 prom 1985, 1987/
FL div 3 prom 1992.

Peter Johnson

JONES, Roger

Role: Goalkeeper 1976-1977
5' 11"
b. Upton, nr Southampton, 8th November 1946

CAREER: Portsmouth app Aug 1963, pro
Nov 1964/Bournemouth June 1965/Blackburn
Rovers Jan 1970 £30,000/UNITED Mar 1976
joint deal with G.Oates £100,000/Stoke City
Feb 1977 free/Derby County July 1980 £25,000
(Birmingham City loan 1981-82)/York City
July 1982 to May 1985, becoming asst-coach/
Sunderland asst-coach Nov 1988 to May 1993.

Debut v West Ham United (h) 13/3/76

With a reputation as one of the top 'keepers in
the lower divisions at that time, Roger Jones
followed United's new manager Gordon Lee
from Ewood Park. Capped by the young
England line-up when with Bournemouth,
Jones went on to break Blackburn's goalkeeper
appearance record with 272 games, once
saving two spot-kicks in one fixture for
Rovers. Although showing excellent
judgement and a mighty throw or kick out,
Jones was unlucky with injuries. He was
dogged by a shoulder knock at St James Park,

an injury severe enough for United to refuse to pay Blackburn the transfer fee. Yet, despite being freed by the black'n'whites, Roger confounded everyone by playing on for another eight years, including a good spell with Stoke City and York. All told Jones amassed almost 800 senior outings in his career, and was skipper of the Minstermen when they won the Fourth Division title. On hanging up his boots Roger had a brief spell as a coach before concentrating on a building business.

Appearances:
FL: 5 apps. 0 gls.
Others: 2 apps. 0 gls.
Total: *7 apps. 0 gls.*
Honours:
2 Eng u23 caps 1968/FL div 3 champs 1975/ FL div 4 champs 1984/FL div 2 prom 1979.

Roger Jones

KEATING, Albert Edward

Role: Inside-right 1923-1925
5' 9"
b. Swillington Common, nr Leeds, 28th June 1902

CAREER: Prudhoe Castle/UNITED Jan 1923 £130/Bristol City Nov 1925 £650/Blackburn Rovers May 1928/Cardiff City Feb 1931/ Bristol City Nov 1932/North Shields 1933/ Throckley Welfare c1935.

Debut v Huddersfield Town (h) 9/2/24

Bert Keating was a consistent reserve goalscorer for United; not one perhaps blessed with cultured ball talents, but a player whose positioning around the danger zone made sure he could find the net. Bert stood in for Cowan and Clark in the schemer's role, and for Neil Harris at centre-forward. He later did exceptionally well at Ashton Gate, poaching 49 goals in only 81 outings, a danger-man when Bristol City won promotion in season 1927-28. His brother Reg, was on United's books and was a much travelled forward of the same era. After retiring, Keating became a local referee, also running a tobacconists and grocer's business in Newcastle.

Appearances:
FL: 12 apps. 3 gls.
Total: *12 apps. 3 gls.*
Honours:
FL div 3(S) champs 1927.

KEEBLE, Victor Albert Williams

Role: Centre-forward 1952-1957
6' 0"
b. Colchester, 25th June 1930

CAREER: Arsenal/King George YC (Colchester)/Colchester Casuals/ Colchester United amat May 1947, pro Sept 1950/UNITED Feb 1952 £15,000/ West Ham United Oct 1957 £10,000/ Retired due to injury 1960/Colchester United development manager c1969/Chelmsford City secretary 1976/Retired 1994.

Debut v Chelsea (a) 12/3/52

An ex rugby player, Vic Keeble's form for Football League newcomers, Colchester United, greatly impressed Newcastle's celebrated scout, Bill McCracken. Keeble grabbed 24 goals in 49 matches and earned a contract at St James Park, signing for the club when he was in the army. A persistent leader, not pretty to watch yet certainly effective, who often took a battering from defenders, Keeble was a menace in the air and as an enthusiast once remarked "would even take a penalty with his head"! Nicknamed 'Camel' by his colleagues, he was deputy to Jackie Milburn or George Hannah at inside-forward during his early days at Gallowgate, but when Milburn moved to outside-right, Vic took over the Number 9 shirt and had two brilliant seasons in 1954-55 and 1955-56 (29 goals). He once netted four times against Huddersfield Town and included was a run to Wembley in which Keeble found the net on five occasions. Joining the Upton Park set-up, Vic proceeded to be a key factor in West Ham's return to the First Division, totalling 49 goals in 80 senior games for the Hammers. Keeble retired due to a back injury, and for a spell became a journalist in Colchester, living in Essex, before concentrating on a long period in charge of administration for Chelmsford City. His son, Chris, joined the Ipswich Town staff in 1995.

Appearances:
FL: 104 apps. 56 gls.
FAC: 16 apps. 11 gls.
Others: 1 app. 2 gls.
Total: *121 apps. 69 gls.*
Honours:
FAC winner 1955/FL div 2 champs 1958.

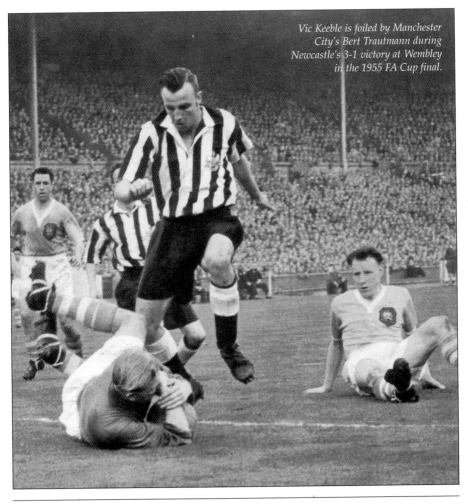

Vic Keeble is foiled by Manchester City's Bert Trautmann during Newcastle's 3-1 victory at Wembley in the 1955 FA Cup final.

KEEGAN, Joseph Kevin O.B.E.

Role: Striker & Manager 1982-1984, 1992-date
5' 8"
b. Armthorpe, nr Doncaster, 14th February 1951

CAREER: Enfield House YC/Peglers Brass Works/Lonsdale Hotel/Scunthorpe United app Dec 1967, pro Dec 1968/Liverpool May 1971 £33,000/SV Hamburg(Germany) June 1977 £500,000/Southampton July 1980 £400,000/UNITED Aug 1982 £100,000/ Retired May 1984/UNITED manager Feb 1992.

Debut v Queens Park Rangers (h) 28/8/82 (scored once)

When Kevin Keegan first joined United during the summer of 1982, the whole of Tyneside was set alight with Keegan-mania. Newcastle were languishing in the Second Division at the time, and manager Arthur Cox saw the former England skipper, and one of the game's superstars, as the man to lead the Magpies back to Division One. From Geordie stock, Keegan's father hailed from Hetton-le-Hole, while his grandfather was a past mine disaster hero at West Stanley, Keegan took immediately to Tyneside and its supporters. With his unique charisma, a special bond between player and fan resulted and helped significantly in revitalising Tyneside's soccer fortunes. After being rejected following trials at Coventry, the dynamic Keegan developed into a world-class star at Liverpool and for England, skippering his country 31 times and scoring 21 goals in his 63 appearances. Operating in midfield or up front, Kevin possessed control, awareness and the ability to create and combine with others as well as a deadly finish. He had lots of courage and was a hard worker on the pitch, appearing on almost 800 occasions in senior football netting 274 goals. Captain of the black'n'whites, he took Newcastle to promotion then announced his retirement, afterwards being employed in television and promotion work while residing for much of the time in Marbella and Hampshire. Then, with the Magpies in a dire predicament as the club's centenary year opened, he was appointed manager at St James Park - his first taste of the football hot-seat. Teaming up with new Chairman, Sir John Hall, the duo began to turn Newcastle United into one of the country's megaclubs. Keegan again acted as a catalyst and United's fans rallied to the call. His judgement as a manager was first-class and he fashioned a series of celebrated line-ups packed with players comfortable on the ball and who wished to play the game in an entertaining fashion. The First Division Championship was achieved in style and then the Premiership was taken by storm. Newcastle had been transformed into a club to rival Manchester United, Liverpool and Arsenal as England's best. Kevin Keegan remains United's finest ever signing, both as a player and as a manager. Keegan was also a successful pop singer, recording three singles during the seventies. For his services to soccer during his playing career, he was awarded the OBE in 1982. To many in the game he epitomises everything that a professional footballer and manager should be.

Appearances:
FL: 78 apps. 48 gls.
FAC: 3 apps. 0 gls.
FLC: 4 apps. 1 gl.
Total: *85 apps. 49 gls.*
Honours:
63 Eng caps 1973-82/1 unoff Eng app. 1976/ 5 Eng u23 caps 1972/FL champs 1973, 1976, 1977/FL div 1 champs 1993(m)/FL div 2 prom 1984/FAC winner 1974/FAC finalist 1977/EC winner 1977/EC finalist 1980/ UEFAC winner 1973, 1976/Bundesliga champs 1979/Footballer-of-the-Year 1976(FWA), 1982(PFA)/European Footballer-of-the-Year 1978, 1979/W.German Footballer-of-the-Year 1978.

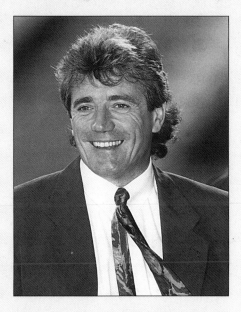

Kevin Keegan celebrates with Chris Waddle during United's promotion winning season of 1983-84.

KEELEY, Glenn Matthew

Role: Centre-half 1974-1976
6' 0"
b. Basildon, Essex, 1st September 1954

CAREER: Ipswich Town app July 1970, pro Aug 1972/UNITED June 1974 £70,000/ Blackburn Rovers Aug 1976 £30,000 (Birmingham City loan 1982-83) (Everton loan 1982-83)/Oldham Athletic Aug 1987 £15,000(Colchester United loan 1987-88)/Bolton Wanderers Sept 1988 to cs 1989/Chorley Aug 1990/Clitheroe 1991.

Debut v Coventry City (h) 17/8/74

Glenn Keeley

Arriving at Gallowgate as a 19 year-old defender who was destined for the top, Keeley had only totalled a mere five senior games for Ipswich Town when United signed him for a substantial fee. However, manager Joe Harvey recognised lots of potential to develop in Glenn who had stood out in youth internationals and Ipswich Town's FA Youth Cup victory. Keeley replaced Magpie skipper Bob Moncur and, although he made a few mistakes - as all youngsters do - Glenn was developing well, reaching the England Under-23 squad until a change in management saw new boss Gordon Lee discard him in favour of Aiden McCaffery. Keeley did, though, gain a place in the black'n'whites' Wembley visit during 1976, but was transferred soon after, to Blackburn where he proceeded to have an exceptional stay at Ewood Park. Glenn spent 11 seasons with Rovers, many as captain, clocking up 413 games and becoming something of a cult figure to local supporters. His transfer from Tyneside later resulted in court proceedings and an FA Inquiry between United and Blackburn. Keeley played only 30 minutes for Everton when on loan, being sent-off in a derby with Liverpool. Glenn's brother, Andy, turned out for both Sheffield United and Tottenham. Latterly, Glenn has been managing a pub in Leyland.

Appearances:
FL: 43(1) apps. 2 gls.
FAC: 8 apps. 0 gls.
FLC: 10 apps. 2 gls.
Others: 11 apps. 0 gls.
Total: *72(1) apps. 4 gls.*
Honours:
Eng youth app. 1973/FLC finalist 1976/FAYC winner 1973/FL div 3 prom 1980.

KEEN, Errington Ridley Liddell

Role: Left-half 1926-1930
5' 8"
b. Walker, Newcastle upon Tyne, 4th September 1910
d. Fulham, London, July 1984

CAREER: Nuns Moor(Newcastle)/UNITED Swifts 1926, pro Sept 1927/Derby County Dec 1930 exch deal for H.Bedford/Chelmsford City player-manager May 1938/Colchester United Nov 1938/Hereford United player-manager July 1939/Notts County war-guest 1940-44/Rochdale war-guest 1940-41/Everton war-guest 1941-42/Fulham war-guest 1941-42/Millwall war-guest 1942-43/ Liverpool war-guest 1942-43/Lincoln City war-guest 1943-44/Charlton Athletic war-guest 1943-44/Leeds United Dec 1945/ Bacup Borough July 1946/Hull City Nov to Dec 1946/IFK Norrkoping(Sweden) 1949/ Later coaching in Hong Kong.

Debut v Derby County (h) 18/10/30

Ike Keen

A promising youngster at St James Park, Errington Keen, generally known as 'Ike', played only once in the first eleven, as deputy for Jimmy Naylor. That outing was against Derby County and the Rams were so impressed with Keen's potential that they soon afterwards took him to the Baseball Ground. It was to the Magpies' regret that the blond-haired Keen developed into a marvellous half-back, talented on the ball and always driving forward, although tending to sometimes dally in defensive situations. The Tynesider was capped by England and played on 237 occasions for Derby. After retiring from the game Ike went into business in Derby, but later was declared a bankrupt when his company collapsed. He was related to James Keen, who was also on United's books a few years earlier, as well as S.J. Graham of Exeter.

Appearances:
FL: 1 app. 0 gls.
Total: *1 app. 0 gls.*
Honours:
4 Eng caps 1933-37/Eng trial app. 1933/ 1 FL app. 1937.

KEEN, James Frederick

Role: Outside-left 1922-1923
5' 7"
b. Walker, Newcastle upon Tyne, 25th November 1897
d. Cleveland, 1980

CAREER: Walker Celtic/Bristol City Apr 1920/UNITED May 1922 £100/Queens Park Rangers May 1923/Hull City July 1924/ Darlington cs 1925/Wigan Borough 1925-26/ Tyneside minor football.

Debut v Birmingham (h) 6/9/22

Uncle of England international 'Ike' Keen, James was also a product of the Welbeck Road school in Newcastle's east-end. A noted professional sprinter, he was extremely fast, the proverbial 'flier' on the touchline. Keen, who could operate on either flank, was only given an opportunity twice during season 1922-23 as reserve to Jimmy Low and Stan Seymour. He later had one good season with QPR, being selected 32 times in the 1923-24 Third Division (South) campaign.

Appearances:
FL: 2 apps. 0 gls.
Total: *2 apps. 0 gls.*

Stan Keery

KEERY, Stanley

Role: Half-back 1952-1957
5' 7"
b. Derby, 9th September 1931

CAREER: Blackburn Rovers amat/
Wilmorton/Shrewsbury Town Aug 1952/
UNITED Nov 1952 £8,250/Mansfield Town
May 1957 £2,500/Crewe Alexandra Oct 1958
to 1965.

Debut v Preston North End (a) 24/1/53

Small and stocky, and a tenacious midfielder
who was an able stand-in during United's
mid-fifties era, Stan Keery's 20 outings were
spread over five seasons, as deputy to either
George Hannah or Jimmy Scoular. He
appeared also at centre-forward where he was
a solid worker who foraged tirelessly for every
kind of ball. At Gresty Road in Crewe, Stan
became a reliable figure playing over 250
matches for the Railwaymen. He later resided
in that town, employed firstly as a bookmaker
and then for the Rolls-Royce company

Appearances:
FL: 19 apps. 1 gl.
FAC: 1 app. 0 gls.
Total: *20 apps. 1 gl.*
Honours:
FL div 4 prom 1963.

KEIR, M.

Role: Outside-right 1893-1894
b. Scotland
Debut v Notts County (a) 14/10/1893

Keir was a lively Scot who arrived on
Tyneside in October 1893 from Dalmuir Thistle
as Newcastle entered the Football League
competition. Making only a single appearance,
as a replacement for Quinn, he sustained an
injury on his debut against Notts County and
wasn't selected again, returning north of the
border before the season was concluded. Keir
arrived along with another Scot, R. Inglis;
neither, though, made an impression on
Tyneside.

Appearances:
FL: 1 app. 0 gls.
Total: *1 app. 0 gls.*

KEITH, Richard Mathison

Role: Right-back 1956-1964
6' 0"
b. Belfast, 15th May 1933
d. Bournemouth, 28th February 1967

CAREER: Boy's Brigade/3rd Old Boys/
Linfield/UNITED Sept 1956 £9,000/
Bournemouth Feb 1964 £3,300/Weymouth
1966 to his death.

Debut v Manchester United (h) 8/9/56

Dick Keith

A one time tinsmith, Dick Keith arrived on Tyneside as one of the most promising youngsters to come out of Ulster. Performing in front of Stan Seymour, he had played out of his skin for Linfield and earned a move to England. Dick was immediately handed a debut against Manchester United and thereafter became a regular for seven seasons, partnering his fellow Irishman, Alf McMichael at full-back. It was an accomplished duo, one that also appeared at international level, including Northern Ireland's positive World Cup campaign of 1958. Keith had a cool, assured manner on the field and attempted to play football from defence whenever possible. His polished style served the Magpies well, being captain of the club as his period at St James Park came to an end after relegation in 1961. Moving to Dean Court, Dick concluded his first-class career with Bournemouth and afterwards appeared for non-league Weymouth. He was killed when sadly only 33 years of age following an accident in a builder's yard whilst dismantling an automatic garage door; Dick's skull was fractured and he died soon afterwards.

Appearances:
FL: 208 apps. 2 gls.
FAC: 11 apps. 0 gls.
FLC: 4 apps. 0 gls.
Total: *223 apps. 2 gls.*
Honours:
23 N.Irel caps 1958-62/1 N.Irel B cap 1958/
4 NIL app. 1956/N.Irel youth app./
NIL champ 1954, 1955/NIC winner
1953/N.Irel Player of the Year 1956.

KELLY, David Thomas

Role: Centre-forward 1991-1993
5' 11"
b. Birmingham, 25th November 1965

CAREER: West Bromwich Albion sch/ Alvechurch/Walsall Dec 1983/West Ham United July 1988 £600,000/Leicester City Mar 1990 £300,000/UNITED Dec 1991 £250,000/ Wolverhampton Wanderers June 1993 £750,000/Sunderland Sept 1995 £1m.

Debut v Port Vale (h) 7/12/91

Hugely impressive during United's last gasp battle to avoid relegation from Division Two in season 1991-92, David Kelly netted 11 vital goals and then proceeded to become the club's top goalgetter with 24 strikes when they earned promotion twelve months later. Not a spectacular striker, but a player's player, honest with lots of effort, deceptively quick around the penalty area and able to take a chance on the ground or in the air. Kelly burst onto the scene as a teenager with Walsall, and after striking 26 goals in season 1986-87 attracted the attention of top clubs, moving on to Upton Park. Kelly, though, had his ups and downs at both

David Kelly

West Ham, and later Leicester, but flourished under Kevin Keegan's inspiration at Gallowgate. Alongside Gavin Peacock and Andy Cole, Kelly became a successful front-line pivot before being somewhat surprisingly discarded as the Magpies entered the Premier League. Kelly had netted a hat-trick in his last match against former club Leicester City, while he also grabbed three on his debut for Eire. Before turning professional at Fellows Park, David had trials with Wolves as well as Southampton and worked at the Cadbury's plant in the Black Country. Kelly appeared in the World Cup finals in the USA during 1994.

Appearances:
FL: 70 apps. 35 gls.
FAC: 5 apps. 1 gl.
FLC: 4 apps. 2 gls.
Others: 4 apps. 1 gl.
Total: *83 apps. 39 gls.*
Honours:
20 Eire caps 1988-date/
1 Eire cap(aban) 1995/
Eire B app./Eire u21 app./
FL div 1 champs 1993, 1996/
FL div 3 prom 1988.

KELLY, Dominic

Role: Centre-half 1938-1946
6' 1"
b. Sandbach, Cheshire, 23rd June 1917

CAREER: Sandbach Ram/Leeds United Sept 1935/UNITED Nov 1938 £1,165 to Mar 1946 free.

Debut v Coventry City (h) 4/2/39

A well built centre-half of Irish decent, Dom Kelly was purchased to rival Jimmy Denmark for the stopper's position just prior to the outbreak of World War Two. Consequently his St James Park career was halted quickly and Kelly entered the army, serving in the Middle East where he appeared in many service fixtures. A great humourist, he returned to Gallowgate once peace was restored but then suffered damage to ligaments which sadly ended his career. Kelly later joined the Newcastle police force.

> **Appearances:**
> *FL: 1 app. 0 gls.*
> *War: 8 apps. 0 gls.*
> **Total:** *9 apps. 0 gls.*

KELLY, Gary A.

Role: Goalkeeper 1984-1989
5' 10"
b. Fulwood, near Preston, 3rd August 1966

CAREER: UNITED app cs 1984, pro 1985(Blackpool loan 1988-89)/Bury loan Oct 1989, pmt Nov 1989 £75,000/(West Ham United loan 1993-94)/Oldham Athletic Aug 1996 £10,000.

Debut v Wimbledon (h) 20/9/86

Gary Kelly has a marvellous football pedigree; his brother Alan Kelly (jnr) is also a goalkeeper - for Sheffield United - while his father, Alan Kelly (snr), was a noted custodian at Preston and for Eire. Graduating in 1985 at St James Park after an apprenticeship, Gary claimed the Number One 'keeper's shirt for season 1987-88 displacing Martin Thomas. As United reached 8th position in the First Division, Kelly showed he was an agile guardian and a good shot stopper, but his lack of height perhaps cost him a senior place in the top division and he was replaced by record purchase Dave Beasant. With Bury, Gary

recorded nearly 300 matches, despite being on strike for a period over a wages dispute. He once appeared for a Republic of Ireland line-up at Under-23 level and faced his brother in the Northern Ireland goal, while he achieved a similar unusual feat when his latter day Newcastle rival, Ulsterman Tommy Wright, was capped and faced Kelly across the field.

> **Appearances:**
> *FL: 53 apps. 0 gls.*
> *FAC: 3 apps. 0 gls.*
> *FLC: 4 apps. 0 gls.*
> *Others: 4 apps. 0 gls.*
> **Total:** *64 apps. 0 gls.*
> **Honours:**
> *1 Eire B cap 1990/Eire u23 app./Eire u21 app./ Eire youth app./FL div 3 prom 1996.*

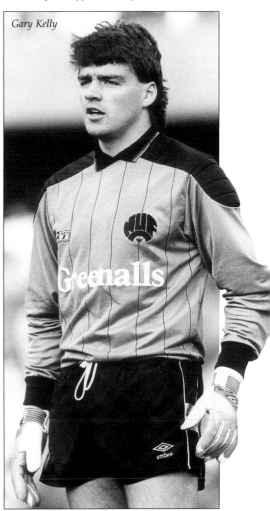

Gary Kelly

KELLY, John

Role: Centre-forward 1933-1935
5' 8"
*b. Hetton-le-Hole, County Durham,
2nd March 1913*

CAREER: Hetton jnrs/Burnley Oct 1930/
UNITED Apr 1933 exch deal with
T.Miller/Leeds United Feb 1935 £1,150/
Birmingham City Jan 1938/Bury cs 1939.

Debut v Derby County (h) 9/9/33

Reserve to Jack Allen at St James Park,
John Kelly was an entertaining player in
United's reserve side, scoring almost a
goal a game for the second string - 22 in
the club's first season of Central League
action during 1933-34. After a handful of
senior outings, John was given a chance
to take over from Allen when he
departed, but soon moved to Elland
Road where he netted 18 goals in 64
games. Before he turned to football,
Kelly had been a butcher's assistant.

Appearances:
FL: 5 apps. 1 gl.
Total: *5 apps. 1 gl.*

KELLY, Peter Anthony

Role: Right-back 1973-1981
5' 7"
b. East Kilbride, 6th December 1956

CAREER: UNITED app 1973, pro July 1974/
Retired due to injury June 1981/London City
(Canada) June 1981/Gateshead 1982.

Debut v Chester (h) 4/12/74 (FLC)

Blond-haired Peter Kelly, an attacking full-
back, came into his own on the departure of
Alan Kennedy and seemed destined for a long
run in the Number 2 shirt. During season
1978-79, Peter showed he could develop into
perhaps another Kennedy, displaying the
same enthusiastic and entertaining bursts
forward and the ability to cause danger in
attack. He was selected for the Scottish
Under-21 squad in 1976 but then tragedy
struck the young defender. Tearing his
cruciate ligament whilst playing against
Luton, the injury was serious enough to keep
him sidelined for months and eventually
caused his
retirement from
first-class
football. Kelly
was later part
of the
Gateshead side
which lifted the
Northern
Premier League
championship
in 1983. He
afterwards ran
a newsagency
business on
Tyneside, for a
period with ex
colleague Terry
Hibbitt.

Peter Kelly

Appearances:
FL: 31(2) apps. 0 gls.
FLC: 3 apps. 0 gls.
Eur: 1 app. 0 gls.
Others: 1 app. 0 gls.
Total: *36(2) apps. 0 gls.*
Honours:
NPL champs 1983.

KELLY, William Bainbridge

Role: Inside-right 1911
5' 9"
b. Newcastle upon Tyne, 1891

CAREER: Benwell Adelaide(Newcastle)/ Balmoral (Newcastle)/Blaydon/North Shields Athletic/Watford 1910/UNITED May 1911 £200/Manchester City Nov 1911 £405/ Blyth Spartans Aug 1913.

Debut v Bolton Wanderers (a) 2/9/11

Bill Kelly joined Newcastle's staff as a 20 year-old with a noted reputation in local football with the North Shields Athletic club, a strong North Eastern League side. He started the 1911-12 season as a first choice, a replacement for the injured Shepherd, but dropped back to the reserve line-up once big signing Billy Hibbert arrived on Tyneside. Kelly was still a useful reserve however, and later did well, returning to the region with Blyth Spartans following a stint at Manchester City.

Appearances:
FL: 6 apps. 0 gls.
Total: *6 apps. 0 gls.*

KELSEY, William J.

Role: Goalkeeper 1906-1908
5' 11"
b. Boldon, County Durham, 1888

CAREER: Boldon jnrs/Boldon Star/UNITED Dec 1906/Boldon Colliery cs 1908.

Debut v Sunderland (a) 20/3/07

Like all reserve goalkeepers on United's books during the early years of this century, the thirteen stone Billy Kelsey was overshadowed by record appearance holder James Lawrence at St James Park. Kelsey was a noted local personality, one biography of the day describing him as: "although of great and ponderous build, he is immensely popular". Appearing only twice for the Magpies, during the club's 1907 championship victory, his debut was in a fever-pitched derby with Sunderland, a 2-0 defeat. He returned to Boldon after United purchased Tom Sinclair as preferred reserve to Lawrence.

Appearances:
FL: 2 apps. 0 gls.
Total: *2 apps. 0 gls.*

KENNEDY, Alan Phillip

Role: Left-back 1971-1978
5' 10"
b. Sunderland, 31st August 1954

CAREER: UNITED app July 1971, pro Sept 1972/Liverpool Aug 1978 £330,000/ Sunderland Sept 1985 £100,000/Hartlepool United cs 1987/Husquvana(Sweden) 1987-88/K Beerschot VAV(Belgium) Nov 1987/Hartlepool United Nov 1987/Grantham Town 1987-88/Sunderland 1987-88/Wigan Athletic Dec 1987/Colne Dynamos Aug 1988/ Wrexham Mar 1990 to Dec 1990/Morecambe Mar 1991/Netherfield player-manager 1991 to Aug 1992/Northwich Victoria/Radcliffe Borough 1992/Netherfield Nov 1993/ Barrow 1994 to 1995-96.

Debut v Stoke City (h) 10/3/73

Alan Kennedy

Another of United's many self-developed full-backs of renown, Alan Kennedy rapidly became a terrace favourite once he had tasted first-team action as a teenager. Brave and tough in the tackle, he never shirked at a 50-50 ball and had a natural instinct to break forward with direct runs at the opposition's box that had the crowd roaring in appreciation. Alan appeared in the 1974 FA Cup final after only a handful of senior outings and afterwards replaced Frank Clark in the left-back position, giving United four years of quality service. Capped at Under-23 and B level with United, he was also selected for a full England place in 1975, but a knee injury prevented his appearance and he didn't get another chance to play for his country for almost a decade. By that time Kennedy had moved on to Liverpool, quitting Gallowgate after relegation in 1978. In 349 senior games for the Reds, Alan won plenty of honours, including two European Cups, netting winners in both finals against Real Madrid and Roma (in a penalty shoot out). He is one of the English game's leading medal winners, possessing over ten major titles from his time at Anfield. Leaving the Football League scene in 1990, Alan played on in non-league football, becoming a local coach and radio personality on Merseyside as well as an accomplished after-dinner speaker. He resides in Ormskirk. His brother Keith Kennedy also played for the Magpies during the same era.

Appearances:
FL: 155(3) apps. 9 gls.
FAC: 21(2) apps. 0 gls.
FLC: 16 apps. 0 gls.
Eur: 2 apps. 0 gls.
Others: 16(1) apps. 1 gl.
Total: *210(6) apps. 10 gls.*
Honours:
2 Eng caps 1984/8 Eng B caps 1978-80/
6 Eng u23 caps 1975/FL champs 1979, 1980,
1982, 1983, 1984/FAC finalist 1974/
FLC winner 1981, 1982, 1983, 1984/
FLC finalist 1976/EC winner 1981, 1984/
EC finalist 1985.

Keith Kennedy

KENNEDY, Keith Vernon

Role: Left-back 1968-1972
5' 7"
b. Sunderland, 5th March 1952

CAREER: UNITED app 1968, pro July 1970/Bury Nov 1972 £3,000/Mansfield Town July 1982 free/Barrow cs 1983/ Morecambe 1986.

Debut v Nottingham Forest (a) 8/4/72

Small, stocky and the elder of the two Kennedy brothers on United's books during the seventies, Keith was the first to show. He claimed a Football League debut in season 1971-72, but it was his younger brother Alan who excelled in the same position, leap-frogging over Keith to replace Frank Clark in the left-back role. Keith departed to a lower grade of football at Gigg Lane and became a solid defender and a model of consistency, turning out in over 400 games for the Shakers.

Appearances:
FL: 1 app. 0 gls.
Total: *1 app. 0 gls.*
Honours:
FL div 4 prom 1974.

KERRAY, James Ridley

Role: Inside-forward 1962-1963
5' 9"
b. Stirling, 2nd December 1935

CAREER: Denny/Dunipace Rovers/Dunipace jnrs/Raith Rovers Aug 1956/Dunfermline Athletic Feb 1960 £2,000/Huddersfield Town Aug 1960 £8,000/UNITED Feb 1962 £10,000 plus L.White/Dunfermline Athletic Apr 1963 £3,000/St Johnstone May 1964 £6,250/Stirling Albion 1966 £6,000/Buxton.

Debut v Southampton (h) 10/2/62 (scored once)

Jimmy Kerray could operate in either inside position and started at St James Park alongside Ivor Allchurch as a replacement for George Eastham. A rather temperamental player, Kerray failed to make a big impact on

Tyneside at a time of rebuilding after relegation shock, although he had netted plenty of goals in Scottish football and been Denis Law's successor at Huddersfield. Kerray had trials at both Sunderland and Dundee before starting his football career with Raith. He later resided in the Huddersfield area, working for ICI and coaching local sides.

Appearances:
FL: 38 apps. 10 gls.
FAC: 1 app. 0 gls.
FLC: 1 app. 0 gls.
Total: *40 apps. 10 gls.*

KETTLEBOROUGH, Keith Frank

Role: Midfield 1966
5' 8"
b. Rotherham, 29th June 1935

CAREER: Rotherham YMCA/Rotherham United Dec 1955/Sheffield United Dec 1960 £15,000/UNITED Jan 1966 £22,500/Doncaster Rovers player-manager Dec 1966 £12,000/ Dismissed as manager May 1967, remaining a player/Chesterfield Dec 1967 £6,000/ Matlock Town Aug 1969.

Debut v West Ham United (h) 8/1/66

Keith Kettleborough was a wise short term purchase by manager Joe Harvey at a time when Newcastle were struggling to steer clear of the First Division

Jimmy Kerray

Keith Kettleborough

relegation zone. Thirty years old and possessing a wealth of experience, the balding Kettleborough had an immediate impact on United's midfield. His ability as a deep lying link-man, with accurate short and long passes, transformed the Magpies' performances and valuable points were picked up to escape the drop. When showing top form with Sheffield United, Kettleborough was called up for England training in 1965 and 1966. Keith also was a fine club cricketer in Yorkshire, appearing as a consistent run maker for Rotherham Town. Kettleborough lives in Rotherham, in Wickersley and for a while ran a milk business before becoming a sports coach and clerk of works at Birkdale Prep School in Sheffield.

Appearances:
FL: 30 apps. 0 gls.
FAC: 2 apps. 0 gls.
FLC: 1 app. 0 gls.
Total: *33 apps. 0 gls.*
Honours;
FL div 2 prom 1961.

KILCLINE, Brian

Role: Centre-half 1992-1994
6' 2"
b. Nottingham, 7th May 1962

CAREER: Notts County app 1978, pro 1979/ Coventry City June 1984 £60,000/Oldham Athletic Aug 1991 £400,000/UNITED loan Feb 1992, pmt Mar 1992 £250,000/Swindon Town Jan 1994 £90,000/Mansfield Town Dec 1995 free, becoming asst coach.

Debut v Barnsley (h) 22/2/92

One of the first tasks Kevin Keegan undertook on his appointment as boss of the Magpies was to tighten United's defence through the purchase of 29 year-old Brian Kilcline. Nicknamed 'Killer', and with the looks of a shaggy-haired marauding Viking to go with it, the powerful defender slipped into the heart of the defence showing a rugged, yet composed, style at centre-half as the club foiled the Second Division trapdoor. His experience as captain did much to ensure Newcastle survived and blossomed in 1992-93, although by that time he had made way for the emerging Steve Howey. Kevin Keegan noted that Brian "more than any other single player helped Newcastle United to stay up". It was at Coventry though that Kilcline had the best spell of his career, making 211 appearances and skippering the Sky Blues to FA Cup victory. Although he was perhaps short of the finer skills, 'Killer' led by example and was an outstanding defender, always grabbing his share of goals (netting over 50)

before he headed for Tyneside. Born of Irish parents, Kilcline was a personality in the English game, characterised by his long hair, walrus moustache, and at Gallowgate, a ponytail; he was quite simply a fearsome sight to strikers.

Appearances:
FL/PL: 20(12) apps. 0 gls.
FAC: 1(2) apps. 0 gls.
FLC: 3(2) apps. 0 gls.
Others: 5 apps. 0 gls.
Total: *29(16) apps. 0 gls.*
Honours:
2 Eng u21 caps 1983/FL div 1 champs 1993/ FL div 2 prom 1981/FAC winner 1987.

Brian Kilcline

KING, George

Role: Centre-forward 1946-1948
6′ 0″
b. Amble, Northumberland, 5th January 1923

CAREER: RAF/UNITED Aug 1946/Hull City
Mar 1948 £750/Port Vale Apr 1949/Barrow
Feb 1950/Bradford City Jan 1952 £3,000/
Gillingham Oct 1952/Kings Lynn June 1954/
Ely City player-coach.

Debut v Tottenham Hotspur (a) 14/9/46

Powerfully built at 6′ 0″ and weighing over 13
stones, George King arrived at St James Park
after serving in the RAF and catching the eye
in services games. With competition for
forward positions fierce at St James Park just
after the war, King had limited opportunities
and was sidelined with injuries. Up against
the likes of Milburn, Donaldson, Stobbart and
Bentley, George had to be content with two
outings during season 1946-47. Yet had King
received that little bit of luck all young
players need, his debut could have catapulted
him onto a different career route. At White
Hart Lane the big striker could easily have
grabbed a hat-trick, but the chances went
astray and King was left to scrape a career
around the lower leagues, notably at Holker

Street where he netted plenty of goals for
Barrow. George's brother, goalkeeper Ray
King, was on United's books at the same time.
George later resided in Ely.

Appearances:
FL: 2 apps. 0 gls.
Total: *2 apps. 0 gls.*

KING, John

Role: Inside-forward 1913-1920
5′ 7″
b. Dykehead, Scotland

CAREER: Partick Thistle/UNITED June 1913
£600/Dykehead Feb 1920/Clydebank Oct 1921
£500.

Debut v Blackburn Rovers (a) 1/9/13

Following good
reports from scouts
north of the border,
United's officials
were impressed with
the ball skills and
potent striking ability
of slightly-built John
King. With Partick
Thistle he had
become one of the
hottest properties on
the Scottish beat,
selected for inter-
league fixtures and
on the verge of a full
cap. Newcastle
moved quickly to
bring King to

John King

Tyneside, but despite having a respectable
record he never hit it off with United's then
critical crowd and rivalled Dixon and Smailes
for either of the schemer's channels. He once
played an entire game as goalkeeper for
United in 1915, after selected 'keeper Bill
Mellor was injured in the pre-match warm up.
King took the shirt and kept a clean sheet,
United drawing the game 0-0 with Tottenham
Hotspur. During World War One he served in
the Scottish Rifles.

Appearances:
FL: 54 apps. 8 gls.
FAC: 7 apps. 2 gls.
Total: *61 apps. 10 gls.*
Honours:
1 SL app. 1913/Scot trial app. 1913.

KING, Raymond

Role: Goalkeeper 1942-1946
6' 1"
b. Amble, Northumberland, 15th August 1924

CAREER: Amble/UNITED Apr 1942 £10/
Leyton Orient Oct 1946 free/Ashington/
Port Vale May 1949/Boston United player-
manager July 1957 £2,500/Poole Town
manager/Sittingbourne manager.

Debut v Barnsley (h) 5/1/46 (FAC)

Ray King

Ray King was a promising heavyweight boxer in the army during the Second World War, but was also highly rated as a goalkeeper by United, joining the Magpies as a youngster and turning out in unofficial war soccer for the club. He shared the Number One shirt for Newcastle with Tom Swinburne during season 1945-46 and received the nod for the important two-legged FA Cup tie with Barnsley. King was a brave but unlucky player when at St James Park. He broke both wrists saving a penalty and played on for several matches without realising the extent of the injury which ultimately led to his release from Gallowgate. Later though, he bounced back to become a celebrated 'keeper in the lower divisions with Port Vale, an important member of their 'Iron Curtain' defence, in a side hailed as cup giant-killers. He was capped at B level for his country and clocked up 275 games for Vale. Brother of United's George King, Ray's other brother, Frank appeared for Everton and Derby. After retiring from the game, Ray later returned to his native Northumberland coastline and settled in Amble practising Shiatsu, a form of physiotherapy.

Appearances:
FAC: 2 apps. 0 gls.
War: 31 apps. 0 gls.
Total: *33 apps. 0 gls.*
Honours:
1 Eng B cap 1954/1 FA app. 1955/
FL div 3 (N) champs 1954.

KINGSLEY, Matthew

Role: Goalkeeper 1898-1904
5' 11"
b. Turton, Lancashire, 1875
d. Atherton, 27th March 1960

CAREER: Edgworth/Turton/Darwen 1896/
UNITED Apr 1898/West Ham United May
1904/Queens Park Rangers cs 1905 to cs 1906/
Rochdale Oct 1907/Barrow.

Debut v Wolverhampton Wanderers (h) 3/9/1898

United's first capped England player when on the St James Park's staff, Matt Kingsley took over the custodian's role during season 1898-99, Newcastle's first in Division One. He was a regular for six seasons before Jimmy Lawrence arrived on the scene. Efficient at his game, Matt was noted for his fisted clearances in the style of the day, and also for a habit of continually swinging his arms to and fro as he was waiting for the action. Somewhat hefty at 14 stones, Kingsley took part in the club's debut in the First Division and once netted two goals when playing as a goalkeeper in a friendly. Noted as the country's most reliable goalkeeper in 1901, Kingsley later resided in the Blackburn area.

Appearances:
FL: 180 apps. 0 gls.
FAC: 9 apps. 0 gls.
Total: *189 apps. 0 gls.*
Honours:
1 Eng cap 1901/Eng trial app. 1901/
3 FL app. 1901-02.

Matt Kingsley

KINSELLA, J.

Role: Inside-left 1897

CAREER: Darwen/UNITED Feb 1897 to cs 1897.

Debut v Walsall (h) 6/3/1897

Purchased from the Darwen club during February 1897 as a player with good pedigree, Kinsella stood in for established names on two occasions during season 1896-97 as the club were striving to join the First Division. Despite being chaired by the critics, he was not held in esteem by the team committee and had departed by the summer.

Appearances:
FL: 2 apps. 0 gls.
Total: *2 apps. 0 gls.*

KIRKCALDY, James William

Role: Left-half 1904-1907
5' 10"
b. Newcastle upon Tyne, 8th November 1885

CAREER: Northern Temperance(Newcastle)/ UNITED Nov 1904 to 1907 when he returned to local football/Kilmarnock on trial Nov to Dec 1908.

Debut v Aston Villa (h) 24/3/06

A reserve player of remarkable stamina and appetite for the ball, James Kirkcaldy was a deputy to the great Peter McWilliam in United's scientific team of the Edwardian era. A different type of player to the Scottish international, Kirkcaldy was a midfield worker as compared to McWilliam's classical style. A former joiner, he appeared on three occasions when the black'n'whites lifted the championship in 1907, then was sidelined for a long period with a knee injury.

Appearances:
FL: 11 apps. 1 gl.
Total: *11 apps. 1 gl.*

KIRKMAN, Alan John

Role: Inside-left 1963
5' 10"
b. Bolton, 21st June 1936

CAREER: Bacup Borough/Manchester City Oct 1955/Rotherham United Feb 1959 £4,000/UNITED Sept 1963 £12,300/ Scunthorpe United Dec 1963 £10,000/Torquay United July 1965/Workington Jan 1967 £1,700/Netherfield player-manager Sept 1968/Rossendale 1970/Retired 1972/Horwich RMI manager 1978 to Oct 1985(in 2 spells).

Debut v Southampton (a) 18/9/63

Alan Kirkman scored twice on his debut for Manchester City and found the net on a regular basis for Rotherham, including a goal in the very first Football League Cup final during 1961. Sturdy and able to snap up the opportunist goal, he joined United as part of manager Joe Harvey's rebuilding plans, but failed to settle on Tyneside and after a handful of outings was soon on the treatment table. His stay at Gallowgate is one of the shortest on record, as he moved to the Old Show Ground at Scunthorpe within four months of his arrival on Tyneside. On leaving the game, Alan, who lives in Bolton, was employed as transport manager for a local haulage company.

Appearances:
FL: 5 apps. 1 gl.
Total: *5 apps. 1 gl.*
Honours:
FL div 4 prom 1966/ FLC finalist 1961.

Alan Kirkman

KITSON, Paul

Role: Striker 1994-date
5' 10"
b. Murton, County Durham, 9th January 1971

CAREER: Leicester City app July 1987, pro
Dec 1988(VS Rugby loan 1987-88)/
Derby County Mar 1992 cash-exch deal
£1.35m/UNITED Sept 1994 £2.25m.
Debut v Aston Villa (a) 1/10/94 (sub)

For much of his stay at St James Park, Paul
Kitson has been on the sidelines. Purchased
for a big fee prior to the shock departure of
Andy Cole, the Durham born striker initially
slipped into Cole's position at centre-forward,
although not an out and out striker. Yet,
Kitson performed with credit in season
1994-95, giving 100%
effort and finding the
net on 12 occasions
in 31 full games. But
the former Derby
County star
couldn't claim
a place in

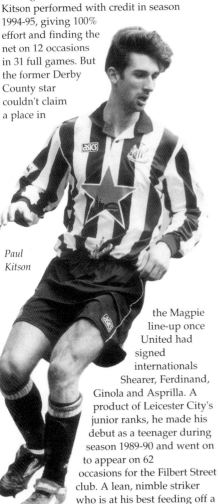

*Paul
Kitson*

the Magpie
line-up once
United had
signed
internationals
Shearer, Ferdinand,
Ginola and Asprilla. A
product of Leicester City's
junior ranks, he made his
debut as a teenager during
season 1989-90 and went on
to appear on 62
occasions for the Filbert Street
club. A lean, nimble striker
who is at his best feeding off a
target man, Kitson works hard chasing and
harrying defenders, a style appreciated by a
Newcastle crowd always willing to applaud a
trier. Paul developed into a young England
player under the guidance of Arthur Cox at
the Baseball Ground and he again found Cox
an influence during his stay at Gallowgate.
Paul was a schoolboy trialist at Ipswich Town,
but was not given a chance at Portman Road.

Appearances:
PL: 26(7) apps. 10 gls.
FAC: 6(1) apps. 3 gls.
FLC: 3 apps. 1 gl.
Total: *35(8) apps. 14 gls.*
Honours:
7 Eng u21 caps 1991-92/FL youth app.

KNOX, Thomas

Role: Outside-left 1965-1967
5' 9"
b. Glasgow, 5th September 1939

CAREER: East Stirlingshire c1958/Chelsea
June 1962 £5,000/UNITED Feb 1965 £10,000/
Mansfield Town Mar 1967 £5,000/
Northampton Town Dec 1967 £5,000/
St Mirren Aug 1969/Tonbridge June 1972.
Debut v Leyton Orient (a) 20/2/65

Joining Chelsea as a
Scot with plenty of
promise, Tommy Knox
didn't make an
impression at Stamford
Bridge but was given
another opportunity
when he arrived on
Tyneside during
United's Second
Division championship
winning season of
1964-65. Arriving to
rival the enigma of

Tommy Knox

Alan Suddick, the Glaswegian again found it
hard to claim a regular place and after a brief
run in each of the next two seasons, was
discarded to join Mansfield. A tricky winger,
rather than one with searing pace, Knox
totalled over 60 games for the Stags and later,
the Cobblers at Northampton.

Appearances:
FL: 24(1) apps. 1 gl.
FLC: 1 app. 0 gls.
Total: *25(1) apps. 1 gl.*

KOENEN, Fransiscus Leonardus Albertus

Role: Midfield 1980-1981
5' 8"
b. Waalwijk, Holland, 4th November 1958

CAREER: SV Hatert(Holland)/NEC Nijmegan (Holland)/UNITED Aug 1980 £80,000 to June 1981 when he returned to Holland/De Treffers (Holland) 1982-83/Diest(Belgium) 1983/ Vitesse Arnhem (Holland) 1984/De Treffers (Holland) 1986-87/GVVV Veenendaal (Holland) 1989 to 1991.

Debut v Sheffield Wednesday (a) 16/8/80

Frans Koenen

After a trial period at St James Park, Dutchman Frans Koenen earned a contract showing neat skills on the ball and a sweet left foot. But the pace and rigours of Second Division English football never suited his style and after the opening weeks of the 1980-81 season the sturdily-built Frans was dropped and selected for the Central League side. A past skipper of the Dutch Under-21 eleven, he returned to the Netherlands on a free transfer when he was unable to find another Football League side.

Appearances:
FL: 11(1) apps. 1 gl.
FLC: 2 apps. 0 gls.
Total: *13(1) apps. 1 gl.*
Honours:
Holland u21 app.

KRISTENSEN, Bjorn

Role: Centre-half 1989-1993
6' 1"
b. Malling, Denmark, 10th October 1963

CAREER: Belder(Denmark)/Malling (Denmark)/Horsens FS(Denmark)/AGF Aarhus(Denmark) app 1982, pro Feb 1983/ UNITED Mar 1989 £260,000(Bristol City loan 1992-93)/Portsmouth Mar 1993 £120,000/ AAB Aalborg(Denmark) July 1995 free.

Debut v Aston Villa (h) 8/4/89

Bjorn Kristensen

A respected and gifted player, Bjorn Kristensen appeared in over 200 games for top Danish side AGF before he moved across the North Sea. Capped by Denmark, 'Benny' showed United's supporters he was a composed defender who liked to use the ball and surge forward. Also able to play at full-back or in midfield, the Dane was a likeable character with European Cup experience and could hit a stinging shot. Following two seasons as a regular with the Magpies, he suffered a serious knee-cap injury which put him on the treatment table for a long period - and at a crucial time during the Keegan-led resurgence. He wasn't part of the new manager's plans and left to rejoin Jim Smith at Fratton Park for a period.

Appearances:
FL: 71(10) apps. 4 gls.
FAC: 6 apps. 0 gls.
FLC: 3 apps. 0 gls.
Others: 6(1) apps. 1 gl.
Total: *86(11) apps. 5 gls.*
Honours:
20 Denmark caps 1987-93/
12 Denmark u21 caps/
7 Denmark youth app./
Denmark Lg champs 1986/
Denmark Cup winner 1987, 1988.

LACKENBY, George

Role: Right-back 1950-1956
6' 0"
b. Newcastle upon Tyne, 22nd May 1931

CAREER: UNITED Sept 1950/Exeter City Dec 1956 £1,500/Carlisle United July 1957 exch deal/Gateshead Aug 1959/Hartlepools United Aug 1960/Ashington 1961.

Debut v Tottenham Hotspur (a) 29/12/51

George Lackenby

Tall and strong, George Lackenby was a play anywhere defender, who made his debut at right-half, then had to wait another four seasons before he gained an extended run in the side. He appeared extensively at right-back during the 1955-56 programme as a temporary replacement for the injured Bobby Cowell and was tenacious on the field, revelling in conflict, and at times stirred the crowd with his biting tackles. After experiencing demotion from the Football League with Gateshead, Lackenby moved to the Victoria Ground in Hartlepool and appeared almost 100 times before heading into non-league football. He later resided in Wallsend.

Appearances:
FL: 19 apps. 0 gls.
Others: 1 app. 0 gls.
Total: *20 apps. 0 gls.*

LAIDLAW, James A.

Role: Outside-left 1900-1901
5' 11"
b. Scotland, 1877

CAREER: Burnley 1893 (Leith Athletic loan 1896-1900)/UNITED Aug 1900 £10/Woolwich Arsenal Aug 1901 to Nov 1901 when he returned to Scotland.

Debut v Stoke (h) 15/9/1900

The purchase of Jimmy Laidlaw was surrounded by controversy. United were fined a guinea and censored by the Football Association after approaching the player in Edinburgh without the permission of his registered club, Burnley. Nevertheless the Scot joined the Gallowgate staff and proceeded to become a useful utility forward for the 1900-01 season. He deputised for fellow Scots, Fraser and Macfarlane at either inside-left or on the wing as the Magpies challenged strongly for the championship. In London with Arsenal, Laidlaw had only three outings, but netted twice and made his debut in a London League derby meeting with Tottenham.

Jimmy Laidlaw

Appearances:
FL: 10 apps. 3 gls.
FAC: 1 app. 0 gls.
Total: *11 apps. 3 gls.*

LANG, Thomas

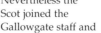

Role: Outside-left 1926-1934
5' 7"
b. Larkhall, nr Motherwell, 3rd April 1906

CAREER: Larkhall Thistle/UNITED Oct 1926 £110/Huddersfield Town Dec 1934 exch with W.Bott/Manchester United Dec 1935/Swansea Town Apr 1937/Queen of the South cs 1938/ Burnbank Athletic war-guest 1943-44/ Ipswich Town Oct 1946/Retired June 1947, becoming Ipswich Town trainer for a period.

Debut v Cardiff City (a) 24/9/27

Tommy Lang was signed by United whilst he was still working on his father's fruit farm in Lanarkshire. He was a noble little winger and an ideal team player. Following in the wake of Stan Seymour in the Number 11 shirt, Lang proved to be a splendid replacement. He had deft footwork with the ball, was accurate with his crosses and possessed a certain style, cutting in from the flank to have a shot at goal. United's official programme notes once described Lang in the words of Kipling "He's little but he's wise, he's a terror for his size". Tommy was a regular for the club over seven seasons, and in 1931-32, the year of FA Cup glory, was an ever-present; in United's semi-final victory over Chelsea the Scot made one goal and scored another to take Newcastle to Wembley. At Ipswich, Lang played on as one of the game's veterans, turning out for the Portman Road club as a 41 year-old.

Appearances:
FL: 215 apps. 53 gls.
FAC: 14 apps. 5 gls.
Others: 1 app. 0 gls.
Total: *230 apps. 58 gls.*
Honours:
FAC winner 1932.

Tommy Lang

LARNACH, Michael

Role: Striker
1977-1978
5' 9"
b. Lybster, Caithness, 9th November 1952

CAREER: Campsie Black Watch(Stirling)/ Clydebank 1972/UNITED Dec 1977 £100,000/ Motherwell Aug 1978 £70,000/Ayr United Sept 1980 £30,000/Stenhousemuir cs 1983/ Clydebank Oct 1983/Kilbowie coach c1986.

Debut v Liverpool (h) 31/12/77

Bill McGarry, after being recently installed as United's boss, signed Michael Larnach in a bid to boost the Magpies' attack. Larnach, having plundered 29 goals for Clydebank in season 1976-77, along with Mark McGhee, were both purchased for large fees, and without apparently being watched by Newcastle's boss. Larnach started the better of the pair in a black'n'white shirt but, thrown into a relegation fight, the young Scot faded and was destined for Central League football and a quick return north of the border. Mike holds an unhappy hat-trick serving United, Clydebank and Motherwell when all three clubs were relegated. With Clydebank in two spells, Larnach netted over 60 goals.

Appearances:
FL: 12(2) apps. 0 gls.
Total: *12(2) apps. 0 gls.*
Honours:
SL div 2 champs 1976/SL div 1 prom 1977.

Mike Larnach

LAUGHTON, Dennis

Role: Centre-half 1973-1975
5' 11"
*b. Dingwall, Ross and Cromarty,
22nd January 1948*

CAREER: Greenock Morton 1967/
UNITED Oct 1973 £20,000/
Retired due to injury June 1975/
Whitley Bay c1980.

Debut v Birmingham City (a) 8/12/73

Dennis Laughton impressed United's officials
when appearing for Morton against the
black'n'whites during the Texaco Cup
tournament, even though he netted an own-
goal. Joining Newcastle as a reserve defender,
he was tall and positive, but was always going
to be a stand-in to the likes of Bob Moncur.
Laughton also operated in midfield and, after
picking up a bad knee injury, later moved to
Gibraltar for a period before returning to
Tyneside where he became a Whitley Bay
hotelier. He was also employed by UK Plant in
the region.

> **Appearances:**
> *FL: 7 apps. 0 gls.*
> *FLC: 0(1) app. 0 gls.*
> *Others: 1(1) apps. 0 gls.*
> **Total:** *8(2) apps. 0 gls.*

LAVERICK, J.

Role: Full-back 1893-1894
5' 9"
b. Tyneside
Debut v Northwich Victoria (h) 13/1/1894

A tough-tackling defender, Laverick appeared
in both full-back positions for United during
their earliest Football League seasons of 1893-
94 and 1894-95. A reserve signing from local
football, he deputised for Rogers and Jeffrey
before moving to Hebburn Argyle in 1894
where he remained for two seasons.

> **Appearances:**
> *FL: 4 apps. 0 gls.*
> **Total:** *4 apps. 0 gls.*

LAW, John H.

Role: Outside-left 1893-1894
b. Scotland

CAREER: Glasgow Rangers/Everton
1893/UNITED Nov 1893 to cs 1894.

Debut v Walsall Town Swifts (a) 26/12/1893

Newcastle's directors
brought John Law from
north of the border in
an effort to improve
a flagging attack
during the club's
first ever Football
League season in
1893-94. He joined
United from
Glasgow Rangers
late in 1893 after a
delay due to the fact
he had signed already
for Everton. Obtaining a
release from Goodison, Law
quickly impressed and the
Newcastle Daily Journal noted

John Law

that he had "showed himself to be a splendid
exponent of the game". However, after a brief
flurry of action over a few weeks, the
moustached Law lost his place and returned
to Scotland.

> **Appearances:**
> *FL: 8 apps. 2 gls.*
> *FAC: 2 apps. 0 gls.*
> **Total:** *10 apps. 2 gls.*

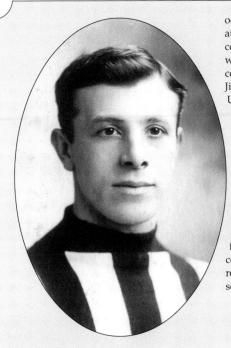

LAWRENCE, James

Role: Goalkeeper 1904-1922
5' 10"
b. Glasgow, 16th February 1885
d. Scotland, November 1934

CAREER: Partick Athletic/Glasgow Perthshire (Hibernian on loan)/UNITED July 1904/South Shields manager May 1922 to Jan 1923/Preston North End manager Feb 1923/Karlsruhe(Germany) trainer Aug 1925/Stranraer director, becoming chairman 1933 to demise.

Debut v Manchester City (h) 1/10/04

In 14 seasons as first choice goalkeeper, the durable and consistent Jimmy Lawrence amassed a record 496 senior outings for United. An intellectual dressing-room joker, Lawrence was at the very heart of United's great Edwardian line-up along with Veitch and McWilliam. In the style of the day, Jimmy rarely caught the ball but fisted away clearances and was always liable to make a stunning save, yet also a costly error - two of which occurred in FA Cup finals. Always attempting to raise spirits, he was cool, confident and extremely popular, both with Tyneside's supporters and his colleagues. A keen politician of the game, Jimmy was a leading figure in the Players' Union at a time when the organisation was struggling to take-off. On the Management Committee for several years, the Scot was appointed chairman in 1921-22 and was an outspoken voice against the establishment in the FA and Football League headquarters. Lawrence was a household name during the years up to World War One, taking part in every one of the Magpies' three successful championship sides and five cup runs to the final. Moving to the continent, Jimmy led Karlsruhe to the regional division title during his first season in Germany.

Appearances:
FL: 432 apps. 0 gls.
FAC: 64 apps. 0 gls.
War: 9 apps. 0 gls.
Others: 2 apps. 0 gls.
Total: *507 apps. 0 gls.*

Honours:
1 Scot cap 1911/
Scot trial app. 1911-12/
FL champs 1905, 1907, 1909/
FAC winner 1910/
FAC finalist 1905, 1906, 1908, 1911.

LEACH, Thomas

Role: Centre-half 1934-1936
5' 10"
b. Wincobank, nr Sheffield, 23rd September 1903
d. Bradford, 1970

CAREER: Wath Athletic cs 1924/
Sheffield Wednesday Oct 1925/UNITED June
1934 £1,100/Stockport County July 1936 £300/
Carlisle United Feb 1937/Lincoln City Sept
1938 to cs 1939.

Debut v Nottingham Forest (a) 25/8/34

Tony Leach

A personality player and one of the big names of the early thirties, Thomas Leach arrived at Gallowgate as a vastly experienced international campaigner who had served Sheffield Wednesday with distinction; 260 league and cup games over eight seasons in which he helped the Owls to two championship victories. Appointed captain of the Magpies, Leach was the pivot around which United's management were going to rebuild their new side following relegation in 1933. For a season that took place, Leach marshalling the black'n'whites but, in 1935-36 'Tony', as he was known, lost his place due to a drop in form and moved down the football ladder. Whilst at Carlisle during season 1936-37 he was involved in scandal when he accepted incentives from a director of Stockport and was banned for four weeks and heavily fined. At the beginning of his career, Leach had a trial at Liverpool and started as a centre-forward.

Appearances:
FL: 51 apps. 2 gls.
FAC: 2 apps. 0 gls.
Total: *53 apps. 2 gls.*
Honours:
2 Eng caps 1931/
1 FL app. 1931/
FL champs 1929, 1930/
FL div 3 (N) champs 1937.

LEAVER, Philip Henry

Role: Centre-half 1977-1982
5' 10"
b. Wirksworth, Derbyshire, 19th October 1961

CAREER: UNITED app June 1977,
pro July 1980/Whitley Bay July 1982 free/
Newcastle Blue Star 1983/North Shields Aug
1985/Washington Nov 1985/Blyth Spartans
Nov 1985.

Debut v Bury (h) 27/8/80 (FLC)

Phil Leaver

Locally brought up although born in Derbyshire, Phil Leaver developed through United's junior sides across the back four and earned a debut in a League Cup tie during the last days of Bill McGarry's reign as boss. With Arthur Cox installed as the new manager, Leaver rivalled Kenny Mitchell and Bruce Halliday - two other United youngsters - but didn't impress and was given a free transfer, afterwards serving various top local clubs.

Appearances:
FLC: 1 app. 0 gls.
Total: *1 app. 0 gls.*

LEE, Robert Martin

Role: Midfield 1992-date
5' 11"
b. Plaistow, London, 1st February 1966

CAREER: Pegasus(Havering)/Sovereign
(Havering)/Hornchurch 1981/
Charlton Athletic app, pro July 1983/
UNITED Sept 1992 £700,000.

Debut v Middlesbrough (h) 23/9/92 (FLC)

After appearing on over 300 occasions for
Charlton Athletic in which he netted more
than 60 goals and was rated as one of the best
performers outside the top division, Robert
Lee made the long journey to Tyneside and

very quickly became one of the top players in the Premier League too. Lee started at St James Park on the right wing during Keegan's 1993 promotion line-up and showed matchwinning ability on the touchline. Very strong in possession, able to withstand tackles and shield the ball, as well as turn quickly, Lee switched to a more conventional midfield role as United started life in the Premier League. Robert's worth to Newcastle became immense as he developed into a terrific midfielder. He was full of energy and work-rate, but also showed considerable panache at linking up front and finding the net with either powerful or placement shots. He fully warranted a regular England squad place, scoring on his debut against Romania and, according to his manager, Lee was arguably the best all round midfield man in the Premiership. Robert registered a hat-trick for United against Antwerp in a UEFA Cup tie during 1994, the only Magpie player to score three goals in European football. Additionally one of his goals in that tie in Belgium is also the quickest on record in a European game for United, netted after only 50 seconds. Brought up in London's East End, before turning professional with Charlton, Lee worked as a shipping clerk and was a turnstile operator at The Valley. An influential figure in Newcastle United's resurgence, it has often been said that when Robert Lee plays well, the Magpies play well too.

Rob Lee

Appearances:
FL/PL: 148 apps. 34 gls.
FAC: 12 apps. 3 gls.
FLC: 12 apps. 3 gls.
Eur: 3 apps. 4 gls.
Total: *175 apps. 44 gls.*
Honours:
7 Eng caps 1995-date/
1 Eng B cap 1994/
2 Eng u21 caps 1986-87/
FL div 1 champs 1993/
FL div 2 prom 1986.

LEEK, Kenneth

Role: Centre forward 1961
5' 10"
b. Ynys y bwl, nr Pontypridd, 26th July 1935

CAREER: Pontypridd Youth Club 1950/
Ynys y bwl jnrs c1951/Northampton Town
pro Aug 1952/ Leicester City Apr 1958
£10,000/UNITED May 1961 £25,000/
Birmingham City Nov 1961 £23,000/
Northampton Town Dec 1964 £9,000/
Bradford City Nov 1965 £9,500/
Rhyl Town player-coach Aug 1968/
Merthyr Tydfil/Ton Pentre/
Retired 1970.

Debut v Walsall (h) 23/8/61

Ken Leek arrived on Tyneside, following
United's relegation from the First Division, as
a new leader to replace the injured Len White.
He made an immediate impact, netting a hat-
trick on his first appearance in a friendly
against Aarhus. With a reputation as a more
than useful goalgetter, Leek had been top
scorer at Filbert Street, but had been
controversially dropped - on the morning of
the game - from their 1961 FA Cup final side
despite the fact he had scored in every round
to Wembley. A front-runner with a robust
style, Ken was seeking a new start at St James
Park. Sometimes played out of position at
Gallowgate, to United's disappointment, he
never settled in the north east and moved on
after only four months of the season. He
returned to the Midlands where he found the
net on a regular basis at St Andrews, scoring
twice in Birmingham's League Cup victory in
1963 when he led the line with zest and
opportunism. Ken totalled almost 200 goals in
his career, 50 of which came in the two seasons
after leaving United. After departing the game
he was employed by the Ford Motor
Company in Daventry and resided in
Northampton.

Appearances:
FL: 13 apps. 6 gls.
FLC: 1 app. 0 gls.
Total: *14 apps. 6 gls.*
Honours:
13 Wales caps 1961-65/
1 Wales u23 cap 1958/
FLC winner 1963/
FL div 2 prom 1965.

Ken Leek

LEIGHTON, William Alexander

Role: Inside-right 1932-1938
5' 9"
*b. Walker, Newcastle upon Tyne,
8th December 1914*
d. 1981

CAREER: Meldon Villa/Walker
Park/UNITED Feb 1932 £25/
Southend United May 1938 £1,000/
Ekco Sports player-manager c1940/
Colchester United 1945 to 1946.

Debut v Chelsea (h) 4/2/33

Well-built, but possessing a
dainty touch on the ball,
Billy Leighton made his
debut for the Magpies

during the club's relegation season in 1932-33. A reserve to Harry McMenemy and Jimmy Richardson, he spent the next five years trying to find a permanent position in the side, but was always recognised as a second choice. Leighton enjoyed good runs in seasons 1934-35 (15 apps.) and 1936-37 (16 apps.) when his expert passing ability showed up for a period. He stepped down a division in an attempt to find regular first-team action, but war intervened and halted his progress.

Appearances:
FL: 39 apps. 8 gls.
FAC: 1 app. 0 gls.
Total: *40 apps. 8 gls.*

LENNOX, Malcolm

Role: Outside or Inside-right 1895-1898
5' 9"
b. Glasgow

CAREER: Glasgow Perthshire/ UNITED Oct 1895/New Brompton 1898/ Later in 1900 returned to Scotland.

Debut v Darwen (a) 9/11/1895

A Trojan individual, and described as "a splendid player", Malcolm Lennox was spotted playing in the highly respected Glasgow local football scene. Joining United during the club's drive to get out of Division Two for the first time, Lennox helped the black'n'whites to build a side that succeeded, and was a regular in the forward line for two seasons. Always willing to work hard, Malcolm also frequently got on the score sheet, netting 12 goals during his first season of 1895-96. By the time Newcastle were pushing for promotion though two years later, he was replaced by Sunderland's veteran John Harvey and moved south. In Gillingham's pioneering side, New Brompton, Malcolm was an ever-present in their Southern League outfit until a badly broken leg sustained in a stormy derby match with Sheppey United put him out of action in 1899. The injury was serious enough to prevent him ever playing senior football again.

Appearances:
FL: 46 apps. 16 gls.
FAC: 3 apps. 1 gl.
Total: *49 apps. 17 gls.*

LIDDELL, Robert

Role: Right-half 1904-1911
5' 8"
b. Blaydon, nr Newcastle upon Tyne, May 1877

CAREER: Heaton Rothbury/ Westwood/UNITED May 1904/ Millwall Athletic June 1911 £150 to 1915.

Debut v Wolverhampton Wanderers (a) 17/3/06

United's reserve team skipper, Bob Liddell, stepped in for star half-back Alex Gardner over five seasons, including the Magpies' championship victories in 1906-07 and 1908-09. Stocky and a power on the field, he was also an expert penalty taker and, when in London with Millwall, was good enough to be chosen for the Southern League Select Eleven. Liddell had a good stay alongside the Thames, totalling 138 games for Millwall. After World War One, Bob returned to Tyneside.

Appearances:
FL: 14 apps. 2 gls.
Total: *14 apps. 2 gls.*
Honours:
4 SnL apps. 1914-15.

LINDSAY, Duncan Morton

Role: Centre-forward 1930-1931
5' 10"
b. Cambuslang, Glasgow, 1907

CAREER: Cambuslang Rangers/East Fife/ Cowdenbeath 1926/UNITED May 1930 £2,700/Bury May 1931 £525(Ashton National loan 1933-34)/Northampton Town Feb 1934/ Hartlepools United cs 1934/Barrow cs 1935/ York City June 1935/Ashton National July 1936.

Debut v Sheffield Wednesday (a) 30/8/30

One of manager Andy Cunningham's replacements for Hughie Gallacher, fellow Scot Duncan Lindsay was a good player but never on the same level as the immortal Gallacher. Short and sturdy, Lindsay had created plenty of headlines north of the border, once netting six goals for Cowdenbeath against Renfrewshire side Johnstone in 1928, and totalling over 80 goals in four seasons. United's scouts watched him on several occasions and brought the tenacious striker into the First Division where he had an excellent, if brief, career in a black'n'white shirt. Given the centre-forward's jersey for part of the 1930-31 season, Lindsay grabbed 12 goals in 19 games, good statistics by anyone's judgement. But he fell out of favour and moved to Bury where he continued his good strike-rate, as he did with every club for whom he appeared.

Appearances:
FL: 19 apps. 12 gls.
Total: *19 apps. 12 gls.*

Duncan Lindsay

LINDSAY, James

Role: Right-back 1899-1900
5' 10"
b. Stockton-on-Tees, 28th August 1880

CAREER: Stockton St Johns/Jarrow/ UNITED amat 1899/Burnley July 1900/ Bury Apr 1901 to c1911.

Debut v Glossop (a) 14/4/1900

Employed as a blacksmith when on United's books as an amateur, Jimmy Lindsay, as could be expected of his trade, was a strong, tough, well-built defender. Brother of Billy Lindsay, who was on United's staff at the same time, he was deputy to his elder brother at St James Park and received few opportunities in the club's first eleven, either in league or cup action, or in friendlies. However, at Gigg Lane with Bury, Lindsay became a noted player and captain of the Shakers when they lifted the FA Cup in 1903. Appearing almost 300 times for the club he was a rock at the back. Marshalling their defence with top class ability, he ensured his team did not concede a single goal whilst reaching the final - and then in the concluding game they romped home with a record 6-0 win against Derby County.

Appearances:
FL: 2 apps. 0 gls.
Total: *2 apps. 0 gls.*
Honours:
FAC winner 1903.

LINDSAY, William A.

Role: Right-back 1898-1900
5' 11"
b. Stockton-on-Tees, 10th December 1872
d. Luton, 27th February 1933

CAREER: Stockton St Johns/Stockton Town/Everton 1893/Grimsby Town May 1894/UNITED Feb 1898/Luton Town May 1900/Watford 1903/Luton Town Apr 1907/Hitchin Town Sept 1907 to c1909.

Debut v Lincoln City (h) 26/2/1898

A past captain of Grimsby Town, Billy Lindsay caught the eye of United's directors with his tenacious defending qualities. After appearing on over 100 occasions for the Mariners, Lindsay moved to Tyneside and took part in the club's run-in to promotion - including the Test Match series - in 1898, and then became an automatic choice for the next two campaigns. Reliable and honest, Billy led

Billy Lindsay

United out for the Magpies' debut in Division One against Wolves and was captain for that historic first season in the top flight. At Luton he became the Hatters' skipper and was at times a controversial character, once spotted at Kempton Races when he should have been playing! His younger brother, James, was also on Newcastle's books during the same era. After leaving the game, Lindsay resided in Luton to his death.

Appearances:
FL: 61 apps. 1 gl.
FAC: 1 app. 0 gls.
Total: *62 apps. 1 gl.*
Honours:
SnL div 2 champs 1904.

LITTLE, John

Role: Right or Left-back 1927-1928
5' 8"
b. Dunston, Gateshead, 18th September 1904
d. Southport, 5th July 1988

CAREER: Leeholme Jnrs/Shildon Athletic/ Crook Town 1926/UNITED Jan 1927/ Southport May 1928 free/Chester Apr 1933/ Le Havre AC(France) player-trainer Sept to Nov 1935/Northampton Town Jan 1936/ Exeter City May 1938 to 1939/Southport war-guest/Fleetwood Hesketh/High Park.

Debut v Cardiff City (a) 24/9/27

John Little was employed as a fitter and mechanic in a local Tyneside colliery when he joined United's staff during the club's championship winning season of 1926-27. Known as 'Jack', he was a reserve to Alf Maitland and Tom Evans at St James Park and played in both full-back roles before moving in an attempt to gain regular first team action. Little developed into one of the lower divisions' best equipped defenders, serving Southport especially well during their Football League years. He was in their side which met the Magpies in the 1932 FA Cup - a three game tussle that ended in a 9-0 United victory. Jack clocked up 251 first team appearances in a sure and fearless manner for Southport. After a period in local Lancashire football, he resided in the west coast resort working at a local gas works for almost 30 years.

Appearances:
FL: 3 apps. 0 gls.
Total: *3 apps. 0 gls.*

LITTLE, Richard

Role: Right-back 1912-1919
5' 8"
b. Ryton, nr Gateshead, 30th May 1895

CAREER: Clara Vale jnrs/Jarrow Croft/UNITED May 1912 £50/Hamilton Academical Aug 1919 £100 to c1922.

Debut v Liverpool (a) 26/12/12

A product of Tyneside's junior clubs, Dick Little was recognised as a "stout little performer" by the media of the day. A good man to have in reserve, Dick was an expert penalty taker in United's reserve side and performed in a brave and honest manner whenever called upon to deputise for household names, McCracken or Hudspeth. But in the main, Little had to be content with North Eastern League football and, due to the First World War, didn't get much opportunity to sample senior football elsewhere. During the hostilities he served as an able seaman in the Royal Navy.

Appearances:
FL: 3 apps. 0 gls.
War: 4 apps. 1 gl.
Total: *7 apps. 1 gl.*

LITTLEFAIR, James

Role: Outside-left
1900-1902
5' 8"
b. Tyneside

CAREER: Burradon/UNITED Apr 1900/ Tyneside local football 1902.

Debut v Sheffield Wednesday (h) 6/4/01

The press of the day wrote that Jim Littlefair was "a dainty little winger", a player who had been quite a handful in Tyneside football at the turn of the century. He was given a chance by United's directors but only managed two outings, both in season 1900-01, as a stand-in for Fraser and Niblo. Jim did, however, pick up medals with United's reserve side in the Northumberland Senior Cup and Northern Alliance.

Appearances:
FL: 2 apps. 0 gls.
Total: *2 apps. 0 gls.*

LIVINGSTONE, Archibald

Role: Inside-right 1935-1938
5' 8"
b. Pencaitland, Lothian, 15th November 1915
d. 16th August 1961

CAREER: Ormiston Primrose/Dundee/
UNITED Mar 1935 £35/Bury June 1938
£500/Rochdale war-guest 1939-40/
Leeds United war-guest 1941-42/
York City war-guest 1942-43/
Liverpool war-guest 1942-43/Wrexham
war-guest 1942-45/Middlesbrough
war-guest 1942-43/Accrington Stanley
war-guest 1944-45/Brentford war-guest
1944-45/Fulham war-guest 1944-45/
Everton May 1946/Southport June 1947/
Glenavon player-coach cs 1948/
Worksop/Dundee.

Debut v Sheffield United (a) 23/11/35
 (scored once)

Although more at home
in the inside-right
berth, Archie
Livingstone was an
entertaining footballer
who appeared in both
inside channels for
United, as well as at
centre-forward. Small
and tricky, with a
lovely body swerve
which he used to good
effect, Livingstone
joined United after a
spell as an apprentice
slater in Scotland and
had a good run in
Newcastle's side
during season 1936-37 when he totalled 15
matches. But St James Park was overspilling
with competition at the time, and Archie
rivalled the likes of Harry McMenemy and
Ed Connelly to start with, then Jimmy
Richardson and Stan Docking, and by the
time England international Ray Bowden
had arrived, Livingstone was resigned to a
move. Later, in 1943, he bagged seven goals
in a single match for Wrexham against
Tranmere.

> **Appearances:**
> *FL: 33 apps. 5 gls.*
> **Total:** *33 apps. 5 gls.*

LOCKEY, James

Role: Right-back 1895-1899
5' 10"
b. Newcastle upon Tyne, 4th January 1874
d. Tyneside, 1955

CAREER: St Thomas'(Newcastle)/ Caxton
(Newcastle)/Trafalgar(Newcastle)/Willington
Athletic/UNITED 1895/Grimsby Town Feb
1899 to Dec 1905/Hebburn Argyle.

Debut v Stoke (a) 23/4/1898 (FL Test Match)

James Lockey didn't
make a big impression
on the Football League
circuit with either
United or with
Grimsby Town, but
was recognised as a
celebrated local
character on Tyneside,
before and after his spell
at St James Park.
A Northumberland
County player, Lockey
stood in for Billy Lindsay
in the controversial Test
Matches during United's
promotion to Division One
in 1898, but only received a
single opportunity in the First
Division before being transferred south. Prior
to signing professional, he had been a brass
finisher by trade. Some sources spell his
surname 'Lockie', however the club's official
record indicates Lockey.

> **Appearances:**
> *FL: 3 apps. 0 gls.*
> **Total:** *3 apps. 0 gls.*

LOGAN, James

Role: Centre-forward 1895-1896
5' 10"
b. Troon, Ayrshire, 24th June 1870
d. Loughborough, 25th May 1896

CAREER: Ayr FC/Sunderland Aug 1891/
Ayr FC Nov 1891/Aston Villa Oct 1892/
Notts County Sept 1893/Dundee Mar 1895/
UNITED Sept 1895/Loughborough Town
Jan 1896 £10 to death.

Debut v Loughborough Town (h) 7/9/1895
(scored once)

James Logan

James Logan holds a celebrated place in football's history, being one of only three players to have grabbed a hat-trick in an FA Cup final, for Notts County against Bolton in 1894. A prolific and cunning goalgetter before the turn of the last century, the stocky Logan started his days wearing a Newcastle shirt in devastating mood, netting in each of his first four games. But he quickly fell out of favour, never getting on too well with the club's directors, and moved on within a few months of his debut. Sadly, only two years after his moment of glory in the country's biggest game, he died after appearing for Loughborough against Newton Heath in April 1896. Without kit - which failed to turn up - he played in torrential rain in his own clothes and had to wear the same attire afterwards. He developed a chill which turned into pneumonia and claimed his life, a sudden and shock demise at the time. Logan also scored on his debut for Scotland, his only cap for his country.

Appearances:
FL: 7 apps. 5 gls.
FAC: 2 apps. 3 gls.
Total: *9 apps. 8 gls.*
Honours:
1 Scot cap 1891/FAC winner 1894.

LORMOR, Anthony

Role: Centre-forward 1987-1990
6' 1"
b. Ashington, 29th October 1970

CAREER: Wallsend Boy's Club/UNITED app 1987, pro Feb 1988(Norwich City loan 1988-89)/Lincoln City Jan 1990 £25,000(Halifax Town loan 1993-94)/Peterborough United Aug 1994 free/Chesterfield Dec 1994 free.

Debut v Tottenham Hotspur (h) 23/1/88 (sub)

Anthony Lormor made his debut for the Magpies when still on a youth training scheme at Gallowgate, standing in for Brazilian international, Mirandinha. Tall and slim, Anth always looked to have the potential to succeed when he pulled on a black'n'white shirt in junior and Central League football, and after scoring on his first two full appearances for the club - against Oxford and Portsmouth - seemed set for a bright future. Yet, after that headlining opening, he rarely received a chance and had to be content to further his career at Sincil Bank. With Lincoln, Anth rattled in 30 goals and was their leading scorer in his first three seasons, while he netted in Chesterfield's play-off final at Wembley in 1994-95. Lormor had recovered from a serious knee injury which wrecked his chances of further progress at Lincoln.

Appearances:
FL: 6(2) apps. 3 gls.
Total: *6(2) apps. 3 gls.*
Honours:
FL div 3 prom 1995.

Anth Lormor

LOUGHLIN, James

Role: Centre-forward 1924-1927
5' 10"
b. Darlington, 9th October 1905

CAREER: Darlington Railway Athletic/
UNITED Nov 1924 £125/West Ham United
May 1927 £650/Coventry City Jan 1929(Bray
Unknowns(Eire) loan cs 1931)
(Dolphins(Dublin) loan cs 1931)(Worcester
City loan 1931-32)(Northwich Victoria loan
1932-33)/Darlington July 1933 to 1934.

Debut v Huddersfield Town (a) 27/12/24

A former blacksmith, Jimmy Loughlin filled in
for Neil Harris and Hughie Gallacher on
occasion during the seasons between United's
FA Cup victory in 1924 and the club's
championship success three years later. In fact
he turned out for four games of that title-
winning season, recognised as a talented
reserve able to find the net in an opportunist
way. He struck five goals in seven games
during season 1925-26 before being picked up
by West Ham where he
again failed to gain a
regular spot. He was,
though, an instant
success with
Coventry, poaching
30 goals - at the time
a club record - in
1929-30. All told
Loughlin's return
with City was first-
class - 39 goals in 65
senior matches - but
he was sidelined with
a bad injury at the
peak of his career.

Appearances:
FL: 12 apps. 5 gls.
Total: *12 apps. 5 gls.*

LOW, James

Role: Outside-right 1921-1928
5' 6"
b. Kilbirnie, Ayrshire, 9th March 1894

CAREER: Elgin City/Heart of Midlothian
1914/Glasgow Rangers 1920/UNITED Oct
1921 £1,300/Retired May 1928.

Debut v Middlesbrough (h) 3/12/21

Jimmy
Low

Jimmy Low was once splendidly described at
the time as "a dapper outside-right whose
pluck and skill is out of all proportion to his
inches". A fine, diminutive winger, he was
signed as a reserve but quickly took over from
fellow Scot Billy Aitken in United's side. A
regular over four seasons before Tommy
Urwin entered the fray, in that period Low
helped win the FA Cup for the Magpies.
Sturdy and consistent without ever being
flamboyant, he had his differences with
Newcastle's management during his period on
Tyneside, twice failing to turn up for fixtures
and by the time the 1927-28 season had got
under way, his stock with the club was at a
low point. Jimmy refused to play for the
second string in the Northumberland Senior
Cup final and United reported the Scot to the
FA and placed him on the list. Before officials
sat to hear the case, Jimmy had left Tyneside
and returned to Elgin, where he had been
brought up. The FA sat in his absence and
suspended the player. During World War One,
Low was commissioned with the Seaforth
Highlanders; he was injured in the fighting
and took some time to recover before entering
football again.

Appearances:
FL: 108 apps. 8 gls.
FAC: 13 apps. 1 gl.
Total: *121 apps. 9 gls.*
Honours:
2 SL app. 1915/FAC winner 1924.

LOW, Wilfred Lawson

Role: Centre-half & Trainer 1909-1933
5' 11"
b. Aberdeen, 8th December 1884
d. Newcastle upon Tyne, 30th April 1933

CAREER: Abergeldie/Montrose on trial/
Aberdeen Sept 1904/UNITED May 1909
£800 exch deal for J.Soye/Fulham
war-guest 1916-19/Retired cs 1924,
becoming asst-trainer and later
groundsman to his demise.

Debut v Bolton Wanderers (h) 1/9/09

Although known as 'The Laughing
Cavalier', Wilf Low was grim in his
methods, a robust destroyer
of the opposition. After his
move from Aberdeen to
Tyneside, the Magpies never
once had reason to regret
enlisting the services of this
wholehearted Scot. With over
100 games to his name with
the Dons, Low, the hero of
many a contest, was a big,
strapping centre-half who
operated in midfield, in the
days before the advent of the
defensive pivot. He was
level-headed, unrelenting
and tough yet, as one critic
remarked, was "an
ornament to the game".
Skipper of United, Wilf is
noted in Newcastle's top ten
list of appearances and,
after he hung up his boots,
looked after the Newcastle
Swifts before taking charge
of St James Park. He
resided in Leazes Terrace,
overlooking the stadium,
until his untimely death as
the victim of a road
accident in the city. Wilf's
brother Harry appeared for
Sunderland, while his son
Norman turned out for
Liverpool and Newport
County, and was on the

field when United recorded their famous
record 13-0 victory in 1946. Another
member of Wilf's family also appeared in
the game with credit; cousin William
served Aberdeen and Barnsley. During the
First World War Wilf enlisted as a sergeant
with the Royal Engineers.

Appearances:
FL: 324 apps. 9 gls.
FAC: 43 apps. 0 gls.
War: 11 apps. 0 gls.
Total: *378 apps. 9 gls.*
Honours:
5 Scot caps 1911-20/
Scot trial app. 1920/
FAC winner 1910/
FAC finalist 1911.

Jerry Lowery

Jerry Lowery impressed several scouts as a 20 year-old in local football and Newcastle fought hard to secure his signature at the end of World War Two. But Jerry found it equally hard to claim the 'keeper's jersey in the immediate peacetime seasons. With severe competition for the one senior place, he found Jack Fairbrother in top form and Jerry's chances were limited to a handful over two seasons. Joining Lincoln however, he found regular football, and claimed over 50 games before heading for the non-leagues and joining up with the Posh. After retiring Lowery became a Cheshire Homes attendant in East Anglia, and later resided in Peterborough.

> **Appearances:**
> *FL: 6 apps. 0 gls.*
> **Total:** *6 apps. 0 gls.*

LOWERY, W.

Role: Goalkeeper 1893-1895
5' 10"
b. Tyneside

CAREER: Trafalgar(Newcastle)/Gateshead NER/Blyth FC/UNITED Sept 1893 to 1895/ Tyneside local football.

Debut v Woolwich Arsenal (h) 30/9/1893

A popular local sportsman, Lowery captivated the local crowd with his marvellous reflex actions in an era of usually ponderous, and somewhat weighty, goalkeepers. Joining United for the club's Football League debut, he took over the custodian's role for their first home fixture, a 6-0 victory over Arsenal, and became first choice goalkeeper for the remainder of the programme before being replaced by Ward for the majority of season 1894-95.

W. Lowery

> **Appearances:**
> *FL: 28 apps. 0 gls.*
> *FAC: 2 apps. 0 gls.*
> **Total:** *30 apps. 0 gls.*

LOWERY, Jeremiah

Role: Goalkeeper 1947-1952
5' 9"
b. Newcastle upon Tyne, 19th October 1924

CAREER: Leicester City amat/CA Parsons Athletic 1945/UNITED June 1947/Lincoln City Feb 1952 £750/Peterborough United July 1954/Barrow June 1956/Crewe Alexandra June 1958/Wisbech Town 1959.

Debut v Huddersfield Town (a) 11/4/50

LOWES, Thomas

Role: Inside-forward 1910-1914
5' 6"
b. Walker, Newcastle upon Tyne, c.1891

CAREER: Walker Church Jnrs/Wallsend Park Villa/UNITED Sept 1910 £25/Coventry City June 1914 £50/Nuneaton Borough cs 1920/Caerphilly Aug 1921/Newport County July 1922/Yeovil Town player-trainer cs 1926, later becoming manager/Barrow trainer, becoming manager 1930/Walsall manager Apr 1937 to Sept 1939/Arsenal scout 1945/Norwich City scout 1961.

Debut v Preston North End (a) 23/12/11

Tommy Lowes

At Gallowgate Tommy Lowes was an understudy to the stars, a rival to Sandy Higgins or Jock King at either inside-right or left. Although a good solid player, he was never to reach the heights of brilliance, except on one mini-run for the black'n'whites in 1911-12 when he netted in three successive fixtures, including a derby with Sunderland. However, Lowes did well with Welsh club, Newport, totalling 125 games and 41 goals and, once he had retired, developed into one of the shrewdest men to occupy the backrooms of football. For over 40 years Tommy was linked with several clubs as a coach or scout, and when based in the north east discovered such stars as Johnny Hancocks (Wolves) and John Barnwell (Arsenal). He also discovered legendary goalkeeper Bert Williams.

Appearances:
FL: 16 apps. 3 gls.
Total: *16 apps. 3 gls.*

LOWRIE, George

Role: Centre-forward 1948-1949
5' 9"
b. Tonypandy, Glamorgan, 19th December 1919
d. Bristol, 3rd May 1989

CAREER: Tonypandy 1933/Swansea Town amat Aug 1936, pro Jan 1937/Preston North End Dec 1937 cash-exch deal/Coventry City June 1939 £1,750/Northampton Town war-guest 1941-42/Lincoln City war-guest 1943-44/UNITED Mar 1948 £18,500/ Bristol City Sept 1949 £10,000/Coventry City Feb 1952/Lovells Athletic July 1953 to 1955.

Debut v Southampton (a) 13/3/48

When he joined the Tynesiders, George Lowrie was the club's record signing and the third most expensive purchase in the game. The Welshman had boasted a tremendous scoring record in wartime football, netting 74 goals for Coventry. Then, in 1946-47 and in the opening months of 1947-48, he crashed home another 47, thereby forcing United to act. Able to operate at inside-left as well, he also netted a headlining hat-trick for Wales against England at Wembley. With a terrific shot and willing to do the fetching and carrying too, Lowrie was rated very highly throughout the country. Arriving at St James Park in a bid to boost United's promotion chances, he began well, but was quickly injured as the 1948-49 season began and was out of action for six months. By the time he was fit again, George Robledo had entered the action for United and Lowrie was surplus to requirements. At Ashton Gate he

George Lowrie

also had cruel luck with injury, a broken leg almost finishing his career. He later was employed by a confectionery firm, and resided for a period in Suffolk before settling in Bristol.

Appearances:
FL: 12 apps. 5 gls.
Total: *12 apps. 5 gls.*
Honours:
4 Wales caps 1948-49/ 9 Wales war caps 1942-46.

LUKE, George Thomas

Role: Outside-left 1950-1953, 1959-1961
5' 8"
b. Newcastle upon Tyne, 17th December 1933

CAREER: UNITED Dec 1950/Hartlepools
United Oct 1953/UNITED Oct 1959
£4,000/Darlington Jan 1961 £2,500/South
Shields c1964.

Debut v Fulham (a) 17/10/59

George Luke

A product of Walkergate schools and a schoolboy international, George Luke spent all of his football career in the north east, including two spells at St James Park as a United player. His first period, as a youngster, was totally overshadowed by the skill and consistency of Scottish international, Bobby Mitchell. But by the time the small but chunky Luke had served Hartlepool with credit - 61 goals in 183 games - he was able to show he had something to offer the top flight. Indeed, in season 1959-60 he took over from the great Scottish maestro on the left wing and looked a penetrating forward at times. However, Newcastle's relegation trauma of the following season led to Luke's departure for a second time, but he again displayed fine form for Darlington, one of the region's lesser clubs. On his retirement George resided in Newcastle, running a furnishings business in Forest Hall. He was cousin to United centre-forward Bill Curry, both playing in the same school team before joining the Newcastle youth set-up.

Appearances:
FL: 27 apps. 4 gls.
FAC: 2 apps. 0 gls.
Total: *29 apps. 4 gls.*
Honours:
Eng schools app./
FL div 3(N) app. 1958.

MAGUIRE, Gavin Terence

Role: Centre-half 1991
5' 10"
b. Hammersmith, London, 24th November 1967

CAREER: Queens Park Rangers Oct 1985/
Portsmouth Jan 1989 £225,000(UNITED loan
Oct 1991)/Millwall Mar 1993 £115,000
(Scarborough loan 1993-94)/USA football
cs 1995.

Debut v Leicester City (h) 12/10/91

Arriving from Portsmouth for a brief one month's loan deal with Newcastle United, Gavin Maguire stepped into the heart of the black and whites' defence with the aim of impressing both manager Ossie Ardiles and the fans. He did well on his first outing showing a competitive instinct and skill on the ball. However, after two more appearances and a knee injury, United sent him back to Fratton Park without the offer of a contract, Ardiles giving young Matty Appleby an extended run-out in his place. However, during his few weeks on Tyneside Maguire, eligible due to his Welsh mother, managed to play for his country as a Newcastle player in the European Championship qualification matches. Whilst with Pompey he appeared on over 100 occasions.

Appearances:
FL: 3 apps. 0 gls.
Total: *3 apps. 0 gls.*
Honours:
7 Wales caps 1990-92/1 Wales B cap 1991.

Gavin Maguire

MAHONEY, Michael James

Role: Goalkeeper 1975-1978
5' 11"
b. Bristol, 25th October 1950

CAREER: Bristol City 1970/Torquay
United Aug 1970 £5,000/UNITED
Mar 1975 £25,000/Chicago Stings(USA)
Nov 1978 £40,000/California Surf(USA)
May 1979/USA indoor soccer, including
Los Angeles Lazers 1982, becoming coach
June 1986/Later with San Bernadino
(USA) 1995.

Debut v Everton (h) 12/4/75

After totalling almost 200 games for
Torquay, Mick Mahoney became first
choice goalkeeper at St James Park
on the retirement of Willie McFaul in
season 1975-76. And for two years
Mahoney displayed fine consistency
and a string of wonderful saves,
notably winning BBC's Match of the
Day's 'Save of the Season' award for one
such effort against Ipswich in 1975. Agile
and popular, Mick was the club's 'keeper as
Gordon Lee's side won their way through to a
League Cup final in 1976 but, by the time Lee
departed and Richard Dinnis had been
installed as boss, Mahoney's form
deteriorated. Newcastle slumped and tumbled
towards the Second Division and new
manager Bill McGarry did not rate Mahoney
highly. Mick was part of an exodus of
players and went overseas to try his
luck in the USA. He played for several
years in that grade of soccer,
appearing in indoor football when in
his forties. Residing in Running
Springs, near Los Angeles, Mahoney
works for a brewery as a delivery driver.
On one occasion playing for the Magpies
against Aston Villa in 1976, Mahoney was
credited with the rare occurrence of a
goalkeeper's own-goal.

Appearances:
FL: 108 apps. 0 gls.
FAC: 12 apps. 0 gls.
FLC: 13 apps. 0 gls.
Eur: 2 apps. 0 gls.
Others: 3 apps. 0 gls.
Total: *138 apps. 0 gls.*
Honours:
FLC finalist 1976.

MAITLAND, Alfred Edward

Role: Right-back 1924-1930
5' 10"
b. Leith, nr Edinburgh, 8th October 1896
d. Leicester, c.1982

CAREER: South Shields cs 1919/
Middlesbrough May 1923 £4,000/
UNITED Oct 1924 £1,000/Jarrow
May 1930/Northfleet Nov 1930/
Salisbury City player-manager
Aug 1933 to May 1935.

Debut v Everton (a) 25/12/24

Starting as an understudy to Frank
Hudspeth at left-back, Alf Maitland
switched to the right-back role and
found a permanent position for
United's championship season of
1926-27. Dashing and fearless, and
sometimes rather erratic according to
contemporary reports, Alf had begun
his career with South Shields. He
appeared in their very first Football
League fixture in 1919 and helped the
Tynesiders on over 150 occasions. The
highly-rated Maitland appeared for
Scotland in trial games during 1923
and also for the Football League, a
rarity for a Scot to turn out for the
English at such a level. Alf was a
controversial character, leaving
Middlesbrough for Gallowgate after a
bust up, while he also fell into dispute
with the Magpies too. Along with
Hughie Gallacher, he was accused of
being drunk on the field when on tour
in Hungary and in 1930 parted
company with United amidst heated
arguments, being put on the transfer
list at such a high fee that no other top
club would buy him. Maitland drifted
into non-league soccer, later residing
in Leicester after a spell as a publican
in North Shields.

Appearances:
FL: 156 apps. 0 gls.
FAC: 7 apps. 0 gls.
Total: *163 apps. 0 gls.*
Honours:
Scot trial app. 1923/
1 FL app. 1923/
FL champs. 1927.

MAKEL, Lee Robert

Role: Midfield 1989-1992
5' 10"
b. Washington, 11th January 1973

CAREER: Springwell jnrs/Hilda Park jnrs/
UNITED sch Feb 1987, app June 1989, pro Feb
1991/Blackburn Rovers July 1992 £160,000
(plus £28,000 from subsequent move)/
Huddersfield Town Oct 1995 £300,000.

Debut v West Bromwich Albion (a) 4/5/91 (sub)

Slightly-built at
only ten stone,
blond-haired Lee
Makel was a
lightweight
midfielder who
possessed a good
touch on the ball
and a silky style.
He was given a
first opportunity
as a 17 year-old in
the Zenith Data
Cup, then a few
outings in league
action during
the reign of
Ossie Ardiles

Lee Makel

and his youthful set-up. However, the
Argentinian's departure and the new batch of
talent brought together by Kevin Keegan saw
Makel very much a promising reserve. Kenny
Dalglish at Blackburn had been impressed
with his attitude and ability and purchased his
talent to compete for a place at Ewood Park.
But again Lee found he was second or third
choice, although he did appear in the
European Champion's League with Rovers
during season 1995-96.
Moving to Huddersfield,
Makel appeared in the
Endsleigh Football League
select team.

Appearances:
FL: 6(6) apps. 1 gl.
FLC: 1 app. 0 gls.
Others: 0(1) app. 0 gls.
Total: *7(7) apps. 1 gl.*
Honours:
1 FL u21 app. 1996.

MALCOLM, Walter Grant Lees

Role: Outside-right 1957-1960
5' 8"
b. Musselburgh, nr Edinburgh,
25th October 1940

CAREER: Dalkeith Thistle/UNITED Oct 1957
£800/Raith Rovers July 1960 £500/Scottish
junior football 1961.

Debut v Nottingham Forest (h) 10/10/59

As an 18 year-old debutant for the Magpies,
Grant Malcolm made what was described as a
"promising right wing display" when he first
pulled on a black and white shirt. He played
well on his only appearance against
Nottingham Forest, despite an early knock
that required a heavily bandaged ankle.
Standing in for Gordon Hughes, Grant
afterwards rarely got close to another first
team outing and returned over the border to
conclude his career in Scotland, prominently
in non-league football.

Appearances:
FL: 1 app. 0 gls.
Total: *1 app. 0 gls.*
Honours:
Scot schools app.

MANNERS, Peter

Role: Midfield 1977-1979
5' 10"
b. Sunderland, 31st July 1959

CAREER: UNITED July 1977/Seiko Sports
(Hong Kong) Dec 1979 to Mar 1980/
Blyth Spartans Mar 1981/Bedlington Terriers
Sept 1983/Seaton Delaval 1985.

Debut v Bristol Rovers (h) 2/5/79

The slimly-built Peter Manners shone in
Central League football and well deserved
his promotion to the senior side during the
latter stages of the 1978-79 season. Coming
in for Mick Martin, he showed plenty of
running ability and potential, but like many
fringe players wasn't given the opportunity
and moved to the Far East for a year before
returning to the region to appear in local
football.

Peter Manners

Appearances:
FL: 2 apps. 0 gls.
Total: *2 apps. 0 gls.*

MARKIE, John

Role: Right-half 1962-1964
5' 10"
*b. Bo'ness, West Lothian,
16th December 1944*

CAREER: Bathgate St Marys/
UNITED Apr 1962/Falkirk May 1964
free/Clyde 1976 to 1977.

Debut v Northampton Town (h) 26/10/63

A past captain of Scotland schoolboys, John
Markie was a bright prospect in United's
junior ranks along with the likes of Bob
Moncur, David Craig and Bryan Robson. He
helped to win the club's first ever FA Youth
Cup victory and manager Joe Harvey handed
the Scot a debut during the 1963-64 season.
But that was always going to be a stop gap
move, and within weeks the headline signing
of England international Stan Anderson from
Roker Park meant John's career development
was blocked. He was released and went on to
serve Falkirk with distinction. In 12 seasons
Markie totalled in excess of 400 games and
twice helped the Bairns to promotion.

Appearances:
FL: 2 apps. 0 gls.
Total: *2 apps. 0 gls.*
Honours:
*Scot schools app./FA Youth Cup winner 1962/
SL div 2 champs 1970, 1975.*

MARSHALL, Gordon

Role: Goalkeeper 1963-1968
6' 1"
b. Farnham, Surrey, 2nd July 1939

CAREER: Balgreen Rovers/Dalkeith Thistle/
Heart of Midlothian July 1956/UNITED June
1963 £18,500/Nottingham Forest Oct 1968
£17,500/Hibernian Apr 1969/Glasgow Celtic
July 1971 free/Aberdeen Jan 1972/Arbroath
June 1972 to July 1975/Newtongrange Star
player-coach 1975/Arbroath 1975/
Newtongrange Star Feb 1980 to cs 1981.

Debut v Derby County (h) 24/8/63

Although born in deepest England when his
father was stationed in Aldershot with the
army, Gordon Marshall was raised in Lothian
and was picked up by Hearts. A tall and
commanding 'keeper, he made a big name for
himself at Tynecastle, claiming 338 first team
matches and earning championship and cup
medals in Scotland. Unspectacular, but safe
and consistent, he was also chosen to
represent England's Under-23 line-up and on
several occasions United watched his progress.
When Newcastle ran into a wages dispute
with first-choice goalkeeper, Dave Hollins,
they moved to sign Marshall for what was
then a hefty fee. Remembered for his bravery
in rushing at forwards' feet, Gordon was an
ever-present as the Magpies lifted the Second
Division title, and a regular as they established
a place in Division One. From a sporting
family, his eldest son is also a goalkeeper
named Gordon and appears for Celtic, while
his younger offspring Scott is on Arsenal's
books and was a member of Scotland's youth
World Cup side in 1989. Additionally his
daughter appeared for the British basketball
side. Gordon played in European Cup football
with Celtic, and after a long playing career
eventually settled in Edinburgh, running a
newsagency and barbers business close to the
capital's famous Princes Street thoroughfare.

Appearances:
FL: 177 apps. 0 gls.
FAC: 6 apps. 0 gls.
FLC: 4 apps. 0 gls.
Total: *187 apps. 0 gls.*
Honours:
*1 Eng u23 cap 1960/FL div 2 champs 1965/
SL champs 1960/SLC winner 1959, 1960,
1963/SLC finalist 1962.*

Gordon Marshall

football for Wisbech, as well as starring during an FA Cup run, he was the target of many Football League clubs and United's manager Charlie Mitten paid a large sum for the untried forward. A rival and second choice to Gordon Hughes on the flank, Marshall never developed in the way Mitten had hoped and was handed a free transfer after three seasons on Tyneside. Returning to semi-professional football, Terry was a noted non-league forward.

Appearances:
FL: 5 apps. 1 gl.
Total: *5 apps. 1 gl.*

Terry Marshall

MARSHALL, Terence William James

Role: Outside-right 1958-1961
5′ 7″
b. Wisbech, Cambridgeshire, 26th December 1935

CAREER: Wisbech Town/ UNITED Dec 1958 £7,000 to June 1961/ Wisbech Town Dec 1962/Hastings United/Bexley United.
Debut v West Ham United (a) 27/3/59

Initially tried at centre-forward in the absence of both Len White and Bill Curry during season 1958-59, Terry Marshall was though, an out and out winger. Catching the eye of United's scouts whilst playing non-league

Dennis Martin

MARTIN, Dennis William

Role: Midfield 1977-1978
5' 11"
b. Edinburgh, 27th October 1947

CAREER: Kettering Town/West Bromwich Albion June 1967/Carlisle United Aug 1970/UNITED Oct 1977 £40,000/Mansfield Town Mar 1978 £25,000/Fremad Amager (Denmark 1979)/Kettering Town cs 1980 to 1981.

Debut v Manchester United (a) 15/10/77 (scored once)

Initially a winger, Dennis Martin developed at The Hawthorns after being purchased from non-league football. At Carlisle, the thinly-framed Martin was converted into an effective midfield player with a neat and skilful touch on the ball. Clocking up 275 games for the Cumbrians, he joined United when the club were struggling to avoid relegation from the First Division. Dennis was given a place for two months, but with results not improving, was destined to spend the remainder of his Gallowgate career in the reserves. He was a

member of Carlisle's successful side when they topped the First Division in 1974. Martin resides in Kettering where he is employed by an insurance company.

Appearances:
FL: 9(2) apps. 2 gls.
Total: *9(2) apps. 2 gls.*
Honours:
FL div 2 prom 1974.

MARTIN, Michael Paul

Role: Midfield & Coach 1978-1983, 1987-1990
6' 0"
b. Dublin, 9th July 1951

CAREER: St Vincents/Reds United/Home Farm/Greenfields-in-Santry/Home Farm/Bohemians 1968/Manchester United Jan 1973 £25,000/West Bromwich Albion loan Oct 1975, pmt Dec 1975 £30,000(Preston North End loan 1978-79)/UNITED Nov 1978 £100,000 to cs 1983/Wolverhampton Wanderers Sept 1983 briefly/Vancouver Whitecaps(Canada) May 1984/Willington Athletic Nov 1984/Cardiff City Nov 1984/Peterborough United Feb 1985/Rotherham United Aug 1985(Preston North End loan 1985-86)/UNITED chief-scout Nov 1987, becoming asst-coach to Oct 1990/Glasgow Celtic coach June 1991 to June 1993.

Debut v Crystal Palace (a) 2/12/78

An effective midfield player for United, tall and graceful on the ball, Mick Martin captained both the Magpies and the Republic of Ireland during his career. Son of Con Martin, also a noted Eire international, Mick exchanged a sports manager's job in Ireland to try his luck in the professional game at Old Trafford. Solid, honest and dependable, Martin began slowly at St James Park but, as he settled, won over Newcastle's supporters with consistent displays in midfield, rarely being the one to hit a pass astray; his performances in seasons 1981-82 and 1982-83 even prompted the crowd to nickname him 'Zico' after the Brazilian ace. Despite his following from the terraces, Mick was discarded just as Arthur Cox's side was set to embark on an entertaining season

Mick Martin

which ended in promotion. Martin was left to wander around the country - and even to North America - to continue his football career. He eventually arrived back on Tyneside and was, for a short time, assistant boss to Colin Suggett during a transitional period in management during October 1988. On leaving the game, the popular Irishman resided in the north east, going into business on Tyneside running a sports shop in Swalwell. He also became a local radio pundit covering United's matches. Mick is one of only a handful of players to have been sent-off in an FA Cup semi-final, when playing for West Bromwich Albion against Ipswich Town in 1978.

Appearances:
FL: 139(8) apps. 5 gls.
FAC: 10 apps. 1 gl.
FLC: 6 apps. 0 gls.
Total: *155(8) apps. 6 gls.*
Honours:
52 Eire caps 1972-83/1 Eire u23 cap/
3 Eire amat app. 1971/All Ireland app. 1973/
1 EL app. 1972/FL div 2 prom 1976.

MATHIE, Alexander M.

Role: Centre-forward 1993-1995
5' 10"
b. Bathgate, 20th December 1968

CAREER: Gairdoch Boys Club/Celtic Boys Club 1981/Glasgow Celtic May 1987/ Greenock Morton Aug 1991 £75,000(Port Vale loan 1992-93)/UNITED July 1993 £275,000/ Ipswich Town Feb 1995 £500,000.

Debut v Sheffield Wednesday (h) 13/9/93 (sub) (scored once)

Newcastle first attempted to purchase Alex Mathie early in 1992, but the move fell through. Yet Kevin Keegan, persistent with all his transfer targets, tried again and clinched the deal almost twelve months later. A Parkhead product, Mathie only appeared rarely for Celtic in senior action, moving to Morton in search of regular football. There he became a prolific scorer and was top goal-getter in his two seasons netting over 40 times;

Alex Mathie

the Cappielaw side eventually cashed in when the Magpies took an interest. The strongly-framed, pacy Mathie arrived at Gallowgate with much to learn but, as Andy Cole's deputy, developed well and by the time he left for Portman Road - again in search of first team soccer - was a much improved player. A regular substitute for the black'n'whites, Alex became an Ipswich Town favourite and a regular on the scoresheet in Division One.

Appearances:
PL: 3(22) apps. 4 gls.
FLC: 2(2) apps. 0 gls.
Total: *5(24) apps. 4 gls.*

George Mathison

cool poise at half-back, George rivalled the tenacious Roddie MacKenzie for places at Gallowgate but, with the exception of a spell during season 1929-30, was usually second choice. Only filling in on injury, Mathison had to be content with North Eastern League soccer where he assisted United to the championship trophy. After a spell with Lincoln, he moved to Gateshead's Football League outfit and gave the Redheugh Park club good service in almost 100 games. His brother also appeared in senior football, while George was the legendary Hughie Gallacher's brother-in-law and played with, and against, the famous Scottish leader. On retirement from football, Mathison resided in Low Fell, Gateshead.

Appearances:
FL: 20 apps. 0 gls.
FAC: 2 apps. 0 gls.
Total: *22 apps. 0 gls.*
Honours:
1 Eng schools app. 1924.

MEGSON, Gary John

Role: Midfield 1984-1986
5' 10"
b. Manchester, 2nd May 1959

CAREER: Frampton Rangers/Parkway jnrs/ Mangotsfield United/Plymouth Argyle app Aug 1975, pro May 1977/Everton Dec 1979 £250,000/Sheffield Wednesday Aug 1981 £130,000/Nottingham Forest Aug 1984 £170,000/UNITED Nov 1984 £110,000/ Sheffield Wednesday loan Dec 1985, pmt Jan 1986 £65,000/Manchester City Jan 1989 £250,000/Norwich City July 1992 free, becoming asst-manager Jan 1994/Lincoln City July 1995 free/Bradford City asst-manager Aug 1995/Norwich City manager Dec 1995 to June 1996/Blackpool manager July 1996.

Debut v Southampton (a) 24/11/84 (sub)

Gary Megson headed for St James Park after a short and controversial stay with Nottingham Forest during which manager Brian Clough did not give the player a first team outing. Newcastle stepped in and Gary ended up on Tyneside, rejoining his previous manager at Hillsborough, Jack Charlton. Ginger-haired Megson had wholehearted commitment; he was a gritty link-man and a player to pass the ball short or long, but one who rarely tried

MATHISON, George

Role: Right-half 1926-1933
5' 8"
b. Walker, Newcastle upon Tyne,
20th December 1909
d. Gateshead, 19th April 1989

CAREER: Walker Celtic/UNITED amat May 1926, pro Dec 1926/Lincoln City Mar 1933 £675/Gateshead Aug 1934/Burnley May 1937 to 1938.

Debut v Bury (a) 19/1/29

A blond-haired teenage star on Tyneside during the mid twenties, George Mathison was a much coveted schoolboy internationalist who eventually signed for the Magpies. With a anything spectacular. During Charlton's one season reign at Gallowgate in 1984-85, Megson found a place in the side, but moved on quickly when a change in the hot seat occurred. He enjoyed a well travelled career but can count himself as being one of the most unlucky players of his era, reaching three FA Cup semi-finals, in 1980, 1983 and 1986, but finding himself on the losing side on each occasion. Gary's father is Don Megson, a formidable defender for Sheffield Wednesday and England.

Appearances:
FL: 21(3) apps. 1 gl.
FAC: 2 apps. 1 gl.
FLC: 1(1) apps. 0 gls.
Total: *24(4) apps. 2 gls.*
Honours:
FL div 2 prom 1984.

Gary Megson

MELLOR, William Gladstone

Role: Goalkeeper 1914-1920
6' 0"
b. Stockport, 1886
d. Burnley, 1995

Bill Mellor

CAREER: Barrow(Rugby Union) 1905/Carlisle United 1908/Norwich City May 1910/ UNITED Jan 1914 £765 to cs 1920.

Debut v West Bromwich Albion (h) 17/1/14

A former rugby player at three-quarter before switching to soccer, Bill Mellor rose to the attention of Newcastle director's when playing for then Southern League club, Norwich City. He was a noted custodian at the Canaries' old Nest ground, but after 73 matches headed for the north and Tyneside. Signed as an eventual replacement for Jimmy Lawrence, the frustrated Mellor had to watch as United's veteran Scottish 'keeper continued to perform at the highest level of consistency. Mellor waited on the sidelines, both before and after the First World War, and never received the opportunity to firmly grasp the first team jersey. He was once described as "a risk taker, but classy nonetheless".

Appearances:
FL: 23 apps. 0 gls.
FAC: 2 apps. 0 gls.
War: 1 app. 0 gls.
Total: *26 apps. 0 gls.*

METCALF, Arthur

Role: Inside-right 1909-1912
5' 8"
b. Seaham, nr Sunderland, 8th April 1889
d. Liverpool, 9th February 1936

CAREER: St Georges/Herrington Swifts/ Hebburn Argyle Aug 1908/North Shields Athletic 1909/UNITED Apr 1909 £100/ Liverpool May 1912 £150/Stockport County Aug 1918/Swindon Town June 1920/ Accrington Stanley June 1922/ Aberdare Athletic June 1923/ Norwich City July 1925.

Debut v Bradford City (a) 9/3/10

A player who claimed a high profile on Tyneside for his positive play in local football, stockily-built Arthur Metcalf earned a professional contract with United. He soon became a more than adequate replacement for internationals Howie and Stewart in the club's line-up, being clever and thoughtful, although somewhat daring with rushes on goal according to contemporary reports. Metcalf was transferred to Anfield where he was part of Liverpool's FA Cup final side just prior to the First World War. He grabbed 23 goals in 52 league games for the Reds and was a forceful and opportunist goalscorer throughout his career, the *Lancashire Daily Post* making a declaration on Arthur's ability: "A likable man who knew the whole alphabet of the game". Later, as skipper of Accrington Stanley, Metcalf occupied all five forward positions. His brother, George, was with Sunderland and Huddersfield Town. Whilst working as a gateman at Anfield, Arthur became ill and was admitted to hospital where he died at the relatively young age of 46.

Appearances:
FL: 12 apps. 2 gls.
Total: *12 apps. 2 gls.*
Honours:
FAC finalist 1914.

Arthur Metcalf

MILBURN, John Edward Thompson

Role: Centre-forward 1943-1957
5' 11"
b. Ashington, 11th May 1924
d. Ashington, 9th October 1988

CAREER: Welfare Rangers/REC Rovers/ Hirst East Old Boys/Ashington YMCA/ Ashington ATC/UNITED Aug 1943/ Sheffield United war-guest 1944-45/ Sunderland war-guest 1944-45/Linfield player-manager June 1957 in a part-exch deal for J.Hill/Yiewsley Nov 1960, becoming player-manager Dec 1960/ Carmel College(Wallingford) coach 1962/ Ipswich Town manager Jan 1963 to Sept 1964.

Debut v Barnsley (h) 5/1/46 (FAC)
(scored twice)

John Edward Thompson Milburn was nationally and internationally known as 'Wor Jackie'. A Geordie idol for over a decade as well as for many a year after he ceased to wear the black and white shirt, and in an era of wonderful centre-forwards, Milburn was widely recognised as one of the best. He had devastating pace - a former pro sprinter with the apt initials of JET - and a lethal shot in either foot. Jackie was especially remembered for his ability to swivel in tight situations to power a drive towards the net. Noted for his many spectacular goals, he relished the big match atmosphere and created headlines over and over again with breathtaking efforts, notably in the 1951 and 1955 FA Cup finals, his latter first minute header being one of the quickest ever in a final. No other United player has scored more goals in all competitions for the Magpies, while he also netted in every round of the 1951 FA Cup run to Wembley. Joining United as a youngster during the war, Jackie worked as a pit apprentice and started his St James Park career on the right wing. He also played in all other forward roles during his long career with United, equally as well as in the famous Number 9 shirt. Milburn could join expertly in approach play, and possessed tremendous ball control running at speed, as well as a marvellous sliding tackle that took the ball from opponents.

'Wor Jackie', a legend on Tyneside, a modest hero who thrilled the Gallowgate crowd for over a decade.

Jackie Milburn

fortunes for over 20 years. A member of the famous Milburn and Charlton footballing family, Jackie was a modest individual and perhaps never quite realised how huge his standing was in the north east. Given a belated testimonial at St James Park in 1967, an astonishing crowd of 45,404 welcomed him home. And his death, due to cancer, was much lamented and was given nationwide media coverage when the whole of Newcastle came to a standstill for his funeral. Jackie Milburn was the working man's hero, Tyneside's favourite son and a character who always had time for his fellow Geordie on the street. He left an impression on everyone who saw him as a player, and everyone who met him as a man. Jackie was made a Freeman of the City, and a statue on Newcastle's main thoroughfare recognises his achievement to the region.

Always in the reckoning for an England place, it was though to Tyneside's anger that he won only half of the caps he should have done. Appearing in the ill-fated 1950 World Cup finals, Jackie grabbed three for his country against Wales and two hat-tricks for the Football League eleven. On leaving United, he became as popular in Northern Ireland, appearing for Linfield in European Cup football and scoring over 100 goals in only two seasons. Jackie sampled management at Portman Road, but was never cut out for that ruthless world. Always a genuine person, a gentleman of the highest order, he returned to Tyneside becoming a respected journalist for the *News of the World*, covering United's

Appearances:
FL: 353 apps. 177 gls.
FAC: 44 apps. 23 gls.
War: 95 apps. 38 gls.
Others: 2 apps. 1 gl.
Total: *494 apps. 239 gls.*
Honours:
13 Eng caps 1949-56/
3 FL app. 1949-50/
4 NIL app. 1958-61/
FAC winner 1951, 1952, 1955/
FL div 2 prom 1948/
NIL champs 1959/
NIC winner 1960/
NIC finalist 1958/
Ulster Footballer of the Year 1958.

MILLER, James

Role: Right or Left-back 1892-1893
5' 8"
b. Scotland

CAREER: Newcastle East End c1888/
UNITED May 1892 to 1893/
Hurlford Town 1894 to 1895.

Debut v Sheffield United (a) 24/9/1892 (NL)

A Northumberland County player, James Miller was once described as "a rattling good back". One of the pioneers of Tyneside football, he turned out for the East End club as captain when they were installed at Heaton and appeared in their first fixture at St James Park against Celtic following the move across the city. Miller operated at right-back during the club's Northern League programme in 1892-93, and moved to the left flank for Newcastle's inaugural Football League season. He took part in United's first senior match against Arsenal in 1893 but soon after was disciplined after declaring in November 1893 that he didn't like training and refused to turn up for action. The club suspended Miller and he never played senior football for Newcastle again. James Miller should not be confused with two other J. (John) Millers who also appeared for Newcastle East End at the same time.

Appearances:
NL: 10 apps. 0 gls.
FL: 9 apps. 0 gls.
FAC: 1 app. 0 gls.
Total: *20 apps. 0 gls.*

MILLER, William

Role: Right-half 1895-1897
5' 9"
b. Kilmarnock

CAREER: Kilmarnock Jan 1894(Glasgow Rangers loan 1894-95)/UNITED July 1895/ Kilmarnock Mar 1897/Jarrow July 1897.

Debut v Loughborough Town (h) 7/9/1895

For a season and a half William Miller was a useful and reliable player in midfield. He had been noted as a man to watch after reaching the Scottish Cup semi-final with Kilmarnock and, following a short stay at Ibrox, moved to Tyneside. Miller slipped into United's Second

Division line-up without causing anyone alarm, except for one notorious incident recorded in the club's official Minutes of Meetings. In December 1895 whilst at Lincoln for a match, he was accused of the theft from the dressing-room of two gold rings, a charge he admitted, and as a result he was suspended for 14 days.

William Miller

Appearances:
FL: 42 apps. 2 gls.
FAC: 6 apps. 0 gls.
Total: *48 apps. 2 gls.*

MILLS, David John

Role: Midfield 1982, 1983-1984
5' 8"
*b. Robin Hood's Bay, nr Whitby,
6th December 1951*

CAREER: Middlesbrough Dec 1968/West Bromwich Albion Jan 1979 £516,720(UNITED loan Jan to May 1982)/Sheffield Wednesday Feb 1983 £30,000/UNITED Aug 1983 in cash-exch deal for I.Varadi/Middlesbrough player-coach June 1984 to May 1986/Whitby Town player-coach/Darlington on trial Aug 1986 to 1987/Dormans Athletic(Teesside) 1994.

Debut v Norwich City (h) 30/1/82 (scored once)

On Newcastle United's staff for two spells, David Mills had long been fancied by Magpie officials during his career. Making a name for himself as an unselfish striker or midfield player who loved to get forward, the Yorkshireman had an impressive record at Ayresome Park of 108 goals in 381 senior games. He became Britain's most expensive player when he moved to The Hawthorns, but only did moderately well with West Bromwich Albion, turning out in 55 league and cup matches. Hard working with a deft touch, a football brain and natural ability to find the net in front of goal, David almost moved to

David Mills

MILNE, William J.

Role: Outside-right 1894-1895, 1897
5' 9"
b. Northumberland

CAREER: Bedlington/Science & Art
(Newcastle)/Rutherford College(Newcastle)
/UNITED 1894/Sunderland 1895/
UNITED 1897 leaving the same year.
Debut v Walsall Town Swifts (a) 29/12/1894

The son of Newcastle United director and
chairman, GT Milne, William was a good all-
round sportsman, celebrated at cricket as well
as football. Milne was an auspicious local
player who represented the Northumberland
county side in 1894. Appearing in the
schemer's role as well as outside-left or right,
he was a regular player in the club's reserve
side and only occasionally was given a first
team call-up. Milne played once during the
Novocastrians' promotion to Division One in
1897-98.

Appearances:
FL: 6 apps. 1 gl.
Total: *6 apps. 1 gl.*

MIRANDINHA, Francisco Ernandi Lima da Silva

Role: Centre-forward 1987-1990
5' 8"
b. Fortaleza, Ceara, Brazil, 2nd July 1959

CAREER: Fortaleza(Brazil)/Maguari(Brazil)/
Ferroviario AC(Brazil)/Botafogo(Brazil) 1980/
Nautico(Brazil) 1982/Portuguese(Brazil) 1985/
Crezero(Brazil) 1985(Santos(Brazil) loan 1985)/
Palmeiras(Brazil) 1986/UNITED Aug 1987
£575,000/Palmeiras(Brazil) loan July 1989, pmt
Feb 1990 £150,000(OS Belenenses (Portugal)
loan 1990-91)/Corinthians(Brazil) Mar 1991/
Shimiza(Japan) 1992/Belmare Hirasuka(Japan)
1993 to 1994/Sao Joao Da Boa Vista(Brazil)
coach 1995/Ferroviario (Brazil) coach 1996.
Debut v Norwich City (a) 1/9/87

The first Brazilian to take to the field in the
Football League, Mirandinha became United's
record purchase when manager Willie McFaul
brought the international centre-forward to
England. With a reputed scorecard of netting
almost 300 goals in Brazil, the deal was a

Gallowgate in 1976, but Gordon Lee's deal fell
through and Mills had to wait for another six
years before he could pull on the black and
white shirt. And then, following an extended
loan deal, United couldn't raise enough cash
to buy him at £100,000, only for the player to
return at a cut price. During the 1983-84
promotion campaign Mills acted as a utility
forward, on the bench more often than not,
but always an experienced head to call upon
and who scored some crucial goals in that
successful season. After quitting the game
Mills was employed as a sales executive with a
printing group based in Bishop Auckland, as
well as becoming a sports journalist for *The
People* newspaper. In 1988 he was seriously
injured in a fatal car accident on Tyneside and
took many months to recover.

Appearances:
FL: 33(6) apps. 9 gls.
FLC: 0(2) apps. 0 gls.
Total: *33(8) apps. 9 gls.*
Honours:
*8 Eng u23 caps 1974-76/Eng schools app./
FL div 2 champs 1974/
FL div 2 prom 1984.*

fascinating one, highly speculative and risky and in the end deemed to fail miserably. Small, with explosive pace over ten yards and nicknamed 'Mira', he packed a powerful shot and did reasonably well during his first year on Tyneside in 1987-88, although rarely producing the Brazilian magic. However, the following season Newcastle were locked into a relegation battle, and Mira was not the type of player for a grim contest on the field. He clashed with new manager Jim Smith who let the South American depart at a big loss to the club; at one stage, following a dispute over money, United's boss was quoted in the local

press as saying "he can rot in Brazil". Mirandinha was nevertheless a popular character on Tyneside, chirpy and somewhat tempestuous. From a family of eight children, as a youngster he had worked down a salt mine, and arrived on Tyneside as the owner of a pig farm in Sao Paulo.

Appearances:
FL: 47(7) apps. 20 gls.
FAC: 4(1) apps. 1 gl.
FLC: 4 apps. 2 gls.
Others: 5(1) apps. 1 gl.
Total: *60(9) apps. 24 gls.*
Honours:
3 (plus) Brazil caps 1987 on/Brazil Olympic app. 1984/1 FL app. 1988.

Mirandinha

Dave Mitchell

impressing Rangers' officials well enough to earn a contract. Big and strong at centre-forward, he had pace and was an awkward bustler up front. Mitchell landed on Tyneside after a spell abroad and two years in Chelsea's reserve side, but was only given two chances to win over manager Jim Smith. Scoring on his debut was a good start, but not enough however and Mitchell was sent back to Stamford Bridge. He qualified to play for Australia, appearing in World Cup preliminary competitions for the Aussies.

Appearances:
FL: 2 apps. 1 gl.
Total: *2 apps. 1 gl.*
Honours:
34(plus) Australia caps/SLC winner 1985/ FL div 1 prom 1993.

MITCHELL, Ian

Role: Outside-left 1970-1971
5' 9"
b. Falkirk, 9th May 1946
d. Broughty Ferry, nr Dundee, 2nd April 1996

CAREER: Woodburn Athletic/Dundee United 1962/UNITED July 1970 £50,000/Dundee United Oct 1971 exch deal for A.Reid/Falkirk Oct 1973 free/Brechin City cs 1974 to 1977.

Debut v Pesci Dozsa (a) 4/11/70 (ICFC) (sub)

Although a respected player on the Scottish beat, Ian Mitchell never fulfilled his potential when he crossed the border as the seventies decade opened. His record of over 100 goals for Dundee United in 239 league matches was a proud achievement, bettered only by two other players at Tannadice. But Ian found the different pace between English and Scottish football too much to handle, his ball playing skills on the wing, or in midfield, being swamped by quick-tackling First Division defenders. Mitchell perhaps wasn't given an extended enough run in United's side, and he quickly returned to the Tay club where he continued to impress north of the Cheviots. When courted as a schools international, the Scot had turned down a string of top clubs, including Manchester United and Spurs and became a regular with Dundee when only 16 years old. When Ian concluded his footballing career, he entered business in Dundee, retailing cash registers. He also coached local Dundee youth sides.

MITCHELL, David Stewart

Role: Centre-forward 1991
6' 1"
b. Glasgow, 13th June 1962

CAREER: Sydney City Hakoah (Australia)/ Glasgow Rangers 1983/Eintracht Frankfurt (Germany) 1985/Feyenoord (Holland) 1987/ Chelsea Dec 1988 £200,000(NEC Nijmegan (Holland) loan)(UNITED loan Jan 1991 to Feb 1991)/ Swindon Town July 1991 £30,000/ Altay Izmir(Turkey) July 1993 £20,000/ Millwall Nov 1993 to cs 1995.

Debut v Blackburn Rovers (h) 12/1/91
(scored once)

Although born in Scotland, Dave Mitchell was brought up in Australia. He eventually paid his own expenses to return to his native Glasgow to appear in trials at Ibrox,

Ian Mitchell

Appearances:
FL: 2(1) apps. 0 gls.
FAC: 1 app. 1 gl.
Eur: 0(1) app. 0 gls.
Total: *3(2) apps. 1 gl.*
Honours:
2 Scot u23 caps 1967/5 Scot amat caps 1963/Scot youth app./Scot schools app.

MITCHELL, Kenneth

Role: Left-back or Centre-half 1975-1981
5' 11"
b. Sunderland, 26th May 1957

CAREER: UNITED May 1975(Greenock Morton loan 1976-77)(Tulsa Roughnecks(USA) loan cs 1978)/Darlington cs 1981/Workington cs 1982 to Sept 1982/Seaham Red Star Aug 1983/Kuusysi Lahti(Finland) 1984/Seaham Red Star cs 1985 to Oct 1985/Gateshead Sept 1986/Newcastle Blue Star Dec 1986/North Shields 1989/Seaham Red Star Mar 1990.

Debut v Manchester City (h) 16/2/77

Originally an out and out striker for United, the tall, blond-haired Kenny Mitchell was converted into firstly, a useful utility player, then a competent left-back and later a central defender. Always eager to move forward and

have a crack at goal, Mitchell was a regular choice in season 1978-79 and had a good run in Arthur Cox's Magpie line-up during 1980-81. When he left England in 1984 to join up with top Finnish club Kuusysi Lahti, the Wearsider appeared in European football and helped to lift the local championship.

Appearances:
FL: 61(5) apps. 2 gls.
FAC: 5 apps. 0 gls.
FLC: 0(1) app. 0 gls.
Others: 1 app. 0 gls.
Total: *67(6) apps. 2 gls.*
Honours:
Finland Lg champs 1984.

Kenny Mitchell

MITCHELL, Robert Carmichael

Role: Outside-left 1949-1961
5' 11"
b. *Glasgow, 16th August 1924*
d. *Newcastle upon Tyne, 8th April 1993*

CAREER: Market-Star jnrs(Glasgow)/Boys Brigade/Third Lanark June 1942/UNITED Feb 1949 £17,000/Berwick Rangers June 1961 free/ Gateshead player-manager May 1963 to Feb 1966.

Debut v Sunderland (h) 5/3/49

Along with Jackie Milburn and Frank Brennan, Bobby Mitchell was the darling of the Tyneside crowd during the club's marvellous immediate post-war years. He cost United a record fee for a winger yet was worth every penny, winning three FA Cup winners' medals with the club and was known throughout football as 'Bobby

Dazzler'. Tall and willowy, he was famed for his immaculate ball control and wing wizardry and scored many an important goal for Newcastle, especially in FA Cup ties, over 100 all told in a career that spanned 13 seasons at St James Park. Always able to raise his game for the important fixture, he thrilled the crowd with magic footwork and ball skills - no other player has played more as a forward for the black'n'whites. He scored on his Scotland debut and would have won far more international honours but for Liverpool's Billy Liddell. Bobby, who was brought up in the shadows of Hampden Park, was the Scottish League's top goalgetter in 1946-47 (22 goals). Operating throughout most of his career in the Number 11 shirt, the Scot did have a spell at left-half during his latter seasons under Charlie Mitten. He was given a testimonial fixture in 1961 and a 40,993 crowd turned up, clear evidence of the affection in which Mitchell was held by

Bobby Mitchell celebrates with George Hannah (left) and Jackie Milburn (right) after United's FA Cup victory over Manchester City in 1955

Bobby Mitchell

MITCHELL, Stewart Anderson

Role: Goalkeeper 1953-1963
5' 9"
b. Glasgow, 3rd March 1933

CAREER: Benburb jnrs/UNITED Sept 1953
£1,050/Third Lanark June 1963 £2,500 to
c 1965.

Debut v Preston North End (a) 4/9/54

Stewart Mitchell's 48 games for United were
spread over seven seasons, 1958-59 being his
best term with 11 outings as the club's senior
goalkeeper. A reserve to Ronnie Simpson and
Bryan Harvey for the majority of his stay, as
well as later to Dave Hollins, the Scot at one
stage had a long spell as United's third team
'keeper. He was unfortunate to break a finger
when he had claimed the guardian's shirt after
an injury to Simpson. Mitchell's transfer fee
back to Glasgow was part settlement of a
match arranged with Third Lanark at the time
of the Dave Hilley transaction - a game which
in fact did not take place.

Appearances:
FL: 45 apps. 0 gls.
FAC: 3 apps. 0 gls.
Total: *48 apps. 0 gls.*

Stewart Mitchell

United's fans. Retiring in 1966, Bobby
became a noted Tyneside celebrity, a
publican for many years in Jesmond (The
Cradlewell) and Heaton (The Lochside). He
lived in Backworth to his death. Mitchell
served as a telegraphist in the Royal Navy
during World War Two, in the
Mediterranean and Pacific.

Appearances:
FL: 367 apps. 95 gls.
FAC: 41 apps. 18 gls.
Others: 2 apps. 0 gls.
Total: *410 apps. 113 gls.*
Honours:
2 Scot caps 1951/
2 SL app. 1947-49/
FAC winner 1951, 1952, 1955.

MITCHELL, Thomas Morris

Role: Outside-left 1920-1926
5' 7"
b. *Spennymoor, Co Durham, 30th September 1899*
d. *November 1984*

CAREER: Parkside United/Tudhoe United/
Spennymoor United/UNITED May 1920
£100/Leeds United Oct 1926 £785/York City
Sept 1931, becoming manager Mar 1937 to Feb
1950(Norway FA coach c 1945)/Later becoming
a York City director cs 1961 to cs 1969.

Debut v Chelsea (a) 5/2/21

Tom Mitchell was lithe, fast on the wing and
hugged the touchline in the style of the day.
Having a good record with Spennymoor,
the Magpies picked him up as the
twenties decade began and he
became a direct rival to Stan
Seymour for the outside-left
role. Tom held the position in
season 1921-22, but then saw
the legendary Seymour take
the limelight thereafter,
although Mitchell was
always on hand to
deputise for the next four
seasons. He was good
enough to represent the FA
Select Eleven, and was the
target of several clubs
before moving to Elland
Road. Mitchell became a
popular character in Yorkshire,
totalling 152 senior games for
Leeds and later assisting York City
in various capacities, captain of their
noted FA Cup giant-killing run to the 6th
Round in 1938. On retiring Tom remained
associated with the game as an FA coach
looking after Yorkshire schools. He also was a
licensee at The Peacock public-house next to
Elland Road for several years, and for a period
opened a sports shop in York. For part of the
war, Mitchell served in the RAF as a pilot
officer stationed predominantly in Norway,
where he later coached for the Norwegian FA.

Appearances:
FL: 60 apps. 5 gls.
FAC: 1 app. 0 gls.
Total: *61 apps. 5 gls.*
Honours:
FA app. 1924/FL div 2 prom 1928.

MITTEN, John E.

Role: Outside-left 1958-1961
5' 9"
b. *Davyhulme, Manchester, 30th March 1941*

CAREER: Mansfield Town amat 1957, pro
Jan 1958/UNITED amat Sept 1958, pro Sept
1960/Leicester City Oct 1961 free/Manchester
United Apr 1963/Coventry City July 1963
free/Plymouth Argyle Jan 1967 £5,000/Exeter
City June 1968/Bath City Aug 1971/Tiverton
Town/Trowbridge/Sidmouth Town to 1980.

Debut v West Bromwich Albion (h) 22/11/58

John Mitten is the son of United manager
Charlie Mitten, and brother to Charles junior
who appeared for United's reserves and
entered league football with Halifax.
John was a noted schools and youth
player, who turned out for his
country several times at that
level, showing the sort of
promise on the wing that
prompted many to claim he
was destined to develop into
a player as good as his
father. But Mitten never
became such an exciting
and penetrating footballer
and perhaps suffered
because of his father's
reputation. At St James Park
he made his debut as a 17
year-old amateur and had the
misfortune of failing with a
penalty on his first outing,
surprisingly being handed the spot-
kick during an atrocious period of
misses by the Magpies. He filled in on the
left wing on a handful of
occasions each season
during his father's reign
on Tyneside, then moved
south, doing well at both
Highfield Road and
Exeter. A natural
sportsman, he also
excelled at cricket,
appearing for
Leicestershire from
1961-1963 as a right-
hand bat and wicket-
keeper. John played for

John Mitten

Nottinghamshire and Lancashire too but without starting a senior fixture. On retiring from the game, Mitten resided in the south west, also assisting his father in a sporting promotion business. His son, John junior, signed for Coventry City during the 1990's.

Appearances:
FL: 9 apps. 3 gls.
FLC: 1 app. 0 gls.
Total: *10 apps. 3 gls.*
Honours:
Eng schools app. 1955/
Eng youth app. 1958-59/
FL div 2 champs 1967.

MOLE, George

Role: Centre-forward 1900
5' 9"
b. Stockton-on-Tees, 1879

CAREER: Stockton St Johns/UNITED Feb 1900/Burnley cs 1900 to c 1902.

Debut v Preston North End (a) 31/3/1900 (scored once)

After moving to St James Park from local football in Teesside, George Mole deputised once for Sandy Macfarlane during season 1899-1900. Although he found the net on his debut against Preston in a 4-1 defeat, the small but stocky player quickly departed, trying his fortune at Turf Moor where he recorded 12 games, netting on three occasions. One of Mole's goals for Burnley was in the 7-0 FA Cup hammering of Manchester United.

Appearances:
FL: 1 app. 1 gl.
Total: *1 app. 1 gl.*

MONCUR, Robert

Role: Centre-half 1960-1974
5' 10"
b. Perth, 19th January 1945

CAREER: UNITED app Oct 1960, pro Apr 1962/Sunderland June 1974 £30,000/Carlisle United player-manager Nov 1976, becoming manager Sept 1977/Heart of Midlothian manager Feb 1980/ Plymouth Argyle manager June 1981 to Sept 1983/Whitley Bay coach Sept 1984/Hartlepool United manager Oct 1988 to Dec 1989.

Debut v Luton Town (a) 30/3/63

Bobby Moncur was one of Newcastle United's finest captains and a superb central defender who marshalled the Magpies during the club's European success and run to Wembley in 1974. A likable Scot off the field, Moncur was a rugged and determined player on it. He began his career on Tyneside as an attacking half-back and scored in United's FA Youth Cup victory over Wolves. But the Scot struggled to claim a first-team place during his first five years with the club and almost departed for a small fee. Moncur though, was determined to turn an average career into a great one and, during season 1965-66, began to concentrate on a central defender's role. Soon he was to dominate the centre-half position as the team's key figure for the next eight seasons. United's most capped Scot, Bobby also skippered his country and was rated highly by several top names in football, including Sir Matt Busby. Dedicated to the black'n'whites' cause, he led Newcastle to a marvellous European victory in 1969, netting a stunning hat-trick over the two legged final with Ujpesti Dosza, the pinnacle of an outstanding career in the game. Before joining the Gallowgate set-up, Bob had trials with Manchester United, Preston and Wolves. After a spell in management, he returned to Tyneside opening a squash club for a period and working with Newcastle United in an insurance business as well as hospitality. He also formed a yachting company on the Tyne. An accomplished sailor, Moncur has taken part in the Round Britain and Fastnet races, as well as transatlantic crossings and the Whitbread Round The

World race in 1993. Moncur excels at most sports, being a fine golfer too, twice winning the footballers' championship.

Appearances:
FL: 293(3) apps. 3 gls.
FAC: 18 apps. 1 gl.
FLC: 10 apps. 0 gls.
Eur: 22 apps. 4 gls.
Others: 15 apps. 2 gls.
Total: 358(3) apps. 10 gls.
Honours:
16 Scot caps 1968-72/
1 unoff Scot app. 1971/
1 Scot u23 cap 1968/
5 Scot schools app./
FAC finalist 1974/
FL div 2 champs 1965, 1976/
ICFC winner 1969/
SL div 1 champs 1980(m)/
FAYC winner 1962.

Bobby Moncur

MONKHOUSE, Alan William

Role: Centre-forward 1953-1956
5' 9"
b. Stockton-on-Tees, 23rd October 1930
d. Teesside, February 1992

CAREER: Thornaby/Millwall Aug 1950/ UNITED Oct 1953 £11,500/York City June 1956 £4,000/South Shields July 1957.

Debut v Cardiff City (h) 7/11/53

Alan Monkhouse

Spotted playing for the army when on National Service, Alan Monkhouse made his debut for Millwall as a teenage amateur and quickly developed into a good striker in the lower divisions. He never settled in London though and, eager to return north, was delighted to join the Magpies, even though not guaranteed a place in United's forward line. Rivalling Milburn, Keeble and occasionally Len White - before his move to the Number 9 shirt - Monkhouse was a strong and effective centre-forward. He perhaps wasn't pretty to watch, but the Teessider's record of 11 goals in 23 matches in a black'n'white shirt is first class and, with United fighting off relegation in season 1953-54, Monkhouse took the weight off Newcastle's playmakers. He won over the fans after a hat-trick against Sheffield United and became a hero after striking two crucial goals in an FA Cup tie with Nottingham Forest the following season, although he missed out on the semi-final and final line-ups in 1955.

Appearances:
FL: 21 apps. 9 gls.
FAC: 2 apps. 2 gls.
Total: *23 apps. 11 gls.*

MOONEY, Edward

Role: Right or Left-half 1919-1927
5' 7"
b. Walker, Newcastle upon Tyne, 22nd March 1897

CAREER: Walker Celtic/UNITED Aug 1919/Hull City June 1927 £500/Scunthorpe United cs 1928/Walker Celtic 1930/Local Tyneside football.

Debut v Huddersfield Town (h) 31/1/20 (FAC)

A versatile midfielder, Edward Mooney was something of a utility player for United over the eight seasons immediately following World War One. He earned a contract having impressed when playing for United's pioneer junior club, Newcastle Swifts, in the Victory League. Operating as a regular at left and right-half, as well as centre-half - in the days before a pivot defender - Mooney was a popular local lad who had graduated to the top of his sport from being a Tyneside shipyard worker. Cheery and always ready to give the side total effort, he was nicknamed 'Peter', had a broad Geordie accent and in many ways was a true son of the Tyne. After taking part in United's FA Cup victory in 1924 and appearing on three occasions during the title success in 1926-27, Mooney was transferred to Humberside, a move tinged with controversy after Hull noted the player was unfit and claimed a reduction in the fee. The Football League committee considered the matter and judged

'Peter' Mooney

in Newcastle's favour. Following a long career in local football, Mooney later was a steward in a Washington social club. He is a great-uncle to television and music star, Jimmy Nail.

Appearances:
FL: 121 apps. 3 gls.
FAC: 14 apps. 1 gl.
Total: *135 apps. 4 gls.*
Honours:
FAC winner 1924

Tom Mooney

Famed for his hard-driven cross too, Mooney was rapidly becoming an exciting talent at St James Park just as war loomed and his blossoming career, like that of many others, was shattered in September 1939 on the outbreak of the Second World War. After leaving the game, Tom resided in the Airdrie area.

Appearances:
FL: 75 apps. 17 gls.
FAC: 5 apps. 2 gls.
War: 1 app. 0 gls.
Total: *81 apps. 19 gls.*
Honours:
2 SL app. 1934-36.

MORAN, Paul

Role: Centre-forward 1991
5' 10"
b. Enfield, London,
22nd May 1968

CAREER: Tottenham Hotspur app July 1984, pro July 1985 (Portsmouth loan 1988-89) (Leicester City loan 1989-90) (UNITED loan Feb 1991) (Southend United loan 1990-91) (Cambridge United loan 1992-93)/Peterborough United cs 1994/Enfield Feb 1996 free.

Debut v Wolverhampton Wanderers (h) 23/2/91

Paul Moran, nicknamed 'Sparrow' at White Hart Lane, was a slightly built, play anywhere striker who found it difficult to break into the Spurs first eleven, although he gained plenty appearances on the substitutes' bench. Arriving on Tyneside in a bid to solve United's goalscoring problems, Moran did not have the happiest of debuts for the Magpies. He missed a glorious chance in front of goal to find the net and to make a name for himself against Wolves, and manager Jim Smith didn't give him another opportunity. Moran attempted to carve out a career at several clubs, but was unable to gain a contract before landing at London Road, Peterborough.

Appearances:
FL: 1 app. 0 gls.
Total: *1 app. 0 gls.*

MOONEY, Thomas

Role: Outside-left 1936-1944
5' 7"
b. Tollcross, Glasgow, 31st October 1910
d. 15th December 1981

CAREER: Royal Albert/Glasgow Celtic/ Airdrieonians 1932/UNITED Oct 1936 £2,650/ Airdrieonians war-guest/Greenock Morton 1944.

Debut v Leicester City (h) 10/10/36

Tom Mooney was in great demand by English clubs following a string of good displays for Airdrie and for the Scottish League side. A match-winner, he was direct and possessed a terrific shot that became his hallmark. He wore only size four boots, but could hit the ball with stinging power towards the net.

Paul Moran

MORDUE, Thomas

Role: Centre-forward 1925-1926
5' 7"
b. Horden, County Durham, 22nd July 1905

CAREER: Herrington Swifts/
Hull City 1923/Horden Athletic 1924/
UNITED Nov 1925 £150/
Sheffield United Sept 1926 £500/
Hartlepools United Sept 1928/
Horden Colliery 1933.

Debut v Sheffield United (h) 9/12/25 (scored once)

Known as 'Tucker' and from a celebrated local
footballing family, Tom Mordue proved to be a
sturdy and aggressive little centre-forward.
Gaining a chance only in season 1925-26 as
Hughie Gallacher's deputy, Mordue
performed admirably and was always well
liked by supporters, whether in senior action
or in the club's reserve side. He bubbled with
enthusiasm and later gave Hartlepool grand
service in over 130 games. At the Victoria
Ground, Tom played alongside two other
members of his family. Another of his relations
was Jack Mordue of Sunderland and England
fame.

> **Appearances:**
> *FL: 5 apps. 2 gls.*
> **Total:** *5 apps. 2 gls.*

MOWATT, Archibald

Role: Outside-right 1891-1893, 1898-1899, 1900
5' 8"
b. South Shields, 1870

CAREER: Wallsend Park Villa/Newcastle East
End 1891/UNITED May 1892 to
1893/Hebburn Argyle 1895/UNITED cs
1898/Lincoln City June 1899/UNITED cs 1900,
leaving in the same year.

Debut v Sheffield Wednesday (h) 17/12/1898

A well-known local personality during the
years at the turn of the century, Archie Mowatt
had three spells attempting a senior career
with United, but managed only a single
outing. Standing in for Joe Rogers in season
1898-99, he was nevertheless very popular
with United's reserve spectators and was a
key figure when Hebburn Argyle lifted the
Northern Alliance trophy in 1897. Mowatt was
also a proficient racing cyclist, in an era when
the sport was very popular in the north east.

> **Appearances:**
> *FL: 1 app. 0 gls.*
> **Total:** *1 app. 0 gls.*

MULGREW, Thomas

Role: Inside-right 1952-1954
5' 6"
b. Motherwell, 13th April 1929

CAREER: Cleland jnrs/Greenock Morton/
Northampton Town July 1949/UNITED Oct
1952 £9,000/Southampton July 1954 £12,500
joint deal with W.Foulkes/Aldershot Aug
1962/Andover Aug 1965.

Debut v Blackpool (a) 8/11/52

Gritty and spirited, Tom Mulgrew was a
player with purpose, having confidence on the
ball. He showed up well during his early
games in a Newcastle shirt during season
1952-53, setting up two goals on his debut
and prompting one report to note he was "a
real top-notcher". At Gallowgate though,
Mulgrew always had stern competition of
international quality for the inside-right berth,
first from Reg Davies and then Ivor Broadis.
As a consequence he moved to The Dell in an
attempt to play regular league football and
immediately made an impression, netting after
only 15 seconds of his first appearance, the

Tom Mulgrew

Keith Mulgrove

fastest goal ever scored at the Saints' stadium. Mulgrew became a crowd favourite with Southampton, scoring over 100 goals in eight seasons and totalling 325 matches. Later Tom resided in Northampton and was employed at a local factory, playing football for the works side.

Appearances:
FL: 14 apps. 1 gl.
FAC: 1 app. 0 gls.
Total: *15 apps. 1 gl.*
Honours:
FL div 3 champs 1960.

MULGROVE, Keith

Role: Left-back 1977-1980
5' 9"
b. Haltwhistle, Northumberland, 21st August 1959

CAREER: UNITED July 1977/Barrow cs 1980 free/Blyth Spartans Mar 1981/Consett 1982.

Debut v Brighton (a) 30/12/78 (sub)

On the fringe of United's first team pool during season 1978-79, Keith Mulgrove was a reserve to either John Brownlie or Kenny Mitchell at full-back. His one and only senior

outing was as substitute at the Goldstone Ground when he came on for Colin Suggett. Being released by manager Bill McGarry, Mulgrove later moved into non-league football.

Appearances:
FL: 0(1) app. 0 gls.
Total: *0(1) app. 0 gls.*

MURRAY, John James

Role: Left or Right-half 1932-1936
5' 9"
b. Saltcoats, Ayrshire, 10th August 1908

CAREER: Glasgow Rangers/UNITED July 1932 £2,500/Albion Rovers Nov 1936 £300.

Debut v Middlesbrough (h) 31/8/32

An ex plumber turned footballer, Jimmy Murray played alongside United's first manager, Andy Cunningham, for Rangers before joining his former colleague at St James Park. Possessing wholehearted endeavour, Murray operated in any role for United in midfield, wearing four different shirts on a regular basis during his four seasons on Tyneside. As the Magpies' skipper on occasion, Murray was a consistent and intelligent performer for the club during a lean period in Newcastle's history.

Appearances:
FL: 92 apps. 10 gls.
FAC: 4 apps. 0 gls.
Total: *96 apps. 10 gls.*

MUTCH, Alexander

Role: Goalkeeper 1922-1958
5' 10"
b. *Inveraray, Argyll, 9th December 1884*
d. *Newcastle upon Tyne, 16th September 1967*

CAREER: Aberdeen Aug 1906/Huddersfield Town May 1910 £400/UNITED Aug 1922 £850/Retired due to injury 1924, becoming groundsman at St James Park until his retirement in July 1958.

Debut v Everton (h) 26/8/22

Alexander Mutch was one of the characters of Gallowgate for many a decade. Known as 'Sandy' and a former Aberdeen shipyard worker, Mutch made a name for himself after assisting Huddersfield when they entered Football League soccer in 1920, taking part in the Terriers' inaugural match. He became one of the

Jimmy Murray

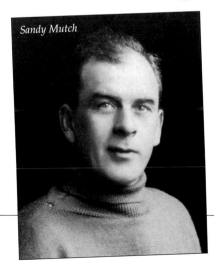

Sandy Mutch

country's most respected goalkeepers, totalling over 250 games for the Leeds Road side. One of his last games for the Tykes was in the 1922 FA Cup final, and soon after he headed for Tyneside to become a rival to Bill Bradley as United's 'keeper. Alex was, by then a veteran, almost 38 years old. He became one of Newcastle's oldest ever debutants and, when over 39, one of the oldest to appear for the Magpies. During season 1923-24, Mutch held the custodian's shirt and would have appeared at Wembley in the FA Cup final for United but for an ironic injury sustained against Aston Villa. With many of United's cup side rested for the league fixture just prior to the final, Mutch was one of only two regulars to appear at Villa Park, but he was carried off with a bad knee injury which forced him to miss the final. Mutch retired soon after due to a knee problem, but continued an association with the black'n'whites for another 34 years as groundsman and popular back stage personality, Jackie Milburn once noting "the players thought the world of him". The name of Mutch was further linked with the club when his son, Alex junior, was appointed assistant-trainer, later becoming United's physio to his death in 1987, with Newcastle for over 50 years.

Appearances:
FL: 36 apps. 0 gls.
FAC: 7 apps. 0 gls.
Total: *43 apps. 0 gls.*
Honours:
FAC winner 1922/FAC finalist 1920/ FL div 2 prom 1920.

McBAIN, Thomas

Role; Centre-forward 1932
5' 9"
b. Whifflet, nr Coatbridge, 1902

CAREER: Whifflet
Emerald/UNITED Feb 1932
£45/Carlisle United Oct 1932 to May
1934, later becoming asst-trainer
1950.

Debut v Portsmouth (a) 16/4/32

Tom McBain, a frequent Scottish
junior goalscorer, caught the eye of
many top clubs as the thirties
decade opened. United brought him
to England, but the small, tricky
leader found it difficult to break into
the Magpies' first eleven. McBain
stood in once for Jack Allen during
season 1931-32, then went on to
serve Carlisle United well for
several years. His debut and sole
outing for the black and whites
resulted in a 6-0 defeat at Fratton
Park.

> **Appearances:**
> *FL: 1 app. 0 gls.*
> **Total:** *1 app. 0 gls.*

McCAFFERY, Aiden

Aiden McCaffery

Role: Centre-half 1975-1978
5' 11"
b. Jarrow, 30th August 1957

CAREER: UNITED app, pro Jan 1975/Derby
County Aug 1978 £60,000/Bristol Rovers Aug
1980 £75,000(Bristol City loan 1981-82)
(Torquay United loan 1984-85)/Exeter City
June 1985 free/Hartlepool United Feb 1987/
Whitley Bay cs 1987/Carlisle United asst
coach Jan 1988, becoming manager Apr 1991
to Sept 1992.

Debut v Ipswich Town (a) 15/3/75

Recommended to United, by then
schoolteacher and former international athlete,
Brendan Foster, Aiden McCaffery was a bright
teenage star who appeared for the Magpies
when he was a 17 year-old. Initially second
choice to Glenn Keeley, the Tynesider was
handed the Number Five shirt for the 1976-77
season and on many occasions looked a solid

defender, alongside Geoff Nulty, with the
potential to reach the top. But during the
club's turmoil and relegation mire the
following season Aiden was one of several
youngsters to suffer. He had a series of rows
with Newcastle's management and was
released to join the Baseball Ground staff.
After a reasonable spell with Derby, McCaffery
had 224 senior outings with Bristol Rovers,
and was also skipper at Eastville.

> **Appearances:**
> *FL: 57(2) apps. 4 gls.*
> *FAC: 5 apps. 1 gl.*
> *FLC: 3(1) apps. 0 gls.*
> *Eur: 3 apps. 0 gls.*
> **Total:** *68(3) apps. 5 gls.*
> **Honours:**
> *Eng youth app. 1976.*

McCALL, William

Role: Outside-left 1948
5' 6"
b. Glasgow, 14th November 1920

CAREER: Aberdeen 1941/UNITED Jan 1948
£8,400/Motherwell Dec 1948 £5,500/
Third Lanark 1950 to 1952.

Debut v Brentford (a) 17/1/48

Willie McCall arrived at St James Park as part
of the cash and exchange deal that saw the
popular Tommy Pearson head for Aberdeen.
A compact, forceful winger, diminutive and
direct in the traditional style of flankers,
McCall took part in the black'n'whites' finale
to win promotion in 1948. But he was replaced
by firstly George Hair, then Bobby Mitchell,
when Newcastle reclaimed their First Division
place. A most popular player in the Granite
City, he allegedly left the Dons under
controversial circumstances after a row over
smoking before fixtures. On leaving the game,
Willie settled in his native Glasgow and was
employed by the Marley Tile Company for
many years.

Appearances:
FL: 16 apps. 4 gls.
Total: *16 apps. 4 gls.*
Honours:
FL div 2 prom 1948/SC winner 1947.

Willie McCall

McCLARENCE, Joseph P.

Role: Centre-forward 1904-1908
5' 10"
b. Newcastle upon Tyne, 1885

CAREER: Wallsend Park Villa/UNITED
Feb 1904/Bolton Wanderers Mar 1908 £350/
Bradford Park Avenue Nov 1908/Distillery
cs 1911.

*Debut v Blackburn Rovers (h) 3/12/04
(scored once)*

An incessant dashing goalscorer in reserve
football, Joe McClarence performed creditably
whenever called upon for first team action. He
filled in for noted forwards, Appleyard and
Orr, covering their absence well, and was
always capable of striking goals himself,
claiming 13 in his limited opportunities. Joe
took a small part in two of United's
championship successes, in 1904-05 (6 apps.)
and 1906-07 (5 apps.), before moving to Bolton
and then Bradford where he continued to bag
goals, netting 33 in 68 senior matches for the
Park Avenue club.

Appearances:
FL: 30 apps. 13 gls.
FAC: 2 apps. 0 gls.
Total: *32 apps. 13 gls.*

PROMINENT FOOTBALLERS.

J. McCLARENCE,
NEWCASTLE UNITED.

McCOLL, Robert Smyth

Role: Centre-forward or Inside-left 1901-1904
5' 9"
b. Glasgow, 13th April 1876
d. Glasgow, 25th November 1959

CAREER: Benmore/Queens Park Jan 1894/
UNITED Nov 1901/Glasgow Rangers Sept
1904/Queens Park Aug 1907/Retired 1910.

Debut v Manchester City (h) 9/11/01 (scored once)

Known as the 'Prince of Centre-forwards'
during his era at the turn of the century, Bob
McColl was a slightly-built forward with
lightning fast acceleration and reflexes.
He became a nationally known
figure after netting three hat-tricks
for Scotland in only five games
(an overall total of 13 goals in
13 games), including one in the
match against England in 1900.
As an amateur, McColl was the
doyen of Scottish football and
many were surprised when he
moved to Tyneside and turned
professional. The local press
reported United had signed "the
smartest dribbler and goalscorer in
Scotland". At Gallowgate, McColl
was recognised as an important
factor in the club's fast-developing
classical Edwardian side; Colin Veitch was to
say he "set the standard". A firm believer in
team play and possession football, Bob was
hugely popular and scrupulously fair on the
field. With the touch of a master on the ball,
McColl captained his country, in the Ibrox
disaster fixture with England, and later went
on to net six goals for Queens Park in 1910
during a single match against Port Glasgow
Athletic. His brother served for a spell in
Newcastle's reserves as well as having a
friendly outing for the senior side in 1902.
Possessed of an astute brain, the Scot later
went into business in Glasgow and founded
the RS McColl newsagents chain which
currently has nationwide outlets.

Bob McColl

Appearances:
FL: 64 apps. 18 gls.
FAC: 3 apps. 2 gls.
Total: *67 apps. 20 gls.*
Honours:
13 Scot caps 1896-1908/1 SL app. 1901/
Scot trial app. 1896-05/SC finalist 1900, 1905.

McCOMBIE, Andrew

Role: Right-back & Trainer 1904-1950
5' 10"
b. Inverness, 30th June 1876
d. North Shields, 28th March 1952

CAREER: Inverness Thistle 1893/Sunderland
Dec 1898/UNITED Feb 1904 £700/Retired Apr
1910, becoming asst-trainer and trainer in Jan
1928 to cs 1930, general assistant to retirement
in 1950.

Debut v Notts County (h) 13/2/04

During his long service of 46 years with the
club, Andy McCombie was a rare defender
who allied brawn with brain. Equally
competent on either flank, he was
tough, yet had a skilful touch. An
automatic choice for five seasons
with Sunderland, totalling 164
games, he assisted in bringing the
championship trophy to Wearside.
The Highlander moved the short
distance to Gallowgate for a record
fee, but amidst rows between
himself and the two clubs, which
ended with an FA Inquiry. After a
court hearing over a dispute of £100 as
a gift or loan, the FA stepped in and
censured Sunderland officials for an
"under the counter" payment.
McCombie partnered fellow international Jack
Carr in United's rearguard and was a key
figure in two title victories for the club, as well
as taking part in another in 1909. He was also
involved as a backstage aid when the Magpies
won their fourth title in 1927. Andy resided in
North Shields to his death and was devoted to
Newcastle's cause to his last day.

Appearances:
FL: 113 apps. 0 gls.
FAC: 18 apps. 0 gls.
Total: *131 apps. 0 gls.*
Honours:
4 Scot caps 1903-05/
Scot trial app. 1901-04/
FL champs 1902, 1905, 1907/
FAC finalist 1905, 1906.

McCRACKEN, William R.

Role: Right-back 1904-1923
5' 11"
b. Belfast, 29th January 1883
d. Hull, 20th January 1979

CAREER: Distillery Dec 1900/UNITED May 1904 £50/Fulham war-guest 1918-19/Hull City manager Feb 1923 to May 1931/Gateshead manager Sept 1932/ Millwall manager May 1933 to Mar 1936/ Aldershot manager Feb 1937 to Nov 1949/ UNITED scout Sept 1951 to c1962/Watford scout to Jan 1978.

Debut v Woolwich Arsenal (h) 3/9/04

Bill McCracken

Andy McCombie

McCORMACK, John Andrew

Role: Centre-half 1906-1909
5' 10"
b. Scotland

CAREER: Johnstone/UNITED May 1906 £25/Everton 1909 £250.

Debut v Sheffield United (h) 26/12/07

A stand-in for the elegant talent of Colin Veitch in United's Edwardian Masters line-up, John McCormack only gained a run-out in midfield during season 1907-08. He was, however, a regular fixture in the Magpies' second eleven, winning the North Eastern League title twice in 1907 and 1908. At Goodison Park McCormack didn't appear in Everton's first eleven.

Appearances:
FL: 2 apps. 1 gl.
Total: *2 apps. 1 gl.*

A celebrated figure in the game, Bill McCracken is recognised as perhaps the greatest and most colourful full-back to wear a United shirt. With a superb tactical mind, Bill perfected the offside game so well that he frustrated the opposition, and supporters, to such an extent that in 1925 football's authorities were compelled to change the rules. His tactical ploy, so cleverly delivered along with Frank Hudspeth, was even put on film in 1920, McCracken demonstrating the infamous offside trap on a silent reel. A player much loved on Tyneside, but the target of abuse elsewhere, McCracken was a controversial personality, often in dispute with the game's authorities, whether his country's FA over international payments or with referees. Indeed his transfer to St James Park ended in an FA Inquiry amidst rumours of illegal approaches and underhand payments. Together with Frank Hudspeth, his colleague for many years, Bill holds a record service of 19 years as a player for the Magpies. Captain of club and country, the Irishman started as second choice to Andy McCombie, but eventually took over the right-back spot and helped Newcastle to three titles and three FA Cup finals. Cousin to Robert McCracken of Crystal Palace and Ireland, Bill was an active scout for almost three decades after he left management. He died nine days short of his 96th birthday. As a player, McCracken represented both United and Ireland when he was over 40 years of age.

Appearances:
FL: 377 apps. 6 gls.
FAC: 55 apps. 2 gls.
War: 10 apps. 0 gls.
Others: 2 apps. 0 gls.
Total: *444 apps. 8 gls.*
Honours:
15 Irel caps 1902-23/1 unoff Irel cap 1903/
2 Irel war caps 1919/5 IL app. 1902-04/
1 FL app. 1918/1 unoff FL app. 1914/
FL champs 1905, 1907, 1909/
FAC winner 1910/FAC finalist 1908, 1911/
IL champs 1903/IC winner 1903/
IC finalist 1902/FA Long Service Medal 1978.

Bill McCracken, one of the game's most celebrated players.

David McCreery

A vastly underrated midfielder, full of fire and determination, David McCreery became United's anchor man as the club won promotion in 1984. A product of the Old Trafford nursery, David was in Manchester United's line-up at 16 years of age and turned out twice at Wembley in cup finals when barely out of his teens. A perpetual substitute for the Reds - coming off the bench on over 50 occasions - he left in search of regular action, and performed in his battling style for Queens Park Rangers and then in America's razzmatazz. Returning to England, he joined up with Arthur Cox's exciting team at Gallowgate, linking perfectly with Terry McDermott in midfield and once noting "my job is to win the ball and give it to somebody else". He aquitted himself most effectively in that role, always going in where it hurt and was a fine foil to the silky skills of Keegan, Beardsley and Waddle. McCreery was a regular for his country, taking part in the 1982 and 1986 World Cup finals. After leaving the game, David resided in Hepscott, Morpeth, near Newcastle. He ran a hospitality company as well as being a European consultant for MLS, the new American soccer organisation.

Appearances:
FL: 237(6) apps. 2 gls.
FAC: 10(1) apps. 0 gls.
FLC: 15 apps. 0 gls.
Others: 4 apps. 0 gls.
Total: *266(7) apps. 2 gls.*
Honours:
67 N.Irel caps 1976-90/1 N.Irel u21 cap 1978/
N.Irel youth app./N.Irel schools app./
FL div 2 prom 1984/FAC winner 1977/
FAC finalist 1976.

McCREERY, David

Role: Midfield 1982-1989
5' 7"
b. Belfast, 16th September 1957

CAREER: Manchester United amat Sept 1972, app Apr 1974, pro Oct 1974/Queens Park Rangers Aug 1979 £200,000/Tulsa Roughnecks (USA) Mar 1981 £225,000 joint deal/UNITED Oct 1982 £75,000/Sundsvaal (Sweden) June 1989/Heart of Midlothian Sept 1989 free/ Hartlepool United player-coach Aug 1991, becoming asst-manager to June 1992/ Coleraine Sept 1992/Carlisle United player-manager Sept 1992 to July 1994/ Hartlepool United manager Oct 1994 to Apr 1995/Barnet scout 1995/Blyth Spartans consultant Sept 1995.

Debut v Leeds United (a) 6/10/82 (FLC)

McCULLOCH, Alexander

Role: Centre-forward 1908
5' 9"
b. Edinburgh 1886

CAREER: Bonnyrigg Rose Athletic/Leith Athletic Apr 1907/ Middlesbrough Feb 1907/ UNITED Feb 1908 £200/Bradford Park Avenue Nov 1908 £100/ Brentford 1909/ Swindon Town 1909/Reading cs 1910/ Swindon Town cs 1911/Coventry City Oct 1912/Raith Rovers cs 1913/Edinburgh St Bernards cs 1915/Alloa Athletic Oct 1915/ Broxburn United 1916/Dunfermline Athletic

Mar 1917/Heart of Midlothian cs 1918 to Feb 1919/Lincoln City July 1919/Aberaman/Merthyr Tydfil cs 1920/Llanelly cs 1921.

Debut v Preston North End (h) 11/3/08

Alex McCulloch arrived at St James Park as a youngster and became an errant traveller during his career, never settling at any club for very long. He stood in once for Bill Appleyard in a United shirt but didn't get another opportunity and was confined to Newcastle's North Eastern League eleven during his ten months on Tyneside. McCulloch later appeared at inside-left for Hearts in the Scottish Victory Cup final of 1919. His club lost 3-0 to St Mirren before a 60,000 crowd at Celtic Park.

Appearances:
FL: 1 app. 0 gls.
Total: *1 app. 0 gls.*
Honours:
SVC finalist 1919.

McCURLEY, John

Role: Inside-forward 1927-1930
5' 8"
b. Kelty, Fife, 17th March 1906

CAREER: Third Lanark/UNITED Dec 1927 £2,500/East Fife Aug 1930/Cowdenbeath May 1933.

Debut v Bolton Wanderers (h) 18/2/28 (scored once)

A relentless midfield worker, able to play on either flank, McCurley was a reserve to Bob McKay and Stan Seymour during his early days on Tyneside. He was then given an extended run in season 1928-29, performing well in the inside-left role when Tom McDonald was injured. However, when his fellow countryman was fit again, 'Jock' as he was commonly known, stepped down and had to be content to substitute in any forward position, as well as at half-back, when the chance came his way. Whilst with Third Lanark, McCurley was good enough to represent the strong Glasgow city select combination, which prompted Newcastle to take a keen interest in the player.

Appearances:
FL: 43 apps. 8 gls.
FAC: 2 apps. 0 gls.
Total: *45 apps. 8 gls.*

McDERMID, Robert

Role: Left or Right-back 1894-1897
5' 7"
b. Scotland, 1870

CAREER: Renton Thistle/Renton/Newcastle West End 1887/Sunderland cs 1888/Sunderland Albion 1890/Accrington 1890/Burton Swifts 1891/Stockton 1892/Lincoln City Apr 1893/Renton cs 1893/Dundee Wanderers/UNITED Oct 1894 £15/Hebburn Argyle Feb 1897/Wormsley Jan 1898/South Shields Sept 1899.

Debut v Burton Wanderers (h) 10/11/1894 (scored once)

Jock McCurley

Bob McDermid

Bob McDermid was a popular and early disciple of the game, especially in the north east where he served on Wearside and with United's pioneers, Newcastle West End. On his day a reliable and occasionally brilliant defender, he was comfortable on the right or left side of the field. Appearing at St James Park for the West Enders when they lifted the Northumberland Senior Cup in 1888, McDermid became a regular for two seasons as the Tynesiders were established as a Football League club in 1894-95 and 1895-96. He later became a publican in South Shields. Some sources spell his surname McDermidd, but club Minute books note it as McDermid.

Appearances:
FL: 56 apps. 2 gls.
FAC: 8 apps. 0 gls.
Total: *64 apps. 2 gls.*

McDERMOTT, Terence

Role: Midfield & Asst-Manager 1973-74, 1982-84, 1992-date
5' 9"
b. Kirby, Liverpool, 8th December 1951

CAREER: Bury app, pro Oct 1969/UNITED Jan 1973 £25,000/Liverpool Nov 1974 £170,000/UNITED Sept 1982 £100,000 to Sept 1984/Cork City Jan 1985 to Mar 1985/Apoel(Cyprus) July 1985 to cs 1987/UNITED asst-manager Feb 1992.

Debut v Manchester United (a) 17/3/73 (sub)

Serving the club in three separate periods, Terry McDermott was first purchased for a bargain fee as a midfielder with potential, then signed again after he had

won everything on offer as a player of special talent with Liverpool and England. Slightly built and full of running, the Merseysider developed quickly at Gallowgate and impressed the Reds' management after his displays for the Magpies in an FA Cup run to Wembley in 1974. A clash with boss Joe Harvey led to his departure to Anfield and Terry was coached into one of the best link men in Europe, totalling 322 games and 75 goals for Liverpool. He was good at short and long passing, and had vision and the willingness to make late penetrating runs into the box. He was also always capable of striking a spectacular goal, several of which helped earn Liverpool trophies, including three European Champions Cups.

Returning to Gallowgate as a 31 year-old, Terry teamed up with Kevin Keegan to lead the club back to Division One, but again fell out with the management, only to return as Keegan's so called 'buffer' in 1992. One of the game's top medal winners, he picked up nine major honours as a player, and, as Kevin Keegan's right-hand man, became a success in management too.

Appearances:
FL: 129(1) apps. 18 gls.
FAC: 13 apps. 4 gls.
FLC: 7 apps. 2 gls.
Others: 18 apps. 0 gls.
Total: *167(1) apps. 24 gls.*

Honours:
25 Eng caps 1978-82/
1 Eng B cap 1978/
1 Eng u23 cap 1974/
FL champs 1977, 1979, 1980, 1982/FL div 2 prom 1984/
FAC finalist 1974, 1977/
FLC winner 1981, 1982/
FLC finalist 1978/EC winner 1977, 1978, 1981/FWA Footballer of the Year 1980/PFA Player of the Year 1980/Cyprus Lg champs 1986/
Cyprus Cup finalist 1986.

Terry McDermott

'Supermac', a cult figure to a
generation of United supporters.

MACDONALD, Malcolm Ian

Role: Centre-forward 1971-1976
5' 11"
b. Fulham, London, 7th January 1950

CAREER: Barnet/Knowle Park jnrs/
Tonbridge July 1967/Crystal Palace/Fulham
Aug 1968/Luton Town July 1969 £17,500/
UNITED May 1971 £180,000/Arsenal Aug
1976 £333,333 (Djurgårdens IF(Sweden) loan cs
1979)/Retired due to injury Aug 1979/Fulham
commercial executive Sept 1979/Fulham
manager Nov 1980, becoming director Aug
1981/Resigned Mar 1984/ Huddersfield Town
manager Oct 1987 to May 1988/South Kinson,
briefly Apr 1990/Also had a short spell with
Lusitano(S.Africa).

Debut v Crystal Palace (a) 14/8/71

Known nationwide as 'Supermac', Malcolm
Macdonald was a phenomenon of the
seventies and hero-worshipped on
Tyneside. Built like a middle-weight
boxer, he was a brash and colourful
centre-forward who lived for hitting the
ball into the back of the net. His style of
play meant excitement, crashing goals
from all distances and all angles. He had
devastating pace, packed a mighty shot
and was deceptively good in the air too.
Possessing verve and confidence,
Macdonald arrived on Tyneside for a record
fee after bagging 58 goals for Luton. At once
the Cockney was taken to by the Gallowgate
faithful, striking a headlining hat-trick on his
home debut against Liverpool. A huge
personality in the region for five years, both
on and off the field, Macdonald departed after
several publicised disagreements with new
manager Gordon Lee. He continued to find
the net at Highbury, claiming 57 goals
for Arsenal before a knee complaint
early in the 1978-79 season caused
problems, an injury that forced his
retirement at only 28 years of age.
Macdonald was the First Division's
leading goalpoacher in 1974-75 (21 goals)
and 1976-77 (25 goals), while he once hit five
goals for England at Wembley against Cyprus
in 1975 to equal an international scoring
record. On retirement from playing, he looked
like developing into a fine manager at Fulham
before a series of personal problems led to
Macdonald's departure from the game. After
running several pubs in the north and south,
as well as working in the media, Malcolm,
always thoughtful and articulate, moved to
Milan in 1991 where he was employed in
sporting telecommunications. For a period he
was also a football agent, assisting in bringing
Brazilian, Mirandinha to Gallowgate. In 1996
he was seen on the after-dinner circuit as a
personality speaker, as well as becoming a
local radio commentator and columnist in the
north east.

Appearances:
FL: 187 apps. 95 gls.
FAC: 23 apps. 14 gls.
FLC: 18 apps. 12 gls.
Others: 29(1) apps. 17 gls.
Total: *257(1) apps. 138 gls.*
Honours:
14 Eng caps 1972-76/4 Eng u23 caps 1972-73/
1 FL app. 1972/FL div 3 prom 1970, 1982(m)/
FAC finalist 1974, 1978/FLC finalist 1976.

McDONALD, John

Role: Inside-left 1895-1899
5' 10"
b. England

CAREER: Glasgow Perthshire 1893/Glasgow Ashfield 1894/UNITED Oct 1895/Lincoln City Nov 1899/Returned to Scotland Jan 1900.

Debut v Leicester Fosse (h) 1/1/1896

A recruit from Scottish junior league football where he was a star with the leading junior side north of the border, John McDonald arrived at the same time as two other Scots - Lennox and McKnight. A reserve forward, John deputised for Andy Aitken during season 1895-96 and also operated at inside-right and centre-forward. McDonald, although originally born in England, had reached the Scotland junior international ranks when with Ashfield. After leaving Tyneside he only made two appearances for Lincoln before moving back to Scotland. John's first action for Newcastle was to run as linesman in the club's reserve fixture against Gateshead NER! His surname is also spelt 'MacDonald' in various sources.

Appearances:
FL: 6 apps. 2 gls.
Total: *6 apps. 2 gls.*
Honours:
2 Scot Junior apps.

McDONALD, John

Role: Outside-left
1912-1914
5' 8"
b. Kirkcaldy, Fife, 1886

CAREER: Wemyss Harp/ Vale of Wemyss/Raith Rovers 1902/Glasgow Rangers Jan 1907 £100/Liverpool cs 1909/UNITED May 1912 £650/Raith Rovers cs 1914 to 1920.

Debut v Bolton Wanderers (a) 2/9/12 (scored once)

John McDonald was a noted player in Liverpool's ranks for three seasons during which he played 78 games before heading for the north east. He took over the outside-left berth at St James Park when fellow Scot, George Wilson moved to a schemer's role and,

although he enjoyed a good season in 1912-13, afterwards became second choice to emerging local lad, Tommy Goodwill. John was sometimes a touch temperamental, once failing to turn up for a United fixture against Derby in 1913; he was fined a week's wages. During the early part of John's career, he was a star of Raith's Scottish Qualifying Cup success in 1907, form which earned him a big move to Ibrox. His Scottish Cup final appearance in 1909 was the occasion of a notorious Hampden Park riot when no trophy was awarded.

Appearances:
FL: 31 apps. 4 gls.
FAC: 5 apps. 0 gls.
Total: *36 apps. 4 gls.*
Honours:
Scot trial app. 1910/SC finalist 1909/ SQC winner 1907.

McDONALD, Neil Raymond

Role: Midfield & Right-back 1982-1988
5' 11"
b. Willington Quay, near North Shields, 2nd November 1965

CAREER: Wallsend Boy's Club/Carlisle United Jan 1980/UNITED Aug 1982 £10,000/ Everton July 1988 £525,000/Oldham Athletic Sept 1991 £500,000/Bolton Wanderers Aug 1994 free/Preston North End Nov 1995 £40,000.

Debut v Barnsley (h) 25/9/82

At one stage Neil McDonald was Newcastle's youngest ever debutant at 16 years 326 days. A past England schools cap, he was a much coveted star with as many as 29 clubs chasing him as a teenager. Neil came into United's side at a time of injury crisis and with only five reserve and junior matches to his name. He performed to the team's requirements and deserved an extended run, an opportunity he eagerly grasped to earn a regular position in midfield, and later at full-back, for the next six seasons. With a strong shot, at one stage Neil was tipped for an England cap, but his progress drifted alarmingly after a big money move to Goodison Park. He never hit it off at Everton, or at Oldham and Bolton where he broke his leg in only his second game, and his promising career deteriorated. A past skipper of the England youth side, Neil was Kevin

Neil McDonald

Keegan's boot-boy at Gallowgate. His father, James, appeared for the Magpies' junior team during the fifties.

Appearances:
FL: 163(17) apps. 24 gls.
FAC: 10(1) apps. 1 gl.
FLC: 12 apps. 3 gls.
Others: 5 apps. 0 gls.
Total: *190(18) apps. 28 gls.*
Honours:
5 Eng u21 caps 1987-88/7 Eng schools app./
2 Eng youth apps. 1983-84/FL div 3 champs
1996/FL div 2 prom side 1984/
FAC finalist 1989.

McDONALD, Robert R.

Role: Centre-forward 1988-1989
6' 3"
b. Hull, 22nd January 1959

CAREER: Hull City app 1976, pro Jan 1977 (Sportclub Cambuur(Holland) loan 1979-80)/ FC Wageningen(Holland) Aug 1980 £19,000/ Tilburg Willem II(Holland) cs 1981/FC Groningen (Holland) June 1982 £75,000/PSV Eindhoven (Holland) cs 1985(Sporting Lisbon (Portugal) loan 1986-87)(FC Groningen (Holland) loan 1986-87)(Racing Jet(Holland) loan 1987-88)(Ikast (Denmark) loan 1987-88)/ Wimbledon trial 1988/UNITED Nov 1988 £150,000/Besiktas(Turkey) Aug 1989 £60,000/ Veendam(Holland) Mar 1990/ Emmen(Holland) asst coach 1992/ Zwolle(Holland) asst coach 1993.

Debut v Millwall (a) 19/11/88

After leaving Humberside to try his luck in the Netherlands, Rob McDonald eventually developed into a potent striker, with his big frame always a handful. He had excellent spells with Groningen and PSV Eindhoven, when he helped the Dutch side to the league championship. In total McDonald netted over 100 goals in Holland and for a spell appeared alongside Ruud Gullit as well as experiencing European Cup and UEFA Cup football. With that healthy pedigree Rob returned to England and to St James Park, but the pace and fiery nature of English soccer never suited his style and he headed for the continent again within a few months.

Appearances:
FL: 6(4) apps. 1 gl.
FAC: 1(3) apps. 0 gls.
Others: 1 app. 1 gl.
Total: *8(7) apps. 2 gls.*
Honours:
Dutch champs 1986.

Rob McDonald

McDONALD, Thomas Henry

Role; Inside-left 1921-1931
5' 8"
b. Inverness, 25th September 1895
d. Newcastle upon Tyne, 1969

CAREER: Inverness/Glasgow Rangers 1919/
UNITED Mar 1921 £2,000/York City May 1931
free/Goole Town Aug 1933/York City
asst-trainer Aug 1934/Usworth Colliery.

Debut v Middlesbrough (a) 5/3/21

Tom McDonald was one of the mainstays of
United's league and cup success during the
entertaining twenties. Forming a fine and
feared understanding with firstly, Stan
Seymour, then fellow countryman, Hughie
Gallacher, on the left flank of Newcastle's
attack, McDonald was an unselfish link man
and a thorough professional. While always
thinking of the team's outcome first and
foremost, he made sure he netted plenty of
goals too, over a century for the club in ten
seasons. A reserve for Scotland, he missed out
on a full cap by a whisker, appearing in three
trial fixtures, but always being one of those
unfortunate not to be selected. A softly spoken
Highlander, Tom was a modest man yet is
recognised in Newcastle's history, along with
Bobby Mitchell, as being present in both

United's top ten appearances and goalscorers'
chart. Blessed with craft and guile, one
contemporary biography noted his style as
"possessing skilful, constructive play and
accurate marksmanship". McDonald served in
the Royal Horse Artillery during World War
One, and after leaving the game settled on
Tyneside where he was employed at the
Vickers Armstrong works. For many years he
also looked after the Gallowgate press-box as a
club steward.

Appearances:
FL: 341 apps. 100 gls.
FAC: 26 apps. 13 gls.
Total: *367 apps. 113 gls.*
Honours:
Scot B app. 1924/Scot trial app. 1922-25/
FL champs 1927/FAC winner 1924.

McDONOUGH, Darron Karl

Role: Midfield 1992-1994
5' 11"
b. Antwerp, Belgium, 7th November 1962

CAREER: Oldham Athletic sch Dec 1977, app
July 1979, pro Jan 1980/Luton Town Sept 1986
£87,000/UNITED Mar 1992 £80,000/Retired
due to injury Apr 1994.

Debut v Grimsby Town (a) 21/3/92

Darron McDonough

Well-built, aggressive and positive with the ball, 29 year-old Darron McDonough joined United's staff as a utility player, able to play in defence or midfield. However, the Belgian-born player was unlucky with injuries, picking up a leg knock which ruled him out of selection for long periods, and this on top of being sidelined at Kenilworth Road with cartilage and ligament problems. Darron had begun his career alongside Mick Quinn in Oldham's ranks, clocking up over 200 games for the Latics before a move to Luton. Missing the Hatters' League Cup final in 1988 due to an injury sustained in the side's last training session before heading for Wembley, McDonough appeared in the final a year later and was hoping for a fresh start on Tyneside. But, after a series of problems both on and off the field, he was forced to quit the scene at the end of the 1993-94 season. Although born on the continent, Darron was brought up in the Manchester area.

Appearances:
FL: 2(1) apps. 0 gls.
Total: *2(1) apps. 0 gls.*
Honours:
FLC finalist 1989.

MacFARLANE, Alexander

Role: Centre-forward or Inside-left 1898-1901
5' 8"
b. Dundee, 1878

CAREER: Baillieston jnrs/Airdrieonians 1895/Arsenal Nov 1896/Airdrieonians cs 1897/UNITED Oct 1898 £30/Dundee Nov 1901/Chelsea Apr 1913/Dundee secretary-manager Mar 1919 to Dec 1924/Charlton Athletic manager May 1925/Dundee manager Dec 1927/Charlton Athletic manager June 1928 to Dec 1932/Blackpool manager July 1933 to July 1935.

Debut v Preston North End (a) 29/10/1898

Alex MacFarlane was an industrious worker with a stout heart and the ability to play across the frontline. Known as 'Sandy' and regarded as a perfectionist, he appeared in all five forward roles and was a regular in the Magpies' combination for three seasons at the turn of the century. MacFarlane fell out of favour on the arrival of Ronald Orr and the emergence of Colin Veitch, but went on to have a marvellous career back in Scotland with

Sandy MacFarlane

Dundee. He played on 333 occasions for the Dens Park club scoring 71 goals and took part in their Scottish Cup victory as well as reaching his country's national side. As a manager, twice in charge of Dundee, Sandy was a highly respected personality of the inter-war era.

Appearances:
FL: 84 apps. 17 gls.
FAC: 2 apps. 0 gls.
Total: *86 apps. 17 gls.*
Honours:
5 Scot caps 1904-11/Scot trial app. 1906/
3 SL apps. 1904-11/SC winner 1910/
FL div 3 (S) champs 1929(m).

McFAUL, William Stewart

Role: Goalkeeper, Coach & Manager 1966-1988
5' 10"
b. Coleraine, 1st October 1943

CAREER: Coleraine 1960/Linfield cs 1963/UNITED Nov 1966 £7,000/Retired 1975, becoming asst-coach then manager Sept 1985 to Oct 1988/Coleraine manager June 1990 to Jan 1992/N.Ireland asst-coach Mar 1994, as well as local coach in Ulster.

Debut v Liverpool (h) 12/11/66

Willie McFaul

After being on Tyneside for trials in his teens, Willie McFaul eventually signed for United after a sparkling display for his club, Linfield against the Magpies, even though he saw seven goals flash past him! Nevertheless, McFaul had still shown he was an acrobatic 'keeper with good reflexes and the potential to develop into a First Division guardian. He took some time to settle, being reserve to Gordon Marshall, but the likable Irishman was established as first choice for the start of the 1968-69 season, coinciding with the club's march on Europe. For the next seven campaigns Willie was an automatic selection and, despite a lack of height, was recognised as one of the First Division's best goalkeepers. McFaul is fondly remembered for three stunning saves in key matches; against Burnley in the FA Cup semi-final, a penalty stop in the Inter Cities Fairs Cup semi-final with Rangers, and a tip-over against Ujpesti Dozsa during the 1969 final. He appeared in every one of United's 24 European ties during the club's early years of action, while McFaul also scored against Pesci Dozsa - in a penalty shoot-out. A part of the Northern Ireland squad for several years, he was unlucky to be around the international scene when Pat Jennings

commanded the 'keeper's position. On Joe Harvey's resignation in 1975, Willie turned to coaching, being appointed caretaker boss twice (in 1977 and 1985) before claiming the hot-seat for himself. For a while his management appeared to work, but costly purchases at the start of the 1988-89 season flopped and he was dismissed. McFaul returned to his native Northern Ireland, and continued to be involved with football in the province. He resides in Coleraine.

Appearances:
FL: 290 apps. 0 gls.
FAC: 23 apps. 0 gls.
FLC: 18 apps. 0 gls.
Eur: 24 apps. 0 gls.
Others: 32 apps. 0 gls.
Total: *387 apps. 0 gls.*
Honours:
6 N.Irel caps 1967-74/3 N.Irel amat caps/ NI youth app/NI champs 1966/ FAC finalist 1974/NIC finalist 1966/ ICFC winner 1969.

McGARRY, Ronald James

Role: Centre-forward or Inside-forward
1962-1967
5' 9"
b. Whitehaven, 5th December 1937

CAREER: Whitehaven(rugby league)/ Workington June 1960/Bolton Wanderers Feb 1962 £10,000/UNITED Dec 1962 £17,500/ Barrow Mar 1967 £3,500/Bolgownie(Australia) player-coach 1968/Gateshead player-manager 1972/Minor Tyneside football.

Debut v Cardiff City (h) 15/12/62

Ron McGarry was a tough, bustling striker who was purchased to replace Jimmy Kerray as manager Joe Harvey was building a side to push for promotion out of Division Two. Versatile in the Number 9 shirt, or in both inside-forward positions, McGarry was a stocky forward, possessing a powerful physique. He took punishment from defenders, but was always able to dish out a fair share of retribution, both

Ron McGarry

in terms of goals and physical retaliation, hence his nickname of 'Cassius', after an infamous fracas with Swansea's Johnson for which McGarry was sent-off. Ron was especially prominent during the Magpies' Second Division title victory in 1965, hitting the net with 16 efforts, the side's top goalgetter. According to his manager, Ron was a "Robledo type of player", but wasn't quite good enough for United's Division One line-up and moved on to Barrow. Always a buoyant though somewhat haughty character, McGarry even had calling cards printed after a contemporary television programme, *Have Goals Will Travel*, which he handed to opposing defenders! McGarry started in the rugby code and was signed initially by Joe Harvey at Workington. He later lived on Tyneside, becoming a bookmaker for a while, then a newsagent.

Appearances:
FL: 118(3) apps. 41 gls.
FAC: 6 apps. 3 gls.
FLC: 5 apps. 2 gls.
Total: *129(3) apps. 46 gls.*
Honours:
FL div 2 champs 1965.

McGHEE, Mark Edward

Role: Striker 1977-1979, 1989-1991
5' 10"
b. Glasgow, 20th May 1957

CAREER: Cumbernauld Burgh/Bristol City 1973/Greenock Morton July 1975/UNITED Dec 1977 £150,000/Aberdeen Mar 1979 £80,000/SV Hamburg(Germany) May 1984 £285,000/Glasgow Celtic Nov 1985 £200,000/ UNITED July 1989 £200,000/IK Braga (Sweden) Apr 1991/Reading player-manager May 1991/Leicester City manager Dec 1994/ Wolverhampton Wanderers manager Dec 1995.

Debut v Leeds United (a) 2/1/78

An extremely clever forward, Mark McGhee possessed marvellous close control and the match-winning ability to weave his way past two or three defenders on one run. He was at

Mark McGhee

Gallowgate for two spells, firstly as a youngster signed from the Scottish League after scoring four goals in front of United officials, then later into his playing career when McGhee had proved himself one of the best strikers in the business. Mark's early period at Newcastle was not a happy one. As a raw kid, he had shown flashes of the brilliance which was to follow, but was in many ways a victim of the Magpies' relegation and internal strife. Moving back north, he linked up with manager Alex Ferguson at Pittodrie and developed into an unorthodox goalpoacher, able to hold the ball up, link well and finish with deadly accuracy from the tightest of chances. With Aberdeen he won

John McGrath

domestic and European honours, scoring 100 goals in 263 senior outings, and earned a big move to German super-club Hamburg. Jim Smith brought the Scot back to Tyneside where he teamed up with Mick Quinn for the 1989-90 season and, thanks to a 59 goal partnership, the black'n'whites almost gained promotion, losing in the play-offs. McGhee showed his true worth in that season and afterwards started on a managerial ladder that appears to be heading for the top. Mark was a trainee architect before moving into full-time football and although he was turned down by Celtic as a trialist, the Parkhead club later paid out a hefty sum to sign him.

Appearances:
FL: 86(11) apps. 29 gls.
FAC: 8(1) apps. 6 gls.
FLC: 5(1) apps. 1 gl.
Others: 3 apps. 0 gls.
Total: *102(13) apps. 36 gls.*
Honours;
4 Scot caps 1983-84/1 Scot u21 cap 1981/
SL champs 1980, 1984, 1986, 1988/
SL div 1 champs 1978/
SC winner 1982, 1983, 1984, 1988, 1989/
SLC finalist 1980, 1987/
ECWC winner 1983/ECWC finalist 1984/
FL div 2 champs 1994(m).

McGOUGH, Richard

Role: Centre-half 1914-1915
5' 9"
b. Cumberland
d. France, 1917

CAREER: Carlisle United 1912/UNITED Dec 1914 £100/Portsmouth 1915 to his death.

Debut v Middlesbrough (h) 10/3/15

Youngster Richard McGough arrived at St James Park from Carlisle United's pre-league outfit. A compact and skilful midfielder, he operated in the middle of the park in the old-fashioned centre-half role. McGough deputised for Wilf Low in Newcastle's first eleven during season 1914-15 before joining up to do battle in World War One. He once scored a goal from his own half for Carlisle! Richard was killed whilst serving as a bombardier in the RSA.

Appearances:
FL: 2 apps. 0 gls.
Total: *2 apps. 0 gls.*

McGRATH, John Thomas

Role: Centre-half 1961-1968
6' 0"
b. Manchester, 23rd August 1938

CAREER: Bolton Wanderers amat June 1953/ Miles Plating Swifts(Manchester)/Bury Oct 1955/UNITED Feb 1961 £24,000 plus R.Stokoe/ Southampton Feb 1968 £30,000(Brighton loan 1972-73)/Southampton coach Sept 1973/ Port Vale manager Dec 1979 to Dec 1983/

Chester manager Jan 1984 to Dec 1984/Preston North End manager June 1986 to Feb 1990/ Halifax Town manager Oct 1991 to Dec 1992/ occasional scout thereafter/Canadian technical director for youth coaching 1996.

Debut v Leicester City (a) 11/2/61

An immense tower of strength during the club's Second Division championship victory in 1965, John McGrath was recognised as a cornerstone of the success along with fellow half-backs Anderson and Iley. Yet McGrath's early years in the north east were of mixed fortune. Arriving as something of a ball-playing central defender, John struggled to settle, was often injured and in his first season the Magpies were relegated. McGrath went on the transfer list for a while but then changed his game style, becoming a more rugged and physical centre-half in the traditional mould; he was successful for three seasons, before and after promotion. Always enduring stiff competition for places during his eight seasons on Tyneside, McGrath eventually lost out to the double rivalry of Ollie Burton and John McNamee, not to mention club skipper, Bobby Moncur. John headed for The Dell where he appeared on 195 occasions winning a Football League cap, and then entered the rocky occupation of football management in the basement of the game. After four jobs in charge, he called it a day, concentrating on a career in entertainment as a noted after dinner speaker, full of football wit and humour. McGrath resides near Manchester.

Appearances:
FL: 169(1) apps. 2 gls.
FAC: 5 apps. 0 gls.
FLC: 6 apps. 0 gls.
Total: *180(1) apps.*
2 gls.
Honours:
2 Eng u23 caps 1961/
1 unoff Eng app. 1969/
1 FL app. 1969/
FL div 2 champs 1965/
FL div 3 champs 1961/
FL div 4 prom 1983(m),
1987(m).

McGUIGAN, John Joseph

Role: Inside or Outside-left 1958-1962
5' 8"
b. Motherwell, 29th October 1932

CAREER: Muirkirk jnrs/Bo'ness jnrs/ St Mirren Nov 1953/Southend United May 1955 free/UNITED June 1958 £2,250 plus W.Punton/Scunthorpe United Jan 1962 exch deal with B.Thomas/Southampton Aug 1963 £10,000/Swansea Town Mar 1965 £6,500 to 1966.

Debut v Everton (a) 30/8/58 (scored once)

A versatile tricky forward, John McGuigan was never perhaps given an extended run in one position during his stay at St James Park. He took the outside-left, inside-left and centre-forward shirts for United, starting off as a replacement for the ageing Bobby Mitchell in season 1958-59, but the Scottish maestro claimed back his jersey and John was tried in a different role. The arrival of new manager Joe Harvey saw an end to the Scot's days on Tyneside, United's ex skipper making room for new blood by releasing McGuigan along

John McGuigan

with several other players. After he left the scene, John became a licensee in Southampton for a period before returning to Scotland and working at the Rolls-Royce plant at Hillington. John's father appeared for Motherwell in inter-war soccer.

Appearances:
FL: 50 apps. 15 gls.
FAC: 3 apps. 1 gl.
FLC: 2 apps. 1 gl.
Total: *55 apps. 17 gls.*

Albert McInroy

McINROY, Albert

Role: Goalkeeper 1929-1934
5' 11"
b. Walton-le-Dale, Lancashire, 23rd April 1901
d. Houghton-le-Spring, 7th January 1985

CAREER: Upper Walton/Coppul Central/High Walton United 1919/Preston North End amat 1921/Great Harwood/Leyland Motors Nov 1922/Sunderland May 1923/UNITED Oct 1929 £2,750/Sunderland June 1934 free/Leeds United May 1935/Gateshead June 1937 to 1939/Stockton c1945.

Debut v Sheffield United (a) 5/10/29

Albert McInroy showed remarkable consistency over a long period between the two world wars, form which made him one of the best 'keepers in the game at the time. Capped by England, he had made his name at Roker Park as a safe, sound pair of hands, totalling 227 games for the Wearsiders before switching to the Tyne and United. Exuding confidence, he was a fabulously witty character, and a central figure in the black'n'whites' journey to Wembley in 1932. However, after being the Magpies regular goalie for five seasons, McInroy fell into dispute with the club's directors over a benefit payment and was handed a free transfer, returning to Sunderland where he always felt at home. On retiring soon after the Second World War, Albert settled in the north east and was for many years a publican in Newcastle, Gateshead and eventually Houghton. At one time during his spell at Newcastle he sustained a poisoned finger, a serious complaint which necessitated talk of amputation. Thankfully, surgery was averted, although Albert was out of action for a long period, a critical loss for the Magpies as they were relegated from Division One.

Appearances:
FL: 143 apps. 0 gls.
FAC: 17 apps. 0 gls.
Total: *160 apps. 0 gls.*
Honours:
1 Eng cap 1927/Eng trial app. 1925/FAC winner 1932.

McINTOSH, Robert A.

Role: Right-half 1920-1924
6' 0"
b. Dundee, 1st August 1892

CAREER: Dundee Fairfield/Dundee 1915/UNITED July 1920 £1,250/Stockport County Oct 1924 £500 to 1925.

Debut v West Bromwich Albion (a) 4/9/20

A tall, slimly-built link-man, calm and assured, Robert McIntosh rarely became flustered even in the most heated contest. Moving to England after good reports from scouts in Scotland, McIntosh immediately

Robert McIntosh

A deadly shot in Newcastle's 'A' team and recognised as a penalty-kick expert, Teddy McIntyre usually appeared at centre-forward for the Magpies' reserves, but in senior action only once turned out in his true position. He deputised in midfield for United's internationals and appeared twice in the Novocastrians' title-winning season of 1904-05. A servant for six years, he won Northern League and Northern Alliance honours, and was given a club benefit game as a token of his loyal service. McIntyre moved on to Craven Cottage, where he helped Fulham lift the Southern League championship. However, during his spell with Plymouth he was involved in controversy which led to him being charged with actual bodily harm. Following a dispute with his trainer in 1909, Teddy ended up breaking his jaw; the trainer, Nicholas Wallis, afterwards died from heart failure but a jury acquitted McIntyre of the charge of manslaughter. Teddy was also a noted athlete and local runner who won contests in the so-called "Morpeth Olympic Games" at the turn of the century.

Appearances:
FL: 6 apps. 1 gl.
Total: *6 apps. 1 gl.*
Honours:
SnL champs 1907.

became a first team midfielder. He was an automatic choice for the three seasons up to 1923-24 but then lost his place just as Newcastle were to embark on a run to Wembley. With Tom Curry and Edward Mooney both pressing for his position, United's director's allowed the Scot to depart for Edgeley Park.

Appearances:
FL: 101 apps. 2 gls.
FAC: 2 apps. 0 gls.
Total: *103 apps. 2 gls.*

McINTYRE, Edward

Role: Right or Left-half 1900-1906
5' 8"
b. Newcastle upon Tyne, 1883

CAREER: Caxton/Allendale Park/ UNITED May 1900/Fulham May 1906/ Plymouth Argyle Aug 1907/ Portsmouth cs 1909/West Stanley cs 1911.

Debut v Everton (h) 1/4/03

Teddy McIntyre

McKANE, Joseph

Role: Left-half 1892-1895
5' 10"
b. Scotland

CAREER: Clydebank/Newcastle East End Jan 1889/UNITED May 1892/Blyth Feb 1895.

Debut v Sheffield United (a) 24/9/1892 (NL)

Joe McKane was a tough competitor, quick to the tackle and a hard-working forager who creditably assisted United and their pioneers, Newcastle East End, during the club's formative years. Arriving on Tyneside from the west of Scotland, Joe appeared in East End's first FA Cup Proper fixture against Nottingham Forest in season 1891-92, then also took part in the inaugural match which took place at St James Park following the East Enders' move from Heaton. McKane was also on the field for the Geordies' Football League baptism a year later and was an ever-present in that historic campaign. He once forced United to play with only ten men at Middlesbrough after he had inadvertently missed the train south.

Appearances:
NL: 8 apps. 0 gls.
FL: 41 apps. 0 gls.
FAC: 3 apps. 0 gls.
Total: *52 apps. 0 gls.*

McKAY, Robert

Role: Inside-right 1926-1928
5' 6"
b. Govan, Glasgow, 2nd September 1900

CAREER: Parkhead White Rose/Vale of Clyde/Parkhead/Neilston Victoria/Greenock Morton 1921/Glasgow Rangers June 1925 £1,750/UNITED Nov 1926 £2,750/Sunderland Oct 1928 in exch for R.Thomson/Charlton Athletic Dec 1930 £1,220/Bristol Rovers Nov 1932 £350/Newport County June 1935/Dundee United manager July 1939 to Oct 1939/Ballymena United manager 1947 to 1949/Charlton Athletic scout.

*Debut v West Bromwich Albion (h) 6/11/26
(scored three)*

An expert schemer, Bob McKay had a marvellous, though short, stay with United after netting a scintillating hat-trick on his debut. Continuing to strike goals throughout his career, the diminutive McKay was a neat and proficient player and a great tactician too. Bob arrived on Tyneside two months into the 1926-27 season and made a big impact on the side, being one of the primary reasons the black'n'whites went on to climb from seventh place to lift the title that year. But a season later, after reaching the Scotland side with United, he fell out of favour and moved the short distance to Roker Park where he again gave good short term service. Totalling almost 600 senior outings in his career, McKay played in all four home countries during his much-travelled period as a player.

Appearances:
FL: 62 apps. 22 gls.
FAC: 4 apps. 1 gl.
Total: *66 apps. 23 gls.*
Honours:
1 Scot cap 1928/
1 SL app. 1926/
FL champs 1927/
SC winner 1922.

Bob McKay

McKAY, William

Role: Centre-forward 1895-1897
5' 10"
b. Scotland

CAREER: Glasgow Rangers/
UNITED cs 1895 to 1897.

Debut v Loughborough Town (h) 7/9/1895

William McKay

William McKay was described as a 'scientific player' of high reputation in Scotland. Although unable to command a regular place at Ibrox, he impressed Newcastle's directors when Rangers visited St James Park in a friendly contest during March 1895. The Glasgow giants won 5-2 and afterwards McKay quickly became a Magpie player. A versatile forward and a utility player during season 1895-96, he appeared at half-back and at inside-right for the club too.

Appearances:
FL: 18 apps. 6 gls.
FAC: 3 apps. 1 gl.
Total: *21 apps. 7 gls.*

McKELLAR, David N.

Role: Goalkeeper 1986
6' 0"
b. Ardrossan, Ayrshire, 22nd May 1956

CAREER: Ipswich Town 1973(Colchester United loan 1975-76)(Peterborough United loan 1975-76)/Ardrossan Winton Rovers cs 1976/Derby County Mar 1978/Brentford Oct 1980/Carlisle United Aug 1983/Hibernian July 1985(Manchester City loan 1985-86)(UNITED loan Feb 1986-May 1986)/Hamilton Academical June 1986 £10,000/Dunfermline Athletic 1987(Hartlepool United loan 1988-89)/Carlisle United Nov 1988/Kilmarnock Mar 1990 £20,000/Glasgow Rangers Aug 1991 £20,000 to cs 1992.

Debut v Ipswich Town (h) 15/3/86

David McKellar was an emergency signing by the black'n'whites towards the end of the 1985-86 season after an injury to first choice goalkeeper, Martin Thomas. A widely travelled and experienced 'keeper, McKellar had been a youth star, winning international honours and helping Ipswich lift the prestigious FA Youth Cup. His potential was perhaps never fully realised and the Scot drifted from club to club, enjoying good spells with Derby County, Brentford and at Carlisle where he played on 151 occasions. He concluded his nomadic career with Scotland's biggest club, Rangers, as understudy to Andy Goram for a period.

Appearances:
FL: 10 apps. 0 gls.
Total: *10 apps. 0 gls.*
Honours:
Scot youth app./FAYC winner 1973.

David McKellar

MacKENZIE, Roderick R.

Role: Right-half 1922-1935
5' 7"
b. Inverness, 22nd May 1901

CAREER: Inverness Thistle/Inverness
Clacknacuddin/UNITED Sept 1922 £100/
Gateshead Aug 1935/Reading briefly.

Debut v Huddersfield Town (h) 7/4/23

Following the likes of
McCombie and
McWilliam from
Inverness, Roddie
MacKenzie signed for
United after a
month's trial. As
dour and as tough as
they come, he was a
hero on several
occasions for United
during his 12 seasons
in the Magpies' first
eleven. Establishing a
place for himself
during
1924-25, the Scot

Roddie MacKenzie

became the side's engine-room in the
middle of the field; tenacious and big
hearted, it was recorded that he would
"tackle anything that moves". Roddie was
an inspiration to his team-mates and
tended to raise his game when he was in a
big match atmosphere,
relishing the contests with
star names. One such duel,
season after season fondly
recalled, was the meeting
with Arsenal's Alex James;
in one clash Roddie is noted
to have spectacularly
flattened the great
international to the floor in
front of Highbury's main
stand. A championship and
FA Cup winner with the
black'n'whites, he was also
in the side when relegation
stunned Tyneside in 1934.
Then at the veteran stage of
his career, MacKenzie lost
his place and moved the
short distance to Redheugh
Park. He later resided on
Tyneside. Although several

sources spell his surname, McKenzie, his
autograph confirms the spelling as
MacKenzie. It is thought he is related to the
United boardroom dynasty of the same
name.

Appearances:
FL: 238 apps. 6 gls.
FAC: 18 apps. 1 gl.
Total: *256 apps. 7 gls.*
Honours:
*FL champs 1927/FAC
winner 1932.*

McKINNEY, William E.

Role: Right-back 1956-1965
6' 0"
b. Newcastle upon Tyne, 20th July 1936

CAREER: Wallsend Rising Sun/Wallsend
St Lukes/UNITED May 1956 £50/
Bournemouth Aug 1965 £2,750/Mansfield
Town June 1966 free/Wellington Town cs 1968.

Debut v Tottenham Hotspur (a) 28/12/57

A mean and solid full-back, Bill McKinney
frequently left forwards knowing they had
been in a physical battle. He was a deputy to
Dick Keith and found it difficult to claim a
regular place in the side, his 94 outings for the
club being spread over eight seasons. A spot-
kick expert, Bill had a good term in season
1960-61 (21 games) the year, alas, when United
were relegated. However, by the time Irish

*Bill McKinney
challenges Jimmy
Greaves.*

international Keith had left the scene McKinney, who was captain of Newcastle on occasion, had the young David Craig as a rival. McKinney was released and concluded his career in the lower divisions. When on national service in 1959, he turned out for the Army eleven. After retiring Bill resided in Dawley, Shropshire.

Appearances:
FL: 85 apps. 6 gls.
FAC: 7 apps. 1 gl.
FLC: 2 apps. 1 gl.
Total: *94 apps. 8 gls.*

McKINNON, Robert

Role: Left-back 1984-1986
5′ 11″
b. Glasgow, 31st July 1966

CAREER: East Kilbride YC/Rutherglen Glencairn/UNITED Oct 1984/Hartlepool United June 1986(Manchester United loan 1990-91)/Motherwell Jan 1992 £150,000/ Twente Enschede(Holland) cs 1996.

Debut v Tottenham Hotspur (a) 7/9/85

Rob McKinnon

In his only outing for the Magpies, youngster Rob McKinnon stood in for Kenny Wharton in a tough away fixture at White Hart Lane. The Scot suffered, along with the rest of his defence, as Spurs inflicted a heavy 5-1 defeat. McKinnon didn't last the 90 minutes and never reached the first team again, being transferred to Hartlepool. However, the ginger-haired Scot developed enormously at the Victoria Ground and on his return to Scotland with Motherwell (over 170 appearances) was established as one of the best defenders north of the border possessing a flair for getting forward. He eventually received a call-up to his country's side too, and was capped at both full and 'B' level.

Appearances:
FL: 1 app. 0 gls.
Total: *1 app. 0 gls.*
Honours:
3 Scot caps 1994-date/2 Scot B caps 1995-96.

McLEAN, David J.

Role: Midfield 1975-1978
5′ 7″
b. Newcastle upon Tyne, 24th November 1952

CAREER: UNITED Aug 1975/Carlisle United loan Mar 1978, pmt May 1978/Darlington Aug 1979 free/Scunthorpe United July 1986 £7,000/Hartlepool United loan 1987-88, pmt July 1988 free/Whitley Bay Aug 1988/Brigg Town to 1996.

Debut v Sheffield United (a) 19/4/76 (sub)

One of a bright crop of youngsters who developed through United's junior side, David McLean was a past England youth player who received an opportunity in the senior team at the end of the 1975-76 programme. Standing in for Rocky Hudson, the auburn-haired midfielder had neat skills and was a compact, tidy player. He was on the fringe

David McLean

of Newcastle's side for three seasons, which included taking part, and being on the bench, for the UEFA Cup ties of 1977-78. With Darlington, the Tynesider totalled over 300 games, an inspiration and skipper when they won promotion in 1984-85. At the end of his career David, as captain, lifted the FA Vase trophy at Wembley for Brigg Town. McLean is employed as a production supervisor for a furnishings business in Scunthorpe, residing in nearby Scotter.

Appearances:
FL: 7(2) apps. 0 gls.
FLC: 1 app. 0 gls.
Eur: 1 app. 0 gls.
Total: *9(2) apps. 0 gls.*
Honours:
Eng youth app./
FL div 4 prom 1985/
FAV winner 1996.

McMENEMY, Harry

Role: Inside-left 1931-1937
5' 9"
b. Glasgow, 26th March 1912

CAREER: Strathclyde jnrs/UNITED July 1931
£475/Dundee July 1937 £1,200/Gateshead
1939 briefly.

Debut v Grimsby Town (a) 5/9/31

Harry McMenemy

A cultured, highly-skilled competitor, Harry McMenemy excelled on the ball and had the ability to strike a telling pass quickly and accurately. An ex-bricklayer who was chased by several top clubs before United won the race, Harry arrived at St James Park as a teenager but won a position in the Magpies' side immediately. He showed much skill and craft, and quickly became a terrace favourite. His first season co-incided with Newcastle's run to Wembley and McMenemy had a big influence on that success. Although dogged by injury after his first two successful seasons in a United shirt, he was also captain of the club for a period. Tipped on more than one occasion for a full Scotland cap, Harry was most unlucky, sustaining an injury and having to drop out of the international side when selected to play in 1933. He was from a large family of noted footballers and it was, ironically, his brother, John of Motherwell, who took his place in that Scotland fixture. His father was the famous 'Nap' McMenemy of Celtic fame, while another brother, Frank turned out for Northampton Town. Harry is also distantly related to Lawrie McMenemy, as well as United coach, Chris McMenemy. After the Second World War, Harry lived and worked in Glasgow.

Appearances:
FL: 138 apps. 34 gls.
FAC: 10 apps. 1 gl.
Others: 1 app. 2 gls.
Total: *149 apps. 37 gls.*
Honours:
FAC winner 1932.

McMICHAEL, Alfred

Role: Left-back 1949-1963
5' 8"
b. Belfast, 1st October 1927

CAREER: Wolfhill Jnrs/Cliftonville 1942/
Linfield 1945/UNITED Sept 1949 joint deal
with G.Hannah £23,000/South Shields
player-manager June 1963 to Feb 1969/
Bangor(N.Ireland) manager Oct 1971.

Debut v Manchester City (h) 17/9/49

Alf McMichael is United's most capped player, captain of both club and country. Possessing excellent positional sense, he was studious at his job and tended to raise his game against the better wingers and for the big occasion, Stanley Matthews once noting that McMichael was "one of the best left-backs I have ever played against". Never too fancy on the ball, McMichael landed on Tyneside as a youngster along with another noted United fifties star, George Hannah. Alf took over from Bobby Corbett and was a regular for 14 seasons, although he missed two of the club's three FA Cup final appearances; in 1951 when he slipped in training and broke a wrist, and then in 1955 when he had ligament trouble. Later in his United career, McMichael partnered fellow Irishman Dick Keith, a duo that also served the international scene, including the 1958 World Cup. One of only seven players to total over 400 matches for Newcastle, McMichael once netted an own-goal after only 32 seconds against West Bromwich Albion in 1951. The Irishman was given a well supported testimonial in 1963 (24,175). After he left the soccer circuit Alf settled in Bangor, County Down, and was employed at the Harland and Wolff shipyard in Belfast.

Appearances:
FL: 402 apps. 1 gl.
FAC: 25 apps. 0 gls.
FLC: 4 apps. 0 gls.
Others: 2 apps. 0 gls.
Total: *433 apps. 1 gl.*
Honours:
*40 N.Irel caps 1950-60/Rest of UK app.
1952/8 NIL apps. 1947-50/
FAC winner 1952/NIC winner 1948.*

Alf McMichael

Big John McNamee was purchased by manager Joe Harvey to add steel to United's flagging defence during a relegation dog-fight in season 1966-67; the cast-iron defender proceeded to do his job with credit. A burly centre-half, gritty and determined, McNamee loved to challenge big name centre-forwards of the era, and became something of a cult figure during his five years with the club. United's supporters quickly took to him, if not for his pure footballing skills - which were limited - then for his reputation as a hard-man stopper. Turned down by Manchester United as a teenager, John joined Celtic and established himself in Scotland. By the time he moved to England though, his rugged style had made him a marked man by opposing fans and also, to a degree, by referees; John was once booked for arguing with Frank Haffey, his own Celtic goalkeeper. After his career closed, McNamee resided in the Lake District, in Cockermouth working as a postman, until a serious car accident in 1988 forced him onto invalidity benefit.

Appearances:
FL: 115(2) apps. 8 gls.
FAC: 6 apps. 0 gls.
FLC: 1 app. 0 gls.
Eur: 7(1) apps. 0 gls.
Total: *129(3) apps. 8 gls.*
Honours:
Scot schools app./SC finalist 1963/
ICFC winner 1969(sub, no app.).

John McNamee

McNAMEE, John

Role: Centre-half 1966-1971
6' 0"
b. Coatbridge, 11th June 1941

CAREER: Bellshill Athletic/Glasgow Celtic Aug 1959/Hibernian June 1964/UNITED Dec 1966 £26,000/Blackburn Rovers Nov 1971 £15,000 to June 1972/Hartlepool United Nov 1973/Greenock Morton Dec 1973 free/ Lancaster City 1974/Workington Town manager, and non-contract player, June 1975 to Dec 1975/Carlisle United asst-coach/ Occasional UNITED scout 1989.

Debut v Tottenham Hotspur (a) 31/12/66

McNEE, John

Role: Outside or Inside-left 1894-1895
5' 4"
b. Renton, Dunbarton

CAREER: Renton c1886/Bolton Wanderers
Sept 1889 £100/UNITED Sept 1894/Gateshead
NER player-trainer Oct 1895/Kingsland
(Norfolk) player-trainer/Watford 1897 to cs
1900/Fulham Aug 1901 to c1902.

*Debut v Burslem Port Vale (a) 6/10/1894
(scored once)*

John McNee

For over a decade
John McNee was a
member of the
famous Renton
combination, a team
from north of the
border that
competed in the
English FA Cup in
season 1886-87.
McNee was in the
side then, and he
also took a
prominent role
when Renton lifted
the Scottish Cup in
1888 by a record 6-1
scoreline. Small and
tricky, perhaps the original traditional Scottish
winger, John was on the field when his club
were crowned unofficial 'Champions of the
World' in May 1888 after that Scottish Cup
win plus victories over English clubs, West
Bromwich Albion and Preston. A true pioneer
of the game, he moved to Bolton where he was
a regular, making 96 appearances (25 goals)
before heading for Tyneside when United
were after new forward blood in their bid to
establish the club as a Football League side.
McNee started well in the Novocastrians' line-
up, netting on his first two outings, but faded
from the scene after a season, although for a
time he was regarded as "a great favourite at
St James Park" by the *Daily Journal*.

Appearances:
FL: 21 apps. 4 gls.
FAC: 2 apps. 0 gls.
Total: *23 apps. 4 gls.*
Honours:
SC winner 1888/
SnL div 2 champs 1900.

McNEIL, Matthew Alexander

Role: Centre-half 1949-1951
6' 3"
b. Glasgow, 28th July 1927
d. Kirkintilloch, 23rd April 1977

CAREER: Hibernian Apr
1947/UNITED Dec 1949
£6,400/Barnsley Aug 1951
£10,500/ Brighton July 1953
£7,000/Norwich City Mar 1956
£3,000/Cambridge United July 1957.

Debut v Middlesbrough (a) 25/12/50

Vastly built centre-half Matthew
McNeil was ideally structured for
the pivot's role, but always played
second fiddle to Frank Brennan at
Gallowgate. Not surprisingly, Matt was
a master in the air, positive and tough,
but his games for Newcastle were
restricted to the 1950-51 season and he
moved to Oakwell for a big fee. McNeil then
made 60 appearances for Brighton and 69 for
Norwich City, and later resided in the west of
Scotland until his early death from lung
cancer.

Appearances:
FL: 9 apps. 0 gls.
FAC: 2 apps. 0 gls.
Total: *11 apps. 0 gls.*

McPHILLIPS, William Pearson

Role: Goalkeeper 1930-1938
6' 1"
b. Musselburgh, nr Edinburgh, 7th June 1910

CAREER: Musselburgh Bruntonians/UNITED
June 1930 £20/Guildford City May 1938/
Bradford City June 1939 £170/
Hartlepools United war-guest 1939-40.

Debut v Liverpool (h) 1/1/34

Tall and thinly-built but a confident
goalkeeper, Bill McPhillips was on
United's staff for almost eight years.
'Scots Wullie', as he was nicknamed
in the dressing-room, made his
debut during the Magpies'
relegation season in 1933-34 but
was always second choice to
either Micky Burns, Norman

Tapken or Tom Swinburne. However, the Scot served the club well whenever called upon, his 34 games spread over five campaigns.

Appearances:
FL: 33 apps. 0 gls.
FAC: 1 app. 0 gls.
Total: *34 apps. 0 gls.*

McTAVISH, John Kay

Role: Inside-right 1912-1913
5' 9"
b. Govan, Glasgow, 7th June 1885
d. 1926

CAREER: Falkirk 1905/Oldham Athletic June 1910/Tottenham Hotspur Jan 1911/UNITED Apr 1912 £650/Partick Thistle May 1913 £500/York City war-guest 1914-15/Goole Town Feb 1915/Falkirk war-guest/East Fife cs 1919/East Stirlingshire cs 1921/Dumbarton c1922/Retired 1924.

Debut v Blackburn Rovers (a) 27/4/12

John McTavish

An excellent ball-player, John McTavish came to prominence at Falkirk when he partnered Scottish legend Jock Simpson and earned an international call-up. McTavish arrived at St James Park after a spell with Spurs where he had totalled 42 senior games. His brother Robert, was also at White Hart Lane, the two playing in the same line-up in 1911. In a black'n'white shirt, McTavish had one good season for the club during 1912-13, before heading back to Scotland. During World War One, he served with the Tyneside Scottish battalion in France, and died after the Great War when he was barely into his forties.

Appearances:
FL: 34 apps. 6 gls.
FAC: 5 apps. 1 gl.
Total: *39 apps. 7 gls.*
Honours:
1 Scot cap 1910/Scot trial app. 1910/
2 SL apps. 1907-08.

McWILLIAM, Peter

Role: Left-half 1902-1911
5' 9"
b. Inveravon, Banffshire, 22nd September 1878
d. Redcar, 1st October 1951

CAREER: Heatherley(Inverness)/Inverness Thistle 1899/UNITED Aug 1902 £10/Retired cs 1911 due to injury/Tottenham Hotspur manager Dec 1912/Middlesbrough manager Jan 1927 to Mar 1934/Arsenal scout cs 1934/Tottenham Hotspur manager Apr 1938/Retired June 1942.

Debut v Middlesbrough (h) 18/10/02

Peter McWilliam was one of the most influential players during Newcastle's formidable Edwardian heyday. Known as 'Peter the Great', the Scot arrived at Gallowgate after being hijacked by United officials when he was on his way to Sunderland for trials to meet an old friend Andy McCombie. He was a raw, but talented schemer to begin with, who actually struggled to claim a first team place. But he came into his own after colleagues persuaded United's directors to give him a chance, and the club never looked back. Newcastle won the title in Peter's first full season and he rapidly developed thereafter as a half-back of exceptional quality. He had a famous body swerve which fooled opponents and characterised his game. Playing with delicacy and distinction, as well as a masterly ease, McWilliam had an acute mind for the tactical side of the game. He didn't tackle too often, but his passes were crisp and precise and he always urged his team-mates forward. Also nicknamed 'Pat', he was a huge crowd favourite on Tyneside for seven successful seasons before a knee ligament injury, sustained whilst playing for Scotland, wrecked his career. Captain of the Scots, that set-back only galvanised Peter to develop as a master manager too. As boss of Spurs especially, he maintained a high standard of football, always wanting his sides to play in the Newcastle style - a passing, possession game. When he guided the Londoners to FA Cup victory, he became one of only a few men to have both managed and played for an FA Cup winning side. For his commitment to soccer Peter was awarded the Football League's Long Service medal in June 1939. On retirement McWilliam resided in Redcar to his death.

Appearances:
FL: 199 apps. 11 gls.
FAC: 41 apps. 1 gl.
Others: 2 apps. 0 gls.
Total: *242 apps. 12 gls.*
Honours:
8 Scot caps 1905-11/
Scot trial app. 1905/
FL champs 1905, 1907, 1909/
FL div 2 champs 1920(m), 1927(m), 1929(m)/
FAC winner 1910, 1921(m)/
FAC finalist 1905, 1906, 1909/
FL Long Service medal 1939.

NAPIER, Christopher Robin Anthony

Role: Centre-forward 1965-1966
6' 0"
b. Dunblane, nr Stirling, 26th September 1943

CAREER: Blackpool Nov 1960/ Preston North End June 1963 £2,000/Workington Nov 1964/ UNITED Nov 1965 £17,500/ Brighton Sept 1966 £8,500/ Blackburn Rovers Aug 1972 £15,000 to May 1974 free/ Durban City(S.Africa) 1974.

Debut v Blackpool (h) 6/11/65

Known as 'Kit', and a prolific scorer in the lower divisions with Workington, 22 year-old Christopher Napier signed for Joe Harvey's side at a time when the black'n'whites were desperate for goals. Tall and slim, Napier was purchased as a promising striker, hopefully to be developed into a

'Kit' Napier

First Division leader who could save United a hefty fee in the transfer market. Although Napier was good with the ball at his feet he wasn't quick enough for Division One football and the plan never materialised. After a handful of run-outs in the senior team, Harvey splashed out on Welsh international Wyn Davies and Napier was transferred to Brighton where he became a big success, firing home 24 goals in season 1967-68 and totalling 291 games with a first-class return of 99 goals all told. He afterwards resided in South Africa entering the motor trade.

Appearances:
FL: 8 apps. 0 gls.
Total: *8 apps. 0 gls.*
Honours:
FL div 3 prom 1972.

NATTRASS, Irving

Role: Right-back 1970-1979
5′ 10″
b. Fishburn, County Durham, 12th December 1952

CAREER: UNITED July 1970/
Middlesbrough July 1979 £375,000/
Retired due to injury June 1986.

Debut v Derby County (h) 27/3/71 (sub)

Cool and refined, Irving Nattrass began his first team career for United in midfield. He later took over from David Craig at right-back and concluded his period with the club in central defence. A product of United's junior structure, Nattrass oozed confidence and was sure and positive in defence, with constructive use of the ball to get his forwards moving. Becoming Newcastle skipper, he was destined to reach full international level before a series of cruel injuries kept him out of action, mishaps that were to follow him for the rest of his career. He missed the 1974 FA Cup run, and later England's tour of South America in 1977 when he was a certainty for his first international appearance. With Newcastle relegated in 1978, Irving's obvious talent was too good for Second Division football and he soon moved back to the top division, signing for Middlesbrough. Although he served Boro' well - 220 league and cup games over seven seasons - perhaps Nattrass would have earned that England opportunity again had he joined a higher profile club. Remaining in the north east after retiring and residing in Washington, Irving went into the retail clothing business in Chester-le-Street and Gateshead.

Appearances:
FL: 226(12) apps. 16 gls.
FAC: 23 apps. 1 gl.
FLC: 22 apps. 3 gls.
Eur: 4 apps. 0 gls.
Others: 25(1) apps. 2 gls.
Total: *300(13) apps. 22 gls.*
Honours:
1 Eng u23 cap 1976/
FLC finalist 1976.

NAYLOR, James

Jimmy Naylor

Role: Right-half 1930-1932
5′ 9″
b. High Crompton, Lancashire, 2nd March 1901
d. Shaw, nr Oldham, 31st August 1983

CAREER: Shawside(Oldham)/Oldham Athletic May 1920/Huddersfield Town Dec 1928 £3,750/UNITED July 1930 £4,000/ Manchester City Oct 1932 £500(Oldham Athletic loan 1932-33)/Macclesfield Town Feb 1934/Nelson Aug 1935/Wigan Athletic Aug 1937.

Debut v Sheffield Wednesday (a) 30/8/30

Although Jimmy Naylor operated mainly on the right side of midfield for United, he was also efficient at left-half. At his peak, Naylor was a splendid attacking player who often produced majestic footwork on the ball and precision passing ability. He read the game well and was a star of the Latics for almost eight years, totalling 237 senior games before joining Huddersfield. At Leeds Road, Jimmy assisted the Terriers in reaching Wembley and was on the fringe of an England call-up. On leaving the game, he returned to his native Lancashire where he lived for the rest of his life.

Appearances:
FL: 30 apps. 0 gls.
FAC: 2 apps. 0 gls.
Total: *32 apps. 0 gls.*
Honours:
FAC finalist 1930/Eng trial app. 1929.

NEALE, Duncan Frederick

Role: Right-half 1959-1963
5' 8"
b. Portslade, nr Brighton, 1st October 1939

CAREER: Ilford/UNITED June 1959/
Plymouth Argyle Aug 1963 £12,000/Plymouth
City 1970.

Debut v Fulham (h) 24/8/60 (scored twice)

Duncan Neale was plucked from the Isthmian
League with Ilford and, after a season of
transition, gained a regular place in First
Division football for the start of the 1960-61
season. A fine attacking player in midfield, the
fair-haired, stocky Neale is noted especially for
two memorable goals on his debut for the
Magpies. But that season ended in relegation
for the Novocastrians, and his form suffered.
A new manager in the shape of Joe Harvey
arrived soon after, and Neale became one of
many players off-loaded in a rebuilding plan.
With Plymouth, Duncan took part in 166
matches operating also at full-back, centre-half
and inside-forward and never failed to give
100%. After football, he ran a building
business in the south west, residing in
Landulph, Cornwall.

> **Appearances:**
> *FL: 88 apps. 8 gls.*
> *FAC: 6 apps. 3 gls.*
> *FLC: 4 apps. 1 gl.*
> **Total:** *98 apps. 12 gls.*

NEILSON, Alan Bruce

Role: Centre-half 1989-1995
5' 11"
b. Wegburg, Germany, 26th September 1972

CAREER: UNITED app 1989, pro Feb 1991/
Southampton May 1995 £400,000.

Debut v Watford (a) 9/3/91 (sub)

Born in Germany while his father was serving
with the RAF, Alan Neilson also lived in
Cyprus before writing to United for a trial. His
hopeful letter was answered positively and he
went on to successfully earn a contract with
the Magpies. A full-back or central defender,
Neilson gained
experience during
season
1991-92 under Ossie
Ardiles, but had to
be content as a
squad player when
Kevin Keegan
started to bring
expensive stars to
Gallowgate.
Capped by Wales at
Under-21 and full
level whilst in the
Magpies' reserve
line-up, Neilson
rarely performed
badly for United
when called upon
to deputise, but had
little option except
to move on in
search of a regular
place. A past
captain of the junior
and second eleven -
skipping the

Alan Neilson

reserves to the Division Two championship in
1995 - he also led out the young Welsh side.
His grandfather, Joseph Neilson was a noted
local player on Tyneside.

> **Appearances:**
> *FL/PL: 35(7) apps. 1 gl.*
> *FLC: 4 apps. 0 gls.*
> *Others: 4 apps. 0 gls.*
> **Total:** *43(7) apps. 1 gl.*
> **Honours:**
> *4 Wales caps 1992-95/1 Wales B cap /*
> *7 Wales u21 caps 1993-94.*

NELSON, James

Role: Right-back 1930-1935
5' 8"
b. Greenock, 7th January 1901
d. Barry, Glamorgan, 8th October 1965

CAREER: St Pauls(Belfast)/Glenarm(Belfast)/
Crusaders/Cardiff City Aug 1921/UNITED
July 1930 £7,000/Southend United June 1935
£250 to May 1939/Ekco Sports(Southend) 1939
to 1945/UNITED scout June 1948.

Debut v Sheffield Wednesday (a) 30/8/30

Jimmy Nelson started his career as a forward,
moved to centre-half, and finally ended up as
a reliable and inspirational right-back of
distinction. Club captain when United lifted
the FA Cup in 1932, Jimmy was recognised as
one of the classiest full-backs of the inter-war
era, capped by Scotland and a member of the
renowned Wembley Wizards combination in
1928. Although born in Scotland, Nelson was
brought up in Northern Ireland and worked as
a boiler-maker before moving to Wales and
signing for Cardiff. At Ninian Park he was
part of a fine City team that reached the FA
Cup final twice, bringing the trophy back to
Wales for the first time in 1927. Possessing rare
powers of anticipation, Newcastle's boss Andy
Cunningham regarded Nelson highly and
brought him to Tyneside for what was a big
fee in 1930. A regular in four campaigns, he
was noted as being "ice-cool and never
flustered". On the club's relegation in 1934
Jimmy moved south and continued to perform
well with his final club, Southend United. He
afterwards became a well known publican
near Roots Hall and later in Cardiff, residing
in Penarth. His son Tony, appeared for Bristol
City, Newport and Bournemouth as an
amateur international, while Jimmy's son-in-
law, Stan Montgomery, played for both
Southend and Cardiff too. Nelson has the
dubious distinction of being the first Cardiff
City player sent-off in the Football league.

Appearances:
FL: 146 apps. 0 gls.
FAC: 13 apps. 0 gls.
Others: 1 app. 0 gls.
Total: *160 apps. 0 gls.*
Honours:
4 Scot caps 1925-30/
Scot trial app. 1928/
Irish Alliance app./
FAC winner 1927, 1932/
FAC finalist 1925/
WshC winner 1923, 1927, 1928, 1930.

*Jimmy Nelson leads the United team
onto the pitch for the 1932 Cup Final
against Arsenal.*

NESBIT, Anthony

Role: Midfield 1985-1987
5' 7"
b. Sunderland, 28th January 1968

CAREER: UNITED app 1985, pro cs 1986 to cs 1987 free/Seaham Red Star/Retired due to injury.

Debut v Charlton Athletic (a) 6/12/86 (sub)

A former schools' international, Tony Nesbit was introduced into top class soccer by manager Willie McFaul. The slightly-built youngster reached the substitutes' bench during season 1986-87 when the black'n'whites were struggling at the bottom of the First Division. Nesbit had good ball control but due to his limited height and build was always going to find it tough in the midfield battleground. He quickly faded and was released the following summer when he started to play local football and was soon forced to quit due to a knee injury. Nesbit later joined the Northumbria Police and lives in Sunderland.

Appearances:
FL: 1(2) apps. 0 gls.
Others: 0(1) app. 0 gls.
Total: 1(3) apps. 0 gls.
Honours:
Eng schools app.

NESBITT, John

Role: Centre-half 1955-1959
6' 2"
b. Washington, 24th September 1933

CAREER: Ashington/South Shields/ UNITED Dec 1955 to cs 1959.

Debut v Sheffield Wednesday (h) 25/9/57

John Nesbitt possessed the perfect physique and temperament for the important role at the centre of the defence. Big and tough, he joined United after being released from the Coldstream Guards, but his three-season career was almost totally restricted to Central League football as an understudy to Bob Stokoe. Appearing on his senior's injury during season 1957-58, Nesbitt also once took over Ronnie Simpson's goalkeeper's jersey during a close season tour. With Simpson not available and no other 'keeper in the party,

John Nesbitt

John wore the Number One shirt for the entire fixture with Rumanians, Petrolul Ploesti in May 1958.

Appearances:
FL: 3 apps. 0 gls.
Total: 3 apps. 0 gls.

NEVIN, George William

Role: Left-back 1925, 1928-1930
5' 11"
b. Lintz, County Durham, 16th December 1907
d. Sheffield, 1973

CAREER: Lintz Colliery/Dipton United/ UNITED Aug 1925/White-le-Head Rangers/ UNITED Dec 1928 £100/Sheffield Wednesday May 1930 free/Manchester United Dec 1933/ Sheffield Wednesday Mar 1934/Burnley May 1935/Lincoln City May 1937/Rochdale June 1939 to c1940.

Debut v West Ham United (a) 9/9/29

Cool under pressure and able to challenge strongly for the ball, George Nevin operated in both full-back roles for United. He stepped in for regulars Bob Thomson and David Fairhurst and was a thoroughly reliable reserve. A former miner in the Durham coalfield, Nevin was robust and solid at over 12 stone, but found it no easy task to claim a permanent position at any of his clubs. His total Football League career record reached a modest 46 games, and only once did he manage a long run

George Nevin

in the first eleven, with Burnley in season 1935-36 (21 matches). His father Ralph played the game to a good standard for Gateshead and Exeter, while three uncles also figured prominently too. His nephew, John Nevin turned out for Crewe Alexandra and York.

Appearances:
FL: 6 apps. 0 gls.
Total: *6 apps. 0 gls.*

NIBLO, Thomas Bruce

Role: Outside or Inside-forward
1898-1902, 1907-1908
5' 9"
b. Dunfermline, 24th September 1877
d. Walker, Newcastle upon Tyne, July 1933

CAREER: Cadzow Oak/Hamilton Academicals/Linthouse Aug 1896/UNITED Apr 1898 £90(Middlesbrough loan 1899-1900)/Aston Villa Jan 1902/Nottingham Forest May 1904/Watford May 1906/UNITED July 1907/Hebburn Argyle player-manager Aug 1908/Aberdeen Dec 1908/Raith Rovers Aug 1909/Cardiff City Dec 1910 £10/Blyth Spartans Feb 1911/Fulham war-guest 1915-16/Crystal Palace war-guest/Isle of Wight football 1919.

Debut v Loughborough Town (a) 11/4/1898

A rare and stylish ball dribbler, Tom Niblo possessed a splendid, and occasionally brilliant, left foot. During his two spells with United he displayed his versatility - especially on the right or left flanks - by appearing in all five forward positions. One contemporary report noted he was "a genuine worker, who is smart in seizing opportunities". As with many talented footballers, the Scot's only

deficiency, was his inconsistency, and the tendency to take on too many players instead of parting with the ball. Nevertheless he was good enough to be selected for his country in 1903-04 when with Aston Villa. Stocky and powerful, Niblo's son Alan also spent a time

Tom Niblo

on United's books without breaking through, while his grandson, Alan junior, captained Wolverhampton Wanderers' reserve side. Wounded during World War One, on his retirement, Tom settled on Tyneside becoming a publican for a period.

Appearances:
FL: 60 apps. 5 gls.
Total: *60 apps. 5 gls.*
Honours:
1 Scot cap 1904/Scot trial app. 1903-04.

NICHOLSON, Benjamin

Role: Left-back 1905-1907
5' 11"
b. Ashington, 1884

CAREER: Morpeth Harriers/UNITED Oct 1905/Luton Town cs 1907/West Stanley Aug 1908.

Debut v Manchester City (a) 16/2/07

Local lad Ben Nicholson joined the club's staff as a reserve half-back who could stand in at full-back too. A consistent player for the second eleven, Ben's time on the Gallowgate staff was confined to Northern League and North Eastern League football, apart from one outing in the senior team as a deputy to Jack Carr. That occurred in 1906-07, the season Newcastle lifted their second championship trophy. After a short period with Luton, where he couldn't claim a place either, Nicholson returned to the region and continued in non-league football.

Appearances:
FL: 1 app. 0 gls.
Total: *1 app. 0 gls.*

Lightly-framed, fair-haired Gary Nicholson graduated from United's junior set-up where he had proved himself as a prolific goalscorer from the wing. Although second choice to the experienced John Connolly, many at St James Park expected the young Tynesider to develop quickly and become a noted player. However, following a handful of Second Division outings spread over three seasons, Nicholson never made the big leap from being a potential star on the sidelines. He moved to the Field Mill stadium and proceeded to total over 100 games for Mansfield. Later in his career Gary became a respected player in local north-eastern soccer.

Appearances:
FL: 7(5) apps. 0 gls.
FAC: 1 app. 0 gls.
FLC: 3 apps. 0 gls.
Total: *11(5) apps. 0 gls.*

NICHOLSON, Gary Anthony

Role: Outside-left 1977-1981
5' 8"
b. Newcastle upon Tyne, 4th November 1960

CAREER: UNITED app 1977, pro Nov 1978/ Mansfield Town Aug 1981 £25,000/York City July 1984 £10,000/Halifax Town June 1985/ Blyth Spartans cs 1987/Whitley Bay June 1988/ North Shields 1989/Guiseley/Gateshead Dec 1993/RTM Newcastle Mar 1994.

Debut v Cambridge United (h) 22/11/78

NOBLE, Peter

Role: Striker 1964-1968
5' 8"
b. Sunderland,
19th August 1944

CAREER: Consett/UNITED Nov 1964 £1,000/ Swindon Town Jan 1968 £8,000/ Burnley May 1973 £40,000/ Blackpool Jan 1980 to Mar 1982.

Debut v Chelsea (a) 25/9/65

Peter Noble (airborne on right) heads Newcastle's equaliser against Fulham in September 1966.

At St James Park, Peter Noble operated mainly as a striker, although he also claimed an odd game in midfield, a position in which he later became a household name. As the Magpies fought to steer away from the relegation zone in seasons 1965-66 and 1966-67, Noble was drafted in to replace Ron McGarry in a search for goals. And the Wearsider gave the club good short term service by netting seven valuable strikes and helping to keep United's First Division place. The arrival though, of Albert Bennett and Wyn Davies, as well as the emergence of Bryan Robson, meant Peter was transferred south. With Swindon he reached Wembley in 1969, a famous giant-killing run by the Robins which ended in a major upset when Arsenal were felled. Noble then served Burnley with distinction, as a hardworking versatile midfield player able to play up front or in defence. He played 300 league and cup matches for the Turf Moor club, a regular for seven seasons. And he always grabbed goals, 80 for Burnley including many from the penalty spot. He once netted four goals in one fixture against Norwich. On hanging up his boots, Peter ran a sportswear business in Burnley.

Appearances:
FL: 22(3) apps. 7 gls.
Total: *22(3) apps. 7 gls.*
Honours:
FLC winner 1969/FL div 3 prom 1969.

NULTY, Geoffrey Owen

Role: Midfield or Centre-half
1974-1978
5' 10"
b. Prescot, Liverpool, 13th February 1949

CAREER: Stoke City July 1967/ Burnley July 1968 free/UNITED Dec 1974 £120,000/Everton July 1978 £45,000/Retired Mar 1980 due to injury, becoming Everton asst-manager/Preston North End asst-manager Dec 1981 to Dec 1983.

Debut v Carlisle United (a) 26/12/74

Although never described as a headlining star, Geoff Nulty was a dedicated professional who fitted into Newcastle's line-up in a manner that held the respect of his team-mates. Joining the club following 152 senior matches for Burnley, Nulty was a utility man at both Turf Moor and St James Park. He started off in midfield, in a marker or destroyer's role, then moved into the centre of the defence where he won the admiration of supporters too. Centre-half was perhaps Nulty's best position and under the leadership of Gordon Lee - and later Richard Dinnis - Geoff became an important figure. He was captain of the side that reached Wembley and then Europe, although he unfortunately missed the League Cup final appointment because of a broken jaw. Soon afterwards the turmoil in which the club found itself as the 1977-78 season began was instrumental in Nulty's move to his native Merseyside to rejoin his former boss Gordon Lee at Goodison Park. The bond between player and manager was strong and, on Nulty's retirement, he was appointed Lee's assistant at both Everton and Preston. Forced to quit the game due to a knee injury sustained in a Merseyside derby clash with Liverpool, at one stage he considered legal action over the incident. Holder of an Open University degree in Social Sciences, Nulty afterwards dealt in property development in the north west, and now runs his own business in Knowsley near Liverpool.

Appearances:
FL: 101 apps. 11 gls.
FAC: 10 apps. 1 gl.
FLC: 10 apps. 2 gls.
Eur: 2 apps. 0 gls.
Others: 4 apps. 0 gls.
Total: *127 apps. 14 gls.*
Honours:
FL div 2 champs 1973.

Geoff Nulty

Graham Oates

OATES, Graham

Role: Midfield 1976-1978
6' 2"
b. Bradford, 14th March 1949

CAREER: Tong Street(Bradford)/
Manningham Mills/Bradford City app
Nov 1969, pro Feb 1970/Blackburn Rovers
June 1974 exch deal/UNITED Mar 1976 joint
deal with R.Jones/Detroit Express(USA)
Mar 1978 £40,000/California Surf(USA) 1981/
Bradford City Jan 1982 briefly/
Lidget Green/Dudley Hill Athletic player-
manager/Scarborough 1987/
Gainsborough Trinity 1988.

Debut v Manchester United (h) 20/3/76(sub)

Graham Oates was purchased by his mentor
Gordon Lee towards the end of the 1975-76
season as a player who could fill both a
defender's and midfielder's role. His United
career began with a much-publicised own-
goal, within four minutes on his first full
home outing against Leeds, Oates sending a
25-yard back-pass into the net. Tall and well-
built, Oates had an uphill struggle at
Gallowgate; he was never taken to heart by
Geordie supporters, either when operating in
defence, or in the centre of the field where he

was drafted in to add some height and grit.
Rarely using his physique to advantage in
midfield, he was cool and composed, but was
ultimately a target of sections of the crowd
who appreciated neither his role nor his effect
on the side. Oates though, had a good record
at Bradford City (175 apps. 21 gls.) and
Blackburn Rovers (86 apps. 11 gls.), winning a
Division Three title medal at Ewood Park. He
later went into business in his native Bradford.

Appearances:
FL: 26(10) apps. 3 gls.
FLC: 3 apps. 0 gls.
Others: 4 apps. 0 gls.
Total: *33(10) apps. 3 gls.*
Honours:
FL div 3 champs 1975.

O'BRIEN, Patrick G.

Role: Right-back 1894-1896
5' 11"
b. Edinburgh, 1873

CAREER: Broxburn Shamrock/Hibernian/
Middlesbrough Ironopolis/Sheffield United
June 1894/UNITED Dec 1894/Hebburn
Argyle 1896 to 1898.
Debut v Walsall Town Swifts (h) 22/12/1894

From early reports, Pat O'Brien appears as one
of the pluckiest players ever to set foot on the
Leazes pitch. The Scot made a good early
impression at St James Park during the club's
second programme of Football League action.
An energetic mover, Pat gloried in the mass
charges at goal during those pioneer days of
the game, but faded after playing in five
different roles. With Hebburn Argyle, O'Brien
helped lift the Northern Alliance
championship in 1896-97 with a string of vital
goals. He remained on Tyneside afterwards
and by 1905 was laid low with illness and in
"destitute circumstances". It is recorded in the
club's Minutes of Meetings that Newcastle
United helped him out by giving him five
guineas.

Appearances:
FL: 9 apps. 2 gls.
FAC: 2 apps. 0 gls.
Total: *11 apps. 2 gls.*

O'BRIEN, William Francis

Role: Midfield 1988-1994
6' 1"
b. Dublin, 5th September 1964

CAREER: Cambridge Boys(Dublin)/Stella
Maris(Drumcondra)/Bohemians 1981/
Shamrock Rovers 1983/Manchester United
Oct 1986 £90,000/UNITED Nov 1988
£300,000/Tranmere Rovers Jan 1994 £350,000.

Debut v Millwall (a) 19/11/88

Known commonly as Liam, injury twice
halted O'Brien's bright progress in United's
line-up over the seven seasons he was on
Tyneside. Although tall and powerfully built,
Liam O'Brien wasn't a physical player, but
more a talented pass-maker with a languid
style who perhaps, had he used his
vast frame to more effect, would
have reached the very top.
Operating in an anchor role, when
in the mood the Irishman could
dominate a game and spray passes
all over the field. He also cracked a
stinging shot that occasionally
found the net with a spectacular
goal. It was caretaker boss Colin
Suggett who brought the Dubliner
to Tyneside after he had failed to
claim a regular spot at Old
Trafford. O'Brien was also in and
out of United's line-up - and absent
due to a broken leg - until Ossie
Ardiles and Kevin Keegan arrived.
On an injury to Paul Bracewell,
Liam stepped in to become a
driving force behind the club's
championship victory in 1993, until
injury sidelined him and Bracewell
returned. Newcastle's elevation to
the Premier League, together with
an influx of stars, meant Liam
moved to Tranmere where he made
over 100 appearances. During the
early part of his career, O'Brien
worked as a fitter and welder, and
experienced European Cup football
with Shamrock. His grandfather
appeared for Shamrock too and his
brother Michael had a spell on
Luton's books. In 1987 Liam was
sent-off within 85 seconds of a First
Division clash for Manchester
United against Southampton - one

of the quickest
dismissals on record
- while in 1994 he
missed a penalty in
a League Cup semi-
final shoot-out that would have earned
Tranmere a place at Wembley.

Appearances:
FL/PL: 131(22) apps. 19 gls.
FAC: 12(2) apps. 1 gl.
FLC: 9 apps. 1 gl.
Others: 9 apps. 1 gl.
Total: *161(24) apps. 22 gls.*
Honours:
15 Eire caps 1986-96/Eire u23 app./
FL div 1 champs 1993/
Eire champs 1984, 1985, 1986/
Eire Cup winner 1985.

Liam O'Brien

O'NEIL, Leslie Arthur

Role: Inside-left 1961-1965
5' 7"
b. Hartford, nr Blyth, 4th December 1943

CAREER: New Hartley jnrs/Blyth Spartans/
UNITED Nov 1961 £200/Darlington Jan 1965
free/Bradford City Mar 1970 £8,000/Carlisle
United May 1972 £6,000/Queen of the South
Aug 1977/Penrith manager/Workington Reds
manager Oct 1989/Swindon Town scout 1992.

Debut v Portsmouth (a) 19/10/63

Youngster Les O'Neil was given very little
amplitude during his days at St James Park. A
teenager who started on the left wing, he was
fast and tricky, shining in the Magpies' FA
Youth Cup victory in 1962. But while some of
his colleagues in that successful line up
graduated to a regular position in United's
side, Moncur and Craig included, O'Neil was
discarded after a single appearance at inside-
forward during season 1963-64. Moving into
the lower
divisions, he
eventually
developed into a
probing
midfielder, an
important player
at Bradford City
(103 games) and to
both Darlington
and Carlisle in
promotion years.
He was an
influential figure
for the Cumbrians
(155 appearances)
as they reached
the First Division.
Les ended his
career with over
500 senior outings
to his name and
later resided in
Carlisle.

Les O'Neil

Appearances:
FL: 1 app. 0 gls.
Total: *1 app. 0 gls.*
Honours:
FL div 2 prom 1974/
FL div 4 prom 1966/
FAYC winner 1962.

O'NEILL, Michael Andrew Martin

Role: Midfield or Striker 1987-1989
5' 11"
b. Portadown, 5th July 1969

CAREER: Coleraine/UNITED Oct 1987
£100,000/Dundee United Aug 1989 £350,000/
Everton trial cs 1992/Middlesbrough trial July
1992/Hibernian Aug 1993 £250,000/
Coventry City July 1996 £300,000.

Debut v Luton Town (a) 7/11/87(sub)

Michael O'Neill
made the journey
from Ireland to
Tyneside as an 18
year-old whizz-kid,
destined by some of
the misguided
media to become
the 'new George
Best'. When he
joined United, the
transfer created a
new record fee from
a Northern Ireland
club. O'Neill was
very much a raw
talent, indeed he
was still studying
for his GCE 'A'
levels, but quickly
made a big impact
on the First
Division scene.
Joining the forward
ranks alongside
Paul Gascoigne and
Paul Goddard,
O'Neill's intricate
style and ball skills
knitted with those
of Gazza and the
press claims
appeared a real
possibility. He was
United's Player of
the Season in 1987-
88 netting 13 goals
in 21 full games.

Michael O'Neill

But then the Irishman was struck by illness
and injury, losing form dramatically. After
being in and out of the side for the following
campaign he was transferred to Scotland - a

talent seemingly lost. O'Neill did resurrect his career north of the border, especially when he moved to Easter Road where he rediscovered much of that talent which had delighted the Tyneside crowd for a season.

Appearances:
FL: 36(12) apps. 15 gls.
FAC: 3(2) apps. 1 gl.
FLC: 2 apps. 0 gls.
Others: 4(1) apps. 1 gl.
Total: *45(15) apps. 17 gls.*
Honours:
29 N.Irel caps 1988-date/
N.Irel u23 caps/
N.Irel youth app./
SLC finalist 1994.

Ronald Orr

ORR, Ronald

Role: Inside-Right or Left
1901-1908
5' 5"
b. Bartonholm, nr Irvine,
6th August 1880

CAREER: Kilwinning Eglinton 1896/St Mirren May 1898/UNITED May 1901 joint deal with R.Bennie/Liverpool Apr 1908 £350/Raith Rovers Jan 1912/South Shields Mar 1913/Fulham war-guest 1916-19.

Debut v Blackburn Rovers (a) 7/9/01

Small in stature but, at eleven and a half stone, not a lightweight, chunky forward Ronald Orr played equally well at inside-left or right. Possessing a power drive, he became a regular in United's side at the turn of the century and grabbed plenty of goals for the Magpies - on one occasion scoring four times in 1901 against Notts County. Appearing in two title campaigns, Orr was an important link-man; a player not to take many headlines, but who dovetailed nicely with the finer skills of McWilliam and Rutherford in midfield, and fed off Bill Appleyard to perfection when up front. Surprisingly perhaps, the Scot was excellent in the air too, despite his size, yet always had trouble in gaining the affection of United's fans. For several seasons he was the unfortunate individual they picked on if performances dipped,

and Ronald moved to Anfield as a direct result of barracking. And he made United suffer very quickly, netting four goals against the Magpies. Orr again performed well for Liverpool over three seasons, claiming 38 goals in 112 games. The *Sportsman's Year Book* of 1905 claims he was also with Glossop before moving to St James Park. However, it is thought this contemporary report is confused with another Scot, William Orr, in action during the same period.

Appearances:
FL: 160 apps. 61 gls.
FAC: 20 apps. 9 gls.
Total: *180 apps. 70 gls.*
Honours:
2 Scot caps 1902-04/
Scot trial app. 1902-06/
FL champs 1905, 1907/
FAC finalist 1906.

OSTLER, John

Role: Centre-half 1896-1900
5' 10"
b. Newarthill, nr Motherwell, 1873
d. Prestonpans, East Lothian, 1958

CAREER: Motherwell/UNITED Dec 1896
joint deal with T.Stewart £200(Middlesbrough
loan 1899-1900)/Retired cs 1900.

Debut v Grimsby Town (a) 26/12/1896

Known as 'Jack', centre-half
Ostler formed the backbone,
along with Stott and Ghee,
of Newcastle's first
promotion side in 1898. A
dominating and unyielding
personality in the centre of
midfield, Jack was an
important character in
United's consolidation
as a top side. He took
part in the club's
inaugural fixture in the
First Division against

Jack Ostler

Wolverhampton Wanderers.
On leaving the game Ostler
returned to Lanarkshire working in a local coal
mine, later moving to Lothian where he was
employed at Rosewell pit.

Appearances:
FL: 71 apps. 3 gls.
FAC: 7 apps. 0 gls.
Total: *78 apps. 3 gls.*
Honours:
FL div 2 prom 1898.

PAILOR, Robert

Role: Centre-forward 1914-1915
5' 10"
b. Stockton, 7th July 1887
d. Hartlepool, 24th January 1976

CAREER: St Oswalds/West
Hartlepool/West Bromwich
Albion Oct 1908/UNITED May
1914 £1,550/Retired due to illness
cs 1915.

Debut v West Bromwich Albion (h) 2/9/14

Bob Pailor signed for Newcastle after an
impressive strike-rate of a goal every two
games for Albion, claiming 47 in 92 senior
fixtures. He helped the Midlands club to the
Second Division title in 1911 and to the FA Cup
final a year later when he scored an extra-time
semi-final winner. The well-built Teessider
possessed pace and agility which made him a
handful in the box but Pailor was an unlucky
player. Firstly he signed for the Magpies just as
war clouds hovered over the nation, then
suffered illness resulting from a kidney
complaint which had previously left him with
only one functioning organ. The former miner
had to call it a day when war forced a football
closedown, and afterwards resided in
Hartlepool where he was employed as a
bookmaker. Even away from the glare of the
game, luck deserted Bob too. Later in life he
had to give up his betting licence when his
sight faded and eventually he became blind.

Appearances:
FL: 11 apps. 2 gls.
FAC: 5 apps. 3 gls.
Total: *16 apps. 5 gls.*
Honours:
FL div 2 champs 1911/FAC finalist 1912.

PAPAVASILIOU, Nikodimos

Role: Midfield 1993-1994
5' 8"
b. Limassol, Cyprus, 31st August 1970

CAREER: Apollon Limassol(Cyprus) 1980/
Arsenal trial 1986/Oldham Athletic 1987/
OFI(Crete) 1988/UNITED July 1993
£125,000/Genoa(Italy) trial July 1994/
OFI(Crete) Dec 1994 £25,000/Apollon
Limassol(Cyprus) 1995.

Debut v Tottenham Hotspur (h) 14/8/93

Niki Papavasiliou

A one-time Arsenal trialist as a teenager, Niki not only has the distinction of having the longest name in United's history, but was also the first player to sign for the club from Mediterranean waters. Relentlessly pursued by manager Kevin Keegan, he impressed in a brief trial period with the club as a small, compact midfield player with an infectious workrate and no little skill with his left foot. After a bright opening in United's colours as the Premier League was encountered for the first time, Papavasiliou lost his place and then was injured in a reserve fixture which put him on the sidelines for a long period. By the time he was fit, a pack of players were fighting for the midfield positions and Niki was destined to be down the list. With national service looming in his native country, the Cypriot returned to Greece to continue his football career. At the time of joining the Magpies, he was much fancied by Monaco, while his career at Boundary Park fell foul of a work permit although he was at Oldham for 12 months. He was so keen to obtain a chance at Gallowgate that he paid his own air fare to Tyneside. Papavasiliou has appeared over 20 times for his country.

John Park

Appearances:
PL: 7 apps. 0 gls.
Total: *7 apps. 0 gls.*
Honours:
24 Cyprus caps 1991-96.

PARK, John Bluey

Role: Outside-right 1936-1941
5' 9"
b. Douglas Water, nr Lanark, 7th October 1913

CAREER: Douglas Water Thistle/Hamilton Academical 1933/UNITED Apr 1936 £1,800 to 1941/Stranraer war-guest/Third Lanark war-guest/Retired 1945.

Debut v Bradford Park Avenue (a) 14/9/36

A rival to Ehud Rogers on the right wing as he joined United, John Park took over the role for the 1937-38 season and at times looked a great prospect. Robust and enthusiastic, the Scot's methods were not always ultra scientific, but he demonstrated that he could be a problem to the opposition. With his bustling style, Park also figured in the centre-forward shirt for United before the Second World War all but ended his football career. John worked in Motherwell's steelworks during the war and remained employed there to his retirement. Since leaving St James Park he has lived in Lesmahagow near Lanark.

Appearances:
FL: 60 apps. 11 gls.
FAC: 1 app. 1 gl.
War: 12 apps. 2 gls.
Total:
73 apps. 14 gls.

PARK, Oswald

Role: Centre-half 1924-1931
5' 11"
b. Darlington, 7th February 1905

CAREER: Darlington Railway Athletic/UNITED Nov 1924 £125(Connahs Quay loan 1929-30 & 1930-31)/Northampton Town May 1931/Hartlepools United cs 1934/North Shields July 1937/Consett player-manager Feb 1938.

Debut v Bolton Wanderers (a) 29/8/25

Clever and versatile, Ossie Park began his career as a midfield player operating in the centre of the pitch, but on the advent of the stopper centre-half changed his role into that of a defensive pivot. As deputy to Charlie Spencer, he appeared on five occasions as the black'n'whites lifted the championship in

1927, then gained an extended run the following season. However, United directors didn't see Park as a long-term replacement for the ageing Spencer, and he was overlooked when the Magpies splashed out heavily on England centre-half Jack Hill in 1928. He spent a long period on loan with Cheshire League club Connah's Quay before moving to Northampton. Ossie later resided in County Durham.

Appearances:
FL: 42 apps. 0 gls.
FAC: 1 app. 0 gls.
Total: *43 apps. 0 gls.*

Ossie Park

PARKINSON, Andrew

Role: Striker 1978-1979
6' 0"
b. Johannesburg, South Africa, 5th May 1959

CAREER: Highlands Park(S.Africa)/Dynamos United(S.Africa)/UNITED Mar 1978/Peterborough United July 1979 free/Philadelphia Fury(USA) cs 1980/Later returning to S.African football.

Debut v Manchester United (h) 11/3/78 (sub)

Tall and somewhat gangling in appearance, Andy Parkinson arrived on Tyneside as a surprise signing from South African soccer. With Newcastle on their way down into the Second Division, it was hoped that Parkinson would prove to be an awkward striker, able to cause mayhem in and around the box. But the youngster, fresh from a sun-soaked landscape, failed to make an impact on his three outings as substitute, although he did possess nice touches on the ball. He lasted only a season with Peterborough, walking out on the Posh to conclude an unhappy period in the Football League.

Appearances:
FL: 0(3) apps. 0 gls.
Total: *0(3) apps. 0 gls.*

Andy Parkinson

PATERSON, Thomas A.

Role: Outside-left 1950-1952
5' 8"
b. Lochore, Fife, 3rd April 1927

CAREER: Raith Rovers/Lochgelly Albert/Leicester City Mar 1948/ UNITED June 1950 £2,500/ Watford July 1952 £750/Berwick Rangers July 1955/Retired due to injury c1957.

Debut v Middlesbrough (a) 25/12/50

A play-anywhere forward, Tom Paterson preferred an inside role, but was generally picked in the outside-left position for Newcastle. Paterson wasn't a regular at either Filbert Street or St James Park - stepping in on only two occasions

for Mitchell and Robledo - but he did have a good run in senior football at Vicarage Road. Tom totalled 45 appearances for Watford before moving to the Scottish League with Berwick. After being forced to quit the game due to a knee injury, he later settled in Gateshead.

Appearances:
FL: 2 apps. 0 gls.
Total: *2 apps. 0 gls.*

Tom Paterson

PATERSON, William Alexander Kennedy

Role: Centre-half 1954-1958
6' 1"
b. Kinlochleven, Argyll, 25th February 1930

CAREER: Inverness Thistle/Ransome & Marles/Doncaster Rovers Mar 1950/UNITED Oct 1954 £22,250/Glasgow Rangers July 1958 £3,500/Greenock Morton Nov 1962 free/Cheltenham Town 1963/Inverness Caledonian 1966/Hamilton(Canada) to 1970.

Debut v Tottenham Hotspur (h) 16/10/54

Purchased by United's directors for a then large fee of £22,250, Bill Paterson was in for a rough ride at St James Park. Bestowed with the hugely popular Frank Brennan's shirt, who was at the time in dispute with the club, Paterson looked anything but a commanding centre-half during his early days at St James Park. A stylish footballer who believed defenders should also play attractive football, he was totally different to the physical Brennan and the supporters did not take to him quickly. Even Paterson himself made the comment that, "I appeared a misfit". Bill's

form plummeted and he lost all the confidence that had earned him international recognition at 'B' level; it was no surprise when he left Tyneside. However, the powerfully-built Scot returned to the big time at Ibrox, regaining his honour in 116 appearances for Rangers, as part of their side winning several trophies in the early years of the sixties. On leaving the game, Paterson became a publican and hotelier in various locations including Goole, Tadcaster, Hythe and Inverness.

Appearances:
FL: 22 apps. 1 gl.
FAC: 5 apps. 1 gl.
Total: *27 apps. 2 gls.*
Honours:
1 Scot B cap 1954/SL champs 1961/ SC winner 1960/SLC winner 1961/ ECWC finalist 1961.

PATON, Harold D.

Role: Inside-right 1921-1922
5' 8"
b. Larkhall, nr Motherwell

CAREER: Clydebank/UNITED May 1921
£410/St Mirren Nov 1922 £600 to 1923.

Debut v Huddersfield Town (a) 27/8/21

Harry Paton

Harry Paton was a nimble player, well known to Scottish fans and regarded as a good prospect during the immediate post-war years. He took an active part in Newcastle's 1921-22 programme, but wasn't retained for the following year. With St Mirren he was again described as "promising", but only appeared on six occasions for the Paisley club. They complained, after the transfer from Tyneside, that Paton was unfit and the dispute went to the Internatioanl League Board for judgement.

Appearances:
FL: 13 apps. 2 gls.
Total: *13 apps. 2 gls.*

PATTEN, John T.

Role: Outside-right & Asst-secretary 1892-1936
5' 9"
b. Tyneside

CAREER: Trafalgar (Newcastle) c1880/
Newcastle West End/UNITED May
1892/Hebburn Argyle 1897 to 1898/UNITED
asst-secretary & reserve manager c1898 to cs
1936/Northumberland FA secretary 1929 to
1947.

Debut v Ardwick (a) 21/10/1893

John Patten was one of Tyneside's foremost football pioneers. Once called a "typically blunt Geordie", he was associated with the West End club before their liquidation in 1892, and then joined East End in readiness for their development into Newcastle United. As a player, Patten was chiefly a reserve operating

John Patten

on the right flank in Northern Alliance football. He was elevated to Football League status only once, in the club's inaugural season. Retiring from the playing side, 'Jack' as he was commonly known, then concentrated on the game's administration. Firstly he acted for United behind the scenes, for many years in charge as secretary of the Magpies' second string in the North Eastern League. He then later became involved with the county association, and was secretary of the Northumberland FA for over 25 years and a member of the FA Council. Patten also refereed and ran the line in reserve games. In a biography published in 1958, Jack was described affectionately as "the grand old man of Tyneside football". Patten lived in Newcastle into his nineties, a staunch United enthusiast to his final day.

Appearances:
FL: 1 app. 0 gls.
Total: *1 app. 0 gls.*

PATTINSON, Daniel

Role: Inside-left 1900-1902
5' 10"
b. Newcastle upon Tyne

CAREER: Malcolm jnrs(Newcastle)/
Rutherford College(Newcastle)/Willington
Athletic/UNITED July 1900/Local football cs
1902.

*Debut v Nottingham Forest (a)
19/3/02 (scored once)*

Youthful forward Daniel Pattinson followed the path of Colin Veitch to United, from Rutherford College and Malcolm juniors in the Heaton district of Newcastle. Although Pattinson played well and netted

on his debut as a reserve to Veitch, he wasn't given another opportunity in senior company. After two seasons of Northern League football, Dan returned to local soccer.

Appearances:
FL: 1 app. 1 gl.
Total: *1 app. 1 gl.*

PAYNE, Lee J.

Role: Outside-left 1988-1989
5' 10"
b. Luton, 12th December 1966

CAREER: Hitchin Town/Dunstable Town/ Luton Town 1987/Barnet/Leicester City trial Sept 1988/UNITED Sept 1988 £25,000/ Reading Mar 1989 £30,000/Veendam (Holland) 1990 £60,000/BV Emmen(Holland) c1991 £110,000/Gateshead July 1993 to Sept 1993.

Debut v Middlesbrough (h) 26/10/88

Lee Payne

After being rejected at Kenilworth Road because of a knee problem, Lee Payne tried to make a comeback with Leicester during a trial period at Filbert Street. His sparkling form alerted Magpie officials after the forward played well against United in a Central League fixture. Manager Willie McFaul took a chance with £25,000 to bring him north - the Irishman's last purchase as Newcastle boss. Exchanging his job from that of finishing foreman on a construction site, had Payne been a success at St James Park, he would have been recognised as the most expensive transfer from non-league football. He needed to total a certain number of appearances for United to earn his previous club another £100,000. Unfortunately the fast and live-wire winger didn't get past seven matches for the Magpies and new manager Jim Smith released Payne to join Reading. Lee is distantly related to Luton's legendary centre-forward Joe Payne, while his father was an amateur goalkeeper with Dunstable.

Appearances:
FL: 6(1) apps. 0 gls.
Total: *6(1) apps. 0 gls.*

PEACOCK, Darren

Role: Centre-half 1994-date
6' 2"
b. Bristol, 3rd February 1968

CAREER: Bristol City/Bristol Rovers/ Newport County app cs 1984, pro Feb 1986/ Hereford United Mar 1989 free/Queens Park Rangers Dec 1990 £350,000/UNITED Mar 1994 £2.7m.

Debut v Norwich City (h) 29/3/94

Darren Peacock became the country's most expensive defender and the Magpies' record purchase when he moved from Loftus Road to Gallowgate in 1994. That headline move was a far cry from his early days in the game with struggling Welsh club Newport County. Apart from picking up a broken leg which needed a bone graft, County's severe financial problems meant Darren was handed a free transfer when the club folded. Moving to Hereford, Peacock quickly established himself as a commanding defender in the lower divisions before being captured by QPR and developed further at Loftus Road. Kevin Keegan made a persistent chase to land the talented player

PEACOCK, Gavin Kevin

Darren Peacock

Role: Midfield or Striker 1990-1993
5' 8"
b. Welling, Kent, 18th November 1967

CAREER: Queens Park Rangers Nov 1984/
Gillingham loan Oct 1987, pmt Dec 1987
£40,000/Bournemouth Aug 1989 £210,000/
UNITED Nov 1990 £450,000 cash-exch deal
with W.Fereday/Chelsea July 1993 £1.25m.

Debut v Leicester City (a) 1/12/90

Gavin Peacock flourished in a Newcastle shirt
and was United's outstanding player during
season 1991-92, the year the club very nearly
tumbled into the old Division Three. A hit
with the fans, had it not been for Peacock's
menace in attack, the Magpies may well have
been doomed before Kevin Keegan arrived to
rescue the side. Always able to fire home
quality strikes from midfield as well, Gavin
was recognised as a Premier League player,
good in controlling the ball,
with vision and a sure
drive when in a scoring
position. He almost
departed to
Middlesbrough as Keegan
took total control, but
changed his mind
when the

and, since joining United's Premier League set-
up, the tough and committed Darren has
given Newcastle's attack-minded side a
touch of grit and stability in defence to
blend with the ball-playing skills.
Although at first United's supporters
had to be convinced he was a top
player, Darren's steely and
determined performances
during season 1994-95 won
over the fans and thereafter he
became a popular player in
United's squad of superstars.
Characterised by his long
flowing hair and pony-tail,
Peacock totalled almost 150
matches in London although
he was rejected as a youngster
at both Bristol City and Rovers.

Hall and
Keegan duo swung
into action. Until injury
put him out of the
selection frame, the past
England schools and
youth player had
taken a major role in
the Magpies'
championship
success in 1993.
Gavin's twisting
runs and quick
turns were in
demand, but after
personal problems
led to an expressed

Gavin Peacock

Appearances:
PL: 77(1) apps. 1 gl.
FAC: 7 apps. 0 gls.
FLC: 9 apps. 2 gls.
Eur: 4 apps. 0 gls.
Total: *97(1) apps. 3 gls.*
Honours:
WshC winner 1990.

wish to return south, United agreed a deal with Chelsea on what was termed compassionate grounds. From a footballing pedigree, his father Keith Peacock - from South Shields - had a long career with Charlton, while he was also in charge of the Gills while Gavin was based in Kent. His debut for United resulted in a remarkable 4-5 defeat at Filbert Street. Two years later, on the same ground, Peacock was the saviour as Newcastle scrambled a win which ensured First Division survival.

Appearances:
FL: 102(3) apps. 35 gls.
FAC: 6 apps. 3 gls.
FLC: 6 apps. 5 gls.
Others: 3 apps. 4 gls.
Total: *117(3) apps. 47 gls.*
Honours:
1 FL app. 1993/
Eng schools app./
Eng youth app. 1985-87/
FL div 1 champs 1993/
FAC finalist 1994.

PEARS, William

Role: Right-half 1936-1941
5' 6"
b. Willington, Co.Durham,
15th November 1918

CAREER: Crook Town/UNITED Sept 1936 £50 to Sept 1941.

Debut v Bury (a) 15/4/39

Starting his career as an inside-forward, Billy Pears stood in for Jimmy Gordon at half-back during the 1938-39 season. A product of Durham schools football and an international at that level, he was a gritty midfielder who knitted determination with a fair degree of skill. However, Pears' development as a Football League player was cut short just when he was making an impact in the club's Central League eleven. War began soon after his senior outings and he joined the army for the duration of the hostilities, a blossoming career in the game over.

Appearances:
FL: 2 apps. 0 gls.
Total: *2 apps. 0 gls.*
Honours:
Eng schools app.

PEARSON, James Findlay

Role: Striker 1978-1980
5' 10"
b. Falkirk, 24th March 1953

CAREER: Gairdoch United/St Johnstone 1969/Everton May 1974 £100,000/UNITED Aug 1978 £75,000/Retired due to injury Feb 1980/Barrow Apr 1980/Gateshead Nov 1981/North Shields player-manager cs 1983/Gateshead July 1984/Workington Oct 1984/Whitley Bay coach Aug 1985/ Blyth Spartans coach Nov 1985 to May 1988/ North Shields manager June 1988/ Gateshead asst-manager 1989 to 1990.

Debut v Millwall (a) 19/8/78

Jim Pearson

A slimly-built, fair-haired Scot, Jim Pearson was able to play as a front runner or a midfield schemer. Skilful and with deft touches, at the peak of his career with St Johnstone and Everton, he was always liable to find the net. Jim made his debut as a 17 year-old in the Scottish League and a record of 39 goals in 96 league outings alerted the Goodison Park club who snapped him up for a six figure sum. Pearson had misfortune with injury in England, but he still managed moments of brilliance in his 116 matches for the Merseysiders. Arriving on Tyneside as part of Bill McGarry's rebuilding plans, knocks continued at St James Park and Jim was more often in the treatment room than on the pitch, eventually leaving the senior game due to a knee injury. He is remembered at Gallowgate for a crucial League Cup penalty shoot-out miss against rivals Sunderland in 1979. Despite this setback, Pearson was a respected professional, who later guided local non-league side Blyth Spartans to two Northern League titles. After leaving the game, Jim worked in insurance, then for sportswear giants Nike, based in Washington.

Appearances:
FL: 11 apps. 3 gls.
FAC: 0(1) app. 0 gls.
FLC: 2 apps. 1 gl.
Total: *13(1) apps. 4 gls.*
Honours:
6 Scot u23 caps 1974-76/
Scot schools app./
Scot youth app./
FLC finalist 1977.

PEARSON, *Thomas Usher*

Role: Outside-left 1933-1948
5' 8"
b. Edinburgh, 6th March 1914

CAREER: Murrayfield Amateurs/ Heart of Midlothian trial 1933/UNITED Mar 1933 £35/Blackburn Rovers war-guest 1940-44/Bolton Wanderers war-guest 1940-41/Tottenham Hotspur war-guest 1941-42/Birmingham war-guest 1942-43/ Liverpool war-guest 1942-43/Blackpool war-guest 1943-45/Stoke City war-guest 1944-45/Walsall war-guest 1944-45/Heart of Midlothian war-guest/Aberdeen Feb 1948 cash-exch deal with W.McCall/ Retired 1953/Aberdeen coach 1959, becoming manager Nov 1959 to Feb 1965/ UNITED scout June 1967.

Debut v Arsenal (a) 14/10/33

Tommy Pearson was a loyal servant to Newcastle United for over a decade and, but for the Second World War, would probably have become a huge international star. The skilful Tommy possessed immaculate ball control and was especially noted for his magical runs on the touchline which featured bamboozling body-swerves and foot shuffles, as well as crowd-pleasing nut-megs. The Scot was quick to develop through United's ranks. He was unorthodox and became a regular for the Magpies in six peacetime seasons, until being unfairly treated by the club during the 1947-48 promotion campaign. Branded a troublemaker by some sections of the management - allegations according to team-mates far from the truth - he left Tyneside with a sour taste, Len Shackleton noting he received "shabby treatment" from the club. Although Pearson was reaching the veteran stage, his departure to Aberdeen opened another door and he became associated with the Dons for over 30 years, as player, coach, manager and local sports journalist. He afterwards returned to the city of his birth, Edinburgh, where he opened a jewellery business as well as becoming a first class amateur golfer, good enough to compete in the Open Championship. Tom is the only player to have appeared for both England and Scotland in international football, turning out for the English in emergency during a wartime fixture on Tyneside. When he made his debut in his country's blue shirt Pearson was over 34 years of age. Serving in the RAF during the war, Tommy was always guaranteed a match on his travels around the country, helping Blackpool to the 1944 North Cup final. His father Tommy senior, was with Hearts, while an uncle, Harry Pearson appeared for Arsenal.

Appearances:
FL: 212 apps. 46 gls.
FAC: 16 apps. 6 gls.
War: 51 apps. 10 gls.
Total: *279 apps. 62 gls.*
Honours:
2 Scot caps 1947/
1 Eng war cap 1940/
1 SL app. 1948/
1 FL app. 1942/
FL div 2 prom 1948.

PEART, John George

Role: Centre-forward 1912-1913
5' 11"
b. South Shields, 3rd October 1888
d. Paddington, London, 3rd September 1948

CAREER: South Shields Adelaide 1905/ Sheffield United May 1907/Stoke June 1911/ UNITED Mar 1912 £600/Notts County Feb 1913 £600/Leeds City war-guest 1916-19/ Rochdale war-guest/Birmingham Nov 1919/ Derby County Jan 1920/Ebbw Vale player-manager Aug 1920/Port Vale Jan 1922/ Norwich City July 1922/Rochdale player-manager Mar 1923/Retired playing May 1924/Bradford City manager July 1930/ Fulham manager May 1935 to his demise.
Debut v Middlesbrough (h) 16/3/12

One of football's most travelled personalities, 'Jack' Peart was a central figure of the game for over 40 years, a player of expert ability and, as a manager, a shrewd judge. Only briefly at Newcastle as one of Albert Shepherd's replacements, the Tynesider was a strong leader with a bustling style. A skilled craftsman in attack, Jack made a name for himself netting 31 goals in 21 games for Stoke during their non-league days. Peart appeared at every level of the Football League, as well as in the Southern and Welsh Leagues, and always he scored goals; 55 for Notts County and 59 for Leeds City. Jack was also often injured, once dubbed, 'the most injured man in football'. He broke his leg twice and fractured his arm, at St James Park being out of action for several weeks too. As a manager, the secretary-manager type of the old school, he took Fulham to an FA Cup semi-final. He also fashioned a side to eventually take the Londoners into the First Division, only to die before his task was achieved.

Appearances:
FL: 17 apps. 6 gls.
Total: *17 apps. 6 gls.*
Honours:
1 FL app. 1914/3 SnL apps. 1912/
FL div 2 champs 1914/
FL Long Service medal 1945.

Jack Peart

PEDDIE, John Hope

Role: Centre-forward 1897-1902
5' 11"
b. Glasgow, 21st March 1877
d. Detroit, USA, October 1928

CAREER: Benburb/Third Lanark June 1895/
UNITED trial Sept 1897, pmt Nov 1897 £135/
Manchester United June 1902/Plymouth
Argyle May 1903/Manchester United May
1904/Heart of Midlothian Jan 1907/
N.American football 1908.

Debut v Newton Heath (a) 13/11/1897

After shining in a friendly match for Third
Lanark against United in April 1897, United
kept a close eye on Glaswegian John Peddie.
Known as 'Jock', it wasn't long before he was
on Tyneside and immediately the free-scoring
poacher started to belt home goals in a
black'n'white shirt. Peddie was a potent
attacker, having a shot of colossal power,
reckoned to be the hardest ever seen at St
James Park during those late Victorian days,
even once shaking the goal net pegs loose with
one terrific shot against Loughborough Town
in 1898. Perhaps Jock can be regarded as
United's first 'Number 9 Hero', contemporary
reports noting he was extremely popular with
supporters, having what can be
regarded today as a cult
following. His power in
attack was the difference
between Newcastle
staying in Division Two,
or tasting the top
league for the first time
in 1898. The moody
Scot appeared in the
club's inaugural
Division One fixture,
but was often in
trouble with the club's
hierarchy for a number
of misdemeanours;
refusing to play, being
absent from training and
ultimately being suspended
sine-die in 1900 (later lifted).
Peddie though could always
claim to be doing his job whilst on the field; 78
goals in 136 games is a fine record by anyone's
standard. When he moved to Old Trafford
many bemoaned his departure. Jock scored
more goals for Manchester United - 58 in 121

Jock Peddie

league and cup matches - and was on the
verge of a Scottish cap on several occasions.
Peddie eventually emigrated to North
America where he spent the rest of his life.

Appearances:
FL: 126 apps. 73 gls.
FAC: 10 apps. 5 gls.
Total: *136 apps. 78 gls.*
Honours:
Scot trial app. 1896-1906/
FL div 2 prom 1898, 1906.

PENMAN, William Salmond Thomson

Role: Inside-left 1963-1966
5' 10"
b. Coaltown of Wemyss, Fife, 7th August 1939

CAREER: St Andrews United/Glasgow
Rangers 1960/UNITED Apr 1963 £11,500/
Swindon Town Sept 1966 £9,800/Walsall
Sept 1970 £6,000/Dundalk cs 1973/Redditch
United 1975.

Debut v Charlton Athletic (h) 3/4/63 (scored once)

As Newcastle challenged for the Second
Division title in 1963-64 and 1964-65, Willie
Penman performed creditably in a black and
white shirt. Although he turned out for
Rangers on only three occasions, he was
effective on Tyneside without being
flamboyant. The Scot linked well in
attack, frequently popping up in the
box and always liable to find the
net. He scored in United's crucial
promotion-winning victory over
Bolton in 1965, but then found
First Division defences much
harder to unlock. He moved to
Swindon where he took part in
the Robins' successful run to
Wembley in the League Cup
during 1968-69. After leaving the
game, Penman went into business in
Walsall where he was employed by a
sports company.

Appearances:
FL: 62(1) apps. 18 gls.
FAC: 2 apps. 0 gls.
Total: *64(1) apps. 18 gls.*
Honours:
FL div 2 champs 1965/FL div 3 prom
1969/FLC winner 1969/SJC winner 1960.

Willie Penman

PHILLIPSON, Thomas William

Role: Centre-forward 1919-1921
5' 8"
*b. Ryton, nr Newcastle upon Tyne,
31st October 1898
d. Wolverhampton, 19th November 1965*

CAREER: Scotswood 1914/UNITED Dec 1919
£500/Swindon Town May 1921 £500/
Wolverhampton Wanderers Dec 1923 £1,000/
Sheffield United Mar 1928/Bilston United
cs 1930/Walsall 1931 to c1932.

Debut v Everton (a) 24/1/20

A broad-shouldered, compact centre-forward,
Tom Phillipson was noted for his first-time
shooting and crowd-rousing sprint in a chase.

Phillipson was a schools' star on Tyneside,
recorded as scoring no fewer than 14 goals
(out of 15) in a single fixture - and getting
another ten in his next match! Tom was at St
James Park when the club was overflowing
with potential stars but was a promising talent
in United's reserve side. However, he never
quite grasped the chances he was given at
Gallowgate immediately after the Great War
and had to prove his worth elsewhere.
Developing into a forceful goalgetter, he
reached his peak at Molineux, where he was
signed by his fellow Geordie and ex United
player, George Jobey. With Wolves, Tom
cracked home 111 goals in only 159 games,
netting a club record 37 league and cup goals
in 1925-26. He was a local hero in the
Midlands town, once scoring five against

Tom Phillipson

Bradford City, and four against Barnsley. On retirement, Phillipson settled in Wolverhampton, entering local business and politics. A pillar of the establishment, Tom became Lord Mayor in 1938 for an extended period. During World War One he served as a sergeant in the West Yorkshire Regiment in Russia.

Appearances:
FL: 14 apps. 4 gls.
FAC: 1 app. 0 gls.
Total: *15 apps. 4 gls.*
Honours:
2 Eng schools apps. 1913/
FL div 3(N) champs 1924.

PINGEL, Frank Mortensen

Role: Centre-forward 1989
6' 1"
b. Resskov, Denmark, 9th May 1964

CAREER: IHF Aarhus(Denmark)/Skovbakken Aarhus(Denmark)/AGF Aarhus(Denmark) July 1987/UNITED Jan 1989 £260,000/ Brondby IF(Denmark) July 1989 £200,000/1860 Munich(Germany) Sept 1992 £250,000/ Bursaspor(Turkey) July 1993/Fenebahce (Turkey) 1993 £300,000/Bursaspor(Turkey) July 1994/Lille OSC(France) 1994-95/Aarhus Fremad(Denmark) Sept 1995.

Debut v Aston Villa (a) 14/1/89 (sub)

A well-travelled striker, Frank Pingel was 24 years old when he joined United to team up alongside Brazilian, Mirandinha in a cosmopolitan-looking Magpie attack. Strong and physical, Pingel was a one-time boxing champion in Denmark. However, manager Jim Smith only briefly tried his continental strike force during the 1988-89 season, before Frank moved back to his native country. The Dane though, developed into a useful centre-foward, firstly winning domestic championship honours and international caps before heading for the Bundesliga. Frank boasts a good record in a Denmark shirt, netting five goals in his 11 international matches.

Appearances:
FL: 13(1) apps. 1 gl.
Total: *13(1) apps. 1 gl.*
Honours:
11 Denmark caps 1992-94/
Denmark FL champs 1990, 1991/
Denmark Cup winner 1988.

Frank Pingel

PRIOR, Kenneth George

Role: Outside-left 1952-1954, 1956-1957
5' 7"
b. Newcastle upon Tyne, 13th October 1932

CAREER: Cambois jnrs/Sunderland amat/UNITED Mar 1952/Millwall May 1954 £100/UNITED July 1956 £1,250/ Berwick Rangers Jan 1957/North Shields 1959/Horden Colliery 1963/ Ashington 1965, becoming manager 1967/Alnwick Town manager Oct 1981.

Debut v Middlesbrough (h) 11/4/52

Ken Prior hailed from football stock, his father George appearing for Sheffield Wednesday, and his brother, Jack for Sunderland and Grimsby. Additionally his brother-in-law was United full-back, Bobby Cowell. Prior had two spells at St James Park in an attempt to break into the senior side, but on each occasion found the talent of Bobby Mitchell blocking his path for the Number 11 shirt. Ken was still a good footballer, despite his lack of first team action. Fast and accurate with his passes and crosses, his best season wearing the black'n'white jersey was in 1951-52 when he deputised for Mitchell on six occasions. Ken later settled in the north east, a prominent official in local football for over two decades.

Appearances:
FL: 10 apps. 3 gls.
Total: *10 apps. 3 gls.*

PUDAN, Albert Ernest

Role: Left-back 1906-1909
5' 11"
b. Canning Town, London

CAREER: Clapton 1899/West Ham United cs 1900/Bristol Rovers cs 1902/UNITED July 1906 £150/Leicester Fosse May 1909 £125/ Huddersfield Town secretary-manager Aug 1910/Leicester Fosse(player) Apr 1912/ Retired 1914/Leicester City director 1919 to Feb 1940 (chairman 1929-31).

Debut v Blackburn Rovers (h) 26/10/07

Known as 'Dick' throughout his career, Pudan was at his peak when on Tyneside, reaching the FA Cup final with the Magpies and appearing, albeit on only three occasions, in United's title side of 1909. He was an excellent passer of the ball

Dick Pudan

and possessed an intelligent footballing brain. Plucked from the Southern League at Bristol Rovers where he appeared in over 100 matches, Dick replaced England international Jack Carr for the 1907-08 season, but himself was replaced by Tony Whitson the following year. Pudan lost his place after an uncomfortable showing in that season's cup final against Wolves, when really he should not have played at all - being bed-ridden a few days before the game with what was called, "a bout of boils". On leaving Tyneside, Pudan was in charge of Huddersfield Town when they entered Football League action, and later had a long spell as director - and chairman - at Filbert Street; he is thought to be the first ex player to reach the boardroom. He was also a successful businessman in the East Midlands running a hosiery manufacturing company.

Appearances:
FL: 24 apps. 0 gls.
FAC: 6 apps. 0 gls.
Total: *30 apps. 0 gls.*
Honours:
FAC finalist 1908/SnL champs 1905.

PUGH, Kevin John

Role: Midfield 1976-1982
5' 7"
b. Corbridge, Northumberland, 11th October 1960

CAREER: UNITED app 1976, pro cs 1977/
Gateshead Aug 1982 free/Darlington Sept
1983/Gateshead 1983/RSC Charleroi
(Belgium) Aug 1984/La Louviere(Belgium)
1994.

Debut v Chelsea (a) 7/11/81 (sub)

Talented teenager Kevin
Pugh was chased by a host of
clubs, including Nottingham
Forest, Aston Villa, Derby
and United. Joining his local
club, Pugh was sturdy and
vigorous on the field. He
made several headlines in
reserve football for United
and was frequently on the
verge of a first team call-up
as the eighties decade began.
But Kevin had to be content with a single
appearance for Newcastle, as a substitute for
Imre Varadi during season 1981-82. He later
settled in Belgium and had a good career on
the continent. When he was with Gateshead,
Pugh helped win the Northern Premier League
championship in 1983 and was called up for
the England non-league squad.

Appearances:
FL: 0(1) app. 0 gls.
Total: *0(1) app. 0 gls.*
Honours:
NPL champs 1983.

PUNTON, William Hamilton

Role: Outside-left 1954-1958
5' 9"
b. Glenkinchie, East Lothian, 9th May 1934

CAREER: Breadalbane/Portadown 1953/
UNITED Feb 1954 £6,000/Southend United
June 1958 exch deal for J.McGuigan/Norwich
City July 1959/Sheffield United Nov 1966
£7,500/Scunthorpe United Jan 1968 £3,000/
Yarmouth Town player-coach June 1969,
becoming manager May 1974/Diss Town
manager May 1990 to 1995.

Debut v Manchester City (h) 3/4/54

Unorthodox in method, Bill Punton arrived on
Tyneside from Ireland after club scouts saw
him score four goals in one match. Strongly-
built and thinning on top, Punton was one of
the many deputies to shadow Bobby Mitchell
through the fifties. His 25 appearances for the
Magpies were spread over four seasons before
he moved on in search of regular senior action.
That he found at Carrow Road where he made
a big name for himself, clocking up an
outstanding record of 256 games and 29 goals
for Norwich. With an all-action style, Bill was
direct and an important figure in the Canaries'
cup success, netting in the 1961-62 League
Cup final. On retirement from the first class
scene, he settled in East Anglia, a respected
personality in football guiding both Yarmouth
and Diss to local success, and in the case of
Diss, to national recognition in the FA Vase of
1994. Bill was also employed by Norfolk
County Council.

Appearances:
FL: 23 apps. 1 gl.
FAC: 2 apps. 0 gls.
Others: 1 app. 0 gls.
Total: *26 apps. 1 gl.*
Honours:
*FLC winner 1962/FL div 3 prom 1960/
FAV winner 1994(m).*

Bill Punton

PYKE, George Woolston

Role: Centre-forward 1913-1922
5' 11"
b. Gateshead, 26th August 1893

CAREER: Rutherford College
(Newcastle)/UNITED Nov 1913 £20/
Durham City war-guest 1918-19/
Blyth Spartans Aug 1922 to 1927/
Local amateur football.

Debut v Derby County (h) 24/9/19

George Pyke was an
extremely popular
character with
supporters at St James
Park immediately
after World War
One. Something of a
local hero, he was
one of many
budding forwards
attempting to claim
a senior jersey in
those post-war
seasons of 1919-20 to
1921-22. Challenging
Andy Smailes and
Neil Harris, he only
graduated to the first
eleven on a few occasions
each campaign, but in
reserve football Pyke was a
pleasure to watch; tall and a threat in
attack, he ravaged North Eastern
League defences. Although good
enough for Football League standard,
George decided to remain in the north
east when it became obvious he wasn't
going to get an extended opportunity at
Gallowgate. He joined Blyth and
proceeded to net 136 goals for the
Spartans, many alongside his brother.
During the First World War George
served in the Middlesex Regiment in
France, and on retirement resided in
Whitley Bay.

> **Appearances:**
> *FL: 13 apps. 3 gls.*
> **Total:** *13 apps. 3 gls.*

QUINN, C.

Role: Outside-right
1893-1894, 1895-96
b. Tyneside

CAREER: Local football/UNITED 1893/
Manchester City Dec 1894/UNITED
1895 to 1896.

Debut v Burton Swifts (a) 23/9/1893

As Newcastle United entered the Football
League in 1893, Quinn was a regular in
the club's forward line during that
historic first season. Appearing
mainly on the right wing, but
also in the inside and outside-
left channels too, he was a
consistent player for the
whole campaign, but afterwards fell out of favour.
Quinn moved to pastures
new in 1896 after missing
the whole of the 1894-95
season, and just one
outing in 1895-96. Even
though the local press
reported him joining
Manchester City, no official
record can be traced of his
transfer.

> **Appearances:**
> *FL: 24 apps. 5 gls.*
> *FAC: 2 apps. 0 gls.*
> **Total:** *26 apps. 5 gls.*

C. Quinn

QUINN, Michael

Role: Centre-forward 1989-1992
5' 10"
b. Liverpool, 2nd May 1962

CAREER: Derby County app 1977/Wigan Athletic Sept 1979/Stockport County July 1982 free/Oldham Athletic Jan 1984 £52,000/ Portsmouth Mar 1986 £150,000/UNITED June 1989 £680,000/Coventry City loan Nov 1992, pmt Dec 1992 £250,000(Watford loan 1994-95) (Portsmouth loan 1994-95)(Plymouth Argyle loan 1994-95)/Hong Kong May 1995/PAOK Salonika(Greece) cs 1995 to 1996.

Debut v Leeds United (h) 19/8/89 (scored four)

A prolific goalscorer since he made an impact with Wigan and Stockport, Mick Quinn moved north from Fratton Park for a fee decided by a league tribunal. United were forced to pay more than they had intended, but in the end the club had signed a player worth every penny. The chirpy Scouser immediately began to repay his fee by hitting four goals in a dramatic debut for the club, then continued to bag a goal every second game for the Magpies. In his opening season as Tyneside's Number 9 hero, Quinn almost took United back into the First Division with his goals - netting 34 in the campaign - the club just missing out on promotion in the play-offs. He was the Football League's top goalgetter in that 1989-90 programme, and one of only a handful of Newcastle players to total over 30 goals in a single season. An opportunist striker, Mick was expert at turning and finding the target in the tightest of situations and even with his back to goal. The Second Division's top scorer in 1986-87 (22 goals) with Pompey, Mick was deceptively lazy in style, once described by manager Jim Smith as, "an ugly duckling player", but Quinn possessed a deadly eye for goal when in the danger zone. The Merseysider's career was also occasionally littered with controversial moments, including 21 days spent in Winchester Prison when with Portsmouth for a motoring offence. On the arrival of Kevin Keegan as boss at Gallowgate, Quinn was sidelined with a bad knee injury

and once fit again was overlooked in favour of David Kelly and record purchase Andy Cole. He only appeared in five league matches during United's 1993 championship season. By the time he ended his domestic career, Quinn had totalled almost 300 senior goals. A keen racehorse enthusiast, in July 1996 he joined Mick Channon's training complex in Hampshire as an assistant trainer.

Appearances:
FL: 112(5) apps. 59 gls.
FAC: 7 apps. 4 gls.
FLC: 7(2) apps. 0 gls.
Others: 6(1) apps. 8 gls.
Total: *132(8) apps. 71 gls.*
Honours:
FL div 2 prom 1987.

RAFFERTY, William Henry

Role: Striker 1979-1980
5' 11"
b. Glasgow, 30th December 1950

CAREER: Port Glasgow Rovers 1967/
Coventry City July 1968/Blackpool Oct 1972
£40,000/Plymouth Argyle Mar 1974 £25,000/
Carlisle United May 1976 £20,000/
Wolverhampton Wanderers Mar 1977 £125,000/
UNITED Oct 1979 £175,000/Portsmouth Dec
1980 £80,000/Bournemouth Feb 1984 £4,000
to cs 1985/Portuguese football 1987.

Debut v Cambridge United (h) 27/10/79

Billy Rafferty arrived
at St James Park with
a good scoring record
at Carlisle and at
Plymouth, where he
formed a productive
partnership with
future England star,
Paul Mariner. Netting
40 goals in 101 games
for the Home Park
club, he made an
uncertain start on
Tyneside, forming a
strikeforce with Peter
Withe and Bobby
Shinton. Rafferty
however, if only for a
few weeks, did look
as though he might
become a noted

Billy Rafferty

striker; he was tall and leggy and able to cause
trouble to defenders. But his relative success
was short lived. He never scored enough goals
over a sustained period and moved south to
Fratton Park where he was a key figure in
Portsmouth's Third Division title victory. Billy
netted 43 times in 111 games for Pompey
before concluding his first class career on the
south coast with Bournemouth. His brother
Stewart appeared in the Scottish League.

Appearances:
FL: 34(5) apps. 6 gls.
FAC: 1 app. 0 gls.
FLC: 2 apps. 2 gls.
Total: *37(5) apps. 8 gls.*
Honours:
FL div 3 champs 1983/
FL div 3 prom 1975.

RAINE, James Edmundson

Role: Outside-right
1905-1906
6' 0"
b. Newcastle upon Tyne, March 1886
d. Davos, Switzerland, 4th September 1928

CAREER: Trinity College(Harrogate)/Rydal
Mount(Colwyn Bay)/Sheffield University/
Scotswood 1903/Sheffield United amat cs
1904/UNITED amat 1905/Sunderland amat
Dec 1906/Bohemians(Newcastle) Mar 1908/
Glossop amat Apr 1908/Percy Park
(Newcastle)(rugby union).

Debut v Middlesbrough (a) 3/3/06

A noteworthy player during the
decade before the First World War,
James Raine toured the world with
amateur combinations, prominently
to South Africa with England in 1910,
and to North America as a member of
the Pilgrims team in 1905. Raine
started his football career when he
attended college and university in
Harrogate and Sheffield, and turned
out in the Football League during
brief spells at Bramall Lane, Roker

James Raine

Park and Gallowgate. A deputy for Jackie Rutherford during season 1905-06 with the black'n'whites, he was a cool and assured player up front, good enough to be a regular for his country and to take part in the prestigious Amateurs v Professionals showpiece in 1906-07. James was also a good cricketer and rugby player, one of the region's finest sportsmen of the Edwardian era. He later settled in the Jesmond suburb of Newcastle, a successful businessman in the north east, managing director of an iron & steel manufacturer in Derwenthaugh. Raine served with the Durham Light Infantry with the rank of major during World War One.

Appearances:
FL: 4 apps. 1 gl.
Total: *4 apps. 1 gl.*
Honours:
10 Eng amat caps 1907-11/
2 unoff Eng app. 1910/
Eng trial app. 1907/1 FL app. 1908.

RAINNIE, Alexander

Role: Left-half 1919-1920
5' 10"
b. Tyneside

CAREER: South Shields/
UNITED May 1919/
Darlington July 1920 £15/
Ashington 1923 to c1924.

Debut v Everton (h) 24/1/20

A stylish half-back, Alex Rainnie gave determined performances for South Shields every time United's directors watched him. He earned a contract at St James Park in the years immediately following the Great War, but found opportunities very limited, being one of several half-backs in contention for a place. Alex never threatened first choice Jock Finlay, only once deputising for the Scot, although he was chosen for the North Eastern select side to play the Central League in 1921-22. Alex later appeared for Darlington and for Ashington during their Football League seasons in the Twenties decade. During the hostilities he served as a chief petty officer in the Royal Navy.

Appearances:
FL: 1 app. 0 gls.
Total: *1 app. 0 gls.*

RAMSAY, Alexander Parrott

Role: Outside-left 1919-1921
5' 8"
b. Gateshead, 1899

CAREER: Spen Black'n'White/Swalwell/
UNITED May 1919 £100/Queens Park
Rangers June 1921 to c1922.

Debut v Liverpool (h) 4/10/19

Alex Ramsay, who had been a gunner in the Machine Gun Corps in France and Egypt during World War One, made a big impact in the opening soccer programme after peace had been restored. A regular on the wing during 1919-20, he was seen as a promising find, fast and direct with an eye for an accurate cross. Although he was well liked by Newcastle's followers, United's officials decided to bring in Stan Seymour from Morton as Alex's replacement and Ramsay left for London. With QPR, he only managed six outings.

Alex Ramsay

Appearances:
FL: 34 apps. 2 gls.
FAC: 3 apps. 0 gls.
War: 5 apps. 3 gls.
Total: *42 apps. 5 gls.*

RAMSAY, Andrew

Role: Goalkeeper 1892, 1893
5' 10"
b. Scotland

CAREER: Newcastle East End 1890/UNITED
May 1892/Stockton May 1892/UNITED July
1893/Dundee Sept 1893/East Benhar.

Debut v Woolwich Arsenal (a) 2/9/1893

Andrew Ramsay was Newcastle United's goalkeeper for their very first Football League game against Arsenal in 1893. That historic fixture was the only official appearance he ever made for the club. Although he took part in several of East End's matches before the Heaton outfit moved to St James Park, Ramsay departed the scene at a time of financial crisis when directors gave players an ultimatum of taking a reduction in wages or finding a new club. He was described as having "height and weight" as well as being "remarkably sure in kicking out low shots".

Appearances:
FL: 1 app. 0 gls.
Total: *1 app. 0 gls.*

Ray Ranson

RANDALL, Charles Edward

Role: Inside-left 1908-1911
5' 10"
b. Burnopfield, County Durham, 1882
d. 27th September 1916

CAREER: Hobson Wanderers/UNITED May 1908 £5(Huddersfield Town loan 1908-09, 1909-10)(Castleford Town loan 1909-10)/Woolwich Arsenal Sept 1911 £400/North Shields Athletic June 1914.

Debut v Bradford City (a) 23/3/09

A robust forward, Charles Randall was quickly captured by United after scoring nearly 50 goals in one local amateur season. Randall made his debut during the Magpies' championship-winning year of 1908-09, being brought back from a loan deal with then non-league Huddersfield. He was a popular character in the club's second string, and in season 1910-11 claimed 16 senior outings, competing with internationals Sandy Higgins and George Wilson. But Randall found himself more often than not on the sidelines, or despatched to appear for the Terriers, or for neighbours Castleford when Huddersfield eventually joined Football League action. Joining Arsenal, he clocked up 44 matches for the Gunners, once scoring a hat-trick against Sunderland.

Appearances:
FL: 18 apps. 6 gls.
FAC: 1 app. 0 gls.
Total: *19 apps. 6 gls.*

RANSON, Raymond

Role: Right-back 1988-1993
5' 9"
b. St Helens, Lancashire, 12th June 1960

CAREER: Manchester City app July 1976, pro July 1977/Birmingham City Nov 1984 £15,000/UNITED Dec 1988 £175,000/ Manchester City Jan 1993 free/Reading Aug 1993 to 1994/Witton Albion player-manager 1995.

Debut v Sheffield Wednesday (a) 26/12/88

Ray Ranson developed quickly as a youngster of note with Manchester City. A regular in the England Under-21 side - including several matches as skipper - Ray's career as a top player looked rosy until a City slump saw his fortunes nosedive. Relegated to the junior team by new manager Billy McNeill, Ranson moved to St Andrews after over 200 games for the Light Blues and then to Tyneside when United were in need of experience and guile in defence. Ray had a difficult early period in a black'n'white shirt but, with accomplished displays, gradually won over the crowd who had been rather hasty in their criticisms of him. But then injury rocked his progress, Ray finding himself in the operating room with a pelvic injury and Achilles tendon problems. He missed over a year of action, and by the time he was back in training Kevin Keegan was in charge and a new batch of Magpie stars were in vogue. It was a cue for Ranson's rather topsy-turvy career to take another turn. On leaving the first-class game he entered an insurance business based in Manchester.

Appearances:
FL: 79(5) apps. 1 gl.
FAC: 10 apps. 0 gls.
FLC: 4 apps. 0 gls.
Others: 3(1) apps. 0 gls.
Total: *96(6) apps. 1 gl.*
Honours:
10 Eng u21 caps 1980-81/
9 Eng schools apps. 1975/
Eng youth app. 1978/FAC finalist 1981/
FL div 2 prom 1985/FL div 2 champs 1994.

REAY, Harry

Role: Outside-right 1892-1893
5' 9"
b. Tyneside

CAREER: Gateshead/Shankhouse Black Watch/Newcastle East End cs 1891/UNITED May 1892/Everton Apr 1893 to 1895.
Debut v Middlesbrough (h) 1/10/1892 (NL)

Harry Reay made a name for himself with one of the north east's noted pioneer clubs, Shankhouse Black Watch. A fabulous winger in his day, Reay thrilled Victorian crowds and by the time he had joined East End was one of the most popular personalities of those early years. A reporter for the *Northerner & Athlete* magazine recorded in 1893 that he was "simply irresistible". Although he did not appear for United in the Football League, Reay took part in the club's Northern League campaign during 1892-93 after East End

moved across the city from Heaton to St James Park. He also was on the field for the Novocastrians' FA Cup fixture in that season too. Harry once scored five goals for United in a friendly against Scottish club, Annbank in March 1893. In fact, he had another two efforts cancelled for 'hands' and 'offside'.

Appearances:
NL: 9 apps. 4 gls.
FAC: 1 app. 1 gl.
Total: *10 apps. 5 gls.*

REDHEAD, William Sylvester

Role: Left-half 1954-1959
5' 8"
b. Newcastle upon Tyne, 10th October 1935

CAREER: George Angus(Newcastle)/ UNITED Aug 1954/Gateshead Aug 1959 free/ South Shields cs 1962/Gateshead c1963/ Queen of the South May 1965 to 1967.
Debut v Sheffield Wednesday (h) 29/12/56

Bill Redhead

Although he was at St James Park for three seasons, Bill Redhead only managed a single match for the Magpies, standing in for Tommy Casey in midfield during 1956-57. He had a nerve-shattering start with United, up against a Sheffield Wednesday wing pair of Albert Quixall and Alan Finney on the top of their form. Newcastle lost the contest 2-1, and Redhead didn't get another chance in senior company. He moved to Redheugh Park across the Tyne and took part in Gateshead's last months as a Football League outfit before concentrating on local non-league soccer, becoming recognised as a fine defender in those circles. He completed his career with a spell in the Scottish League.

Appearances:
FL: 1 app. 0 gls.
Total: *1 app. 0 gls.*

REID, Alex Dennis

Role: Midfield 1971-1973
5' 8"
b. Glasgow, 2nd March 1947

CAREER: Glasgow Perthshire/Glasgow Rangers Apr 1964/Dundee United June 1968 free/UNITED Oct 1971 exch deal for I.Mitchell/Greenock Morton Oct 1973 £20,000/Dundee United Dec 1975/Ayr United Oct 1976/Retired due to injury 1977.

Debut v Nottingham Forest (h) 20/11/71

Only appearing twice at Ibrox, Alex Reid was snapped up by Dundee United and developed into one of the best club players north of the border. He made a deep impression on United manager Joe Harvey after displaying top form against the Magpies in European ties for the Tannadice club in 1969. Ginger-haired Reid had a cultured left foot and could prompt and create from midfield, being very capable on the ball but also a player who could turn to a spoiling role. Entering action in England for season 1971-72, he found it a struggle to adapt to the much faster and more competitive First Division. Although the Scot showed flashes of excellent play, he was always in and out of the black'n'whites line-up and quickly moved back north. Reid continued to be a more than competent midfielder in Scotland, playing on until a knee injury forced him to leave the game. He later moved to Canada, residing in the Vancouver area.

Alex Reid

Appearances:
FL: 15(8) apps. 0 gls.
FAC: 0(2) apps. 0 gls.
Others: 1 app. 0 gls.
Total: *16(10) apps. 0 gls.*

REID, O.

Role: Right-half 1895-96

CAREER: Rotherham/UNITED Dec 1895 £20 to 1896.

Debut v Manchester City (a) 4/1/1896

Reid was elevated to the first eleven for two outings as a replacement for the injured Miller during season 1895-96, United's third season of Football League action but did not enjoy a rewarding period in United's line-up. In his two games, Newcastle lost twice and conceded ten goals to Manchester City and Grimsby Town. He quickly returned to the 'A' side and played out the remainder of his short Newcastle career in the Northern Alliance.

Appearances:
FL: 2 apps. 0 gls.
Total: *2 apps. 0 gls.*

REID, William

Role: Inside-left 1899-1900
5' 6"
b. Mauchline, Ayrshire, 1876
d. Scotland, 12th April 1923

CAREER: Stevenston Thistle/
Kilmarnock Athletic 1894/Kilmarnock
May 1897(UNITED loan Mar 1899
to early 1900)/Partick Thistle Dec 1900
£30/Galston cs 1902/Thornhill Aug
1906/Kilmarnock Oct 1906/Galston
Nov 1906.

Debut v Derby County (h) 25/3/1899
(scored once)

Nicknamed 'Roggie' in his native
Ayrshire, Billy Reid was a classy inside-
forward. He had caught the eye of
United's directors when an influential
member of Kilmarnock's Scottish Cup
and Second Division title side just
before the turn of the century. Always
able to create an opening with his skill
on the ball, he was on the verge of
international recognition at one stage in
his career. Reid arrived on Tyneside in a
loan deal, on a trial period which, if he
fitted into the Magpies' line-up, would
earn him a long term contract. He began
well, netting on his debut, however his
form never matched his displays in the
Scottish League. He returned north and
continued his football career with both
senior and local clubs, appearing in 68
games for Kilmarnock, grabbing 30
goals.

Appearances:
FL: 4 apps. 1 gl.
Total: *4 apps. 1 gl.*
Honours:
Scot trial app. 1898/
SC finalist 1898/
SL div 2 champs 1898, 1899.

George Reilly

REILLY, George Gerard

Role: Centre-forward 1985
6' 4"
b. Bellshill, nr Motherwell, 14th September 1957

CAREER: Corby Town/Northampton Town
June 1976/Cambridge United Nov 1979
£140,000/Watford Aug 1983 £90,000/UNITED
Feb 1985 £200,000/West Bromwich Albion Dec
1985 £150,000/Cambridge United cs 1988/
Barnet 1989/Retired due to injury Mar 1990.

Debut v Luton Town (h) 23/2/85

Tall, strongly-built and aggressive, George
Reilly learnt the game the hard way, in the
basement with Northampton and Cambridge.
Moving to England from his native Scotland
when two years old, the former bricklayer
made an impact when he joined Watford,
fitting into Graham Taylor's long ball game at
Vicarage Road to perfection. Reilly netted the
goal that sent Watford to Wembley in 1984 and
became a handful for every defence he faced.
Joining Newcastle as the club searched for a
new forward combination, he was Jack

Charlton's target man, being fed by playmakers Beardsley and Waddle. But Reilly never grabbed enough goals to become a big hit at Gallowgate, only three in his first season and seven in 1985-86. Although fairly popular with the terraces, at one stage being given the nickname of 'Rambo' for his honest and wholehearted displays, George was replaced by Billy Whitehurst and moved on to The Hawthorns. He was eventually forced to quit the football scene due to a back injury. Along with Dave Beasant and Shaka Hislop, at 6'4" he is one of the tallest players to appear for the Magpies.

Appearances:
FL: 31 apps. 10 gls.
FAC: 2 apps. 0 gls.
Total: *33 apps. 10 gls.*
Honours:
FAC finalist 1984.

RENDELL, Thomas

Role: Left-half 1894-1895
5' 8"
b. Tyneside

CAREER: Shankhouse Black Watch/ UNITED Aug 1894/ Shankhouse Black Watch cs 1895.

Debut v Darwen (a) 1/9/1894

A former Shankhouse Black Watch player, Tom Rendell joined the United staff in the close season of 1894 and was used as a utility player during the 1894-95 programme. Operating mainly at left-half, he also turned out at left and right back, as well as centre-half and right-half. A regular for that Second Division campaign, the *Daily Journal* noted Tom as "a worthy sub for Jeffrey". He remained for the season before returning to local Tyneside soccer.

Appearances:
FL: 23 apps. 0 gls.
FAC: 2 apps. 2 gls.
Total: *25 apps. 2 gls.*

RICHARDSON, Edward

Role: Outside-left 1922-1923
5' 9"
b. Easington, County Durham

CAREER: South Shields 1919/UNITED Aug 1922/Huddersfield Town Dec 1923/Sheffield Wednesday Dec 1924 to 1925/Local north east soccer, including Whitburn 1932.

Debut v Preston North End (h) 23/9/22

One of the club's reserves to Stan Seymour on the left wing, Eddie Richardson made a name for himself with South Shields' Football League side. At Gallowgate though, he rarely pushed the consistent Seymour for a first team place, deputising for the legendary figure twice during season 1922-23. After spells at Leeds Road and Hillsborough, where he also struggled to claim a regular spot, Richardson returned to his roots and played local football. On Huddersfield's staff when the Yorkshire club won championship titles in both 1923-24 and 1924-25, Richardson was a reserve to Town's many star names of the period.

Appearances:
FL: 2 apps. 0 gls.
Total: *2 apps. 0 gls.*

Jimmy Richardson (see overleaf)

RICHARDSON, James Robert

Role: Inside-right 1928-1934, 1937-1938
5' 7"
b. Ashington, 8th February 1911
d. Bexley, London, 28th August 1964

CAREER: Blyth Spartans 1925/UNITED
Apr 1928 £200/Huddersfield Town Oct 1934
£4,000/UNITED Oct 1937 £4,500/Millwall Mar
1938 £4,000/Fulham war-guest 1941-42/
Aldershot war-guest 1941-42/Charlton Athletic
war-guest 1942-43/Leyton Orient war-guest
1944-45/Leyton Orient player-trainer Jan 1948,
becoming trainer June 1951 to June 1955/
Millwall asst-trainer Nov 1956 to 1957

*Debut v Blackburn Rovers (h) 4/9/29
(scored once)*

A motor engineer when he joined United's
staff, Jimmy Richardson had displayed a
special talent when appearing for Blyth
Spartans, one that was richly developed by the
Magpies. Very fast over ten yards, he had
tremendous close control of the ball and his
dribbling one-man runs attacking defenders
were a feature of United's play during the
early thirties. A workhorse as well, Richardson
became a popular character and one of the
central figures of Newcastle's FA Cup victory
in 1932, at the focus of attention when he
crossed the ball for the infamous 'Over the
Line' goal against Arsenal at Wembley. At his
peak with United the following season - 1932-
33 - he was capped by England, netting two
goals in his two appearances. With the club's
relegation in 1934, Jimmy soon moved on, to
Huddersfield where he again proved a good
servant, claiming 32 goals in 125 games for the
Tykes. Following a brief second stint at
Gallowgate at the end of his career, he settled
in London and was Millwall's trainer until ill
heath forced him to leave. His brother, John
Richardson appeared for Oldham.

> **Appearances:**
> *FL: 150 apps. 46 gls.*
> *FAC: 13 apps. 7 gls.*
> *Others: 1 app. 0 gls.*
> **Total:** *164 apps. 53 gls.*
> **Honours:**
> *2 Eng caps 1933/*
> *2 Eng schools apps./*
> *1 FL app. 1937/*
> *FAC winner 1932/*
> *FL div 3(S) champs 1938.*

RICHARDSON, Joseph

Role: Right-back & Trainer 1929-1977
5' 8"
b. Bedlington, Northumberland,
19th August 1908
d. Newcastle upon Tyne, 14th June 1975

CAREER: New Delaval Villa/Blyth Spartans/
UNITED May 1929 joint deal £250/Retired
1945, becoming asst-trainer to his death.

Debut v Brighton (h) 15/2/30 (FAC)

Devoted to United's cause for most of his life,
Joe Richardson became one of the real Geordie
characters of St James Park for almost 50
years. A former blacksmith and strong as the
proverbial ox, as a full-back he was a gritty
defender, possessing all the traditional tenacity
of his local Bedlington terrier. Unruffled and
robust, but fair, he rivalled Alf Maitland as a
youngster, then was a reserve to Jimmy
Nelson before claiming
the shirt for himself in
season 1934-35.
Throughout the years
leading up to the
outbreak of war,
Richardson was a
permanent fixture in
the side. He skippered
United for a period
during the war seasons,
then turned to coaching
the reserves and young
players through three
decades. Joe was a
jovial figure and a
popular backroom aid
at Gallowgate. He
holds record service of
48 years as a player and
trainer.

> **Appearances:**
> *FL: 208 apps. 1 gl.*
> *FAC: 15 apps. 0 gls.*
> *War: 114 apps. 0 gls.*
> **Total:**
> *337 apps. 1 gl.*
> **Honours:**
> *1 Eng war cap 1940/*
> *Eng schools app.*
> *1925.*

Joe Richardson

RICHARDSON, Ord

Role: Inside-right 1902-1903
5' 10"
b. Tyneside

CAREER: Wallsend Park Villa/
UNITED May 1902/
Local football 1903.

Debut v Wolverhampton Wanderers (a) 1/11/02

Tynesider Ord Richardson stood in once for
Scottish international forward Ronald Orr
during season 1902-03. It was Richardson's
only taste of senior action, his remaining time
at St James Park being restricted to Northern
League football. Ord later became a worthy
North Durham cricketer, appearing in local
matches up to the Second World War.

Appearances:
FL: 1 app. 0 gls.
Total: *1 app. 0 gls.*

RIDLEY, James

Role: Outside-left 1907-1911
5' 9"
b. Tyneside

CAREER: Byker East End/
Willington Athletic/
UNITED Feb 1907 £50/
Nottingham Forest Feb 1911 £150/
Wallsend Sept 1919.

Debut v Everton (h) 7/12/07

James Ridley was an efficient member of the
United 'A' side which dominated local football
during the Edwardian era. Winning the North
Eastern League title on four occasions, Ridley
was reserve to George Wilson during his time
on United's staff. He appeared on a handful of
occasions in each of his four years with the
club, having five outings when Newcastle
lifted the championship trophy in 1909. He
always gave a good display, being very fast
with what were noted as, "electric dribbles"
being a feature of his game. The swiftest man
on the Magpies' books at the time, Ridley once
won the Morpeth Handicap and other
prominent races of the day.

Appearances:
FL: 17 apps. 2 gls.
Total: *17 apps. 2 gls.*

ROBERTS, Richard James

Role: Outside-left 1901-1904
5' 7"
b. Bromsgrove, nr Redditch, 1878
d. 1931

CAREER: Redditch Excelsior/West
Bromwich Albion Apr 1899/UNITED
May 1901/ Middlesbrough Apr 1904
£450/Crystal Palace cs 1905/Retired
due to injury 1909.

Debut v Blackburn Rovers (a) 7/9/01

Joining Newcastle from the
Midlands, Richard
Roberts very quickly
became a favourite
of United's
supporters. He
was a fast and
direct winger
who proved he
could score goals
from the flank,
claiming 12 in his
first campaign for
the black'n'whites.
Consistent over two
seasons, he was
surprisingly replaced by
Bobby Templeton, a move
which to start with caused dismay
among the Newcastle crowd.
However, when Scottish international
Templeton began to weave his magic,
the furore over Roberts' loss was soon
forgotten. He later concluded his
career briefly on Teesside, then as part
of Crystal Palace's Southern League
line-up (74 apps., 25 gls.) including
helping to defeat the Magpies in a
1907 giant-killing act. When at The
Hawthorns Roberts reached the FA
Cup semi-final but saw his side
relegated, hence a move to St James
Park.

Appearances:
FL: 51 apps. 17 gls.
FAC: 4 apps. 0 gls.
Total: *55 apps. 17 gls.*

ROBERTSON, John Grant

Role: Striker 1988
5' 7"
b. Edinburgh, 2nd October 1964

CAREER: Tartan·Boys Club/Salvesens/Edina Hibs/Heart of Midlothian app Sept 1980, pro Jan 1981/UNITED Apr 1988 £750,000/Heart of Midlothian Dec 1988 £750,000.

Debut v Everton (a) 27/8/88

John Robertson

John Robertson was tracked by a host of clubs including Arsenal, Nottingham Forest and Leeds, before signing for his home team at Tynecastle where former United skipper Bob Moncur was manager. Very quickly the small, compact and lightning-fast striker began to show why he was in demand. With Hearts, Robertson became one of the top goalgetters in Scotland. Possessing a natural touch in front of goal, he netted almost 150 times for Hearts in five years until United paid out a club record fee to bring him to Tyneside. But at St James Park he was never played in his free role up front by manager Willie McFaul, his style clashing with that of Mirandinha who was at Gallowgate at the same time. Many followers of the club were totally perplexed as to why such a quality player only managed seven full outings in a black and white shirt before returning north. He was out of action for a period with a persistent muscle problem, but Newcastle's side at the time was crying out for a player of Robertson's ability in front of goal. When he returned to Scotland, John immediately started to bang the ball in the net again, eventually winning full caps for his country and scoring on his national debut. He rivals only Ally McCoist as the most efficient striker in the modern Scottish League, amassing nearly 250 goals to the end of the 1995-96 season.

Appearances:
FL: 7(5) apps. 0 gls.
FLC: 0(2) apps. 0 gls.
Others: 2 apps. 0 gls.
Total: *9(7) apps. 0 gls.*
Honours:
16 Scot caps 1991-date/
1 unoff Scot app. 1990/
2 Scot B caps 1990-96/2 Scot u21 caps 1985/
Scot schools app./Scot youth app./
Scot Young Player of the Year 1984/
SC finalist 1986, 1996.

ROBINSON, David John

Role: Striker 1986-1992
6' 0"
b. Walkergate, Newcastle upon Tyne,
27th November 1969

CAREER: Wallsend Boys Club/UNITED app 1986, pro cs 1988(Peterborough United loan 1990-91)/Reading Apr 1992 free/Blackpool cs 1992/Gateshead Aug 1994/Bishop Auckland June 1995/Lincoln City trial Nov 1995/Cambridge United 1995 to cs 1996.

Debut v Arsenal (h)
12/11/88 (sub)

After overcoming a bad knee ligament injury as a junior, Dave Robinson was a live-wire centre-forward in Central League football. He was on the fringe of United's first eleven over four seasons, but never made the starting line-up except in friendly contests. Once netting six goals in six games during a pre-season tour of Sweden, much was expected of the tall and unorthodox target man. Robinson netted as a substitute on his second outing against Reading in an FA Cup tie, but could not break into the team in a sustained way. He tried his luck with Peterborough, Reading and Blackpool, but rarely made headlines.

Appearances:
FL: 0(8) apps. 0 gls.
FAC: 0(1) app. 1 gl.
FLC: 0(1) app. 0 gls.
Total: *0(10) apps. 1 gl.*

ROBINSON, James Walter

Role: Centre-half 1931
6' 0"
b. Ruyton (or Ryton)

CAREER: Stargate/Burnley cs 1923/ Nelson cs 1925/Doncaster Rovers 1929/ Scarborough 1930/UNITED Jan 1931 £300 to June 1931.

Debut v Manchester United (h) 17/1/31

A deputy to the injured Dave Davidson and transfer-listed Jack Hill, for a few months during season 1930-31 James Robinson was a tough and rugged centre-half, typical of the pivot's role during the thirties. After an unspectacular Football League career, he had performed well for non-league Scarborough in FA Cup runs in front of watching United scouts, but didn't stay long on Tyneside, moving after only five months. *The Journal's* 'Castellion' commented on his appearance in United's side in the absence of Hill, "There is very little room for comparison", while Colin Veitch wrote in his column that he was "far from being impressive". The policy of leaving out Hill was not a favoured one and Robinson was perhaps unfairly compared with the England pivot. The transfer deal from Scarborough was the second transaction within a week by the Magpies, Alec Betton having already arrived from the Yorkshire club.

Appearances:
FL: 1 app. 0 gls.
Total: *1 app. 0 gls.*

ROBINSON, Mark James

Role: Right-back 1993-1994
5' 9"
b. Manchester, 21st November 1968

CAREER: West Bromwich Albion app 1985 to May 1987 free/Barnsley Jan 1988/UNITED Mar 1993 £450,000/Swindon Town Aug 1994 £600,000.

Debut v Charlton Athletic (h) 10/3/93

After an unsuccessful spell at The Hawthorns where he made a teenage debut, Mark Robinson spent six seasons in the ranks of Barnsley totalling over 140 matches before being given the chance of a big-time career at St James Park. Stockily built, Mark was solid in the tackle and fast in recovery, performing

Mark Robinson

at full-back - as cover for Barry Venison - and in midfield. Helping United in the final push for promotion in 1992-93 (9 apps.), Robinson was unluckily injured in a pre-season friendly before the black'n'whites began their assault on the Premiership. He was out of action for most of the season and by the time he returned to something near full fitness Robinson had several players ahead of him in the first team pecking order. Kevin Keegan released Mark, making a good short term profit for the Magpies.

Appearances:
FL/PL: 14(11) apps. 0 gls.
FAC: 1 app. 0 gls.
Total: *15(11) apps. 0 gls.*
Honours:
FL div 2 champs 1996

ROBINSON, Raymond Wilson

Role: Outside-right 1919-1920
5' 7"
b. Blaydon, nr Newcastle upon Tyne, 1895
d. Newcastle upon Tyne, 6th January 1964

CAREER: Scotswood/Grimsby Town war-guest 1915-16/UNITED May 1919 £400/ Sunderland Aug 1920 £750/Grimsby Town May 1921/Sunderland June 1922/ Eden Colliery Oct 1922/ Lancaster Town/ Liverpool Police July 1924/Shirebrook/ Silverwood Colliery Sept 1928.

Debut v Arsenal (a)
30/8/19

At around 13 stones in weight, Ray Robinson was quite a hefty-looking winger, but nevertheless made a big impact on the club's side during the first season of action after World War One. A regular at outside-right that campaign, for most of the programme the Tynesider performed well, able to penetrate

Ray Robinson

defences from the flank. Yet for all his efforts it wasn't enough to stop United's directors bringing in Scot Billy Aitken to take over his role. Robinson moved to Wearside and on to Blundell Park, but never gained an automatic place in either side. Ray had been a corporal in the Tank Corps in France during World War One, and later resided in Newcastle until his death.

Appearances:
FL: 27 apps. 4 gls.
FAC: 2 apps. 0 gls.
Total: *29 apps. 4 gls.*

ROBINSON, Robert

Role: Goalkeeper 1952-1954
5' 11"
b. Newbiggin by the Sea, nr Ashington, 23rd June 1923

CAREER: Burnley amat/Newbiggin/ Sunderland Feb 1947/UNITED Aug 1952 £2,500 to June 1954.

Debut v Burnley (a) 6/9/52

Sunderland's reserve goalkeeper, United purchased Bobby Robinson when senior guardian Ronnie Simpson, was out of action. Bobby only filled in for the Scot on a handful of occasions during the 1952-53 season and left the club after two years to return to local football. At Roker Park he was also deputy to another noted goalkeeper in John Mapson, although Robinson totalled 18 appearances in a good run during season 1951-52.

Bobby Robinson

Appearances:
FL: 5 apps. 0 gls.
Total: *5 apps. 0 gls.*

ROBINSON, Stuart

Role: Outside-left 1975-1980
5' 9"
b. Middlesbrough, 16th January 1959

CAREER: Murton Colliery/UNITED Nov 1975/Aldershot July 1980 free to cs 1983.

Debut v Leicester City (h) 3/12/77

Stuart Robinson

Slimline winger Stuart Robinson gained a fine youth record, appearing for his country and developing through United's junior structure. He was given a chance in the first eleven during season 1977-78, but unfortunately his break in senior company coincided with a torrid relegation year for the Magpies. Newcastle dropped from the First Division and Robinson's long-term opportunities thereafter were limited. He attempted a career with Aldershot but after 86 games left the Football League scene.

Appearances:
FL: 11(1) apps. 2 gls.
FAC: 2 apps. 1 gl.
Total: *13(1) apps. 3 gls.*
Honours:
Eng youth app.

ROBLEDO, Eduardo Oliver

Role: Left-half 1949-1953
5' 9"
b. Iquique, Chile, 26th July 1928
d. Persian Gulf, 6th December 1970

CAREER: Barnsley 1943/ UNITED Jan 1949 £3,500/ Colo-Colo(Chile) May 1953 joint deal with G.Robledo/ Notts County Sept 1957 to 1958.

Debut v Aston Villa (a) 31/12/49

The younger of the two Robledo brothers at St James Park during the immediate post-war years, Ted's career in the game followed the same path as his more famous counterpart. Nevertheless, while he was something of a makeweight in the deal that brought George to Gallowgate, Ted became a valued squad player and earned a regular position in midfield during season 1951-52. Honest and hardworking at left-half, he rivalled Charlie Crowe and gained a place for the Wembley team in 1952. Dark-haired and handsome, like his brother, Ted returned to Chile in 1953, but attempted a come-back in the Football League with the other Magpies, alongside the Trent in Nottingham. That didn't last long, and Robledo eventually left the game, gaining employment with an American company in the oil business. His untimely death in 1970 was surrounded by controversy; Ted was assumed dead after being reported missing overboard in the Persian Gulf from a tanker, the *Al Sahn*, returning him home to Lowestoft from a Dubai oil-rig. After an investigation by Interpol, the captain of the boat was later charged with murder, but ultimately acquitted. No trace of Robledo's body was ever found.

Appearances:
FL: 37 apps. 0 gls.
FAC: 8 apps. 0 gls.
Others: 2 apps. 0 gls.
Total: *47 apps. 0 gls.*
Honours:
FAC winner 1952.

Ted Robledo

ROBLEDO, George Oliver

Role: Inside-forward 1949-1953
5' 9"
b. Iquique, Chile, 14th April 1926
d. Vina Del Mar, Chile, 1st April 1989

CAREER: Dearne Valley Old Boys/Brampton
Welfare/Barnsley amat 1942/Huddersfield
Town amat 1943/Barnsley Apr 1943/Lincoln
City war-guest 1943-44/UNITED Jan 1949
joint deal with E.Robledo £23,000/Colo-
Colo(Chile) May 1953 joint deal with
E.Robledo £15,000/O'Higgins(Chile)
1959/Retired 1961, later becoming a director of
both Colo-Colo and O'Higgins clubs.

Debut v Charlton Athletic (h) 5/2/49

George Robledo was brought up in Yorkshire
of an English mother after the family had
emigrated from South America following the
Chilean revolution in 1932. A pit worker at
Wath, the stocky inside-forward-cum-striker
gained a place in Barnsley's wartime side and
quickly built up a reputation as a deadly
goalgetter. George, who netted a hat-trick on
his Football League debut, was admired and
coveted by Newcastle's Stan Seymour and
manager George Martin, and the pair finally
succeeded in acquiring his services once the
club had gained promotion into Division One.
He teamed up with Jackie Milburn and Bobby
Mitchell and this Magpies' forward
combination became one of the most feared in
the country. Robledo was the grafter, always
chasing for the ball, tackling, and lethal
whenever an opening came his way. Bobby
Mitchell once remarked, "He used to blast
them in from all directions - and they went
like a bullet". In season 1951-52, when he
netted the late winner in the FA Cup final
against Arsenal, George equalled Hughie
Gallacher's scoring record of 39 goals and was
Division One's leading scorer. Extremely
popular on Tyneside, he was also a regular for
his country, taking part in the 1950 World Cup
finals in Brazil. Fêted as a hero in Chile, on
several occasions George was enticed back to
his native country to help develop the game,
and he eventually left Tyneside for a hefty
financial package when 27
years old and at his peak.
In 1962 Robledo acted as
liaison officer to England
and was on the organising
committee during the
World Cup in Chile.
Nicknamed 'Pancho' by his
colleagues, George later
was employed by a mining
company, and was head of
sport at St Peters school in
Vina Del Mar where he
resided to his death.
Robledo holds Newcastle's
individual scoring record
in any fixture, netting
seven times against Border
Province of South Africa
whilst on tour in July 1952.

Appearances:
FL: 146 apps. 82 gls.
FAC: 18 apps. 9 gls.
Others: 2 apps. 0 gls.
Total: *166 apps. 91 gls.*
Honours:
34 caps Chile 1950-c59/
1 FA app. 1948/
FAC winner 1951, 1952/
Chile Lg champs 1956.

Bryan Robson (see overleaf), a junior product at St. James Park who developed into a potent striker.

ROBSON, Bryan Stanley

Role: Striker 1962-1971
5' 8"
b. Sunderland, 11th November 1945

CAREER: Clara Vale jnrs/UNITED Nov 1962 £75/West Ham United Feb 1971 £120,000/ Sunderland June 1974 £145,000/West Ham United Oct 1976 £80,000/Sunderland June 1979 £45,000/Carlisle United player-coach Mar 1981 £10,000/Chelsea player-coach July 1982 (Carlisle United loan 1982-83)/Sunderland player-coach July 1983 free/Carlisle United July 1984, later becoming asst-manager and manager Aug 1985/Gateshead Oct 1985/ Newcastle Blue Star Sept 1986/Manchester United scout 1987, becoming School of Excellence coach 1988/Hartlepool United asst-manager Oct 1988/Sunderland community officer Nov 1988/Hartlepool United 1989/ Manchester United asst-coach cs 1991/ Sunderland asst-coach 1995.

Debut v Charlton Athletic (a) 1/9/64 (scored once)

Bryan Robson

Although youngster Bryan Robson found the net on his debut for United, it took the small and chunky forward several seasons to become a deadly goalpoacher who would later be rated as the best uncapped striker in England. A fixture in Joe Harvey's plans from 1964 to 1967, Robson never found the net too often, and it wasn't until he teamed up with Welshman, Wyn Davies for the 1968-69 season that 'Pop', as he was known, started to bang the ball into the net. The 'Little and Large' duo combined perfectly as the Magpies stormed Europe. Robson was sharp, quick on the turn and revelled in the space that Davies created. He also could strike the ball sweetly from long range, hitting several quite spectacular efforts often in a big match atmosphere, and especially in European ties. Bryan was tipped for full England honours, but after a controversial war of words with manager Joe Harvey over the lack of professionalism within the corridors of St James Park, he transferred to Upton Park for a record club fee. The Wearsider enjoyed two marvellous spells at West Ham, scoring 104 goals in 254 matches, while Pop also served Sunderland with distinction too, over five different periods. He was the Football League's leading scorer in season 1972-73 (28 goals), and by the time he retired when in his 40's, had scored over 300 goals. A fine golfer, Robson is a past winner of the footballers' championship; he also ran a newsagency on Tyneside before concentrating on a career in coaching at Old Trafford and then on Wearside.

Appearances:
FL: 205(1) apps. 82 gls.
FAC: 10 apps. 4 gls.
FLC: 4 apps. 2 gls.
Eur: 24 apps. 9 gls.
Total: *243(1) apps. 97 gls.*
Honours:
3 Eng u23 caps 1967-69/
1 FL app. 1970/
FL div 2 champs 1965, 1976/
ICFC winner 1969/
FL div 3 prom 1982.

ROBSON, Keith

Role: Striker 1971-1974
5' 11"
b. Hetton-le-Hole, Co. Durham,
15th November 1953

CAREER: UNITED May 1971/West Ham
United Sept 1974 £60,000(Team Hawaii(USA)
loan May 1977)/Cardiff City Aug 1977
£25,000/Norwich City Feb 1978 £25,000/
Leicester City Sept 1981 £30,000(Carlisle
United loan 1982-83)/Hong Kong Sept 1983/
Wroxham(Norwich) Aug 1984/Norwich
Busmen/Corinthians(Norwich)/Wroxham
1986/Mackintosh(Norwich)/Wroxham
Aug 1988, becoming asst-manager 1993.

Debut v Chelsea (h) 24/3/73

Keith Robson

Tall and well
built, Keith
Robson was a
promising
striker
developed by
the Magpies.
However, he
was unlucky to
be at Gallowgate
at the time of
the Macdonald-
Tudor
partnership up
front and
consequently his
chances on first
team duty were
limited,
although he did
manage 13
games during
season 1973-74
when Supermac was out injured. Robson was
a good deputy and on moving to Upton Park,
provided the Hammers with a skilful left-
sided attacker. He totalled 87 games for West
Ham, hitting 19 goals, including a number in
successful cup runs during the mid 1970's,
although he missed out on the 1975 FA Cup
final. Keith did though, figure in the
Londoners' European final the following year,
netting in the showpiece with Anderlecht and
a spectacular effort in the semi-final that
clinched victory over Eintracht Frankfurt.
Sometimes aggressive, and temperamental on
the field, whilst at Carrow Road he gave some
exuberant performances too. Robson later
settled in the Norwich area becoming heavily
involved in local football.

> **Appearances:**
> *FL: 14 apps. 3 gls.*
> *FLC: 1 app. 2 gls.*
> *Others: 3 apps. 1 gl.*
> **Total:** *18 apps. 6 gls.*
> **Honours:**
> *ECWC finalist 1976.*

ROBSON, Thomas Henry

Role: Outside-left 1966-1968
5' 8"
b. Gateshead, 31st July 1944

CAREER: Redheugh Boys Club/Northampton
Town Aug 1961/Chelsea Nov 1965 £30,000/
UNITED Dec 1966 £13,000/Peterborough
United Oct 1968 £20,000/Nuneaton Borough
cs 1981/Stamford 1982/Northampton Town
Oct 1984/Chatteris 1985/Peterborough United
Nov 1986 asst-coach.

Debut v Tottenham Hotspur (a) 31/12/66

Tynesider Tommy Robson had limited
opportunities at Stamford Bridge due to the
sparkling form of Bobby Tambling. But when

Tommy Robson

he was brought home by manager Joe Harvey, as a wide player to replace Alan Suddick, Robson himself began to sparkle in a black'n'white shirt. A dedicated professional, Tommy always gave the side 100% effort; nimble and quick on the left wing, he is remembered for his tip-toe sorties at the opposition. He had one excellent season for the black'n'whites, in 1967-68, when he scored 11 goals in 40 games, helping the club into European football for the first time. But Harvey then discarded the cheery winger and Robson moved to Peterborough where he became something of an institution for the next decade and more. He clocked up a record total of 559 matches for the Posh and scored an impressive 128 goals. Robson resides in Peterborough, working for the local newspaper, *The Herald & Post*.

Appearances:
FL: 46(2) apps. 11 gls.
FAC: 1 app. 0 gls.
FLC: 1 app. 0 gls.
Total: *48(2) apps. 11 gls.*
Honours:
Eng youth app. 1962/
FL div 4 champs 1974/
FA Vase finalist 1984.

ROCHE, David

Role: Midfield 1986-1993
5' 11"
b. Daisy Hill, Wallsend, 13th December 1970

CAREER: Wallsend Boys Club/UNITED app 1986, pro Aug 1988(Gateshead loan 1992-93) (Peterborough United loan 1992-93)/ Doncaster Rovers Oct 1993 £25,000/Southend United Mar 1995 £55,000 to 1996.

Debut v Arsenal (a) 15/4/89 (sub)

As a juvenile, David Roche played in front of a 30,000 crowd at St James Park in a pre-match schools six-a-side game. And, after being chased by Arsenal, Sunderland and Leicester, he was soon to be appearing for Newcastle United in a similar atmosphere. A tough tackling midfield player, David was the club's youth team skipper and was rapidly given a first team debut as a teenager, then a regular place by Ossie Ardiles on the departure of ex Scotland captain Roy Aitken. Roche gained valuable experience in the Argentinian's eleven, a side however which plummeted

down the Second Division table. The Tynesider went through a torrid few months as Newcastle struggled and by the time Kevin Keegan had been installed at St James Park, David was destined for a career in the game elsewhere. Off the field, Roche went through several controversial moments; he was once shot in the leg and sprayed with ammonia in a Tyneside night-spot. Then at Newcastle Crown Court in March 1996 he was convicted of wounding with intent following a city centre attack and sentenced to four years imprisonment which effectively ended his football career.

Appearances:
FL: 23(13) apps. 0 gls.
FAC: 1 app. 0 gls.
FLC: 2 apps. 0 gls.
Others: 1(2) apps. 0 gls.
Total: *27(15) apps. 0 gls.*

David Roche

ROEDER, Glenn Victor

Role: Centre-half 1983-1989
6' 1"
b. Woodford, Essex, 13th December 1955

CAREER: Arsenal sch/Orient Oct 1973/
Queens Park Rangers Aug 1978 £250,000(Notts
County loan 1983-84)/UNITED Dec 1983
£120,000 to May 1989 free/Watford July 1989/
Leyton Orient player-coach Jan 1992/
Gillingham player-manager Oct 1992/
Watford coach June 1993, becoming manager
July 1993 to Feb 1996.

Debut v Blackburn Rovers (h) 26/12/83

Stylish, assured on the ball and tinged with a
touch of arrogance, Glenn Roeder was Arthur
Cox's final piece in the team building which
ensured United's promotion to the First
Division in 1984. Originally a midfield man,
Glenn moved into the back line and became a
commanding central figure in defence. An
elegant, upright player who could always use
the ball well and almost continental
style, make menacing progress
forward. Having a crowd-pleasing
double shuffle in possession which
confounded opponents, Roeder
was a past skipper of Orient and
QPR, leading out the Loftus Road
club at Wembley in 1982. But
Glenn unluckily missed the
replayed final with Spurs due to
suspension following a dismissal
in a league game. Totalling 181
matches for Rangers and on the
fringe of a full England cap, he
was also captain of the Magpies
and served United with credit
for six seasons. His father
appeared in semi-
professional football in the
Southern League.

Appearances:
FL: 193 apps. 8 gls.
FAC: 11 apps. 1 gl.
FLC: 11 apps. 1 gl.
Others: 4 apps. 0 gls.
Total: *219 apps. 10 gls.*
Honours:
6 Eng B caps 1978-80/
FL div 2 champs 1983/
FL div 2 prom 1984/
FAC finalist 1982.

Glenn Roeder

ROGERS, Ehud

Role: Outside-right 1936-1939
5' 6"
b. Chirk, 15th October 1909
d. Chirk, 25th January 1996

CAREER: Weston Rhyn/Llanerch Celts
(Rhosllanerchcrugog)/Chirk/Oswestry Town
1933/Wrexham May 1934/Arsenal Jan 1935
£2,600/UNITED June 1936 £2,500/Swansea
Town May 1939 £700/Wrexham war-guest
1939-41/Everton war-guest 1943-44/Lovells
Athletic war-guest/Aberaman war-guest/
Wrexham Dec 1945/Oswestry Town 1947/
Later became Chirk coach c1962.

Debut v Barnsley (h) 29/8/36

Ehud Rogers was a Welsh
amateur international
before he caught the eye
of Arsenal in 1935. Light,
fast and described as
"plucky", he possessed
more than a touch of finesse
on the ball. At Highbury
he was largely confined
to being a reserve to the
Gunners' famous stars,
however he grabbed five
games in the 1935 title-
winning season.
Whenever he did get a chance
though he played well, form which
alerted United. Known as 'Tim'
because apparently his colleagues were
unable to pronounce his biblical
christian name, he joined the Magpies'
Second Division attack where he was
lively and dangerous for two
seasons, fading just before the
outbreak of the Second World War
when he was replaced by another
former Highbury reserve, Ralph
Birkett. At St James Park, as well
as at Highbury, he often treated
his colleagues to a Welsh song,
tunefully rendered before leaving
the dressing-room. Rogers
served with the RAF in Egypt
for a time during the
fighting, while he also
appeared for his country
at full level during the
hostilities. On leaving
the game he resided

347

in Chirk and ran a newsagency. His brother, Joe, appeared for Manchester City and Shrewsbury Town.

Appearances:
FL: 56 apps. 10 gls.
FAC: 2 apps. 0 gls.
Total: *58 apps. 10 gls.*
Honours:
2 Wales war caps 1941-45/
1 Wales amat cap 1934/1 WL app. 1935/
1 Wales & Ireland combined app. 1935.

ROGERS, Joseph James

Role: Outside-right 1898-1901
5' 11"
b. Coventry 1876
d. Meriden 1955

CAREER: Stoke United/Macclesfield c1880/Southampton St Marys Dec 1894/ Grimsby Town May 1896/UNITED Apr 1898/ Preston North End Jan 1901/Germany playing and coaching c1902/Tivoli(Grimsby) c1906.

Debut v Stoke (a) 24/9/1898

Joe Rogers was attracted to Newcastle United after a spell with the Mariners in which he bagged 23 goals in 53 league outings. Joining United for the 1898-99 season - the Magpies' first in Division One - he became a popular player, effective when in sight of goal and good enough to become the club's first international player. Joe was chosen to represent the FA eleven to tour Germany at the turn of the century, in all but name an international appearance. He had a field day on the continent, netting seven goals on the tour, five in one fixture. Following a time spent coaching in Germany, he returned to England and resided in the Grimsby area for a period. At the beginning of his career with the Saints, Rogers once netted ten goals in a single game during 1895, but was afterwards used in the full-back position!

Appearances:
FL: 54 apps. 10 gls.
FAC: 3 apps. 1 gl.
Total: *57 apps. 11 gls.*
Honours:
3 unoff Eng caps 1900.

ROGERS, Thomas

Role: Left-back 1893-1895
5' 9"
b. Scotland

CAREER: Perth Jnrs/UNITED Jan 1893 to 1895.

Debut v Liverpool (h) 25/11/1893

Initially joining Newcastle United early in 1893, Tom Rogers arrived on Tyneside from local Perth football. He was described in the *Newcastle Daily Chronicle* as "a young Scotch player"...."who has favourably impressed the committee with his powers". First choice left-back, Rogers had a good run in the club's senior eleven during season 1893-94, gaining notable praise for that first season of league action. After six outings the following term he lost his place and departed in 1895. Some sources have his name as, 'Rodgers', but official club records note Rogers.

Appearances:
FL: 22 apps. 0 gls.
FAC: 2 apps. 0 gls.
Total: *24 apps. 0 gls.*

ROSS, Eric Williams

Role: Midfield 1967-1969
5' 9"
b. Belfast, 19th September 1944

CAREER: Glentoran/UNITED Aug 1967 £5,250/Northampton Town Oct 1969 £15,000 (Hartlepool United loan 1971-72)/Canadian football cs 1976/North Shields Oct 1976.

Debut v Lincoln City (a) 13/9/67 (FLC)

A great favourite in Ireland with Glentoran, Eric Ross showed he was a probing midfield player with an accurate pass and shot. Joe Harvey gave him a chance to establish himself in England, but Eric struggled to record an impact on the First Division scene. Making two appearances in each of seasons 1967-68 and 1968-69, Ross was capped by Northern Ireland when in United's reserve side, but was

Eric Ross

Tall and moustached in the style of the day, Tom Rowlandson was a typical gent of the Edwardian era. A distinguished scholar, he was a noted amateur international player of the establishment, a Cambridge Blue and Corinthian personality. At St James Park only briefly as an amateur, he deputised for Jimmy Lawrence just once, but did get 12 outings in Sunderland's senior line-up. Also a full-back, Tom played for the Corinthians on 75 occasions, once against the Magpies in the 1906-07 FA Charity Shield fixture. Residing in Barton, Yorkshire, he was honoured during the First World War being awarded the Military Cross for his exploits with the Yorkshire Regiment. He sadly though became another victim of the conflict and was killed in action in France.

Appearances:
FL: 1 app. 0 gls.
Total: *1 app. 0 gls.*
Honours:
2 Eng amat caps 1907/
Eng trial app. 1906.

Tom Rowlandson

transferred to Northampton where he totalled over 50 games. Bespectacled, Ross wore contact lenses on the field and later resided in Canada for a period.

Appearances:
FL: 2 apps. 0 gls.
FLC: 2 apps. 0 gls.
Total: *4 apps. 0 gls.*
Honours:
1 N.Irel cap 1969/1 N.Irel u23 cap 1967/
N.Irel youth app./1 NIL app. 1967/
NIC finalist 1967.

ROWLANDSON, Thomas Sowerby

Role: Goalkeeper 1905-1906
5' 11"
b. Darlington, 1880
d. France, 15th September 1916

CAREER: Charterhouse School/Trinity Hall College, Cambridge University 1903/Preston North End amat/Sunderland amat Dec 1903 to Dec 1904/UNITED amat 1905 to 1906/Old Carthusians 1907/Member of the Corinthians side 1903-1910.

Debut v Bury (h) 21/10/05

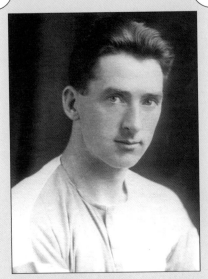

ROXBURGH, Robert

Role: Right-back 1920-1924
5' 11"
b. Morpeth, Northumberland, 5th February 1896
d. Leeds, 20th November 1974

CAREER: Morpeth Comrades/UNITED Nov 1920 £50/Blackburn Rovers May 1924 £375 to 1931/Holland coaching c1935/Leeds United asst-trainer 1938 to Nov 1957.

Debut v Arsenal (h) 30/4/21

During four seasons at St James Park Robert Roxburgh was resigned to be the great Bill McCracken's deputy. Appearing on 24 occasions during those campaigns, Robert performed well, especially in season 1922-23 when he was in the side on 11 occasions. A safe defender who rarely took risks, however he had little option but to depart in order to guarantee first team action; this he achieved at Ewood Park, claiming 127 matches for Blackburn when Rovers were a top First Division side. Afterwards Robert had a 19-year spell on the Elland Road staff.

Appearances:
FL: 24 apps. 0 gls.
Total: *24 apps. 0 gls.*

RUSSELL, Samuel R.

Role: Full-back 1920-1925
5' 8"
b. Downpatrick, Co Down, 2nd January 1900

CAREER: Distillery/Old Park Corinthians/ UNITED Aug 1920 £200/ Shelbourne May 1925/ Bradford City Dec 1926/ Derry City June 1931.

Debut v Manchester City (a) 2/5/21

A hard-tackling defender, Sam Russell operated at both right and left-back positions for the Magpies. After crossing the Irish Sea to give a good showing on trial at Gallowgate in 1920, he earned himself a contract.  Sam stepped in for established players, Hudspeth, Hampson or McCracken over five seasons for Newcastle before moving back to Ireland to claim honours and then on to Bradford City where he also found conspicuous success. At Valley

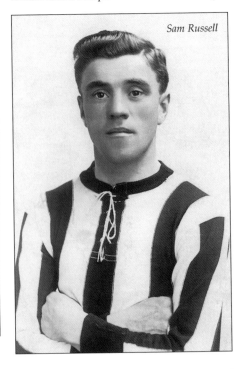

Sam Russell

Parade, Sam made 145 appearances, helped City to the Third Division title and was chosen for his country. He was once selected for the English FA side, but had to withdraw when officials became aware of his Irish nationality.

Appearances:
FL: 28 apps. 0 gls.
FAC: 3 apps. 0 gls.
Total: *31 apps. 0 gls.*
Honours:
3 N.Irel caps 1930-32/
FL div 3(N) champs 1929/
Eire champs 1926.

RUSSELL, Thomas

Role: Left-back 1934-1937
5' 9"
b. Cowdenbeath, 23rd November 1909

CAREER:
Cowdenbeath/Glasgow Rangers Feb 1933/UNITED Aug 1934 £650/ Horden Colliery Welfare May 1937.

Debut v Plymouth Argyle (a) 22/9/34

A reserve fixture at Ibrox who took part in Rangers' title victories in both 1934 (3 apps.) and 1935 (5 apps.), Tom Russell moved to Tyneside hoping to break into United's side and make an impression in England. However, even with Newcastle in the Second Division, he still found gaining a regular place difficult. Second choice to David Fairhurst, the Scot appeared during the 1934-35 season before moving into North Eastern League soccer with Horden.

Appearances:
FL: 7 apps. 0 gls.
Total: *7 apps. 0 gls.*

Jackie Rutherford

RUTHERFORD, John

Role: Outside-right 1902-1913
5' 9"
b. Percy Main, nr Newcastle upon Tyne, 12th October 1884
d. Neasden, London, 21st April 1963

CAREER: Percy Main 1897/Willington Athletic 1900/UNITED Jan 1902 £75/ Woolwich Arsenal Oct 1913 £800/Chelsea war-guest 1918-19/Stoke player-manager Mar to Aug 1923/Arsenal Sept 1923/ Retired cs 1925/Arsenal Jan 1926/ Clapton Orient Aug 1926/Retired cs 1927/Tufnell Park trainer c1929.

Debut v Bolton Wanderers (h) 1/3/02 (scored once)

Jackie Rutherford was one of United's most outstanding forwards of any era. A huge favourite with Geordie supporters, Rutherford had an unusually long career as a player; he made his debut as a 17 year-old for United - when he netted and became the club's youngest ever scorer and, at the time, the youngest debutant. And he did not retire from playing until he was into his 40's. Known as 'Jock' or 'Jackie', the Tynesider rapidly climbed to fame, starting as a centre-forward or inside-forward but switching to the right-wing for the 1903-04 season. Before he was 20 years old he had been capped by England, one of the youngest-ever internationals, and he continued playing for his country for over a decade. Jackie was a key personality in every one of United's championship and cup final sides during their marvellous Edwardian period. For over 12 seasons he romped along the touchline with style, speed, control and, most important of all, consistency. He could always bag goals too - netting nearly 100 for Newcastle. Without doubt Jackie was one of the game's biggest names during the years before and after the Great War but, towards the end of his stay on Tyneside, the prematurely balding Rutherford fell into dispute with the club over benefit payments. Approaching 30, Jackie moved to Arsenal, and many thought it would be his final fling in the game yet Jackie appeared for the Gunners on 323 occasions! Scoring two goals for Chelsea in the wartime Victory Cup final during 1919, he only tasted management briefly with Stoke, as their first ever boss. Rutherford came from a large footballing family; his brothers Sep and Bob both had notable careers in the game too, while another brother, Andrew was on United's books for a while. His son John James was also with Arsenal, and amazingly appeared for the North London side during the same 1925-26 season as his father. Jackie was nicknamed 'The Newcastle Flier' during his heyday, and had a superstition whereby he always ran last out of the tunnel. On leaving the game, Rutherford became an off-licensee in Neasden, London to his death.

Appearances:
FL: 290 apps. 78 gls.
FAC: 44 apps. 14 gls.
Others: 2 apps. 2 gls.
Total: 336 apps. 94 gls.
Honours
11 Eng caps 1904-08/
Eng trial app. 1907-08/
2 FL apps. 1904-22/
FL champs 1905, 1907, 1909/
FAC winner 1910/
FAC finalist 1905, 1906, 1908, 1911/
FAVC winner 1919.

RUTHERFORD, R.E.

Role: Centre-half 1905-1906
Debut v Liverpool (a) 9/4/06

One of the club's promising youngsters, Rutherford was given a single opportunity in Football League action during season 1905-06. United's team committee had problems with six senior men on international duty. Pushed up front to an inside-forward role, 'Ixion' in *The Daily Journal* remarked: "This was carrying the experimental game to extremes". Rutherford had just played reserve football against Bishop Auckland, then two days later faced the First Division leaders at Anfield. Although the Magpies lost 3-0, Rutherford applied himself well according to contemporary reports of the match.

Appearances:
FL: 1 app. 0 gls.
Total: 1 app. 0 gls.

RYAN, John B.

Role: Left-back 1983-1984
5' 10"
*b Ashton-under-Lyne, nr Manchester,
18th February 1962*

CAREER: Oldham Athletic app June 1978, pro
Feb 1980/UNITED Aug 1983 £225,000/
Sheffield Wednesday Sept 1984 cash-exch for
P.Heard plus £40,000/Oldham Athletic Aug
1985 £25,000/Mansfield Town Oct 1987
£25,000/Chesterfield June 1989/Rochdale July
1991 free/Bury Dec 1993/Stalybridge Celtic
1994/Radcliffe Borough cs 1996.

Debut v Leeds United (a) 27/8/83

John Ryan

Reports by several
football
commentators
considered John
Ryan to be a
future England
full-back after a
string of
impressive
displays for
Oldham. Reaching
the Under-21 side
before he moved
to Tyneside, Ryan
possessed lovely
ball skills and
attacking flair,
characteristics of
the modern style of full-back. Arthur Cox
swooped to bring him to St James Park in a
double full-back signing, Ryan joining
United's staff at the same time as Malcolm
Brown. While Brown was unluckily injured
almost immediately, Ryan stepped into Cox's
promotion-chasing side looking potent in
attack, but occasionally fragile in defence. He
was replaced by Kenny Wharton half-way
through the 1983-84 season, then Wes
Saunders took over his role when Newcastle
started a new spell in Division One. Ryan
faded dramatically from the scene, moving to
Hillsborough and back to Boundary Park
where he totalled 100 games for Oldham. A
double fracture of his leg in 1986 further
interrupted a blossoming career that had
promised much. John is now a partner in a
small construction and development company
in Manchester.

Appearances:
FL: 28 apps. 1 gl.
FAC: 1 app. 0 gls.
FLC: 2 apps. 0 gls.
Total: *31 apps. 1 gl.*
Honours:
1 Eng u21 cap 1983/FL div 2 prom 1984.

RYDER, Isaac

Role: Inside-left 1893-1895
b. Tyneside
Debut v Woolwich Arsenal (h) 30/9/1893

From a popular local footballing family, Isaac
Ryder was related to Joseph, also at St James
Park at the same time. An early footballing
stalwart of Tyneside, Ryder came into the side
only once, but in what was to become an
historic fixture - United's first Football League
victory, a 6-0 win at Gallowgate over Arsenal.
During his stay with the club, Isaac was
restricted mainly to Northern Alliance football
and once earned criticism from local reporters
for "dilly-dallying" on the ball.

Appearances:
FL: 1 app. 0 gls.
Total: *1 app. 0 gls.*

RYDER, Joseph

Role: Goalkeeper 1892-1895
5' 10"
b. Tyneside

CAREER: Newcastle Albion/Newcastle West
End/Newcastle East End 1892/UNITED May
1892/Hebburn Argyle 1895/South Shields 1897.

Debut v Burton Swifts (a) 23/9/1893

Joining United's founder club, Newcastle East
End, Joe Ryder had to compete with several
players for the goalkeeper's position during
those early days at St James Park. Newcastle
tried four other custodians - Whitton, Lowery,
Ramsay and Ward - and Ryder only managed
two matches for the club. He was though a
respected local character, good enough to
appear for Northumberland County in 1893.
Related to Isaac Ryder, he later served other
Tyneside clubs with distinction.

Appearances:
FL: 2 apps. 0 gls.
Total: *2 apps. 0 gls.*

SANSOM, Kenneth Graham

Debut v Sheffield Wednesday (a) 26/12/88

Role: Left-back 1988-1989
5' 7"
b. Camberwell, London, 26th September 1958

CAREER: Crystal Palace app 1973, pro Dec 1975/Arsenal Aug 1980 £1.35m/UNITED Dec 1988 £300,000/Queens Park Rangers May 1989 £340,000/Coventry City Mar 1991 £100,000/Everton Feb 1993 free/Brentford Mar 1993/Barnet Aug 1993/Partick Thistle trial Sept 1993/Chertsey Town Dec 1993/Watford player-coach cs 1994, becoming asst-manager to Feb 1996.

Ex England skipper Kenny Sansom joined Newcastle as an accomplished 30 year-old defender with almost 700 senior games to his name. Short and compact, Sansom boasted a great left foot, was accurate in his distribution of the ball and a tough little competitor. The former Arsenal favourite provided experience for United's struggling line-up as they battled to steer away from the drop into Division Two. But Sansom's purchase was too late to save the Magpies' hide, although Kenny himself showed all the qualities that saw him recognised as one of the country's top players.

Appearing in both the 1982 and 1986 World Cup finals, the Londoner made a name with Crystal Palace after being handed a debut as a 16 year-old. He totalled 197 games for Palace before a multi-exchange deal saw him move to Highbury where he went on to play in 394 games for the Gunners. Sansom had trials with Leeds before joining the Selhurst Park set-up, while he remains one of England's most capped players with 86 full internationals to his credit. Kenny now lives in Bromley, Kent.

Kenny Sansom

Appearances:
FL: 20 apps. 0 gls.
FAC: 4 apps. 0 gls.
Total: *24 apps. 0 gls.*
Honours:
86 Eng caps 1979-1988/
2 Eng B caps 1979/
8 Eng u21 caps 1979-80/
1 Eng youth app. 1977/
Eng schools app. 1974/
1 FL app. 1988/
FL div 3 prom 1977/
FL div 2 champs 1979/
FLC winner 1987/
FLC finalist 1988/
FAYC winner 1977.

Wes Saunders

Saunders looked a sound player in the centre of the defence, however he fell from favour following a succession of managerial changes. Wes proceeded to have excellent spells in a lower grade of football, with Carlisle, Dundee and Torquay especially, but a series of knee problems necessitating five operations forced him to quit the game. Saunders later returned to East Boldon, playing local football and was employed in the family's clothing business in County Durham.

Appearances:
FL: 79 apps. 0 gls.
FAC: 6 apps. 1 gl.
FLC: 8 apps. 0 gls.
Total: *93 apps. 1 gl.*
Honours:
Eng youth app./
FL div 2 prom 1984/
FL div 4 prom 1991.

SAUNDERS, Wesley

Role: Left-back or Centre-half 1980-1985
5' 11"
b. Boldon, Co.Durham, 23rd February 1963

CAREER: UNITED app 1980, pro June 1981 (Bradford City loan 1984-85)/Carlisle loan Aug 1985, pmt Nov 1985 £20,000/Dundee Feb 1988 £100,000 (£50,000 to Newcastle)/Torquay United July 1990 £60,000, becoming caretaker-manager Apr 1991/Retired due to injury cs 1993/Spennymoor United Sept 1993.

Debut v Chelsea (a) 7/11/81

United brought Wes Saunders, one of the region's top schools players, through their junior ranks to replace Davies and Johnson at left-back as Arthur Cox was building the side to regain First Division status. Despite a few misdemeanours as a teenager, he impressed as a tall and powerful player. And Wes effectively switched to centre-half for the 1983-84 promotion season playing a part in that successful campaign. To many Newcastle supporters

SCANLON, Albert Joseph

Role: Outside-left 1960-1962
5' 10"
b. Manchester, 10th October 1935

CAREER: All Saints/Manchester United amat 1950, pro Dec 1952/UNITED Nov 1960 £17,500/Lincoln City Feb 1962 £2,000/ Mansfield Town Apr 1963/Belper Town Aug 1966 free to Oct 1966.

Debut v Blackburn Rovers (h) 26/11/60

A survivor of the Munich Air Disaster in 1958 Albert Scanlon recovered from a badly broken leg sustained in the crash, this after having just established himself in the Reds' side a few weeks before that fateful day in Germany. He appeared in the Old Trafford club's title victories in both 1955-56 and 1956-57 as deputy to David Pegg. One of the famous Busby Babes, Scanlon was twice

Albert Scanlon

an FA Youth Cup winner with Manchester United and showed he was a direct and fast winger. Totalling 127 games for the Old Trafford side, he got back into the Reds' team and was rated as one of the country's top young stars in season 1958-59 when he became an England Under-23 player. But his blossoming career stagnated due to a lack of consistency and by the time he joined his uncle, Charlie Mitten, on Tyneside, he was in need of a career boost. St James Park though, never really suited Scanlon. United were on their way into Division Two and after only one and a half seasons contesting the Number 11 shirt with Liam Tuohy, Scanlon moved on. Afterwards he played on 116 occasions for the Stags at Mansfield before leaving the first class game. He was later employed in a number of roles including dock worker, security officer and warehouseman for Colgate Palmolive in the Manchester area.

Appearances:
FL: 22 apps. 5 gls.
FAC: 4 apps. 1 gl.
FLC: 1 app. 0 gls.
Total: *27 apps. 6 gls.*
Honours:
6 Eng u23 caps 1959/
1 FL app. 1960/
FL div 4 prom 1963/
FAYC winner 1953, 1954.

SCOTT, George

Role: Outside-left 1929-1930
5' 6"
b. Blackhill, County Durham

CAREER: Crawcrook/White-le-Head Rangers/South Shields Mar 1927/ UNITED Apr 1929 £1,250/ Gillingham May 1930/ North Shields Mar 1932/ Wigan Athletic June 1933.

Debut v Middlesbrough (h) 25/12/29

George Scott appeared in 65 league games for South Shields during their Football League days at Horsley Hill. He joined United's staff as cover on the flank for either Tommy Lang or Tommy Urwin. All his outings for the Magpies were in season 1929-30 before moving south to join Gillingham. Slightly built, he was like many of the touchline fliers of the era, tricky and fast.

Appearances: *George Scott*
FL: 7 apps. 2 gls.
FAC: 3 apps. 0 gls.
Total: *10 apps. 2 gls.*

SCOTT, James

Role: Midfield or Outside-right 1967-1970
5' 9"
b. Falkirk, 21st August 1940

CAREER: Denny Rovers/Falkirk/Bo'ness United/Hibernian 1958/UNITED Aug 1967 £35,000/Crystal Palace Feb 1970 £20,000/ Falkirk Jan 1972/Hamilton Academical cs 1973 to 1974.

Debut v Southampton (h) 19/8/67
(scored once)

Jim Scott came from a noted footballing family. His father turned out for Falkirk and Burnley, while his brother, Alex appeared for Rangers and Everton; both Jim and Alex also were capped by Scotland. Scott was a player with a delicate touch, able to operate on the flank or in midfield. After establishing himself as a noted craftsman at Easter Road, Jim gave United two very good seasons, as Newcastle qualified for Europe in 1967-68, and the following term when the Inter Cities Fairs Cup was secured. He is credited with netting the club's first ever goal in European competition,

Jim Scott

SCOTT, James Adamson

Role: Midfield 1976-1980
5' 8"
b. Newcastle upon Tyne, 28th February 1960

CAREER: UNITED July 1976(Carlisle United loan 1979-80)/Berwick Rangers cs 1980 free/Ashington Dec 1980/Blyth Spartans c1981/Brandon United Nov 1982.

Debut v Chelsea (a) 18/3/78

Known as 'Jamie' and possessing plenty of stamina, grit and effort, Scott was introduced into United's midfield during a time of crisis as Newcastle slipped nearer to the relegation trapdoor in season 1977-78. With new blood needed, the Tynesider was given a chance but, although he gave one hundred per cent effort, could not change results. Scott remained a squad player for another season before being released.

Appearances:
FL: 9(1) apps.
0 gls.
Total:
9(1) apps.
0 gls.

against Feyenoord, and during that memorable season Jim linked with Bryan Robson and Wyn Davies to good effect. He often struck important goals, one in the Fairs Cup semi-final, and another in the final against Ujpesti Dozsa. On ending his career back in Scotland, Scott teamed up with his brother and ran a long-established public house with a footballing theme in Falkirk.

Appearances:
FL: 70(4) apps. 6 gls.
FAC: 4(1) apps. 1 gl.
FLC: 4 apps. 0 gls.
Eur: 14(1) apps. 5 gls.
Total: *92(6) apps. 12 gls.*
Honours:
1 Scot cap 1966/
Scot jnr app./
ICFC winner 1969.

Jamie Scott

SCOTT, John George

Role: Outside-left 1910-1913
5' 6"
b. Rosehill, Wallsend, 1890

CAREER: Wallsend Slipway/UNITED May 1910 £25/Grimsby Town May 1913 £50 to 1915 free.

Debut v Woolwich Arsenal (h) 1/4/11

A reserve to 'Wee Geordie' Wilson at outside-left, John Scott deputised during three seasons. He appeared on six occasions in 1911-12, one outing being a derby meeting with Sunderland at Roker Park. A late replacement, the press recorded his appearance, "with timidity and trepidation"! Yet Jack, as he was more commonly known, was the hero of the day; he netted a late winner, scoring with the "essence of coolness", lobbing the Sunderland 'keeper from 12 yards with only three minutes left on the referee's watch. Small, yet well built, he grabbed a chance of first team soccer at Blundell Park, but events did not turn out as expected and after only 49 games he was given a free transfer on the condition he moved, as it was noted, to, "any club but a league outfit".

Appearances:
FL: 8 apps. 1 gl.
Total: *8 apps. 1 gl.*

Jack Scott

SCOTT, Kevin Watson

Role: Centre-half 1984-1994
6' 2"
b. Easington, Co Durham, 17th December 1966

CAREER: Easington jnrs/ Middlesbrough app 1983/Sherburn 1984/Eppleton CW/UNITED Dec 1984/Tottenham Hotspur Feb 1994 £850,000(Port Vale loan 1994-95).

Debut v Sheffield Wednesday (h) 6/9/86 (scored once)

Rejected at Ayresome Park, Kevin Scott was handed a lifeline by Magpies manager Jack Charlton and the youngster went on to prove he was worth another chance. A key figure alongside Gazza in Newcastle's FA Youth Cup victory, on his senior debut for the black'n'whites Kevin found the net, but then was promptly dropped and had to wait a couple of seasons before being able to claim a regular place in defence. Under firstly Jim Smith, then Ossie Ardiles, Kevin became United's first choice centre-half and skipper. Built for the position, he could be a positive and dominating defender, but sometimes lacked the finer skills necessary to set attacks going. Although he played well during the Magpies' First Division title success, Scott afterwards found himself replaced as Kevin Keegan fashioned a side to challenge for the Premiership. He earned a big move though, to rejoin Ardiles at White Hart Lane and his career looked to be taking off. But Scott found a place in Tottenham's side difficult to hold down, especially after the South American was sacked.

Appearances:
FL/PL: 229 apps. 8 gls.
FAC: 15(1) apps. 1 gl.
FLC: 18 apps. 0 gls.
Others: 10(2) apps. 2 gls.
Total: *272(3) apps. 11 gls.*
Honours:
FL div 1 champs 1993/
FAYC winner 1985.

Kevin Scott

Malcolm Scott had to play second fiddle to Bob Stokoe for five seasons at St James Park. A solid defender nevertheless, Scott was big, somewhat ungainly and recorded his first outing when still a part-timer at the club. Sharing his football with a career as an engineer, Scott made his debut in an emergency after Stokoe had dropped out just before a game at Old Trafford. Travelling through the night, Malcolm arrived in time to face England leader Tommy Taylor and had a harrowing baptism, the Reds winning 6-1. His best season was 1958-59 (16 games), while he was also tried at centre-forward on a few occasions; once against Leeds he netted twice when up against Jack Charlton. The press of the day noted he "proved well worthy of a prolonged run as leader of the attack". Scott was also a fine cricketer, with Durham and on Northamptonshire's books for a decade. He scored over 2,000 runs and took 457 wickets in his 183 senior county matches. A spin bowler, he was once banned in 1967 for a bowling action which contravened the rules.

Appearances:
FL: 25 apps. 2 gls.
FAC: 1 app. 0 gls.
Total: *26 apps. 2 gls.*

SCOTT, Malcolm Ernest

Role: Centre-half 1955-1961
6' 1"
b. South Shields, 8th May 1936

CAREER: Cleadon jnrs/UNITED Sept 1955 £15(Northampton Town loan 1961-62)/ Darlington Oct 1961 £2,200/York City Oct 1963 to 1965/Northamptonshire cricketer 1959-69.

Debut v Manchester United (a) 12/1/57

Malcolm Scott

SCOTT, Matthew McLintock

Role: Left-back 1900-1901
5' 10"
b. Airdrie, 11th July 1872

CAREER: Airdrieonians Sept 1890/UNITED
Oct 1900/Airdrieonians cs 1901/Albion
Rovers 1902/Retired due to injury 1903.
Debut v Sheffield United (a) 8/12/1900

A strapping and experienced full-back Matt Scott kicked the ball long and with purpose, as well as specialising in off the line clearances. At his peak with Airdrie, Scott was capped by Scotland and was signed by United's directors as cover for Dave Gardner for the 1900-01 season. He infrequently gained a place in the side, by accounts of the day being a touch slow when against a winger with pace. His brother Robert was also a Scottish international with Airdrie. Scott was forced to retire from the game after a nasty injury when playing for Albion Rovers against Renton in February 1903.

Appearances:
FL: 5 apps. 0 gls.
Total: *5 apps. 0 gls.*
Honours:
1 Scot cap 1898.

SCOTT, William

Role: Centre-forward 1938-1946
5' 10"
b. Bucksburn, nr Aberdeen, 10th October 1916
d. Bridge of Don, August 1994

CAREER: Aberdeen 1935/UNITED Sept 1938
£3,750/Linfield war-guest/Consett July 1946
free.
Debut v Brentford (a) 7/1/39 (FAC)

United officials were suitably impressed when they watched Willie Scott fire in five goals for Aberdeen reserves as a 21 year-old. Not a regular with the Dons, claiming only 27 appearances in three seasons, a deal was settled on the spot with the Pittodrie club, and Willie travelled to Tyneside to bid for one of the forward positions. Rivalling Cairns and Stubbins, tragedy struck for the tearaway striker when he soon broke a leg and by the time he was fit again, war had been declared and his career was curtailed. Scott did, however, play wartime football for the Magpies. He joined up with the local Tyneside Scottish battalion and was one of the many caught up in the evacuation at Dunkirk, captured and imprisoned in Germany. It is recorded by the club that the directors sent him "a parcel of comforts" during his incarceration. On retiring, Willie worked at Consett steelworks, before moving to Kincorth and Bridge of Don near Aberdeen. He was for the latter part of his life a 'lollipop man' in Aberdeen. His son Jocky, was a noted Scottish League player and recent Hibernian coach.

Appearances:
FL: 6 apps. 2 gls.
FAC: 3 apps. 0 gls.
War: 10 apps. 4 gls.
Total: *19 apps. 6 gls.*

SCOTT, William H.

Role: Centre-forward 1923-1926
5' 8"
b. Scotland

CAREER: Larkhall Thistle/
Airdrieonians/UNITED Mar
1923 £800/Retired due to injury May 1926.
Debut v West Bromwich Albion (a) 14/3/23

William Scott

A star of junior football north of the border, William Scott possessed all the qualities to become a hit in England. He had pace, ball control and a shoot-on-sight instinct. A reserve to Neil Harris, Scott became a popular forward in the club's North Eastern League line-up, but was out of action for several months with a bad leg injury he picked up in season 1923-24. He actually called a halt to his career in October 1924, but made a comeback only for the injury to break down again, finally forcing Scott out of football.

Appearances:
FL: 4 apps. 0 gls.
Total: *4 apps. 0 gls.*
Honours:
Scot jnr app.

SCOULAR, James

Role: Right-half 1953-1961
5' 7"
b. Livingston, West Lothian, 11th January 1925

CAREER: Livingston Station/Edinburgh Waverley/Gosport Borough 1943/Portsmouth Dec 1945/UNITED June 1953 £22,250/ Bradford Park Avenue player-manager Jan 1961 £1,300 to May 1964/Cardiff City manager June 1964 to Nov 1973/Aston Villa scout/ Wolverhampton Wanderers scout/Newport County manager Feb 1976 to Jan 1977/ Swansea City scout/UNITED scout occasionally.

Debut v Sunderland (h) 22/8/53

One of the biggest characters of the immediate postwar years, Jimmy Scoular was a daunting midfield player to oppose. He was as tough as they come, but also possessed dainty skills and the expert passing ability to send a perfect 40 yard cross field pass. Respected throughout the game, Jimmy had developed as Portsmouth lifted two titles and he gave the

Jimmy Scoular holds the FA Cup at Wembley in 1955 flanked by, (left to right) Hannah, Smith, Mitchell, Milburn, Casey and Batty.

Fratton Park club grand service in 285 games. Scoular was a fighter, never one to admit defeat, and he joined the black'n'whites for a big fee to replace Joe Harvey as skipper. With the same driving qualities as his noted predecessor, Scoular led United to Wembley in 1955 when he dominated the game against Manchester City and snuffed out the menace of the much vaunted 'Revie Plan'. On that occasion Charlie Buchan recorded, "I have never previously seen a wing-half display as good as that of Scoular's in any big game". Jimmy was a formidable friend and foe; he fell out with individuals along the way, but nobody could argue with his contribution to the game, clocking up over 600 matches. During the war years, Scoular served in the Royal Navy, on HMS Dolphin at Gosport, while his father, Alec appeared for several Scottish clubs. After a fluctuating spell in management, Jimmy was employed by a chemical firm as well as running a guest-house in Cardiff before retiring to live in the South Wales area.

Appearances:
FL: 247 apps. 6 gls.
FAC: 24 apps. 0 gls.
Others: 1 app. 0 gls.
Total: *272 apps. 6 gls.*
Honours:
9 Scot caps 1951-53/
FL champs 1949, 1950/
FAC winner 1955/
FL div 4 prom 1961(m).

Jimmy Scoular

SELLARS, Scott

Role: Midfield 1993-1995
5' 7"
b. Sheffield, 27th November 1965

CAREER: Leeds United sch Dec 1981, app July 1982, pro July 1983/Blackburn Rovers July 1986 £25,000/Leeds United July 1992 £800,000/UNITED Mar 1993 £600,000/ Bolton Wanderers Dec 1995 £750,000.

Debut v Charlton Athletic (h) 10/3/93

Scott Sellars arrived on Tyneside as a replacement for the ageing Kevin Sheedy. With a left foot as sweet as the former Everton midfielder, Sellars had not seen regular first team action for a year, having been unable to break fully into a Leeds side - his second spell at Elland Road - despite a big move from Ewood Park. Slipping into Newcastle's left flank, the Yorkshireman quickly began to show the Geordie crowd his delicate skills which would give United's promotion side balance and vision, and the slightly built Sellars became an influential figure as the black'n'whites entered the Premiership. He was accurate with his passing and always a danger at pulling the ball back for Andy Cole to pounce. A bad cartilage injury though, put Scott out of action for many months, and by the time he was fully fit he had the presence of David Ginola to contend with; he subsequently moved to Burnden Park in search of regular action. During the early part of his career, Sellars was chased by both Sheffield Wednesday and Manchester United as a teenager, and made his Football League debut as a 17 year-old for Leeds. A free-kick expert around the box, Scott appeared in four promotion play-offs with Blackburn, succeeding at Wembley in 1992.

Appearances:
FL/PL: 56(5) apps. 5 gls.
FAC: 3 apps. 0 gls.
FLC: 6(1) apps. 2 gls.
Eur: 4 apps. 1 gl.
Total: *69(6) apps. 8 gls.*
Honours:
3 Eng u21 caps 1988/
FL div 1 champs 1993/
FL div 2 prom 1992.

Scott Sellars

seasons as a goalscoring winger of merit. He linked stylishly with Tom McDonald at first, then with Hughie Gallacher, as the Geordies lifted the FA Cup and the championship three years later, an ever-present in both successes, scoring at Wembley as well as grabbing 18 goals in the title campaign. On the fringe of a full England cap, Seymour did win unofficial honours during a tour of Australia in 1925. His retirement from the Magpies was surrounded in controversy; Stan was in dispute with the club over benefit payments, and thereafter he concentrated on an outfitter's business as well as becoming a journalist in the city. Yet in 1938 with United in a dire situation, he was surprisingly invited to join the board to give the club fresh zest and the benefit of his experience from the playing side. Despite it being quite a rarity in football for a top player to become a director, Seymour began to fashion the next great United line-up. After the war, the Magpies became one of the major attractions in the country and much of the credit was down to Seymour's vision. He was, for many of those successful years during the fifties, manager in all but name. And when the club did have a boss, Seymour continued to be tremendously influential in team affairs. Possessing unrivalled contacts in the game both north

SEYMOUR, George Stanley

Role: Outside-left, Manager & Director
1920-1929, 1938-1978
5' 7"
b. Kelloe, Co Durham, 16th May 1893
d. Newcastle upon Tyne, 24th December 1978

CAREER: UNITED amat c1909/Shildon Town/Coxhoe/Bradford City Sept 1911 £150/Greenock Morton Feb 1913/UNITED May 1920 £2,500/Retired cs 1929/UNITED director June 1938 to Apr 1976, becoming Honorary Manager Sept 1939 to Mar 1947 and Dec 1950 to Dec 1954/Chairman 1954-56/Vice President Apr 1976 to death.

Debut v West Bromwich Albion (h) 28/8/20 (scored once)

One of the most distinguished names in United's history, Stan Seymour was associated with the club for almost 50 years and was known throughout the football community as 'Mr Newcastle'. After being rejected as a teenager by the Magpies, he returned to dominate the outside-left position for eight

Stan Seymour

Stan Seymour

and south of the border, Seymour was a
director who never appeared to be world's
apart from either the players or spectators and
often stood on the terraces to gauge
supporters' opinions. A formidable figure,
Stan could be controversial and frequently had
well-publicised differences with fellow board
members. Seymour ran a sports shop in
Newcastle, while his son, Stan jnr also took the
Chairman's position at St James Park. Another
son, Colin, appeared for United in wartime
football.

Appearances:
FL: 242 apps. 73 gls.
FAC: 24 apps. 11 gls.
Total: *266 apps. 84 gls.*
Honours:
2 unoff Eng caps 1925/
1 unoff war app. 1918/
Eng trial app. 1921-26/
2 FL apps. 1925-28/
1 FL war app. 1918/
FL champs 1927/
FAC winner 1924.

SHACKLETON, Leonard Francis

Role: Inside-left or Inside-right 1946-1948
5' 8"
b. Bradford, 3rd May 1922

CAREER: Kippax United/Horton Banktop(Bradford)/Arsenal amat Aug 1938/London Paper Mills/Enfield/Dartford/Bradford Park Avenue Dec 1940/Huddersfield Town war-guest 1940-45/Bradford City war-guest 1940-42/UNITED Oct 1946 £13,000/Sunderland Feb 1948 £20,050/Retired May 1958 due to injury.

Debut v Newport County (h) 5/10/46 (scored six)

Len Shackleton

Many supporters, as well as ex players, who watched and played with Len Shackleton, consider there has never been a player quite like him before or since. A complete showman who could perform every trick in the book, and many more never seen at all, Shackleton was a truly brilliant inside-forward. Possessing skills galore, Len made a name with his home town club, Bradford. With a tremendous record in wartime football and the immediate peacetime seasons, Shackleton joined United for a record fee after 217 outings and 171 goals for Bradford. And what a debut awaited the Yorkshireman at St James Park; Newcastle won 13-0 to create a Football League record and Shack netted a double hat-trick to make headlines throughout the country. But Len's relationship with Newcastle's management was never to be too fruitful. He only stayed for a season and a half before moving to Roker Park for another record fee. Yet in that time he still became a huge crowd favourite on Tyneside for his playmaking. With Sunderland he bedded in well, staying at Roker Park until

Len Shackleton

retiring through an ankle injury and after totalling 348 senior games, scoring 101 goals. A sorcerer of a player, he at times destroyed opponents with dribbling and passing ability. Yet, like many of his vision and style, often confounded team-mates who were not on his wave-length. He later settled in the region, for many years a sports journalist for the *Daily Express* then *Sunday People*. Once when commenting on his old club at St James Park, Len noted, "I've heard of players selling dummies, but this club keeps buying them"! Shackleton had a way with words, and produced one of the most famous books on the game, his autobiography, *Clown Prince of Soccer*, which had a chapter entitled, "The average director's knowledge of football" - and the page was left blank! On leaving the newspaper world in 1983, Shackleton semi-retired and later resided in Grange-over-Sands. A fine cricketer too, he appeared for Northumberland, and on the soccer field during 1940, played for two different clubs on the same day - for Bradford Park Avenue in the morning, then for Bradford City in the afternoon!

Appearances:
FL: 57 apps. 26 gls.
FAC: 7 apps. 3 gls.
Total: 64 apps. 29 gls.
Honours:
5 Eng caps 1949-55/
1 unoff Eng cap 1946/
1 Eng B cap 1950/
1 FA app. 1946/
Eng schools app. 1936/
1 Eng over 30 app. 1954/
2 FL apps. 1949/
FL div 2 prom 1948.

SHANKLEY, Robert

Role: Inside-forward 1934-1935
5' 6"
b. Douglas, Lanark, 1912

CAREER: Hull City/Rutherglen Glencairn/
UNITED June 1934/Aldershot July 1935
free/Barrow 1936/Clapton Orient 1937 to
1943.

Debut v Nottingham Forest (a) 25/8/34

Developed initially at Hull City by former
United favourite Bill McCracken, Bob
Shankley didn't break fully into the Football
League on Humberside and returned to
Glasgow. But with noted junior club
Rutherglen Glencairn, he impressed United
and was given a second chance in England at
St James Park. Deputising in midfield, on the
right or left of the field, during season 1934-35,
Shankley couldn't gain a regular place but was
a force in the club's Central League line-up.
Bob moved to Aldershot, Barrow and then
Clapton Orient where he gained a place
infrequently, mainly at centre-forward,
appearing on 13 occasions for the Londoners.

> **Appearances:**
> *FL: 6 apps. 0 gls.*
> **Total:** *6 apps. 0 gls.*

SHEEDY, Kevin Mark

Role: Midfield 1992-1993
5' 9"
b. Builth Wells, Wales, 21st October 1959

CAREER: Hereford Lads Club/Hereford
United app 1975, pro Oct 1976/Liverpool June
1978 £80,000/Everton June 1982 £100,000/
UNITED Feb 1992 free to May 1993/Blackpool
June 1993 free to cs 1995/Blackburn Rovers
asst-coach 1995/Tranmere Rovers asst-coach
June 1996.

Debut v Barnsley (h) 22/2/92

After a modest start in the game, by the time
Kevin Sheedy had retired he was recognised
as one of the finest midfield players of the
eighties. Picked up by Liverpool from the
lower divisions, Sheedy had a frustrating
period at Anfield unable to break into their
side. Everton took him across Stanley Park
and very quickly Kevin's career took off. With
a quality left foot, he linked alongside Peter

Reid, Trevor Steven and Paul Bracewell - later
a colleague at Newcastle - in the Blues'
midfield as Everton went through a period of
much glory. Sheedy joined up with Kevin
Keegan at a time when the Magpies needed
his guile and experience. He served Newcastle
well in a short spell, assisting them to steer
clear of relegation then becoming a key figure
as promotion was secured the following
season. With a thundering shot, Sheedy was a
dead-ball expert, and totalled nearly 400
senior games for Everton. Born of an Irish
father and Welsh mother, he was a regular for
the Republic of Ireland side, appearing in the
1990 World Cup finals. Kevin took part in
three FA Cup finals with the Goodison club,
but found himself on the losing side on each
occasion.

> **Appearances:**
> *FL: 36(1) apps. 4 gls.*
> *FAC: 2(1) apps. 1 gls.*
> *FLC: 4 apps. 0 gls.*
> *Others: 4 apps. 1 gl.*
> **Total:** *46(2) apps. 6 gls.*
> **Honours:**
> *45 Eire caps 1984-93/Eire u21 app./*
> *Eire youth app./FL champs 1985, 1987/*
> *FL div 1 champs 1993/FL div 3 champs 1976/*
> *FAC finalist 1985, 1986, 1989/*
> *FLC finalist 1984/ECWC winner 1985.*

Kevin Sheedy

SHEPHERD, Albert

Role: Centre-forward 1908-1914
5' 8"
b. Great Lever, Lancs, 10th September 1885
d. Bolton, 8th November 1929

CAREER: Bolton St Marks/Bolton Temperance/Bolton Wanderers amat/ Blackburn Rovers amat/Bolton Wanderers amat cs 1902/Bolton St Lukes 1902/Bolton Wanderers cs 1904/UNITED Nov 1908 £850/ Bradford City July 1914 £1,500/Retired 1916.

Debut v Nottingham Forest (a) 28/11/08 (scored once)

An unselfish, astute leader of the attack who became noted for his rip-roaring dashes through the middle, Albert Shepherd possessed lightning speed off the mark and a lethal shot. Not a big man for the centre-forward's role, he had a one way to goal approach to the game and following a big transfer to St James Park, very quickly became a crowd hero. An international when he moved to Tyneside, scoring on his England debut, Shepherd for some unknown reason was never a hit with the national side's committee, although Charlie Buchan rated him as the best player in the leader's role before 1925. He was top scorer in the First Division in 1905-06 (26 goals) as well as 1910-11 (25 goals) and arrived at St James Park with an impressive record of 90 goals in 123 senior games for Bolton. Albert continued in that vein for the Magpies until an injury in April 1911 put him on the sidelines for almost two years forcing him to miss that season's FA Cup final. Shepherd recorded the fateful moment in his own words, "I was doing one of my mad rushes, as some people call them, when I collided with the Rovers custodian, and had to be carried from the field". He scored four goals for the Football League in a single match, as well as on five occasions for United, while his home debut for the black'n'whites coincided with the remarkable 1-9 reverse at the

Albert Shepherd

hands of neighbours Sunderland. Shepherd was also a colourful character, often in the news for one reason or another, once agreeing with United's directors that if he netted a hat-trick, he could leave the field early to catch a train - this he duly did in a match against Notts County in 1909! A championship and cup winner for the club, his performance in the 1910 final victory over Barnsley was outstanding, Shepherd netting twice, including the very first penalty in a FA Cup final. After leaving the scene Albert resided in Bolton and became a well known landlord at the Crown & Cushion public-house.

Appearances:
FL: 104 apps. 76 gls.
FAC: 19 apps. 16 gls.
Total: *123 apps. 92 gls.*
Honours:
2 Eng caps 1906-11/Eng trial app. 1911/ 2 FL apps. 1906-11/FL champs 1909/ FL div 2 prom 1905/FAC winner 1910.

SHIEL, John

Role: Centre-forward 1936-1938
5' 11"
b. Seahouses, Northumberland, 13th May 1917

CAREER: Seahouses/UNITED Dec 1936 £10/North Shields May 1938 free/ Huddersfield Town Oct 1938 to July 1939/ Seahouses.

Debut v Barnsley (a) 6/9/37

Jack Shiel began with his home town club of Seahouses in the North Northumberland leagues, but then caught United's attention and was given a chance at professional football. He was at St James Park for less than two seasons and was given only a single opportunity in United's senior eleven, as a stand-in for centre-forward Jack Smith during the 1937-38 campaign. Shiel later had another chance at Football League action, this time at Leeds Road, but again only managed one appearance for Huddersfield. During World War Two, John served on Royal Navy minesweepers, and after leaving football resided in Seahouses running a family fishing boat on the Northumberland coast.

Appearances:
FL: 1 app. 0 gls.
Total: *1 app. 0 gls.*

SHINTON, Robert Thomas

Role: Striker 1980-1982
5' 8"
b. West Bromwich, 6th January 1952

CAREER: Lye Town/Walsall Feb 1972/
Cambridge United Mar 1974 £22,000/
Wrexham July 1976 £15,000/Manchester City
June 1979 £300,000(Millwall loan 1979-80)/
UNITED Mar 1980 £175,000/Millwall loan Jan
1982, pmt Feb 1982/Worcester City player-
manager Aug 1983 free/Weymouth Feb 1985.

Debut v Cambridge United (a) 8/3/80

Bobby Shinton

Bobby Shinton was a slightly-framed striker
who rose to prominence with Wrexham during
seasons 1977-78 and 1978-79; the Welsh club's
historian noted that Shinton had "mesmerised

the opposition" in many of his 175 games for
the Robins. Bobby fired in 56 goals before
heading for Maine Road in a record deal.
However, he never quite lived up to his top
billing when he pulled on Manchester City's
blue shirt alongside international names and
ended up at St James Park with his career in
need of a boost. With Newcastle searching for
a new strike-force combination, Shinton
teamed up with Ray Clarke for the 1980-81
season, but the duo failed miserably, Shinton
ending up top scorer with a mere seven goals,
the lowest total for a season in United's
history. The genial Brummie suffered a medial
ligament injury and moved on soon after, later
setting up his own glazing business in
Worcester, a trade in which Bobby had trained
before turning professional with Walsall.

Appearances:
FL: 41(1) apps. 10 gls.
FAC: 3(1) apps. 0 gls.
FLC: 3 apps. 0 gls.
Total: *47(2) apps. 10 gls.*
Honours:
*FL div 3 champs 1978/WshC winner 1978/
WshC finalist 1979.*

SHOULDER, Alan

Role: Striker 1978-1982
5' 5"
b. Bishop Auckland, 4th February 1953

CAREER: Leeholme jnrs/Bishop Auckland
1972/Blyth Spartans 1977/UNITED Dec 1978
£20,000/Carlisle United June 1982 free/
Hartlepool United June 1985 free/Retired Feb
1988 due to injury/Ferryhill Athletic Dec
1988/Gretna asst-manager/Newcastle Blue
Star coach June 1992/Coundon manager/
Crook Town manager Dec 1993.

Debut v Stoke City (h) 9/12/78

Alan Shoulder was a brilliant short term
purchase by United. Exchanging a career at
Horden pit for the comparative luxury of a
footballer's lifestyle, Alan arrived from non-
league football with Blyth Spartans at the late
age of 25 and his spirited play captured the
hearts of United's crowd. Having become
something of a star name during Spartans'
famous run to the 6th Round FA Cup draw in
1978, Alan was signed by manager Bill
McGarry after relegation from Division One
and successfully partnered Peter Withe for two

Alan Shoulder

SIBLEY, Albert

Role: Outside-right 1947-1950
5' 10"
*b. West Thurrock, nr Grays, Essex,
6th October 1919*

CAREER: Southend United Aug 1937/Arsenal war-guest 1940/Fulham war-guest 1941-42/Tottenham Hotspur war-guest 1941-42/Aldershot war-guest 1941-42/Chelsea war-guest 1941-42/Crystal Palace war-guest 1941-42/Millwall war-guest 1941-42/Queens Park Rangers war-guest 1941-45/UNITED Feb 1947 £6,500 plus E.Brown/Southend United July 1950 £2,000/Retired May 1956.

Debut v Southampton (h) 15/2/47

Known as 'Joe' throughout his football career, Sibley had been a favourite in Essex before heading north to Tyneside. Scoring six goals in 24 games for Southend, Joe had a good track record, but took time to settle at Gallowgate. Jockeying for the outside-right position with Tommy Walker, he had a good run in the side during United's promotion campaign of 1947-48, then was recognised as second choice to Walker. He also was in the treatment room for many weeks due to a succession of knocks.

Described by one pen picture of the day as "purposeful and fast", by the time he had retired from the game his total appearances for Southend had risen to 226. Sibley afterwards resided in the Essex resort.

Appearances:
FL: 31 apps. 6 gls.
FAC: 1 app. 0 gls.
Total:
32 apps. 6 gls.
Honours:
FL div 2
prom 1948.

seasons. A breath of fresh air to United's flagging side, he scored 21 goals in season 1979-80, many through sheer persistence and a lethal shot from the penalty spot. But once his partner had returned to the First Division, Shoulder's influence faded dramatically. On picking up an eye injury, he later returned to local football, assisting several clubs in an equally wholehearted fashion. He entered the family timber business near Bishop Auckland, as well as having an interest in a poultry farm nearby. When at Gretna, Shoulder helped guide the side to the First Round of the FA Cup, the first Scottish club to play in the competition for 100 years.

Appearances:
FL: 99(8) apps. 35 gls.
FAC: 3(1) apps. 1 gl.
FLC: 4(2) apps. 2 gls.
Total:
106(11) apps. 38 gls.

Joe Sibley

SIMM, William

Role: Outside-right 1893-1894
b. Tyneside

CAREER: Newcastle Rangers c1882/
Trafalgar(Newcastle) 1893/UNITED 1893/
Local football 1894/Hebburn Argyle 1900
to 1901.

Debut v Small Heath (h) 28/10/1893

William Simm was a prominent Geordie
player during the earliest years of the sport on
Tyneside. Capped for Northumberland
County, Simm was described by the *Daily
Journal* in 1893 as being "one of the best local
forwards". He had played for Newcastle
Rangers, a pioneer outfit in the city, appearing
in the very first Northumberland Senior Cup
final during the 1883-84 season. At St James
Park for only a short period, he assisted the
club once in Football League action before
returning to local competition. His brother,
Richard Simm was also a distinguished
Tyneside player during the same era.

> **Appearances:**
> *FL: 1 app. 0 gls.*
> **Total:** *1 app. 0 gls.*

SIMPSON, Neil

Neil Simpson

Role: Midfield 1990-1991
5' 10"
b. London, 15th November 1961

CAREER: Middlefield Wasps/Aberdeen 1978/
UNITED July 1990 £100,000/Motherwell
Aug 1991/Cove Rangers player-commercial
manager Aug 1993.

Debut v Port Vale (a) 15/9/90 (sub)

With a robust and competitive style in
midfield, Neil Simpson joined his former
Scotland skipper Roy Aitken at St James Park
in readiness for a promotion assault in season
1990-91. However Neil's stay on Tyneside was
anything but productive; he was dogged by
injury and in the end only made a single
appearance from the kick-off for the Magpies,
and that lasted only 36 minutes. Neil never
showed the rich talent he had displayed in
over 250 games for Aberdeen. With a
determined attitude, Simpson was a
formidable player in Scotland, helping the
Dons to much success including European

glory under Alex Ferguson at Pittodrie.
Although remembered for his battling
powerhouse qualities, he also displayed a
delightful touch on the ball. An Englishman
by birth but brought up near Aberdeen, he is
one of only a few players to have been capped
by the Scots although born over the border.

> **Appearances:**
> *FL: 1(3) apps. 0 gls.*
> *FLC: 0(1) app. 0 gls.*
> **Total:** *1(4) apps. 0 gls.*
> **Honours:**
> *4 Scot caps 1983-88/*
> *11 Scot u21 caps 1982-85/*
> *Scot youth app./*
> *SL champs 1984, 1985/*
> *SC winner 1982, 1983, 1984/*
> *SLC winner 1986/*
> *SLC finalist 1988, 1989/*
> *ECWC winner 1983.*

SIMPSON, Ronald Campbell

Role: Goalkeeper 1951-1960
5' 10"
b. Glasgow, 11th October 1930

CAREER: Queens Park amat June 1945/Third Lanark July 1950/UNITED Feb 1951 £8,750/Hibernian Oct 1960 £2,100/Glasgow Celtic Sept 1964 £3,000/Retired May 1970 due to injury/Glasgow Celtic asst-coach/Hamilton Academical manager Oct 1971 to Sept 1972/St Johnstone asst-coach 1990/Partick Thistle asst-coach 1990/Dunfermline Athletic asst coach.

Debut v Bolton Wanderers (h) 29/8/51

Ronnie Simpson is a player with a quite remarkable career. Making his debut in the senior game when only 14 years 304 days old with Queens Park, he became a noted 'keeper for United during the fifties then, after injury threatened his career, bounced back to win everything on the Scottish scene, as well as the coveted European Cup and a Scotland cap. He was by then 36 years 196 days old, the oldest international debutant for his country. Not a tall or physically imposing goalkeeper, Simpson though possessed cat-like agility with spectacular reflexes which made up for his

small stature. Ronnie took over from Jack Fairbrother between the Magpies' posts for the 1951-52 season and was an automatic choice for seven campaigns, including runs to Wembley in 1952 and 1955. A serious muscle injury finally kept him out of the side, and after many months of treatment it appeared he would hang up his gloves. But Simpson didn't give in and instead moved back to Scotland to start on the second part of his rewarding career. Linking up with Jock Stein, he became a veteran 'keeper at Parkhead as Celtic gathered every trophy they competed for in 1966-67, totalling 188 senior games for the Bhoys. Retiring due to a shoulder injury when over 40, Ronnie then began on a life which took in many occupations from publican in Edinburgh, to local councillor, sports shop owner, as well as specialised goalkeeper coach. In 1972 he became a member of the Pools Panel, a regular attendee at meetings on match-days into the 1990's. His father Jimmy appeared for Rangers and for Scotland, making the Simpsons a rare family international pair. A fine golfer too, Ronnie is a past winner of the Footballers Championship. He resides in Scotland's capital.

Ronnie Simpson

Appearances:
FL: 262 apps. 0 gls.
FAC: 33 apps. 0 gls.
Others: 2 apps. 0 gls.
Total: *297 apps. 0 gls.*
Honours:
5 Scot caps 1967-69/2 Scot B caps 1953-57/
3 Scot amat caps 1950/Scot youth app./
1 SL app. 1969/4 GB amat Olympic app. 1948/
FAC winner 1952, 1955/SL champs 1966,
1967, 1968, 1969/SC winner 1967/
SLC winner 1966, 1967, 1968/
EC winner 1967/Scot Player of the Year 1967.

SINCLAIR, John Evens Wright

Role: Outside-right or left 1967-1969
5' 6"
b. Culross, Fife, 21st July 1943

CAREER: Blairhall Colliery/Dunfermline
Athletic cs 1960/Leicester City May 1965
£25,000/UNITED Dec 1967 £67,500/Sheffield
Wednesday Dec 1969 exch for D.Ford
(Chesterfield loan 1972-73)(Durban(S.Africa)
May 1973 loan)/Stenhousemuir cs 1975 to
cs 1976.

Debut v Nottingham Forest (h) 13/1/68

Jackie Sinclair cost the Magpies a near record
fee when purchased to solve a problem wing
position, and with the hope of giving service
to the menace of Wyn Davies at centre-
forward. Having a good record at Filbert
Street alongside Derek Dougan - 53 goals in
113 matches - Sinclair's pedigree was a good
one, yet the little Scot never quite reached the
heights expected of him and in the final
analysis disappointed many. Possessing killing
pace and a telling shot, though he rarely used
these on Tyneside, Jackie had a good spell in a
black'n'white shirt as the Fairs Cup was
secured in 1969, netting a crucial goal in the
semi-final battle with Rangers. Joe Harvey,
however, exchanged him for David Ford the
following season and Sinclair did well at
Hillsborough (109 games) before returning to
his roots in Fife. He later was employed by the
National Coal Board, residing in Dollar. Jackie
is a nephew of Sunderland's Tommy Wright,
also a Scottish international, while his brother
Willie turned out for Falkirk and Huddersfield
and his cousin, another Tommy Wright also
appeared for Leicester. Sinclair's son Chris was
on Dunfermline's books and took part in the
1991 Scottish League Cup final.

Appearances:
FL: 42(1) apps. 6 gls.
FAC: 1(1) apps. 0 gls.
FLC: 1 app. 1 gl.
Eur: 4(2) apps. 1 gl.
Total: *48(4) apps. 8 gls.*
Honours:
1 Scot cap 1966/ICFC
winner 1969/
SC finalist 1965.

Jackie Sinclair

SINCLAIR, Thomas S.

Role: Goalkeeper 1907-1912
5' 11"
b. Glasgow

CAREER: Rutherglen Glencairn 1900/
Greenock Morton June 1903/Glasgow Rangers
Oct 1904(Glasgow Celtic loan 1906-07)/
UNITED Mar 1907 £375 to May 1912/
Dumbarton Harp Dec 1912/Dunfermline
Athletic Apr 1913/Stevenston United July
1916/Kilmarnock Feb 1917/Stevenston United
Mar 1917/Retired cs 1919.

Debut v Stoke (h) 29/3/07

A fine custodian, Tom
Sinclair was one of
the many deputies
to United stalwart,
Jimmy Lawrence.
Having played in
the 1905 Scottish
Cup final for
Rangers, Sinclair
became one of
the few players
to appear for
both Glasgow
giants when he
helped out Celtic
after their regular
'keeper Davie Adams
had been injured. Tom in
fact never conceded a
goal and won a

Tom Sinclair

Glasgow Cup medal with the green and
whites then made the trip to Tyneside,
United's scouts having been suitably
impressed with his form for the Old Firm.
After helping Celtic to a Scottish League win,
in 1906-07 (6 appearances), Sinclair then made
three appearances for Newcastle
during their title victory in the
same season, but deputised only
rarely thereafter during his six
seasons on the St James Park
staff. Tom later settled in
Glasgow and ran a billiards hall
in the city.

Appearances:
FL: 8 apps. 0 gls.
Total: *8 apps. 0 gls.*
Honours:
SC finalist 1905.

SLOAN, Scott Mark

Role: Forward 1990-1991
5' 10"
b. Wallsend, 14th December 1967

CAREER: Ponteland United/
Berwick Rangers Dec 1989 £1,000/
UNITED July 1990 £65,000/Falkirk
Nov 1991 £50,000(Cambridge
United loan 1993-94)/Hartlepool
United Aug 1994 free to May
1995/Kalmar (Sweden) Feb 1996.

*Debut v Oxford United (a) 13/10/90
(sub)*

Scott Sloan

A United supporter as a lad, Scott
Sloan swopped a career with
Cadbury's to join the professional
staff at St James Park. A part-
timer for Berwick Rangers,
Newcastle had followed Sloan's
progress after he struck 17 goals
in the Scottish League during
season 1989-90. Appearing in
various forward positions for the
Magpies, on the right and left flank especially,
Sloan found the big jump from Berwick to
English Second Division football too much
and never came to terms with the faster pace.
He moved to Brockville Park where he helped
Falkirk to promotion.

Appearances:
FL: 11(5) apps. 1 gl.
FAC: 1 app. 0 gls.
Others: 1 app. 0 gls.
Total: *13(5) apps. 1 gl.*
Honours:
SL div 1 champs 1994.

SMAILES, Andrew

Role: Forward 1919-1922
5' 9"
*b. Radcliffe, nr Amble, Northumberland,
21st May 1895*
d. Shepton Mallet, Somerset, October 1978

CAREER: Blyth Spartans/UNITED Oct 1919
£300/Sheffield Wednesday Oct 1922 £1,500/
Bristol City Oct 1923/Rotherham United Aug
1929, becoming trainer 1934 and manager Aug
1952 to Oct 1958/ Middlesbrough scout/
Scarborough manager Feb 1959 to 1961.

Debut v Sheffield United (a) 6/12/19

Well built and strong, but
very fast too, Andy
Smailes scored goals on a
regular basis throughout
his career. In either the
central or inside roles, he
was direct and possessed
an ever-dangerous first-
time shot. Newcastle
picked Andy up from
Blyth straight after World
War One, and he quickly
became a regular in the
Geordies' attack. He was
first choice during seasons
1919-20 and 1920-21 and
was voted best inside-left in
the country by *Topical Times*
in 1920. Smailes once netted
a hat-trick against
Sunderland, but the
combined arrival of Tom
McDonald and Billy Aitken
pushed him from the
limelight and he moved to
Yorkshire, then to Bristol
where he appeared on 162 occasions for City.
Later joining the Millmoor set-up at
Rotherham, Andy spent 30 years in their
service, guiding the Tykes to their highest ever
position in the Football League in 1954-55.
Related to the famous Milburn and Charlton
footballing dynasty through his wife, Hannah,
Andy lived in Shepton Mallet on retiring.

Appearances:
FL: 73 apps. 30 gls.
FAC: 4 apps. 0 gls.
Total: *77 apps. 30 gls.*
Honours:
FL div 3(S) champs 1927.

*Andy
Smailes*

Tony Smith

SMELLIE, Richard

Role: Centre-forward 1896-1897
5' 10"
b. Scotland

CAREER: Albion Rovers/Nottingham Forest c1894/UNITED cs 1896 to cs 1897.

Debut v Small Heath (a) 5/9/1896

A cool-headed and determined goalpoacher, Dick Smellie spent one terrific season on Tyneside. Replacing Willie Thompson as the club's centre-forward, during his term of action Smellie struck 15 goals and looked to be a brilliant capture. He was noted in the *Newcastle Daily Journal* as a "sturdy athlete", who was "fast, a good shooter, and will be a dangerous opponent". He scored four goals in a single match against Darwen, but by the summer had surprisingly left the Magpies and didn't appear in Football League soccer again. With Forest, Smellie claimed three goals in 17 outings.

> **Appearances:**
> *FL: 26 apps. 15 gls.*
> *FAC: 1 app. 0 gls.*
> **Total:** *27 apps. 15 gls.*

SMITH, Anthony

Role: Defender or Midfield 1975-1979
5' 11"
b. Sunderland, 20th February 1957

CAREER: UNITED July 1975/Peterborough United Mar 1979 joint deal with A.Guy £10,000/Halifax Town Aug 1982 free/ Hartlepool United cs 1984 to May 1989/ Newcastle Blue Star.

Debut v Wolverhampton Wanderers (a) 12/11/77 (sub)

Tony Smith was introduced into Newcastle's line-up during the Magpies' relegation season in 1977-78, a year the club used a record number of players. A past England Under-19 schoolboys' captain, Smith was tall and dark, and a powerful and composed defender in Central League football. He wasn't given a long run in the senior side, although he was on the bench for the UEFA Cup contest with Bastia. Tony drifted into the lower divisions where he made over 400 appearances for the Peterborough, Halifax and Hartlepool. On leaving the scene, Smith returned to the north east and was employed at the Nissan complex in Sunderland.

> **Appearances:**
> *FL: 1(1) app. 0 gls.*
> *Others: 1 app. 0 gls.*
> **Total:** *2(1) apps. 0 gls.*
> **Honours:**
> *Eng youth app.*

SMITH, David

Role: Outside-right 1935-1936
5' 7"
b. South Shields, 12th October 1915

CAREER: Middle Docks/Reyrolles/UNITED Oct 1935 £35/South Shields May 1936/ Glasgow Rangers war-guest/Derby County war-guest 1942-43/Northampton Town war-guest 1943, pmt cs 1945, becoming secretary 1951 and manager July 1954/ Aldershot manager July 1959, becoming secretary-general manager Mar 1967 to 1972.

Debut v Burnley (h) 8/2/36

Newcastle United were impressed with Dave Smith's appearances as an amateur playing for the Reyrolles works side on Tyneside. He was

Dave Smith

given a trial in the Magpies' reserve eleven and helped to secure six goal victories in each of his two games. A stand-in for Wilf Bott during the Second Division programme of 1935-36, Smith was granted only a single game in senior company, and was out of action due to injury for 12 months. Dave was, though, a permanent fixture with Northampton. He played for the Cobblers over 150 times before moving into the managerial side of the game.

Appearances:
FL: 1 app. 0 gls.
Total: *1 app. 0 gls.*

Jack Smith

SMITH, Jack

Role: Centre-forward 1934-1938
5' 11"
b. Batley, Yorkshire, 17th February 1915

CAREER: Whitehall Printers(Leeds)/ Dewsbury Moor Welfare/ Huddersfield Town amat June 1932, pro Oct 1932/UNITED Sept 1934 £2,500/ Manchester United Feb 1938 £6,500/ Burnley war-guest/Blackburn Rovers Mar 1946 £3,000/Port Vale May 1947 to cs 1948/Macclesfield Town.

Debut v Plymouth Argyle (a) 22/9/34 (scored once)

An astute piece of transfer business was recorded by Newcastle United when Jack Smith arrived at St James Park for a modest £2,500. Purchased as a 19 year-old, he was immediately plunged into the Second Division fray and showed an energetic and goal hungry ambition. He scored the winning goal on his debut, then netted another 14 times in the next 20 games to establish himself as a new hero. He totalled 16 goals in his first season, then another 26 and 24 in subsequent programmes. Smith was quick off the mark and could use both feet to hit shots with power and once scored four in a single match against Doncaster. By the time he moved into the First Division after signing for promotion-bound Manchester United, Jack had a 65% goals per game strike-rate level; only Ferdinand, Cole, Gallacher and Shepherd in the Magpies' history can better that. His transfer was not taken kindly by the United faithful and there was much uproar at the time. At Old Trafford, Smith did not hit the net with the same authority, striking only 15 goals in 42 matches before war called a halt to his career.

Appearances:
FL: 104 apps. 69 gls.
FAC: 8 apps. 4 gls.
Total: *112 apps. 73 gls.*
Honours:
2 Eng schools apps. 1929/ FL div 2 prom 1938.

SMITH, James

Role: Midfield 1969-1976
5' 11"
b. Glasgow, 20th January 1947

CAREER: Benburb jnrs/Aberdeen 1965/
UNITED July 1969 £80,000(Glasgow Celtic
loan 1975-76)/Retired due to injury July
1976/Whitley Bay Aug 1976 briefly.

Debut v Sheffield Wednesday (a) 20/8/69 (sub)

A master craftsman, 'Jinky' Jimmy Smith
could send the crowd into raptures when he
was in the mood, and infuriate his manager
when not. The Scot had a languid, lazy style
but also a tantalising right foot featuring the
piece de resistance of the Smith 'nutmeg',
(slipping the ball through his opponents' legs),
a showpiece which was the talk of Tyneside.
Making a name for himself at Pittodrie, Jimmy
played on 140 occasions (37
goals) before moving to
Tyneside for what was
reported as a £100,000 deal,
the first six-figure fee paid by
United. However, details
indicate the transfer was
much less, with only add-ons
increasing the overall
amount. At 22 years-old and
already capped by Scotland,
Smith took time to adapt to
the different English game,
but by season 1971-72 had
settled and become the
darling of the fans, able to hit
a match-winning pass with
the most delicate through-
balls and chips. Missing a
year with a cartilage injury,
on his return he enjoyed two
and a half seasons displaying
many magical performances
before another knee
complaint put him on the
sidelines. And after new
manager Gordon Lee had
sent the Scot on loan to
Parkhead, his knee failed
again and Smith was forced
to halt his career. Jinky was
once sent-off in a Texaco Cup
fixture against Birmingham
after only 53 seconds in
December 1973, one of the

fastest dismissals of all time. At St James Park
in 1978 Jimmy had a testimonial which
attracted a crowd of 17,428. He later went into
a trophy business in Newcastle, but it failed
controversially, and he also went through a
disturbing period with a betting addiction. A
hero to a generation of supporters, including
Peter Beardsley, Smith lives on Tyneside and
was a taxi driver for a spell. His brother Joe,
also turned out for Aberdeen.

Appearances:
FL: 124(5) apps. 13 gls.
FAC: 14(1) apps. 0 gls.
FLC: 9(1) apps. 0 gls.
Eur: 5 apps. 0 gls.
Others: 18(2) apps. 3 gls.
Total: *170(9) apps. 16 gls.*
Honours:
*4 Scot caps 1968-74/1 Scot u23 cap 1967/
Scot jnr app./1 SL app. 1968/
FAC finalist 1974/SC finalist 1967.*

'Jinky' Jimmy Smith

SMITH, John

Role: Forward 1894-1896
5' 9"
b. Ayrshire
d. Newcastle upon Tyne,
3rd February 1911

CAREER: Kilmarnock cs
1885/Newcastle East
End 1887/Kilmarnock 1887 to June 1888/
Sunderland Aug 1889/Liverpool May 1893/
Sheffield Wednesday 1893/UNITED cs 1894
to 1896.

Debut v Darwen (a) 1/9/1894

A well known and popular early player in the
north east, 'Jock' Smith served United's
pioneers, East End before moving into the
Football League with Sunderland, Liverpool
and Sheffield Wednesday. Tricky and
hardworking, he returned to Tyneside for the
1894-95 season as an experienced campaigner
and was used as a utility player; he appeared
in every forward position for the club, as well
as at right-half during that season. He left the
following year and later became a licensee in
Byker. On the news of his sudden death due to
illness, the Magpies gave his widow a benefit
match at St James Park. On Wearside, Smith
helped Sunderland to the league title.

Appearances:
FL: 25 apps. 10 gls.
FAC: 2 apps. 0 gls.
Total: *27 apps. 10 gls.*
Honours:
FL champs 1892.

SMITH, Thomas

Role: Centre-half 1941-1952
5' 11"
b. Horden, County Durham, 2nd February 1923
d. Durham, 31st March 1993

CAREER: Horden Colliery Welfare/UNITED
Mar 1941/Annfield Plain Aug 1952 free,
becoming trainer and manager/Horden
Colliery Welfare manager 1956 to 1957.

Debut v Barnsley (h) 5/1/46 (FAC)

Although at Gallowgate for over a decade,
'Tot' Smith only managed ten senior games,
seven of which were in season 1946-47. The
purchase of Scottish international Frank

Brennan saw Smith as his deputy and chances
were few and far between due to his rival's
consistency. Nevertheless, Smith was a good
defender who skippered United's side to the
Central League championship in 1948, the
only occasion the black'n'whites have lifted the
reserve title. In wartime football Smith was a
regular and only Albert Stubbins played more
for the club during those years. During his
footballing days at Newcastle, Tot had an
artificial cartilage inserted into his knee, one of
the first operations of its kind at the time. He
played at both Luton and Wolves briefly, on
trial, before joining United. Smith had two
other brothers in the game, George and
Robert, who both also signed for the Magpies
in World War Two. On leaving local football,
Smith ran a betting shop near Durham.

Appearances:
FL: 8 apps. 0 gls.
FAC: 2 apps. 0 gls.
War: 145 apps. 0 gls.
Total: *155 apps. 0 gls.*

SMITH, William

Role: Inside-left 1898-1899
5' 9"
b. Scotland, 1873

CAREER: Hibernian
c1893/UNITED Feb
1898 to 1899.

Debut v Luton Town (a)
19/2/1898

William Smith was signed in time for United's
promotion run-in during season 1897-98, and
the noted Scot had a major say in the outcome
of the season. With lots of experience playing
north of the border, taking part in Hibs' first
league season and ending as top scorer in
1895-96, Smith fitted in well and netted six
important goals in his 19 outings, including
two strikes in Test Matches which decided the
club's elevation to the First Division. *The Daily
Journal* commented in 1898 that he could
"dribble past several opponents in a
meritorious style", although he carried a hefty
frame, and was described as a, "heavyweight". Smith remained on Tyneside for part
of the following season, running out for the
inaugural fixture in Division One, but then
was replaced by the talent of Willie Wardrope.
He took part in the Scottish Cup final of 1896

at Logie Green in Edinburgh, the game with Hearts being the first, and only, final to be played outside Glasgow.

Appearances:
FL: 19 apps. 6 gls.
Total: *19 apps. 6 gls.*
Honours:
SC finalist 1896.

SORLEY, Jock

Role: Inside-left or Centre-forward 1892-1893
5' 10"
b. Scotland

CAREER:
Newmilns/Newcastle East End Jan 1891/UNITED May 1892/Middlesbrough 1893/Blackburn Rovers Sept 1893/Burton Swifts May 1895/Hebburn Argyle 1896 to 1899.

Debut v Sheffield United (a) 24/9/1892 (NL) (scored once)

Jock Sorley was a prominent member of the Newcastle East End club, both at their previous home of Chillingham Road, and when they moved to St James Park. Described in the *Daily Chronicle* as as being "popular amongst the followers of football during his residence in Newcastle", when he left the club he was awarded "a handsome gold medal". Captain for a period, Jock took part in United's first game at St James Park and their inaugural Football League match, scoring too, and only left the region becaue of a financial crisis at St James Park; Sorley wouldn't take a reduction in wages and moved to further his career on Teesside. When on form, few defenders could cope with his darting runs and eye for goal. Later returning to Tyneside, Jock assisted Hebburn Argyle to the Northern Alliance title in 1897 netting 30 goals. He once scored five goals for Newcastle in a friendly against West Bromwich Albion during 1893.

Appearances:
NL: 8 apps. 8 gls.
FL: 1 app. 1 gl.
FAC: 1 app. 0 gls.
Total: *10 apps. 9 gls.*

SOULSBY, John

Role: Centre-forward 1914-1919
5' 10"
b. Tyneside

CAREER: Rodsley(Gateshead)/UNITED cs 1914/Blyth Spartans 1919/Ashington cs 1922 to c1924.

Debut v Middlesbrough (h) 10/3/15

John Soulsby

A rival to Bob Pailor and Tom Hall for the leader's role at Gallowgate, John Soulsby was spotted scoring goals for Rodsley and given a contract with the Magpies. The First World War put a stop to his progress, and he joined up with the Light Infantry, serving as a corporal in the trenches in France. He didn't gain a chance once peace was restored although moving to Ashington, Soulsby helped in the Portland Park club's Football League days. He totalled 32 league appearances for Northumberland's other black'n'whites from the inside-right or outside-right positions.

Appearances:
FL: 1 app. 0 gls.
Total: *1 app. 0 gls.*

SOYE, James

Role: Inside-left 1906-1909
5' 8"
b. Govan, Glasgow, 14th April 1885

CAREER: Rutherglen Glencairn/Belfast Celtic/Hibernian on trial/Distillery/Southampton cs 1905/UNITED May 1906/Aberdeen May 1909 exch deal for W.Low/Non-league Scottish football 1919.

Debut v Everton (h) 15/9/06

An electrical engineer by trade, Jimmy Soye appeared at centre-forward and in both inside channels for United, including a single appearance as a deputy for Bill Appleyard in the title winning season of 1906-07. Always considered a reserve at St James Park, Soye

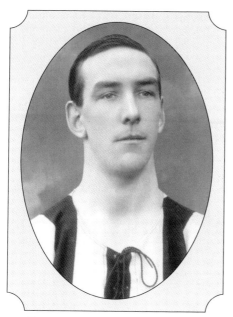

Jimmy Soye

found a regular place with the Dons, moving north as part of the deal that brought Wilf Low to Tyneside. In Scotland he developed into a potent outside-left, with flair and the habit of scoring spectacular goals. Totalling 201 senior matches for Aberdeen over six seasons, he netted on 25 occasions reaching the fringe of the Scotland side.

Appearances:
FL: 7 apps. 2 gls.
Total: *7 apps. 2 gls.*
Honours:
1 SL app. 1912.

SPEEDIE, Finlay Ballantyne

Role: Inside-left 1906-1908
5' 9"
b. Dumbarton, 18th August 1880
d. Dumbarton, 5th February 1953

CAREER: Artizan Thistle(Dumbarton)/ Clydebank jnrs/Dumbarton 1897/Glasgow Rangers Oct 1900/UNITED Sept 1906 £600/ Oldham Athletic June 1908 joint deal with W.Appleyard/Bradford Park Avenue Apr 1909/Dumbarton Sept 1909 to 1920, later becoming trainer in 1933.

Debut v Sheffield Wednesday (h) 29/9/06 (scored twice)

Although Finlay Speedie usually operated at inside-left, he appeared in all areas of the field for United; in defence, midfield and in attack. Used as the club's utility man, Speedie was a distinguished player having won several Scottish honours at Ibrox, including netting two goals in the 1904 cup final. He was cool, assured and steady, apparently able to cruise through a match with supreme nonchalance, yet still be a star performer. Only at St James Park for two seasons, Speedie became a crowd favourite after scoring twice on his debut, but was allowed to leave when the club had a mini rebuilding period in the summer of 1908. Scoring on his debut for Scotland as well, Finlay served with the Argyll & Sutherland Highlanders during World War One and was wounded during battle, being awarded the Military Medal. A witty and buoyant character, Speedie came from a footballing family; his brother Willie, and nephew, also Finlay, both played for Dumbarton too.

Appearances:
FL: 52 apps. 13 gls.
FAC: 7 apps. 1 gl.
Others: 1 app. 0 gls.
Total: *60 apps. 14 gls.*
Honours:
3 Scot caps 1903/1 unoff Scot app. 1903/ Scot trial app. 1903/1 SL app. 1905/ FL champs 1907/FAC finalist 1908/ SL champs 1901, 1902/SL div 2 champs 1911/SC winner 1903/SC finalist 1904, 1905.

Finlay Speedie

SPENCER, Charles William

Role: Centre-half 1921-1928
5' 11"
b. Washington, 4th December 1899
d. York, 9th February 1953

CAREER: Glebe Rovers(Washington) 1915/ Washington Chemicals 1919/UNITED Oct 1921/Manchester United July 1928 £3,250/ Tunbridge Wells Rangers player-manager May 1930/Wigan Athletic player-manager Aug 1932/Grimsby Town manager Mar 1937 to Apr 1951/Hastings United manager 1951/ York City manager Nov 1952 to his demise.

Debut v Bolton Wanderers (h) 11/3/22

During his early days at St James Park, Charlie Spencer was a creative half-back. However, on the advent of the stopper centre-half role following the offside rule change in 1925, he was converted to a commanding defender, arguably the first exponent of the new tactic. Never showy, but consistent at his game, Charlie was a player's player, colleague Stan Seymour once noting that he was "a

magnificent clubman". With a temperament for the big occasion, auburn-haired Spencer was a solid performer in both the Magpies' FA Cup and title victories during the twenties decade. He was described as "lithe and graceful", reaching the England set-up at his peak in 1925 and captaining the Football League eleven two years later. Entering management, Charlie was a respected boss, but was dogged by illness. He started as a goalkeeper with colliery side, Glebe Rovers, and during World War One served in the Royal Engineers Signals.

Appearances:
FL: 161 apps. 1 gl.
FAC: 14 apps. 0 gls.
Total: *175 apps. 1 gl.*
Honours:
2 Eng caps 1924-25/
5 unoff Eng app. 1925/
Eng trial app. 1926/
2 FL apps. 1926-28/
FL champs 1927/
FAC winner 1924.

SPINK, James

Role: Right-half 1913-1919
5' 8"
b. Dipton, nr Consett, County Durham

CAREER: Craghead United/UNITED Mar 1913/Hartlepools United 1919 to c1921.

Debut v West Bromwich Albion (h) 17/1/14

Youngster Jimmy Spink emerged in the seasons prior to the Great War and promised much. A rival to Bob Hewison in midfield, Spink made excellent progress and earned a rapid elevation to Newcastle's Division One side, selected on 15 occasions in season 1914-15. Having a good and sure touch on the ball, Jimmy was destined for a bright future until war clouds put a stop to football at the end of that programme. With the Durham Light Infantry during the hostilities, Spink later appeared for Hartlepool during their North Eastern League days just before their entry into the Football League in 1921. His brother Tom appeared for Fulham.

Appearances:
FL: 20 apps. 0 gls.
FAC: 4 apps. 0 gls.
Total: *24 apps. 0 gls.*

Charlie Spencer

SRNICEK, Pavel

Role: Goalkeeper 1990-date
6' 2"
*b. Bohumin, nr Ostrava, Czechoslovakia,
10th March 1968*

CAREER: Victoria Bohumin Jnrs(Czech)/ZD
Bohumin(Czech)/Dukla Tabor(Czech) 1986/
Dukla Prague(Czech) 1987/Banik Ostrava
(Czech)/Leicester City trial Oct 1990/
UNITED trial Dec 1990, pmt Jan 1991
£350,000.

Debut v Sheffield Wednesday (h) 17/4/91

A former Eastern Block soldier, Pavel
Srnicek's arrival on Tyneside in 1990
co-incided with some of the poorest
Newcastle performances on record as
the Magpies struggled in Division
Two. The tall goalkeeper could speak
little English at first, and had a torrid
early period in Newcastle's side.
However, Pavel was determined to
succeed. He gradually settled in the
north east, learnt the language and
improved his all round goalkeeping
skills immensely, especially at
collecting crosses safely. His progress
was such that when Kevin Keegan
took over the reigns at Gallowgate,
Srnicek claimed the Number One
shirt, even although Mike Hooper
was soon purchased as a first choice.
Acrobatic and with exceptional shot-
stopping ability, Pavel earned
something of a cult following with
United's Toon Army; the Czech
making a series of spectacular saves
as United lifted the First Division
championship then embarked on a
bid for the Premier title. One such
stop against Everton in which he
twisted in mid-air prompted Gordon
Banks to note that it was in his "all
time top ten great saves". Srnicek
holds a French passport and was
Ludo Miklosko's deputy in the Banik
team in Czechoslovakia. Pavel
followed the path of Miklosko to
England, and into his country's side
too, being a member of the successful
Euro '96 squad in England. In June
1992, Srnicek had trials with Marseille
when he was in dispute with United
over payments.

Appearances:
*FL/PL: 125(1) apps. 0 gls.
FAC: 11 apps. 0 gls.
FLC: 9(1) apps. 0 gls.
Eur: 4 apps. 0 gls.
Others: 6 apps. 0 gls.*
Total: *155(2) apps. 0 gls.*
Honours:
*4 Czech Republic caps 1994-date/
3 Czech u21 caps/FL div 1 champs 1993.*

STARLING, Ronald William

Role: Inside-forward 1930-1932
5' 9"
b. Pelaw, Gateshead, 11th October 1909
d. Sheffield, 17th December 1991

CAREER: Washington Colliery/Hull City amat 1925, pro 1927/UNITED May 1930 £3,750/Sheffield Wednesday June 1932 £3,250/Aston Villa Jan 1937 £7,500/Walsall war-guest 1939-42/Nottingham Forest war-guest 1939-42/Northampton Town war-guest 1939-40/Sheffield Wednesday war-guest 1940-41/Nottingham Forest trainer July 1948 to June 1950.

Debut v Sheffield Wednesday (a) 30/8/30

Tragically United's directors allowed the talented Ron Starling to slip through their fingers and become a huge star elsewhere. Rejected firstly as a youngster by Newcastle, he was developed initially by Bill McCracken at Hull and then sold to the Magpies. Possessing all the midfield skills to become a

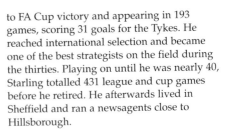

schemer of outstanding ability, he replaced Tom McDonald and became a regular for season 1930-31, but the emergence of Jimmy Richardson and Harry McMenemy persuaded United's directors to let the mercurial, wavy-haired Starling move on. An inside-forward of many tricks, one biography noted he was a "ball playing genius". Ron could captivate the crowd with his artistry, but on occasion would over-elaborate and frustrate many. At Villa Park and Hillsborough he was a big favourite, captaining the Owls

Ron Starling

to FA Cup victory and appearing in 193 games, scoring 31 goals for the Tykes. He reached international selection and became one of the best strategists on the field during the thirties. Playing on until he was nearly 40, Starling totalled 431 league and cup games before he retired. He afterwards lived in Sheffield and ran a newsagents close to Hillsborough.

Appearances:
FL: 51 apps. 8 gls.
FAC: 2 apps. 0 gls.
Total: *53 apps. 8 gls.*
Honours:
2 Eng caps 1933-37/Eng trial app. 1933/
FL div 2 champs 1938/
FL war(N) champs 1944/FAC winner 1935.

STENHOUSE, Henry

Role: Outside-right 1902-1905
5' 7"
b. Blyth, Northumberland

CAREER: Blyth Spartans/UNITED May 1902/Ashington 1905/Blyth Spartans late 1905.

Debut v Aston Villa (a) 29/11/02

Harry Stenhouse became the first Blyth Spartans player to turn out in the Football League. Joining United as a direct winger who possessed a big reputation in local football, he had a cracking shot and, following a series of good displays in the club's Northern League side, was elevated to the first team in place of Willie Stewart. His debut, however was not a memorable afternoon. United lost 7-0 to Villa, for a period the club's heaviest defeat.

Appearances:
FL: 6 apps. 0 gls.
Total: *6 apps. 0 gls.*

STEPHENSON, Paul

Role: Outside-right 1984-1988
5' 10"
b. Wallsend, 2nd January 1968

CAREER: St Marys Boys Club/UNITED app 1984, pro Dec 1985/Millwall Nov 1988 £300,000(Gillingham loan 1992-93)/Brentford Mar 1993 £30,000/York City Aug 1995 £35,000.

Debut v Southampton (h) 14/12/85

Paul Stephenson

STEVENSON, James

Role: Inside-right 1898-1900
5' 8"
b. Paisley, 1876

CAREER: Clyde 1894/Derby County Jan 1895/UNITED Oct 1898 £225/Bristol City cs 1900/ Clyde cs 1901/Grimsby Town Sept 1901/Leicester Fosse Jan 1902/Clyde Oct 1902 £27.

Debut v Liverpool (h) 5/11/1898

Jimmy Stevenson was a raider who possessed plenty of craft and ball control. With Derby County, he played alongside Steve Bloomer and enjoyed a good record as a marksman with the Rams, scoring 31 goals in 73 league games. He appeared in the 1898 FA Cup final before United made a bid to sign the diminutive Scot. Noted as a master dribbler, he was, as one contemporary report claimed, "a wizard with the leather". After a good season for the black'n'whites in 1898-99, United's first in the top league, he was unlucky with injury at St James Park and was superceded by the emergence of Alex Gardner. Stevenson almost gained a Scotland cap on several occasions, but had to be content with trial games. James later went into business in Glasgow.

A youth international, Paul Stephenson made his debut for the Magpies as a 17 year-old and almost capped a sparkling display with a goal, only for his headlining effort to be controversially chalked off by the referee. With pace and skill, the Geordie appeared to be heading in the right direction for stardom, but following two seasons as a new face on the First Division scene during 1985-86 and 1986-87, Stephenson lost his momentum and place in the side. Moving to London, he had a useful stay at The Den, providing service for the combination of Sheringham and Cascarino to feed off. Paul's father played for Gateshead.

Appearances:
FL: 58(3) apps. 1 gl.
FAC: 2 apps. 0 gls.
FLC: 3(1) apps. 0 gls.
Others: 3(1) apps. 0 gls.
Total: *66(5) apps. 1 gl.*
Honours:
Eng youth app. 1986.

Appearances:
FL: 33 apps.
12 gls.
FAC: 4 apps. 1 gl.
Total:
37 apps. 13 gls.
Honours:
Scot trial
1897-1903/
FAC finalist 1898.

Jimmy Stevenson

STEWART, Ian Edwin

Role: Outside-left 1985-1987
5' 7"
b. Belfast, 10th September 1961

CAREER: Queens Park Rangers May 1980
(Millwall loan 1982-83)/UNITED Aug 1985
£150,000/Portsmouth Dec 1987(Brentford loan
1987-88)/Leicester City trial Dec 1988/
Aldershot Jan 1989/Colchester United 1992/
Harrow Borough Nov 1992.

Debut v Luton Town (h) 21/8/85

Early impressions at St James Park of Ian
Stewart's talent were most favourable. With
control and a clever, but direct style, the
Irishman, who had impressed with his
performances in 82 games for Rangers, looked

a good purchase by
manager Willie
McFaul. Stewart
could provide a
dangerous cross
and was able on
occasion to hit a
powerful shot. But
by the time of his
last outing for
United, during
season 1986-87, he
had been labelled
with the
inconsistent tag.
Taking part in the
1986 World Cup
finals, Ian never
fulfilled his
potential after

Ian Stewart

bright openings for QPR, United and Northern
Ireland - hitting a stunning goal against West
Germany during an early international
appearance. Once he left Tyneside Stewart's
career declined, and he rarely showed the skill
that had taken him almost to the top.

Appearances:
FL: 34(8) apps. 3 gls.
FAC: 2(1) apps. 0 gls.
FLC: 4(1) apps. 0 gls.
Total: *40(10) apps. 3 gls.*
Honours:
31 N.Irel caps 1982-87/
N.Irel schools app./
N.Irel youth app./
FL div 2 champs 1983.

STEWART, James

Role: Inside-left or right 1908-1913
5' 9"
b. Gateshead, 1883
d. 23rd May 1957

CAREER: Todds Nook(Newcastle)/
Gateshead NER/Sheffield Wednesday May
1902/UNITED Aug 1908 £1,000/Glasgow
Rangers Sept 1913 £600/North Shields
Athletic player-manager May 1914.

Debut v Bradford City (h) 2/9/08

Known as 'Tadger' from his early days in
local Tyneside football, Jimmy Stewart
delighted many fans during his career
with a repertoire of delicate skills and an
ability to regularly hit the back of the net.
Another of United's many international
stars of the Edwardian era, Stewart
returned to his area of birth after a
rewarding period at Hillsborough. In 141
games for Sheffield Wednesday he scored

59 goals, including a run to FA Cup glory in which he bagged vital strikes in both the semi and final rounds. That form earned Jimmy an England cap and a big move back to Tyneside. Replacing Ronald Orr in United's ranks, Stewart operated in both schemers' positions as well as at centre-forward. Winning title honours with the Magpies, he missed the 1910 final but played in the showpiece a year later. The local favourite though, did have his differences with United's hierarchy, and was once suspended indefinitely for using bad language to the club's officials. On retiring from the game, Stewart resided in Gateshead and was employed as a commercial traveller.

Appearances:
FL: 121 apps. 49 gls.
FAC: 17 apps. 4 gls.
Total: *138 apps. 53 gls.*
Honours:
3 Eng caps 1907-11/
Eng trial app. 1907-11/
4 FL apps. 1910-11/
FL champs 1904, 1909/
FAC winner 1907/
FAC finalist 1911.

Jimmy 'Tadger' Stewart (left) enjoying a game of billiards with team mate Albert Shepherd early this century.

STEWART, Thomas

Role: Right-back 1896-1898
5' 10"
b. Lanarkshire

CAREER: Motherwell/ UNITED Dec 1896 joint deal with J.Ostler £200/ Grimsby Town cs 1898 to 1899.

Debut v Grimsby Town (a) 26/12/1896

Stout defender Tom Stewart came into United's side half way through the 1896-97 campaign. Hard and physical with little finesse, Stewart was described in the *Newcastle Daily Journal* as a "full-back with excellent credentials" who "tackled with resolution and coolness, and kicked with great power and judgement". Despite this glowing report though, he was replaced by Billy Lindsay as Newcastle embarked on their final push for promotion during the following season. With Grimsby, Tom played on only one occasion.

Appearances:
FL: 27 apps. 0 gls.
FAC: 3 apps. 0 gls.
Total: *30 apps. 0 gls.*
Honours:
FL div 2 prom 1898.

STEWART, William Graham

Role: Outside-right 1901-1903
5' 8"
b. Glasgow, 29th February 1876

CAREER: Third Lanark/Queens Park
1897/UNITED June 1901 to cs 1903.

Debut v Stoke (h) 14/9/01

Forward Willie Stewart boasted a first class reputation in Scotland, capped by his country and a cup finalist in 1900. An amateur, he had played alongside Bob McColl in the Queens Park eleven and was a fine, athletic-

Willie Stewart

looking player who combined admirably with his team-mates for a season at St James Park. An automatic choice in United's ranks during 1901-02, he was left out of the side for patches during the following campaign and was eventually replaced by Turner and Rutherford. Thinning on top, Willie had an excellent turn of speed and possessed ability to cut in or go outside his full-back.

Appearances:
FL: 37 apps. 4 gls.
FAC: 4 apps. 1 gl.
Total: *41 apps. 5 gls.*
Honours:
2 Scot caps 1898-1900/SC finalist 1900.

STIMSON, Mark Nicholas

Role: Left-back 1989-1992
5' 11"
b. Plaistow, London, 27th December 1967

CAREER: Orient sch/Queens Park Rangers sch/Tottenham Hotspur app July 1984, pro July 1985(Orient loan 1987-88)(Gillingham loan 1988-89)/UNITED May 1989 £150,000/ Portsmouth loan Dec 1992, pmt July 1993 £95,000(Barnet loan 1995-96)/ Southend United Mar 1996 £25,000.

Debut v Leicester City (a) 26/8/89

Blond-haired Mark Stimson was unheard of by most United supporters when Jim Smith signed him from Spurs. An attacking full-back, Stimson claimed the left-back role for three seasons as the Magpies strove hard to get out of the Second Division. A resilient character, he had his highs and lows at Gallowgate, both chastised and hailed by the fans. As a schoolboy, Mark was offered opportunities by six London clubs before choosing White Hart Lane, but found that manager Terry Venables would never give him a run in the first team despite being on the bench several times. Possessing a good shot and turn of pace, he followed Jim Smith to Fratton Park and made over 50 appearances for Pompey.

Appearances:
FL: 84(4) apps. 2 gls.
FAC: 7 apps. 1 gl.
FLC: 5 apps. 0 gls.
Others: 4 apps. 0 gls.
Total: *100(4) apps. 3 gls.*

Mark Stimson

STOBBART, George Campbell

Role: Forward 1946-1949
5' 7"

b. Pegswood, Northumberland, 9th January 1921
d. Newcastle upon Tyne, 3rd January 1995

CAREER: Netherton jnrs/Middlesbrough May 1939/North Shields war-guest/Darlington war-guest 1943-44/UNITED Sept 1946 £4,650/ Luton Town Oct 1949 £11,000/Millwall Aug 1952/Brentford Sept 1954 to 1956.

Debut v Coventry City (h) 11/9/46 (scored twice)

George Stobbart

Versatile in any forward position, George Stobbart was a valuable member of United's promotion side in 1947-48 netting several crucial goals in the finale to the season. Strong and stocky, George was a tremendous grafter up front, and had good pace over a 20 or 30 yard chase for the ball. Scoring plenty of goals for Middlesbrough during, and just after, the war, 121 in total, Newcastle paid what was a big fee for his all-round ability. George had an eventful start for the Magpies, netting twice on his debut, but picked up an ankle injury which kept him on the sidelines for a few weeks. When he moved to Kenilworth Road, Stobbart became Luton's most expensive signing and once scored four goals in an eight-minute burst for the Hatters against Blackburn in 1949. On leaving the game, he resided in the Forest Hall district of Newcastle to his death.

Appearances:
FL: 66 apps. 21 gls.
FAC: 6 apps. 1 gl.
Total: *72 apps. 22 gls.*
Honours:
FL div 2 prom 1948.

STOKOE, Robert

Role: Centre-half 1947-1961
6' 0"

b. Mickley, nr Gateshead, 21st September 1930

CAREER: Wylam Boys' Brigade 1944/ Army Cadets 1945/Spen jnrs 1946/ UNITED Sept 1947 £10/Bury Feb 1961 cash-exch deal for J.McGrath, becoming player-manager Dec 1961/Charlton Athletic manager Aug 1965/Leyton Orient asst-coach 1967/Rochdale manager Oct 1967/Carlisle United manager Oct 1968/ Blackpool manager Dec 1970/Sunderland manager Nov 1972 to Oct 1976/Bury manager Nov 1977/Blackpool manager May 1978 to Aug 1979/Carlisle United scout/Rochdale Nov 1979/Carlisle United manager Sept 1980 to Aug 1985, returning in Oct 1985 to May 1986/Sunderland caretaker-manager Apr to June 1987, becoming consultant to May 1989/UNITED occasional asst-coach June 1989/Bury part-time asst-coach 1991/Chelsea scout cs 1991/Swindon Town scout Dec 1993 to cs 1994/Bury consultant to May 1996.

Debut v Middlesbrough (a) 25/12/50
(scored once)

Although Bob Stokoe made his first appearance for United in the Number 9 shirt, when he found the net, he was first and foremost a half-back who liked to attack, but who found it difficult to break into the side in his favoured role. Featuring as a utility defender during the first four seasons of the fifties decade, he was 12th man at Wembley in 1951. With the club for almost 14 years, Stokoe was often frustrated at his lack of opportunities during the first half of his Magpie career, and made several transfer requests. But Bob eventually claimed the centre-half position in season 1954-55 and at last gained the regular role he aspired to. Stokoe was outstanding at the centre of the back line as Newcastle lifted the FA Cup that year, becoming a sound and dependable back line anchor for the next five seasons. Determined in the tackle and good in distribution, Stokoe skippered the side on many occasions during that period and when he left to start a long career in management at Bury, Stokoe had served the club with distinction. One of only a handful of men to have played in a winning FA Cup team, then manage a side to victory - with Sunderland in 1973 - Stokoe became one of the modern game's most travelled managers, and most respected. Yet he never got the opportunity to be boss of the Magpies, despite being linked with the job several times. He resided in Carlisle until the summer of 1991 when he moved to Lancashire, although in 1996 he returned to his native north east to live in Hexham.

Bob Stokoe challenges for a high ball at St James Park. He spent almost 14 years at Gallowgate.

Appearances:
FL: 261 apps. 4 gls.
FAC: 26 apps. 1 gl.
Others: 1 app. 0 gls.
Total: *288 apps. 5 gls.*
Honours:
FAC winner 1955, 1973(m)/
FL div 3 champs 1961/
FL div 2 prom 1976(m)/
FL div 3 prom 1982(m)/
FL Long Service Medal 1984.

STOTT, James

Role: Left-half 1895-1899
5' 10"
b. Middlesbrough, 1871
d. Gosforth,
Newcastle upon Tyne,
8th October 1908

CAREER: South Bank/
Middlesbrough c1891/Liverpool
Aug 1893/Grimsby Town June 1894/
UNITED June 1895 £15/Middlesbrough
Sept 1899 to 1900.

Debut v Loughborough Town (h) 7/9/1895

Appointed captain of Newcastle United
shortly after arriving on Tyneside, Jimmy Stott
was an inspiring half-back. Clever and swift,
he was a good all rounder, and especially,
afraid of no man in the tackle. Stott could be
tough as they come, and was censored by the
club board in 1896 for "continual fouling of his
opponents"! Part of Liverpool's first promotion
line-up, he repeated the feat at St James Park,
one of the stalwarts in that successful 1897-98
season. Said to be something of a snappy
dresser, he often wore a top-hat on Sundays
and on leaving football became a popular
publican at The Star Hotel on Westgate Road.
Stott died in Newcastle Lunatic Asylum, the
sad victim of a brain tumour.

Appearances:
FL: 117 apps. 9 gls.
FAC: 14 apps. 2 gls.
Total: *131 apps. 11 gls.*
Honours:
FL div 2 champs 1894/
FL div 2 prom 1898.

STUBBINS, Albert

Role: Centre-forward 1936-1946
5' 11"
b. Wallsend, 13th July 1919

CAREER: Sunderland amat 1935/Whitley &
Monkseaton 1935/UNITED amat Mar 1936,
pro Apr 1937/Sunderland war-guest 1941-42/
Liverpool Sept 1946 £12,500/Ashington Sept
1953/Retired 1954/Liverpool scout 1954-60/
New York Americans (USA) coach 1960,
returning to Tyneside in the same year.

Debut v Luton Town (a) 7/5/38

A legendary figure of the game, red haired
Albert Stubbins was brought up in the States
as a youngster, moving in 1923 to New York
and later Detroit. He returned to the north
east though, and developed into a promising
inside forward. Joining United, Albert was
quick to gain a first team opportunity and
by season 1938-39 such was his progress
that pundits championed him for an
England place. Tall and forceful, he would
run at defenders, and scare them to death
with his ability, possessing frightening pace
and a mighty shot from his size 11 boots.
Yet Stubbins was most unfortunate to be
poised on the brink of stardom when war
intervened. Remaining in the area on
essential work in local shipyards as a
draughtsman, Albert made the best of a
raw deal by becoming the country's most
potent goalscorer. Stubbins bagged goals

Albert Stubbins

by the hatful. He scored over 230 goals for the Magpies in seven seasons; 42 in 1942-43, and 43 each in season 1943-44 and 1944-45. Included in these figures were 29 hat-tricks, and Albert once netted five in a single match. Defenders had no answer and by the time peace was restored and football was back to normal in 1946, Stubbins was a big name, capped by England and the Football League, later netting five times against the Irish League in 1950. He then decided a move would be in his best interests, and a record sale to Liverpool was arranged. At Anfield Stubbins again became a legendary figure, winning title and cup honours with the Reds. Albert scored more goals, 83 in 180 games, before leaving the first class game. Once nicknamed "The Smiling Assassin", Stubbins was a gentleman of the game. He is featured on The Beatles' famous album cover, *Sergeant Pepper's Lonely Hearts Club Band*, while he has also been honoured at the House of Commons. Afterwards Albert returned to Tyneside, becoming a well known journalist for *The People*, as well as a local radio broadcaster, to his retirement in 1984. Stubbins resides in Wideopen on the outskirts of Newcastle.

Alan Suddick

Appearances:
FL: 27 apps. 5 gls.
FAC: 3 apps. 1 gl.
War: 188 apps. 231 gls.
Total: *218 apps. 237 gls.*
Honours:
1 unoff Eng cap 1946/
1 Eng war cap 1941/
2 FA apps. 1947/
4 FL apps. 1947-51/
FL champs 1947/
FAC finalist 1950/
WrC finalist 1942.

SUDDICK, Alan

Role: Forward 1961-1966
5' 11"
b. Chester-le-Street, Co Durham, 2nd May 1944

CAREER: Chester Old Boys/UNITED Oct 1961/Blackpool Dec 1966 £63,000/Stoke City Dec 1976/Bury Oct 1977(Southport loan 1977-78)/Barrow Sept 1978/Lancaster City Nov 1979/Blackpool Apr 1982/Workington 1984/Runcorn Apr 1985/Morecambe/ Blackpool Wren Rovers 1994.

Debut v Charlton Athletic (h) 7/10/61

Introduced as a 17 year-old teenager during season 1961-62, one of the club's youngest-ever players, Alan Suddick became the golden boy of St James Park. During his opening games in a black'n'white shirt, Suddick ran the show as the Magpies won 4-1, 7-2 and 5-0. Manager Joe Harvey saw in Suddick's special talent a player with a top class international future, but alas in the end he did not to reach that lofty pinnacle. Suddick was versatile across the forward-line, appearing in the Number 7, 8 or 11 shirt, but always with freedom to roam up front and display his ball talents and stunning shooting ability. An entrancing player when in the mood, he was cheeky, yet erratic. Suddick had a huge terrace following, often inspiring headlines, but was an enigma to boss Harvey, who agonisingly couldn't get the best from his genius. Sold to raise funds at a time of relegation crisis, Alan's departure to Blackpool caused a huge outcry. He remained at Bloomfield Road for a decade and was equally popular, registering 348 games (76 goals) for the Seasiders. His two sons, Jarryd and Fraser, both played local north east football, while Alan had a succession of occupations after retiring from the game; he ran a hotel, was a retailer and later became a decorator.

Appearances:
FL: 144 apps. 41 gls.
FAC: 4 apps. 1 gl.
FLC: 4 apps. 1 gl.
Total: *152 apps. 43 gls.*
Honours:
2 Eng u23 caps 1963/Eng youth app. 1962/ FL div 2 champs 1965/FL div 2 prom 1970/ FAYC winner 1962.

SUGGETT, Colin

Role: Midfield & Coach 1978-1994
5' 8"
b. Washington, 30th December 1948

CAREER: Sunderland app 1964, pro Jan 1966/West Bromwich Albion July 1969 £100,000/Norwich City Feb 1973 £75,000/ UNITED Aug 1978 £60,000 to June 1981, becoming asst-coach/coach Sept 1985/ caretaker-manager Oct to Dec 1988/asst-coach Dec 1988 to Feb 1994/Bolton Wanderers scout 1994/Berwick Rangers scout and local coach 1994/Ipswich Town director of youth Mar 1995.

Debut v West Ham United (h) 23/8/78

Colin Suggett

The first north east player to be transferred for a six figure sum, Colin Suggett began his career as a striker with lightning speed and reflexes around the box. He had good positional sense and very quickly became a teenage star at Roker Park, making 98 appearances and scoring 25 goals, before his move to the Midlands. At the Hawthorns, Colin switched roles to become a midfielder, without losing the knack of putting the ball in the net. He was highly efficient in more than 100 outings for the Baggies before settling at Carrow Road where he became a firm favourite. Suggett was their Player of the Year in 1974-75, totalled 243 games and had an eventful time with Norwich, experiencing both relegation and promotion, while he also reached Wembley. Bill McGarry brought him back to his native region when United were in need of experience and solidity after the turmoil of relegation in 1978. Suggett though, was past his best and an ankle ligament injury towards the end of the 1978-79 season ended his career. Always keen to work with youngsters, he moved into the coaching side of the game. At Gallowgate for over ten years in that capacity, although he was in charge of first-team affairs for a while, Colin saw his kids win the FA Youth Cup in 1985 and players like Gascoigne, Howey, Clark and

Watson all develop into international talent. Leaving the club after a dispute over policy with Kevin Keegan, Suggett took up a similar appointment with Ipswich Town.

Appearances:
FL: 20(3) apps. 0 gls.
FLC: 1 app. 0 gls.
Total: *21(3) apps. 0 gls.*
Honours:
Eng schools app. 1964/
Eng youth app. 1965-67/
FL div 2 prom 1975/
FLC finalist 1970, 1975/
FAYC winner 1966, 1967.

SWAN, Christopher Samuel

Role: Inside-forward 1919-1923
5' 8"
b. Byker, Newcastle upon Tyne, 4th December 1900
d. Bournemouth, 1979

CAREER: Tyneside jnrs/UNITED May 1919/ Stockport County cs 1923 free/Hull City Aug 1925/Crystal Palace May 1929 to 1931/ Scarborough 1932.

Debut v Burnley (a) 2/4/20

Chris Swan

Bright schools product Chris Swan reached his country's international side before the close-down due to the First World War. He was given a contract at St James Park on the resumption of soccer, but struggled to claim a first team opportunity, being restricted to three games during April 1920 and one single outing two seasons later. Swan appeared in both inside-forward roles for United as well as outside-right and later had a fine stay with Hull City, claiming almost 100 senior games for the Humberside club.

Appearances:
FL: 4 apps. 0 gls.
Total: *4 apps. 0 gls.*
Honours:
2 Eng schools apps. 1915.

SWEENEY, Paul Martin

Role: Left-back 1989-1990
5' 8"
b. Glasgow, 10th January 1965

CAREER: St Kentigerns/Tynecastle Boys Club/Raith Rovers 1981/UNITED Mar 1989 £100,000/St Johnstone Mar 1990 £100,000/ Gateshead July 1993 free/Hartlepool United Aug 1994/Gateshead Sept 1994/Durham City Dec 1994/Morpeth Town 1995, becoming coach 1996/South Shields Sept 1996.

Debut v Southampton (a) 1/4/89 (sub)

Paul Sweeney

With a fiery style, flame-haired Glaswegian Paul Sweeney landed on Tyneside as an unknown although he had proved to be a tenacious and noted defender in the hustle and bustle of lower division Scottish football. He was given the backing of the fans at St James Park due to his all-action determination and 100% attitude, but Sweeney lacked the finer skills, a factor which manifested itself when in better quality company. Surviving a nasty car crash when on United's books, the Scot later suffered a bad knee injury which put him out of action for many weeks. Nicknamed 'Toddy' by his colleagues, as a part-timer in Scotland, Sweeney totalled almost 200 games for Raith.

Appearances:
FL: 28(8) apps. 0 gls.
FAC: 3 apps. 0 gls.
FLC: 2(1) apps. 0 gls.
Others: 2 apps. 0 gls.
Total: *35(9) apps. 0 gls.*
Honours:
Scot youth app./SL div 2 prom 1987.

SWINBURNE, Thomas Anderson

Role: Goalkeeper 1934-1947
5' 9"
b. East Rainton, Co Durham, 9th August 1915
d. Durham City, 1969

CAREER: East Rainton/Hull City briefly/
Herrington Colliery/UNITED Apr 1934/
Grimsby Town war-guest 1940-41/Notts
County war-guest 1940-41/Bolton Wanderers
war-guest 1941-42/Rochdale war-guest
1941-42/Southport war-guest 1941-42/
Consett June 1947 free/Horden CW Sept 1951.

Debut v Blackpool (h) 12/9/34

Tom Swinburne

Tom Swinburne
appeared for the
black'n'whites both
before and after
World War Two,
during an era when
the Magpies had
three or even four
professional
goalkeepers chasing
for the Number One
jersey. A pipe-
smoking goalkeeper,
he had as rivals
for the position
Tapken, McPhillips and Theaker before
the war, then Garbutt, Theaker and
Fairbrother after the fighting had ended.
He was a sound and trusty guardian at
times, although it was noted he
could lose the occasional soft
goal, while he also had
problems with repeated finger
dislocations. Serving with the
RAF during the war years,
Tom was capped by England
during the hostilities. His two
sons also played football
between the posts, Alan for
Oldham, and Trevor for Carlisle;
both attempted careers at St
James Park in the sixties.

Appearances:
FL: 77 apps. 0 gls.
FAC: 7 apps. 0 gls.
War: 51 apps. 0 gls.
Total: 135 apps. 0 gls.
Honours:
1 Eng war cap 1940.

TAIT, Alexander

Role:
Centre-forward
1952-1960
5' 11"
b. West Sleekburn, nr Bedlington,
Northumberland, 28th November 1933

CAREER: UNITED Sept 1952/Bristol City
June 1960 £5,000/Doncaster Rovers June
1964/Burton Albion cs 1965, later becoming
manager.

Debut v Everton (h) 11/4/55

Red haired, skilful and full of dash, Alex Tait
was a bright teenage star who chose to become
a part-time professional at St James Park when
training to become a teacher. The first north
east player to appear for the England youth
side, Tait netted four goals in a 6-0 victory
over Wales in March 1952. Making his debut
in season 1954-55, Tait had a few outings the
following campaign then really made a big
impression in 1956-57. Given a mini-run in
place of Vic Keeble, he displayed first class
anticipation around the penalty area and
always gave tenacious displays which
thrilled the Gallowgate crowd. Also
operating on the right wing, he scored
a well remembered hat-trick for the
Magpies in a derby match with
Sunderland during 1956 and much was
expected of this new find. Yet Tait was
to drift from the scene, although
he became a great favourite at
Ashton Gate. Totalling 136
games and scoring 44 goals
for Bristol City, Alex
concluded his career in non-
league football with Burton
Albion. Residing in Tutbury,
Tait became a teacher in the
Trentside town. He was also
for a spell Loughborough
College sports coach.

Appearances:
FL: 32 apps. 8 gls.
FAC: 2 apps. 2 gls.
Total: 34 apps. 10 gls.
Honours:
Eng youth app. 1952.

Alex Tait

TAPKEN, Norman H.

Role: Goalkeeper 1933-1938, 1942-1943
5' 10"
b. Wallsend, 21st February 1914
d. June 1996

CAREER: Wallsend Thermal Welfare/
UNITED May 1933 £25/Manchester United
Dec 1938 £850/Sunderland war-guest
1942-43/UNITED war-guest 1942-43/
Darlington war-guest 1943-46/Aldershot
war-guest 1944-45/Brighton war-guest
1944-45/Chester war-guest 1944-45/
Darlington Apr 1947/Shelbourne 1948 to
1949/Stoke City asst-trainer July 1952 to c1960.

Debut v Bradford City (h) 17/11/34

Although not a spectacular goalkeeper,
Norman Tapken was a safe and confident
teamster to have as the last line of defence. His
judgement and anticipation were good and he
took over from Micky Burns for the 1934-
35 season at St James Park. Newcastle's
first choice 'keeper for three years, as a
schoolboy he had been a black'n'white
fan who fulfilled an ambition of
playing for the Magpies, this after an
early injury had threatened his career.
Losing his place to Tom Swinburne,
Tapken was later at Old Trafford
(16 apps.), then crossed the
Irish Sea to appear in the
Republic with
Shelbourne, a short but
rewarding stay which
brought him plenty of
honours in Ireland.
Apart from reaching
the cup final,
Norman also helped
win the Republic's
Shield and Leinster
Cup in 1949.

Appearances:
FL: 106 apps. 0 gls.
FAC: 7 apps. 0 gls.
War: 9 apps. 0 gls.
Total: *122 apps. 0 gls.*
Honours:
2 EL apps. 1949/Eire
Cup finalist 1949.

TATE, Isaac Holliday

Role: Goalkeeper 1923-1927
5' 7"
b. Gateshead, 28th July 1906

CAREER: Marley Hill/UNITED Aug 1923 £5/
West Ham United May 1927 free/Doncaster
Rovers cs 1929, becoming asst-trainer
Sept 1935.

Debut v West Ham United (h) 17/9/24

Isaac Tate became the youngest goalkeeper in
the Football League when he was plunged
into United's side during season 1924-25. At 18
years old he stood in for the injured Bill
Bradley when rival Alex Mutch was also on
the sidelines. Known as 'Ike' to his colleagues,
he did well against West Ham United, but
only managed a handful of games for the club
thereafter. Despite his small build, the
Hammers' directors had been suitably
impressed and promptly signed the
Tynesider. At Upton Park, Tate
became a deputy to international
goalkeeper Ted Hufton appearing
on only 14 occasions for the
Londoners. Returning north
with Doncaster he gained first
team soccer, helping Rovers to a
Third Division title success in
1935. All told Isaac
made 135 outings for
the Yorkshiremen.

Appearances:
FL: 4 apps. 0 gls.
Total: *4 apps. 0 gls.*
Honours:
FL div 3(N) champs
1935.

Norman Tapken

TAYLOR, Allan

Role: Goalkeeper 1925-1926
5' 11"
b. North Shields, 1st December 1905
d. North Tyneside, 1981

CAREER: North Shields/UNITED cs
1925/South Shields cs 1926/Tottenham
Hotspur July 1929/Hartlepools United May
1937/Retired cs 1938.

Debut v Notts County (h) 5/9/25

A rival to Isaac Tate for the reserve 'keeper's position at St James Park, Allan Taylor was another Tynesider who had a teenage baptism for the Magpies and, like Tate, couldn't break into the senior side fully. Standing in only once for first choice Willie Wilson in season 1925-26, Taylor moved to South Shields where he became a regular at Horsley Hill during their days as a Football League force, including a spell in the Second Division. Joining Spurs after a trial, Allan remained in North London for eight years claiming 69 league and cup appearances. He later returned to his native Tyneside and resided in North Shields.

Appearances:
FL: 1 app. 0 gls.
Total: *1 app. 0 gls.*

TAYLOR, Colin

Role: Outside-left 1963-64
5' 8"
b. Stourbridge, 24th August 1940

CAREER: Stourbridge/Walsall
Feb 1958/UNITED May 1963
£20,000/Walsall Oct 1964 £10,000/
Crystal Palace May 1968/Walsall
Sept 1969/Kidderminster Harriers
cs 1973.

Debut v Derby County (h) 24/8/63
(scored once)

A ginger haired, thick-set winger, Colin Taylor will be remembered for his deadly left-foot. Known as 'Cannonball' for the power of his shooting, he had a reputation as a goalscorer, netting 33 league strikes for Walsall in season 1960-61. Taylor took over from Jimmy

Colin Taylor

Fell in United's ranks and for a season appeared a good purchase, but during the opening weeks of the 1964-65 programme manager Joe Harvey allowed the bustling player to return to the Midlands in a surprise move. Pulling on Walsall's shirt once more, Taylor became a noted servant at Fellows Park, and by the end of his career had totalled almost 500 senior games. He also continued to bag plenty of goals, more than 200, holding the Saddlers' aggregate goals record with 184 league strikes. On retiring from the game, Colin resided in the Midlands becoming a decorator for a period and later a brewery representative. His brother Brian also appeared for Walsall as well as Shrewsbury and Rotherham.

Appearances:
FL: 33 apps. 7 gls.
FAC: 3 apps. 0 gls.
Total: *36 apps. 7 gls.*
Honours:
FL div 4 champs 1960/FL div 3 prom 1961/FL div 2 prom 1969.

Colin Taylor (right) trains with Ollie Burton & Gordon Marshall

TAYLOR, Ernest

Role: Inside-forward 1942-1951
5' 4"
b. Sunderland, 2nd September 1925
d. Birkenhead, 9th April 1985

CAREER: Hylton Colliery jnrs/UNITED Sept
1942 £10/Plymouth Argyle war-guest
1945-46/Blackpool Oct 1951 £25,000/
Manchester United Feb 1958 £6,000/
Sunderland Dec 1958 £6,000/Altrincham
Sept 1961/Derry City Nov 1961/
Retired Feb 1962/New Brighton
(New Zealand) coach Feb 1964/Later, Heswall
(Cheshire) consultant/Also had a spell with
Carlshalton Athletic.

Debut v Barnsley (a) 9/1/46 (FAC)

Known as the 'Tom Thumb' of football during
the fifties, Ernie Taylor was barely 10 stones
and at only 5' 4" was a titch among giants on
the football field. Wearing only size 4 boots,
Taylor though had the skill and the eye for a
telling pass that made him one of the most
productive schemers in the country. A
submariner during the hostilities, he was one
of Stan Seymour's bright hopefuls as war
ended in 1945. Taylor only figured in a
handful of games when the Magpies won
promotion in 1948, but was given a place for
the club's rebirth in the First Division. For
three seasons he was an influential member of
the side that attempted to lift the
championship trophy. And in season 1950-51
Ernie had his best term with the
black'n'whites, reaching Wembley and setting
up a marvellous Jackie Milburn goal with a
gloriously deft back-heel. But after the joy of
FA Cup sucess, Taylor's ability was largely
overlooked. Often the player to drop out if the
team did badly, many supporters were
perplexed when he was sold to Blackpool for
a large fee. Teaming up with Mortensen and
Matthews, Taylor showed off
all the talents Newcastle had let
go. Totalling 242 games for
Blackpool, he reached Wembley
again with the Seasiders, then
amazingly did it for a third
time when with Manchester
United, signed by the Old
Trafford club after the fateful
Munich crash in 1958. Ernie
deservedly won an England
call-up too, and was frequently
among the goals as well,
netting almost 100 in his career.
On returning from a period in
New Zealand, Taylor later
settled on Merseyside,
employed at the Vauxhall car
plant at Hooton. His brother
Eddie appeared for Willington
in the 1950 FA Amateur Cup
final.

Ernie Taylor

Appearances:
FL: 107 apps. 19 gls.
FAC: 10 apps. 2 gls.
War: 26 apps. 7 gls.
Total: *143 apps. 28 gls.*
Honours:
1 Eng cap 1954/
1 Eng B cap 1956/
1 unoff Eng app. 1957/
FAC winner 1951, 1953/
FAC finalist 1958.

TAYLOR, John Henry

Role: Outside-right 1952-1960
5' 7"
b. Crawcrook, nr Gateshead, 6th October 1935

CAREER: Crawcrook/UNITED Nov 1952
(Fulham loan 1956-57 & 1957-58)/Chelmsford
City June 1960 free/Cambridge United 1962.

Debut v Sheffield United (a) 1/1/55

Harry Taylor was on United's books for seven
seasons after arriving from junior football on
south Tyneside with Crawcrook. His career at
Gallowgate started as a deputy to Len White,
but was interrupted by a spell in London
when on National Service. Joining Fulham on
loan, Taylor made 28 appearances for the
Cottagers before returning to Tyneside. And in
the following season he had his best year in a
Magpie jersey. Taylor claimed 16 outings on
the wing during 1958-59 when a rival to
Gordon Hughes for the Number 7 shirt.
However, in the final reckoning he lost out to
Hughes for the position and moved to non-
league football in the south, joining up with
another former Newcastle reserve, Jimmy
Gibson. Taylor later returned to the area, being
employed by Newcastle Breweries. He is an
uncle to Howard Kendall, of Preston, Everton
and Sheffield United.

> **Appearances:**
> *FL: 28 apps. 5 gls.*
> *FAC: 1 app. 0 gls.*
> **Total:** *29 apps. 5 gls.*

Harry Taylor

TEMPLETON, Robert Bryson

Role: Outside-left 1903-1904
5' 9"
b. Coylton, nr Ayr, 22nd June 1879
d. Kilmarnock, 2nd November 1919

CAREER: Irvine Heatherbell/Westmount/
Kilmarnock Roslin 1896/Neilston Victoria/
Kilmarnock (rugby) 1896/Hibernian Apr
1898/Aston Villa Mar 1899 £250/UNITED Feb
1903 £400/Woolwich Arsenal Dec 1904
£375/Glasgow Celtic May 1906 £250/
Kilmarnock Oct 1907/Fulham July 1913 £50/
Kilmarnock Apr 1915/Retired May 1915.

Debut v Liverpool (a) 7/3/03

One of the biggest
characters in the
game before the
Great War, Bobby
Templeton became
a legend on and
off the field,
mesmerising
defenders, as well
as spectators, with
his play down the
wing. Tall and
handsome, he also
became a
fashionable
Edwardian dandy,
often in the news
with his extrovert
antics, once in
1908 entering a
lion's cage at a

Bobby Templeton

circus and placing his head inside the beast's
mouth! But first and foremost, Templeton was
a football artiste. He could be a matchwinner
when in the mood, the type of skilful
entertainer who could make the ball talk.
Often inconsistent though, Bobby still
delighted the Tyneside crowd over three
seasons and on his day was dazzling. William
Pickford wrote in 1905: "To watch Templeton
at his best is a sight for the gods, to watch him
at his worst was to see at a glance the frailty of
things human". After appearing in ten games
of United's 1905 title season, Bobby moved on,
always finding it hard to remain at one club
for long. United's fans were not happy,
especially when his replacement, Bert Gosnell,
possessed a style in direct contrast to the Scot's
flamboyant showmanship. Scoring on his

Scotland debut, it is thought that the terrible Ibrox disaster of 1902 was indirectly attributable to the crowd's swaying to watch one of Templeton's weaving dribbles. Later a publican in Kilmarnock, Bobby died of heart failure following the fierce epidemic of influenza that hit the whole country at the end of World War One. He was also the footballers' billiards champion when on Tyneside, along with team-mate Bill Appleyard.

Appearances:
FL: 51 apps. 4 gls.
FAC: 1 app. 1 gl.
Total: 52 apps. 5 gls.
Honours:
11 Scot caps 1902-13/
1 unoff Scot app. 1902/
Scot trial app. 1900-12/
Scot jnr app./
3 SL apps. 1910-11/
FL champs 1900, 1905/
SL champs 1907/
SC winner 1907.

THAIN, John William

Role: Outside-right 1921-1922
5' 9"
b. Pelaw, Gateshead, 1903

CAREER: Pelaw jnrs/UNITED Nov 1921 £10/Brentford cs 1922 free/Peterborough & Fletton United 1923/Grimsby Town May 1924 to 1925.

Debut v Aston Villa (h) 17/12/21

Young forward John Thain found claiming a place in United's side immediately after World War One extremely difficult. He deputised only once, for Jimmy Low during season 1921-22 and played all his other football for the club in the North Eastern League. Thain did resurrect his career when he joined Grimsby Town after a spell in non-league football. He made 26 appearances for the Mariners in season 1924-25.

Appearances:
FL: 1 app. 0 gls.
Total: 1 app. 0 gls.

Cam Theaker

THEAKER, Clarence Alfred

Role: Goalkeeper 1938-1947
6' 0"
b. Spalding, Lincolnshire, 8th December 1912
d. Hartlepool, 7th February 1992

CAREER: Spalding Town/ Grimsby Town May 1934/ UNITED Nov 1938 £1,250/ Darlington war-guest 1939-40/ Lincoln City war-guest 1942-43/ Hartlepools United June 1947 to 1948.

Debut v Cardiff City (a) 21/1/39 (FAC)

Known as 'Cam' during his career, Theaker was signed by United to rival Tom Swinburne at St James Park just before the outbreak of World War Two. A reserve fixture at Blundell Park, he turned out in 15 games for Newcastle before war put a halt to first class soccer. He continued between the posts for the club during wartime football and returned to the fold for the resumption of Football League action in 1946-47. Tom Swinburne though was selected ahead of him and Theaker was transferred to Hartlepool where he concluded a career ravaged by war. He later resided in the Durham coastal town to his death.

Appearances:
FL: 13 apps. 0 gls.
FAC: 3 apps. 0 gls.
War: 65 apps. 0 gls.
Total: 81 apps. 0 gls.

THOMAS, Andrew Mark

Role: Midfield 1986-1988
6' 0"
b. Eynsham, nr Oxford, 16th December 1962

CAREER: Oxford United app 1978, pro Dec 1980(Fulham loan 1982-83)(Derby County loan 1982-83)/UNITED Sept 1986 £100,000/ Bradford City June 1988 £80,000/Plymouth Argyle July 1989 £80,000/Retired due to injury 1991/Thame United 1992/Oxford City cs 1993, becoming manager.

Debut v Wimbledon (h) 20/9/86

A midfielder with a reputation for scoring goals, Andy Thomas became a noted player with Oxford, totalling 150 league and cup games claiming 45 goals as the Headington club became a force during the 1980s. But a broken leg in 1984 hindered his progress and by the time United made a move to bring him to Tyneside, Andy was ready for a new challenge. Tall and slimly built, he operated just behind a front duo for Newcastle and in his first season, 1986-87, looked very effective at times. He scored seven goals that year in United's First Division eleven, but the following season Thomas did not figure in manager Willie McFaul's plans and he moved to Bradford City at the end of the campaign. Forced to retire from the first class scene due to a back injury when at Home Park, Thomas returned to his native Oxfordshire where he served Oxford City, reaching the FA Vase final at Wembley. He works for a printing company.

Andy Thomas

Appearances:
FL: 24(7) apps. 6 gls.
FAC: 3 apps. 1 gl.
FLC: 1 app. 0 gls.
Others: 1 app. 2 gls.
Total: *29(7) apps. 9 gls.*
Honours:
FL div 3 champs 1984/FLC winner 1986(sub)/FAV finalist 1995.

THOMAS, Barrie Ernest

Role: Centre-forward 1962-1964
5' 10"
b. Measham, Leicestershire, 19th May 1937

CAREER: Measham Imperial/Leicester City July 1954/Mansfield Town June 1957 free/Scunthorpe United Sept 1959 £20,000/UNITED Jan 1962 £45,000/Scunthorpe United Nov 1964 £20,000/Barnsley Nov 1966/Retired due to injury cs 1968/Measham Swifts manager 1968.

Debut v Huddersfield Town (h) 20/1/62

A formidable goalscorer, Barrie Thomas netted over 250 goals in his career, boasting a tremendous strike ratio of goals per games. Thomas was a natural goalpoacher, no great artist with the ball, but a hearty leader who tore into defences. After being jettisoned by Leicester following a teenage debut in the First Division, he developed a scoring habit with Scunthorpe and cost United a record fee when he moved to the north east. Although Barrie was often in and out of the treatment room at St James Park, he still managed to hit the net on a regular basis and only a handful of other centre-forwards in United's history claim a better strike-rate than his 65%. Sometimes erratic in front of goal, he was nevertheless selected for the full England squad training session at Lilleshall in 1962, only for injury to prevent his appearance. After hitting the net on 21 occasions in season 1963-64, Thomas was surprisingly released to rejoin Scunthorpe as United embarked on their promotion

Barrie Thomas

winning programme the following year. At the Old Show Ground he grabbed more goals, scoring five in a single game against Luton in 1965. Barrie holds Scunthorpe's goals record for a season, 31 in 1961-62. Retiring due to a knee injury, Thomas resided in the Barnsley area running a transport business before moving to Netherseal near Burton on Trent.

Appearances:
FL: 73 apps. 48 gls.
FAC: 2 apps. 1 gl.
FLC: 3 apps. 1 gl.
Total: *78 apps. 50 gls.*
Honours:
Eng youth app. 1955/
FL div 4 prom 1968.

THOMAS, John William

Role: Inside-right 1911-1912
5' 9"
b. Sacriston, County Durham, 1891

CAREER: Spennymoor United/Brighton cs 1910/UNITED June 1911 £25/Spennymoor United May 1912.

Debut v Manchester City (a) 27/1/12

At United's Gallowgate headquarters for only the 1911-12 season, Jack Thomas played once for the first eleven, stepping in when the Magpies' forward-line was disrupted due to injury. A rival to Tommy Lowes in the battle to deputise for United's international first teamers, the local press noted when he moved back to the region that "He has the reputation of being very speedy". However, John made little impression at St James Park and moved

to North Eastern League football with Spennymoor on the conclusion of that season's programme. A teenager at The Goldstone, Thomas suffered from ill health and only managed a single appearance for Brighton.

Appearances:
FL: 1 app. 0 gls.
Total: *1 app. 0 gls.*

THOMAS, Martin Richard

Role: Goalkeeper 1983-1988
6' 1"
*b. Senghenydd, nr Pontypridd,
28th November 1959*

CAREER: Bristol Rovers app, pro Sept 1977(Cardiff City loan 1982-83)(Tottenham Hotspur loan 1982-83)(Southend United loan 1982-83)/UNITED loan Mar 1983, pmt July 1983 £50,000(Middlesbrough loan 1984-85)/Birmingham City loan Oct 1988, pmt Nov 1988(Aston Villa loan 1992-93)(Crystal Palace loan 1992-93)/ left Birmingham City June 1993 free/ Cheltenham Town 1994/Later becoming a specialised goalkeeping coach for Birmingham City, Norwich City, Swindon Town and the FA at Lilleshall.

Debut v Barnsley (a) 4/5/83

Established as a goalkeeper of quality with Bristol Rovers, Martin Thomas made almost 200 appearances for the Eastville club before losing his place due to a badly dislocated finger that kept him out of action for almost a year. Tall and positive, Thomas then went on a series of loan deals which eventually earned him a contract at St James Park. As a rival to Kevin Carr, Newcastle possessed two goalkeepers of similar style and ability. The pair jockeyed for the position, sharing the role during the black'n'whites' promotion success in

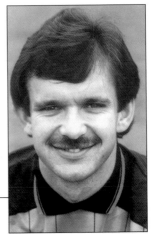

Martin Thomas

1983-84. But as Newcastle reached the First Division, Thomas soon became the Number One choice. Capped by Wales, Martin was understudy on the international scene to Everton's Dai Davies, while his brother David, played for the Wales B side at rugby union. Thomas had a career that was often disrupted by injury, but showed the Tyneside public that on his day he could be a splendid goalkeeper. In season 1982-83, he unusually appeared for five different clubs.

Appearances:
FL: 118 apps. 0 gls.
FAC: 5 apps. 0 gls.
FLC: 7 apps. 0 gls.
Others: 1 app. 0 gls.
Total: *131 apps. 0 gls.*
Honours:
1 Wales cap 1987/
2 Wales u21 caps 1979-81/
Wales youth app./
FL div 2 prom 1984/
FL div 3 prom 1992.

THOMPSON, Alan

Role: Midfield 1989-1993
6' 0"
b. Newcastle upon Tyne, 22nd December 1973

CAREER: UNITED sch cs 1989, pro Mar 1991/
Bolton Wanderers July 1993 £250,000.

Debut v Swindon Town (a) 2/11/91 (sub)

Alan Thompson made a remarkable recovery after sustaining terrible injuries in a car accident which placed several of United's youth stars in hospital during 1990. Thompson suffered a broken neck and back, undergoing two operations that threatened a promising career before it had really started. However, the Tynesider battled to fitness and showed he possessed a cultured left foot, able to cross a dangerous curling ball into the box or hit a vicious shot. Appearing at full-back for the Magpies as well as in his more accustomed midfield role, Alan took part in the European youth tournament for England and had also captained his country's school eleven. Following a few outings in Newcastle's senior line-up during season 1991-92, he was replaced by more experienced professionals, but was always recognised as a future star. Manager Kevin Keegan though, found it increasingly difficult to satisfy the youngster's

ambition and allowed Thompson to leave for Burnden Park where he became a noted midfielder reaching the England Under 21 set-up. Once sent-off for the young England side in 1996, Thompson attended school with Steve Watson and on one occasion played for three different United sides within three days; the junior eleven, the club's reserve team and the senior line-up.

Appearances:
FL: 13(3) apps. 0 gls.
FAC: 1 app. 0 gls.
Others: 3 apps. 0 gls.
Total: *17(3) apps. 0 gls.*
Honours:
2 Eng u21 caps 1995-96/Eng youth app./
Eng schools app./FL div 1 prom 1995/
FLC finalist 1995.

Alan Thompson

THOMPSON, Frank

Role: Centre-forward 1923-1925
5' 8"
b. Birtley, nr Gateshead

CAREER: St Peters Albion 1921/UNITED
Nov 1923 £150 to May 1925.

Debut v Birmingham City (a) 5/4/24

A prominent local player, Frank Thompson
was described as being "a consistent performer
in the Tyneside League" and several clubs
were eager to sign him before United stepped
in. Deputising for Scottish international centre-
forward Neil Harris during season 1923-24,
young Thompson displayed form on his
senior baptism. He was fast and eager, but
destined to spend the majority of his stay with
the black'n'whites in North Eastern League
football, although he went on tour to Spain
with the first team in May 1924. With
Newcastle having a settled side, winning the
FA Cup during the period he was at St James
Park, Thompson found it difficult to break
through and moved on at the end of the 1924-
25 programme.

Appearances:
FL: 2 apps. 1 gl.
Total: *2 apps. 1 gl.*

THOMPSON, George Alfred

Role: Outside-right 1903-1905
5' 9"
b. Wolverhampton, 1878
d. North Shields, 17th October 1943

CAREER: Halesowen/UNITED May 1903/
Crystal Palace cs 1905/Carlisle United 1906/
Newcastle City secretary.

Debut v Nottingham Forest (a) 9/4/04

Arriving on Tyneside from the Midlands,
George Thompson found himself in the
shadows of the great Jackie Rutherford on
Tyneside. He did appear once during the
club's championship season of 1904-05, albeit
in a FA Cup tie, and took part in two reserve
title successes in the Northern League. A local
athlete of merit too, he had excellent sprinting
ability, but didn't have any chance of
dislodging England international Rutherford
from his wing position. Thompson moved to
London and assisted Crystal Palace in their

Southern League campaign. Later George
returned to the north east settling in
Tynemouth, for many years a sign and poster
writer in Newcastle.

Appearances:
FL: 1 app. 0 gls.
FAC: 1 app. 0 gls.
Total: *2 apps. 0 gls.*

THOMPSON, Henry

Role: Left-back 1908-1910
5' 10"
b. Tyneside

CAREER: North Shields Athletic/UNITED
May 1908 £50/Crystal Palace Oct 1910 £25
to c1911.

Debut v Preston North End (h) 3/1/10

A solid defender for North Shields in local
football, Henry Thompson was added to the
staff as cover in the full-back role. He
deputised for Tony Whitson during season
1909-10, but found the competition in front of
him overwhelming. Apart from the cultured
play of Whitson, the Magpies also had on the
staff Carr, McCracken, Pudan, Waugh and
another up and coming youngster, Frank
Hudspeth. Thompson moved to Crystal Palace
where he took part in their 1910-11 Southern
League campaign (4 apps.).

Appearances:
FL: 2 apps. 0 gls.
Total: *2 apps. 0 gls.*

John Thompson

THOMPSON, John Henry

Role: Goalkeeper 1950-1957
5' 10"
b. Newcastle upon Tyne, 4th July 1932

CAREER: UNITED Sept 1950/Lincoln City
May 1957 £2,500/Horden Colliery Welfare cs
1960/Annfield Plain/Retired 1964.

Debut v Manchester United (a) 23/10/54

Learning much from Jack Fairbrother when a
teenager at St James Park, John Thompson
then found himself as second choice to Ronnie
Simpson when Fairbrother departed. His
chances were limited to a handful of games
during seasons 1954-55 and 1955-56, although
he did get on the team-sheet for the Charity
Shield contest with Chelsea in
September 1955. Like Simpson,
he was not a tall or imposing
'keeper, John being relatively
small, yet agile. Thompson was
a regular at Sincil Bank with
Lincoln during season 1957-58.
On leaving the game, he
became self-employed, running
a betting outlet on Tyneside
and residing in Forest Hall,
Newcastle.

    Appearances:
    FL: 8 apps. 0 gls.
    Others: 1 app. 0 gls.
    Total: *9 apps. 0 gls.*

THOMPSON, Thomas

Role: Inside-right 1946-1950
5' 6"
b. Fence Houses,
nr Houghton-le-Spring,
Co Durham, 10th November 1928

CAREER: Lumley YMCA/
UNITED Aug 1946 £25/Aston
Villa Sept 1950 £15,000/
Preston North End June 1955
£25,000/Stoke City June 1961
£2,500/Barrow Mar 1963/
Retired due to injury Aug
1964/Preston North End
asst-coach briefly.

Debut v Coventry City (a)
21/2/48

Small but strongly built, Tommy Thompson
developed into one of the fifties' top inside-
forwards. With plenty of stamina, he
possessed delicate touches and speed off the
mark that eventually saw him turn into a
potent schemer and attacker always able to
score goals, netting over 300 in his career. But
during his early days at St James Park,
Thompson was given only a few chances to
impress. Blooded in the promotion season of
1947-48, he then had Stobbart, Gibson, Taylor
and Robledo all ahead of him in the ranking.
But Tommy blossomed at Villa Park as a free
scoring inside-forward, good enough to earn
England recognition. Nicknamed 'Topper', he
grabbed 76 goals for Villa in 165 games before
moving to Deepdale where he joined up with
Tom Finney in Preston's forward line. Scoring

over 100 goals in
Lancashire, he then
formed another good
partnership with
Stanley Matthews at
Stoke when nearing the
end of his career.
Aware of his
colleagues' positioning
and always willing to
have a go himself, he
netted 34 goals in the
First Division during
season 1957-58 when
Preston finished as
runners-up. Tommy
also scored four goals
for the Football League
against Eire in 1951.
Retiring after a knee
complaint, Thompson
returned to his original
joinery trade, living in
Preston.

Appearances:
FL: 20 apps. 6 gls.
Total:
20 apps. 6 gls.
Honours:
2 Eng caps 1952-57/
1 Eng B cap 1957/
2 FL apps. 1952-57/
FL div 2 champs 1963.

Tommy Thompson

THOMPSON, William

Role: Centre-half 1957-1967
5' 11"
b. Bedlington, Northumberland, 5th January 1940

CAREER: UNITED Jan 1957/ Rotherham United June 1967 £15,000/ Darlington Mar 1968/South Shields cs 1970.

Debut v Chelsea (a) 5/11/60

Making his debut for the Magpies during the relegation season of 1960-61, Bill Thompson shared the centre-half role with John McGrath during his early years at St James Park. A former miner, Bill was long-legged and a tall, commanding defender at his best. In fact he had developed a top reputation during 1961-62 and 1962-63, gaining a call-up to the England under 23 squad only for a leg knock to prevent his appearance. Plagued by injury yet on the club's staff for a decade, Thompson never quite established himself as a first team regular, having later additional competition from McNamee and Moncur. Bill also had an outing at centre-forward for Newcastle before moving to Millmoor in 1967. He returned to his native Northumberland, to Stakeford, being employed at the Wilkinson Sword complex nearby.

Appearances:
FL: 79(1) apps. 1 gl.
FAC: 6 apps. 0 gls.
FLC: 3 apps. 0 gls.
Total: *88(1) apps. 1 gl.*

THOMPSON, William K.

Role: Centre-forward 1892-1897
5' 7"
b. North Seaton, Northumberland, 1862

CAREER: Bedlington Burdon 1880/ Shankhouse Black Watch/Newcastle East End Dec 1889/UNITED May 1892/Jarrow July 1897/Ashington c1898.

Debut v Sheffield United (a) 24/9/1892 (NL)

Willie Thompson was a dashing goalgetter during the pioneering years of Tyneside football. Popular with all his clubs, Thompson wasn't too big, but was swift and possessed a telling shot in either foot, as well as a magnificent moustache in the style of the day. A Northumberland County player, Willie took part in United's initial Football League fixture against Arsenal in September 1893, while he is registered as scoring the club's first hat-trick, also against the Londoners later the same month. A formidable player in United's first three years of senior action, Thompson grabbed 46 goals, a goal every second match for the Tynesiders. He later suffered from injury, being described as having, "a dodgy knee" by the local press. Thompson is also registered as scoring the very first penalty for East End during 1892.

Appearances:
FL: 80 apps. 33 gls.
NL: 7 apps. 6 gls.
FAC: 11 apps. 7 gls.
Total: *98 apps.*
46 gls.

Willie Thompson

THOMSON, James Arnott

Role: Midfield 1968-1971
5' 6"
b. Glasgow, 28th June 1948

CAREER: Petershill jnrs/UNITED Aug 1968 (Barrow loan 1970-71)/Grimsby Town June 1971 free/Greenock Morton cs 1972/ Gateshead/Evenwood Town Sept 1976/ Newcastle Blue Star/Minor Tyneside football 1978/Berwick Rangers manager 1988 to Sept 1988.

Debut v Burnley (a) 1/11/69

Jimmy Thomson

A fierce competitor in midfield, small and well built, Jimmy Thomson was spotted playing for Scottish junior side, Petershill by United's Glasgow scouts. During season 1969-70, he deputised for Dave Elliott in the anchor role in the middle of the park, then was transferred to Blundell Park where he recorded 32 appearances for the Humberside black'n'whites, winning Fourth Division title honours. Converted to full-back and back on Tyneside with Blue Star, he reached Wembley in the 1978 FA Vase. He resides on Tyneside, for a period a publican in Felling and later employed by Vaux Breweries.

Appearances:
FL: 4(1) apps. 0 gls.
Total: *4(1) apps. 0 gls.*
Honours:
FL div 4 champs 1972/FAV winner 1978.

THOMSON, Robert W.

Role: Left-back 1928-1934
5' 9"
b. Falkirk, 24th October 1905

CAREER: Lauriston Villa/Falkirk Amateurs/ Falkirk 1925/Sunderland Apr 1927 £5,000/ UNITED Oct 1928 exch for R.McKay/Hull City July 1934 £340/Racing Club de Paris (France) cs 1935/Ipswich Town July 1936/ Retired due to injury 1937/Ipswich Town asst-trainer 1937, becoming trainer to June 1950.

Debut v Leeds United (h) 6/10/28

Bob Thomson

Originally a half-back, Bob Thomson moved into a full-back's role and enjoyed conspicuous success. With Falkirk he won Scotland honours against the Auld Enemy, England, before earning a big move to the First Division south of the border at Roker Park. Small but tough and persistent in defence, he also showed considerable grace when on the ball, even to the point where at times he appeared rather lazy. Wearing the red and white of Sunderland on only 22 occasions, he then moved to Tyneside in an exchange deal with Bob McKay. Replacing Frank Hudspeth in United's defence, Thomson was first choice for two and a half seasons before losing out to Dave Fairhurst. He then spent a long period in Newcastle's reserve line-up as the club competed for membership of the Central League. During a spell in Paris, Bob was on the Racing Club's staff when they lifted the French league and cup double in season 1935-36. Retiring due to a broken leg suffered when at Ipswich, he afterwards helped out behind the scenes at Portman Road for several years. During World War Two, the Scot served in the RAF in the Middle East and was a member of the famous Eagle Squadron.

Appearances:
FL: 73 apps. 0 gls.
FAC: 7 apps. 0 gls.
Total: *80 apps. 0 gls.*
Honours:
1 Scot cap 1927/1 SL app. 1927.

THORN, Andrew Charles

Role: Centre-half 1988-1989
6' 0"
b. Carshalton, Surrey, 12th November 1966

CAREER: Wimbledon app, pro 1984/UNITED July 1988 £850,000/Crystal Palace Nov 1989 £650,000/Wimbledon Oct 1994 free to cs 1996/ Heart of Midlothian Sept 1996/ Tranmere Rovers Sept 1996 free.

Debut v Everton (a) 27/8/88

Andy Thorn became Newcastle's joint record purchase at £850,000 along with his Wimbledon colleague Dave Beasant. Moving to Tyneside as a 21 year-old defender who had shown he had all the qualities to reach the top, Thorn was to be a key figure in manager Willie McFaul's rebuilding programme at Gallowgate. Quick and strongly built, Andy began with a 0-4 drubbing at Goodison Park, but then netted on his home debut and although the team failed to knit together, dropping into Division Two, Thorn's own performances were sound if not spectacular. With a new manager taking charge in the shape of Jim Smith, the Londoner figured for the early weeks of the 1989-90 season, but was sold back to the capital in a bid to raise cash to fund another restructuring programme in the dressing-room. At Selhurst Park, Thorn became the cornerstone to Palace's defence for seven seasons, appearing on over 150 occasions. He reached Wembley with the Eagles, repeating the feat he had achieved as a member of the Wimbledon fairy story, when they defeated Liverpool in the FA Cup final of 1988.

Appearances:
FL: 36 apps. 2 gls.
FLC: 4 apps. 1 gl.
Others: 3 apps. 0 gls.
Total: *43 apps. 3 gls.*
Honours:
5 Eng under 21 caps 1988/
FAC winner 1988/
FAC finalist 1990/
FL div 2 prom 1986/
FL div 1 champs 1994.

TILDESLEY, James

Role: Right-back 1903-1906
5' 11"
b. Halesowen, nr Birmingham, 7th October 1881
d. Newcastle upon Tyne, January 1963

CAREER: Halesowen St John/UNITED Feb 1903/Middlesbrough Sept 1906 £200 to 1907/ Luton Town 1908/Leeds City Dec 1909 to c1910/UNITED scout.

Debut v Wolverhampton Wanderers (h) 31/10/03

Picked up from local Midlands football, Jimmy Tildesley acted as a reserve to either Jack Carr or Bill McCracken, two international backs at St James Park. A more than able defender himself, he claimed 16 games in season 1903-04 and took part in two Northern League title successes for the Magpies' reserve side. Broad-shouldered and a tough

Jimmy Tildesley

competitor, the local press of the day recorded he tackled with, "astounding power and success". His brother T. Tildesley was also on the club's books at the same time and appeared once in senior action during a friendly in 1904-05. After retiring from the playing side of the game, Jim became a noted scout, uncovering Micky Burns and Robert Roxburgh for the club. He later settled in Newcastle.

Appearances:
FL: 21 apps. 0 gls.
FAC: 1 app. 0 gls.
Total: *22 apps. 0 gls.*

TINNION, Brian

Role: Left-back 1984-1989
6' 0"
b. Burnopfield, Co Durham, 23rd February 1968

CAREER: UNITED app 1984, pro Feb 1986/
Bradford City Mar 1989/Bristol City Mar 1993
£180,000.

Debut v Everton (a) 20/4/87

Brian Tinnion

Making his senior debut for United in midfield, Brian Tinnion slipped into the left-back role for a long spell during season 1987-88. Fired with a determined attitude, he rivalled both John Bailey and Kenny Wharton at Gallowgate and looked like seeing off his more experienced colleagues until United went through a bad patch of results which affected his confidence. With a quality left foot, at the peak of his early development Tinnion was elevated to the England Under-21 squad in May 1988, but unluckily had to withdraw from a tour of Brazil due to injury. Brian moved to Bradford City and then to Bristol City, making a major contribution at both clubs. Reverting back to midfield, he netted the goal which gave the Ashton Gate club a memorable FA Cup giant-killing knock-out over Liverpool at Anfield in 1994. Tinnion totalled more than 150 games for the Bantams and over 100 with Bristol City.

Appearances:
FL: 30(2) apps. 2 gls.
FLC: 5 apps. 0 gls.
Others: 3(1) apps. 0 gls.
Total: *38(3) apps. 2 gls.*
Honours:
FAYC winner 1985.

TODD, Kevin

Role: Striker 1981-1983
5' 9"
b. Sunderland, 28th February 1958

CAREER: Grindon WMC/Ryhope CA/
UNITED Aug 1981(Darlington loan 1981-82)/
Darlington Sept 1983 £5,000/Newcastle Blue
Star July 1985/Kuusysi Lahti(Finland) 1987/
Whitley Bay Oct 1988/Berwick Rangers Aug
1990 £18,000/Bishop Auckland July 1992/
Spennymoor United Sept 1996.

Debut v Derby County (h) 10/10/81 (sub)

Scoring almost 200 goals in local football within three seasons was form which spurred United to offer Wearsider Kevin Todd a trial period at St James Park; he impressed and was handed a full-time contract. Although Kevin wasn't a tall or battling type of striker, he had a good touch and liked to use his pace and ability on the ball, as well as intelligent positioning. Netting twice on his first full game for the black'n'whites, he rubbed shoulders with the likes of Kevin Keegan and Terry McDermott during his stay at St James Park. Todd made a handful of appearances just before United gained promotion in season 1983-84, then snapped ligaments and lost his chance in the big-time, moving to Darlington soon after. Todd quickly returned to non-league football where he became a distinguished player for a decade and more. He reached international selection and while briefly in Finland, lifted that country's domestic cup. He also entered business in the north east, running a trophy shop in Sunderland.

Kevin Todd

Appearances:
FL: 5(2) apps. 3 gls.
FAC: 2(1) apps. 0 gls.
FLC: 1 app. 0 gls.
Total:
8(3) apps. 3 gls.
Honours:
Eng(non-lg) app. 1988/
FA(non-lg) app. 1990/
Finland Cup winner 1988/
FL div 4 prom 1985.

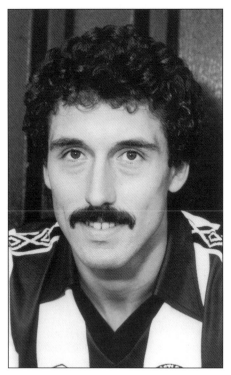

TREWICK, John

Role: Midfield 1980-1984
5′ 9″
b. Stakeford, Northumberland, 3rd June 1957

CAREER: West Bromwich Albion July 1972/
UNITED Dec 1980 £250,000(Oxford United
loan 1983-84)/Oxford United July 1984 free/
Birmingham City Sept 1987/Bromsgrove
Rovers cs 1989/Hartlepool United Oct 1989/
Barnet 1989/Gateshead Oct 1990 to Jan 1991/
West Bromwich Albion community-officer
June 1992, becoming asst-coach 1992.

Debut v Bristol City (h) 20/12/80

From a footballing family, John Trewick's
father, George, and cousin, Alan, both played
for Gateshead during their Football League
days. Developed from a schoolboy at the
Hawthorns, John was an England player as a
youth but after appearing on 128 occasions for
Albion, assisting in a promotion success in
1975-76, he moved back to the north east for a
record club fee. Possessing good vision in
midfield with the capacity for hard work,
Trewick rarely hit a bad pass and was in many
ways an ideal anchor man. But John did not

settle quickly at St James Park. He was injured
for a long spell and United's fans did not see
the best of his talent until after a loan spell at
Oxford. Arriving back at Gallowgate for a
promotion run-in, Trewick was lodged in a
midfield role alongside McDermott and
McCreery and played an important part in
regaining the club's First Division status in
1983-84. Surprisingly though, Trewick was
then released, going back to the Manor
Ground (142 apps.), where he yet again won
promotion from the Second Division as well as
taking part in Wembley glory. On hanging up
his boots, Trewick linked up with West
Bromwich Albion once more, serving at the
Hawthorns in various capacities, including a
spell as caretaker manager in October 1994. He
totalled 128 league and cup games for Albion.

Appearances:
FL: 76(2) apps. 8 gls.
FAC: 7 apps. 0 gls.
FLC: 2 apps. 0 gls.
Total: *85(2) apps. 8 gls.*
Honours:
Eng schools app./
Eng youth app. 1975/
FL div 2 champs 1985/
FL div 2 prom 1976, 1984/
FLC winner 1986.

TUDOR, John A.

Role: Striker 1971-1976
5′ 10″
b. Ilkeston, Derbyshire, 24th June 1946

CAREER: Stanley Common Welfare/
Cotmanhay United/Middlesbrough amat/
Ilkeston Town/Coventry City app Jan 1965,
pro Jan 1968/Sheffield United Nov 1968/
UNITED Jan 1971 exch deal for J.Hope &
D.Ford/Stoke City Oct 1976 £30,000/AA Gent
(Belgium) Aug 1977/Retired due to injury cs
1978/North Shields coach, becoming manager
Oct 1979/Gateshead Dec 1980/Bedlington
Terriers Nov 1982/Derbyshire coaching
school/Minnesota(USA) coaching school
June 1994.

Debut v Burnley (a) 30/1/71

After serving both Coventry and Sheffield
United in an honest and professional manner,
John Tudor arrived at St James Park to boost
United's strike-force. His first season was
unspectacular and at times he fought a

John Tudor challenges West Ham's Clyde Best at Upton Park in December 1972.

running battle with sections of the crowd. But on the signing of Malcolm Macdonald in readiness for the start of the 1971-72 season, Tudor's career was set to explode as a near-perfect partner to Supermac. Blond-haired John had aerial power, worked intelligently at his game, and proved an ideal foil for Macdonald. For the next four seasons the duo were United's cutting edge, and few partnerships in the top division could better them. Newcastle's previously critical fans now accepted the likable Tudor, who showed both courage and dedication in abundance. He became a genuine favourite and was a regular until injury and a change in manager, as well as the departure of Macdonald, led to his own transfer. Retiring from the first class game due to a knee problem, Tudor later returned to the north east where he became a publican in Bedlington for a spell before moving back to his native Ilkeston. He started to become involved in coaching schools, moving to the States in 1994. A late developer in the game, John worked as a welder, truck driver and tile-maker before turning professional at Jimmy Hill's Coventry. He had short spells at Sheffield United, Derby, Notts County, Chesterfield and Forest before hand, while John signed for Middlesbrough for a year, but only appeared for the second string.

Appearances:
FL: 161(3) apps. 53 gls.
FAC: 15 apps. 4 gls.
FLC: 8 apps. 1 gls.
Others: 32(1) apps. 15 gls.
Total: *216(4) apps. 73 gls.*
Honours:
FL div 2 champs 1967/
FL div 2 prom 1971/
FAC finalist 1974.

TUOHY, William

Role: Outside-left 1960-1963
5' 7"
b. Dublin, 27th April 1933

CAREER: Dublin St Marys/Shamrock Rovers 1951/UNITED May 1960 £9,500/Shamrock Rovers Aug 1963, becoming coach/Eire manager Sept 1971 to Nov 1972/Shelbourne manager 1982/Eire youth manager to Feb 1986/UNITED scout 1989.

Debut v Preston North End (a) 20/8/60

One of the top performers in the Republic of Ireland, Liam Tuohy arrived in England with a big reputation as a skilful winger who could score goals. Purchased as Bobby Mitchell's successor in the Number 11 shirt, the Irishman made a good start with the Magpies, showing plenty of spirit, but then suffered, like many of his colleagues, when the side became entangled in a relegation dog-fight during 1960-61. Tuohy was a regular for the following season, then lost his place to Jimmy Fell and returned to Dublin, rejoining Shamrock Rovers. Liam remained associated with Irish soccer in several roles for the next 20 years and more.

Appearances:
FL: 38 apps. 9 gls.
FAC: 1 app. 0 gls.
FLC: 3 apps. 0 gls.
Total: *42 apps. 9 gls.*
Honours:
8 Eire caps 1956-65/
2 Eire B caps 1958-59/
24 EL apps. 1955-66/
EL champs 1954, 1957, 1959, 1964/
Eire Cup winner 1955, 1956, 1964, 1965.

TURNER, Arthur D.

Role: Outside-right 1903-1904
5' 8"
b. Hartley Wintney, nr Farnborough, June 1877
d. Hartley Wintney, nr Farnborough, 4th April 1925

CAREER: Aldershot North End 1892/South Farnborough/Camberley St Michaels/Brentford trial/Reading trial/Southampton St Marys May 1899/Derby County May 1902/UNITED Jan 1903/Tottenham Hotspur Feb 1904 £150/Southampton May 1904(Bristol City loan 1904-05)/Retired cs 1905/South Farnborough Athletic.

Debut v Notts County (a) 31/1/03

Arthur Turner was an opportunist player, quick to capitalise on an opening. Known as 'Archie', he possessed an excellent turn of speed and showed a flair that excited supporters. Playing his best football for Southampton in the Southern League, Turner totalled 98 senior games for the Saints and netted 30 goals, many alongside his brother, Harry. He appeared in two FA Cup finals for Southampton and was chosen for the England side on two occasions at his peak at the turn of the century. Following a brief stay at the Baseball Ground, Archie ended up on Tyneside, although he again found his stay in the First Division a short one. He managed only 13 games for the Magpies before the emergence of Jackie Rutherford saw him move on again, to White Hart Lane. On leaving the game, Archie entered his family's business in Farnborough. Turner was also a fine cricketer at club level in Hampshire.

Archie Turner

Appearances:
FL: 13 apps. 1 gl.
Total: *13 apps. 1 gl.*
Honours:
2 Eng caps 1900-01/
Eng trial app. 1900/
1 SnL app. 1900/
FAC finalist 1900, 1902/
SnL champs 1901.

TURNER, David John

Role: Right or Left-half 1960-1963
5′ 9″
b. Retford, 7th September 1943

CAREER: UNITED amat Aug 1960, pro Oct 1960/Brighton Dec 1963 £4,500(Portsmouth loan c1972)/Blackburn Rovers Aug 1972 free/Sheffield United asst-coach cs 1974/Aldershot coach, becoming asst manager/Toronto Blizzard (Canada) coach 1979/Aldershot coach Sept 1990.

Debut v Leeds United (h) 28/4/62

On the St James Park staff from schools football, Dave Turner helped the Magpies lift the FA Youth Cup for the first time in 1962, but found claiming a Football League place near impossible during his four seasons on Tyneside. A competent wing-half, he was given a chance in the last game of the programme for both seasons 1961-62 and 1962-63 and was noted in *The Journal* as being a "top class prospect". Apart from a League Cup outing, Dave couldn't find a place thereafter and moved to Brighton where he did prove a capable midfield player, skipper of the Seagulls in many of his 338 games. He was a stalwart player at the Goldstone Ground for nine seasons. Turner then had a period associated with Aldershot with a ten-year stint residing in Canada. Recently he has been living in Nottinghamshire.

Appearances:
FL: 2 apps. 0 gls.
FLC: 1 app. 0 gls.
Total: *3 apps. 0 gls.*
Honours:
FL div 4 champs 1965/
FL div 3 prom 1972/
FAYC winner 1962.

URWIN, Tom

Role: Outside-right
1924-1930
5′ 6″
b. Haswell, nr Sunderland, 5th February 1896
d. Tynemouth, 7th May 1968

CAREER: Fulwell/Lambton Star/Shildon 1913/Middlesbrough amat Feb 1914, pro May 1914/Fulham war-guest 1915-16/UNITED Aug 1924 £3,200/Sunderland Feb 1930 £525/Retired May 1934/Sunderland asst-trainer.

Debut v Blackburn Rovers (h) 10/9/24

Tom Urwin is one of only a handful of players to have received benefits from all three of the north east's senior clubs. A great servant to the region, he appeared on 200 occasions for Middlesbrough before heading to Tyneside after a row over payments. Bill McCracken actually poached him at Newcastle Central Station when the player was on his way to meet Manchester United officials. A midget winger full of craft, one pen picture of the twenties described him as being, "little but good, he has the speed and cunning and puts centres in the right place every time". Tom was in United's first eleven for six seasons and took part during the club's championship success in 1926-27 while he was also capped for his country when at St James Park. Operating mainly on the right-wing, he also played on the left touchline in a sprightly fashion too. Moving to Wearside in 1930 on the last leg of his regional crusade, Tommy was connected with the Roker side for many years as trainer to the Reds' youngsters. He later was employed as an accounts clerk in Sunderland Royal Infirmary and lived at Monkseaton. During World War One, Urwin served in the Royal Artillery.

Appearances:
FL: 188 apps. 23 gls.
FAC: 12 apps. 1 gl.
Total: *200 apps. 24 gls.*
Honours:
4 Eng caps 1923-26/Eng trial app.
1921-26/Eng schools app. 1910/
12 FA app. 1931-32/
1 FL app. 1927/
FL champs 1927.

Tom Urwin

VARADI, Imre

Role: Centre-forward 1981-1983
5' 9"
b. Paddington, London, 8th July 1959

CAREER: Letchworth Town/FC 75 (Hitchin)/
Sheffield United Apr 1978/Everton Feb
1979 £80,000/Benfica(Portugal) trial July
1981/ UNITED Aug 1981 £125,000/
Sheffield Wednesday Aug 1983 £150,000/
West Bromwich Albion June 1985
£285,000/Manchester City Oct 1986/
Sheffield Wednesday Sept 1988 exch for
C.Bradshaw/Leeds United Feb 1990
£50,000(Luton Town loan 1991-92)(Oxford
United loan 1992-93)/Rotherham United
Mar 1993/Boston United cs 1995/
Mansfield Town Aug 1995/Scunthorpe
United Oct 1995/Matlock Town
player-manager Nov 1995.

Debut v Watford (h) 29/8/81

Well travelled, and a favourite at all his
ports of call, Imre Varadi scored goals
throughout his career. Quicksilver fast,
and always snapping at defenders' heels,
he joined United after impressing Arthur
Cox in limited appearances for Everton.
Swarthy, dark-haired and known as 'Ray',
he in fact almost joined Benfica (one trial
game) before heading for Tyneside, but
that spectacular deal fell through and he
pulled on the black'n'white shirt for the
start of the 1981-82 season. Although
erratic in his finishing, Varadi had an
explosive shot and bagged 20 goals in his
first year for United, then another 22 the
following campaign when he partnered
Kevin Keegan in attack. He also once hit
five goals in a friendly against Hartlepool.
To the shock of all United's supporters
though, Cox then sold the striker to
Sheffield Wednesday, later replacing him
with the more skilful Peter Beardsley.
Born of a Hungarian father and Italian
mother, Varadi continued to find the net
nevertheless and by the end of his career
in the first class game had scored almost
200 goals. When at Elland Road he
appeared on three occasions in Leeds' title
winning season of 1991-92. His brother
Fernando was on Fulham's staff, and as a
youngster Ray had brief spells on trial
with Tottenham and Cambridge United.

Appearances:
FL: 81 apps. 39 gls.
FAC: 5 apps. 2 gls.
FLC: 4 apps. 1 gl.
Total: *90 apps. 42 gls.*
Honours:
FL div 2 champs 1990/FL div 2 prom 1984.

Imre Varadi

VEITCH, Colin Campbell McKechnie

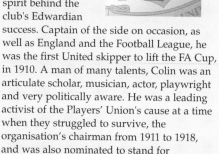

Role: Half-back & Trainer 1899-1926
5' 6"
b. Heaton, Newcastle upon Tyne, 22nd May 1881
d. Berne, Switzerland, 27th August 1938

CAREER: Larkspur jnrs(Newcastle)/Dalton jnrs(Newcastle)/Malcolm jnrs(Newcastle)/Rutherford College(Newcastle) 1895/UNITED amat Jan 1899, pro Apr 1899/Retired cs 1915, becoming asst-trainer to cs 1926/ Bradford City manager Aug 1926 to Jan 1928.

Debut v Wolverhampton Wanderers (h) 28/10/1899

One of the most eminent names, not only in United's past, but in the game's history, Colin Veitch was a true great. He was a complete footballer, able to operate in any position, appearing for United in every role apart from goalkeeper, left-back and outside-left. He also turned out for England in four different roles and was the most versatile player in the country before World War One, a factor which went against him in international selection, leaving Veitch a constant reserve for a decade. Appearing also for United under the pseudonym of 'Hamilton' when at college, Colin took part in 16 seasons of football for the club. Veitch preferred midfield, at centre-half, and was a player of few frills, yet controlled the game with his straightforward ability. Ivan Sharpe noted that "Veitch played with the supreme ease of a man who is the master of his job". He was a thoughtful player, an expert tactician and always had control of the ball and used it to good purpose. He also often found the net

for the Magpies and can be identified as perhaps the leading spirit behind the club's Edwardian success. Captain of the side on occasion, as well as England and the Football League, he was the first United skipper to lift the FA Cup, in 1910. A man of many talents, Colin was an articulate scholar, musician, actor, playwright and very politically aware. He was a leading activist of the Players' Union's cause at a time when they struggled to survive, the organisation's chairman from 1911 to 1918, and was also nominated to stand for Parliament as a socialist. Married to an actress, he was heavily involved in the Newcastle Playhouse, Newcastle Operatic Society and Clarion Choir, and counted George Bernard Shaw among his close friends. Colin's association with Newcastle United came to a bitter end in 1926 when he was sacked as manager of the club's recently formed junior set up, the Newcastle Swifts. Afterwards he became a shrewd, and at times, highly critical journalist for the *Newcastle Chronicle* and was once banned from St James Park for his stinging remarks regarding the club. Veitch died whilst convalescing in Switzerland after having contracted pneumonia. During World War One, Colin rose to the rank of 2nd Lieutenant.

Appearances:
FL: 276 apps. 43 gls.
FAC: 45 apps. 6 gls.
Others: 1 app. 0 gls.
Total: *322 apps. 49 gls.*

Honours:
6 Eng caps 1906-09/
Eng trial app. 1906-07/
4 FL apps. 1906-11/
FL champs 1905, 1907, 1909/
FAC winner 1910/
FAC finalist 1905, 1906, 1908, 1911.

VENISON, Barry

Role: Defender or Midfield 1992-1995
5' 10"
b. Consett, 16th August 1964

CAREER: Sunderland app May 1979, pro Jan 1982/Liverpool July 1986 £250,000/UNITED July 1992 £250,000/Galatasary(Turkey) June 1995 £750,000/Southampton Oct 1995 £850,000.

Debut v Southend United (h) 15/8/92

A product of schools football at Roker Park, Barry Venison was a teenage star for Sunderland (206 apps.), skippering the

Barry Venison

Wearsiders at Wembley in 1985 when only 20 years of age. Moving in a big deal to Anfield, Venison took part in title and FA Cup victories with Liverpool before returning to the north east for a bargain fee. One of manager Keegan's inspired signings during the summer of 1992, Venison marshalled United's defence from the right-back spot as the Magpies stormed to the First Division championship. Also stepping in at centre-half, he was comfortable on the ball, able to distribute passes accurately, and was also totally committed, showing determination and inspirational qualities that rallied both his colleagues and supporters. Barry quickly became a favourite and as the club tackled Premiership football he developed into an international player. Moving into a holding midfield role, Venison was selected for a deserved England cap showing the talent to cover ground, win the ball with steely aggression and release a pass from a position just in front of the defence. Venison played with immense pride in his shirt during a three year spell on Tyneside, during which time he skippered the side, as he had done at Roker Park, and also the England Youth and Under-21 elevens. A dedicated follower of fashion, the blond-haired Barry was characterised by his flowing locks and flamboyant attire during his spell at Gallowgate.

Appearances:
FL/PL: 108(1) apps. 1 gl.
FAC: 11 apps. 0 gls.
FLC: 9 apps. 0 gls.
Eur: 1 app. 0 gls.
Others: 3 apps. 0 gls.
Total: *132(1) apps. 1 gl.*
Honours:
2 Eng caps 1995/
10 Eng u21 caps 1983-86/
Eng youth app. 1983/
FA PL app. 1994/
FL champs 1988, 1990/
FL div 1 champs 1993/
FAC winner 1989/
FLC finalist 1985, 1987.

WADDLE, Christopher Roland

Role: Forward 1980-1985
6' 0"
b. Heworth, Gateshead, 14th December 1960

CAREER: Pelaw jnrs/Whitehouse SC/Mount Pleasant SC/HMH Printing Co/Pelaw SC/Leam Lane SC/Clarke Chapman/Tow Law Town cs 1978/UNITED July 1980 £1,000/Tottenham Hotspur July 1985 £590,000/Olympique Marseille (France) July 1989 £4.25m/Sheffield Wednesday July 1992 £1m/Falkirk Sept 1996/Bradford City Oct 1996 free.

Debut v Shrewsbury Town (h) 22/10/80

Chris Waddle exchanged a labourer's job at a seasoning factory making sausages and pies for a chance in professional football at St James Park. The down to earth Tynesider made rapid progress, eventually becoming one of the game's biggest names commanding, at the time, the third highest transfer fee ever, behind Maradona and Gullit when he moved to France. At first Waddle never looked to be a quality footballer. He possessed an awkward, lumbering style but, under the guidance of Arthur Cox and Kevin Keegan at Gallowgate, a hidden talent was developed. With rare ability to go past defenders using a body-swerve and deceptive pace, Chris quickly claimed a regular place in United's first eleven. At centre-forward or on either wing, Waddle roamed across the front line and, during the Magpies' promotion to Division One in 1983-84, he became a noted player. Along with Keegan and Beardsley up front, United had a forward trio of some style. Waddle could place a dangerous swerving cross and had an eye for goal too, producing a vicious bend on many shots. Chris could beat men in tight situations and became a matchwinner, soon destined to be in the England Under-21 and full England squads. But with Newcastle's lack of success forcing him to move south, it was with Tottenham that Waddle became a regular for his country. He appeared in the 1986 and 1990 World Cup finals, missing a crucial penalty kick in the semi-final shoot-out with West Germany in Italy. After 173 games (42 goals) for Spurs, he then made that record move to Marseille where Waddle's career flourished even further. He became a megastar in Provence alongside top names like Papin and Boli. The Geordie's showmanship and magic on the ball was loved by the French, being nicknamed 'Le Dribbleur Fou'. Chris won league championship medals with Marseille as well as reaching the European Cup final in 1991. Returning to England, he joined

Chris Waddle

up with Sheffield Wednesday where Chris again showed his native public what a splendid player he was, although he was dogged by injury at Hillsborough. Waddle once had a hit record cut along with Glenn Hoddle entitled Diamond Lights. Chris was rejected by both Sunderland and Coventry after trials, while United also took a look at him as a young teenager only to let him go. His cousin, Alan Waddle appeared for Liverpool, Swansea and Newport.

Appearances:
FL: 169(1) apps. 46 gls.
FAC: 12 apps. 4 gls.
FLC: 9 apps. 2 gls.
Total: *190(1) apps. 52 gls.*
Honours:
62 Eng caps 1985-92/
1 Eng u21 cap 1985/
1 FL app. 1988/
FL div 2 prom 1984/
FAC finalist 1987, 1993/
FLC finalist 1993/
French Lg champs 1990, 1991, 1992/
French Cup finalist 1991/
EC finalist 1991/
FWA Footballer of the Year 1993.

WAKE, Henry Williamson

Role: Right-half 1919-1923
5' 7"
b. Seaton Delaval,
nr Newcastle upon Tyne,
21st January 1901
d. 19th July 1978

CAREER: Bigges Main/ Birtley/UNITED May 1919/ Cardiff City May 1923 £200/ Mansfield Town June 1931 £250/Gateshead July 1932 to c1933.

Debut v Manchester City (h)
17/4/20

Harry Wake

A prominent schoolboy footballer on Tyneside and captain of the club's junior set-up, Newcastle Swifts, Harry Wake was introduced into United's senior eleven towards the end of the 1919-20 season. But the youngster always had fierce competition for a half-back place at St James Park, with Finlay, Curry, Mooney and McIntosh all ahead of him in selection. Wake wasn't big and tough, more a waif-like figure in midfield. Harry possessed lots of honest endeavour, ability when on the ball and found a good home at Ninian Park, breaking through into first team soccer. He helped Cardiff reach two FA Cup finals in 1925 and 1927, and made headlines on both occasions. Against Sheffield United in 1925 he unfortunately lost the ball on the edge of the box for Fred Tunstall to net the only goal of the game, while two years later he scored in the semi-final but had to miss the final due to a kidney injury. Wake also helped the Welshmen to runners-up spot in the First Division during 1923-24 and totalled over 150 appearances for Cardiff. He later took part in Mansfield Town's first League game in 1931. Harry was related to William Wake who was on United's books in 1906-07 and later with Exeter, Plymouth and Queens Park Rangers.

Appearances:
FL: 3 apps. 0 gls.
War: 1 app. 0 gls.
Total: *4 apps. 0 gls.*
Honours:
2 Eng schools apps. 1915/
1 WL app. 1927/
FAC finalist 1925/
WshC winner 1930/
WshC finalist 1929.

Andy Walker

Walker also holds the ball up well and can bring others into the game. He scored nearly 70 goals in almost 200 games for the Parkhead club, before moving to Bolton after his unsuccessful stay on Tyneside. At Burnden Park Andy returned to his best, hitting 33 goals in season 1992-93. Unfortunately, injury halted his exciting progress and Walker found himself back in Glasgow, but in a second spell with the Celts found it difficult to recapture his earlier sparkle.

Appearances:
FL: 2 apps. 0 gls.
FLC: 1 app. 0 gls.
Total: *3 apps. 0 gls.*
Honours:
3 Scot caps 1988-95/1 Scot u21 cap 1988/
SL champs 1988/SL div 1 champs 1985/
SC winner 1988/SC finalist 1990/
SLC finalist 1995/FL div 2 prom 1993.

WALKER, Leonard

Role: Right-half 1963-1964
5' 11"
b. Darlington, 4th March 1944

CAREER: Middlesbrough amat 1959/ Spennymoor United 1962/UNITED May 1963 £250/Aldershot June 1964/Charterhouse School part-time coach/Darlington player-coach Aug 1976, becoming coach 1977, manager Oct 1978 to June 1979/Aldershot coach 1980, becoming manager Apr 1981 to Nov 1984, and, June 1985 to Mar 1991, being appointed general-manager/Fulham asst-manager July 1994.

Debut v Preston North End (h) 25/9/63 (FLC)

WALKER, Andrew F.

Role: Striker 1991
5' 8"
b. Glasgow, 6th April 1965

CAREER: Partick Thistle jnrs/Toronto Blizzard(Canada)/Baillieston jnrs 1983/ Motherwell July 1984/Glasgow Celtic July 1987 £350,000(UNITED loan Sept 1991)/Bolton Wanderers Feb 1992 £160,000/Glasgow Celtic June 1994 £550,000/Sheffield United Feb 1996 £500,000.

Debut v Millwall (a) 21/9/91

Only at St James Park for a brief spell on loan, Andy Walker didn't solve Ossie Ardiles' problem of finding a dangerous front man. The Scot never recaptured the form that had made him a potent attacker in Scotland, one of Celtic's heroes during their double victory in 1988 and Scotland's top goalgetter with 26 strikes. At his peak, Walker was an excellent poacher, small, yet quick and with good positional sense as well as the finish of a natural marksman.

After making only a single Football League appearance, plus a League Cup outing, for Newcastle during season 1963-64, Len Walker moved south to become one of the lower divisions' most noted players during the sixties and seventies. He was given little scope to impress under Joe Harvey's regime at Gallowgate, being in the shadows at half-back to Jim Iley, Stan Anderson and Ollie

Len Walker

Burton. But joining Aldershot was the break Walker needed and the gritty, competitive midfielder proceeded to total over 500 senior games for the Hampshire club. Also playing at full-back, Len became the Shots' record appearance holder and was club skipper for several seasons. Later, as manager, he guided the Recreation Ground club to promotion in 1987. On his retirement from the playing side of the game Walker again became a highly respected coach in the basement of professional football.

Appearances:
FL: 1 app. 0 gls.
FLC: 1 app. 0 gls.
Total: *2 apps. 0 gls.*
Honours:
FL div 4 prom 1973, 1987(m).

WALKER, Nigel Stephen

Role: Midfield 1977-1982
5' 10"
b. Gateshead, 7th April 1959

CAREER: Whickham/UNITED Apr 1977 (Plymouth Argyle loan 1981-82)/San Diego (USA) May 1982 free/Sunderland on trial Dec 1982/Crewe Alexandra Jan 1983/Sunderland July 1983(Blackpool loan 1983-84)/Chester June 1984/Hartlepool United June 1985 free/ Blyth Spartans cs 1987, becoming manager Jan 1992/Dunston Fed Nov 1992/RTM Newcastle Aug 1995.

Debut v Bristol City (h) 5/11/77

A skilful midfield player, Nigel Walker was blooded in United's relegation season from the First Division in 1977-78. With flair and style on the ball, and despite the test of playing in a desperate side, Nigel proved to the Geordie supporters in 14 outings that he was very much a discovery who had the potential to become a quality player. Walker developed further in United's Second Division line-up over the next three seasons, but again in a mediocre side. He did show flashes of genius, able to glide past two or three defenders in some exciting runs from midfield. However, United's coaching staff could never quite develop the Tynesider into a midfielder who, after this brilliant approach play, could deliver the final telling pass or shot. Under Arthur Cox's management, he was discarded and Walker drifted around the country, and across

the Atlantic, before returning to Tyneside where he concentrated on local football. He also studied computer sciences at Northumbria University gaining a first class honours degree and is currently a mathematics teacher at Lanchester Grammar School. As a schoolboy, Walker captained the county youth side at rugby union.

Appearances:
FL: 65(5) apps. 3 gls.
FAC: 3 apps. 0 gls.
FLC: 1 app. 0 gls.
Total: *69(5) apps. 3 gls.*

Nigel Walker

WALKER, Thomas Jackson

Role: Outside-right 1941-1954
5' 10"
*b. Cramlington, nr Newcastle upon Tyne,
14th November 1923*

CAREER: Netherton jnrs/UNITED Oct 1941/
Oldham Athletic Feb 1954 £2,500/Chesterfield
Feb 1957 £1,250/Oldham Athletic July 1957/
Retired Apr 1959.

Debut v Coventry City (h) 11/9/46

Tommy Walker began his career at centre-half,
but as wartime football came to a close had
developed into a pacy winger who could
operate on both flanks. Fast and direct, he
tended to pick the ball up deep and storm
down the touchline and proved a very
effective forward, especially
when in direct contrast to
the tricky ball-play of
Bobby Mitchell on the
opposite wing. In
season 1946-47 he was
a rival to Jackie
Milburn for the
Number 7 shirt, then
he had competition
from Sibley, Stobbart
and Hair at outside-
left. Tommy only
managed eight games
during United's promotion
campaign the following
season due to a broken arm, but by the start
of the 1948-49 season was installed as a
regular at outside-right. Walker was at his
peak as the Magpies
reached Wembley
twice in 1951 and
1952 when his
penetrating sorties
into the opponents'
box were a feature of
United's play. On
leaving Tyneside,
Tommy also served
Oldham well, turning
out in 164 matches
(23 goals) for the
Latics during two
spells. On retiring
Walker settled in the
Manchester area,
running a newsagents
in Middleton. A
methodist lay
preacher for a period,
Walker took part in
several sprint
handicaps, including
the famous
Powderhall meeting
in Edinburgh.

Appearances:
*FL: 184 apps. 35 gls.
FAC: 20 apps. 3 gls.
War: 29 apps. 2 gls.
Others: 2 apps. 0 gls.*
Total: *235 apps. 40 gls.*
Honours:
*FAC winner 1951,
1952.*

Tommy Walker

WALLACE, Joseph

Role: Forward 1890-1895
5' 10"
b. Ayrshire

CAREER: Glenbuck/Newmilns 1888/
Newcastle East End Jan 1891/UNITED
May 1892/Rendel (Newcastle) cs 1895.

*Debut v Sheffield United (a) 24/9/1892
(NL)*

Joseph Wallace

Joseph Wallace was a formidable Scot whose career commenced with the marvellously named Glenbuck 'Cherrypickers' side in Ayrshire. Enticed to Tyneside by East End's management he soon became a firm favourite of the small crowds that watched Newcastle United's embryo clubs. Wallace was a play-anywhere forward, appearing for United on either flank as well as in both inside-forward and wing roles. One of the mainstays of the club's first Football League season in 1893-94 (25 apps.), Joe netted six times in the first six league matches and ended top scorer with 15 goals. He not only took part in the club's first game against Arsenal, but also the initial game at St James Park with Celtic. Remaining on Tyneside for much of his life after leaving the football scene, Wallace later ran into financial difficulties. It is recorded in the club's official Minutes of Meetings that in March 1933 he was in dire straits, the club purchasing clothes and gifting him money.

Appearances:
NL: 8 apps. 6 gls.
FL: 42 apps. 19 gls.
FAC: 3 apps. 2 gls.
Total: *53 apps. 27 gls.*

WARBURTON, John

Role: Left-back 1894-1895
b. Tyneside

CAREER: UNITED 1894/Hebburn Argyle
1895 to 1899.

Debut v Leicester Fosse (h) 1/1/1896

Hailing from a popular local footballing family, Warburton came into United's side for three games in succession during the New Year period in season 1895-96. Deputising for international defender Bob Foyers, he didn't receive a further opportunity in Football League soccer, but gave the club's reserve side in the Northern Alliance good service. He joined another Alliance side, Hebburn Argyle in 1895 helping them win the title in 1896-97. Warburton left Hebburn in 1899 and afterwards appeared for several other local combinations.

Appearances:
FL: 3 apps. 0 gls.
Total: *3 apps. 0 gls.*

WARD, Edward

Role: Inside-right 1920-1922
5' 8"
b. Cowpen, Blyth, 16th June 1896

CAREER: Blyth Spartans/UNITED May 1920
£300/Crystal Palace June 1922 £250/Nelson
June 1923 to c1924.

Debut v West Bromwich Albion (h) 28/8/20

Newcastle United were attracted to Ted Ward after he impressed in a local cup final against the Magpies' reserve eleven. United's directors quickly snapped up the inside-forward and he just as rapidly made a name for himself in the First Division. Ward rivalled Ed Dixon at inside-right, but received the nod for much of the 1920-21 programme as the club challenged for the championship. Possessing pace, and a good touch of the ball, as well as a stinging shot, Ward looked to be a find. However, within 12 months Ted had been despatched south to join Crystal Palace where he recorded only four games for the Londoners before returning north to appear with Nelson during their Football League sojourn. His stay in London resulted in Palace requesting a refund on the transfer fee due to Ward being

Ted Ward

sidelined with a persistent knee complaint and he was eventually handed a free transfer.

Appearances:
FL: 21 apps. 5 gls.
FAC: 4 apps. 0 gls.
Total: *25 apps. 5 gls.*

WARD, W. A.

Role: Goalkeeper 1894-1896

CAREER: Loughborough Town/UNITED Sept 1894 to 1896.

Debut v Grimsby Town (h) 15/9/1894

A one-time inside-forward who began his career with Loughborough Town, Ward arrived at St James Park in September 1894 for the opening games of what was only the club's second programme in the Football League. He was installed as first choice goalkeeper and at one stage was described by the *Newcastle Daily Journal* as being "safe as the proverbial bank". Ward took over from Lowery and Ryder, but had taken part in both Newcastle's worst league defeat (0-9 to Burton Wanderers) and heaviest FA Cup reverse (1-7 to Aston Villa). By the end of the season United's team committee decided he was not the answer to a goalkeeping problem that continued for some years. Ward lost his place to Henderson and left the club in 1896.

Appearances:
FL: 18 apps. 0 gls.
FAC: 3 apps. 0 gls.
Total: *21 apps. 0 gls.*

WARDROPE, William

Role: Outside-left 1895-1900
5' 6"
b. Wishaw, Lanarkshire, 1876

CAREER: Dalziel Rovers/Motherwell amat/ Linthouse/UNITED May 1895/ Middlesbrough loan Apr 1900, pmt May 1900/ Third Lanark May 1902/Fulham cs 1904/ Swindon Town cs 1906/Hamilton Academical Sept 1907/Third Lanark 1908/ Raith Rovers cs 1908/USA & Canada coaching Sept 1910.

Debut v Loughborough Town (h) 7/9/1895 (scored once)

Willie Wardrope hit the scene in a major way during season 1895-96. With United's side just starting to develop after a couple of seasons of struggle, it was players like Wardrope who took the club forward to a different level of football. The Scot netted 20 goals in 36 games in his first season, all from the left-wing position, and proved a formidable opponent. Weighing in at 12 stone, Wardrope was small yet decidedly well built. He was also astute and skilful as well as the possessor of a terrific shot. During his opening campaign of 1895-96 Willie struck 13 goals in nine successive matches. For the next four seasons Wardrope continued to be a key player in United's cause, helping the black'n'whites to promotion in 1898. He was an international trialist just before the turn of the century, although later he was suspended by the Scottish FA for alleged irregularities. On leaving Tyneside, he appeared for several clubs, notably Third Lanark where he starred as the Glasgow club won the Scottish title, and for Fulham during their Southern League days, netting 32 goals in 70 appearances. Wardrope's brother Alex, turned out for Middlesbrough, Portsmouth and Airdrie. In 1910 Willie emigrated to the USA, residing for a period in Pittsburgh.

Willie Wardrope

Appearances:
FL: 131 apps. 45 gls.
FAC: 14 apps. 7 gls.
Total: *145 apps. 52 gls.*
Honours:
Scot trial app. 1899/1 SL app. 1903/ 1 Scot jnr app./FL div 2 prom 1898, 1902/ SL champs 1904/SnL champs 1906.

WARE, Harry

Role: Inside-right 1935-1937
5' 10"
b. Birmingham, 22nd October 1911
d. Stoke, 28th October 1970

CAREER: Hanley St Lukes/Cobridge Celtic/
Stoke St Peters/Stoke City amat Dec 1927, pro
Dec 1929/UNITED Sept 1935 £2,400/Sheffield
Wednesday May 1937 £1,700/Norwich City
Nov 1937/Northampton Town war-guest
1940-42/Nottingham Forest war-guest
1940-41/Stoke City war-guest 1940-41/
Crystal Palace war-guest 1942-43/Watford
war-guest 1942-44/Northwich Victoria
manager Sept 1946/EDO Haarlem(Holland)
trainer Aug 1948/Northwich Victoria
manager 1950 briefly/Port Vale
trainer 1956/Crewe Alexandra
manager June 1958 to May
1960/Stoke City asst-trainer
June 1960, later becoming scout
to his demise.

Debut v Fulham (h) 28/9/35
(scored once)

A play-anywhere
midfielder, Harry Ware
arrived at St James
Park as a schemer to
provide quality service
for centre-forward Jack
Smith. Winning a
promotion medal with
Stoke under the
guidance of Tom Mather,
his new boss at St James
Park, Harry was a slim
playmaker who could
create an opening.
Totalling 53 league
matches for City, he made
an impact during season
1935-36 when he rivalled
Billy Leighton for the inside-
right channel. But after that
early promise the Brummie
was injured, lost form and
faded from the scene moving
to Hillsborough. During World
War Two, Ware served as a
sergeant in an anti-tank platoon
and was wounded in the chest

Harry Ware

during the *Overlord* operation, an injury which
eventually forced his retirement from the first
class game. The son of a former boxing British
and European bantamweight champion, Harry
competed as a useful middleweight himself
and worked in the Potteries before turning
professional with Stoke. He later became an
American citizen after marrying into a New
Jersey family.

Appearances:
FL: 44 apps. 9 gls.
FAC: 5 apps. 0 gls.
Total: *49 apps. 9 gls.*
Honours:
FL div 2 champs 1933.

WATKIN, George

Role: Centre-forward 1962-1963
6' 0"
b. Chopwell, nr Gateshead,
14th April 1944

CAREER: Chopwell/UNITED
Apr 1962 £25/Kings Lynn July
1963/Chesterfield July 1964
£250/Gateshead cs 1965.

Debut v Bury (a) 1/12/62

George Watkin joined the
Magpies from a local junior
side and proceeded to
impress in the club's youth
and reserve line-ups. A
member of United's
successful FA Youth Cup
eleven in 1962, he was quick
off the mark at that level and
a threat up front. Deputising
once for Barrie Thomas in
Newcastle's centre-forward
shirt, Watkin came into a
much changed front line and
faced former United stalwart,
Bob Stokoe at Gigg Lane.
Watkin was up against it all
afternoon, Ivor Broadis
reporting in *The Journal* noted
George "had the sort of debut
that could well set him back a
bit". The raw youth showed
bags of guts but could get
nowhere against the
experienced Stokoe. Manager
Joe Harvey found little

requirement for the youngster thereafter and George moved into non-league football, re-appearing in the Football League for Chesterfield. He had seven outings for the Spireites before returning to Tyneside and joining up with Gateshead.

Appearances:
FL: 1 app. 0 gls.
Total: *1 app. 0 gls.*
Honours:
FAYC winner 1962.

WATSON, John

Role: Right-back 1902-1903
5' 11"
b. Newarthill, Lanarkshire

CAREER: Clyde/UNITED Nov 1902 £200/New Brompton/Brentford cs 1903/Leeds City July 1908/Clyde cs 1910.

Debut v Sheffield United (a) 15/11/02

With a big reputation in Scotland, John Watson was a popular character with Clyde and it was reported that there was much unrest in Glasgow when he moved to England. Appearing for the Glasgow select eleven, Watson was a well built and powerful defender who was purchased in an attempt to fill a problem right-back position. Newcastle had tried Davidson, Bennie, Wilson and Tildesley as well as Watson, but couldn't find a consistent player until Scottish international Andy McCombie arrived on the scene. John managed only a handful of games during season 1902-03 before he tried his luck south. A success with Brentford, he played on 169 occasions in Southern League football for the London club. Later Watson turned out in 45 league matches for Leeds City before continuing his career back on Clydeside.

Appearances:
FL: 3 apps. 0 gls.
Total: *3 apps. 0 gls.*

WATSON, John Ian

Role: Forward 1990-1993
5' 9"
b. South Shields, 14th April 1974

CAREER: Wallsend Boys Club/UNITED app June 1990, pro Apr 1992 to May 1993 free/ West Bromwich Albion trial cs 1993/ Scunthorpe United July 1993/Gateshead Feb 1994.

Debut v Hull City (h) 11/5/91 (sub)

A friend and contemporary of his namesake Steve Watson at both Burnside School and the renowned Wallsend Boys Club, both players developed through the junior ranks at St James Park, but went very different ways. While Steve became a noted star, John found it difficult to break into the first eleven following a brief appearance as substitute against Hull City on the last day of the season, and another flirtation during the Anglo-Italian Cup in 1992-93. A utility forward, operating in the centre-forward's role originally, Watson was handed a free transfer and managed only a handful of games for Scunthorpe before heading back to the region when he signed for Vauxhall Conference side Gateshead. John proceeded to become a regular fixture in the Tyneside club's line-up. When a junior with the black'n'whites, John was injured in serious car accident along with his colleagues on the A1 when returning from a match.

John Watson

Appearances:
FL: 0(1) app. 0 gls.
Others: 0(1) app. 0 gls.
Total: *0(2) apps. 0 gls.*

WATSON, Peter

Role: Right-back 1892-1893
b. Scotland

CAREER: Newmilns/Newcastle East End Jan 1891/UNITED May 1892/Rotherham Town Feb 1893 to 1894.

Debut v Middlesbrough Ironopolis (a) 19/11/1892 (NL)

Peter Watson was a capable full-back who arrived from Scotland along with Joe Wallace in 1891. First choice until the arrival of Harry Jeffrey, he was then reserve to Jeffrey during the club's earliest period at St James Park. Watson made only three appearances for the club during the Northern League season of 1892-93, but had little hope of shifting Jeffrey from the first eleven. Moving to join up with Rotherham's pioneer club, Watson took part in Town's first ever Football League season and faced Newcastle United as they entered senior action too, in 1893-94. Rotherham though, failed miserably in that testing debut campaign; they ended next to bottom of the table and had to seek re-election. Peter had become something of a local hero on Tyneside when he rescued a policeman in Byker from a gang during 1892.

> **Appearances:**
> *NL: 3 apps. 0 gls.*
> **Total:** *3 apps. 0 gls.*

WATSON, Stephen Craig

Role: Right-back 1989-date
6' 0"
b. North Shields, 1st April 1974

CAREER: Wallsend Boys Club/ UNITED sch cs 1989, app July 1990, pro Apr 1991.

Debut v Wolverhampton Wanderers (a) 10/11/90 (sub)

On many occasions Steve Watson has held his own in United's side of internationals. A versatile player who has been linked with the Magpies since he was a ten-year-old schoolboy, Watson operates in midfield, at right-back, in central defence or even in attack. He is also a more than adequate goalkeeper in emergency. Tall and powerful, Steve has skill on the ball and ability to find the net, striking several spectacular efforts for United. An England Under-21 regular, Watson was introduced as a teenager, the club's youngest ever player at 16 years and 223 days, when he appeared against Wolves in 1990.

Before he was 20 the Tynesider had made almost 100 appearances for the club he had supported since a schoolboy at Burnside. Steve had to take a back seat for the first period of Keegan's resurgence of the Magpies, but then claimed a permanent place on the bench. At times though the popular local product had long and impressive runs in the first team in a number of roles, settling more and more into a right-back spot where he rivalled big-money signing Warren Barton. Energetic with loads of enthusiasm, he also possesses a dangerous long throw, which was executed in his younger days with a somersault! Watson also had trials with Sunderland and Huddersfield before signing forms for United and has represented his country as a youth international

Steve Watson

in two World Cup tournaments, in Portugal and Australia. Curiously Steve once played for England's Under-21 eleven in the same week as he turned out in Newcastle's Northern Intermediate League line-up!

Appearances:
FL/PL: 112(24) apps. 10 gls.
FAC: 8(2) apps. 0 gls.
FLC: 8(4) apps. 1 gl.
Eur: 1(2) apps. 1 gl.
Others: 3(1) apps. 0 gls.
Total: 132(33) apps. 12 gls.
Honours:
12 Eng u21 caps 1993-date/Eng youth app.

WATTS, Charles

Role: Goalkeeper & Trainer 1896-1908
5' 9"
b. Middlesbrough, 1872
d. Newcastle upon Tyne,
23rd November 1924

CAREER: Middlesbrough Ironopolis 1892/Blackburn Rovers June 1893/ Burton Wanderers 1894(Blackburn Brooks loan 1895-96)/UNITED May 1896/Retired cs 1906, becoming asst-trainer to Apr 1908.

Debut v Small Heath (a) 5/9/1896

Taking over from John Henderson in United's goal, Charlie Watts can be recognised as the club's first custodian of note. A regular for two seasons as the Magpies claimed a First Division place, he was a robust 'keeper, agile for his era, with a reputation for punching the ball a long distance in the style of the day. He created several headlines; once in 1897 at Turf Moor, Charlie saved the same Burnley penalty kick three times. Yet like many goalkeepers of the early years, Watts was prone to error and as a consequence United's directors made a wide search for a new rival, signing Matt Kingsley in readiness for Newcastle's debut in the top flight. Charlie Watts though, remained at Gallowgate for another eight seasons, a loyal servant, rarely being given an extended run, especially when Jimmy Lawrence entered the action. He did however appear on four occasions during the black'n'whites title winning season in 1904-05. On retirement Watts assisted on the coaching staff at St James Park, but then left the game, afterwards being a noted racing enthusiast on Tyneside.

Charlie Watts

A loveable personality, it was remarked that he won and lost three fortunes as both a race-horse owner and tipster. Charlie was also a gambler during his playing career, in 1898 winning a then huge amount of £600 in prize money in a *Sporting Chronicle* racing skills competition. His death occurred under tragic circumstances; reports indicated he committed suicide by cutting his own throat in the back lane of his home after being in a desperate state following an unsuccessful bet to win £3,000 in order to clear mounting debts. His son was also found with wounds and a fractured skull, injuries received in an apparent domestic dispute. At the inquest, Newcastle's former 'keeper's sad demise was recorded as "suicide during temporary insanity".

Appearances:
FL: 93 apps. 0 gls.
FAC: 8 apps. 0 gls.
Total: *101 apps. 0 gls.*
Honours:
FL div 2 prom 1898.

WAUGH, Kenneth

Role: Right-back 1952-1956
5' 6"
b. Newcastle upon Tyne, 6th August 1933

CAREER: East End Rangers/Film Renters/ UNITED Aug 1952 £10/Hartlepools United Dec 1956 £680/Retired May 1962.

Debut v Arsenal (a) 15/10/55

With Bobby Cowell's career being shortened due to injury, the right-back spot in United's side was contested by four players, one of which was local product Ken Waugh. He rivalled George Lackenby, Arnold Woollard and the experienced Ron Batty until the arrival of Irishman Dick Keith settled the issue in no uncertain terms. Waugh was given a run in the side during season 1955-56, but wasn't considered First Division quality at that time. Ken was transferred soon after, moving down the east coast to the Victoria Ground where he topped 200 senior games for Hartlepool. On retiring from the game, he later emigrated to Australia.

Appearances:
FL: 7 apps. 0 gls.
Total: *7 apps. 0 gls.*

WAUGH, Robert

Role: Right-back 1908-1912
5' 8"
b. Newcastle upon Tyne

CAREER: Newcastle Bentonians/UNITED Jan 1908/Derby County cs 1912 £100 to 1915/ Hartlepools United war-guest 1919/ Jarrow Sept 1919.

Debut v Aston Villa (h) 11/12/09

An engineer by trade, Bob Waugh rendered useful service to the Magpies without ever threatening his rival in the senior side. That was the great Bill McCracken, so it wasn't unexpected that Waugh only collected a handful of games for the club, his best haul being eight matches during 1909-10. But on the odd occasion he did win a place in McCracken's absence through injury or international duty, Waugh pleased the crowd immensely, one local press report making the comment that he "has the ability and the temperament to reach the heights". Moving to Derby, Bob appeared on 29 occasions for the Rams before returning to the north east, initially with Hartlepool in the Northern Victory League immediately after World War One, then for a lengthy spell in North Eastern League football.

Appearances:
FL: 11 apps. 1 gl.
Total: *11 apps. 1 gl.*
Honours:
FL div 2 champs 1915.

Bob Waugh

WAYMAN, Charles

Role: Centre-forward 1941-1947
5' 6"
b. Bishop Auckland, 16th May 1921

CAREER: Chilton Colliery/Spennymoor United/UNITED Sept 1941/Portsmouth war-guest 1944-45/Southampton Oct 1947 £10,000/Preston North End Sept 1950 £10,000 plus E.Brown/Middlesbrough Sept 1954 £8,000/Darlington Dec 1956/Retired Apr 1958 due to injury/Evenwood Town coach briefly.

Debut v Barnsley (h) 5/1/46 (FAC)

Charlie Wayman was a consistent goalscorer throughout his career, netting over 300 goals. Small, cool and skilful with the ball, Wayman

Charlie Wayman

developed through wartime football at St James Park after writing to Stan Seymour for a trial. He was to quickly become a feared striker as United attempted to gain promotion as soon as peacetime soccer returned in 1946. With a lethal left foot, he was mobile and twice scored four goals in a single match for the Magpies. During season 1946-47 he grabbed 34 goals, but was at the centre of an unsavoury dispute with club officials on the eve of Newcastle's FA Cup semi-final with Charlton Athletic. Top scorer Wayman was dropped, United lost 0-4 and afterwards also missed a promotion place. Charlie was then quickly transferred, for a club record fee, to Southampton where he became a most popular centre-forward, hitting 77 goals in only 107 senior outings. In one match against Leicester during 1948 the explosive and quick-thinking Number 9 struck five goals. And at Deepdale with Preston, Wayman again registered a first-class goals record, netting in every round of their run to Wembley in the FA Cup of 1954. Several observers of the era reckoned it was only a lack of inches that stopped him winning an England cap, while Wayman was the Football League's divisional top goalgetter in 1946-47, 1948-49 and 1952-53. During wartime service, Charlie served as an able seaman in the Royal Navy then entered essential work in the Durham coalfield. On retiring from the game due to a knee injury, Wayman was employed by Scottish & Newcastle Breweries, residing in his native area of Bishop Auckland, at Coundon near Shildon. His brother Frank appeared for Chester.

Appearances:
FL: 47 apps. 32 gls.
FAC: 6 apps. 4 gls.
War: 71 apps. 35 gls.
Total: *124 apps. 71 gls.*
Honours:
FL Div 2 champs 1951/FAC finalist 1954.

Charlie Wayman

WEAVER, Samuel

Role: Left-half 1929-1936
5' 9"
b. Pilsley, Derbyshire, 8th February 1909
d. Mansfield, 15th April 1985

CAREER: Pilsley Red Rose/Sutton Junction
on trial/Sutton Town 1926/Hull City Mar
1928 £50/UNITED Nov 1929 £2,500/Chelsea
Aug 1936 £4,166/Southampton war-guest
1939-40/Fulham war-guest 1939-44/
Notts County war-guest 1942-43/
Derby County war-guest 1942-43/
West Ham United war-guest 1943-44/
Mansfield Town war-guest 1945-46/
Wrexham war-guest 1945-46/
Leeds United war-guest 1944-45/
Stockport County Dec 1945/Retired cs 1947/
Leeds United asst-trainer 1947/Millwall
trainer June 1949/Oxo Sports Club(Bromley)
Jan 1954/Mansfield Town trainer Sept 1955,
becoming manager June 1958 to Jan 1960
when he reverted to asst-trainer to 1967, then
scout to Oct 1980/Also appeared as a cricketer
for Somerset(1939) and Derbyshire(1934),
becoming county masseur in 1956.

Debut v Arsenal (a) 30/11/29
(scored once)

Sam Weaver was a polished and powerful
wing-half who became a household name
during the thirties. Although remembered in
the game's history as a player who mastered a
prodigious long-throw - considered to be the
longest in the game at the time - Weaver's
ability was much more than producing a

S. WEAVER.

Sam Weaver

touch-line fling. He was a formidable midfielder who established himself as an England player as Newcastle lifted the FA Cup at Wembley in 1932. Netting on his debut at Highbury for United, then also on his first home appearance, Sam possessed a marvellous engine coupled with stamina and a driving power that ran the Magpies' midfield for seven seasons. And when his flowing black head of hair reached the penalty area it always meant problems for the opposition. Captain of the club on many occasions, Weaver tumbled with United into the Second Division in 1933, but remained loyal to the black'n'whites in a bid to regain their top flight status. But after two seasons of failure, Weaver's undoubted talent was stagnating and no-one was surprised when he moved back into Division One following a big move to Stamford Bridge. At Chelsea he again became a popular character, totalling 125 games for the Blues, and also skippering the Londoners before the Second World War halted his career. Weaver though, remained connected with the game for many years thereafter. Associated with his local club, Mansfield Town for over 25 years, he was a noted football personality right up to his death. Sam was also a fine cricketer although, due to his football commitments, only managed two first-class games in the County Championship as a lower order batsman and left arm bowler. When he died in 1985, Sam Weaver's ashes were scattered over the Field Mill pitch at Mansfield.

Appearances:
FL: 204 apps. 41 gls.
FAC: 25 apps. 2 gls.
Others: 1 app. 0 gls.
Total: *230 apps. 43 gls.*
Honours:
3 Eng caps 1932-33/
Eng trial app. 1932-34/
FA app. 1934/
2 FL apps. 1933-34/
FAC winner 1932.

WHARTON, Kenneth

Role: Left-back & Midfield 1978-1989
5' 8"
b. Blakelaw, Newcastle upon Tyne, 28th November 1960

CAREER: St Marys Boys Club/Duke of Northumberland/Dodds Arms/Hull City trial/Grainger Park Boys Club/UNITED app Jan 1978, pro Jan 1979/Retired due to injury May 1989/Middlesbrough trial July 1989/Carlisle United Aug 1989/Bradford City trial Sept 1989/West Bromwich Albion trial Oct 1989/Berwick Rangers Oct 1989/Whitley Bay Dec 1989/Winnipeg Furies(Canada) Apr 1990, later becoming player-manager/Gateshead Jan 1992/Whitley Bay Dec 1992/St Johnstone coach Dec 1992 to Nov 1993/Middlesbrough asst-coach July 1994/Also appeared in local Tyneside Sunday football, for Blakelaw SC.

Debut v West Ham United (a) 24/3/79 (sub)

A former captain of Newcastle schoolboys, Kenny Wharton was nicknamed 'Bones' due to his slight frame. Although he was not physically imposing, Kenny was a furious competitor, never shirking a challenge against a much bigger opponent. Wharton also possessed

Kenny 'Bones' Wharton

talent on the ball, able to operate in the left-back position as well as in midfield, roles he filled in equal parts for United. With skill to deliver accurate passes and an ability to find the net, Wharton proved a valuable player for the club over the 11 seasons he was a member of the first team squad, remarkably surviving six changes of manager during that period. A regular from season 1980-81, he filled both defensive and midfield positions as Newcastle won promotion in 1983-84, while Kenny had his best season under the guidance of Jack Charlton the following year. An injury to his cartilage ended a career in the first class game, although he attempted several comebacks elsewhere. Kenny was granted a testimonial in 1989 when a crowd of 20,899 turned up at Gallowgate, and afterwards he assisted several clubs in a bid to get back into football before settling in a role at Ayresome Park coaching youngsters. His son Paul, an England youth player, is with Hull City, while Kenny is married to the grand-daughter of United pioneer, Tommy Ghee.

Appearances:
FL: 268(22) apps. 26 gls.
FAC: 22 apps. 0 gls.
FLC: 13(2) apps. 1 gl
Others: 8 apps. 0 gls.
Total: *311(24) apps. 27 gls.*
Honours:
FL div 2 prom 1984.

WHITE, John

Role: Right-back 1896-1898
5' 10"
b. Galston, nr Kilmarnock

CAREER: Kilmarnock/St Mirren 1894/Clyde 1895/UNITED May 1896 to cs 1898/Dundee 1898/Leicester Fosse 1899 to 1900.

Debut v Small Heath (a)
5/9/1896

A strong and sturdy full-back, John White turned out on both flanks for United during his two seasons of service. Following Newcastle's promotion into the First Division, White

John White

moved back to Scotland appearing in Dundee's first game at Dens Park in August 1899. He later had a brief excursion with Leicester, without making their Football League side.

Appearances:
FL: 48 apps. 1 gl.
FAC: 5 apps. 0 gls.
Total: *53 apps. 1 gl.*
Honours:
FL Div 2 prom 1898.

WHITE, Leonard Roy

Role: Centre-forward 1953-1962
5' 7"
b. Skellow, nr Doncaster, 23rd March 1930
d. Huddersfield, 17th June 1994

CAREER: Upton Colliery/Rotherham United May 1948/UNITED Feb 1953 £12,500/Huddersfield Town Feb 1962 exch for J.Kerray plus £10,000/Stockport County Jan 1965 £4,000/Altrincham cs 1966/Sligo Rovers/Ossett Town/Brown Tractors/Elland United/Huddersfield YMCA and other local Yorkshire non-league sides/Bradford City asst-coach briefly.

Debut v Liverpool (h) 21/2/53

Initially purchased by United as cover for Tommy Walker on the right wing, during the first few seasons of his career at St James Park Len White operated as a versatile forward, playing across the front line. While he had a few games in the Number 9 shirt up to season 1957-58, it was the departure of Jackie Milburn and Vic Keeble that led to a permanent switch for White into the leader's role. And what a success the stocky Yorkshireman made of the opportunity. In his first season he netted 25 goals, then hit the target on a regular basis thereafter, scoring 25, 29, and 29 times in the next three campaigns. Once grabbing four goals in a single game for United, he had terrific strength on the ball, weaving in and out of challenges at speed and was able to finish with a power-packed shot. White loved to attack defences on his own and he set the Gallowgate crowd roaring with many a spectacular goal. No-one on Tyneside doubted his quality, and there was much anger when Len was continually overlooked for the England side, especially after he had shown top

Len White - only Jackie Milburn has scored more goals for United in league and cup football.

Len White celebrates a United goal against Manchester City.

form in his country's shirt at Football League level, striking an eight minute hat-trick against the Irish in 1958. A former plate layer at Bullcroft and Burradon pits, White's Newcastle career was halted as the Magpies battled for points in their relegation season of 1960-61. In a clash with Dave Mackay of Spurs, Len was carried from the field and sidelined for almost six months. By the time he returned to the fray United were in Division Two and former team-mate Joe Harvey was installed on a rebuilding programme. White was not part of his plans and he moved to firstly, Huddersfield, then Stockport, where he enjoyed a fruitful swansong to his career, totalling almost 300 goals by the time he left senior football. In fact, White didn't stop playing the game he loved until well into his 50's, appearing for several pub and works teams in the West Yorkshire area. Len resided in Huddersfield and worked in manufacturing to his death. Several brothers

of his large family also played soccer to a good level; Fred, Albert and John all appearing in the Football League. With only the legendary Jackie Milburn scoring more goals than Len in United's past, White can be recognised in Newcastle's history as the finest forward not to gain a full England cap. He was also worshipped during the late 1950's almost as much as 'Wor Jackie' had been in the years before.

Appearances:
FL: 244 apps. 142 gls.
FAC: 22 apps. 11 gls.
FLC: 3 apps. 0 gls.
Others: 1 app. 0 gls.
Total: *270 apps. 153 gls.*
Honours:
2 FL apps. 1959-60/
FA app./
FAC winner 1955/
FL div 3 (N) champs 1951.

WHITEHEAD, Robert

Role: Right-back 1954-1962
5' 9"
b. Ashington, 22nd September 1936

CAREER: Fatfield/UNITED Dec 1954
(Cambridge City loan 1961-62)/Darlington
July 1962 £600 to c1964.

Debut v Burnley (a) 28/9/57

Bob Whitehead spent eight seasons on
United's staff after signing as a youngster. He
was though, only considered for selection in
Football League action for three of those years,
making his debut during 1957-58. He stepped
in for Dick Keith in the right-back role on 19
occasions during the next two seasons and
was a capable and sound reserve, but had
little chance of permanently dislodging the
Northern Ireland international. After a period
in non-league football with Cambridge City,
he returned north to serve Darlington in
almost 50 matches. After leaving the game,
Whitehead settled in Stakeford and was
employed by an electrical manufacturer in
Bedlington.

Appearances:
FL: 20 apps. 0 gls.
Total: *20 apps. 0 gls.*

WHITEHURST, William

Role: Centre-forward 1985-1986
6' 1"
b. Thurnscoe, nr Barnsley, 10th June 1959

CAREER: Retford Town/Bridlington Trinity/
Mexborough Town/Hull City Oct 1980
£1,800/UNITED Dec 1985 £232,500/Oxford
United Oct 1986 £187,500/Reading Feb 1988
£120,000/Sunderland Sept 1988 £100,000/Hull
City Dec 1988 £150,000/Sheffield United Feb
1990 £35,000(Stoke City loan 1990-91)/
Doncaster Rovers Mar 1991 free(Crewe
Alexandra loan 1991-92)/Hatfield Main/
Kettering Town/Goole Town/Stafford
Rangers 1992/Mossley/South China (Hong
Kong)/Glentoran Jan 1993/Frickley Athletic
1993, becoming manager Nov 1994.

Debut v Luton Town (a) 7/12/85

A whole-hearted striker, powerfully built at 6'
1" and over 14 stones, Billy Whitehurst caught
the eye of manager Willie McFaul when
United's boss was hunting for a new centre-
forward. In his first spell with Hull City,
Whitehurst had scored over 50 goals in a little
over 200 league and cup games for the Tigers
and the ex bricklayer was given a chance in
First Division football at St James Park.
Although not the most subtle or mobile striker
the club has fielded, Billy stuck gallantly to his
task in a short period wearing the
black'n'white shirt. But scoring seven goals in
21 appearances during season 1985-86 wasn't
deemed good enough for Division One action
and he was replaced by Paul Goddard in the
next campaign. Playing the game hard, but fair,
Billy then moved around the circuit, helping
Oxford during their historic
period in the top flight.
Whitehurst later continued
his career in the Unibond
League as manager of
Frickley Athletic.

Billy Whitehurst

Appearances:
FL: 28 apps. 7 gls.
FAC: 1 app. 0 gls.
FLC: 1(1) apps. 0 gls.
Total:
30(1) apps. 7 gls.
Honours:
FL div 3 prom 1985/
FL div 4 prom 1983/
FL div 2 prom 1990.

WHITSON, Thomas Thompson

Role: Left-back 1905-1919
5' 8"
b. Cape Town, South Africa, 1885
d. Walker, Newcastle upon Tyne,
10th January 1945

CAREER: Walker Athletic/Walker Parish/
UNITED Feb 1905 £65/Carlisle United
player-trainer Oct 1919 to 1924.

Debut v Notts County (a) 14/4/06

Nicknamed 'Tony' and born in South Africa
when his Geordie parents were working in
Cape Town, Whitson was a lightweight
defender, something of a rarity on United's
books during the glory years up to World War
One. But he was tough and
durable and, once he had
claimed a place for the
1908-09 title winning
season when he was
voted best left-back
in the country,
became difficult to
dislodge from the
full-back position
until Frank
Hudspeth
entered the fray.
Whitson had
accurate
distribution from
defence, and as a
consequence fitted
into United's
classical passing
style with ease. He
was remembered for a
well-timed sliding tackle,
a typical feature of his play,
and whilst at his peak in
1910 and 1911, Tony reached
the fringe of the international set-up. He
unluckily missed the 1910 FA Cup final replay
due to injury, although he appeared in six of
the earlier games and the initial clash with
Barnsley at the Crystal Palace. As war
approached in 1914, Whitson had the
distinction of winning the first army training
session at St James Park, a rifle range
competition set-up on the pitch! During a
period at Carlisle, he coached and skippered
the Cumbrians to a North Eastern League
championship win in 1922. During the inter-

'Tony' Whitson

war years, Tony resided in Walker, employed
as an engineer at Swan Hunter's and Parson's
works on the Tyne.

Appearances:
FL: 124 apps. 0 gls.
FAC: 21 apps. 0 gls.
Others: 1 app. 0 gls.
Total: *146 apps. 0 gls.*
Honours:
Eng trial app. 1911/
1 FL app. 1909/
FL champs 1909/
FAC finalist 1910(first game), 1911.

WHITTON, David

Role: Goalkeeper 1892-1893
b. Tyneside

CAREER: Newcastle West End 1889/
UNITED May 1892 £10/
Shankhouse Black Watch cs 1893.

Debut v Sheffield United (a) 24/9/1892
(NL)

Small in stature for a goalkeeper,
Dave Whitton was the club's first
guardian following the change in
venue from Heaton to St James
Park during the summer of 1892.
An established 'keeper on Tyneside
during the Victorian pioneering
days of the game, Whitton was
described by the local press as "a
bundle of energy". He appeared for
the club during the 1892-93 Northern
League programme just prior to the
club's entry into the Football
League, while he also took part
in the first game on the
Leazes' turf, against Celtic.
By the time Newcastle
were voted into the
Second Division, Dave had
departed for local rivals,
Shankhouse. Whitton
additionally took part in
Newcastle West End's first
ever FA Cup proper fixture
against Grimsby Town in 1890.

Appearances:
NL: 10 apps. 0 gls.
FAC: 1 app. 0 gls.
Total: *11 apps. 0 gls.*

Dave Whitton

WILKINSON, Jack

Role: Outside-left 1930-1932
5' 7"
*b. Wath upon Dearne,
Yorkshire, 13th June 1902
d. April 1969*

CAREER: Dearne Valley Old Boys/Wath Athletic Feb 1925/ Sheffield Wednesday Oct 1925 £250/ UNITED May 1930 £3,000/Lincoln City Sept 1932 £600/Sunderland Jan 1935/ Hull City Oct 1936/Scunthorpe United Aug 1937 to 1939/Ransomes & Marles manager Dec 1947.

Debut v Sheffield Wednesday (a) 30/8/30

Fast, small and weighing only 9 stones, Jack Wilkinson, who was known as 'Ginger', was a noted schoolboy player in Yorkshire, a trialist for his country at that level. He netted 100 goals from the wing in non-league football, form which alerted the attentions of Yorkshire clubs. He entered senior football with Sheffield Wednesday as a teenager and scored on his debut during season 1925-26. In that year Jack inspired the Owls to promotion from Division Two but, following a bright opening in the higher level, faded from the scene at Hillsborough. Newcastle stepped in and gave Wilkinson an opportunity to rival Tommy Lang for the outside-left position. He claimed the shirt in 1930-31 with some stylish displays in Newcastle's forward line, then lost his place to the Scot. Moving to Sincil Bank, Wilkinson assisted Lincoln to the Midland League championship.

Appearances:
FL: 30 apps. 7 gls.
FAC: *2 apps. 0 gls.*
Total: *32 apps. 7 gls.*
Honours:
FL div 2 champs 1926.

Jonathan Wilkinson

WILKINSON, Jonathan Montague

Role: Centre-forward 1927-1929
5' 8"
*b. Esh Winning, Co. Durham, 18th July 1908
d. Newcastle upon Tyne,
19th September 1979*

CAREER: Esh Winning/Durham City/Crook Town 1927/UNITED May 1927 £250/Everton June 1929 £675/Blackpool Mar 1931/Charlton Athletic Feb 1933 £550 to c1940.

Debut v Aston Villa (a) 29/10/27

Auburn-haired local starlet Jonathan Wilkinson was hot property as a youngster in Durham football. Nimble of foot, he was quickly captured by Newcastle's scouts and entered action at St James Park as an understudy to Hughie Gallacher. An ex pit boy, he was given the nickname 'Monte' and showed delightful touches in attack when given an opportunity, stepping in for Gallacher during his periods of international action and suspension. In 1927-28 Wilkinson grabbed nine goals in 16 outings, and on occasion switched to inside-right, linking up with 'Wee Hughie' to good effect. He once netted an unforgettable hat-trick in 1928 against Aston Villa during one of the most enthralling tussles seen at St James Park, a fixture which ended in United's favour by 7-5! Supporters considered Monte deserved a better deal at Newcastle, but he was sold to Everton where he amazingly found himself reserve to the game's other legendary centre-forward, Dixie Dean! With Charlton, Jon at last claimed a regular place and netted 50 goals in 235 senior matches. He played an important part in the Londoners' rise from Division Three to runners-up spot in the First Division in 1936-37. Wilkinson served in Burma during World War Two, and later resided in Lincoln for a period before returning to the north east. He became a cinema manager in Washington.

Appearances:
FL: 27 apps. 11 gls.
Total: *27 apps. 11 gls.*
Honours:
*FL div 3 (S) champs 1935/
FL div 2 prom 1936.*

Ron Williams

WILLIAMS, Ronald

Role: Centre-forward 1933-1935
5' 8"
b. Llansamlet, nr Swansea, 23rd January 1907
d. Swansea, 30th March 1987

CAREER: National Oil Refinery(Skewen)/
Bethel jnrs/Swansea Town cs 1929(Llanelli
loan)/UNITED Nov 1933 £1,500/Chester Apr
1935 £800/Swansea Town May 1936/ Chester
cs 1939/Swansea Town war-guest 1940-
43/Lovells Athletic/Milford Haven.

Debut v Aston Villa (a) 25/11/33 (scored once)

Ron Williams was purchased by Newcastle in
a bid to get United out of relegation trouble in
Division One after FA Cup hero Jack Allen
had lost pace and form during season 1933-34.
Williams had been converted from the wing at
the Vetch Field and proved a dashing leader
with a robust style. He was difficult to knock
off the ball and arrived on Tyneside after
hitting plenty of goals for the Welshmen,
including a hat-trick on his Christmas Day
debut in 1929. Ronnie was one of the earliest
Welshmen to pull on a Newcastle shirt and
began like a man inspired, striking ten goals in
ten games. But then the Magpies became
bogged down in a tense relegation struggle
and the goals dried up. Capped by Wales
when at St James Park, Williams had in fact
appeared for the club's 'A' team against local
works outfit Reyrolles, then travelled to play
for his country against England a few days

later. He departed from the north east soon
after the club's First Division status was lost,
later returning to the Swans where he totalled
187 games and 51 goals. A fine cricketer,
Ronnie appeared for Swansea, and during the
Second World War served as a policeman. He
resided in the South Wales town, employed by
Swansea Council housing department.
Williams was also a bowls player of some
note, being capped by Wales in 1976.

Appearances:
FL: 35 apps. 14 gls.
FAC: 1 app. 0 gls.
Total: *36 apps. 14 gls.*
Honours:
2 Wales caps 1935/
3 WL apps. 1930-33/
WshC winner 1932.

WILLIS, David L.

Role: Right or Left-half 1907-1913
5' 7"
b. Byker, Newcastle upon Tyne, July 1881
d. New Southgate, London, 26th May 1949

CAREER: Gateshead LNER/Sunderland
1901/Reading May 1903/Sunderland cs
1904/UNITED May 1907 £100/Reading May
1913 to 1915/Palmers(Jarrow) 1919/Raith
Rovers trainer 1920/Nottingham Forest trainer
July 1925/Derby County trainer June 1933 to
June 1947/Derbyshire CCC masseur May 1949
to death.

Debut v Nottingham Forest (h) 28/9/07

One of only a handful of players to have
joined United from Sunderland where he
made 53 appearances, Dave Willis returned to
his native Tyneside as a utility half-back, able
to operate in any midfield role. With plenty of
talent at St James Park already, Willis still
managed to claim conspicuous success,
gaining regular selection in seasons 1907-08,
1908-09, when the title was secured, and
1911-12. He also came into United's FA Cup
final side after an injury to Peter McWilliam in
1911. Cool-headed with a broad Geordie
accent, Dave gave plenty of effort on the field
for six seasons. On retiring from the game
after the First World War, he began a coaching
career in football. At Raith he was associated
with the early development of the great Alex
James - the famous Scot married his daughter -
and once installed at the Baseball Ground he

Dave Willis

trained the Rams to a Wembley FA Cup victory over Charlton in 1946. Additionally, when based in the Midlands, Willis was masseur to the Indian cricket side when they visited Trent Bridge and died shortly after a match at The Oval. He passed away at the home of his son-in-law, Alex James.

Appearances:
FL: 95 apps. 3 gls.
FAC: 12 apps. 1 gl.
Others: 1 app. 0 gls.
Total: *108 apps. 4 gls.*
Honours:
FL champs 1909/FAC finalist 1911.

WILLIS, Robert

Role: Inside-right 1893-1895
5' 10"
b. Northumberland

CAREER: Shankhouse Black Watch/UNITED amat Dec 1893/Shankhouse Black Watch 1895.
Debut v Small Heath (a) 16/12/1893 (scored once)

The *Newcastle Daily Chronicle* described Bobby Willis as a "well known forward" when he joined United's staff for the Christmas programme of 1893. A noted amateur player, he had already appeared for the Northumberland County side and, as the local press recorded, "proved a great acquisition".

Coming into United's forward line during the Tynesiders' first Football League season, Willis struck a goal on his debut and in a derby encounter with Middlesbrough Ironopolis over the New Year celebrations, scored twice as United hammered the Tees' club 7-2. Bobby did well the following season too, hitting 14 goals in only 20 games, but then left the club to return to semi-amateur football.

Appearances:
FL: 34 apps. 19 gls.
FAC: 2 apps. 0 gls.
Total: *36 apps. 19 gls.*

WILLS, Thomas

Role: Left-back 1903-1906
5' 9"
b. Kilmarnock
d. Johannesburg, South Africa, February 1912

CAREER: Ayr/UNITED Nov 1903/Crystal Palace 1906/Carlisle United 1908 to c1910/ Johannesburg(S.Africa) player-coach to demise.
Debut v Bury (h) 28/11/03

After showing up well in Scottish junior football, several clubs were interested in Thomas Wills' defensive qualities when he moved across the border to sign for Newcastle. Replacing the experienced William Agnew at left-back during the 1903-04 season, he wasn't an immediate success and the club's team committee elevated local product Jack Carr to the position within a few months. Wills though, did appear twice in United's championship winning season the following year, but moved to Crystal Palace soon after. He was with Carlisle for only a brief period before emigrating to South Africa where he played and coached the game in Johannesburg until his death.

Thomas Wills

Appearances:
FL: 18 apps. 0 gls.
FAC: 1 app. 0 gls.
Total: *19 apps. 0 gls.*

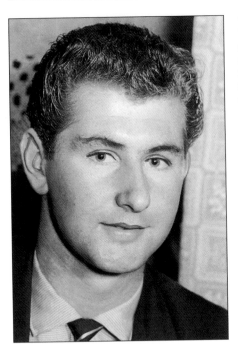

WILSON, Carl Alan

Role: Centre-forward 1958-1959
6' 0"
b. Lanchester, Co Durham, 8th May 1940

CAREER: Crookhall jnrs/Derwent Valley jnrs/Delves Lane jnrs/UNITED Feb 1958/Gateshead Dec 1959 £410/Doncaster Rovers July 1960/Millwall July 1961 to 1963/Sparta Rotterdam (Holland) July 1962/Weiss Essen (Germany) cs 1963 to cs 1964.

Debut v Blackpool (a) 25/8/58

A strong and muscular centre-forward who worked at Crookhall pit near Consett, and the son of United centre-half Joe Wilson (1927-30), Carl Wilson was handed a league baptism when 18 years old as a 24-hour replacement for Len White. That match was Wilson's only taste of senior football for United and the robust leader was given a good report, *The Journal* noting "all credit went to Wilson for the fighting effort". Carl had an unlucky career as a youth at Gallowgate, breaking his wrist as well as his ankle and finding another opportunity proved difficult. Appearing for Gateshead during their last days of Football League soccer and briefly at Millwall (5 apps.)

when they lifted the Division Four title in 1962, Carl struggled to find consistent form at any of his English based clubs, but after moving to the continent he developed into a noted striker, once scoring a hat-trick for Sparta in a European Cup Winners' Cup tie during 1962. After his career, Wilson returned to the area of his birth, settling in Hurbeck near Consett. He became involved in the haulage business as well as having an involvement in a landholding.

Appearances:
FL: 1 app. 0 gls.
Total: *1 app. 0 gls.*

WILSON, George W.

Role: Outside-left 1907-1919
5' 6"
b. Lochgelly, nr Dunfermline, 1884
d. Canada, 2nd June 1960

CAREER: Buckhaven/Cowdenbeath 1902/Heart of Midlothian May 1903/Everton May 1906 £800(Distillery loan 1907-08)/ UNITED Nov 1907 £1,600/Raith Rovers cs 1919 £250/East Fife 1920/Albion Rovers/ Raith Rovers manager cs 1926 to Feb 1927/ St Andrews(Vancouver, Canada).

Debut v Liverpool (a) 14/12/07 (scored twice)

George Wilson was one of the country's biggest names when he signed for United for a new nationwide record fee. Although known as 'Smiler', he was a dour Scot, cunning on the ball, and making up for his lack of inches with extra pounds. Wilson made a name for himself at Tynecastle in Edinburgh, winning Scotland caps before a joint move to Everton along with his brother, David, developed his career further. His stay at Goodison Park was a stormy one though, as George never hit it off with the Everton directors and, after vehement remarks concerning the side's style of play, he was dropped from their FA Cup final side after starring in six successful games leading up to the final. Afterwards he was disciplined and despatched to Belfast to appear for Distillery. Newcastle stepped in and thereafter started a marvellous association with the Magpies. Noted by one commentator as a, "purest football gem", for eight seasons "Wee Geordie" served the club at outside-left and inside-left, and the chunky little Scot became a much loved personality at Gallowgate.

Newcastle's attractive style of play suited his talent; he was tricky and fast, becoming an important figure in the black'n'whites successful side that won the title in 1909 and reached three FA Cup finals. Towards the end of his career, younger wingers Goodwill and Booth pushed him hard for a place as the First World War approached, and after serving in the Royal Navy, Wilson moved back to Fife. George is one of only a few footballers to have

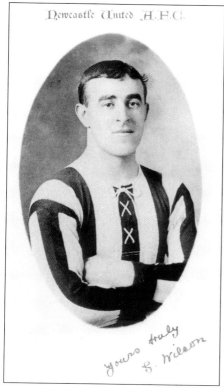

won both a Scottish and English cup winners medal. He netted Hearts' only goal of the 1906 Scottish Cup final against Third Lanark, while he was also influential as United lifted the FA Cup for the first time in 1910. Wilson later emigrated to Canada where he died in 1960.

Appearances:
FL: 176 apps. 25 gls.
FAC: 41 apps. 8 gls.
Others: 1 app. 0 gls.
Total: *218 apps. 33 gls.*
Honours:
6 Scot caps 1904-09/1 SL app. 1906/1 IL app. 1908/FL champs 1909/FAC winner 1910/ FAC finalist 1908, 1911/SC winner 1906.

WILSON, James

Role: Outside-left 1959-1962
5' 6"
b. Newmilns, nr Kilmarnock, 20th April 1942

CAREER: Shotts Bon Accord/UNITED Sept 1959 £750/Greenock Morton June 1962 £1,500/ Aberdeen May 1965 £10,000/Motherwell Dec 1967/Dundee cs 1970 exch deal/Falkirk Mar 1975 to 1976/Later becoming Keith manager to 1982/Cove Rangers manager June 1996.
Debut v Cardiff City (h) 1/10/60

When he was purchased from junior football north of the border, Jimmy Wilson was described by one journalist as a "bony braw Scotsman". A raw talent, Wilson came in on the right flank for Gordon Hughes during Newcastle's relegation battle in season 1960-61, but it was the following year that the Scot had his best spell for United. On the left-wing, he rivalled Liam Tuohy and for a few weeks claimed a place before the emergence of teenager Alan Suddick put both Wilson and Tuohy in the shade and led to their joint departure. Jimmy returned to Scotland where he became a good club player, especially for Morton and Dundee (91 league apps.). At Cappielaw, Wilson helped Morton to the Scottish Second Division championship, while he reached inter-league selection during season 1966-67. Wilson resides in the Aberdeen area, running a public house in the Granite City.

Appearances:
FL: 12 apps. 2 gls.
FLC: 1 app. 0 gls.
Total: *13 apps. 2 gls.*
Honours:
Scot jnr app./
1 SL app. 1967/
SLC finalist 1964/
SL div 2 champs 1964.

WILSON, Joseph Alexander

Role: Inside-right 1933-1936
5' 6"
b. High Spen, Co Durham, 23rd March 1911
d. Brighton, 3rd April 1984

CAREER: Spen Black & White/ Winlaton Celtic/Tanfield Lea Institute/ UNITED amat May 1933, pro Sept 1933/ Brighton May 1936 £450/Aldershot war-guest/Reading war-guest/Tottenham Hotspur war-guest 1944/Retired as Brighton player May 1947, becoming trainer, chief-scout, asst-manager and on occasion, caretaker-manager (1963)/ Retired May 1974.

Debut v Hull City (h) 25/12/34 (scored once)

Joe Wilson worked his way through United's junior and reserve elevens to claim a first team place during season 1934-35. That was no easy task in pre-war days as, with a large staff of professionals, competition was intense for the 11 senior places. With Newcastle dropping from the First Division in 1934, he was given a chance as the club attempted to rebuild and jump back to the top division. A grafter and forager in midfield and up front, Wilson was small but had a pleasing unselfish style. He was noted for occasional penetrating runs into the box, but after two seasons of being in and out of the Magpie eleven, the signing of Harry Ware saw him move on. It was with Brighton on the south coast that Wilson found regular action, becoming a much loved personality at the Goldstone Ground for the next 30 years and more. Appearing 351 times, he was associated in various capacities to his retirement. His younger brother, Glen, also played for Brighton, and was appointed skipper of the Seagulls; he had been on United's books as a youngster and went on to total over 400 games for the south coast club.

> **Appearances:**
> *FL: 28 apps. 5 gls.*
> *FAC: 2 apps. 0 gls.*
> **Total:** *30 apps. 5 gls.*

WILSON, James H.

Role: Goalkeeper 1912-1914
5' 9"
b. Newcastle upon Tyne

CAREER: Newcastle Bentonians/UNITED May 1912 £10/North Shields Athletic June 1914.

Debut v Liverpool (h) 1/1/13

The son of a distinguished Newcastle policeman, James Wilson impressed almost everyone who watched him playing for amateur side Bentonians. Included in these spectators were Newcastle officials and they took on the local goalkeeper as an understudy for Jimmy Lawrence and Sid Blake. Making his debut in a New Year's Day clash with Liverpool in 1913, Wilson only rarely was given a chance due to Lawrence's consistency. He was between the posts when the club's home record FA Cup defeat occurred at St James Park against Sheffield United in 1914, a 0-5 reverse. For several years after he left St James Park, Wilson remained involved in local football on Tyneside.

> **Appearances:**
> *FL: 3 apps. 0 gls.*
> *FAC: 1 app. 0 gls.*
> **Total:** *4 apps. 0 gls.*

WILSON, John Thomas

Role: Centre-forward 1919-1920
5' 9"
b. Leadgate, Co Durham, 8th March 1897

CAREER: Leadgate St Ives/Leadgate United/ UNITED May 1919/Leadgate Park player-manager cs 1920/Durham City Feb 1922/ Stockport County June 1922/Manchester United Sept 1926 £500/Bristol City June 1932 to May 1933.

Debut v Arsenal (a) 30/8/19

Known as 'Jack' and from the heartland of Durham, Wilson served as a bombardier during the hostilities and began the new era of football after World War One as a promising centre-forward, being given a chance for the opening games of the 1919-20 season. At the time United had a problem finding an adequate replacement for pre-war star Albert Shepherd and Wilson filled the role along with several others until Neil Harris landed on

Tyneside. The highlight of Jack Wilson's brief flurry with the Magpies was a two goal strike against Arsenal at St James Park in September 1919, but he was soon after relegated to North Eastern League football. Jack was unlucky with injuries during his period with the black'n'whites, twice breaking a leg. His senior career appeared to be over when he moved back to Leadgate soccer, but Wilson received another chance when he joined Durham City's line-up at a time when they were in Division Three (N), their first in the Football League. He eventually ended up at Old Trafford, captaining Manchester United from the left-half position. By then he had developed into a rugged half-back who served the Reds well over five seasons in which he totalled 140 games. On leaving the game, Wilson resided in Leadgate and for a period was employed in the licensing trade in the north east.

Appearances:
FL: 7 apps. 2 gls.
War: 2 apps. 1 gl.
Total: *9 apps. 3 gls.*

WILSON, Joseph William

Role: Centre-half 1927-1930
5' 11"
*b. West Butsfield, nr Tow Law, Co Durham,
29th September 1910*
d. Shotley Bridge, County Durham, 3rd April 1996

CAREER: Crook Town/Annfield Plain/ Stanley United/UNITED Dec 1927 £50/ Southend United Aug 1930 £500/Brentford July 1935/Reading Aug 1939/York City war-guest 1941-45/Barnsley July 1945 to Apr 1947/ Blyth Spartans player-manager Mar 1948/ Consett trainer cs 1950.

Debut v Aston Villa (h) 7/12/29

A formidable defender in his prime, Joseph Wilson played the game hard, and sometimes rough. A County Durham schoolboy player in 1923-24, he joined United's staff following a noted career in local football where his father had appeared for Tow Law Town. Joe was on the club's payroll for the first time when United were reigning League Champions, but it took him a while to make his senior debut, with firstly Charlie Spencer, then England skipper Jack Hill ahead of him in selection for the defensive anchor role. Joe stepped in for a single outing during season 1929-30, but then

moved to Southend soon after his only appearance. Noted as "one of the finest pivots in Division Three", Wilson gave his all in the slog of basement football. He clocked up 172 games for Southend, then 60 for Brentford, being a most popular character at Griffin Park when the Bees were in the First Division. Nicknamed 'Farmer Joe' by his colleagues, he was once fined £1 at Chelmsford Police Court for poaching during his days in Essex. During the Second World War he was a PE instructor, and after retiring enjoyed a colourful life back in the north east, employed in various occupations from insurance salesman, horse-trainer(at Alnwick), small holding farmer and Consett steel worker. The charming Joe resided in Crookhall near Consett to his death, fathering no fewer than ten children; seven were boys, of whom six played football and one son, Carl, played for Newcastle United's senior eleven too.

Appearances:
FL: 1 app. 0 gls.
Total: *1 app. 0 gls.*

Joe Wilson

WILSON, Terence

Role: Midfield 1992
6' 0"
b. Broxburn, West Lothian, 8th February 1969

CAREER: Nottingham Forest July 1985
(UNITED loan Jan 1992)/Retired due to injury
Mar 1994/Dunfermline Athletic trial cs 1996.

Debut v Oxford United (a) 1/2/92

Terry Wilson's short period at Gallowgate
coincided with an historic moment in the
club's annals. Making his debut at Oxford on
the first day of February 1992, his loan period
was perhaps manager Ossie Ardiles' last
attempt to turn the tide of bad results. Wilson,
and his manager, did not have a happy day at
the Manor Ground, United losing 5-2, a dire
result which very soon marked the end for the
Argentinian and a dramatic entry of Kevin
Keegan to St James Park. Newcastle's new
supremo immediately wielded the axe and
Wilson was relegated to the bench, a decision
he did not like and as a consequence he was
quickly despatched back to Forest. Prior to his
trial at St James Park, the Scot had been a most
promising youngster under Brian Clough at
the City Ground, capped at Under 21 level by

Scotland, but he was continually hampered by
injury and had to call a halt to his career
following a bad knee ligament complaint
when only 25 years of age.

Appearances:
FL: 2 apps. 0 gls.
Total: *2 apps. 0 gls.*
Honours:
4 Scot u21 caps 1988-90.

WILSON, William

Role: Goalkeeper 1925-1929
5' 10"
*b. Port Seaton, nr Edinburgh,
7th September 1900*

Willie Wilson

CAREER: Peebles
Rovers/UNITED Sept 1925 £600/
Millwall June 1929 £700 to cs 1934 when he
returned to Scottish football.

Debut v Blackburn Rovers (h) 9/9/25

Joining Newcastle on a months trial from
borders side, Peebles Rovers, Willie Wilson
had the opportunity to impress and earn a
contract at St James Park. With Bill Bradley's
goalkeeping position up for grabs, Wilson had
a most remarkable start for the
Magpies. On his debut against
Blackburn, United fell on home soil
by the amazing scoreline of 1-7.
Nevertheless, Wilson was not
blamed and went on to gain a
professional contract, developing
into a safe 'keeper, a near perfect
ever-present as the Magpies won the
Division One title the following
season. With plenty of confidence,
the ex miner was Newcastle's regular
custodian for three seasons, until
Micky Burns and the arrival of
Albert McInroy led to his departure
to Millwall. At The Den he again
performed well for a period, playing
in more than 100 consecutive games
for the Lions and all told making 156
league and cup appearances over
five seasons.

Appearances:
FL: 127 apps. 0 gls.
FAC: 7 apps. 0 gls.
Total: *134 apps. 0 gls.*
Honours:
FL champs 1927.

Terry Wilson

WILSON, William

Role: Right-back 1900-1903
5' 9"
b. Tyneside

CAREER: South Shields Athletic/UNITED
May 1900/Bradford City Aug 1903 £50/
Local Tyneside football cs 1905.

Debut v Bury (a) 13/12/02

Billy Wilson was one of several players tried
in a problem right-back role during the first
campaigns of the twentieth century. Given a
trial run-out during season 1902-03, the club's
directors considered Wilson "promising", but
quickly put him back in the Northern League
'A' team. With the headline signing of Scottish
international Andy McCombie, he didn't get
another opportunity in the side and moved to
join Bradford City, taking part in the Bantams'
first ever Football League match, against
Grimsby in 1903. Wilson proceeded to appear
on 63 occasions for City as they entered senior
action in Division Two during 1903-04 and
1904-05.

> **Appearances:**
> *FL: 4 apps. 0 gls.*
> **Total:** *4 apps. 0 gls.*

WILSON, William Sykes

Role: Right-half 1960-1962
5' 8"
b. Peebles, 16th March 1943

CAREER: Walkerburn jnrs(Peebles)/
UNITED Mar 1960 to June 1962 free.

Debut v Sheffield United (h) 11/10/61 (FLC)

A young Scot, Billy Wilson stood in for Duncan
Neale in one of the club's earliest Football
League Cup matches against Sheffield United at
Gallowgate in 1961. Although the Magpies lost,
Billy was described as being "competent and
cool" and "fully justified his senior baptism".
With the right-half position up for grabs, Wilson
was in contention along with Neale, Wright and
Franks. Noted as a "useful teenager" by *The
Newcastle Journal's* analyst, Wilson did not
develop further and by the end of the 1961-62
season was appearing for United's third eleven.

> **Appearances:**
> *FLC: 1 app. 0 gls.*
> **Total:** *1 app. 0 gls.*

WINSTANLEY, Graham

Role: Centre-half 1964-1969
5' 11"
b. Croxdale, Co Durham, 20th January 1948

CAREER: UNITED app July 1964, pro Dec
1965/Carlisle United Aug 1969 £7,000/
Brighton Oct 1974 £20,000/Carlisle United July
1979 to May 1980, becoming asst-coach/
Penrith Town, becoming manager May 1982.

Debut v Leeds United (h) 24/12/66 (sub)

Graham Winstanley

Bespectacled,
slim and with a
quiet nature,
Graham
Winstanley
showed
considerable
promise as a
defender during
his period at St
James Park.
Arriving at the
club from
schools' football,
Graham had
plenty of
competition
ahead of him,
notably seniors,
Burton, McNamee, McGrath and Moncur. But
he pushed for contention during season 1966-
67 and thereafter was in Joe Harvey's squad,
often on the substitute's bench without
getting onto the field. Winstanley appeared in
European football for the Magpies, against
Sporting Lisbon in Portugal and was up to the
task, having a fine game against some of the
continent's top forwards. Moving to Brunton
Park, Graham became a key figure in
Carlisle's rise to the First Division, totalling
over 200 matches for the Cumbrians in his
two spells with the club. Winstanley
afterwards settled in Carlisle, running a
building supply business then working for
The Cumberland News.

> **Appearances:**
> *FL: 5(2) apps. 0 gls.*
> *FAC: 1 app. 0 gls.*
> *Eur: 1 app. 0 gls.*
> **Total:** *7(2) apps. 0 gls.*
> **Honours:**
> *FL div 2 prom 1974.*

WITHE, Christopher

Role: Left-back 1979-1983
5' 10"
b. Speke, Liverpool, 25th September 1962

CAREER: UNITED app 1979, pro Oct 1980/
Bradford City June 1983 free/Notts County
Oct 1987 £20,000/Bury July 1989 £40,000
(Chester loan 1990-91)/Mansfield Town loan
Jan 1991, pmt Mar 1991 exch deal/Shrewsbury
Town Aug 1993 free/Boston United July 1996
free.

Debut v Shrewsbury Town (h) 22/10/80

Chris Withe made his Football League debut
only 11 days after turning professional with
United in 1980. Brother of England
international Peter Withe who was also on the
club's books at the same time, Chris didn't
possess his more famous relation's height and
build, but had neat skills on the ball and when
he first appeared for the black'n'whites in
season 1980-81 appeared to have the qualities
necessary to become an established defender.

Chris Withe

As a rival to Peter
Johnson and Ian
Davies, Withe
didn't develop as
envisaged, and
allowed another
junior product,
Wes Saunders, to
leap ahead of him
for first team
action. Chris was
transferred to
Bradford City
where he claimed
a regular place in
lower division
football. Winning
promotion with
City, Withe made
over 150 outings

for the Tykes, while he also made an
impression at his other ports of call too; at
Notts County he was Player of the Year in
1988-89.

Appearances:
FL: 2 apps. 0 gls.
Total: *2 apps. 0 gls.*
Honours:
FL div 3 champs 1985, 1994/
FL div 4 prom 1992.

WITHE, Peter

Role: Centre-forward 1978-1980
6' 2"
b. Liverpool, 30th August 1951

CAREER: Smiths Coggins(Liverpool)/
Southport amat cs 1970, pro Aug 1971
(Skelmersdale loan)/Barrow Dec 1971 free/
Port Elizabeth City(S.Africa) 1972/Arcadia
Shepherds(S.Africa) c1973/Wolverhampton
Wanderers Oct 1973 £13,500/Portland Timbers
(USA) May 1975/Birmingham City July 1975
£40,000/Nottingham Forest Sept 1976 £42,000/
UNITED Aug 1978 £200,000/Aston Villa June
1980 £500,000/Sheffield United June 1985
(Birmingham City loan 1987-88)/Huddersfield
Town asst-player-manager July 1988/Aston
Villa asst-manager Jan 1991/Wimbledon
manager Oct 1991 to Jan 1992/Evesham Feb
1992/Aston Villa youth development officer
1995, chief-scout Oct 1996.

Debut v Luton Town (h) 26/8/78

A much-travelled striker, Peter Withe didn't
reach great heights in the game until he
teamed up with Brian Clough at Nottingham
Forest. Brave and strong, Withe was an
unselfish target man up front, expert at
holding and laying the ball off. All left foot,
and never a really consistent scorer, Withe was
nevertheless a menace in the box, his aerial
prowess always able to cause problems for
defenders. At the City Ground he helped
Forest to the First Division championship
before surprisingly dropping a division to join
Bill McGarry's rebuilding plans at St James
Park as United's record purchase. Immediately
Withe became a big favourite with his never-
say-die attitude. He was undoubtedly too
good for Second Division football and his
continued presence in a black and white shirt
rested on United's quick promotion. In 1978-79
and 1979-80 that didn't materialise and Withe
soon moved back to Division One, joining
Aston Villa where he again helped win the
title (netting 20 goals), as well as the European
Cup in 1982; Peter slotted home the winner in
that epic match against Bayern Munich in
Rotterdam. Goals flowed for Withe at Villa
Park as he registered 90 in 232 games, form
which also earned him England recognition. A
bubbly personality, Withe later assisted Villa
on the coaching staff after a brief spell in
management at Wimbledon, while he is also
an occasional BBC radio summariser. Peter

was an apprentice electrician in Liverpool's dockside before turning to professional football. His brother Chris also appeared for Newcastle, while his son, Jason, had spells with Huddersfield Town and West Bromwich Albion.

Appearances:
FL: 76 apps. 25 gls.
FAC: 4 apps. 2 gls.
FLC: 3 apps. 0 gls.
Total: *83 apps. 27 gls.*
Honours:
11 Eng caps 1981-85/FL champs 1978, 1981/ FL div 2 prom 1977/FLC winner 1978/ EC winner 1982.

Peter Withe

WOOD, Edmund Eli

Role: Centre-half 1928-1930
6' 0"
b. Stairley, Warwickshire, 10th February 1903

CAREER: Northampton Town/Birmingham 1926/Rhyl Athletic 1928/UNITED May 1928 £750 to May 1930.

Debut v Burnley (h) 29/8/28

Tall and well built, Ed Wood arrived at St James Park as a defender, at a time when the centre-half role was up for grabs. Coming into the side for Ossie Park when the Magpies had defensive problems, he did not have a memorable start in a black'n'white shirt. Facing Burnley's centre-forward George Beel, his opponent netted a hat-trick as the visitors won 7-2 and Wood chased his heels all afternoon. Newcastle directors immediately increased the search for a commanding pivot, Jack Hill soon arriving on Tyneside. Wood was one of the new skipper's deputies thereafter and left during the summer of 1930.

Appearances:
FL: 9 apps. 0 gls.
Total: *9 apps. 0 gls.*

Ed Wood

WOODBURN, James

Role: Right or Left-half 1935-1948
5' 9"
b. Rutherglen, Glasgow, 29th January 1917

CAREER: Kilsyth Emmett/Coltness United/
UNITED amat 1935, pro Feb 1938 £100/
Liverpool war-guest 1940-41/Wrexham war-
guest 1940-41/Northampton Town war-guest
1941-42/Bolton Wanderers war-guest
1943-44/Doncaster Rovers war-guest
1944-45/Hibernian war-guest/Gateshead
player-trainer Sept 1948 £750/Retired June
1952.

Debut v Coventry City (a) 1/10/38

United discovered former
electrician Jimmy Woodburn
in Scotland on one of the
club's many scouting trips
north of the border.
Purchased as a teenager to
groom for the future, Woodburn developed in
the years just before the outbreak of the
Second World War and was most unlucky to
have broken through into United's senior
eleven just as the clouds of war descended.
With exceptional positional sense on the field,
he worked tirelessly and read the game well,
appearing in all half-back roles for Newcastle,
as well as in the inside-forward positions too.
After serving in the Cameron Scottish Rifles
during the war, taking part in the D-Day
landings, Jimmy returned to the fold in 1946
and competed along with Joe Harvey and
Duggie Wright as United strived for a
promotion spot. He was used largely as a
utility player in midfield, appearing on 17
occasions as the Magpies returned to the First
Division in 1948. Woodburn's father turned
out for St Mirren in Scottish football.
Remaining in the region after a spell with
Gateshead (132 lge apps.), Jimmy became a
house-master at an approved school in
Durham.

Jimmy Woodburn

Appearances:
FL: 44 apps. 4 gls.
FAC: 3 apps. 0 gls.
War: 49 apps. 4 gls.
Total: 96 apps. 8 gls.
Honours:
FL div 2 prom 1948.

WOODS, Charles Morgan Parkinson

Role: Inside-right 1959-1962
5' 6"
b. Whitehaven, 18th March 1941

CAREER: Keels Boys Club/
Cleator Moor Celtic/UNITED
May 1959 £25/Bournemouth
Nov 1962 £5,000/Crystal
Palace Nov 1964/Ipswich
Town July 1966/Watford June
1970 (Colchester United loan
1971-72)/Blackburn Rovers
July 1972/Ipswich Town asst-
coach 1973, becoming coach
Aug 1982, asst-manager 1991,
then scout and chief-scout
1995.

*Debut v Fulham (a) 31/8/60
(scored once)*

Charlie Woods had the daunting task of filling George Eastham's boots when the future England player fell into dispute with United. Then only a raw youngster, Woods was plunged into United's side for a relegation fight during season 1960-61. Small and compact, and a fixture at inside-right, he showed plenty of talent with the ball and could strike a stinging shot, but United's overall

Charlie Woods

performances in that programme were dire, and the young Woods suffered as a consequence. Newcastle fell into Division Two and a change in management saw Jimmy Kerray arrive and Charlie move south, eventually becoming a loyal servant at Portman Road. As a player he appeared on 89 occasions, then turned to coaching, being associated with the East Anglian club for more than 20 years.

Appearances:
FL: 26 apps. 7 gls.
FAC: 3 apps. 3 gls.
FLC: 1 app. 0 gls.
Total: *30 apps. 10 gls.*
Honours:
FL div 2 champs 1968.

WOODS, Harold

Role: Inside-right
1922-1923
5' 8"
b. St Helens, Lancs,
12th March 1890

CAREER: St Helens Recreational/Ashton Town/St Helens Town/Norwich City June 1911/South Shields Aug 1919/UNITED Jan 1922 £2,600/Arsenal June 1923 £575/Luton Town Aug 1926/North Shields 1930.

Debut v Arsenal (a) 4/2/22

A versatile player, Harry Woods could play in any forward position and appeared across the front line for United. Having taken part in the old South Shields' club's first Football League

Harry Woods

game in August 1919, Harry made an impression at Horsley Hill and his ability was noticed a few miles down the Tyne at St James Park. He joined United as a reserve with plenty of experience; 151 outings for Norwich in the Southern League and almost 100 for Shields. Well balanced, clever on the ball and able to use possession to advantage, he was one of several forwards tried in the months immediately after World War One. But the purchase from Scotland of Billy Aitken pushed Woods out of the picture and he moved to Highbury. In London, Harry played some of his best football, and was top scorer for the Gunners in 1923-24 and 1924-25. He scored 22 goals in 75 fixtures, making his debut for Arsenal against Newcastle. Woods was a glass worker before turning to football, and served in the Tank Corps in France during the First World War.

Appearances:
FL: 14 apps. 2 gls.
FAC: 2 apps. 0 gls.
Total: *16 apps. 2 gls.*

WOOLLARD, Arnold James

Role: Right-back 1952-1956
6' 0"
b. Pembroke, Bermuda, 24th August 1931

CAREER: Hamilton(Bermuda)/Bermuda Athletic Ass/Northampton Town Aug 1949/Peterborough United cs 1952/ UNITED Dec 1952 £5,000/Bournemouth June 1956 £2,000/Northampton Town Mar 1962 to cs 1963.

Debut v Portsmouth (a) 18/4/53

Arnold Woollard caught the eye of Newcastle officials following outstanding performances for Peterborough in a giant-killing FA Cup run during 1952-53. A fine all round defender, Woollard stepped into United's back-line, initially as deputy to Frank Brennan at centre-half during 1952-53, then more often as a reserve to Bobby Cowell. When Cowell was injured, Arnold had the opportunity of a more regular place in the Magpies' side, but lost out to Ron Batty. He did though, become one of the soundest full-backs in the lower divisions appearing for Bournemouth in over 160 matches and then returning to Northampton where he appeared on 31 league occasions. Woollard helped the Cobblers to the Third Division title in 1962-63. On leaving the game, Arnold resided on his home island of Bermuda, employed in government service.

Appearances:
FL: 8 apps. 0 gls.
FAC: 2 apps. 0 gls.
Total: *10 apps. 0 gls.*
Honours:
FL div 3 champs 1963.

WRIGHT, Brian George

Role: Right-half 1956-1963
5' 11"
b. Sunderland, 19th September 1939

CAREER: UNITED Sept 1956/Peterborough United May 1963 £7,500 to cs 1972/ Scarborough cs 1972 to cs 1973.

Debut v Nottingham Forest (a) 23/4/60

Brian Wright joined United's junior set-up from schools football and quickly made an impression as he worked his way through the ranks. Tall and well built, he skippered the Magpies' youth team and when he first appeared for the senior side at the City Ground against Forest, turned on a grand performance. Strong and industrious, with control of the ball in midfield, he also possessed bite in the tackle. Wright was given a few outings at half-back in season 1960-61 and after the club's relegation that year, received an extended run for the following term. But the appointment of Joe Harvey as boss saw wholesale changes to the playing staff. Duncan Neale took his place, then Ollie Burton became a big

Arnold Woollard

Brian Wright

purchase and Wright was frozen out. He moved to Peterborough where he proceeded to appear for the Posh for the next eight seasons, totalling 322 matches. Only four players have topped that figure for Peterborough, one of them Tommy Robson, another ex Magpie. Brian later resided on Wearside after hanging up his boots.

Appearances:
FL: 45 apps. 1 gl.
FAC: 1 app. 0 gls.
FLC: 1 app. 0 gls.
Total: *47 apps. 1 gl.*

WRIGHT, John Douglas

Role: Left-half 1938-1948
5' 11"
b. Rochford, nr Southend on Sea, 29th April 1917
d. Bedlington, 28th December 1992

CAREER: Chelmsford City 1935/Southend United July 1936/UNITED May 1938 £3,250/ Southend United war-guest 1939-40/Swansea Town war-guest 1942-43/Hamilton Academical war-guest/Lincoln City Dec 1948 £600/Blyth Spartans player-trainer Dec 1954, becoming player-manager cs 1955, then secretary May 1957 to Nov 1960.

Debut v Plymouth Argyle (h) 27/8/38

A player who possessed captivating artistry on the ball, Duggie Wright graced United's midfield for only two Football League seasons immediately before and after the Second World War, but made a huge impression on both colleagues and spectators. Slimly built with a mop of wavy hair, he had a master's touch of the ball and a distinguished air on the field. Wright also had a rapid rise to fame, signing for the black'n'whites after only 34 games for his first league club Southend. Recommended to United by ex

Duggie Wright

captain, Jimmy Nelson, Duggie made such an impact that he became Newcastle's playmaker-in-chief in a Seymour-led resurgence. Wright was picked for his country, in a game against Norway at St James Park, but then his whole career was sadly wrecked by Hitler's invasion of Poland. Like most footballers, Duggie served abroad, with the noted Tyneside Scottish Black Watch regiment. He was wounded, almost losing his life at Dunkirk and took part in *Operation Overlord*. A sergeant in the artillery, he was mentioned in dispatches for his "heroic" exploits. Wright regained his place for season 1946-47, but was a long term injury casualty and by then it was clear perhaps a few too many years had passed. Despite being highly praised for his ice-cool on field contributions by team-mates like Joe Harvey and Len Shackleton, he was discarded to Lincoln, rather too hastily according to many fans. At Sincil Bank, Wright played a major part in their promotion in 1952, an inspirational skipper of the Imps. The midfielder totalled over 200 outings for Lincoln before returning to the north east when he joined the Blyth Spartans staff.

Afterwards Duggie settled in that town, at Newsham, a noted personality to his death. He worked at Blyth power station for nearly 25 years before retiring. Wright's father Jocky appeared for several clubs, including Bolton and Sheffield Wednesday, while his brother, Bill, was Reading's captain.

Appearances:
FL: 72 apps. 1 gl.
FAC: 10 apps. 0 gls.
War: 24 apps. 0 gls.
Total: *106 apps. 1 gl.*
Honours:
1 Eng cap 1939/
FL div 3 (N) champs 1952.

WRIGHT, Thomas James

Role: Goalkeeper 1988-1993
6′ 1″
b. Belfast, 29th August 1963

CAREER: Grange Rangers(Ballyclare)/ Brantwood(Belfast)/Linfield/UNITED Mar 1988 £30,000(Hull City loan 1990-91)/ Nottingham Forest Sept 1993 £450,000 (Reading loan 1996-97).

Debut v Aston Villa (a) 14/1/89

Tommy Wright followed the path of former Northern Ireland international goalkeeper Willie McFaul to St James Park. A highly rated 'keeper from Linfield, like McFaul, Tommy took time to claim a regular place on Tyneside arriving initially to compete for the vacant Number One jersey after the departure of Dave Beasant to Chelsea. Rivalling fellow Irishman Gary Kelly initially, and also John Burridge, Wright gained the position for season 1989-90 then was sidelined through injury. Bouncing back, he again claimed the shirt for season 1991-92 but was again injured after a string of brilliant

Tommy Wright

displays. Tommy saw Pavel Srnicek take-over the position as United won promotion the following year. When Newcastle started life in the Premier League, Wright made only a fleeting appearance before the purchase of Mike Hooper saw his departure to Forest. Between the posts as Frank Clark guided the Reds back into the Premier League, Wright has experienced an unlucky career, constantly battling against injury both at Gallowgate and at the City Ground in Nottingham. Tommy was also a proficient athlete as a teenager, being chosen for his country at the cross-country event. He was All-Ireland champion and was offered a lucrative athletics scholarship in the States, but chose to stay in Northern Ireland as a publican. With Linfield Wright appeared in the European Cup.

Appearances:
FL/PL: 72(1) apps. 0 gls.
FAC: 4 apps. 0 gls.
FLC: 6 apps. 0 gls.
Others: 1 app. 0 gls.
Total: *83(1) apps. 0 gls.*
Honours:
22 N.Irel caps 1989-94/N.Irel u23 app./
N.Irel u21 app./1 FL app. 1993/
FL div 1 champs 1993/FL div 1 prom 1994.

WRIGHT, William John

Role: Outside-left 1958-59
5' 11"
b. Blackpool, 4th March 1931

CAREER: Blackpool May 1950/Leicester City Aug 1955 £1,500/UNITED July 1958 £7,500/ Plymouth Argyle July 1959 £5,150/Hull City Aug 1961/Millwall Aug 1961/Tonbridge cs 1962.

Debut v Blackpool (a) 25/8/58

Fair-haired Billy Wright was a direct winger who played in any forward position. Understudy to the great Stanley Matthews at Bloomfield Road, he moved to Leicester in search of more regular action and for a season did well at Filbert Street, helping City to promotion from the Second Division. A record of ten goals in 29 games from the flank was first-class and Newcastle picked him up for a small fee during the summer of 1958. He was given a chance at the start of the following season, at centre-forward as well as on the touchline and in a schemer's role. Scoring twice in an amazing match that took place with Chelsea which ended 6-5 in the Blues' favour, Wright picked up an injury and couldn't hold his place, being transferred before the new programme started. He afterwards drifted around the lower divisions without making a huge impact - a player whose potential was never fulfilled.

Billy Wright

Appearances:
FL: 5 apps. 3 gls.
Total: *5 apps. 3 gls.*
Honours:
FL div 2 champs 1957/FL div 4 champs 1962.

WRIGHTSON, Jeffrey G.

Role: Midfield 1985-1987
5' 11"
b. Walker, Newcastle upon Tyne,
18th May 1968

CAREER: Wallsend Boys Club/UNITED app 1985, pro May 1986/Preston North End June 1987 free/Darlington trial July 1992/Blackpool trial Aug 1992/Gateshead Aug 1992.

Debut v Everton (h) 26/12/86

As a junior Jeff Wrightson helped United lift the FA Youth Cup alongside Paul Gascoigne in 1985. Tall and positive, he was called up to the senior

Jeff Wrightson

eleven at a time of near panic in United's ranks. With the Magpies fighting at the bottom of the First Division during season 1986-87, the young Tynesider was thrown into the cauldron during the Christmas and New Year programme. Stepping into David McCreery's anchor role in midfield, Wrightson was up against it and saw Everton inflict a heavy defeat on his Football League baptism. Nevertheless, Wrightson gave his all, but was unlucky to be handed his opportunity in senior football at the wrong time. He later spent five seasons in Preston's ranks, a noted defender in Division Three and Four. Wrightson clocked up over 150 games for the Deepdale club before joining Gateshead where he became a commanding player in the Vauxhall Conference.

Appearances:
FL: 3(1) apps. 0 gls.
Total: *3(1) apps. 0 gls.*
Honours:
FAYC winner 1985.

David Young

YOUNG, David

Role: Midfield 1964-1973
5' 10"
b. Newcastle upon Tyne, 12th November 1945

CAREER: UNITED Sept 1964/Sunderland Jan 1973 £20,000/Charlton Athletic July 1974 £27,000/Southend United Sept 1976 free/ Dartford Dec 1978 to May 1980.

Debut v West Bromwich Albion (a) 14/3/70

Lean and leggy, David Young spent almost a decade on United's staff as a professional without ever really commanding a first-team place. He did have one productive season in 1970-71 when he appeared on 29 occasions, mainly in a midfield marker role. A players' player, Young rarely caught the eye, was efficient rather than spectacular and went through a game giving plenty of effort, covering lots of defensive ground. Also able to play at centre-half, he took part in United's Inter Cities Fairs Cup campaigns of 1969-70 and 1970-71 before heading for Roker Park. With rivals Sunderland, David found himself part of the famous Wearside FA Cup march on Wembley in 1973, a substitute as the Reds defeated Leeds United. Young went on to make 89 appearances for Charlton, and was captain at The Valley when the Londoners gained promotion to Division Two. After retiring from the game, Young remained in the south; he was employed in sports centre management in Orpington, Bexleyheath and Gillingham.

Appearances:
FL: 41(2) apps. 2 gls.
FLC: 4 apps. 0 gls.
Eur: 5(1) apps. 0 gls.
Others: 2(1) apps. 0 gls.
Total: 52(4) apps. 2 gls.
Honours:
FL div 3 prom 1975/
FL div 4 prom 1978/
FAC winner 1973(sub, no apps.)

SHEARER, Alan

Role: Centre-forward 1996-date
6' 0"
b. Gosforth, Newcastle upon Tyne,
13th August 1970

CAREER: Cramlington jnrs/Wallsend Boys'
Club 1983-86/Cramlington jnrs 1985-86/
Southampton sch Sept 1984, app July 1986, pro
Apr 1988/Blackburn Rovers July 1992 £3.6m/
UNITED July 1996 £15m.

Debut v Everton (a) 17/8/96

The world record £15 million purchase of Alan
Shearer during July 1996 took Newcastle
United's commitment to establish the Magpies
as one of the top clubs in Europe to a different
level. Newcastle saw off the challenge of their
rivals, Manchester United, to sign the
Blackburn and England striker with the
advantage of knowing that Shearer very much
wanted to play for his home-town side. A
supporter of the black'n'whites, and of Kevin
Keegan, as a teenager, Alan was once at
St James Park for trials, but ended up in
goal for part of the time and his talent
was lost to Southampton. Netting a hat-
trick on his first full league outing for the
Saints against Arsenal he became, at 17
years old, the youngest player to do so in
the top flight. By the time he had
developed into an up and coming young
striker at Southampton, claiming a
record 13 goals for the England Under-21
side, United tried to take him back to
Tyneside during 1992 with a £3 million
bid. That attempt failed, but Kevin
Keegan never lost his admiration for the
player described as the ultimate all-
round centre-forward. Shearer is strong,
aggressive and intelligent leading the
front line. He possesses power in both
feet, is clinical close in and quite
spectacular from long range. Alan has a
searing turn of pace and is quite
outstanding in the air, but plays a team
game too. It was Blackburn Rovers who
eventually gained his transfer and at
Ewood Park Shearer hit 130 goals, almost
a goal a game over four seasons; 22
(1992-93), 34 (1993-94), 37 (1994-95) and
37 (1995-96). He was very much the key
man who won the Premier League
Championship for Rovers in 1995 and

rapidly the Geordie became a regular for the
full England side, appointed skipper recently
under new coach Glenn Hoddle. Netting on
his debut for his country, Shearer went on to
become leading scorer in the Euro '96
tournament with a devastating burst of
finishing. His reputation as Europe's best
striker was cemented further and United
stepped in to smash the previous highest fee
paid for Lentini and Ronaldo on the continent.
Alan Shearer returned home to a rapturuous
welcome to become not only the last piece in
Kevin Keegan's 'dream-team' but also to
hopefully become established as Newcastle
United's biggest ever Number 9 hero.

Honours:
28 Eng caps 1992-date/
1 Eng unoff app. 1996/
1 Eng B cap 1992/
11 Eng u21 caps 1991-92/
England Youth app./
PL champs 1995/
FWA Footballer of the Year 1994/
PFA Player of the Year 1995.

Alan Shearer, United's current No. 9 hero and the most expensive player in the world.

STOP PRESS...ADDITIONS

BOWDEN, R. (p49):
9 FA apps. on tour to N. America 1931.

CARR, F.A. (p74):
Joined Reggiana (Italy) Oct 1996 free.

DAVIES, E.R. (p108):
Coach to Balga (Australia) to c1994.

DENNISON, R.S. (p113):
died Gillingham, 19th June 1996.

HOOPER, M.D. (p190):
Joined Portsmouth cs 1996.

HUCKERBY, D. (p196):
Joined Coventry City Nov 1996 £1m.

PEACOCK, G. (p318):
Joined QPR on loan 1996-97.

LAWRENSON, Mark Thomas
(b. Preston, Lancs, 2nd June 1957)
Joined United as defensive coach Nov 1996. Eire international (38 caps), former Preston North End, Brighton and Liverpool defender. Mark totalled over 250 games for the Anfield club (1981-1988) after signing for a club record £900,000. Later became Oxford United manager in 1988. Won domestic and European honours with Liverpool, several alongside Terry McDermott and Peter Beardsley. His father appeared for Preston North End and Southport.

Mark Lawrenson on the air in his role as a BBC 'Radio Five Live' football summariser.

APPLEBY, Richard Dean
(1991-1995)
Midfield, b. Middlesbrough 1975
Career: UNITED sch cs 1991, pro 1992/Ipswich Town loan Nov 1995, pmt Dec 1995/Swansea City 1996.
An England youth international, Richie Appleby at one stage of his career at St James Park looked to have a bright future. Possessing lovely skills, he appeared for the Magpies in Anglo-Italian fixtures. Playing alongside his brother Matty against the Italians during the 1992-93 season, his early progress was rapid, despite a broken ankle. At 5' 10", he operated on the wing, up front or in midfield for the club's junior and reserve teams, Appleby however lost his way and was given another chance by Ipswich Town.
2 apps. 0 gls.

BELL, George W. (1918-1920)
Full-back, b. Sunderland
Career: UNITED amat 1918, pro May 1919/Malay Straits 1920.
Able to play on both flanks in defence, George Bell served as a sergeant during World War One and returned to his native north east to sign amateur forms for United. He appeared for the Magpies in the wartime Newcastle District League and then was given a debut in the senior line-up for the Northern Victory League clash with local rivals Sunderland in March 1919 when he deputised for Frank Hudspeth. On the club's books for the resumption of Football League soccer in 1919-20, he couldn't break through and soon left the club.
3 apps. 0 gls.

BLACK, Neville (1949-1953)
Inside-left, b. Pegswood 1931
Career: Pegswood/UNITED Sept 1949/Exeter City Jan 1953/ Rochdale 1953 to 1956.
Neville Black's only appearance in senior company was in the 1952 FA Charity Shield clash with Manchester United at Old Trafford. A tall (5' 11") inside-forward who was described as having "great promise", Black possessed a turn of speed that troubled defenders. Following his debut the local press remarked that Stan Seymour had, "a fatherly talk with the lad and gave him an expert critique". Due to the mass of stars at St James Park during that era, Neville never reached the first eleven again, although he did well at Rochdale claiming over 50 appearances.
1 app. 0 gls.

BLACKBURN, Maurice
(1939-1941)
Inside-right, b. Prudhoe 1919
Career: Backworth/UNITED amat June 1939 to 1941.
A local pit-worker who was unlucky enough to be spotted by the club just prior to the outbreak of World War Two. Joining the club as an amateur, the diminutive 5' 5" tall schemer appeared for the black'n'whites in wartime football, scoring on his debut against Leeds in June 1939. Blackburn didn't resume his career on the cessation of hostilities in 1945.
12 apps. 1 gl.

BROADY, Percy Kent
(1942-1945)
Half-back, b. Tyneside
Career: UNITED May 1942 to 1945.
Another player to have his career halted by Hitler's invasion of Europe. Broady was spotted by United's excellent scouting network and was given an opportunity in the club's wartime eleven making his senior debut in an amazing 5-5 draw against York City during May 1943. That absorbing encounter was Broady's only outing for the club's first eleven.
1 app. 0 gls.

BROWN, Ernest Charles
(1945-1947)
Inside-forward,
b. South Shields 1921
Career: South Shields/UNITED Dec 1945/Southend United Feb 1947/Hartlepools United 1951 to c1952/Whitburn/Later becoming a Blackpool scout.
Picked up by Stan Seymour after impressing in South Shields' ranks at the end of the Second World War, Ernie Brown's highlight in a black'n'white shirt occurred when he netted twice in a 3-0 victory at Leeds during April 1946. A rival to Ernie Taylor, he found it hard to establish himself in United's senior squad once league action began in season 1946-47. He moved to Southend as part of the deal that brought Joe Sibley to St James Park, but made only a handful of appearances in Essex before heading for Hartlepool.
12 apps. 4 gls.

BROWN, Joseph (1919)
Centre-forward
A striker who deputised for Curtis Booth in United's forward-line during the Northern Victory League programme of 1919. Scoring on his only appearance for the Magpies against Scotswood, Brown wasn't offered a full-time contract once Football League action started later in the same year.
1 app. 1 gl.

CALDER, Neil Alexander
(1942-1943)
Goalkeeper, b. Tyneside
Career: Ryton jnrs/UNITED Dec 1942 to 1943.
Joining United from Tyneside junior club Ryton, Neil Calder pulled on the goalkeeper's jersey on only one occasion for the Magpies, for a meeting against Leeds United during January 1943. The youngster had a harrowing senior baptism as the Tykes fired 7 goals past the debutant. He failed to impress and spent his short stay with the club in United's wartime reserve league.
1 app. 0 gls.

Billy Wilson

Players to have appeared for the club in a first-class senior competitive fixture, but who have not made their debut in league or cup football for United. Competitions classified as 'first-class' in this section are; Texaco Cup, Anglo-Scottish Cup, Anglo-Italian Cup, Wartime League and Cup competitions, FA Charity Shield and Full Members Cup matches as well as Simod, Zenith and Mercantile Credit tournaments.

CHAMBERS, Colin
(1975-1978)
Outside-left or Midfield,
b. Newcastle upon Tyne 1958
Career: UNITED app 1975, pro cs
1976 to May 1978/Whitley Bay
1978/Later Orwin manager.
One of Gordon Lee's youngsters
thrown into a controversial Anglo-
Scottish Cup meeting with Ayr
United during September 1976.
United's boss fielded a reserve
line-up to show that he wanted no
truck with the competition and
Chambers was part of a side that
fell 0-3, being substituted after 75
minutes. As a consequence
Newcastle were heavily censored
and fined. Skipper of United's
juniors, Chambers did get another
opportunity in a friendly contest,
but couldn't claim a league or cup
debut for the Magpies, or for any
other side. Chambers afterwards
resided in Forest Hall in Newcastle
and was involved in local football.
1 app. 0 gls.

COOK, John (1918-1920)
Inside-left, b. Sunderland
Career: UNITED amat 1918, pro
May 1919/Scotswood Apr 1920.
Taking part in the Northern
Victory League for Newcastle,
John Cook had a single outing
against Middlesbrough in United's
centre-forward shirt although
more often figuring in the inside-
forward role in reserve football. He
was offered a professional contract
when peacetime soccer started
once more for season 1919-20, but
couldn't push for a First Division
place and moved to local Tyneside
soccer with the strong Scotswood
outfit.
1 app. 0 gls.

COPELAND, Edward
(1939-1946)
Outside-right, b. Hetton 1921
Career: Hartlepools United
1938/Easington CW/UNITED
amat June 1939/Huddersfield
Town wg 1942-43/UNITED Aug
1943/Hartlepools United wg
1945-46, pmt cs 1946 to 1948.
Briefly with United before the
Second World War erupted, Eddie
Copeland returned to St James
Park and appeared on a regular
basis for the club during season

1943-44. Rivalling a young Tommy
Walker on the wing, Copeland was
5' 8" tall and quick, while he could
be a match-winner too. He netted
twice as Newcastle defeated
Gateshead 3-1 at Redheugh Park in
a wartime derby match during
December 1943. Copeland played
for Hartlepools' senior line-up
both before and after the hostilities
totalling 40 league matches.
20 apps. 3 gls.

COULSON, William J.
(1971-1973)
Midfield, b. Winlaton 1950
Career: Consett Town/North
Shields 1970/UNITED Sept
1971/Southend United Oct 1973
(Aldershot loan 1974-75)
(Huddersfield Town loan
1975-76)/Darlington 1976/
Hong Kong Rangers 1978/
Frankston City(Australia) c1982.
Fair haired Billy Coulson
impressed many United
supporters in a string of stirring
displays for United's Central
League side during season
1971-72. Able to get forward and
become an extra striker, Coulson
earned a first-team call up for a
Texaco Cup semi-final meeting
with Derby County in December
of that season. He again played
well and indications were at the
time that Joe Harvey had found a
gem. But Coulson wasn't given a
further opportunity, although he
was on the subs bench in Football
League matches. He moved to
Southend for £10,000 and totalled
over 50 games before moving to
Australia where he played
alongside several famous names,
Martin Chivers and Martin Peters
included.
1 app. 0 gls.

CUMMINGS, H. (1918-1919)
Outside-left
Career: UNITED amat 1918
to cs 1919.
A teenager who was handed a
single game for Newcastle during
the celebratory Northern Victory
League competition on the
conclusion of World War One.
Coming in for Alex Ramsay on the
left wing, Cummings was blooded
in a Tyne-Wear confrontation
during March 1919 at Roker Park.

United lost 2-1 to their rivals and
Cummings wasn't offered terms
during the summer months.
1 app. 0 gls.

DESWART, Walter Poole
(1940-1941)
Right-half, b. Pelton
Career: Ouston jnrs/
UNITED 1940 to 1941.
Of Belgian extraction, Walter
Deswart was a big and powerful
half-back who stood in for Jimmy
Gordon for a North Regional
League fixture with Grimsby Town
during January 1941. That game
was played at Scunthorpe due to
war difficulties and Deswart didn't
have a convincing afternoon as
United fell 4-0.
1 app. 0 gls.

DIXON, John Thomas
(1943-1944)
Inside-forward, b. Hebburn 1923
Career: Boys Brigade/Reyrolles/
UNITED May 1943/Hull City wg
1944-45/Middlesbrough wg
1944-45/Sunderland wg 1944-45/
Aston Villa cs 1944 to 1961 when he
became asst-coach to 1967.
While Johnny Dixon failed to
appear in league or cup football for
the black'n'whites, he was to prove
an exceptional footballer elsewhere,
one of Aston Villa's post-war stars.
Scoring a brace on his United
debut in December 1941, Dixon
had his best season at St James
Park during 1943-44 when he
totalled 24 appearances (7 goals).
He rivalled Ernie Taylor at
Gallowgate and lost out to the little

Johnny Dixon

schemer as peacetime approached. Moving to Villa Park, Dixon developed into an inspirational leader, a dignified skipper of the Midland side when they lifted the FA Cup in 1957. Appearing on 430 occasions for the claret and blues, he was an attack minded schemer, netting 144 goals for Villa over 15 seasons. He had a long stride and friendly personality and later ran an ironmongers business in the Sutton area.
38 apps. 13 gls.

DONALDSON, Robert Stone
(1943-1947)
Left-half, b. South Shields 1921
Career: South Shields Ex Schoolboys/UNITED Jan 1943/ Hartlepools United July 1947, becoming trainer 1951/North Shields trainer.
Hard tackling and tenacious, Bobby Donaldson was a regular in United's wartime line-up for two seasons, 1943-44 and 1944-45. Operating on both sides of the half-back line, he partnered Tot Smith. On the fringe of making United's Football League side during 1946-47, he joined Hartlepool during the close season and proceeded to total over 150 games for the Victoria Ground club, later serving them behind the scenes too. Donaldson started out in the same junior side in South Shields as Stan Mortensen.
87 apps. 2 gls.

DONNELLY, John W.
(1918-1920)
Outside-left,
b. Newcastle upon Tyne
Career: UNITED amat 1918, pro May 1919 to cs 1920 free.
A regular for the Magpies second eleven in the local Newcastle District League during season 1918-19, John Donnelly earned a place in the opening games of the Northern Victory League competition during 1919. Scoring on his senior debut against Scotswood, John was a rival to Ed Cooper and Alex Ramsay on the wing. Donnelly was retained when a normal format of soccer reappeared in August 1919, but couldn't push his way through the wall of talent at Gallowgate.
5 apps. 1 gl.

DORAN, John Francis
(1918-1919)
Centre-forward, b. Belfast 1896, d. Sunderland 1940
Career: Newcastle Empire/ Coventry City 1914/UNITED amat 1918/Brentford 1919/ Norwich City 1919/Brighton 1920/Manchester City 1922/ Crewe Alexandra 1924/Mid-Rhondda 1924/Shelbourne 1924/ Fordsons 1925/Boston Town 1925 to 1927.
Although born in Northern Ireland, Jack Doran was brought up a Geordie after his family had moved to Northumberland. Appearing for the county side, this well built, 5' 11" tall, curly haired striker was soon destined for a notable career in the game. Appearing for United in the 1918-19 District League campaign, he made his senior appearance for the club in the Victory League derby contest with Sunderland during March 1919 when he found the net. But Doran wasn't recruited and he moved south to eventually find a place in Brighton's line-up. With a stinging shot, he scored 55 goals in only 85 games, form which saw him capped by Ireland (3 apps.). A big move to Manchester City followed, but his stay at Maine Road wasn't a success and he later became a publican after leaving the game. During the First World War, Jack served in the RAOC and won the Military Medal and DCM. He was though the victim of a gas attack on the Somme and Cambrai battlefield, and after settling in Sunderland, he died of a respiratory illness at an early age.
4 apps. 1 gl.
Note: *Although Newcastle United's official record indicates Doran appeared in four games, local press reports suggest a player called Johnson may have replaced him in three fixtures. No record of Johnson exists.*

ENGLISH, Andrew (1940-1943)
Centre-forward,
b. Newcastle upon Tyne
Career: Coxlodge jnrs/UNITED Sept 1940 to 1943/Gateshead wg 1942-43.
From Fawdon, Andrew English worked as a brass fitter at a local

engineering works on Tyneside and joined United's staff after scoring plenty of goals in junior league football for Coxlodge. A centre-forward who possessed dash and craft, he had a good run in the club's side during season 1940-41 when he held the No 9 shirt, with regular centre-forward Albert Stubbins moving to inside-forward. Also assisting neighbours Gateshead during wartime football, English didn't enter the Football League scene when the post-war boom started in 1946.
23 apps. 6 gls.

FAIRIER, Charles (1918-1920)
Outside-right, b. Newcastle upon Tyne 1894, d. Newcastle upon Tyne 1982
Career: UNITED amat 1918, pro May 1919/Ashington Aug 1920 free/Gateshead.
Lightly framed, fast and tricky on the ball, Charles Fairier was a regular contender for the wing spot in the club's local and Victory League competitions during 1918-19. The *Newcastle Daily Journal* noted that he showed, "proof of his qualification as an aspirant for a place on the First League team". By the time Division One football had returned, Fairier earned a contract for the 1919-20 season. However he didn't progress as expected and moved to Ashington. He was also a noted boxer and professional sprinter under the pseudonym of 'Charlie Bradley'. He once topped the bill at St James Hall and was a favourite at the renowned Powderhall meeting in Edinburgh. Fairier was later employed at a local colliery and at Parson's Heaton works.
7 apps. 0 gls.

GILHOLME, Alan George
(1939-1942)
Inside-right, b. Whitley Bay 1922, d. Monkseaton 1992
Career: Backworth/UNITED amat Mar 1939 to 1942/Horden CW/ Bishop Auckland 1946 to c1951.
A most useful schemer who joined United's ranks as a teenager just before the outbreak of World War Two. Having showed talent in local Tyneside football, United's

boss Tom Mather signed the 5' 6" midfielder with the aim to groom the youngster as a future star. But war ruined Gilholme's chances of a decent career in the game, although making his debut during season 1939-40, he appeared on 17 occasions for the black'n'whites in 1940-41. On the restoration of peace, Alan moved to non-league football where he reached Wembley as part of Bishop Auckland's FA Amateur Cup side in 1950. He later resided in Monkseaton, working as an insurance executive.
21 apps. 3 gls.

GOLDING, William (1944-1945)
Goalkeeper,
b. Newcastle upon Tyne 1922
Career: Burradon Welfare/
UNITED Sept 1944 to 1945.
A local goalkeeping talent signed by Newcastle as cover during season 1944-45. Stepping in for regular choice, on loan international 'keeper Dave Cumming of Middlesbrough, Golding had a debut to savour. He appeared at Ayresome Park in a Tyne-Tees derby and helped United to a convincing 8-2 victory. By the time United's professional custodians were returning to the fold on the conclusion of the Second World War, Golding was released.
2 apps. 0 gls.

GREEN, Stanley (1936 to 1941)
Inside-forward,
b. Newcastle upon Tyne
Career: Heaton Stannington/
Ashington/UNITED amat July 1936 to 1941.
Tall and rangy, Stan Green appeared in United's Central League side during the years leading up to the outbreak of World War Two. Tenacious and good on the ball, he was a jovial character in United's dressing-room. Green deputised for Harry Clifton at inside-right, and for Jimmy Gordon at right-half during season 1939-40 before joining the RAF in 1941.
2 apps. 0 gls.

HARNBY, Donald Reed
(1944-1947)
Right-back, b. East Hetton 1923
Career: Darlington ATC/UNITED May 1944 to June 1947/Middlesbrough wg 1944-45/Hull City wg 1944-45/York City 1947/Spennymoor United 1947/Grimsby Town 1949 to 1952/Grimsby Borough Police.
Making his debut for United against Gateshead in August 1944, Don Harnby was a strong tackler and rugged defender. Filling in for the veteran Joe Richardson at right-back, he had a rival in Bobby Cowell for the Number Two shirt and ultimately Cowell was to win the race. At 5' 11" he was a tall full-back who became a regular in the club's Central League line-up for 1946-47 before moving to York and Grimsby where he totalled 37 outings.
8 apps. 0 gls.

HART, William Robert
(1940-1944)
Right-half,
b. Newcastle upon Tyne 1923
Career: Willington Quay/
UNITED Sept 1940 to 1944/
North Shields/Chesterfield 1946/Bradford City 1947 to 1949.
Bill Hart was described by one colleague as, "the ultimate terrier". A player who revelled in a contest, he was small and slim, a ball winning wing-half, tough as they come. In contention for a place during seasons 1939-40 to 1942-43, in the 1941-42 campaign Hart was chosen on 22 occasions for United across the half-back line, but wasn't retained and he moved to local football with North Shields. Picked up by Chesterfield, he made his Football League debut with the Spireites, before claiming 30 matches for Bradford City.
38 apps. 1 gl.

HENDERSON, Henry B.
(1943-1944)
Outside-right,
b. Newcastle upon Tyne
Career: Throckley Welfare/
UNITED Oct 1943 to 1944.
Able to operate on both wings, Henderson rivalled Eddie Copeland and Charles Woollett, as well as Tommy Walker, for the

flankers position at St James Park during wartime football. And he was often 4th choice having to appear in the club's reserve side in the Northern Combination League. But on his few outings in senior company, Henderson played well and provided several telling crosses which resulted in goals for Albert Stubbins.
5 apps. 0 gls.

HIGHMOOR, George Wilfred
(1942-1946)
Outside-right,
b. Clara Vale 1924
Career: Clara Vale jnrs/UNITED Sept 1942 to 1946/Halifax Town wg 1942-43.
George Highmoor has the distinction of pulling on the shirt of the great Tom Finney for his three games as a Newcastle United player. A war-guest from Preston, Finney couldn't make the side for a trio of games in October 1942 and Highmoor stepped in to face Bradford City (2 matches) and Gateshead. Finney returned the following week and Highmoor concluded his career with the Magpies in the Northern Combination.
3 apps. 0 gls.

HINDMARSH, Edward
(1942-1943)
Half-back, b. Sunderland 1921
Career: Hylton jnrs/UNITED Sept 1942 to Aug 1943/Sunderland c1944/Carlisle United 1946 to 1947.
Making his debut in a thrilling fixture with Leeds United in September 1942 which ended in a 5-3 defeat for the Tynesiders, Ed Hindmarsh appeared at both right-half and left-half during the club's brief period in the club's first eleven. Attempting a career with his local club, Sunderland, Hindmarsh found a home at Brunton Park for a season where he entered Football League and FA Cup contests and totalled 15 senior matches.
6 apps. 0 gls.

HOPE, George (1943-1946)
Inside-right,
b. Newcastle upon Tyne
Career: Scotswood/UNITED Mar 1943 to 1946.

Hope's only game in a black'n'white jersey was against Hartlepools United at St James Park in October 1943. A substitute for John Dixon, he was only at Gallowgate during a brief spell at home on army leave. Hope was resigned by the club in the close season of 1945 but failed to break into the Magpies' senior eleven.
1 app. 0 gls.

HOWDON, Stephen (1941-1943)
Inside-forward, b. Prudhoe 1922
Career: Ryton jnrs/UNITED Aug 1941 to Dec 1943/Gateshead 1945/Hexham Hearts c1947.
On United's books for three seasons and an automatic choice in United's Northern Combination line-up, Howdon came into the Football League North side on an injury or unavailability of senior men. Operating at either inside-right or left, his debut was against Bradford City during August 1941 and he later took part in peacetime football for Gateshead in the Third Division(North).
10 apps. 1 gl.

HUBBLE, Leonard (1940-1946)
Left-back, b. Horden 1920
Career: Horden CW jnrs/UNITED Sept 1940 to 1946/Middlesbrough wg 1943-44/Leicester City wg 1944-45/Charlton Athletic wg 1944-45.
Playing alongside Tot Smith at Horden, Len Hubble made the same journey to St James Park to join his former team-mate within United's ranks. Although he was on Newcastle's staff for five seasons, Hubble only managed three games in the first eleven in 1941-42 and 1945-46, two of which were against Sheffield Wednesday. He did though play many more games for United's second string in the Northern Combination, but by the time peace was restored was overshadowed by Bobby Corbett at Gallowgate.
3 apps. 0 gls.

HUDSON, John (1940-1945)
Outside-right,
b. Blaydon 1921
Career: Clara Vale jnrs/UNITED Aug 1940 to 1945/West Stanley/Chesterfield 1946

(Bangor City loan 1953)/Shrewsbury Town 1953/Buxton 1955.
Known as Jackie, Tynesider John Hudson became a key figure in Chesterfield's ranks during the immediate post-war years. Appearing at centre-forward and inside-forward for the Derbyshire club, he totalled 173 games netting 33 goals at a time when Chesterfield were a Second Division force, for a period in 1946-47 close rivals for promotion with United. Hudson's stay at St James Park was one largely confined to the reserve team, although he managed a handful of fixtures on the wing in season 1939-40 and 1940-41.
3 apps. 0 gls.

HUGHES, Joseph (1938-1943)
Right-back, b. Hetton-le-Hole 1918
Career: UNITED Dec 1938 to 1943.
Developed through United's 'A' team and 5'7" tall, Joe Hughes was a young reserve who stood in for the experienced Joe Richardson at right-back during season 1942-43. His debut occurred against Bradford Park Avenue during August 1942, a 4-1 defeat.
2 apps. 0 gls

HUNTER, Isaac (1918 to 1919)
Left-half.
Career: UNITED 1918 to cs1919.
Isaac Hunter appeared in the opening fixture of the Northern Victory League against Hartlepools United in January 1919. That turned out to be his only senior outing for the Magpies, his place taken by noted Scot, Jock Finlay. Hunter nevertheless was a regular in the club's District League side for season 1918-19.
1 app. 0 gls.

HUTCHINSON, Robert (1918-1920)
Inside-left, b. Ashington
Career: Gosforth/St Mirren/UNITED amat 1918, pro May 1919/Ashington Nov 1920/Nelson 1922/Stockport County 1923/Chesterfield 1924/Barrow c1925.
Bob Hutchinson had an unlucky spell at Newcastle. Apart from

having his early footballing career ruined by World War One, he underwent cartilage surgery in 1919 which cost him an opportunity to push for a place at St James Park at a crucial time. Hutchinson's single appearance came in a Victory League clash with Scotswood, a deputy for Ed Dixon, while later in his career he took part in Nelson's Third Division(North) championship success in 1922-23. Prior to that, 12 months earlier Hutchinson took part in Ashington's first season in the Football League.
1 app. 0 gls.

HUTTON, Thomas Osborne (1939-1942)
Full-back, b. Gateshead 1922
Career: Sleekburn Welfare/UNITED 1939 to 1942/Red Rose (Army)/Accrington Stanley 1944/Carlisle United 1947/Rochdale 1949/Nelson 1950/Tranmere Rovers 1950/Chorley player-trainer 1951.
Described as, "sound rather than spectacular", Tom Hutton was a hardworking, tall (5' 11") defender who could also play at half-back. A joiner by trade, he came into United's team as a replacement for Jimmy Denmark at centre-half for a Christmas Day meeting with Middlesbrough in 1940. All Tom's appearances with the club were in that 1940-41 season, but then he soon after joined the army and later had a decent career in the lower divisions during immediate post-war football, appearing on 44 occasions for Carlisle.
3 apps. 0 gls.

LAW, John Alfred (1937-1944)
Left-back, b. Gateshead 1917
Career: Washington Colliery/UNITED Aug 1937 to May 1944.
With a robust style, John Law came into United's side as a replacement for Bobby Ancell for a clash with York City during April 1940. One commentator noted him as, "a nippy full-back and strong tackler". 5' 8" tall and on the fringe of his Football League debut for United just before the outbreak of the Second World War, his career was wrecked by the hostilities. Law worked for

G.Angus and Company in Newcastle during the war, and appeared frequently for the club in the Magpies' reserve eleven.
1 app. 0 gls.

LEE, R. (1943-1944)
Goalkeeper
A player on United's staff for the 1943-44 wartime season and who was third choice 'keeper behind Dave Cumming and Ray King. Lee appeared twice for the Novocastrians, his debut an absorbing thriller against Hartlepools United at the Victoria Ground in October 1943 which ended in a 5-4 defeat for the black'n'whites.
2 apps. 0 gls.

LIGHTFOOT, Lawrence
(1943-1946)
Outside-left,
b. Waterhouses 1923
Career: Waterhouses/UNITED Sept 1943/Consett July 1946.
Operating at both outside-left and occasionally outside right, Lawrence Lightfoot shared the number 11 shirt with Charles Woollett during season 1943-44. His debut occurred in a tussle with Bradford Park Avenue during September 1943, and although he was on Newcastle's staff to the end of the war, it was Woollett and later Tommy Pearson, as well as George Hair, who pushed him from the scene.
10 apps. 0 gls.

LITCHFIELD, Eric Brimley
(1937-1943)
Outside-right,
b. Liverpool 1920
Career: Bedford Town/UNITED amat July 1937, pro Jan 1939 to 1943/Leeds United wg 1941-42/ Reading wg 1942-43/Millwall wg 1942-43/York City wg 1943-44/ Northampton Town wg 1943-44.
The son of a clergyman, Eric Litchfield was a young budding star on United's books before the outbreak of the Second World War. Recognised as a, "promising talent", he took part in Central League football, but his career was torn apart by the five year conflict. His two senior games for the Magpies occurred in seasons

1939-40 and 1942-43 before he served in South Africa during the war. As a guest player for Northampton, he once scored four goals in a 9-1 victory over Nottingham Forest. In 1952 Eric emigrated to South Africa becoming a sports writer on the *Rand Daily Mail.*
2 apps. 0 gls.

McCORMACK, James Henry
(1942-1947)
Outside-right, b. Spennymoor
Joining United in April 1942 from local junior football, Jim McCormack was associated with the Magpies for five years as an amateur, not leaving until the end of the 1946-47 season. He was always recognised as a reserve, only taking part in two games of the Football League North competition, yet he played well on each occasion, netting in both games. Firstly in a 3-3 draw with York City in October 1942, then in a 5-4 defeat at Leeds.
2 apps. 2 gls.

McQUADE, George (1942-1946)
Inside-forward,
b. Scotland 1918
Career: Annan/UNITED Aug 1942 to May 1946.
Although wartime football curtailed normal football activity, United's scouting network still operated, and with notable success. George McQuade was one such find, spotted when playing for Annan in the south of Scotland. An inside-forward, he was blooded on the wing as a replacement for Woollett in a derby fixture with Sunderland during May 1942, but the Scot didn't get another opportunity.
1 app. 0 gls.

McVAY, Thomas Lloyd
(1939-1941)
Goalkeeper,
b. North Shields 1923
A former England schools international, capped against Ireland in 1937, Tom McVay signed for United in July 1939, but just had a few short months on Newcastle's Football League payroll before all contracts were cancelled on the outbreak of the

Second World War. Before joining the RAF, he had one outing in Tom Swinburne's position, against Leeds in June 1940.
1 app. 0 gls.

MILBURN, John Nicholson
(1940 to 1946)
Outside-left, b. Crook
Career: Crook Town/Stanley United/UNITED amat Nov 1940 to 1946.
The first Milburn to play for Newcastle United, and one hardly known to Magpie supporters. John Milburn pulled on the black and white shirt almost three years before 'Wor Jackie' stepped onto the turf, competing in the home clash with Grimsby Town in December 1940. Not related to his more famous namesake and although Milburn appeared in Northern Combination soccer for the club, that was his only first-class outing, being second choice to Laurie Nevins for most of his period at St James Park. Joining the RAF, he later became an electrician working for the local council, residing in Crook.
1 app. 0 gls.

MOSES, George (1939-1946)
Inside-right, b. Tow Law 1916
Career: UNITED Aug 1939/ Port Vale wg 1944-45/ Hartlepools United Aug 1946 to 1947.
Slightly built George Moses only clocked up nine games for the Magpies, yet he had the excellent record of netting six goals. Scoring on his debut against Darlington in November 1939, he was a fast, blond striker who played in a traditional centre-forward's role or as a schemer, quick to support the attack. An apprentice engineer in Scotswood's armaments factory during the war, Moses joined Hartlepool for the 1946-47 Football League programme and totalled 19 league games in first-class football.
9 apps. 6 gls.

MYERS, James (1940-1941)
Inside-right,
b.County Durham 1922
Joining the St James Park staff in August 1940 from the Ferryhill

club, Jimmy Myers was another player whose career never took off after being a promising junior. War service restricted him to a single game for the Magpies, in May 1941 against Leeds on Tyneside, a scoring debut for the teenager.
1 app. 1 gl.

NEVINS, Laurence (1940-1947)
Outside-left, b. Gateshead 1920
Career: UNITED Sept 1940/
Middlesbrough wg 1940-45/
Brighton June 1947/Hartlepools
United 1948 to 1949.
In between duty as a submariner during World War Two, Laurie Nevins pulled the black and white shirt on during three seasons from 1939-40. A regular in 1940-41 when he totalled 30 games, Nevins showed he could be an effective left winger, quick and with a telling cross. But war ruined his career and Nevins only briefly tasted Football League action with Brighton (5 apps.) and Hartlepools United (18 apps.). On leaving the game during the fifties he settled on Tyneside.
33 apps. 5 gls.

O'NEIL, Thomas Henry
(1942-1948)
Right-back, b. Spennymoor 1925,
d. Newport 1978
Career: Spennymoor United
1942/UNITED Sept 1942/
Leeds United wg 1943-44/
Newport County Apr 1948/
Spennymoor United 1949.
A young rival to Joe Richardson during his early seasons at Gallowgate, Tom O'Neil managed only one game in United's senior eleven, against Huddersfield Town in September 1942. Moving to Wales for a small fee of £150 in attempt to catch a period in league football with Newport, O'Neil was unfortunate to break his leg which restricted his first-class record to 10 matches. He later resided in the South Wales town to his death.
1 app. 0 gls.

OWENS, Mel (1975-1977)
Left-back, b. Durham
Career: UNITED app 1975, pro
1976 to cs 1977 free.
A junior product of Gordon Lee's management at St James Park, Mel

Owens signed apprentice forms for the Magpies during the summer of 1975 and very quickly figured in a senior Newcastle team sheet. Selected for the ill fated and controversial trip to face Ayr United in the much maligned Anglo-Scottish Cup during Sept 1976, Owens had to fight a rearguard action for most of the evening as the Geordie's reserve line-up fell by 3 goals. The England youth international failed to make the grade afterwards and drifted out of professional football.
1 app. 0 gls.

PORTER, Leslie (1944-1949)
Right-half, b. Gateshead 1923
Career: Redheugh Steelworks/
UNITED Aug 1944/Hereford
United wg 1945-46/York City Apr
1949 to 1953/North Shields 1954.
Starting as a winger, Leslie Porter took part in four seasons of wartime football for Newcastle, making his debut during the 1942-43 campaign. At 5' 9" tall, it was with York City that he was elevated to the Football League scene in 1949, eventually totalling 37 games for the Tykes.
16 apps. 2 gls.

PORTER, W. (1942-1946)
Right-half, b. County Durham
Career: Shotton Colliery/
UNITED Sept 1942/
Hartlepools United 1946.
A player to take part in just one Football League North fixture during World War Two, that a Tyne derby with Gateshead at Gallowgate during April 1943. He was retained on United's large professional staff for the big peacetime kick-off in August 1946 but moved to the Victoria Ground, Hartlepool in an attempt to secure a first-team place. He managed only two matches for 'Pool.
1 app. 0 gls

PRICE, Arthur (1939-1944)
Wing-half, b. Rowlands Gill 1922
Career: Spen Black & White/
UNITED amat Aug 1939, pro Aug
1940 to 1944/Consett/
Leeds United 1945 to 1946.
Red haired and only 5' 6" tall, Arthur Price was a compact and

neat midfielder who played on either side of the field. He had two good seasons in United's ranks, in 1940-41 and 1941-42, although he was registered with the club for five years, war service restricted his time in the region. Moving to Elland Road for a period, Price recorded 7 games for Leeds.
43 apps. 1 gl.

REED, F.T.W. (1918-1920)
Centre-half, b. Seaton Burn
Career: Seaton Burn/Gateshead/
UNITED 1918 to cs 1920/
Durham City wg 1919.
Related to the noted West Bromwich Albion inter-war defender Fred Reed, his Newcastle United cousin did not make the grade in Football League soccer after appearing once for the club against Sunderland in the Northern Victory League during January 1919. As a deputy to Wilf Low, he did have a good 90 minutes on that occasion, the local press noting that Reed, "fearlessly and successfully tackled the Sunderland forward celebrities".
2 apps. 0 gls.

ROBSON, Ralph (1939 to 1942)
Inside-left, b. Walkergate 1922
Career: Parsons jnrs/UNITED
May 1939 to 1942.
Signed on amateur forms from local works side Parsons, Ralph Robson was a diminutive player at only 5' 4" tall. Able to play wide on the left touchline, or in midfield, he found the promise of a professional career in soccer destroyed by the declaration of war 4 months after joining the Gallowgate staff. Robson was selected on a handful of occasions during seasons 1939-40 and 1941-42.
5 apps. 1 gl.

RUSHTON, George (1944-1946)
Outside-right, b. Coxhoe 1927
Career: Shotton jnrs/UNITED
amat Sept 1944, pro Nov 1945
to 1946/Horden CW.
Stan Seymour's scouting network during the latter years of the Second World War made sure a steady stream of young north eastern talent ended up at St James Park. George Rushton was

one of many teenagers who tried to earn a long term contract. Standing in on the wing for another of those budding soccer stars, Jackie Milburn, during December 1945, Rushton never quite made the grade and left the scene in 1946.
1 app. 0 gls.

RUTHERFORD, Robert
(1944-1946)
Inside-left, b. South Shields 1922
Career: Wallsend St Lukes/
UNITED Mar 1944/Gateshead
1946 to 1953.
Known as Bobby, his highlight during two years on the Gallowgate staff was a derby fixture with Sunderland when Rutherford scored twice in a 3-0 victory. In and out of the side during seasons 1943-44 and 1944-45, Rutherford later joined Gateshead where he accumulated 10 games in the Third Division(North). On leaving football he became a draughtsman in the north east.
19 apps. 2 gls.

RUTHERFORD, Thomas V.
(1938-1944)
Goalkeeper, b. Tyneside
Career: Scotswood/UNITED
May 1938/Ashington 1940/
UNITED 1940 to 1944/
Hartlepools United wg 1944-45.
Tom Rutherford's brief period as United's goalkeeper coincided with some remarkable results in wartime football. His debut against Gateshead on Christmas Day 1942 ended in a 6-6 draw, while he also took part in a 9-0 victory over Leeds, a 7-3 success against Middlesbrough and another fascinating draw, 5-5 with York City. Rivalling Norman Tapken and Ray King, his outings were confined to seasons 1942-43 and 1943-44.
25 apps. 0 gls.

SALES, Ronald Duncan
(1942-1947)
Centre-half, b. South Shields 1920
Career: Reyrolles/UNITED July 1942/Middlesbrough wg 1944-45/Leyton Orient May 1947/Hartlepools United 1950/South Shields 1951.
Possessing a good left foot, Ron

Sales started in the same works side as another wartime player, Johnny Dixon. Taking over from Tot Smith in the pivot's role for an extended period in 1942-43, Sales showed he could develop into a good defender, strong and positive. It was in London though that he made his breakthrough, recording 48 senior games for Leyton Orient before moving to the Victoria Ground, Hartlepool.
42 apps. 0 gls.

SALTHOUSE, W. (1940-1941)
Outside-left
A forward who only made a single outing for the Magpies, in a Tyne-Tees derby fixture on Christmas Day 1940. He came into the side for Laurie Nevins and had an ineffective afternoon as United fell 3-1.
1 app. 0 gls.

SCARR, Raymond (1942-1944)
Inside-forward,
b. County Durham 1921
Career: Chester-le-Street Old Boys/UNITED Nov 1942 to 1944.
A regular in the Northern Combination League during season 1942-43, Raymond Scarr was promoted to first-team action in the Football League North, filling in across the forward line during seasons 1942-43 and 1943-44 when senior players were out of action.
7 apps. 0 gls.

SEYMOUR, Colin Matthew
(1939-1943)
Inside-left,
b. Newcastle upon Tyne,
d. Yorkshire 1943
Career: Heaton Stannington 1939/Gateshead amat 1939/UNITED amat 1939 to 1943.
The son of ex United star winger, and director, Stan Seymour, Colin was a former Royal Grammar School pupil and a schoolboy international at rugby and cricket. Taking part in a few games during the 1939-40 and 1942-43 seasons, as well as more frequently in the club's reserve wartime outfit, Seymour tragically lost his life during a training flight in Yorkshire.

Joining the RAF, he became a flying officer and served in bombing operations over Germany. On one such sortie his aircraft crashed at Bedale in Yorkshire on return to base in Lossiemouth.
3 apps. 0 gls.

SIMPSON, Thomas Graham
(1941-1943)
Centre-forward
A young deputy for the potent attacking skills of Albert Stubbins, Simpson found himself in the Number 9 role on a handful of occasions during seasons 1941-42 and 1942-43, his debut being against Rotherham United in a League War Cup fixture during February 1942.
4 apps. 0 gls.

SLOAN, James (1945-1946)
Centre-forward,
b. Newcastle upon Tyne 1924
Career: North Shields/Parsons Athletic/UNITED Feb 1945/Middlesbrough wg 1944-45/Hartlepools United Nov 1946 to 1952.
A product of St Aloysius School, the young leader was blooded in United's line-up against Middlesbrough during January 1945 and had a great start in a black'n'white shirt. In the first minute he went off on a penetrating run and made a goal for Charlie Wayman. Reserve to Albert Stubbins for his stay at Gallowgate, Sloan moved to Hartlepool in an exchange deal involving J.Brown and he proceeded to total 83 first-class matches scoring 28 goals in the Football League.
7 apps. 0 gls.

SMITH S. (1918-1919)
Outside-left
From Tyneside, Smith had been just demobbed from the Great War when he joined the United staff as an amateur during 1918. And he soon pushed his way into the club's senior side at the time, for a Northern Victory League fixture with Darlington Forge Albion. Deputising for Ed Cooper on the wing, he was unconvincing in attack and

wasn't part of the squad when the club's directors were drawing up their retained list for the new 1919-20 season.
1 app. 0 gls.

SPIKE, Septimus (1940-1942)
Right-back,
b. Willington Quay 1921
Career: Willington Athletic/ UNITED 1940 to 1942/Leeds United wg 1940-42.
Sep was an automatic selection for United's reserve line-up in the Northern Combination during season 1941-42. He was upgraded to take Joe Richardson's Number Two shirt in September 1941 for a few games before having a handful of outings with Leeds in the Football League North competition.
3 apps. 0 gls.

STEEL, William (1939-1942)
Outside-left,
b. Newcastle upon Tyne 1920
From the Walker district of the city, Billy Steel was an apprentice engineer at the giant Parson's works during the Second World War. His only match for the Magpies was a trip to Leeds Road to face Huddersfield Town in September 1941. United, and Steel, didn't have a happy afternoon as the black'n'whites fell heavily by 5-0.
1 app. 0 gls.

TAYLOR, James Davis
(1939-1940)
Centre-forward,
b. Sunderland 1920
A shipwright on Tyneside, Jim Taylor joined United from the Hylton Colliery side in April 1939 and only claimed a single game for United's first eleven as a replacement for Billy Cairns. However, in a good performance against Bradford City at the end of the 1939-40 season, he netted twice as the Magpies lost narrowly 4-3 to the Yorkshire club. Described as a clever ball player with a constructive urge.
1 app. 2 gls.

THOMPSON, Matthew
(1939-1941)
Outside-right
On the club's books as war was declared in September 1939, Matt Thompson only occasionally received a call to appear for the senior team, once in 1939-40 and again on a single outing the following term. He was employed at a local coal-mine in Bedlington for a period.
2 apps. 0 gls.

THOMPSON, William Nesbit
(1940-1941)
Outside-right, b. Bedlington 1921
A former Ashington player, Bill Thompson joined the United roll-call in Aug 1940, but only remained for a little over 12 months, leaving due to service commitments in October 1941. A pit-lad in the Ashington coalfield, he took part in a marvellous 4-3 defeat against Middlesbrough for his debut in February of that year.
1 app. 0 gls.

TULTHORPE, George
(1918-1919)
Inside-left
A local player who joined United's staff during 1918 at a time when members of the Magpies' professional staff were scattered around the country due to war service. Tulthorpe scored on his debut for Newcastle, against Scotswood in January 1919, and took part in the first half of the Northern Victory League programme. He was replaced once Curtis Booth and Billy Hibbert had arrived back at St James Park.
6 apps. 1 gl.

VARTY, Thomas Heppell
(1940-1945)
Outside-left,
b. Hetton-le-Hole 1921
Career: Vickers Works/UNITED 1940/Darlington 1945/Watford 1950 to 1951.
Employed in the giant Vickers armament factory on Tyneside, Tom Varty was given a chance at Gallowgate during season 1941-42. Although appearing often for United's wartime second string, he was handed only one game in

senior company, against Leeds United at Elland Road in November 1941. Later though, Varty made a name for himself within Darlington's ranks, claiming over 160 matches for the Quakers. He later went into business in that town.
1 app. 0 gls.

WALL, George H. (1918-1919)
Inside-right, b. Ouston 1897,
d. Newcastle upon Tyne 1919
Career: Perkinsville/UNITED amat 1918, pro May 1919 to death in Sept 1919.
An England schools international, George Wall came into United's First World War celebration side in February 1919 against Middlesbrough and was regarded as "a promising player" by the local press. Deputising for Ed Dixon, Wall had an unhappy afternoon on Tees-side as the Magpies fell 3-0, but he still impressed in local football and was highly rated. After being given a contract for the 1919-20 First Division season, the Tynesider died suddenly after a short illness when only 22 years old which saddened everyone at the club. Six of his team-mates acted as underbearers at his funeral in Ouston.
1 app. 0 gls.

WHITTLE, Ernest (1944-1946)
Inside-left, b. Lanchester 1925
Career: Quaking Houses jnrs/ UNITED Nov 1944 to 1946/ Seaham CW/West Stanley/ Lincoln City 1950/Workington 1954/Chesterfield 1956/Bradford Park Avenue 1957/Scarborough 1958/Ruston Bucyrus(Lincoln) 1961/Lincoln Claytons 1966/ Lincoln City asst-coach 1966.
After leaving St James Park, Ernie Whittle developed into a snappy midfielder of some note in the lower divisions. Claiming over 150 games for Lincoln, and more than 100 at Workington, he won a Third Division(North) championship medal when at Sincil Bank in 1952 when he netted 19 goals. With a stocky 5' 6" frame, he received little opportunity when at Gallowgate, stepping in once for Charlie Wayman in February 1945

against Hartlepool. Later residing in Lincolnshire, Whittle's son and grandson were both on Lincoln's books.
1 app. 0 gls.

WILLITTS, Joseph (1941-1943)
Right-back, b. Shotton 1924
Career: Shotton CW/UNITED Nov 1941 to Aug 1943/ Hartlepools United 1945 to 1956.
A miner at Shotton colliery, Joe Willitts came into United's side for Joe Richardson in defence for a journey to face Sheffield Wednesday during December 1941. A regular in the Northern Combination side that season, he wasn't promoted to the black'n'whites' first eleven again. Like several of United's wartime players, he moved to the Victoria Ground in search of senior action and he totalled over 250 games for Hartlepool. Joe was recognised as a penalty king, once netting three times from the spot in a match against Darlington.
1 app. 0 gls.

WILSON, William Arthur (1913-1922)
Forward,
b. Newcastle upon Tyne 1896,
d. Newcastle upon Tyne 1996
Career: UNITED Swifts 1913, amat 1918, pro May 1919/Myrthyr Town May 1922/West Stanley 1923/Carlisle United 1925/Retired 1925.
Connected with Newcastle's early junior development programme for several years, Billy Wilson was well built and powerful at 14 stone and 5'9" tall. A play-any-where forward, once noted during 1920 in the *Newcastle Daily Chronicle*, "as one of the finest youngsters on the club's books....and if given the chance could blossom out as England's winger". Unfortunately Wilson was rarely given an opportunity, appearing twice during the Victory League in 1919, and in a handful of friendly contests, including a tour to Spain and France in 1921. A regular for the Magpies' reserve side from 1917 to 1922, Billy had severe competition for places in the immediate post-war years, both in attack and at half-back where he

also figured. A celebrated sprinter too, he served in the Royal Navy during the war. Moving to Wales to appear for Merthyr's Football League side, Wilson soon returned to Tyneside where he ran a furniture making business and then worked as a turner at Vicker's and Parson's works. From a large family, his brother Arthur was also on United's books without making the grade, but had a fine career with Southampton and West Ham United. Billy is recognised as becoming the oldest United footballer on record, surviving to a few days before his 100th birthday. He died in High Heaton during March 1996.
2 apps. 0 gls.

WOOD, George Andrew (1944-1946)
Goalkeeper, b. Gateshead 1923
Career: Blucher United/ UNITED 1944 to 1946.
George Wood filled the boots of regular goalkeeper Dave Cumming only occasionally during the 1944-45 and 1945-46 seasons. His debut for the Magpies was in a derby tussle with Sunderland during April 1945 and although United lost 3-0, Wood's highlight was the return meeting the following month. Newcastle thrashed the Wearsiders 5-0 and George was also on the field for one of the easiest games any United 'keeper has taken part in, an 11-0 mauling of Middlesbrough during May 1945.
7 apps. 0 gls.

WOODS, Patrick Bede (1943-1945)
Left-half
Joining United from local side Bedewell in November 1943, Pat Woods gained a run in United's Football League North line-up in each of three seasons up to 1946. He also guested for Hartlepools United joining the Victoria Ground set-up permanently in October 1945. Pat didn't graduate to Football League status once a peacetime programme was restored during the summer of 1946.
16 apps. 0 gls.

WOOLLETT, Charles (1942-1946)
Outside-left, b. Murton 1921
Career: Eppleton CW/UNITED Nov 1942/Middlesbrough wg 1944-45/Hartlepools United wg 1945-6/Bradford City Aug 1946/ York City 1949 to 1950.
One of the mainstays of wartime football at St James Park, Charlie Woollett *(pictured above)* ran the touchline with distinction. Very fast, he linked with Stubbins at centre-forward in a highly productive way over four seasons. Scoring on his debut against Middlesbrough in December 1941, a 7-0 victory, Woollett later also guested for 'Boro against the Magpies, such was the strange format of wartime soccer. He later made 44 league and cup appearances for Bradford City, costing the Tykes a fee of £600 when he moved from Gallowgate.
75 apps. 13 gls.

YEATS, John (1940-1942)
Centre-half, b. Gateshead
Career: Whitehall jnrs/UNITED Aug 1940 to 1942/Middlesbrough wg 1941-42.
Appearing for the Magpies during the first three seasons of wartime football, John Yeats slipped into Newcastle's side as a deputy pivot for Jimmy Denmark and Tot Smith. A frequent member of the second eleven, he worked as a turner at the Parson's engineering works on Tyneside.
4 apps. 0 gls.

ANDERSON, Ronald J. (1941)
Bury
Inside-right,
b. Newcastle upon Tyne
Career: Bury c1939/UNITED wg
1940-42/Millwall wg 1941-42/
Crystal Palace 1947 to c1948.
Appearing as a schemer as well as
in the Number 9 shirt for United,
Ron Anderson hailed from the
Fenham area of the city and took
part in a handful of fixtures when
he returned home. Scoring in his
second match for Newcastle,
against Bradford City during
September 1941, he later
attempted a career at Selhurst
Park but failed to make the
Football League eleven.
3 apps. 1 gl.

BAINBRIDGE, R. (1943)
Grimsby Town
Centre-forward
On United's staff for season
1943-44, R. Bainbridge appeared
only once for the club, as a deputy
for Albert Stubbins against
Bradford Park Avenue in
September 1943. Although official
club records indicate he was on
Grimsby Town's books, no trace
of this player has been found. It is
suspected he is in fact Bill
Bainbridge of Ashington who
hailed from Gateshead and
appeared for United when on
Tyneside. Bill also played for
Hartlepools United, Manchester
United and Tranmere Rovers.
1 app. 0 gls.

BALMER, John (1941-1942)
Liverpool
Inside-right, b. Liverpool 1916,
d. 1984
Career: Collegiate Old Boys/
Everton amat/Liverpool 1935/
Brighton wg 1940-41/UNITED wg
1941-42/Retired 1952.
An England wartime international
in November 1939, Jack Balmer
had a noted spell at Anfield,
totalling 313 games and netting
111 goals. Liverpool skipper, he
was a highly skilled goalpoacher
who teamed up with Albert
Stubbins in the Reds' side that
won the championship in 1946-47.
5' 10" tall and a great opportunist
up front who possessed a stinging
shot, Balmer once struck three

consecutive hat-tricks for
Liverpool in 1946. From a
footballing family, his uncles
William and Robert both played
for Everton. During his short stay
with United during season
1941-42, he first developed an
understanding with Stubbins that
was to serve Liverpool so well
after the Second World War.
6 apps. 1 gl.

BARRON, James (1944-1945)
Blackburn Rovers
Goalkeeper, b. Burnhope 1913,
d. Newcastle upon Tyne 1969
Career: Durham City/Blyth
Spartans 1933/Blackburn Rovers
1935/UNITED wg 1944-45/
Darlington 1946 to 1947.
Only appearing once for the
Magpies, against Huddersfield
Town during December 1944, Jim
Barron had been the first choice
'keeper at Ewood Park before the
outbreak of World War Two. In
the region on essential work in the
steel industry, he was called-up by
Newcastle's officials due to the
unavailability of another guest
player, Dave Cumming of
Middlesbrough. All told Barron
totalled 83 games for Blackburn in
a sound, if not spectacular career.
He helped lift the Second Division
championship in 1939 and
reached the War Cup final the
following year. Barron's son, Jim
(junior) appeared prominently for
Nottingham Forest and
Wolverhampton Wanderers.
1 app. 0 gls.

BATEY, Robert (1943)
Preston North End
Half-back, b. Greenhead 1912,
d. Chorley 1988
Career: Greenhead South Tyne
Rangers/Carlisle United 1931/
Preston North End 1934/
Liverpool wg 1940-41/UNITED
wg 1942-43/Gateshead wg
1943-44/Hartlepools United wg
1943-44/Millwall wg 1943-44/
Southport wg 1943-44/Barrow
wg 1945-46/Leeds United
1945/Southport 1947/Annfield
Plain player-trainer 1948/Leyland
Motors 1949/Chorley ass-player-
trainer 1952.
Prior to World War Two, Bob
Batey was in and out of Preston

Frank Soo

**During World War Two
clubs were allowed to
field guest players from
other sides to supplement
their staff. Newcastle
United took on several
established stars during
the war programme, many
stationed in the north-east
or resident for a period in
their native area.**

*War guests career spans
noted are the seasons the
player spent at each club,
eg 1940-41 means 1940-41
season, or 1940-42 means
seasons 1940-41 and
1941-42. For easy reference,
the club noted at the
beginning of the biography is
each player's base club.*

North End's fine side, yet he still topped over 100 matches and appeared at Wembley in the 1938 FA Cup final when the Lancastrians defeated Huddersfield to lift the trophy. A sturdy defensive figure, he came into United's side during the spring of 1943 when serving in the RAF, his last game for the black'n'whites being a marvellous 5-5 draw with York City. On leaving the game, Batey worked for Leyland Motors to his retirement in 1977.
8 apps. 0 gls.

BELL, William (1943) *Kilmarnock*
Goalkeeper, b. Kilmarnock
Career: Shawfield jnrs/
Kilmarnock 1939/UNITED wg
1942-43/Halifax Town wg
1943-44/Ayr United 1946.
A Scottish junior international goalkeeper, Willie Bell also took part in the 1939 Scottish Junior Cup final before joining his local club, Kilmarnock. He was unfortunate to have been given his chance in professional football just before war was declared. Although only 5' 8" tall, Bell possessed good anticipation coupled with a steady pair of hands. A stylish custodian, his two games in United's colours both ended in victories, 3-1 at Leeds and 2-0 against Gateshead.
2 apps. 0 gls.

BILLINGTON, Hugh John R.
(1940-1941) *Luton Town*
Centre-forward,
b. Ampthill 1916, d. Luton 1988
Career: Luton Cocoa Works/
Chapel St Methodists/
Waterlows/Luton Town 1938/
UNITED wg 1940-41/York City
wg 1943-44/Chelsea 1948/
Worcester City 1951.
A potent centre-forward, especially for Luton Town where he grabbed 63 goals in only 86 league games, and also after the Second World War in the blue shirt of Chelsea. With a record of 32 goals in 90 appearances for the Stamford Bridge club, Hugh ended his long career on a high note. Having a terrific shot, he collected many of his goals from long range efforts and during his

brief period at St James Park had a first-class tally also. Not of big build, Hugh was only 5' 9", but caused all sorts of problems for defenders.
4 apps. 3 gls.

BOYES, Walter Edward (1942)
Everton
Outside-left,
b. Killamarsh 1913, d. 1960
Career: Woodhouse Mills United/
West Bromwich Albion 1931/
Everton 1938/UNITED wg
1941-42/Middlesbrough wg
1941-42/Brentford wg 1942-43/
Clapton Orient wg 1942-43/
Sunderland wg 1942-43/Millwall
wg 1942-43/Leeds United wg
1942-44/Aldershot wg 1944-45/
Preston North End wg 1944-45/
Manchester United wg 1944-45/
Linfield wg/Notts County player-
trainer 1949/Scunthorpe United
player 1950/Retford Town player-
manager 1953/Hyde United
manager 1958/Swansea Town
trainer 1959 to 1960.
A distinguished pre-war England international winger who won three caps for his country and appeared twice for the Football League side. A splendid little player, at 5' 4" tall, Wally was tricky and always was able to score goals as well as create openings. He appeared on 73 occasions for Everton before and after World War Two and took part in the Goodison club's title success in 1938-39. He also reached the FA Cup final with West Bromwich Albion in 1935, a day at Wembley which saw him find the net. An errant traveller during the war, Boyes landed at Gallowgate during February and March 1942 and took the place of Charlie Woollett on the left touchline.
2 apps. 0 gls.

CARR, Edward Miller
(1942-1945) *Arsenal*
Centre-forward,
b. Wheatley Hill 1917
Career: Wheatley Hill CW/
Arsenal 1935/Margate 1936/
Arsenal 1937/Bradford Park
Avenue wg 1940-44/UNITED
wg 1942-45/Middlesbrough wg
1942-43/Darlington wg

1943-44/Huddersfield Town
1945/Newport County 1946/
Bradford City 1949/Darlington
1953, becoming trainer 1954,
manager 1960 to 1964/Tow Law
Town manager 1964/UNITED
scout 1969.
An ex miner who, after establishing himself as a promising striker at Highbury, returned to County Durham to work down the pits during the hostilities. Carr became, next to Albert Stubbins, Newcastle's most potent forward during the era, boasting an impressive 80% strike-rate. Sturdy, but not tall at 5' 6", Eddie was deputy in the main to Ted Drake in London, but he had some excellent performances for the Gunners, helping them to the championship in 1938 before a knee operation threatened his career. On one occasion in the black and white stripes of the Magpies, Carr hit six goals in an 11-0 romp over Bradford City during 1944. In post-war football Eddie continued scoring goals, for Newport (55 goals) and Bradford City (56 goals) before returning to settle in his native County Durham.
70 apps. 56 gls.

CHILTON, Allenby C. (1943)
Manchester United
Centre-half, b. South Hylton 1918,
d. Southwick 1996
Career: Hylton Colliery jnrs/
Seaham Colliery/Liverpool 1938/
Manchester United 1938/Cardiff
City wg 1941-42/UNITED wg
1942-43/Charlton Athletic wg
1943-44/Hartlepools United wg
1944-45/Middlesbrough wg
1944-45/Reading wg 1945-46/
Airdrieonians wg/Resumed with
Manchester United 1946/Grimsby
Town player-manager 1955 to
1959/Wigan Athletic manager
1960/Hartlepools United scout
1961, becoming manager 1962
to 1963.
A key defensive figure for Manchester United after the Second World War, Allenby Chilton was recognised as one of the finest players of his time, tough, yet highly creative with the ball. A tall and powerful pivot, he

claimed 390 games for the Old Trafford club, many as captain and totalling 179 consecutive appearances (1951-55) to create a club record. Winning two England caps, he secured both a title and FA Cup winners medal with Manchester United, as well as wartime honours for the Reds and at Charlton. As player-boss of Grimsby, he took the Mariners to the Third Division (North) title in 1956. Playing in the last two games of the 1942-43 season for Newcastle, he served in the Durham Light Infantry and was wounded during the Normandy landings at Caen. Allenby later ran a shop and worked at a steelworks. He returned to his native Wearside, residing in Seaburn.
2 apps. 0 gls.

CONNOR, John (1943)
Bolton Wanderers
Left-back,
b. Ashton-under-Lyne 1914
Career: Mossley/Bolton Wanderers 1934/UNITED wg 1942-43/Tranmere Rovers 1947 to 1949.
Making his Football League debut against Port Vale during February 1935, John Connor took part in 36 senior contests for Preston. At St James Park he stepped in for Doug Graham during November 1942, facing Gateshead in a double Football League North meeting. And Connor helped United to a 7-4 victory over their Tyneside rivals in one of the derby clashes. Resuming his career with Tranmere, John totalled 46 league matches for the Merseyside outfit.
2 apps. 0 gls.

COYDE, Norman
(1936-1938,1942-1943)
Southend United
Outside-right, b. Wallsend 1918, d. Newcastle upon Tyne 1985
Career:
Wallsend/Sunderland/UNITED May 1936 free/North Shields May 1938 free/Southend United 1939/Gateshead wg 1941-42/UNITED wg 1942-43.
A teenage friend of Albert Stubbins at Carville School,

Norman Coyde first joined the St James Park staff at the same time as his more famous colleague in 1936. However he couldn't break through United's pre-war ranks and moved south to try his luck with Southend United. A fast winger, Coyde wasn't a regular with the Shrimpers and returned to Gallowgate for wartime action; the highlight of his stay being a goal in the amazing 6-6 draw with Gateshead on Christmas Day 1942. Illness curtailed his career and later he was employed as a shipyard plumbing manager in Wallsend. Norman was also an excellent golfer and local cricketer. He resided in Walker to his death.
7 apps. 1 gl.

CUMMING, David Scott
(1943-1945) *Middlesbrough*
Goalkeeper, b. Aberdeen 1910
Career: Hall Russell jnrs/Aberdeen 1930/Arbroath 1933/Middlesbrough 1936/UNITED wg 1943-45/Retired 1948.
A Scottish international goalkeeper, capped in season 1937-38, Dave Cumming was a regular with the Magpies during seasons 1943-44 and 1944-45. Also winning a wartime cap for his country when at St James Park in October 1944, Cumming was a hearty player with quick reflexes. When he moved from Scotland to head for Teesside for £3,000, Dave was recognised as one of the most expensive 'keepers to cross the border. A good servant to 'Boro, he totalled 157 games for the Ayresome Park side and actually appeared on several occasions for the Magpies against his registered club. 5' 10" tall, he retired from the game following a dislocated knee-cap.
56 apps. 0 gls.

DIMOND, Stuart (1943)
Manchester United
Centre-forward, b. Chorlton 1920
Career: Manchester United 1939/UNITED wg 1942-43/Notts County wg 1943-44/Leicester City wg 1943-44/Swansea Town wg 1944-45/Stockport County wg 1944-45/Bradford City 1945/Winsford United 1948.
Only appearing on a single

occasion for United during March 1943, Stuart Dimond deputised for Albert Stubbins in the leader's role for a journey to face Leeds United at Elland Road. Dimond found the net in a terrific contest that ended 5-4 to the home side. Unable to make the first-team at Old Trafford, Stuart entered Football League action with Bradford City, but managed only nine appearances.
1 app. 1 gl.

DUFFY, Robert McFarlane Davidson (1944-1945)
Glasgow Celtic
Left-half, b. Dundee 1913
Career: Dundee St Josephs 1932/Lochee Harp 1933/Glasgow Celtic 1935/Dundee wg 1939-40/Blackpool wg 1940-41/Bradford City wg 1941-42/Fulham wg 1941-42/Hamilton Academical wg 1941-42/Huddersfield Town wg 1941-43/Rochdale wg 1942-43/Dundee United wg 1943-44/Port Vale wg 1944-45/Swansea Town wg 1944-45/UNITED wg 1944-45/Leeds United wg 1945-46/Resumed with Celtic 1945 to 1947.
Known as Bertie, during the Second World War he worked as a physical trainer instructor for the RAF and travelled the country as a consequence. Duffy's football career followed him around, landing at various ports of call up and down the length of England and Central Scotland. At 5' 8", he was a solid half-back, a reserve to Celtic's stars at Parkhead, and as a result Bertie managed only four games for the Glasgow club. But he produced some good performances in wartime soccer which had several pundits tip him for a Scotland cap in 1944-45, the season he turned out for Newcastle.
21 apps. 0 gls.

DUNS, Leonard (1933, 1939-1942)
Sunderland
Outside-right,
b. Newcastle upon Tyne 1916, d. Ponteland 1989
Career: West End Albion/Newcastle West End/UNITED amat 1933/Sunderland 1933/UNITED wg 1939-42/Aldershot wg 1939-44/Bristol City wg

1941-42/Reading wg 1941-42/
Notts County wg 1942-43/West
Bromwich Albion wg 1943-44/
Wrexham wg 1944-46/
Shrewsbury Town wg 1945-46/
Resumed with Sunderland
1946/Ashington 1952.
A formidable player with
Sunderland, Len Duns totalled
247 senior games for the Roker
Park club, finding the net on 54
occasions. After being rejected by
United as a youth, he went on to
lift both the title (1936) and FA
Cup (1937) in a red and white
shirt before the Second World
War. At 5' 9" tall, he was strong
and sturdy, a fast and direct
winger, lethal if he gained a sight
of goal. With the Royal Artillery
during the hostilities, Duns
guested for several clubs,
including a rewarding spell with
the Magpies on and off over three
seasons.
20 apps. 8 gls.

EASTHAM, Henry (1942)
Liverpool
Inside-right, b. Blackpool 1917
Career: Blackpool 1933/Liverpool
1936/Southport wg 1939-40/New
Brighton wg 1939-40/Leicester
City wg 1939-40/Brighton wg
1940-44/Bolton Wanderers wg
1941-42/UNITED wg 1941-42/
Leeds United wg 1941-43/
Blackpool wg 1944-45/Distillery
wg/Resumed with Liverpool
1946/Tranmere Rovers 1948/
Accrington Stanley 1953/
Netherfield 1955/Rolls Royce to
1955.
Uncle to Newcastle's George
Eastham, this member of the
famous Eastham clan was noted
for his excellent vision, control
and accurate distribution, a ball
player in the family tradition.
Able to play anywhere in attack,
Harry took part in a derby War
Cup meeting with Sunderland for
United in January 1942 and later
assisted Liverpool to the League
Championship in 1947 alongside
Stubbins. He totalled 69 games for
the Reds before moving across the
Mersey where he clocked up over
150 matches for Tranmere. A knee
injury halted his career, Eastham
afterwards ran a pub near Bolton.
1 app. 0 gls.

FAGAN, William (1942)
Liverpool
Inside-left, b. Musselburgh 1917,
d. Wellingborough 1992
Career: Balgonia Scotia/Wellesley
jnrs 1934/Glasgow Celtic 1934/
Preston North End 1936/
Liverpool 1937/Aldershot wg
1939-44/Leicester City wg
1940-41/Northampton Town wg
1940-45/Glasgow Celtic wg
1941-42/UNITED wg 1942-43/
Chelsea wg 1943-44/Millwall wg
1944-45/Reading wg 1944-45/
Crystal Palace wg 1945-46/
Resumed with Liverpool to 1951,
becoming asst-trainer/Distillery
player-manager 1952/Weymouth
player-manager 1952 to 1955.
A Scotland wartime cap in 1945,
Bill Fagan took part in two FA
Cup finals, one either side of war
in 1937 and 1950. Another player
to play alongside Albert Stubbins
in Liverpool's title-winning side
during 1946-47, he also appeared
in the War South Cup in 1944 for

Chelsea, during one of his many
sojourns during wartime soccer.
Red-haired and well built, the
Scot began as an intelligent
schemer who during his later
days moved to half-back. Fagan
turned out for the Anfield club on
161 occasions, scoring 47 goals
and cost a sizable £8,000 when he
moved across Lancashire from
Preston. Serving in the RAF
during the war, Bill later worked
at a borstal in Dorset. His uncle
'Jean' McFarlane appeared with
Celtic and Middlesbrough.
2 apps. 0 gls.

FINNEY, Thomas O.B.E. (1942)
Preston North End
Outside-right, b. Preston 1922
Career: Preston North End
1937/UNITED wg 1942-43/
Southampton wg 1942-43/Bolton
Wanderers wg 1942-43/Resumed
with Preston North End/retired
1960, becoming a Preston director
and later President.

Tom Finney

One of the most famous players in English football, Tom Finney pulled on the black and white shirt for six games during the 1942-43 season. And on one occasion he scored a memorable hat-trick for the Magpies against Gateshead during November 1942 as United won an epic match 7-4. Winning 76 caps for his country (30 goals), Finney was also selected on 17 occasions for the Football League, and was twice named Footballer of the Year (1954 & 1957). Slightly built at 5' 8", Tom was a genius on the ball; he served with the Tank Corps during the war and after a marvellous career of 569 first-class matches (249 goals) Finney settled in his native Preston running a plumbing and electrical business. He remains associated with Preston North End as President.
6 apps. 3 gls.

FORSTER, Leslie James (1943)
Blackpool
Outside-right,
b. Newcastle upon Tyne 1915
Career: Walker Celtic/Blackpool 1938/UNITED wg 1942-43/York City 1946/Gateshead 1947 to 1948.
Born and bred in Byker, Leslie Forster took over the right wing position at St James Park for a period during the spring of 1943. Having made his Football League debut for Blackpool during the season prior to war breaking out, his promising career was devastated by the hostilities. He totalled only three league games at Bloomfield Road, 10 with York and 15 for Gateshead before leaving the stage.
3 apps. 0 gls.

GALLACHER, Patrick (1939)
Stoke City
Inside-left, b. Bridge of Weir 1909, d. Greenock 1992
Career: Linwood St Connels/ Bridge of Weir/Sunderland 1927/Stoke City 1938/UNITED wg 1939-40/Notts County wg 1940-41/Leicester City wg 1942-43/Weymouth player-manager.
Like Len Duns, Patsy Gallacher was another noted Sunderland player from their successful pre-war side to appear in Magpie

colours. A Scottish international schemer in 1934-35, Gallacher was also capped in wartime football and was a most effective forward. Winning title and FA Cup honours, he claimed 108 goals in 307 games for the Wearsiders, a regular for ten seasons at Roker Park. Quick thinking on the ball and 5' 8" tall, his stay at Gallowgate was all too brief, only a single game against York City in October 1939. Gallacher served in the RAF during the war years and appeared for several clubs as a passing guest. After leaving the game Patsy entered business in London before returning to Scotland.
1 app. 0 gls.

GLASSEY, John Robert (1944)
Mansfield Town
Inside-left,
b. Chester-le-Street 1914,
d. Durham 1984
Career: Horden Colliery/ Liverpool 1933/Stoke City 1936/Mansfield Town 1939/ Hartlepools United wg 1939-40/ UNITED wg 1943-44/Third Lanark wg/Stockton 1945/ Horden CW/Blackburn Rovers scout.
Bobby Glassey only appeared occasionally at all his Football League clubs, although during his stay at Anfield did well for Liverpool, netting four goals in nine matches. Arriving at St James Park towards the end of the 1943-44 season, he stepped into Johnny Dixon's role at inside-forward for fixtures against Darlington and Sheffield United.
2 apps. 0 gls.

GRAY, Robert (1940-1945)
Gateshead
Goalkeeper,
b. Newcastle upon Tyne 1923
Career: Whitehall jnrs/UNITED amat 1940/Gateshead 1941/ Millwall wg 1941-42/UNITED wg 1944-45/Resumed with Gateshead 1945 to 1959/Ashington/North Shields 1959.
Appearing between the posts on two occasions for United, once when on the club's books as an amateur in season 1939-40, the other in 1944-45 after he had

signed for neighbours Gateshead. Taking part as a regular in Newcastle's reserve side during 1940-41, Gray developed into an outstanding goalkeeper for the Redheugh club, one of the best in the lower divisions of the Football League in post-war soccer. He totalled over 450 league and cup matches for Gateshead, and was a 6' 0" tall, commanding custodian. It was a surprise to many that a top club didn't take him into First Division football such was his reputation. Bob appeared for the Football League North side in 1956-57.
2 apps. 0 gls.

GRAY, Thomas David (1945)
Dundee
Right-half, b. Dundee
Career: Greenock Morton/ Dundee 1944/UNITED wg 1945-46/Resumed with Dundee 1945-46/Arbroath 1949, becoming manager 1955/Dundee United manager 1957 to 1958.
Briefly on Tyneside during the winter of 1945, Tommy Gray deputised for Donaldson and Gordon at right-half and took part in an absorbing derby tussle with Sunderland on Boxing Day in front of a 40,311 crowd at St James Park. Just starting to make a name for himself at Dens Park, Gray took part in a 3-1 victory before heading back to Tayside. He proceeded to appear on over 100 occasions for Dundee before having a healthy spell as a player and manager at Arbroath. His brother David turned out for Rangers, Preston North End and Blackburn.
1 app. 0 gls.

HERD, Alexander (1940-1941)
Manchester City
Inside-forward, b. Bowhill 1911,
d. Dumfries 1982
Career: Hearts of Beith/Hamilton Academical/Manchester City 1933/Manchester United wg 1939-40/UNITED wg 1940-41/ Chelsea wg 1944-45/ Middlesbrough wg 1945-46/ Stockport County wg 1945-46/ Resumed with Manchester City 1946/Stockport County 1948 to 1951.

Another noted star who appeared for the Magpies in wartime soccer, Alex Herd had an immensely successful period with Manchester City prior to the Second World War, reaching two FA Cup finals and playing a major part in their title victory in 1937. He claimed 290 games for the Maine Road club and netted 124 goals, additionally recording 90 wartime fixtures for the Sky Blues. A player who could cause menace to defences with his late runs and piledriver shots, Alex hailed into a footballing family. His brother Andrew was capped by Scotland when with Hearts, while his son, David appeared with credit for Manchester United and also for Scotland. Alex himself claimed a wartime cap in 1942 and appeared alongside his son for Stockport during season 1950-51. In Newcastle's ranks Herd impressed on a short but productive stay. He netted three goals over the winter period of season 1940-41. For several years Herd was a representative of an asphalt company.
4 apps. 3 gls.

HOWE, Donald (1939)
Bolton Wanderers
Inside-forward,
b. Wakefield 1917
d. Bolton 1978
Career: Whitehall Printeries/ Bolton Wanderers 1933/UNITED wg 1939-40/Norwich City wg 1940-42/Resumed with Bolton 1945 to 1953.
Don Howe had a remarkable single outing for Newcastle, netting all of five goals against York City during October 1939. A quality all round footballer, Howe remained at Burnden Park all of his Football League career totalling 286 appearances for Bolton and grabbing 35 goals. Lightweight and versatile, he was intelligent and a good club player. During the war he served with Bolton's footballing 53rd Territorial RA reaching the rank of sergeant-major. Later he worked for a paper merchant in Bolton.
1 app. 5 gls.

Don Howe

HUNTER, James Boyd (1941)
Preston North End
Outside-right,
b. Dunfermline 1913
Career: Wheeldons United 1928/ Stanton Ironworks 1929/Ilkeston United 1930/Fulham trial 1932/Ripley Town 1934/ Mansfield Town 1934/Plymouth Argyle 1935/Preston North End 1939/UNITED wg 1941-42/ Mansfield Town wg 1939-43/ Nottingham Forest wg 1940-41/ Blackburn Rovers wg 1943-44/ Plymouth Argyle wg 1945-46/ Aldershot wg 1945-46.
An established pre-war winger or inside-forward, Jimmy Hunter was born a Scot, but raised in England after his family moved in search of work. And during

World War Two, Hunter found himself aiding the war effort at Wallsend, employed in the shipyards for a period. Taking part in the early months of the 1941-42 Football League North programme, he later appeared for several clubs on his travels around the country but did not see senior action after World War Two. Hunter totalled 98 games for Plymouth during the thirties.
8 apps. 0 gls.

JULIUSSEN, Albert L. (1944)
Huddersfield Town
Inside-right, b. Blyth 1920
Career: East Cramlington jnrs/ Huddersfield Town 1938/ Bradford Park Avenue wg 1939-40/Dundee United wg 1941-45/UNITED wg 1943-44/ Dundee 1945/Portsmouth 1948/ Everton 1948/Consett/Berwick Rangers 1951/Dundee United/ Brechin City 1953.
Of Scandinavian extraction, Albert Juliussen was brought up in Northumberland and was a feared striker for Dundee in the years after World War Two. A terrace favourite, he had a great left foot and possessed explosive shooting, netting almost 90 goals for the Dens Park club in three years, and another 83 for near rivals Dundee United. That record saw him move south to Portsmouth for a big fee of £10,500, but Juliussen never quite recaptured his deadly form south of the border. The former Northumberland Boys player, took to the St James Park field only once during season 1943-44, facing Hartlepool. He created headlines when in two successive Scottish League fixtures during 1947 he found the net on 13 occasions; seven against Dunfermline and six against Alloa! During the hostilities Albert served with the Black Watch regiment.
1 app. 0 gls

KINGHORN, William John Darroch (1942) *Liverpool*
Outside-left, b. Strathblane 1912
Career: Queens Park/Liverpool 1938/Leicester City wg 1939-40/ Brighton wg 1940-44/

Manchester City wg 1941-42/
UNITED wg 1941-42/Leeds
United wg 1942-43/Blackburn
Rovers wg 1944-45/Burnley wg
1944-45/Resumed with Liverpool
1945 to 1946.

Another Anfield personality to
don the black'n'white stripes
during wartime football, Bill
Kinghorn was just establishing
himself in Liverpool's ranks as
war clouds hovered in 1939. A
past Scottish amateur
international winger with Queens
Park, Kinghorn joined up at the
Merseyside club with a career in
top football at his feet. War
though, prevented that and he
made only 19 appearances for the
Reds all told in first-class football.
He stepped in for Charles
Woollett on each of his outings for
United.
2 apps. 0 gls.

LEWIS, David Jenkin (1944)

Crystal Palace
Outside-right or left,
b. Merthyr Tydfil 1912
Career: Gellyfaelog amat/
Swansea Town 1929/Bury 1936/
Crystal Palace 1937/Bath City/
Blyth Shipyard/UNITED wg
1943-44/Llannelli & Aberaman.
Although club records note Lewis
being on Swansea's staff when he
guested for Newcastle, research
indicates the player was actually
with Crystal Palace. Twice capped
by Wales in 1933 when he was
earlier with the Swans, Lewis was
a lightweight on the wing
possessing a rasping shot and
was, when on form, quite a
handful. Known as Dai, he served
with the Welsh Regiment as a
training instructor and spent a
period in the north east when he
pulled on the black'n'white shirt
against Gateshead during January
1944. Later he worked for ICI,
afterwards employed as a
postman in Swansea.
1 app. 0 gls.

LOCKIE, Alexander J. (1940)

Sunderland
Centre-half, b. South Shields 1915
Career: South Shields Youth
Club/Sunderland 1935/UNITED
wg 1940-41/Notts County 1946
to c1947.

Tall, strong and commanding in
the air, Alex Lockie was described
by a colleague as being able to
"tackle like a tank". A
draughtsman in the Tyne
shipyards during the war, he
appeared only sparsely for
Sunderland after war was
declared, claiming 52 games for
the Roker side, a regular in 1938-
39. He moved to the other
Magpies in Nottingham on
peacetime football being restored
and totalled 26 matches for
County. His one occasion in
United's eleven was as deputy to
Jimmy Denmark for a trip to face
York City in November 1940.
1 app. 0 gls.

McCORMACK, Cecil James

(1945) *Gateshead*
Centre-forward,
b. Newcastle upon Tyne 1922,
d. 1995
Career: Gateshead 1938/
Sunderland wg 1941-42/York City
wg 1942-43/UNITED wg
1944-45/Chester wg 1944-46/
Manchester City wg 1945-46/
Middlesbrough wg 1945-46/
Ipswich Town wg 1945-46/
Aldershot wg 1945-46/Resumed
with Gateshead 1946/
Middlesbrough 1947/Chelmsford
City 1948/Barnsley 1950/Notts
County 1951/Kings Lynn 1956/
Polish White Eagles(Canada) 1957
to 1962.
Gateshead's Cec McCormack
filled in the Number 9 role for
Albert Stubbins once during April
1945 and is another post-war
celebrity to have pulled on
Newcastle's shirt. Classy and of
slight built at centre-forward,
McCormack proved to be a first
rate opportunist who scored goals
at all his clubs. In the war leagues
he netted over 100 times for
Gateshead as he thrilled
spectators at Redheugh Park.
With Barnsley McCormack
became the Second Division's top
marksman in season 1950-51 with
33 goals, a post-war club record.
After a £20,000 deal took him to
Notts County, Cec found the net
on 36 occasions in only 85 games
for Notts County, another noted
achievement. McCormack served
in the RAF and hailed from

Scotswood Road in Newcastle. He
later emigrated to Canada,
employed as a fitter for De
Havilland in Toronto. He also
appeared for a Canadian Select XI
later in his career.
1 app. 0 gls.

McINNES, James Sloan (1941)

Liverpool
Left-half, b. Ayr, d. Liverpool 1965
Career: Third Lanark 1935/
Liverpool 1938/Brighton wg
1940-43/York City wg 1941-42/
UNITED wg 1941-42/Luton Town
wg 1942-43/Millwall wg 1942-43/
Queens Park Rangers wg
1942-43/Fulham wg 1942-43/
Leeds United wg 1942-43/
Manchester United wg 1944-45/
Retired 1946, becoming Liverpool
asst-secretary and secretary 1955
to demise.
A talented wing-half, Jimmy
McInnes was not only a fine
player, totalling over 50 games for
Liverpool, but also a highly
educated man, holding a BSc
gained at Edinburgh University.
His education helped him to
move from the playing side of the
game into Anfield's management
after war had interrupted his
career. Part of Liverpool's
administrative team for over a
decade, he helped rebuild the club
during the days of Bill Shankly.
McInnes reached the Scottish Cup
final in 1936 with Third Lanark
and played his only game for
United against Sheffield
Wednesday on Boxing Day 1941.
1 app. 0 gls.

McINTOSH, Alexander (1941)

Wolverhampton Wanderers
Inside-forward,
b. Dunfermline 1916
Career: St Mirren/Folkestone/
Wolverhampton Wanderers
1937/UNITED wg 1940-41/
Watford wg 1941-42/Cardiff City
wg 1943-44/Birmingham City
1947/Coventry City 1948/
Kidderminster Harriers 1949/
Bilston United 1951.
Alex McIntosh lost the best years
of his career to the war era. As
fighting broke out, the Scot was a
regular in the Wolves side that
had just completed a league and
FA Cup runners-up double. At 23

years of age he would have faced a period at the top, but instead, McIntosh was stationed at Netherwitton near Morpeth with the 2nd Battalion Bucks Regiment. Consequently he was attracted to St James Park and appeared in United's War Cup challenge during 1941, scoring three goals in a run that ended at the semi-final stage of the competition.
3 apps. 2 gls.

McKERRELL, Daniel (1941)
East Fife
Outside-left, b. Blantyre
Career: Hamilton Academical/ Falkirk/East Fife loan 1938, pmt 1938/UNITED wg 1941-42/ Middlesbrough wg 1941-42/ Resumed with East Fife to 1947. Known as Danny, the Scot had a swift rise to fame just prior to war being declared in 1939. Joining East Fife, he made a dramatic debut in the Scottish Cup semi-final replay against St Bernards during April 1938 and ended up scoring the winner in a 2-1 success. Then he took part in the Hampden Park victory over Kilmarnock, netting the first and last goals in the final. McKerrell became an overnight hero in Fife. Billeted in the north east when on RAF service, the small and darting winger came into United's side during the early part of the 1941-42 season.
2 apps. 0 gls.

MEEK, Joseph (1939-1942)
Swansea Town
Inside-forward, b. Hazlerigg 1910, d. Hazlerigg 1976
Career: Newcastle Co-op/Seaton Delaval/Middlesbrough amat/ Gateshead 1931/Bradford Park Avenue 1934/Tottenham Hotspur 1936/Swansea Town 1939/ UNITED wg 1939-42/Lincoln City wg 1940-42/Middlesbrough wg 1940-41/Southport wg 1940-41/ Grimsby Town wg 1941-42/ Nottingham Forest wg 1941-42/ Burnley wg 1945-46/Rochdale wg 1945-46/Retired 1945. Rejected by Liverpool after a trial for being too small at 5' 5", Joe Meek developed into a character of the immediate pre-war years. He had two good seasons for

Spurs, scoring a hat-trick on only his second outing in March 1936 and claiming 51 appearances all told. From the outskirts of Newcastle, he returned home on the declaration of war and pulled on the United shirt twice, netting in each of his matches against Hartlepool and Leeds. On leaving the game, Joe resided on Tyneside to his death.
2 apps. 2 gls.

MORTENSEN, Stanley Harding (1943) *Blackpool*
Centre-forward, b. South Shields 1921, d. Blackpool 1991
Career: South Shields Ex Schoolboys/Blackpool 1937/ Huddersfield Town wg 1941-43/ UNITED wg 1942-43/Bath City wg 1942-44/Aberdeen wg 1942-44/Swansea Town wg 1942-43/Sunderland wg 1943-44/ Arsenal wg 1944-46/Watford wg 1945-46/Resumed with Blackpool 1946/Hull City 1955/Southport 1957/Bath City 1958 to 1959/ Lancaster City 1960/Retired 1962/Blackpool manager 1967 to 1969.

Capped on 25 occasions for England, Stan Mortensen (above) is one of Tyneside's most famous sons, recognised as one of the most dangerous forwards during the immediate post-war era. A legend at Bloomfield Road, he teamed up with Stanley Matthews to form an electrifying attack. With a tremendous burst of speed and deadly marksmanship, Stan was a lion-heart in the Number 9 shirt for Blackpool and England. He scored a hat-trick in the 1953

FA Cup final and netted 222 goals in 354 matches for the Seasiders. He additionally recorded 23 goals in his 25 matches for his country, striking four on his debut in Lisbon. Apart from appearing for the England B and wartime side as well as Football League eleven, Mortensen also took to the field for Wales in a war international during 1943. Reaching another two Wembley finals in 1948 and 1951 (against Newcastle), on his single appearance for the black'n'whites, Stan netted twice in a resounding 9-0 defeat of Leeds during January 1943. On leaving the game, Mortensen ran a card shop on Blackpool's Golden Mile and additionally owned sports and betting outlets. For a period he was a local councillor in Blackpool too, as well as sitting on the Pools Panel for many years. During the war years he served in a Wellington bomber and survived a plane crash in Scotland.
1 app. 2 gls.

MULLEN, James (1942-1943)
Wolverhampton Wanderers
Outside-left, b. Newcastle upon Tyne 1923, d. Wolverhampton 1987
Career: Wolverhampton Wanderers 1937/Leicester City wg 1940-41/UNITED wg 1942-44/ Darlington wg 1943-46/Reading wg 1942-43/Middlesbrough wg 1945-46/Resumed with Wolves 1946/Bromsgrove 1960. Another celebrated Tynesider, Jimmy Mullen joined the Wolves staff straight from St Aloysius School and rapidly developed into a top winger, both before and after the war. An England schools player and captain of Newcastle and Northumberland Boys, he could well have become a United player had his parents not moved south, but it was at Molineux that he fully realised his special schoolboy talent. 5' 10" tall, fast moving with a long stride, Mullen spent 23 seasons pulling on the gold shirt for Wolves, totalling 486 senior matches and scoring 112 goals. A PT instructor during the hostilities, Jimmy partnered Jackie Milburn during 'Wor Jackie's'

United debut, and his displays for Newcastle were as eyecatching as everything in his career. Playing 12 times for England, Mullen won three titles and the FA Cup with Wolves, together with Football League, B and wartime honours. Jimmy was awarded a Football League Long Service medal in 1961. On retiring from football he opened a sports shop in Wolverhampton.

15 apps. 4 gls.

NICHOLSON, William Edward
OBE (1943-1944)
Tottenham Hotspur
Right-half, b. Scarborough 1919
Career: Scarborough Working Mens Club/Scarborough Young Liberals/Tottenham Hotspur amat 1936/Northfleet/Tottenham Hotspur 1938/Hartlepools United wg 1939-40/Manchester United wg 1939-40/UNITED wg 1942-44/Sunderland wg 1942-43/Middlesbrough wg 1942-43/Fulham wg 1942-43/Darlington wg 1944-45/Resumed with Tottenham 1946, becoming trainer 1955, asst-manager 1957, manager 1958 to 1974/West Ham United scout & managerial consultant 1974/Tottenham Hotspur managerial consultant 1976, becoming President 1991.
One of post-war football's most eminent figures. Bill Nicholson travelled around the north east when serving in the Durham Light Infantry as a training instructor during wartime soccer and guested for all the region's clubs. On peacetime he quickly established himself in the fine Spurs side that won the Second Division championship in 1950. He went on to win the title at White Hart Lane, and an England cap together with B and Football League honours. Once his solid playing career as a rugged half-back was concluded after 345 first-class games for Spurs, Nicholson moved into management in North London, leading Tottenham to a succession of honours, a record unrivalled by few, and in an entertaining style to please all. For his services to the game Bill was awarded the OBE in 1975.

19 apps. 0 gls.

Bill Nicholson

OSBORNE, Frederick (1940)
Aston Villa
Inside-forward,
b. Rotherham 1915.
Career: Thurnscoe Victoria 1934/Aston Villa 1937/UNITED wg 1940-41/Middlesbrough wg 1942-43/Coventry City 1946/Denaby United 1948 to 1955.
At 6' 0", Fred Osborne was a tall and leggy schemer who was on the fringe of the Villa side just as war was declared. A regular scorer, almost 100 goals, for the claret and blues' second string in 1937-38 and 1938-39, war halted his promising progress. Unable to claim a place at Coventry either, Osborne later resided in Yorkshire and was employed by ICI. During World War Two he saw action in France, Holland and Germany as part of the nation's forces.

1 app. 0 gls.

Fred Osborne

PARR, Jack (1944) *Derby County*
Left-back, b. Derby 1920,
d. Littleover 1985
Career: Long Eaton United/
Holbrook St Michaels/Derby
County 1937/Notts County wg
1940-44/Cardiff City wg 1941-
42/Lincoln City wg 1941-42/
Mansfield Town wg 1941-42/
Nottingham Forest wg 1943-44/
UNITED wg 1943-44/Resumed
with Derby County 1945/
Shrewsbury Town 1953/
Gresley Rovers/Burton
Albion/Belper Town.
Always a steady and reliable
player, Jack Parr was a solid 6' 1"
and 13 stone full-back who
registered 134 appearances for
Derby and 116 for Shrewsbury. He
was unlucky to miss the 1946 FA
Cup final, after playing in every
round to Wembley, because of a
broken arm. In the north east on
service during season 1943-44, he
appeared against Sheffield United
for the Magpies. Parr was selected
for the England B side to face the
Army in 1946-47.
1 app. 0 gls.

PEARSON, Stanley Clare
(1941-1942) *Manchester United*
Inside-forward, b. Salford 1919
Career: Adelphi Lads Club/
Manchester United 1935/Grimsby
Town wg 1939-40/Middlesbrough
wg 1940-41/Brighton wg 1941-43/
UNITED wg 1941-42/Queens
Park Rangers wg 1943-44/
Folkestone wg/Resumed with
Manchester United 1946/Bury
1954/Chester 1957, becoming
manager 1959 to 1961/Prestbury
manager.
An inside-forward of immense
power who could create and hit
goals season after season. Capped
on eight occasions by England,
Stan Pearson was an influential
player in Manchester United's FA
Cup success in 1948 and their title
victory in 1952. His record of 149
goals in 345 games for the Reds is
evidence enough of his
contribution, while he also
grabbed five goals in his limited
appearances for his country, as
well as a hat-trick for the Football
League side. 5' 9" tall and dark-
haired, Pearson was stationed in
Shildon with the South Lancs

regiment for a period and landed
at St James Park for a few games
during season 1941-42. In a long
career, Stan played on until he
was over 40 years of age. He later
ran a newsagents business in
Prestbury.
5 apps. 0 gls.

Jackie Robinson

PEPPITT, Sydney (1941)
Stoke City
Outside-right, b. Stoke 1919
Career: Stoke City 1935/
Middlesbrough wg 1940-41/
UNITED wg 1941-42/Millwall wg
1943-44/Queens Park Rangers wg
1945-46/Linfield wg/Resumed

with Stoke City 1946/Port Vale
1950 to 1951.
A former England schools player
in 1934, Syd Peppitt appeared
twice for the Magpies, in a double
header with local rivals
Sunderland in the autumn of 1941.
Attending the same school in
Hanley as the legendary Stanley
Matthews, Peppitt developed
through Stoke's ranks alongside
the maestro, making his Football
League debut as a 17 year-old. He
was a versatile forward, appearing
across the front line. By the time
he had left the Victoria Ground,
Syd had totalled almost 100
matches for Stoke.
2 apps. 0 gls.

ROBINSON, John Allan (1942)
Sheffield Wednesday
Inside-right,
b. Shiremoor 1917, d. 1972
Career: Shiremoor/Sheffield
Wednesday 1934/UNITED wg
1941-42/Middlesbrough wg
1940-41/Sunderland 1946/Lincoln
City 1949 to 1950.
One of several full England
internationals to pull on the
Magpie strip during wartime
soccer, Jackie Robinson was
capped on four occasions during
the thirties, making his debut for
his country as a 19 year-old.
Remembered for his pace and
graceful play, Robinson could go
past defenders, pass well and
shoot with menace. A great all
round forward, including wartime
matches, he totalled more than
230 senior games for the Owls,
netting over 130 goals. Returning
home to Tyneside for a few
months during 1942, he pulled on
Newcastle's colours for a home
fixture with Middlesbrough in
February. 5' 10" tall, Jackie also
appeared for the Football League
side and was forced to quit the
game due to a broken leg.
1 app. 0 gls.

SCOTT, Frederick H. (1945)
York City
Outside-right, b. Fatfield 1916,
d. Nottingham 1995
Career: Fatfield jnrs/Bolton
Wanderers c1936/Bradford Park
Avenue 1937/York City 1937/
Gateshead wg 1941-43/UNITED

wg 1944-45/Charlton Athletic wg 1943-44/Nottingham Forest 1946 to 1956.

An England schools international, Fred Scott hailed from a mining background in County Durham. He joined Bradford Park Avenue as a teenager and developed as an exciting 5' 6" winger with pace and a telling cross. Serving in the RAF during World War Two, Scott took part in several matches for United towards the end of the conflict on the continent in 1945 and later served Nottingham Forest well, this after 167 outings for York. At the City Ground he became the oldest player to turn out for Forest, wearing the red shirt 20 days short of his 40th birthday. In all Fred registered 322 games for the Trent club as they climbed from the lower reaches of the Football League. Later in his career, Scott became a noted scout for Sunderland, Sheffield Wednesday, Southampton and Blackpool. He was connected with football to 1983, residing in Nottingham.
6 apps. 1 gl.

SHORT, John D. (1940-1943)
Leeds United
Inside-right, b. Gateshead 1921
Career: St Hilda's/Leeds United 1937/Halifax Town wg 1939-40/UNITED wg 1940-43/Sunderland wg 1942-43/Bradford Park Avenue wg 1942-43/Hartlepools United wg 1943-46/Middlesbrough wg 1944-45/Millwall 1948, becoming asst-coach 1955, coach 1956 to 1960/Huddersfield Town coach 1960/Sheffield United coach 1961, becoming asst-coach 1969/Gillingham asst-coach c1978, becoming chief-scout and physio/Chesterfield physio c1982/Notts County asst-coach 1983, becoming physio to 1986.
One of the mainstays of United's early wartime seasons, John Short was a blond-haired, 6' 0" half-back or inside-forward who possessed a quick football brain. Stylish but with a battling attitude, Short crashed home plenty of goals for the Magpies over three seasons, claiming 35 in only 43 matches. He once netted four times against Middlesbrough

during December 1941. With Leeds he claimed 55 goals in 102 games, while at The Den, Short recorded 272 appearances over eight seasons before moving into a long spell as a coach and physio.
43 apps. 35 gls.

SMALLWOOD, Frederick (1943)
Reading
Outside-left, b. Wrexham 1910
Career: Llanerch Celts/Wrexham amat 1933/Chester 1934/Macclesfield Town 1935/Southampton 1936/Reading 1938/Wrexham wg 1939-42/UNITED wg 1942-43/Sunderland wg 1941-43/Hartlepools United 1943-45/Retired 1945.
A former pit worker in the Wales coalfield, Fred Smallwood was a diminutive (5' 5") quick flanker, typical of the pre-war style of winger. Resident in the north east for much of the 1939-1945 war era, Smallwood appeared frequently for the region's clubs, twice for Newcastle in a double meeting with York City in March 1943. A Welsh amateur international, he started well in his Football League career after joining Southampton, but was sidelined due to injury. Fred totalled 49 games for the Saints and was something of a dressing-room joker. On match days it was said he carried a lucky rabbit's foot in his football shorts! Later Smallwood played in a dance-band in the north east, settling in the Sunderland area.
2 apps. 0 gls.

SMIRK, Alfred H. (1940)
Southend United
Outside-right, b. Pershore 1917
Career: Sunderland Bus Co/Sheffield Wednesday/Southend United 1938/UNITED wg 1940-41/Colchester United wg/Gateshead 1948 to 1949.
A product of Chester-le-Street schools and an England international at that level, Alf Smirk was once targeted by Stan Seymour and Tom Mather as a purchase just prior to the Second World War. But with a £6,000 fee quoted, United backed off and the player remained in Essex only

to find himself at St James Park as a war guest in the autumn of 1940 when he was stationed in Corbridge with the Essex regiment. Smirk had a rewarding spell with Southend, claiming 114 games in which he scored 32 goals. He then again headed back north when he signed for Gateshead where he proceeded to total 11 matches for the Redheugh club. After leaving the game, Alf became a denizen of football's press box.
1 app. 0 gls.

SOO, Frank (Hong Y) (1941)
Stoke City
Left-half, b. Buxton 1914
d. Cheadle 1991
Career: West Derby Boys Club/Prescot Cables/Stoke City 1933/UNITED wg 1941-42/Millwall wg 1941-46/Blackburn Rovers wg 1941-42/Everton wg 1941-42/Reading wg 1942-44/Chelsea wg 1942-43/Brentford wg 1943-45/Shrewsbury Town wg 1945-46/Burnley wg 1945-46/Crewe Alexandra wg 1945-46/Port Vale wg 1945-46/Colchester United wg/Leicester City 1945/Luton Town 1946/Chelmsford City asst-player-manager 1948/St Albans City manager/Padova (Italy) coach 1950/Palermo (Italy) coach 1951/Thereafter many Swedish appointments as coach and manager 1952 to 1972 with a spell as Scunthorpe United manager 1959-1960.
One the outstanding players of wartime soccer, Frank Soo was capped on nine occasions by England during the hostilities and was something of a wing-half artiste. Discovered by future United boss Tom Mather when he was in charge of Stoke City, Soo was a confident player with plenty of craft and vision. Of mixed descent, his father originated from China, Frank was garrisoned at Whitley Bay for a period in the RAF and took to the St James Park field as a replacement for Norman Dodgin. Once peace was restored Soo helped both Leicester and Luton before entering a much travelled career as a continental coach of repute. With Djurgardens he lifted

the Swedish championship and his team appeared in the European Cup, while Frank also had a spell in charge of the Swedish national side.
2 apps. 0 gls.

SPUHLER, John Oswald (1944)
Sunderland
Outside-right, b. Sunderland 1917
Career: Sunderland 1934/ Hartlepools United wg 1939-40/ Carlisle United wg 1939-40/ Middlesbrough wg 1940-41/ UNITED wg 1943-44/ Middlesbrough 1945/Darlington 1954/Spennymoor United player-manager 1956/Stockton manager 1957/Shrewsbury Town manager 1958.
A good servant to north east football, Johnny Spuhler appeared on 35 occasions for Sunderland, 241 for Middlesbrough and over 70 for Darlington. He wore the black'n'white of United briefly during April 1944. An England schools international in 1932, he had just proved a new find in Sunderland's talented line-up before war was declared. Claiming 21 appearances in the Reds' 1937-38 campaign, he was described by one colleague as being fast and direct, "like a whippet". At Ayresome Park, Spuhler was converted into an effective centre-forward, scoring 81 goals before he moved to Feethams. On retiring from the game, Johnny ran a post-office in Yarm, later residing in Barnard Castle.
2 apps. 1 gl.

STEWART, Alan V. (1944)
Huddersfield Town
Centre-half,
b. Newcastle upon Tyne 1922
Career: Huddersfield Town 1940/UNITED wg 1943-44/York City 1949 to 1957.
Appearing at left-back for United during March 1944, Alan Stewart only totalled 15 games for Huddersfield due to the war ruining his early career. But on signing for York City for the start of the 1949-50 season, he found a home as a solid lower division defender. Tall and commanding at the centre of York's defence, he took part in City's famous FA Cup

run to oppose Newcastle in the FA Cup semi-final of 1955 and made 231 appearances for the Minstermen. Stewart later became a representative for a York brewery.
2 apps. 0 gls.

SURTEES, John (1941-1942)
Nottingham Forest
Inside-right,
b. Newcastle upon Tyne
Career: Bournemouth/Sheffield Wednesday 1934/Nottingham Forest 1936/York City wg 1940-41/UNITED wg 1941-42/ Resumed with Forest 1946.
An FA Cup winner in 1935 with Sheffield Wednesday, Jack Surtees was a big, strong schemer. Scoring two goals on his first outing for Newcastle against Leeds, Jack later resided in North Shields following a career with Sheffield Wednesday and Forest which had seen him take part in 146 senior matches. His brother had a spell with Aston Villa.
2 apps. 2 gls.

TAYLOR, Philip Henry
(1941-1942) *Liverpool*
Right-half, b. Bristol 1917
Career: Bristol Rovers 1932/ Liverpool 1936/Bristol Rovers wg 1939-40/Brighton wg 1940-44/ UNITED wg 1941-42/Leeds United wg 1942-43/Resumed with Liverpool 1946, becoming coach 1954, manager 1956 to 1959.
A polished half-back and a pass master, Phil Taylor skippered Liverpool in their 1950 FA Cup final appointment and was recognised as one of the top names of the immediate post-war boom. Capped by England at schools, B, Football League and full level (3 apps.), he also was a key figure in the title trophy ending up at Anfield in 1947 and totalled 345 games for the Reds. Cool and composed, the 5′ 10″ Taylor was a stylist and he took part in a string of United games during season 1941-42. He was also a fine cricketer, turning out in one first-class county fixture for Gloucestershire during 1938. After being succeeded by Bill Shankly at Anfield, he became a sales representative.
7 apps. 0 gls.

WALLACE, John L. (1942)
Partick Thistle
Centre-forward, b. Glenbuck
Career: Saltcoats Victoria/Cumnock jnrs/Partick Thistle 1935/UNITED wg 1942-43/Ayr United 1946.
Taking part in a single fixture for United when on army service, a 0-4 defeat at Huddersfield in September 1942, John Wallace had been a prominent striker north of the border. In the three seasons up to the declaration of war, Wallace netted 26, 23 and 28 goals per campaign for Thistle in the Scottish League. Had it not been for Hitler's invasion, a bright career would no doubt have followed for this Caledonian sharp-shooter.
1 app. 0 gls.

WALSHAW, Kenneth (1941)
Sunderland
Outside-left, b. Tynemouth 1918
Career: North Shields/ Sunderland 1939/UNITED wg 1941-42/Resumed with Sunderland 1944/Lincoln City 1947/Carlisle United 1947/

Phil Taylor

Bradford City 1950 to 1951/North Shields manager 1954.

Although he failed to make the Football League side at Roker Park, Ken Walshaw did appear in the FA Cup competition for the Wearsiders in 1946. At 5' 9", he was small and crafty on the wing, although Ken operated in the centre-forward's shirt for United during season 1941-42. At Lincoln he claimed 17 outings, while at Brunton Park Walshaw did better, totalling 50 games and netting 15 goals for Carlisle.

4 apps. 0 gls.

WATSON, John F (1941) *Bury*
Centre-half, b. Hamilton 1917
Career: Douglas jnrs/Bury 1936/ UNITED wg 1941-42/Fulham 1946/Real Madrid(Spain) player-coach 1948/Crystal Palace 1949/ Canterbury City 1951.

A stopper centre-half from the football hotbed of Lanarkshire, Jock Watson turned out on six occasions for Bury before war interrupted his progress. Taking the inside-forward's shirt for the Magpies, he continued his career with Fulham (72 games) and later had a spell with the great Real Madrid club, albeit a decade before they reached the top of the European game. A season later he was appointed Crystal Palace skipper and totalled 63 matches for the Londoners before leaving the Football League circuit.

1 app. 0 gls.

WATTERS, John (1941)
Glasgow Celtic
Inside-forward, b. Waterside 1919
Career: Glasgow Celtic jnrs 1935/ St Rochs 1936/Glasgow Celtic 1937/UNITED wg 1941-42/ Airdrieonians 1947/Pollock trainer-physio 1949/Sunderland physio 1956 to 1982.

Johnny Watters netted on his debut for United against York City when he was stationed at a Royal Navy centre. During the war he took part in the D Day invasion, serving on HMS Warspite and by the time he had returned to peacetime football, couldn't claim a regular place at Parkhead. Playing for the Celts on only ten occasions, he had though

appeared in front of the biggest league attendance in Britain when 118,730 watched the Rangers v Celtic contest in January 1939. For over 25 years Watters was connected to Sunderland as a respected physiotherapist.

2 apps. 1 gl.

WESTWOOD, Raymond William
(1939) *Bolton Wanderers*
Inside-left, b. Brierley Hill 1912, d. Brierley Hill 1982
Career: Stourbridge/Brierley Hill Alliance/Bolton Wanderers 1928/UNITED wg 1939-40/ Chester 1947/Darwen 1949.
Like his Bolton colleague Don

Ray Westwood

Howe, Ray Westwood also had a noted single appearance for the Tynesiders. When stationed at Alnmouth he came into the side against York City and the England international crashed home a marvellous hat-trick as United won 9-2. Selected for the Football League too, Westwood was a swift mover and was recalled for his direct runs at goal. A delicate player, but very forceful at the same time, he was always willing to work and could frequently bag goals; he netted 144 for Bolton in 333 matches, and on many occasions was a matchwinner. Nephew to David Stokes, also a celebrated player for Bolton, Ray served in the army at Dunkirk and in Egypt. Later he ran a fishmongers then a newsagency in his home town in Staffordshire.

1 app. 3 gls.

AITKEN, Ralph Allan
(1886-1887, 1889-1890) *West End*
One of the most celebrated players
to have landed on Tyneside during
Victorian times, Ralph Aitken (b.
1863) was an established Scottish
international from Renfrew who
joined the West End club in October
1886. A star outside-left with
Dumbarton, Aitken appeared for
his country on two occasions and
was recognised as a most popular
figure, always full of tricks on the
ball. He scored twice on his debut
for the West Enders, in a city derby
encounter with East End at St James
Park. Moving back to Dumbarton in
January 1887, Ralph was also on the
scoresheet in the 1887 Scottish Cup
final and after a brief return to
Tyneside during 1889-90, later
appeared with Southampton St
Marys. For several years Aitken was
employed as a plater in a Fife
shipyard. He died in 1928.
10 apps. 5 gls.

ARMSTRONG, John (1881-1886)
East End
A pioneer half-back with the
Stanley club, the embryo side of
Newcastle East East and ultimately
Newcastle United, John Armstrong
played in their first-ever fixture
against the Elswick Leather Works
2nd XI and became an early
skipper of the East End outfit in
Byker. Armstrong hailed from that
district and was a joiner by trade.
He became one of the club's
original shareholders and
appeared on East End's first
director list in February 1890.
57 apps. 5 gls.

ANGUS, J. (c1885-1888, 1889)
West End
A forward who netted the first
ever FA Cup goal at St James Park,
scoring the winner against
Sunderland in the First Round
replay during October 1886. On
the West End staff for two spells,
he had a period with Sunderland
Albion, Everton (5 apps.) and
Gainsborough Trinity before
returning to Tyneside during
August 1889. His spell on
Merseyside co-incided with
Everton's first Football League
season in 1888-89.
57 apps. 26 gls.

ARNOTT, Walter (1887) *West End*
Another noted personality of the
early game, Scottish international
Wattie Arnott appeared once for
the club in a fixture against
Shankhouse during December
1887. From Pollokshields, the Scot
was something of a freelance
player turning out for a string of
clubs including Kilmarnock,
Linfield, Third Lanark and St
Bernards, as well as Celtic, Notts
County, Queens Park and the
famous Corinthians eleven.
Capped on 14 occasions for his
country at full-back, he was fast
and kicked the ball long and hard.
Sporting a magnificent
moustache, Arnott's appearance
in Newcastle was a big coup for
the early development of soccer in
the region, and even if he ended
up leaving the field 20 minutes
into the second-half to catch a
train home, his visit was still a
welcome sight. Arnott took part in
five Scottish Cup finals and was
dubbed 'the greatest back in the
world' at the time. He was born in
Glasgow during 1863 and died in
1931.
1 app. 0 gls.

BLACKETT, William (1883-1889)
East End
Capped a number of times for the
Northumberland side when inter-
county football was well
respected, William Blackett also
appeared for a select Newcastle &
District eleven which faced up to
The Corinthians in 1887. He
served East End at wing-half with
honour for six years.
72 apps. 1 gl.

CAMPBELL, T. (1887-1888)
East End
Joining East End from local outfit
Boundary in 1887, Campbell was
a regular at full-back for a year
and represented Northumberland
against Durham and Cleveland
during season 1887-88.
20 apps. 0 gls.

CHARD, William (1886-1888)
East End
East End's first choice goalkeeper
for two seasons following a move
from Newcastle FA to
Chillingham Road during

December 1886. Chard later
became a noted referee in the
region.
34 apps. 0 gls.

CONNOLLY, J. (1891-1892)
East End & West End
Arriving in Heaton from the
Stockton club during the close
season of 1891, Connolly operated
in the forward-line and once
registered four goals during a
friendly against Queen of the
South Wanderers. His career on
Tyneside was colourful, being
sent-off in the very next fixture for
striking an opponent. Connolly
moved to St James Park in
January 1892 joining rivals West
End, but found the club in a
perilous financial state and didn't
stay long.
3 apps. 5 gls.

COOK, J.P. (1881-1886) *East End*
One of the Stanley club's
enthusiasts, the well-built 6' 0"
Cook was a half-back and
forward. He later became
secretary of East End for a period,
succeeding founder WA Coulson
in 1882.
45 apps. 12 gls.

COULSON, W.A. (1881-1884)
East End
The founder of Stanley, and
therefore the man responsible for
Newcastle United too. A forward,
Coulson was on the pitch for
Stanley's very first game and
scored in the 5-0 victory over the
Elswick Leather Works 2nd XI. He
was also the club's first captain
and was awarded a gold scarf pin
as a mark of his dedication to East
End in 1883. He eventually
became secretary of the club in
that same year. Coulson was also
a fine local cricketer for the
Stanley club.
17 apps. 1 gl.

COUPE, Joseph (1888-1889)
East End
A former Blackburn Olympic half-
back, Joseph Coupe signed for
East End in September 1888 and
made a good impression on
Tyneside. He represented
Northumberland in March 1889
and also appeared for the

Newcastle & District combination. Contemporary reports made the comment that he always, "made his presence felt" on the field.
46 apps. 3 gls.

DOYLE, Daniel (1888)
East End
One of several distinguished Scots to briefly appear on Tyneside during the game's formative years. Left-back Dan Doyle was noted as a giant of the game, some judges recognising him as arguably the greatest defender of his time. Born in Paisley during 1864, like many Scots of his era, he turned out for a number of clubs, a 'soldier of fortune' in England. He landed at Hibs, Sunderland, Hearts, Grimsby and Bolton, as well as Everton (45 apps.) and Celtic (133 apps.), where he won many honours, including eight Scotland caps. At Goodison Park Dan helped lift the League Championship in 1891. Skipper of his country too, Doyle spent a brief period in Heaton with East End between September and December 1888 and, like his fellow Scots who ventured to Tyneside, did much to enlighten the public that football had taken root in the area. After leaving the game Doyle resided in Strathclyde, a man of several occupations to his death in 1918.
Note: Doyle's appearances and goals total cannot be traced; it is judged from articles compiled by him that he used a pseudonym.

John Armstrong

Prominent players to have appeared for Newcastle United's pioneer clubs, Newcastle East End and Newcastle West End.

Note: Contemporary information on this period in the club's history is scarce and as a result little is known on most of the players to have helped form the Magpies. Appearances and goals noted are not comprehensive, but indicate as far as research allows the totals each player has made with either East or West End. Due to the late introduction of competitive football in the shape of the Northern League during this era, totals also include friendly matches as well as games for Stanley Football Club, the forerunner to Newcastle East End.

FENWICK, J. (1881-1886)
East End
A stalwart full-back with Stanley and East End, Fenwick was a noted personality in Byker as Newcastle United's pioneer clubs took shape.
48 apps. 2 gls.

FINDLAY, William (1881-1884)
East End
The first secretary of Stanley, prominent in the formation of the club during 1881, he became skipper of the side a year later. A forward, Findlay scored one of the goals in their first fixture and was captain of the side when they changed the name of the club to East End. William's brother R Findlay also appeared for the East Enders.
28 apps. 3 gls.

HISCOCK, Edward (1883-1889)
East End
A crowd-pleasing forward, and a ball dribbler in the style of the day. Nicknamed 'Ned' on Tyneside, Hiscock scored almost 40 goals for United's pioneers and became the first East End player to be selected for Northumberland, in 1884 against Durham. He also registered the first hat-trick, claiming four goals in a 9-0 friendly victory over Hibernia during the same year. It is thought that team-mate Matt Hiscock was his brother.
76 apps. 37 gls.

HISCOCK, Matthew K.
(1883-1885) *East End*
A solid full-back who became prominent in forging a soccer base along with a group of players on the east side of Newcastle. Hiscock was also appointed secretary of East End for a short time in 1885. A shipwright who lived in Byker, Matt was an early shareholder of the club.
28 apps. 0 gls.

HOBAN, Thomas (1884-1889)
East End
A former Newcastle Rangers player at St James Park, Tommy Hoban gained several honours at representative level for both the city and county sides. An outside-

left of note, he was a hugely popular character on Tyneside and totalled almost 100 games for United's pioneers. *The Northern Magpie* magazine of the day humourously noted that he, "has played since the days of stage coaches and is about as fast as one". A player who thrilled the Victorian supporters with his attacking ability, Hoban succeeded Alec White as captain of East End in 1888. Tommy also had a spell with Hibernian.
95 apps. 35 gls.

JARDINE, William (1890-1892)
West End
A goalkeeper who joined Newcastle West End in July 1890, Jardine served the St James Park club well during their last years on Tyneside before the club's disbandment during the summer of 1892.
41 apps. 0 gls.

KELSO, Robert Robinson
(1888-1889) *West End*
Born in Dunbartonshire during 1865 and a star player with Renton, Bob Kelso arrived on Tyneside during the summer of 1888 as a signing which showed that football was developing fast in the region. A Scottish international right-half (8 caps), Bob was a player of sure judgement and a gritty style. He once was nicknamed the 'Renton Ruffian' for his formidable defending. Winning Scottish Cup honours, Kelso turned out for West End for one season before pulling on the colours of Everton (103 apps.), Preston, Dundee and Bedminster. He won both League Championship and FA Cup honours in England. Uncle to Tom Kelso, also a Scottish international player, Bob died in 1942.
28 apps. 3 gls.

MACK, P. (1888-1889) *East End*
A centre-forward signed from Edinburgh Hibernians in December 1888, and one of many Scots to head for Tyneside during Victorian pioneer years.
27 apps. 13 gls.

McCURDIE, Alec (1889-1892)
East End & West End
A big favourite on Tyneside, Alec McCurdie joined East End from Clydebank in January 1889 and operated in midfield with distinction during the years up to the historic move by the Heaton club to St James Park. Appearing for the county side, he in fact was transferred to West End in January 1892 a few months before they became defunct. The *Newcastle Daily Chronicle* of the day complimented McCurdie: "few finer lads have graced the football field".
100 apps. 5 gls.

McINNES, Thomas (1890-1891)
West End & East End
A potent outside-left during the Victorian era of football, Glaswegian Tommy McInnes served both of United's pioneer clubs and became a distinguished player elsewhere. Scoring the first

Bob Kelso

ever FA Cup hat-trick for East End, against Shankhouse in November 1890, he was poached by rivals West End the following January before moving back to Scotland with Clyde. McInnes, who was capped by his country when with Cowlairs in 1889, joined Nottingham Forest in June 1892 and proceeded to perform with much credit in 185 games (55 gls.). He was regarded as one of the best wingers in the Football League. Tom reached the 1898 FA Cup final and received a winners medal before being transferred to Lincoln City in 1900.
61 apps. 34 gls.

Note: There has been much confusion over McInnes, as another player of the same name appeared for Notts County, Everton and Luton during the same era. He was also born in Glasgow in the same year. However contemporary records indicate that the Newcastle player is linked to Nottingham Forest.

MUIR, A. (1887-1889) East End
From Heaton, Muir proved a prolific goalscorer for East End at times, once claiming five goals in a competitive fixture with Point Pleasant in January 1888, yet amazingly he wasn't top scorer on the day, White grabbing seven in a 19-0 victory. Muir also hit four in the same competition, the Northumberland Challenge Cup, against Ovingham in February 1889.
39 apps. 15 gls.

MUIR William (1885-1891) East End
Thought to be related to A Muir, he also hailed from the east of the city and originally started playing the game with Tyne Association and the Newcastle Rangers club, the first tenant of St James Park. Selected for Northumberland and the Newcastle District select combination, Muir registered East End's first goal in the FA Cup against South Bank in October 1887. He emigrated to South Africa in 1891 to take up a prominent position in athletics and later skippered Rangers, a well known South African football team.
37 apps. 13 gls.

NICHOLSON, Thomas
(1887-1890, 1892) West End
A free scoring centre-forward who had two periods with West End. Tom once scored four goals in a 15-0 romp over the North Eastern club during 1888, while he also found his shooting boots on three occasions in an FA Cup tie with South Bank a year later. Nicholson moved to West Manchester in the summer of 1890, but returned to St James Park during March 1892 for the last weeks of West End's existence.
83 apps. 43 gls.

RAYLSTONE, J. (1886-c1889)
West End & East End
Noted in the local press as a "tough, uncompromising player", Raylstone was an imposing character who served both East and West End. He appeared at St James Park from 1886 to 1888 and was capped for Northumberland during that period. At centre-half he was also capped when with East End signing for the Chillingham Road outfit in the close season of 1888.
103 apps. 22 gls.

SCOTT, D. (1883-1888) East End
Another who was a regular with Northumberland during seasons 1885-86 and 1886-87, Scott appeared in the forward line and was a regular scorer for the Chillingham Road outfit. He also appeared for a Newcastle XI against The Corinthians in a prestige friendly during those seasons.
65 apps. 16 gls.

SCOTT, Matthew (1889-1892)
East End
A prominent goalkeeper for East End who was signed from Elswick Rangers in October 1889, Matt Scott later had a spell with Sunderland, joining the Roker Park staff in November 1892. He made a single appearance for the Reds in the Football League during season 1893-94 and departed Wearside in May 1897 to South Shields, this after a long period as a reserve to the famous Ted Doig. With East End he was a sound 'keeper and is one of only a

few players to total over 100 games for the club's pioneers. Scott played on several occasions for Northumberland and had a brief spell on Newcastle United's staff in 1895, appearing for the A side.
112 apps. 0 gls.

SMITH, J. (1888-1889) East End
Captain of East End, succeeding Tommy Hoban in September 1888, Smith was a dependable forward who, like many of his Heaton colleagues, was capped for Northumberland.
46 apps. 6 gls.

SPENCE, J. (1891-1892) East End
Purchased from Sunderland during July 1891, Spence totalled just four games for the Wearsiders in the First Division, but had a good return of goals, claiming three altogether, including two on his debut against Burnley, Sunderland's first ever game in the Football League. He is noted in the Roker club's annals as an historic figure, one of his strikes being Sunderland's first registered goal. A Scot, he landed on Wearside from Kilmarnock in October 1889.
35 apps. 5 gls.

TAYLOR, J. (1885-1890) West End
A grand servant to West End's cause at full-back, J Taylor was a dependable player who also helped off the field to further the cause at St James Park. He later had a benefit match staged for him in April 1892 when a local Scotland combination faced up to a local English eleven. In 1893 he was playing for Benwell club, Rendall.
111 apps. 1 gl.

TIFFEN, William (1882-1889)
West End
The founder of West End FC, Billy Tiffen was not only a player, but also acted as secretary and treasurer for a period. Always cheerful and optimistic, Tiffen represented Northumberland and later became secretary of the regional Football Association in 1889 and a member of the powerful FA Council. The early

text, *Association Football And The Men Who Made It* described Tiffen as giving "ardent, energetic and tireless work" to the area's football development. He died during November 1925.
74 apps. 10 gls.

TINLIN, Charles (1887-c1895)
East End
Originally Charles Tinlin was a player and administrator for the Cheviot club, and when they merged with East End his services were captured by the Byker side before they moved the short distance to Heaton. Operating only occasionally on the field as a forward, Tinlin however also acted as match secretary in 1887 and financial secretary from 1888 to 1891. A determined individual behind the scenes in developing East End into a soccer force, he once scored a hat-trick against Elswick Rangers in the Northumberland Challenge Cup during 1891. Charles is noted in official club Minutes as still being involved in 1893 as East End developed into Newcastle United.
4 apps. 3 gls.

WHITE, Alec H. (1882-1892)
East End
Without doubt the player to have made the biggest impact during Newcastle United's pioneering years. A schoolmaster who resided in Heaton, Alec White hailed from Glamis in Scotland and initially played for Newcastle Rangers, joining the city's foremost club at the time in 1880. He twice won the Northumberland & Durham Challenge Cup (in 1881 and 1882) before joining East End and quickly White became regarded as "the life and soul of the team". Tough, but clever on the field, he operated in midfield from the centre-half position. Alec was appointed captain in 1885 and became a regular for the County side. Such was his reputation that he was also chosen as a reserve for the national North v South challenge match in 1886, a tremendous accolade considering that football on Tyneside was still very much in its infancy. White

was also honoured by being selected to appear for The Corinthians a year later, while when appearing at centre-forward for East End, he once scored seven goals in a 19-0 victory over Point Pleasant in 1888 - still a club record! An original shareholder with Newcastle, the Scot retired during the summer of 1888 but remained associated with the East End club as an administrator and director, playing the occasional match, his last being against Blackburn Rovers in February 1892. Afterwards White became a distinguished local figure with the Northumberland FA, appointed Treasurer from 1913 to 1938 and holding a seat on the local FA Council for 50 years. He was nominated several times without success for a Newcastle United board posiiton between 1925 and 1930. Alec was also awarded the FA's Long Service medal. He died on Tyneside during March 1940.
107 apps. 34 gls.

WATSON, Thomas (c1883-1889)
West End & East End
While Tom Watson never kicked a ball in anger for either of United's pioneers, he gave both clubs fine service as secretary and manager before making a huge name for himself in charge of Sunderland and Liverpool. Born in Heaton in April 1859, he appeared for Rosehill and Willington before joining West End. After a period establishing the St James Park club, Tom moved across the city in the summer of 1888 to team up with the red and whites at Chillingham Road. Silver-tongued and a shrewd administrator, Watson helped form the Northern League in 1889 which was a major factor in the development of soccer in the region. The *Newcastle Daily Chronicle* noted that he had "proved himself a true judge of style" and he did

such a good job on Tyneside that Tom was lured to join Sunderland in the close season of 1889, at the time a club far more advanced than either East End or West End. Sunderland went on to lift the League Championship in 1892, 1893 and 1895 under Watson's guidance, while he was also appointed to the League's influential Management Committee. At one point in 1895, and before the appointment of Frank Watt, Watson applied for the vacant United secretary's post. A year later, during August 1896 the Tynesider moved to Liverpool and again developed a fine set-up in a spell of 19 years with the Reds, the Anfield club winning title and FA Cup honours in 1901, 1906 and 1914. Tom was awarded the Football League's Long Service medal in 1910. He died on Merseyside in May 1915.

Tom Watson

ARDILES, Osvaldo Cesar (1991-1992)
b. Cordoba, Argentina, 3rd August 1952

Career: Red Star Cordoba(Argentina)/
Instituto de Cordoba(Argentina) 1971/
Huracan(Argentina) 1975/Tottenham Hotspur
1978(Paris St-Germain(France) loan 1982-83)
(Blackburn Rovers loan 1987-88)/Queens Park
Rangers 1988/Fort Lauderdale Strikers(USA)
1989/Swindon Town 1989, becoming manager
1989/UNITED manager Mar 1991 to Feb
1992/West Bromwich Albion manager 1992/
Tottenham Hotspur manager 1993 to 1994/
Guadalajara(Mexico) manager 1995/Shimizu
S-Bulse(Japan) manager 1996.

An established star with Argentina, winning
the World Cup in 1978, the small, frail-looking
Ossie Ardiles collected 42 caps for his country
and had a marvellous career combining skill
with non-stop workrate to perfection. He was
taken to White Hart Lane for a £325,000 fee by
former United coach Keith Burkinshaw, and
became a huge favourite with Spurs' fans,
totalling 311 senior games and winning FA
Cup and European honours with the
Londoners. He proved himself as a manager
with Swindon, allowing his side to play
possession football with an attacking flair. The
Robins gained a place in the First Division,
only for administrative financial irregularities
to rob Ardiles of his triumph. Arriving at St

APPENDIX FOUR
MANAGERS

MANAGERS

1892-1930: Directors' Committee
1930-1935: Andy Cunningham *(qv)*
1935-1939: Tom Mather
1939-1947: Stan Seymour *(qv)*/Committee
1947-1950: George Martin
1950-1954: Stan Seymour *(qv)*/Committee
1954-1956: Doug Livingstone
1956-1958: Directors' Committee
1958-1961: Charlie Mitten
1961-1962: Norman Smith
1962-1975: Joe Harvey *(qv)*
1975-1977: Gordon Lee
      1977: Richard Dinnis
1977-1980: Bill McGarry
1980-1984: Arthur Cox
1984-1985: Jack Charlton
1985-1988: Willie McFaul *(qv)*
1988-1991: Jim Smith
1991-1992: Ossie Ardiles
1992-date: Kevin Keegan *(qv)*

Caretaker managers: W.McFaul (Feb 1977),
J.Harvey (Aug 1980), W.McFaul (Aug 1985),
C.Suggett (Oct-Dec 1988), R.Saxton
(Mar 1991). All *qv*.

Note: qv = see biography in players' or
trainers' section.

James Park in a blaze of publicity, Ossie began the task of getting Newcastle into Division One by discarding Jim Smith's experienced players and bringing in youth. While supporters liked his fresh approach to the game, and movement going forward, Ardiles never could develop a rearguard. Without a solid defence, Newcastle struggled. And without experience in the side they stumbled to the bottom of the Second Division and Ossie found himself staring the Third Division in the face. United's boardroom acted and, as Sir John Hall took control, Ardiles was sacked after only 10 months in charge with Kevin Keegan brought in to save the club from disaster. The Argentinian proceeded to do a good job at The Hawthorns, but faced similar defensive problems when in charge of Tottenham and did not last long.

CHARLTON, John OBE (1984-1985)
b. Ashington, 8th May 1935

Career: Ashington YMCA/Ashington Welfare/Leeds United 1950/Middlesbrough manager 1973/Sheffield Wednesday manager 1977 to 1983/Middlesbrough caretaker-manager 1984/UNITED manager June 1984 to Aug 1985/Eire manager 1986 to 1995.

A member of the north east's most famous sporting family, Jack Charlton was recommended to Leeds by his uncle Jim Milburn. At 6' 2" tall, leggy and tough, Charlton developed into a formidable centre-half who played at Elland Road for 20 seasons creating a record appearance total of 770 league and cup games. Always capable at hitting goals from set pieces, Charlton netted almost 100 for the Tykes. Success came to Jack late into his career as part of Don Revie's resurgence at Elland Road. Winning title, League Cup, FA Cup and European honours, he also reached England's team alongside his brother Bobby, winning 35 caps. A member of the immortal 1966 World Cup winning eleven, he was FWA Footballer of the Year in 1967. Jack then entered management where he became a forthright boss, taking both Middlesbrough and Sheffield Wednesday to promotion. Manager of the Year in 1974, he had always been a Newcastle United supporter, often tipped as taking over the Magpie hot-seat. That occurred when Arthur Cox departed and 'Big Jack', as he was known, had a short and stormy period in charge of affairs at Gallowgate. Charlton was never keen

to use the transfer market as a manager, being a grafter and unspectacular in his actions. When United's fans clamoured for new blood on the departure of star Chris Waddle, Charlton resisted any headline buys. He sensationally quit on the eve of the 1985-86 season after being taunted by the crowd during a pre-season friendly. Yet Charlton had consolidated the Magpies on their return to the First Division, heading the table early into the programme and few knew of the financial problems at the club, which in fact restricted any use of the transfer market. But his tactical no-frills style of play, so successfully employed at Ayresome Park and Hillsborough, was not appreciated by United's masses. Charlton spent time working for television before taking the Republic of Ireland manager's position in 1986. Again he adopted the same tactics on the field and Jack successfully guided the country to World Cups and European Championships, becoming a hugely respected figure in Ireland, honoured with the Freedom of Dublin in 1994. Residing in Stamfordam, near Newcastle, Charlton remains associated with the game as a media expert and, despite his experience in charge of United, still holds a deep affection for the club he supported as a kid. Jack remains equally as popular with Newcastle supporters who hold no grudge against one of their own.

Jack Charlton

COX, Arthur (1980-1984, 1994-date)
b. Southam, Warwickshire, 14th December 1939

Career: Coventry City 1955/Retired due to injury, becoming asst-coach 1958/Walsall asst-coach/Aston Villa asst-coach 1968/Preston North End coach 1970/Halifax Town coach cs 1970/Sunderland coach 1973, becoming asst-manager/Galatasary(Turkey) coach 1976/Chesterfield manager 1976/UNITED manager Sept 1980/Derby County manager June 1984 to 1993/UNITED asst-coach May 1994, becoming chief scout July 1996.

Arthur Cox

Arthur Cox's early career in the game was wrecked after he sustained a broken leg when only 18 years of age. The injury was critical enough to force his retirement without breaking into Coventry's senior side. But an opportunity arose for the youngster to enter coaching at Highfield Road and following a learning period with a number of clubs, Arthur gained recognition after being assistant to Bob Stokoe as Sunderland lifted the FA Cup in 1973. In charge of Chesterfield, Cox further enhanced his reputation by building a good side in the lower divisions and when United were searching for a new manager to replace Bill McGarry in 1980, Cox was the choice. Not a household name and never flamboyant, Cox was a surprise appointment to many, but his workmanlike, no-nonsense attitude slowly produced the goods at St James Park. Above all he will be remembered as the manager who made one of the club's greatest ever signings by bringing Kevin Keegan to Gallowgate. That transfer coup was a master stroke. Keegan's

influence attracted other players to Cox's squad and United gained promotion to Division One with attractive, entertaining football. In the process, Arthur also brought in another huge Newcastle star to be, Peter Beardsley, to play alongside Keegan and the rapidly developing Chris Waddle. That should have been the start of a long association for Cox as Newcastle's manager, but just as the promotion celebrations died down he sensationally quit after a dispute over his contract and the direction of the club's strategy. Moving to the Baseball Ground, Arthur spent almost a decade with Derby County, steering them from Division Three to Division One, but also tasting relegation. He departed after being troubled by a back injury, later returning to Gallowgate as one of Kevin Keegan's assistants.

DINNIS, Richard Ramsey (1975-1977)
b. Blackburn, 1941

Career: Burnley amat/Blackburn Rovers asst-coach 1969/Burnley asst-coach/Blackburn Rovers coach 1971, becoming caretaker-manager 1974-75/UNITED coach June 1975, becoming manager Feb 1977 to Nov 1977/Philadelphia Furies(USA) coach 1978/Blackburn Rovers coach 1979/Occasional scout for Bristol City, Arsenal, Middlesbrough among others/Al Ittihad(Saudi Arabia) coach 1985 briefly/Accrington Stanley coach 1992/Barrow manager 1992 to 1993.

Richard Dinnis had brief periods on the books of both Blackburn and Burnley as a player, but never graduated to first-team football. A Darwen schoolteacher, dividing his time between geography and PE, Dinnis had a short and stormy reign as Newcastle's manager. Without the experience of playing the game to any high standard, Dinnis nevertheless developed into a respected coach. Teaming up with Gordon Lee at Ewood Park, the partnership landed on Tyneside in 1975 and began to bond with United's players. When Lee walked out on the club, Richard was the player's choice as United's new boss but then a stormy period of players against director power erupted at the club. The club's hierarchy wanted to appoint a big name,as did most supporters, but United's players backed Dinnis to the point that even strike calls were made. Newcastle's directors had to back down and offer Richard control, albeit a temporary position. Dinnis led the club to a lofty position

Richard Dinnis

in the First Division and into the UEFA Cup for season 1977-78. More contract wrangling followed, but Dinnis remained in charge as the Magpies started the new season, yet the opening weeks of that campaign proved a disaster. They were knocked out of the UEFA Cup and slumped to bottom of the division after ten defeats in a row. Dinnis was sacked after little more than five months in the job. Afterwards he attempted to stay in the game, but also returned to teaching. Dinnis resides in the Blackburn area.

LEE, Gordon Francis (1975-1977)
b. Pye Green, Hednesford, Staffs, 13th July 1934

Career: Hednesford Town 1951/Aston Villa 1955/Shrewsbury Town player-coach 1966/Port Vale manager 1968/Blackburn Rovers manager 1974/UNITED manager June 1975/Everton manager Feb 1977/Preston North End manager 1981 to 1983/Occasional scout/KR Reykjavik(Iceland) coach 1984/Leicester City asst-manager 1988, becoming caretaker-manager 1991(to May 1991).

A resourceful left-back or left-half with Aston Villa, Gordon Lee totalled 142 games for the Midland side and appeared in the 1961 and 1963 Football League Cup finals. Tall and angular-faced, Lee took to coaching at Shrewsbury and eventually found his way to Tyneside after guiding both Port Vale and Blackburn to promotion success. Rated the best young manager out of the First Division, Lee's reign at Gallowgate was tinged with controversy from start to finish; his appointment was the centre of a tug of war between United and Rovers, but he fashioned United into a hard-working, professional combination to the joy of supporters who had for years struggled with an apparent lack of professionalism. As a manager he could develop and motivate, yet Lee never found a place for flair and artistry in his team, and disliked the star system. That brought him into conflict with one of the biggest of that breed, Malcolm Macdonald. Although the club reached Wembley in the League Cup during 1975-76 and had a good challenge for both the FA Cup and a European place, there was an undercurrent of feuding within the camp. Supermac was sensationally sold to Arsenal and soon after Lee sold himself to Everton, leaving the club stunned. At Goodison he initially did well, but then Gordon's regime fell apart and he was dismissed. Since then, Lee has struggled to regain a top job. He resides in Lytham occasionally scouting for Premiership and Football League clubs.

Gordon Lee

LIVINGSTONE, Dugald (1954-1956)
b. Alexandria, nr Dumbarton, 25th February 1898
d. Harlow, Bucks, 18th January 1981

Career: Parkhead 1915/Ashfield 1916/Glasgow Celtic 1917/Dumbarton Harp wg 1917-21/Clydebank wg 1918-19/Everton 1921/Plymouth 1926/Aberdeen 1927/Tranmere Rovers 1930/Exeter City trainer 1935/Sheffield United trainer 1936/Sheffield Wednesday manager 1947/Sparta Rotterdam (Holland) coach 1949/Eire national coach 1951/Belgium national coach 1953/UNITED manager Dec 1954/Fulham manager Jan 1956/Chesterfield manager 1958 to 1962.

As a player, Duggie Livingstone was regarded as a model professional, a cool and calculated full-back who did well at Everton (100 apps.) and Tranmere (88 apps.) after starting with Celtic where he totalled 47 games. Entering coaching at Exeter, Livingstone made a name for himself when he was in charge of the Belgian national side for the 1954 World Cup, his team recording a memorable victory over the holders West

Germany. Newcastle's directors, none too keen at the time to enter the modern style of appointing a manager, had nevertheless been considering a change from the Team Committee. Livingstone was appointed just before the club embarked on another FA Cup run that ended at Wembley in 1955. He arrived at St James Park bristling with modern coaching techniques, but his stay was not a happy one.

Duggie Livingstone

Attempting to bring in continental ideals, now accepted but then unheard of in the north east, caused much raising of eyebrows. He tried to coach United's established stars and Jackie Milburn once remarked, "Frankly we needed new training like a hole in the head". Yet some players appreciated Livingstone's football philosophy; Bob Stokoe noted that Duggie "was first-class and of great benefit". Livingstone also had the formidable Stan Seymour to contend with. United's director made sure he had a say in team affairs and Livingstone was obliged to submit his selections to the board for approval, and his FA Cup final team was suitably changed by Seymour when it did not contain Milburn. After that success at Wembley, Livingstone's role was diminished. He was told to look after the juniors and it was no surprise when he moved to Fulham. On leaving the game, he resided in Marlow to his death.

McGARRY, William Harry (1977-1980)
b. Stoke on Trent, 10th June 1927

Career: Northwood Mission/Port Vale 1945/ Huddersfield Town 1951/Bournemouth player-manager 1961/Watford manager 1963/ Ipswich Town manager 1964/Wolverhampton Wanderers manager 1968/United Arab Emirates coach/Saudi Arabia national coach 1976/UNITED manager Nov 1977 to Aug 1980/Brighton scout/Power Dynamo(Zambia) coach/Zambian national coach/S.African director of coaching 1984/Wolverhampton Wanderers manager 1985(to Nov 1985)/ Botswana coaching 1993.

United needed a tough, steadying figure after the turmoil left in the wake of successive managements of Gordon Lee and Richard Dinnis; that man was former England international wing-half Bill McGarry. A disciplinarian, he joined the club as they were destined for the Second Division but was unable to stop the slide. McGarry underwent a massive rebuilding process, discarding those players at the centre of the player-power tactics and bringing in experienced pros from around the country. For one season Bill appeared to have blended a decent team together, spearheaded by Peter Withe during the 1979-80 campaign. But after heading the table the Magpies fell away and a promotion chance was lost. As a player, McGarry was tough and aggressive, and revelled in a hard-man tag. He made 381 appearances for Huddersfield when they were a top side, winning four caps for England. During his early days as a manager he had good periods at Portman Road and Molineux, reaching domestic and European finals.

Bill McGarry

George Martin

MARTIN, George Scott (1947-1950)
b. Bothwell, nr Hamilton, 14th July 1899
d. Luton, 1972

Career: Cadzow St Annes/Hamilton Academical 1920(Bo'ness loan)(Bathgate loan)/Hull City 1922/Everton 1928/Middlesbrough 1932/Luton Town 1933, becoming trainer 1937, manager 1939/UNITED manager May 1947/Aston Villa manager Dec 1950 to 1953/Luton Town chief scout 1960, becoming manager 1965 to 1966.

Smart and elegant, George Martin took control of Newcastle in a push to achieve First Division status immediately after World War Two. However his early months in charge received wholesale criticism after a succession of player changes, including the sale of terrace favourite Len Shackleton to Sunderland. Yet Martin quickly developed a new side and promotion was achieved the following season, in 1948. Success brought a new crop of heroes to the field; Milburn, Brennan, and Mitchell included. Martin though didn't remain long afterwards. Aston Villa lured him south, but again it was a short period in charge and after a spell out of football he returned to Luton Town, a club where he was always held in affection. As a player George was part of First and Second Division title sides at Goodison Park, appearing as an inside-forward alongside Dixie Dean. A stylish schemer, he was a sharp-shooter and totalled 218 games for Hull City during the twenties. Also skilled at bowls, tennis and golf, Martin was famed for his sculpting as well as tenor singing, making broadcasts away from the football scene.

MATHER, Thomas (1935-1939)
b. Chorley, 1888
d. Stoke-on-Trent, 29th March 1957

Career: Bolton Wanderers asst-secretary 1910, becoming secretary and later manager 1915/Manchester City asst-secretary 1919/Southend United manager 1920 to 1922/Stoke City manager 1923/UNITED manager June 1935 to Oct 1939/Leicester City manager 1945 to 1946/Kilmarnock manager 1947 to 1948.

A genial personality, Tom Mather built a fine side at Stoke winning the Third and Second Division titles and introducing Stanley Matthews to senior football. Arriving at St James Park in a bid to revive the club's sagging fortunes, he soon attempted to sign Matthews for the Magpies, a deal that fell through, although plenty of other noted players did end up at Gallowgate. Mather was just beginning to forge a successful partnership with new director Stan Seymour when war was declared and he soon moved on. Always impeccably dressed and often wearing a bowler hat, Mather was from the old school of managers, brought up in office administration, yet he maintained tactical discussion at St James Park and instilled confidence in youngsters; Albert Stubbins being one such teenager to find an opportunity at Gallowgate. Mather later worked in the catering industry in the Potteries.

Tom Mather

MITTEN, Charles (1958-1961)
b. Rangoon, Burma, 17th January 1921

Career: Dunblane Rovers/Strathallan
Hawthorn/Manchester United 1936/Tranmere
Rovers wg 1939-41/Cardiff City wg 1941-42/
Southampton wg 1943-44/Chelsea wg 1943-
45/Wolverhampton Wanderers wg 1944-45/
Independiente Sante Fe(Colombia) 1950/
Fulham 1951/Mansfield Town player-manager
1956/UNITED manager June 1958 to Oct
1961/Altrincham manager 1962.

Charlie Mitten

One of the most controversial characters in
post-war football, Charlie Mitten was also one
of the top wingers of his day. Born on an army
base in Burma, at outside-left he was a strong
and forceful player, once selected by Sir Matt
Busby in his 'greatest ever team'. His Old
Trafford career was severed by war, but he still
managed to total 161 matches and have a
noteworthy return of goals, 61 from the flank;
he netted four, including a hat-trick of
penalties, in one game against Aston Villa.
Winning an unofficial England cap in 1946 and
an FA Cup medal at Old Trafford, Mitten
caused headlines when he moved to Bogota
and broke the maximum wage rule, earning a
small fortune in the process but also FA
suspension. After 160 games for Fulham,

Charlie headed for St James Park as an
appointment destined to bring United into a
rapidly modernising football world. Mitten's
management was young and bright; his
colourful style and sharp wit brought a
freshness to Gallowgate. He changed many
things; from training methods and junior
development to streamlining the club's kit.
Some of the changes were for the better, some
controversial, and always he never quite got
the backing of a feuding boardroom, split in
support of the manager. His mentor William
McKeag backed him to the hilt, but others,
notably Stan Seymour did not have the same
view. And that was never for the good of the
team, Mitten once commenting that
"Newcastle was unmanageable because of the
boardroom intrigue". He signed some good
players, Ivor Allchurch included, but had to
contend with many problems, not least George
Eastham's dramatic stand. By the start of the
sixties, United were struggling to avoid the
drop from Division One. Mitten could not stop
a slide and he was dismissed, interestingly
enough at a time when the powerful McKeag
was out of the country. Charlie found it
difficult to claim a job in football after that and
being a dog racing enthusiast, ran the White
City greyhound stadium in Manchester for a
period. He was also a UEFA licensed agent for
a while too, organising soccer tours around the
world. Latterly Mitten has settled in the
Manchester area. His son John was also at
Newcastle, while Charles junior operated in
the Football League too.

SMITH, James Michael (1988-1991)
b. Sheffield, 17th October 1940

Career: Newcross United/Oaksfield/Sheffield
United 1957/Aldershot 1961/Halifax Town
1965/Lincoln City 1968/Boston United player-
manager 1969/Colchester United player-
manager 1972/Blackburn Rovers manager
1975/Birmingham City manager 1978/Oxford
United manager 1982/Queens Park Rangers
manager 1985/UNITED manager Dec 1988 to
Mar 1991/Middlesbrough asst-coach 1991/
Portsmouth manager 1991/FL Managers
Association chief-executive 1995/
Derby County manager 1995.

Although never reaching lofty heights as a
player, Jim Smith developed into one of the
most highly respected managers on the circuit,
one who tasted football throughout upper and
lower divisions. A hardworking and

Jim Smith

SMITH, Norman (1938-1962)
b. Newburn, Newcastle upon Tyne,
12th December 1897
d. Newcastle upon Tyne, 18th May 1978

Career: Mickley/Ryton United/Mickley/
Huddersfield Town 1923/Sheffield
Wednesday 1927/Queens Park Rangers
1930/Retired 1932/Kreuzlingen(Switzerland)
player-trainer/St Gallen(Switzerland)
trainer/UNITED trainer July 1938, becoming
manager Oct 1961 to June 1962.

After a playing career as a reserve wing-half
for Huddersfield on 24 occasions when they
lifted a hat-trick of titles during the twenties,
Norman Smith was Stan Seymour's choice to
become his right-hand man when the club was
being overhauled from top to bottom just
before World War Two. Speaking fluent
German, he had a successful spell coaching in
Switzerland before settling back on his native
Tyneside, and immediately after the war his
influence was such that United's side
developed into one of the nation's best. At the
very heart of the club for over 20 years, he
stepped into the managerial role on the

enthusiastic wing-half as a player, he guided
Colchester, Birmingham and Oxford to
promotion, and then steered QPR to a good
position in the First Division and to Wembley
in the League Cup. Joining United on the
departure of Willie McFaul,
Smith's wheeling and dealing
style of management
immediately went into action.
Loving the transfer market he
brought in many faces during
his period in charge, Mick
Quinn and Roy Aitken
included. And the 'Bald Eagle'
as he was nicknamed, very
nearly succeeded in taking
Newcastle back into the First
Division, just missing
promotion in the play-off of
1990. Tough and outspoken at
times, eventually though
Smith found the minefield of
politics at St James Park and
the immense pressure to
succeed too much and he
resigned, taking up a much
more relaxed position at
Fratton Park. Smith later led
Derby County into the
Premier League in 1996.

dismissal of Charlie Mitten, very much as a
long term caretaker. That temporary role was
concluded when Joe Harvey walked through
the St James Park gates in 1962. Afterwards
Norman retired
from the game and
watched United
from the stand,
dying suddenly
after a visit to St
James Park,
collapsing on his
way from the
stadium. During his
career Smith had
trained both the
England and
Football League
sides. United player
Duggie Graham
was his son-in-law.

Norman Smith

BAYLES, W. (1892-1894)

A veteran trainer of United's pioneer club, Newcastle East End. Bayles took charge of the fitness routines during the club's days at Chillingham Road in Heaton, joining the East Enders in February 1891 for a salary of "10 shillings per week". He moved across the city to a St James Park base along with the rest of East End in May 1892 and continued looking after the players until the arrival of Harry Kirk in December 1894. During 1892, Bayles also took over the groundsman's duties.

Keith Burkinshaw

BURKINSHAW, Keith H. (1968-1975)
b. Higham, nr Barnsley, 23rd June 1935
Career: Wolverhampton Wanderers amat/Denaby United/Liverpool 1953/Workington 1957, becoming player-manager 1964/Scunthorpe United 1965/Zambia coaching 1968/UNITED asst-coach cs 1968, becoming coach cs 1971 to May 1975/Tottenham Hotspur coach 1975, becoming manager 1976/Bahrain national coach 1984/Sporting Lisbon manager 1986/Gillingham manager 1988 to 1989/England asst-coach 1990/Swindon Town chief-scout 1991/West Bromwich Albion asst-manager 1992, becoming manager 1993 to 1994.
A much respected and noted coach who did a good job at St James Park working alongside Joe Harvey to develop a flamboyant and exciting side. United's board of directors were heavily criticised on Burkinshaw's dismissal

APPENDIX FIVE
SENIOR COACHES, TRAINERS & ASSISTANT MANAGERS

1892-1894: W Bayles
1894-1895: Harry Kirk
1895-1896: J Pears
1896-1897: W Leach
1897-1903: Tom Dodds
1903-1928: James McPherson (snr)
1928-1930: Andy McCombie *(qv)*
1930-1937: James McPherson (jnr)
1937-1938: Harry Bedford *(qv)*
1938-1962: Norman Smith *(qv)*
1962-1966: Jimmy Greenhalgh
1966-1968: Ron Lewin
1968-1971: Dave Smith
1971-1975: Keith Burkinshaw
1975-1977: Richard Dinnis *(qv)*
1978-1979: Peter Morris
1979-1981: Willie McFaul *(qv)*
1981-1982: Tommy Cavanagh
1981-1985: Willie McFaul *(qv)*
1985-1987: Colin Suggett *(qv)*
1987-1988: John Pickering
1988-1991: Bobby Saxton
1991-1992: Tony Galvin
1992-1995: Derek Fazackerley
1995-date: Chris McMenemy
1992-date: Terry McDermott *(qv)*

Note: qv = see biography in players' or managers' section.

after the departure of Harvey, many players and the majority of supporters seeing him as a figure who could have served the club well over a sustained period. Keith proceeded to be appointed boss at White Hart Lane and the Yorkshireman brought top quality players like Ardiles and Villa to Tottenham. He fashioned a side to reach Wembley on three occasions, twice as winners of the FA Cup, as well as a team good enough to lift the UEFA Cup. But after that success Burkinshaw's career took a downward spiral, surprisingly not being able to land another top position despite a first-class track record. As a player Keith was a solid wing-half who spent seven years at Anfield claiming only a single outing. He then appeared over 300 times in the lower divisions for Workington. Burkinshaw resides in Welwyn.

CAVANAGH, Thomas H. (1981-1982)
b. Liverpool, 29th June 1928
Career: Preston North End 1949/Stockport County 1950/Huddersfield Town 1952/Doncaster Rovers 1956/Bristol City 1959/Carlisle United 1960/Cheltenham player-manager 1961(5 months)/Brentford coach, becoming manager 1965/Nottingham Forest coach 1966/Hull City coach 1971/Manchester United coach 1972, becoming asst-manager 1977 to 1980/UNITED asst-manager July 1981 to Oct 1982/Rosenborg Trondheim(Norway) coach 1982 to 1983/Burnley asst-manager 1985, becoming manager to 1986/Wigan Athletic coach 1988 to 1989.

Tommy Cavanagh

One of football's errant travellers, Tommy Cavanagh possessed a no-nonsense attitude, yet a witty and jovial character. With a wealth of experience in the game, firstly as a midfielder who totalled over 400 games, then as a coach reaching the heights of success at Old Trafford and guiding Forest to runners-up position in the First Division, Tommy moved to Gallowgate as Arthur Cox was attempting to restructure the club. With a colourful personality, Cavanagh only stayed on Tyneside for a little over a year before continuing his journey around the football scene. During his playing days, Cavanagh tasted relegation with Huddersfield, Bristol City and twice at Doncaster. He was a team-mate of Bill McGarry at Leeds Road when the Terriers won promotion in 1953. He was also assistant coach with the Northern Ireland squad for a period.

DODDS, Thomas J. (1897-1903)
b. Bishop Auckland, 1859
d. Darlington, 24th January 1909
Career: Sunderland trainer 1891/UNITED May 1897/Leyton May 1903/Liverpool. A major influence on Sunderland's formidable side before the turn of the century, Tom Dodds left Wearside following rows with Chairman JP Henderson over a lack of player discipline. A bearded and zealous character, he was in charge of the Magpie players as they moved into Division One for the first time in 1898. Dodds played his part in the club's consolidation as a major force in the game during the following years.

Tom Dodds

Being dismissed in May 1903, he later resided in Tyne Dock for a period and died of pneumonia.

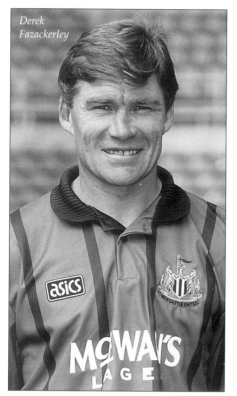

Derek Fazackerley

GALVIN, Anthony (1991-1992)
b. Huddersfield, 12th July 1956

Career: Hull University/Goole Town/ Tottenham Hotspur 1978/Sheffield Wednesday 1987/Swindon Town 1989, becoming asst-manager 1991/UNITED asst-manager Mar 1991 to Feb 1992/Gateshead occasionally as a player 1991.

Newcastle United's assistant-manager under Ossie Ardiles, the pairing had originally bonded together during their successful spell at White Hart Lane as players, then with Swindon Town in management. A graduate in Russian Studies at Hull University, Galvin had 10 seasons with Spurs, claiming 273 games as a hard working winger operating in a deep lying position. He was one of

Tony Galvin

the Londoners unsung heroes as Tottenham lifted the FA Cup (twice) and UEFA Cup, but a very effective player who appeared on 29 occasions for the Republic of Ireland. Tony was actually on United's books as a player, but didn't see first-class action although he did turn out in a friendly. His brother Chris, appeared for Leeds, Hull and Stockport.

FAZACKERLEY, Derek William (1990-1995)
b. Preston, 5th November 1951

Career: Blackburn Rovers 1969/Chester player-coach 1987/York City player-coach 1988/Bury 1989/Darwen/Kumu(Finland) player-coach 1990/UNITED asst-coach Oct 1990, becoming coach Feb 1992/Blackburn Rovers coach Sept 1995.

A great favourite at Ewood Park, Derek Fazackerley spent the majority of his playing career with Blackburn, totalling a record 674 senior games over 17 seasons for the Lancashire club. A tough central defender, quick and forceful, Fazackerley was a near perfect professional and brought those qualities to the coaching side of the game. Given an opportunity at St James Park by Jim Smith, he was promoted to look after the first-team squad by Kevin Keegan and assisted in the development of the Magpies as one of the Premier League's top sides. Derek only departed due to a wish to reside in his native Lancashire.

GREENHALGH, James Radcliffe (1962-1966)
b. Manchester, 25th August 1923

Career: Newton Heath Loco/Hull City 1946/ Bury 1950/Wigan Athletic 1955/Gillingham asst-player-coach 1956/Lincoln City asst-coach 1959/UNITED coach June 1962/Darlington manager July 1966/Middlesbrough asst-coach 1968, becoming coach/Sunderland chief-scout 1980 to 1982/Later a scout for several clubs.

A uncompromising wing-half as a player, predominately with Hull (167 games), Jimmy Greenhalgh was appointed as Joe Harvey's chief aid as the Magpies made a sustained bid to regain their First Division status. Jimmy was something of a fitness fanatic and hard

task master. Greenhalgh also held an astute tactical appraisal of the game and linked well with Harvey's motivation qualities. It was a partnership that took United to the Second Division championship in 1965. After spells as manager and coach elsewhere, Greenhalgh became a respected scout.

Jimmy Greenhalgh

LEACH, W. (1896-1897)

At St James Park for only a brief period, W Leach arrived to succeed Harry Kirk in August 1896 from Derby County. Leach had a sound reputation at the time and *Ixion* of the *Newcastle Daily Journal* wrote that he had been instrumental in taking the Rams from the bottom of the league to runners-up spot in Division One during 1895-96. It was noted that Leach would get the players, "in the pink of condition". He didn't remain long on Tyneside though, departing during the close season of 1897 and being replaced by Tom Dodds.

LEWIN, Ronald Dennis

(1966-1968, 1974-1976)

b. Edmonton, London, 21st June 1920

d. Cockermouth, 24th September 1985

Career: Enfield Town 1936/Bradford City 1943/Stockport County wg 1943-44/Fulham 1946/Gillingham 1950/Chatham 1955/Skeid Oslo(Norway) coach/Norway national coach/Cheltenham Town manager 1958/Wellington Town manager 1962/Everton asst-coach 1962/UNITED coach Aug 1966/Walsall manager July 1968 to 1969/UNITED asst-coach cs 1974 to July 1976/Kuwait, Greece & Iceland coaching/Brandon United coach 1981/Gateshead youth-officer 1983/Workington Town coach 1985 to death.

A member of Fulham's Second Division championship side in 1948-49, Ron Lewin was a good club player, a sound right-back who also did well at Gillingham where he totalled almost 200 matches. On retiring from the playing aspect of soccer, Lewin began a long and varied coaching career which took him all over Europe and beyond, and to all levels of the

Ron Lewin

game. He was brought into Joe Harvey's organisation on the departure of Jimmy Greenhalgh, and was prominent as the club qualified for Europe for the very first time. Lewin took up the manager's job at Fellows Park before the black'n'whites embarked on that inaugural and successful season in Europe. During the Second World War, Lewin spent six years as a physical training and parachute instructor.

KIRK, Harry (1894-1897)

A former trainer at Notts County since 1890, Harry Kirk was appointed in December 1894 after a period alongside the Trent. Kirk was sacked from his position at Meadow Lane following the Notts Magpies relegation at the end of the 1892-93 season. Kirk spent his period at St James Park during the initial building of a side good enough for Football League soccer. He was replaced by Pears in 1895, although Kirk remained connected with the club in other capacities to May 1897. He later was a pavilion attendant at Nottinghamshire's Trent Bridge cricket ground.

Chris McMenemy

McMENEMY, Christopher (1993-date)

b. Gateshead, 1st August 1961

Career: Southampton 1977/Retired due to injury 1979/Salisbury City 1981/Romsey Town/Southampton asst-coach 1982/Sunderland asst-coach 1985/Chesterfield coach 1988, becoming asst-manager and manager 1992 to 1993/Tottenham Hotspur scout/UNITED chief-scout July 1993, becoming asst-coach Feb 1994 & director of youth football, and coach Sept 1995.

Chris McMenemy took control of youth football at Gallowgate during February 1994 following a period in charge of Chesterfield when he was recognised as the youngest manager in the game at 29 years-old. From a family with a rich footballing pedigree, his father Lawrie is noted in Southampton's history, while he also had a brief spell on United's books as a player. Chris is also distantly related to the famous pre-war Scots McMenemy clan of which Harry appeared for Newcastle in the 1932 FA Cup final. Starting his career as an apprentice under his father's influence at The Dell, he never made the senior side and moved into coaching. On the departure of Derek Fazackerley, Chris moved into the senior position at St James Park.

McPHERSON, James Quar (senior)
(1903-1932)
b. Kilmarnock, 1862
d. Newcastle upon Tyne, 6th December 1932
Career: Berliner(Germany)/Kilmarnock trainer c1890/UNITED trainer cs 1903/Retired Jan 1928, becoming masseur to his death.
A former athlete in Victorian Britain, James McPherson entered soccer by way of a position in Berlin keeping players fit and ready for action. Known as 'Sandy', he arrived at St James Park just as the club was ready to take off and become Edwardian England's top side. Jolly and with an abundance of tact and spirit, he became an important backstage aid at Gallowgate for the next 25 years. Hailing from a noted sporting family, several of his relations played football and became accomplished in athletics. James and John both appeared for Kilmarnock, the latter, known as 'Kytie' being capped by Scotland. His son also carried on the McPherson name within the corridors of St James Park, while another relation, David, also played for Kilmarnock. Additionally he was also related by marriage to Edwin Dutton, on United's staff

James McPherson Snr.

and who appeared for the German national side in 1909. Sandy also trained both the England and Scotland teams during his career. Residing in Jesmond, when he died in 1932, one obituary noted that, Jimmy had, "lived for the club".

McPHERSON, James Quar (junior)
(1930-1937)
b. Scotland
Career: North Shields Athletic/Houghton Rovers/Vitesse Arnhem(Holland) c1920/Later, UNITED trainer July 1930 to cs 1937.
Son of United's celebrated trainer Sandy McPherson and a 'chip off the old block', James junior took charge of United's senior players as Andy Cunningham arrived as manager of the club. He was the former Rangers stars aid as the Magpies reached Wembley in 1932 and lifted the FA Cup. Yet the club didn't not progress after that success and McPherson left St James Park after relegation and on the arrival of a new management team at board level in the shape of Stan Seymour. His son Bob also became a trainer in the game.

MORRIS, Peter John (1978-1979)
b. New Houghton, Derbyshire, 8th November 1943
Career: New Houghton/Ladybrook Colts/ Langwith Boys Club/New Houghton/ Mansfield Town 1959/Ipswich Town 1968/ Norwich City 1974, becoming asst-coach/ Mansfield Town player-manager 1976/ UNITED asst-manager Feb 1978/ Peterborough United manager Feb 1979 to 1982/Crewe Alexandra manager 1982/Southend United manager 1983 to 1984/Nuneaton Borough manager 1985/Aajar Sporting(Saudi Arabia)/ Leicester City coach 1987, becoming caretaker manager and asst-coach 1988/ Kettering Town manager 1988/Boston United manager 1992/Northampton Town asst-manager 1993/ Kings Lynn manager 1995. Peter Morris was more than once linked with a transfer to St James Park as a player. A strong midfielder, he tasted promotion success with Ipswich, Mansfield and Norwich and

totalled 365 games for the Stags as well as 258 at Portman Road. A non-stop worker in midfield, he was a highly respected professional who linked up with Bill McGarry at St James Park in 1978. At that time Peter was also registered as a player, but only took part in friendly action for the black'n'whites. Like many of United's modern coaches, Morris has landed at many ports of call on his travels, his only trophy success being with Mansfield where he lifted the Third Division championship in 1976-77.

PEARS, J. (1894-1896)
First appointed to Newcastle's staff in 1894, he was elevated to the post of first-team trainer in August 1895 at a salary, according to the club's Minutes, of "35 shillings per week". However within a year United's directors were expressing dissatisfaction with his methods and Pears was sacked in March 1896, being replaced in a temporary role by W.Thompson.

PICKERING, John (1962-1965, 1986-1988)
b. Stockton-on-Tees, 7th November 1944
Career: Stockton jnrs/UNITED app 1962, pro Apr 1963/Halifax Town Sept 1965/ Barnsley 1974/Blackburn Rovers asst-coach 1975, becoming asst-manager 1979/Bolton Wanderers coach 1979/ Carlisle United coach 1980/Lincoln City asst-manager 1981, becoming manager 1985/Queens Park Rangers scout 1986/ Cambridge United scout 1986/UNITED asst-coach June 1986, becoming coach Sept 1987/Lincoln City asst-manager Nov 1988/Middlesbrough coach 1990, becoming asst-manager 1992, asst-coach 1994.
On United's books as a youngster, John Pickering couldn't break into the Magpies first eleven as a player apart from a single appearance in a friendly against St Johnstone. He had tough competition for a central defenders position in the shape of Moncur, Burton, McGrath and Thompson. John though, moved to Halifax for a £1,250 fee and became the cornerstone of Town's defence for almost a decade, making a record 367 league appearances for the Shay club. Moving into the coaching scene, he was respected by his players and when at Carlisle, Peter Beardsley once remarked that he was the best coach the England player had worked with. Pickering

made a sentimental return to St James Park in the summer of 1986 under Willie McFaul's management. At that time John was out of football and the chance at Gallowgate allowed the Teessider to return to soccer, although his stay on Tyneside was to be a short one. Pickering stood in as caretaker-manager at both Blackburn(1979) and Middlesbrough(1994).

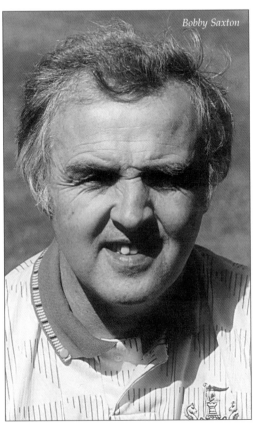

Bobby Saxton

SAXTON, Robert (1988-1991)
b. Bagby, nr Thirsk, 6th September 1943
Career: Wolverhampton Wanderers/Denaby United/Derby County 1962/Plymouth Argyle 1968/Exeter City 1975, becoming player-manager 1977/Plymouth Argyle manager 1979/Blackburn Rovers manager 1981 to 1986/Preston North End coach 1987/York City manager 1987/Blackpool coach 1988/UNITED asst-manager Dec 1988, becoming caretaker-manager Mar 1991(1 game) to Mar 1991/ Manchester City chief-scout 1991/Blackpool chief-scout, becoming asst-manager 1994/ Sunderland asst-coach 1995.

Bobby Saxton had a respectable if not spectacular playing career in the lower divisions. A centre-half with resolve, he played on over 400 occasions, captain at Plymouth in many of his 256 outings for the Pilgrims. Wholehearted and enthusiastic, he brought those qualities to St James Park when he was appointed as Jim Smith's aide in December 1988. Saxton almost helped guide United back into the First Division on the club's relegation, but a play-off disappointment was the runners-up prize for a season of hard work in 1989-90. He later though assisted Peter Reid in taking Sunderland into the Premier League for the first time in 1996. As a manager with Exeter in 1977, Saxton won promotion from the Fourth Division.

SMITH, David B. (1967-1971)
b. Dundee, 22nd September 1933
Career: Ashdale amat/East Craigie/Burnley 1950/Brighton 1961/Bristol City 1962/Burnley asst-coach c1962/Libya national coach/ Sheffield Wednesday asst-coach 1965, becoming coach/UNITED asst-coach June 1967, becoming coach July 1968/Arsenal asst-coach cs 1971/Mansfield Town manager 1974/ Southend United manager 1976 to 1983/ Plymouth Argyle manager 1984/Dundee manager 1988/Torquay United manager 1989 to 1991/Cyprus coaching 1993.

Dave Smith

A former Scottish youth and amateur international, as a player Dave Smith had the misfortune to break his leg on no fewer than five occasions and therefore had a career on the field that never developed. As a coach Smith became a likable and jovial character, popular with his players, but tough and forceful with a competitive Scottish edge. Replacing Ron Lewin as United's first-team coach in the close season of 1968, he was on the bench throughout the club's Inter Cities Fairs Cup success during the following season, but soon afterwards departed for Highbury. Smith later was in charge of lower division clubs, having success at Southend, Mansfield and at Plymouth where he was within a whisker of taking Argyle into the top division. Latterly Dave has been coaching local youngsters in the Devon area as well as an occasional scout for senior clubs.

ARCHIBALD, George Greig
(Chair 1913-1915; Dir 1897-1920)
b. 1851
d. Newcastle upon Tyne 1927
Joining United's **board** in June 1897, George Archibald was, **like the** majority of Newcastle's Chairmen, a distinguished Tyneside figure. An engin**eer** in his younger days, **he** was an enthusiastic supporter of the club's cause during the earliest days of the game **on** Tyneside and by **the time** he was appointed **to** United's directorate **had** switched trades, becom**ing** a successful wine **and spirit** merchant. The elaborately moustached Archibald was **also** a local politician, being elected to **the city** council in May 1894 and becoming Alderman in 1914. He had a keen **interest** in municipal matters and was **Chair**man of the city's Fire Brigade Comm**ittee.** George was appointed Chair**man** of Newcastle United in 1913 **and held** the post until the First World **War put** a stop to football in 1915. Archibald left the board in 1920 **and resid**ed in the Rye Hill district **of New**castle to his death.

BELL, Joseph
(Chair 1908-1909; Dir 1892-1909)
b. Newcastle upon Tyne c.1835
d. Newcastle upon Tyne 1909
Known as 'Uncle Joe' and Chairman of the Magpies for two years in 1908 and 1909, Joseph Bell was at the very heart of United's great Edwardian set-up, striking a unique player-director relationship. Often leading the team out during that successful era, Bell was seldom away from the players and in days before the introduction of a manager, was a positive factor in the club's development as a top side. A jovial character, Bell hailed from Heaton where he owned a grocery business and he was an original backer of the Newcastle East End outfit, one of the leading shareholders in 1890. During those formative years, Joe loaned the club much needed funds and it was at his residence in Rothbury Terrace that the now historic meeting took place in 1892 between officials of East and West End which led to the East Enders moving to St James Park and with it the start of Newcastle United. Bell was an original director, but left the board in 1897 only to rejoin shortly afterwards. Appointed to the Chair in August 1908, Joseph died when Chairman in 1909 at the height of the club's mastery. He was related to John William Bell, also a director of United during the same period.

Joseph Bell

CAMERON, John
(Chair 1894-1895, 1904-1908; Dir 1892-1916)
b. Perthshire
d. Newcastle upon Tyne 1916

John Cameron came south with his family from Scotland to seek work and settled on Tyneside during the 1870s, employed in the clothing business on an apprenticeship with Bainbridge & Company. He later worked for a Leeds clothier and developed his own business, residing in the East End heartland of Heaton. A supporter of East End's cause, his family were original shareholders possessing one of the biggest stakes in Newcastle United's pioneers. Cameron joined the club's board a year before the move to St James Park in 1892 and soon became an influential figure. John was heavily involved in the development of local football. He founded the North Eastern League and encouraged the Northern Alliance competition, while he became the first United director to sit on the country's governing body, the Football League Management Committee, from 1907 to 1916. Appointed Chairman of the Magpies in two spells, briefly before the turn of the century, and then from June 1904 to August 1908 when United had become the nation's most feared side. The *Newcastle Daily Journal* noted Cameron as being "largely responsible for cultivating the scientific game which has characterised the career of Newcastle United". A well known lay preacher too, Cameron died in July 1916 only months after taking over the management of the County Hotel in Jarrow. He left a widow and eight children and the club assisted their well-being by raising £768. Two other members of the family, James and Daniel Cameron, were also directors of the club during the same era.

John Cameron

1892-1893: **Alex Turnbull**
1893-1894: **D. McPherson**
1894-1895: **John Cameron**
1895: **Alex Turnbull**
1895-1901: **William Nesham**
1901-1904: **James Telford**
1904-1908: **John Cameron**
1908-1909: **Joseph Bell**
1909-1911: **James Lunn**
1911-1913: **George T. Milne**
1913-1915: **George G. Archibald**
1915-1919: **John Graham**
1919-1928: **John P. Oliver**
1928-1929: **David Crawford**
1929-1941: **James Lunn**
1941-1949: **George F. Rutherford**
1949-1951: **John W. Lee**
1951-1953: **Robert Rutherford**
1953-1955: **G. Stanley Seymour** (*qv*)
1955-1958: **Wilf B. Taylor**
1958-1959: **William McKeag**
1959-1964: **Wallace E. Hurford**
1964-1978: **Lord Westwood**
1978-1981: **Robert J. Rutherford**
1981-1988: **Stanley Seymour**
1988-1990: **W. Gordon McKeag**
1990-1991: **George R. Forbes**
1991-date: **Sir John Hall**

Note: qv = see biography in players' section.

David Crawford

FORBES, George Robert
(Chair 1990-1991; Dir 1983-1992)
b. Coldstream 1945

George Forbes was appointed Chairman of Newcastle United at the height of the 'share-war' and raging battle for control of the club as the nineties decade opened. From the Scottish borders, Forbes took over from Gordon McKeag once Sir John Hall's camp gained a foothold in the boardroom. Acting as something of an intermediary between the two warring factions, Forbes had the difficult task of pulling the club together. Newcastle United was in turmoil at the time; a poor side on the pitch, increasing debts off it, and a split boardroom. Despite working tirelessly and unobtrusively to find a compromise between rivals, Forbes was no match for Sir John's determination and financial muscle and eventually stepped down in December 1991 as the Cameron Hall Group took control in all but name. As a youngster George played soccer for noted border club Chirnside United while his uncle, John Johnston, was on United's books during the thirties. Always a supporter, he was invited to join the boardroom in October 1983 but left the club completely during July 1992. He runs an auction business in the north east as well as a 200 acre farm on the England-Scotland border. Forbes was once a noted rally driver.

CRAWFORD, David
(Chair 1928-1929; Dir 1904-1929)
b. unknown
d. Tyneside 1929

Another local Tyneside dignitary to be associated strongly with the rise of football in the city. David Crawford settled in Jesmond, living in Holly Avenue and was linked to the East End club during the 1880s. His brother Bob Crawford was a local player of repute, appearing for the Newcastle Rangers eleven and later becoming an umpire (in days before referees) for Newcastle East End. Crawford became a shareholder of the club on the introduction of an equity in 1890 and remained closely associated with Newcastle United's growth over the next 40 years. A chemical manufacturer in the region, he joined the board in June 1904 remaining in that capacity to his death in 1929 at the time of his chairmanship. Crawford was Northumberland FA President from 1886 to 1889.

George Forbes

GRAHAM, John

(Chair 1915-1919;
Dir 1892-1893, c.1895-1934)
b. unknown
d. Newcastle upon Tyne c.1934

From the Newcastle West End camp, John Graham was one of the organisers of football in the west of the city at St James Park. The club's treasurer during those Victorian days, he became one of the earliest appointed directors at Gallowgate, on the board in 1890 when the West End club became a limited company. Graham represented the West Enders' somewhat hopeless cause at the meeting with East End during the spring of 1892 which saw his club fold and East End move across the city. John was invited to join his rivals' management and remained connected to the club until 1934, a continuous director apart from a brief period during the 1890s. Graham also acted as secretary to United's A (reserve) side from July 1896 for a time and was Chairman during the years of the First World War. He resigned his post as a director in May 1934 and died shortly afterwards.

John Graham

HALL, John Sir

(Chair 1991-date; Dir 1990,
1991-date)
b. North Seaton 1933

Without doubt, Sir John Hall will go down in history as the Chairman who has made the biggest impact on Newcastle United Football Club. Perhaps the most powerful man in the north east, Sir John stepped in and rescued an ailing giant during 1990 and 1991, and with his substantial financial backing, business acumen and enthusiastic drive, has turned the club into an organisation to rival not only the best in Britain, but also in Europe. A former NCB surveyor, Sir John later became a highly successful property developer, making his fortune from the Gateshead Metro Centre shopping complex. Knighted in July 1991, by that time he was committed to gaining hold of the Magpies and in a sometimes bitter confrontation with United's establishment, eventually gained a controlling interest. He installed Kevin Keegan as manager and, since critically escaping relegation into Division Three in 1992, the club has grown from strength to strength on and off the park. Acting very much as a visionary and strategist, he guided Newcastle from a modest single figure turnover to a highly successful business with a turnover approaching £50 million. He has also completely redeveloped St James Park and set up the Newcastle Sporting Club on the lines of such multi-themed giants as Barcelona and Sporting Lisbon. Appointed initially to the board for a brief period in March 1990, he soon resigned his post due to infighting, but returned in November 1991 when he almost had full control of affairs. Sir John became Chairman a month later and has become the most popular football Chairman in United's history, Newcastle supporters being appreciative of his worth in the club's total transformation. A Millennium Commissioner, Sir John resides at Wynyard Hall, the former estate of the Londonderry family. His son Douglas is also a United director.

Sir John Hall

HURFORD, Wallace Edwin
(Chair 1959-1964; Dir 1950-1967)
b. Newcastle upon Tyne 1889
d. Newcastle upon Tyne 1967
A dental surgeon by profession,
Wallace Hurford's family had links
with the club going back to the days of
Newcastle East End. From a teenager
he was a supporter of the Magpies
and a season-ticket holder, while he
also played football himself for
Armstrong College. A shareholder too,
he was first nominated for a position
on the board in 1930, but it took
Wallace another 20 years to become
appointed, in April 1950. With a
friendly manner and common sense
approach, Hurford was largely
responsible for developing the club's
postwar youth set up under the
banner of the N's. He was elected
Chairman in October 1959 but had to
preside over a difficult period in the
club's history; relegation from
Division One, the sacking of Charlie
Mitten and a rebuilding period
thereafter. He
suffered ill-health
during 1964 and
Lord Westwood
took over the
Chair in October
of that year.
Hurford
remained a
director to his
death in Jesmond
during January
1967. During the
First World War
he served in the
Royal Medical
Corps, while he
was also a
prominent bridge
player, once
winning the
North of England
championship.

Wallace Hurford

LEE, John W.
(Chair 1949-1951; Dir 1934-1954)
b. Whitley Bay 1887
d. Newcastle upon Tyne 1954
John Lee was a successful Tyneside
businessman who ran an egg importing and
poultry merchants
operation. Possessing a
vibrant personality he
was an inspiration and
a tonic within United's
ranks, Stan Seymour
once remarking that he
"created an atmosphere
of welcome and
fellowship". Becoming a
director of the club in
June 1934 after being
first nominated four
years earlier, Lee
reached the Chairman's

John Lee

seat in December 1949 and was in charge for
two years, including the period when the
Magpies lifted the FA Cup in 1951. He was
also a director of several other companies in
the region as well as Chairman of the Crown
Building Society. Lee died when still a director
of the black and whites in November 1954.

LUNN, James
(Chair 1909-1911, 1928-1941;
Dir 1896-1941)
b. Newcastle upon Tyne 1860
d. Newcastle upon Tyne 1941
A celebrated local politician who ran a
building contractors business in the
region, James Lunn was first elected to
the city council in 1909 and went on to
hold the post of Sheriff of Newcastle
upon Tyne (1922) and Alderman (1927). A
United shareholder since July 1895, Lunn
joined the club's board during the
summer of 1896 and was a strong voice in
club matters for the next 40 years and
more. Chairman in two spells, from 1909
to 1911, and then for a long period from
December 1928 to his death in March
1941, Lunn saw his club lift the FA Cup twice
during the period he was in charge, in 1910
and 1932. He was also a Justice of the Peace as
well as being Chairman of the Royal Arcade
Building Society. James resided initially in
Eldon Square, then in Gosforth to his death.
His brother was another prominent
Novocastrian, Sir George Lunn.

James Lunn

directors. That sometimes brought conflict between the two men who did not always see eye to eye. In some quarters William McKeag was also known as 'Mr Newcastle' just as Seymour was. He was Chairman of the club during 1958 and 1959, while he was also a governor of the RVI and Royal Grammar School and was honoured by becoming a Freeman of Newcastle upon Tyne in 1966. Father of Gordon McKeag, later Chairman of the club, he served in both world wars reaching the rank of major. As a youth McKeag was a useful footballer and boxer, as well as running under an assumed name at the Powderhall sprints in Edinburgh. William McKeag died during October 1972 when still a member of United's board.

William McKeag

McKEAG, William
(Chair 1958-1959; Dir 1944-1972)
b. Durham 1897
d. Whitley Bay 1972

The son of a pit worker, William McKeag was one of the most prominent figures to serve the region during the last century. A solicitor and initially a Liberal MP for Durham City (1931-1935), he became a Newcastle councillor in 1936 and was an outspoken local politician for the next 25 years. Alderman of the city and twice Lord Mayor, McKeag was an instantly recognisable character, sporting a monocle as well as having the gift of colourful oratory, Churchillian in style. Before he became associated with Newcastle United, William was on the board of Durham City and had a love of football from an early age. He was first suggested for a seat on the Magpie hierarchy in 1930 and in fact became something of a rebel shareholder, a fierce critic of the club during the troubled years of the mid thirties. He was eventually elected in May 1944, and together with Stan Seymour (senior), the club possessed two forthright and powerful

McKEAG, William Gordon
(Chair 1988-1990; Dir 1972-1991)
b. Whickham 1929
Gordon McKeag took over the family position in Newcastle's boardroom in November 1972 on the death of his father. Educated at the Royal Grammar and Durham Schools and later Cambridge University, McKeag studied law and followed in his father's footsteps in the family's Gosforth solicitors' practice. Always interested in local sport, Gordon captained Percy Park rugby club and appeared for Northumberland.
He also appeared for the county at squash and was a fine cricketer as well as a tennis player of repute. McKeag was brought up with Newcastle United in his blood, a fervent supporter who eventually became a force in the boardroom, reaching the Chairman's seat on the resignation of Stan Seymour (junior) in June 1988. His reign though was one of bitter feuding and determined defence against a takeover challenge from the

Gordon McKeag

Magpie Group and Sir John Hall. A three-year battle for control raged in which Gordon eventually conceded, but on leaving the scene he departed with integrity and respect. Always showing a vein of bulldog resistance as well as a wry sense of humour, McKeag vacated the Chair in December 1990 and left the board during November 1992. He did though retain his post of President of the Football League, a position achieved in January of that year. His links with both the FA and FL grew stronger as he left St James Park, being a member of various committees administrating the game.

McPHERSON, D.
(Chair 1893-1894; Dir 1893-1894)
Associated with the early days of Newcastle United's development, D. McPherson was only a director of the club for a short period. He was elected to the board early in 1893 just after Newcastle East End moved to St James Park. A local businessman, he became Chairman in October of that year, but had stepped down on his first anniversary in charge of the Magpies and left the football scene soon afterwards.

MILNE, George Taylor
(Chair 1911-1913; Dir 1895-1917)
b. Alnwick 1845
d. Newcastle upon Tyne 1917
Father of United player William Milne and a senior representative of the well known John Sinclair cigarette and tobacco company on Tyneside, George Milne was a director of Newcastle United for 22 years. From the Northumberland county town of Alnwick, Milne first joined the board in 1895 and remained a valued member of the club to his death in September 1917. Very well respected in north east sporting circles, he was also an enthusiastic follower of Northumberland cricket, his two sons appearing for the county side. A Newcastle West End supporter originally, George had been connected with the St James Park club for some years before their liquidation in 1892. Milne didn't join the new East End organisation immediately, but was asked to participate within three years. Chairman at Gallowgate for two years from 1911, he was also President of the Northumberland FA from 1902 to 1917, while George was also a Life Governor of the RVI. He died after attending a Newcastle United Swifts game in 1917, contracting pneumonia which proved fatal.

William Milne

NESHAM, William
(Chair 1895-1901; Dir 1892-1901)
b. Newcastle upon Tyne
d. Newcastle upon Tyne 1901
Newcastle West End's first Chairman, William Nesham owned the lease of St James Park which he sold to the West Enders in December 1890. Residing in Leazes Terrace, he was one of the driving enthusiasts in the region as the game struggled to take-off. Along with John Black, Nesham did much to see that West End survived for a decade and enjoyed some early success before a cash crisis eventually saw their demise. Nesham was then invited to join the East End board and for almost a decade served Newcastle United with esteem. A wealthy local dignitary, he held the Chairmanship from August 1895 to his death in January 1901. Nesham was also President of the Northumberland FA at the time of his demise, while the Tynesider was a highly respected cricketer as well. A doctor and merchant, several sources spell his name as 'Neasham' although official club documentation confirms Nesham.

John Oliver

OLIVER, John Peel
(Chair 1919-1928; Dir 1902-1928)
b. 1860
d. Newcastle upon Tyne 1928
A wine and spirit merchant and owner of several public-houses in the region, John Oliver was one of three of the Oliver family to sit on United's board of directors. Joining the club's management during the close-season of 1902, he remained in a very active role for 26 years. John was Chairman of the club when they won the FA Cup in 1924 and saw the First Division title arrive at St James Park three years later. Well known in football circles, he was "highly respected for his integrity" and had a position on the Football League Management Committee. It was just before one of the meetings of football's rulers in 1921 that Oliver suffered a heart attack and had to be rushed to Euston hospital. His activities were restricted afterwards, but Oliver remained a loyal servant to Newcastle United's cause to his death in December 1928, shortly after visiting St James Park. Oliver

married a sister of Newcastle East End pioneer Tom Watson and is related to Cumbrian huntsman John Peel, made famous in the celebrated folk song, *"D'ye ken John Peel"* written by John Graves.

RUTHERFORD, George F.
(Chair 1941-1949; Dir 1925-1949)
b. Tyneside
d. Tyneside 1949
One of three members of the Rutherford dynasty to have held the Chairmanship of Newcastle United, George Rutherford was the first to be elected as a figurehead of the Magpies, replacing James Lunn in March 1941. A coal merchant in the north east, he held control throughout World War Two and saw the club return to the First Division in 1948. A long-standing shareholder of the club, George was first nominated to become a director in 1923, joining the board two years later. He was remembered as an unselfish and hospitable individual, a steady influence around the table. From Gosforth, he sat on the Football League Management Committee from 1938 to 1942 and was Vice-President of the Football League thereafter to his death in 1949. Also related to another United Chairman, John Oliver, by marriage.

RUTHERFORD, Robert
(Chair 1951-1953; Dir 1930-1959)
b. Wallsend 1881
d. Newcastle upon Tyne 1959

A distinguished surgeon, Robert Rutherford started his professional career as a doctor in Cardiff. He moved back to Tyneside taking the post of Deputy Medical Officer of Health for Newcastle upon Tyne in 1911 and later moved to become Medical Officer of Health, and Schools Medical Officer for Wallsend. By that time Rutherford had been nominated to join his brother George on United's board. He was first put forward in 1927 but not co-opted until 1930. Noted as a "loveable character", he was known affectionately as 'Dr Bob' and was a great raconteur on United's travels. Rutherford could be blunt and direct at times, he was a true United supporter often travelling with the team, especially after retiring from his medical

post in 1947. He was Chairman from November 1951 to 1953, but unfortunately missed the Wembley victory in 1952 having to undergo an operation in London. During World War One, Rutherford served in the Medical Corps and was honoured with the Military Cross. Residing in Jesmond, he died during December 1959 when still on the club's board.

Dr Robert Rutherford

RUTHERFORD, Robert James
(Chair 1978-1981; Dir 1950-1981)
b. Newcastle upon Tyne 1913
d. Newcastle upon Tyne 1995

The son of past Chairman Dr Robert Rutherford, he was elected into Newcastle's inner sanctum in April 1950 and spent 31 years on the club's executive. Educated at The Royal Grammar School and Durham University, he followed his father into the medical profession, also becoming an eminent surgeon. Although Robert witnessed all of Newcastle's victorious fifties era, by the time he was elevated to the Chairmanship in January 1978, the club was in rapid decline. Being Lord Westwood's deputy for over a decade prior to his appointment, Rutherford shunned the public spotlight and suffered from supporters' criticism at the club's lack of

professionalism and modern success. At a critical point in United's history during March 1981, he resigned both his post as Chairman and director along with Lord Westwood, when he was asked to increase a financial guarantee to the club's bankers. An outstanding golfer, Rutherford resided in Gosforth to his death in August 1995.

SEYMOUR, Stanley (junior)
(Chair 1981-1988; Dir 1976-1991)
b. Greenock 1916
d. Birmingham 1992

Stanley Seymour junior was born in Scotland when his father was playing for Greenock Morton. But he soon moved to Tyneside along with the family and began a long association in north east football. Not surprisingly he followed Newcastle United with dedication as a supporter, first being nominated for a boardroom post in 1959. Running the family's sports outfitters business in the centre of Newcastle, Seymour was also a keen rugby enthusiast and became involved in the administration of the Northern Alliance league as well as the Northumberland FA. By the time he became the region's NFA President, Stan had reached the United boardroom, appointed a director in succession to his famous father in April 1976. He took over as Chairman on the resignation of Rutherford and Westwood in March 1981 and presided over one of the most thrilling periods in United's history when he was instrumental in bringing Kevin Keegan to Tyneside during 1982. Seymour always fought hard for the development of local youngsters at St James Park and guided United into a new era of commercialism and

Stanley Seymour jnr

sponsorship. A tremendous character, although he liked to keep a low profile, Stan resigned in June 1988 just before the 'share war' erupted in earnest although he remained connected to the club he loved as President. He died suddenly after attending a United fixture at St Andrews, Birmingham during November 1992.

TAYLOR, Wilfred Burns
(Chair 1955-1958; Dir 1941-1971)
b. North Shields 1888
d. Newcastle upon Tyne 1971
Wilf Taylor was a miller of repute in the region, a director of local enterprise Hindhaughs. From good Tyneside stock, Wilf's uncle was the first Lord Mayor of Newcastle upon Tyne and he became a United official during the Second World War, in November 1941. That appointment to the board was after several years of trying to gain a seat, initially a nomination in 1936. Thin and frail looking, Taylor possessed a wise head and he became Chairman following the 1955 FA Cup final. Wilf remained in charge until the summer of 1958 when he resigned at a time of boardroom feuding. During the fifties decade Taylor became an influential figure in the wider administration of football, a member of the Football League Management Committee from 1956 to 1964 and Vice President of the League for six years, to 1970. His reign on United's board ended shortly after, on his death during February 1971.

Wilf Taylor (left) holds the 1955 FA Cup with Jimmy Scoular and Stan Seymour (Snr).

TELFORD, James
(Chair 1901-1904; Dir
1892-1904)
b. Scotland
A shrewd businessman
who was involved in
the drapery trade, John
Telford is credited with
changing the whole
outlook on football on
Tyneside. The Scot can
claim to have been a
major influence in
putting the name of
Newcastle United on
the soccer map during
the first decade of the
club's existence. *The
Newcastle Daily Journal*
noted that Telford,
"established the
financial success of the
club". Residing in
Westgate Road, he was

Baron Westwood

a West End supporter becoming a director
during 1892 and Chairman in January 1901. A
powerful, eloquent character, at times even
domineering, James had a personality that
ensured results. He was involved in most of
the club's early transfers being a good judge of
a player, bringing many of Newcastle's
Edwardian stars to St James Park. Yet the Scot
lost his director's place after a boardroom
coup in June 1904, a shock to Tyneside at the
time. His departure was not liked in the
dressing-room with Bob McColl one of several
players who publicly opposed the decision.
Colin Veitch recorded that Telford had
received treatment of a "scurvy nature".

TURNBULL, Alexander
(Chair 1892-1893, 1895; Dir 1892-1901)
The club's first Chairman following the East
End and West End combination in 1892. Alex
Turnbull was very much an East Ender.
Residing in Heaton, he was one of the
Chillingham Road outfit's original
shareholders, indeed his family held the
largest stake in the company with 35 shares
and not surprisingly was one of the club's
founding directors at the first AGM in 1890. A
business representative travelling the country,
as well as running the East End Hotel on
Chillingham Road, Turnbull remained as the
club's figurehead until October 1893. During
that year he spoke with passion for United's

corner when they were
seeking votes for election
into the Football League.
He did have another
short period as Chairman
from May to August
1895, while he left the
boardroom completely
during 1901.

**WESTWOOD, William;
Baron, Lord Westwood**
(Chair 1964-1978;
Dir 1960-1981)
*b. Newcastle upon Tyne
1908*
*d. Newcastle upon Tyne
1991*
Apart from Sir John Hall,
the Second Baron
Westwood is Newcastle
United's most celebrated
figure to have taken
control of the boardroom.
Son of a past Newcastle United director who
rose to fame as a union leader in the
shipyards, Lord Westwood was a true gent,
noted as being firm, but fair in his attitudes to
life, business and to football. Bill Westwood
made his own way, very much like Sir John
Hall. He started as a railway clerk, became a
company secretary, then by the time he was
appointed to the Magpie boardroom in
August 1960 was a director of a host of
companies, including a toy manufacturing
giant. Westwood was both distinguished and
distinctive with silvery wavy hair and a
famous black patch over one eye, the legacy of
a car accident. Taking over the Chair at
Gallowgate on the illness to Wally Hurford,
Westwood controlled the club at a time of
fluctuating fortunes; promotion, a European
victory, Wembley appearances, but then slump
and financial collapse. By the time of his
resignation as Chairman in January 1978 his
reign had turned sour and when asked to help
fund mounting debts in March 1981
Westwood resigned. A magistrate, Lord
Westwood was also a servant of the Football
League, on the Management Committee from
1970, becoming President in 1974 to his
resignation from United's board. Bill
Westwood died in Gosforth in November
1991, another United Chairman, Gordon
McKeag, said on his death that he was, "a man
of wit, dignity and charm".

CLUB OFFICIALS
DIRECTORS
Archibald, G.G.
Auld, J.R.
Bates, S.F.
Bell, J.
Bell, J.W.
Bennie, R.B.
Bennett, T.L.
Black, J.
Bowman, Sir G.
Bramwell, W.
Braithwaite, F.
Cameron, D.
Cameron, James
Cameron, John
Carmichael, M.
Catesby, W.P.
Cowan, J.
Crawford, D.
Cushing, R.
Davis, H.
Dickson, H.H.
Dickson, G.R.
Dougan, J.
Dunn, E.
Forbes, G.R.
Forster, G.R.
Fox, A.
Good, W.
Graham, J.
Hall, D.
Hall, Sir J.
Henderson, R.
Hudson, W.R.
Hurford W.E.
Johnson, R.
Jones, R.
Lee, J.W.
Lewis, J.
Lilburn, W.
Lunn, J.
Mallinger, P.C.
Matthews, G.R.
Milne, G.T.
Molineux, W.
McConachie, G.
McKeag, W.
McKeag, W.G.
McKenzie, R.
McKenzie, R.R.
McKenzie, R.W.

McVickers, D.
MacPherson, D.
Nesham, W.
Nevin, R.W.
Neylon, J.
Oliver, J.P.
Oliver, R.
Oliver, T.
Peel, J.E.
Rush, J.
Rutherford, G.F.
Rutherford, R.
Rutherford, R.J.
Salkeld, D.V.
Sanderson, W.J.
Seymour, G.S.
Seymour, S.
Shepherd, F.
Simpson, R.W.
Stableforth, A.G.
Strother Stewart, R.
Taylow, W.B.
Telford, J.
Turnbull, A.
Westwood, Lord Snr
Westwood, Lord Jnr
Young, R.
Zollner, L.

PRESIDENTS
Bennett, T.L.
Braithwaite, F.
Seymour, S.
Westwood, Lord Jnr

CHIEF EXECUTIVES
Stephenson, D.
Fletcher, F.

SECRETARIES
Barker, J.D.
Cushing, R.
Ferguson, J.S.
Hall, E.
Golding, W.H.
Hoole, M.G.
Neylon, J.
Watt, F.G. Snr
Watt, F.G. Jnr

Freddie Fletcher - Newcastle's current Chief Executive.

Russell Cushing (above) and Frank Watt (below) two of United's administrators to serve the club with distinction.

1	Sir JOHN HALL, (Chairman, NUFC)
2	D. HALL (Director, NUFC)
3	F. SHEPHERD (Director, NUFC)
4	T. L. BENNETT (Director, NUFC)
5	R. JONES (Director, NUFC)
6	F. FLETCHER (Chief Executive, NUFC)
7	R. CUSHING (Secretary, NUFC)
8	KEVIN KEEGAN (Manager, NUFC)
9	PAUL JOANNOU
10	E. JOANNOU
11	R. GREEN
12	R. BORTHWICK, Leicester
13	J. EDMINSON, Corebridge
14	A. CANDLISH, Newcastle
15	S. CORKE, Newcastle
16	P. TULLY, Hexham
17	DAVID HEWSON, Typestyles, Gateshead
18	TONY HARDISTY, Newcastle
19	TONY HILL, Oakham, Rutland
20	JOHN A. HARRIS, Southgate, London
21	EUGENE MacBRIDE, Grantham, Lincs
22	JOHN LAWSON, Nottingham
23	HARRY STANIFORTH, Anstey, Leics
24	NEILL STANIFORTH, Leicester
25	BRIAN JOHN JONES, Kings Park, Glasgow
26	FREDERICK LEE, Plymouth, Devon
27	IAN GRIFFITHS, Saltney, Chester
28	RAYMOND SHAW, Sutton-in-Ashfield, Notts
29	GERALD MORTIMER, Ilkeston, Derbyshire
30	GEORGE PAINTER, Castle Cary, Somerset
31	GEOFF ALLMAN, Essington, Wolverhampton
32	MOIRA & FREDERICK FURNESS, North Shields
33	NEVILLE FURNESS & HELEN CHAMBERS, Wallsend
34	CAROL & WILLIAM WILSON, North Shields
35	KRIS ANDREW FURNESS, Tynemouth
36	TONY FIDDES, Newcastle upon Tyne
37	JOE FIDDES, Newcastle upon Tyne
38	MALCOLM BLAKEY, Felpham, Bognor Regis
39	MARK THOMPSON, Burnopfield
40	ANTONY VAUGHAN, Ashford, Middlesex
41	ROSS ALEXANDER BOWMAN, Walkerdene, Newcastle upon Tyne
42	IAN ATHEY, Killingworth, Newcastle
43	NEIL McQUEEN, Forest Hall, Newcastle upon Tyne
44	JOHN ROBINSON, Burnham on Sea, Somerset
45	DAVID ALBANY STEWART, Whitburn, Sunderland
46	MICHAEL HOGG, Bugbrooke, Northamptonshire
47	MICHAEL ROBERT SLATER, Clay Cross, Chesterfield
48	DEREK HYDE, Llanishen, Cardiff
49	WES GARGETT, Coxhoe, Co Durham
50	GLEN D. MARSHALL, North Anston, Sheffield
51	GARETH KING, Wednesbury, West Midlands
52	STEWART P. FLEMING, Wallsend, Tyne & Wear
53	KEITH TALBOT, Twyford, Reading
54	LANCE ROBSON, Belford, Northumberland
55	STEVEN J. SLATER, Low Fell, Gateshead
56	ANTHONY TAYLOR, Moorside, Sunderland
57	PHILIP H. BROWN, Darlington, Co Durham
58	LES RUFFELL, Little Haywood, Staffs
59	T. BROWNE, Denton Burn, Newcastle
60	DALE LAND, St Albans, Herts
61	JOSEPH TAYLOR, Ryton
62	JONATHAN STEWART, London
63	KEVIN GREY (12 yrs), North Shields, Tyne & Wear
64	PETER S. BLACK, Boxmoor, Hemel Hempstead
65	JONNY STOKKELAND, Kvinesdal, Norway
66	PAUL, DAVID & MARK CARPENTER, Usworth, Washington
67	DAVID KEATS, Thornton Heath, Surrey
68	JOHN RINGROSE, Romford, Essex
69	JENNIFER ELIZABETH VICKERS, Wallsend
70	PAULINE MORRALLEE, Prudhoe, Northumberland
71	MICHAEL PESCOD, London EC2
72	MALCOLM SCOTT, Tweedmouth, Northumberland
73	B.S. CARTER, Hadrian Park, Wallsend
74	JOHN W. BRADLEY, Holton-Le-Clay, Grimsby
75	MICHAEL J.P. GAFF, Houghton-Le-Spring
76	MICHAEL JONES, Birtley, Chester-Le-Street
77	COLIN TAYLOR, Whickham, Newcastle upon Tyne
78	COLIN EDWARDS, Great Lumley, Co Durham
79	L. LAMBERT, Blyth, Northumberland
80	VICTORIA ELIZABETH LAWINS, Blyth
81	ALISTAIR GOODWIN, Shipcote, Gateshead
82	COLIN JARVIS, Low Moorsley, Hetton-Le-Hole
83	MARTIN PALLETT, Morpeth, Northumberland
84	JOHN J. WILSON, Ouston, Chester-Le-Street
85	CHARLES DOCHERTY, Hebburn, Tyne & Wear
86	D.K. WILLIAMS, Pinner, Middlesex
87	BARRY STOKER, New Malden, Surrey
88	ROBERT STOKER, Whickham, Tyne & Wear
89	RAYMOND WALTON, Cockermouth, Cumbria
90	DAVID LUMB, Bromley Cross, Bolton
91	ROBERT SMAIL, Loughborough, Leics
92	JOHN ROBSON, Wallsend, Tyne & Wear
93	DAVID WINDER, Carlisle, Cumbria
94	COLIN STRAUGHAN, Chapel Park, Newcastle
95	GLENN CARVER, Woodford Green, Essex
96	R.T. COLLINSON, Carlisle, Cumbria
97	JOHN A. ALDER, Gateshead
98	JOHN A. ALDER, Gateshead
99	GEORGE R. DICKSON, Newcastle upon Tyne
100	EDWIN MOIR, Widdrington, Morpeth
101	GEOFF & JON BUFFEY, Heapey, Chorley, Lancs
102	NIGEL ION, Holy Cross, Wallsend
103	PETER BLOOMER, Prudhoe, Northumbria
104	KEV HILL, Gateshead
105	GEORGE E. STOKES, Carleton Park, Penrith
106	DOUGLAS G. STOKES, Penrith, Cumbria
107	WILLIAM ARMSTRONG, Penrith, Cumbria
108	MARK WILLIAM DAWSON, Benton, Newcastle
109	D.E. BANKS, Todwick, Sheffield
110	J.E. FLECK, Paddington, London
111	A.R. CURRY, Kenilworth, Warwickshire
112	IAN SHANKS, Amble, Morpeth
113	MATTHEW MANKELOW, London E2
114	BILL McCARTHY, Woodley, Reading
115	PAUL SEBASTIAN KIERAN, Mossley, Lancs
116	BILL COOK, Randlay, Telford, Shropshire
117	PHIL & PAM CARRICK, Forest Hall. Newcastle
118	L.A. ZAMMIT, Fareham, Hampshire
119	JACK FRASER SMITH, Cheadle Hulme, Cheshire
120	GRAHAM DI DUCA, Little Weighton, East Yorks
121	LEONARD DI DUCA, Scunthorpe, North Lincs
122	TREVOR SMITH, Tanfield Lea, Stanley, Co Durham
123	NORMAN ERNEST BENNETT, Glebe, Washington
124	ROB OVERTON, East Holborn, South Shields
125	Miss MARGARET PETRIE, Newcastle upon Tyne
126	HUGH COLLINGWOOD, East Molesey, Surrey
127	CERI & DAVID LOW, Shenley, Herts
128	COLIN J. McINNES, Pitlochry, Perthshire
129	TONY MORLEY, Timperley, Altrincham, Cheshire
130	A.N. OTHER, Hertfordshire

131 ÖRJAN HANSSON, Helsingborg, Sweden	196 K.A. ARTHUR, Gosforth, Newcastle
132 JOHN E. ELLIS, Shrewsbury, Shropshire	197 PETER G. COATES, Gosforth Newcastle
133 DOUGLAS LAMMING, North Ferriby, N. Humberside	198 JOHN MALCOLM VEALE, Forest Hall, Newcastle
134 MARK WADDELL, Lowestoft, Suffolk	199 ROBERT ERNEST GLENWRIGHT, South Bents, S'Land
135 MORGAN DAVID COOK, Southport	200 LIAM HUGH LAVELLE, Whitley Bay
136 ANDREW BARR, Bow Brickhill, Milton Keynes	201 RICH WILSON, Whitby, N. Yorkshire
137 ROB DUDDING, Fenham, Newcastle	202 DAVID HUGHES, Godden Green, Kent
138 CHRISTOPHER GAVIN DONNELLY, Caversham, Reading	203 MELVYN HUGHES, Godden Green, Kent
139 JOHN GAVIN DONNELLY	204 RICHARD HUGHES, Godden Green, Kent
140 NEIL FOWLER, Pontcanna, Cardiff	205 CHRIS CABLE, Lytham, Lancashire
141 TONY PORTER, North Shields	206 RON BRUNTON, Maidenhead, Berks
142 DAVID DODD, Felling, Tyne & Wear	207 DAVID KIRSOPP, Bishop Auckland
143 NEIL BROWN, Menston, Ilkley, Yorkshire	208 IAN SPARK, Fenham, Newcastle
144 DAVID WALKER, Montagu Estate, Newcastle	209 BERNIE LAMB, Benton, Newcastle
145 JOHN FENWICK, Felling, Tyne & Wear	210 DAVID PETE LANNING, Gosforth, Newcastle
146 PAUL C. HESLOP, Slough, Berkshire	211 KENDRA LONGTHORNE, Bishops Green, Spennymoor
147 A.E. WILLIAMSON, Gateshead, Tyne & Wear	212 A.G. BARBER, Gomersal, Cleckheaton
148 MARK MOFFITT, Pinner, Middlesex	213 JOHN T. EWART, Acomb, York
149 TONY RYMER, Gosforth, Tyne & Wear	214 Dr. KEITH BEVERIDGE, Sedgefield, Co Durham
150 JACK WILLIAM TURNER, West Denton, Newcastle	215 JORDAN THOMAS JOHN LISLE, Tynemouth
151 ALLAN J. GRAHAM, Silloth, Cumbria	216 GEOFFREY DAWSON, Heysham, Morecambe
152 JOE T. PORTHOUSE, Torry, Aberdeen	217 JIM McGUIGGAN, Coalisland, Dungannon, Co Tyrone
153 LESLIE USHER, Whickham, Newcastle	218 JONATHAN MILLER, Seaton Sluice, Whitley Bay
154 RICHARD MILLS, Chester-le-Street	219 JAMES HART, Heaton, Newcastle
155 PETTERI WALLENIUS, Lahti, Finland	220 IAN MUDIE, Bingham, Notts
156 ROBERT TREVOR JORDAN, Dudley, Cramlington	221 NEIL GRAY, Fairfield, Stockton on Tees
157 S.D. REDPATH, Churchdown, Glos	222 MARTIN SIMONS, Bekkevoort, Belgium
158 T.D. REDPATH, Wooler, Northumberland	223 N.A. HEWETT, Prudhoe, Northumberland
159 K. SLATTER, Akrotiri, Cyprus	224 TONY & MICHAEL RODGERS, Hounslow, Middx
160 MARK GRAHAM, West Lavington, Devizes	225 LOUIS AZZOPARDI, Rabat, Malta
161 MICHAEL GOLDSMITH, Sandyford, Newcastle	226 CLAVERING MAGS, Hartlepool
162 PAUL ATKINSON, St Johns, Newcastle	227 PETER CLARK, Newsham, Blyth
163 ROSS ATKINSON, Great Whittington, Northumberland	228 JOHN WILLIAM NICHOL, Gateshead
164 GARY THOMPSON, Wallsend, Tyne & Wear	229 MIKE LANCASTER, Enfield, Middlesex
165 ELIZABETH S. HENZELL, Killingworth Village	230 ROBERT ANTHONY YOUNGS, Hessle, Yorkshire
166 COLIN RUDD, Moortown, Leeds	231 J.W. WESLEY BLAKEY, Westerhope, Newcastle
167 J. PARWANI, Gillingham, Kent	232 DAVID ANDREW LAND, East Boldon, Newcastle
168 JOE CARPENTER, Longbenton, Newcastle	233 CRIS CONNOR, Comberford, Staffs
169 DEREK FORSTER, Darras Hall, Ponteland	234 KEN, KAREN & RACHEL QUINN,
170 TREVOR MEAD, Parkeston, Harwich, Essex	Heddon on the Wall, Newcastle
171 TOM STODDART, Woodham, Newton Aycliffe	235 DES BUTTON, Hayle, Cornwall
172 PAUL EDEN, Newport, Shropshire	236 DAVID G. BROWNLOW, Newcastle
173 DAVID GREAVES, Bishopthorpe, York	237 ADRIAN C.T.B. PALMER, JADE Y. & MICHELLE FERGUSON,
174 KEITH DOUGLAS, Gosforth, Newcastle	Malton, N. Yorks
175 DAVID JACKSON, Barmston, Washington	238 JARED & LINDA ROBINSON, Adwick-Le-Street, S. Yorks
176 JOHN E. GRAY, Scunthorpe, Lincs	239 WILLIAM MARSH, Adwick-Le-Street, S. Yorks
177 STEVEN RELPH, Walkerdene, Newcastle	240 TIM BELL, High Wycombe, Bucks
178 MARK JONES, Blythewood, Ascot, Berks	241 PAUL COLIN WARREN, Wallsend, Tyne & Wear
179 MICKI IANNOTTA, Banbury, Oxon	242 JONATHAN HALL, Henleaze, Bristol
180 DOUGLAS RAWLINSON, Lemington, Newcastle	243 STUART SHAKA ARKLEY, Selby, N. Yorks
181 GEORGE M. STEPHENSON, Rock, Alnwick	244 K.G. McQUEEN, Hebburn, Tyne & Wear
182 ANTHONY DINSDALE, Darlington	245 DAVID TICEHURST, Lancing, West Sussex
183 RICHARD SHANNON, Newcastle Upon Tyne	246 MICHAEL HOOD, Eighton Banks, Gateshead
184 ARTHUR BARKER, Pendower Est., Newcastle	247 ELLEN PINCHARD, Walker, Newcastle
185 PHILIP PRICE, Esh Village, Co Durham	248 STEVE WOOD, Newcastle upon Tyne
186 PHILIP PRICE, Esh Village, Co Durham	249 NEIL WOOD, Newcastle upon Tyne
187 JOHN ALDERSON, Duston, Northampton	250 PHIL WOOD, Manchester
188 JOSEPH WILLIAM FOSTER, Gateshead	251 DAVID RIDLEY, Newcastle upon Tyne
189 JAMES R. O'NEILL, Cramlington, Northumberland	252 JOHN CLARK, Canvey Island, Essex
190 BOB ASHBURN, Amble, Morpeth	253 ALAN WOOD, Newcastle upon Tyne
191 DAVID TWIZELL, Tynemouth, Tyne & Wear	254 SHARON N. MAY, North Greetwell, Lincoln
192 LES O'NEIL, Byker, Newcastle	255 PETER & SHONA WATSON, Haswell, Co Durham
193 MICHAEL PAUL TAYLOR, Edmonton, London	256 ANDREW BLAIN, Chilwell, Nottingham
194 PAUL DIXON, Newton on Ouse, York	257 DAVID STEPHEN BAGGALEY, Prudhoe
195 J.T. MOODY, Usworth Village, Tyne & Wear	258 DAVID EARNSHAW, Belper, Derbyshire

259 ANDREW & JOHN M. BRODIE, Sutton Bonington, Leics
260 JOHN BYRNE, Barrhead, Glasgow
261 DAVE McPHERSON, Colchester, Essex
262 BARRY BARKES, Harestock, Winchester
263 J. HURLEY, Abertillery, Gwent
264 MICHAEL PENSON, Notholt, Middx
265 G. SPEIGHT, Eastmoor, Wakefield, W. Yorks
266 DAVID SULLIVAN, Bethnal Green, London
267 RICHARD STOCKEN, Holmes Chapel, Crewe
268 WILLIAM KILMURRAY, Dublin, Eire
269 STEVEN McINTOSH, Cleadon, Sunderland
270 ALFRED BRWON, Wheatbottom, Crook, Co Durham
271 THOMAS WILLIM HALL, Morpeth, Northumberland
272 RORY STUART ADAMSON, Benton, Newcastle
273 COLIN CAMERON, Sidcup, Kent
274 STEVE EMMS, Evesham, Worcs
275 MARTIN JARRED, York
276 PETER STEVENS, Windsor, Berkshire
277 DAVE WINDROSS, Barlby, Selby, N. Yorks
278 DONALD NOBLE, Dunkeld, Perthshire
279 MICHAEL MALONEY, St Leonards on Sea, E.Sussex
280 RICHARD WELLS, St Marks Hill, Surbiton
281 PHIL HOLLOW, Lipson, Plymouth, Devon
282 BRIAN CRAWFORD, St Johns Wood, London
283 STEPHEN TANSEY, Farndon, Notts
284 DUNCAN WATT, Sleaford, Lincs
285 GEORGE EASTON-KYLE, Langworth, Lincs
286 GORDON SMALL, Penwortham, Preston
287 ROGER PHILLIP IAN BLAIR, Guildford
288 PAUL G. PATTINSON, Salem, Oldham
289 MALCOLM FERGUSON, Newton Hall, Durham
290 D.N. DURNIE, Bellerby, Leyburn, N. Yorks
291 RAY STEINBERG, Blaydon-on-Tyne
292 STEWART FELL, Radcliffe, Manchester
293 GAVIN HAIGH, Chester-le-Street, Co Durham
294 MICK GRAYSON, Handsworth, Sheffield
295 BILL CANTWELL, Llandudno (ex Walker)
296 BILL STAINTON, Worcester Park, Surrey
297 STEPHEN BROOKE, Cookridge, Leeds
298 MICHAEL ANTHONY O'DONNELL, Bermondsey, London
299 ERIC HOGG, Fairfield, Stockton
300 CHRISTER SVENSSON, Ödeshög, Sweden
301 ANTONI GADOMSKI, Kingston Park, Newcastle
302 D.W. LOWREY, Northburn Dale, Cramlington
303 KEN PRIOR, Bitterne, Southampton
304 J. JACKSON, Oakhill, Stoke on Trent
305 JOHN DIAMOND, Hebburn, Tyne & Wear
306 ANDREW IAIN WALKER, Stokesley, Cleveland
307 TIFFANY & MICK PILCH, Watton, Thetford, Norfolk
308 LEE HODGKINSON, Toronto, Ontario, Canada
309 DENIS MCDONALD, Malahide, Co. Dublin, Eire
310 W.D.J. McGILLIVRAY, Greenlaw Mains, Penicuik
311 JOHN McMULLEN, Walker, Newcastle
312 STATSBIBLIOTEKET, Aarhus, Denmark
313 FRANK E. EVANS, Sundorne Grove, Shrewsbury
314 ADAM WALLER, Hartlepool
315 BRIAN A. O'KELLY, Hall Green, Birmingham
316 GORDON V. SCOTT, Basildon, Essex
317 TREVOR SCOTT, Basildon, Essex
318 ALAN DAVISON, WATERSHED PICTURES, London SW18
319 SUE WRATTEN (née Blythe), Saul, Glos
320 RICHARD WRATTEN, Saul Glos
321 BOBBY GREENLAND, Fulham, London
322 COLIN SMITH, Rise Park, Romford, Essex
323 STU FORSTER, Hexham, Northumberland

324 SIMON HILDREY, Colliers Wood, London SW19
325 WILLIAM JOHN DIMMICK, Stanley, Co Durham
326 JOHN EMMERSON, Chester-le-Street, Co Durham
327 KENNY CROW, Shipcote, Gateshead
328 SARAH & JOHN JOBLING, Cramlington
329 STEVE WILKES, Cardiff
330 GEOFF BELL, Fenham, Newcastle
331 JANE FRANCES WOOD, Shoreham-by-Sea, W. Sussex
332 JOHN FORD, Leith, Edinburgh
333 MARK FIELD, Preston, Lancs
334 JULIAN FIELD, London N13
335 MALCOLM FLETCHER, Basildon, Essex
336 PHILIP C. RICE, York
337 ALAN DORMER, Consett, Co Durham
338 COLIN ANDERSON, Whitley Bay
339 NORMAN HICKIN, Low Fell, Gateshead
340 ANDREW GEORGE, Roath Cardiff
341 ROGER TALBOT, Sandbach, Cheshire
342 MICHAEL BATEY, Hetton-le-Hole, Tyne & Wear
343 ARTHUR WALKER, Hexham, Northumberland
344 DENIS LESLIE SMITH, North Heaton, Newcastle
345 LIAM MOFFATT, Etherley Dene, Bishop Auckland
346 ANDREW DOWLING, Skelmorlie
347 DUNCAN MACINTYRE, Greenock
348 MICHAEL HICKS, Seaton Burn, Newcastle
349 DARRELL HAWKSWORTH, Marsh, Huddersfield
350 JOHN TINDLE, Alvechurch, Worcs
351 QUENTIN DAVID McGILL, Sutton Coldfield
352 DOMINIC MATTHEW DAVID McGILL, Sutton Coldfield
353 K. PINK, Salisbury, Wiltshire
354 CHRIS ALEXANDER, Houghton-le-Spring
355 ALAN HINDLEY, Maghull, Merseyside
356 KEITH MAUGHAN & JENNIFER WRIGHT, Crawcrook, Ryton
357 R. BAILLIE, Benton, Newcastle
358 EMMA BAILLIE, Benton, Newcastle
359 SARAH BAILLIE, Benton, Newcastle
360 DAVID J. GODFREY, Raglan, New Zealand
361 JASON S.K. DICKINSON, High Green, Sheffield
362 MICHAEL A. CRAGGS, Watford, Herts
363 GARETH M. DAVIES, Holyhead, Anglesey
364 TONY BROWN, Beeston, Nottingham
365 GEOFF DICK, Pegswood, Morpeth
366 STEPHEN DEREK BROWN, Tulse Hill, London
367 ROGER WASH, Newmarket, Suffolk
368 GEORGE M. STEPHANIDES, Limassol, Cyprus
369 GARY HORNBY, Droitwich, Worcs
370 PETER HORNBY, London
371 PAUL GOWANS, Ashington, Northumberland
372 GEORGE W. BLAIR, Alnwick, Northumberland
373 PAUL LUNNEY, Glasgow
374 COLIN CAMPBELL, Nunthorpe, Middlesbrough
375 ANDREW JAMES CAMPBELL, Nunthorpe, Middlesbrough
376 STEVEN KEMPSTER, Middleton, Manchester
377 Dr D SMITH, Darley Abbey, Derby
378 LESLIE ROBSON, Curzon Park, Chester
379 PETER EDWARD LITTLE, Cleator Moor, Cumbria
380 TERRY FROST, Baildon, Shipley
381 JOHN A. HANN, Helensburgh, Argyll & Bute
382 DICK BARTON, Lexden, Colchester, Essex
383 BERT GREEN, Horwich, Bolton
384 PHILLIP RUDKIN, Syston, Leicester
385 GERALD TOON, Thurnby, Leicester
386 JULIAN BASKCOMB, Leicester